Every Decker book is accompanied by a CD-ROM.

The disk appears in the front of each copy, in its own sealed jacket. Affixed to the front of the book will be a distinctive BčD sticker **"Book *cum* disk"**.

The disk contains the complete text and illustrations of the book, in fully searchable PDF files. The book and disk will be sold *only* as a package; neither will be available independently, and no prices will be available for the items individually.

BC Decker Inc is committed to providing high quality electronic publications that will compliment traditional information and learning methods.

We trust you will find the Book/CD Package invaluable and invite your comments and suggestions.

Brian C. Decker
CEO and Publisher

D1218191

American Cancer Society
Atlas of
Clinical Oncology

Published

Blumgart, Fong, Jarnagin	*Hepatobiliary Cancer (2001)*
Cameron	*Pancreatic Cancer (2001)*
Char	*Tumors of the Eye and Ocular Adnexa (2001)*
Eifel, Levenback	*Cancer of the Female Lower Genital Tract (2001)*
Shah	*Head and Neck Cancer (2001)*
Silverman	*Oral Cancer (1998)*
Sober, Haluska	*Skin Cancer (2001)*
Wiernik	*Adult Leukemias (2001)*
Willett	*Cancer of the Lower Gastrointestinal Tract (2001)*
Winchester, Winchester	*Breast Cancer (2000)*

Forthcoming

Carroll, Grossfeld, Reese	*Prostate Cancer (2001)*
Clark, Duh, Jahan, Perrier	*Endocrine Tumors (2002)*
Droller	*Urothelial Cancer (2002)*
Fuller	*Uterine and Endometrial Cancer (2003)*
Ginsberg	*Lung Cancer (2001)*
Grossbard	*Malignant Lymphomas (2001)*
Ozols	*Ovarian Cancer (2002)*
Pollock	*Soft Tissue Sarcomas (2001)*
Posner, Vokes, Weichselbaum	*Cancer of the Upper Gastrointestinal Tract (2001)*
Prados	*Brain Cancer (2001)*
Raghavan	*Germ Cell Tumors (2002)*
Steele, Richie	*Kidney Tumors (2003)*
Volberding	*Viral and Immunological Malignancies (2003)*
Yasko	*Bone Tumors (2002)*

American Cancer Society
Atlas of
Clinical Oncology

Editors

GLENN D. STEELE JR, MD
Geisinger Health System

THEODORE L. PHILLIPS, MD
University of California

BRUCE A. CHABNER, MD
Harvard Medical School

Managing Editor

TED S. GANSLER, MD, MBA
Director of Health Content, American Cancer Society

American Cancer Society

Atlas of
Clinical Oncology

Cancer of the Female Lower Genital Tract

Patricia J. Eifel, MD

Professor
Department of Radiation Oncology
University of Texas
M.D. Anderson Cancer Center
Houston, Texas

Charles Levenback, MD

Associate Professor and Deputy Chairman
Department of Gynecologic Oncology
University of Texas
M.D. Anderson Cancer Center
Houston, Texas

DISCARD

2001

BC Decker Inc

Hamilton • London

BC Decker Inc
20 Hughson Street South
P.O. Box 620, LCD 1
Hamilton, Ontario L8N 3K7
Tel: 905-522-7017; 1-800-568-7281
Fax: 905-522-7839; 1-888-311-4987
E-mail: info@bcdecker.com
Website: www.bcdecker.com

ISBN 1–55009–107-7
Printed in Canada

Cover illustration created by Monique LeBlanc

Sales and Distribution

United States
BC Decker Inc
P.O. Box 785
Lewiston, NY 14092-0785
Tel: 905-522-7017; 1-800-568-7281
Fax: 905-522-7839; 1-888-311-4987
E-mail: info@bcdecker.com
Website: www.bcdecker.com

Canada
BC Decker Inc
20 Hughson Street South
P.O. Box 620, LCD 1
Hamilton, Ontario L8N 3K7
Tel: 905-522-7017; 1-800-568-7281
Fax: 905-522-7839; 1-888-311-4987
E-mail: info@bcdecker.com
Website: www.bcdecker.com

Foreign Rights
John Scott & Company
International Publishers' Agency
P.O. Box 878
Kimberton, PA 19442
Tel: 610-827-1640
Fax: 610-827-1671
E-mail: jsco@voicenet.com

U.K., Europe, Scandinavia, Middle East
Harcourt Publishers Limited
Customer Service Department
Foots Cray High Street
Sidcup, Kent
DA14 5HP, UK
Tel: 44 (0) 208 308 5760
Fax: 44 (0) 181 308 5702
E-mail: cservice@harcourt_brace.com

Australia, New Zealand
Harcourt Australia Pty Limited
Customer Service Department
STM Division
Locked Bag 16
St. Peters, New South Wales, 2044
Australia
Tel: 61 02 9517-8999
Fax: 61 02 9517-2249
E-mail: stmp@harcourt.com.au
Website: www.harcourt.com.au

Japan
Igaku-Shoin Ltd.
Foreign Publications Department
3-24-17 Hongo
Bunkyo-ku, Tokyo, Japan 113-8719
Tel: 81 3 3817 5680
Fax: 81 3 3815 6776
E-mail: fd@igaku.shoin.co.jp

Singapore, Malaysia, Thailand, Philippines, Indonesia, Vietnam, Pacific Rim, Korea
Harcourt Asia Pte Limited
583 Orchard Road
#09/01, Forum
Singapore 238884
Tel: 65-737-3593
Fax: 65-753-2145

Contributors

DIANE C. BODURKA, MD
Assistant Professor
Department of Gynecologic Oncology
University of Texas
M.D. Anderson Cancer Center
Houston, Texas
Post-treatment Surveillance

KEVIN R. BRADER, MD
Assistant Professor
Department of Obstetrics & Gynecology
Division of Gynecologic Oncology
Vanderbilt University
Nashville, Tennessee
Chemotherapy in Curative Management

MOLLY A. BREWER, DVM, MD, MS
Assistant Professor
Department of Gynecology
University of Texas
M.D. Anderson Cancer Center
Houston, Texas
Treatment of Squamous Intraepithelial Lesions

THOMAS W. BURKE, MD
Professor
Department of Gynecologic Oncology
University of Texas
M.D. Anderson Cancer Center
Houston, Texas
Surgical Treatment of Invasive Cervical Cancer

HIGINIA R. CARDENES, MD
Clinical Assistant Professor
Department of Radiation Oncology
Indiana University School of Medicine
Indianapolis, Indiana
Management of Vaginal Cancer

SILVIA D. CHANG, MD
Clinical Instructor
Department of Radiology
University of British Columbia
Vancouver, British Columbia
Diagnostic Imaging

ROBERT L. COLEMAN, MD
Associate Professor & Vice Chairman for
    Gynecologic Services
Department of Obstetrics & Gynecology
Division of Gynecologic Oncology
University of Texas
Southwestern Medical Center
Dallas, Texas
Anatomy and Natural History

NATHAN D. COMSIA, BA
Research Assistant
Department of Radiation Oncology
University of Washington Medical Center
Seattle, Washington
*Radical Management of Recurrent Cervical
    Cancer*

CHRISTOPHER P. CRUM, MD
Professor
Department of Pathology
Division of Women's & Perinatal Pathology
Harvard Medical School
Brigham & Women's Hospital
Boston, Massachusetts
Pathology

PATRICIA J. EIFEL, MD
Professor
Department of Radiation Oncology
University of Texas
M.D. Anderson Cancer Center
Houston, Texas
Invasive Carcinoma of the Cervix
Radiation Therapy for Invasive Cervical Cancer
Late Complications of Pelvic Radiation Therapy

BENJAMIN GREER, MD
Professor
Department of Obstetrics & Gynecology
Director
Division of Gynecologic Oncology
University of Washington Medical Center
Seattle, Washington
Radical Management of Recurrent
  Cervical Cancer

KATHRYN MCCONNELL GREVEN, MD
Professor
Department of Radiation Oncology
Wake Forest University Baptist Medical Center
Winston Salem, North Carolina
Acute Effects of Radiation Therapy

HEDVIG HRICAK, MD, PHD
Professor
Department of Radiology
Cornell University
Chairman
Department of Radiology
Memorial Sloan-Kettering Cancer Center
New York, New York
Diagnostic Imaging

ANUJA JHINGRAN, MD
Assistant Professor
Department of Radiation Oncology
University of Texas
M.D. Anderson Cancer Center
Houston, Texas
Radiation Therapy for Invasive
  Cervical Cancer

JOHN J. KAVANAGH, MD
Professor and Chief
Section of Gynecologic Medical Oncology
Division of Cancer Medicine
University of Texas
M.D. Anderson Cancer Center
Houston, Texas
Palliative Care

JEFFREY T. KEATING, MD
Clinical Fellow
Department of Pathology
Division of Women's & Perinatal Pathology
Harvard Medical School
Brigham & Women's Hospital
Boston, Massachusetts
Pathology

WUI-JIN KOH, MD
Associate Professor
Department of Radiation Oncology
Adjunct Associate Professor
Department of Obstetrics & Gynecology
University of Washington Medical Center
Seattle, Washington
Radical Management of Recurrent
  Cervical Cancer

EVANTHIA KOSTOPOULOU, MD
Pathologist
Department of Pathology
Hippokrateion General Peripheral Hospital
  of Thessaloniki
Thessaloniki, Greece
Pathology

CHARLES LEVENBACK, MD
Associate Professor & Deputy Chairman
Department of Gynecologic Oncology
University of Texas
M.D. Anderson Cancer Center
Houston, Texas
Surgery for Vulvar Cancer
Late Complications of Pelvic Radiation Therapy

KATHERINE Y. LOOK, MD
Associate Professor
Department of Obstetrics & Gynecology
Division of Gynecologic Oncology
Indiana University School of Medicine
Indianapolis, Indiana
Management of Vaginal Cancer

KAREN LU, MD
Assistant Professor
Department of Gynecologic Oncology
University of Texas
M.D. Anderson Cancer Center
Houston, Texas
Surgical Treatment of Invasive Cervical Cancer

LAILA I. MUDERSPACH, MD
Associate Professor
Department of Obstetrics & Gynecology
Division of Gynecologic Oncology
USC Keck School of Medicine
USC & LAC Women's & Children's Hospital
Los Angeles, California
Epidemiology

ADNAN R. MUNKARAH, MD
Associate Professor
Department of Obstetrics & Gynecology
Director
Division of Gynecologic Oncology
Wayne State University
Karmanos Cancer Institute
Detroit, Michigan
Screening for Neoplasms

PAMELA J. PALEY, MD
Assistant Professor
Department of Obstetrics & Gynecology
Division of Gynecologic Oncology
University of Washington Medical Center
Seattle, Washington
Radical Management of Recurrent
*   Cervical Cancer*

MARCUS E. RANDALL, MD
William A. Mitchell Professor & Chair
Department of Radiation Oncology
Indiana University School of Medicine
Indianapolis, Indiana
Management of Vaginal Cancer

LYNDA ROMAN, MD
Associate Professor
Department of Obstetrics & Gynecology
Division of Gynecologic Oncology
USC Keck School of Medicine
USC & LAC Women's & Children's Hospital
Los Angeles, California
Epidemiology

ANTHONY H. RUSSELL, MD
Associate Professor
Department of Obstetrics & Gynecology
University of California Davis School
    of Medicine
Division of Radiation Oncology
Radiological Associates of Sacramento
Sacramento, California
Radiation Therapy for Vulvar Cancer

JUDITH K. WOLF, MD
Assistant Professor
Department of Gynecologic Oncology
University of Texas
M.D. Anderson Cancer Center
Houston, Texas
Molecular Biology

Contents

Preface

This volume of the American Cancer Society Atlas of Oncology is intended to provide clinicians, students, and scientists with an integrated analysis and review of the biology, diagnostic evaluation, and treatment of cancers of the lower female genital tract. Recent changes in the accepted treatment for invasive cervical cancer, and in many aspects of the epidemiology, diagnosis, and evaluation of these cancers, make this discussion particularly timely.

Carcinomas that involve the cervix, vagina, or vulva have many features in common, particularly with respect to their epidemiology, biology, pathology, and diagnostic evaluation. We have addressed these subjects in individual chapters that draw on literature and data relevant to carcinomas arising in any of these sites. Where locoregional treatments diverge to address technical challenges that are specific to individual sites, separate discussions have been included.

Invasive cancers involving the vagina and vulva are rare. As well, these cancers require specialized methods for successful treatment because of their proximity to the bladder and rectum. Carcinoma of the cervix also is relatively uncommon in the United States, whereas breast, lung, colon, and ovarian cancers are much more frequent causes of death. This low incidence is partially owing to the remarkable success of cytologic screening, which detects most abnormalities in their preinvasive stages. However, cervical cancer continues to be the most frequent cause of cancer-related deaths in women who live in the developing countries of Central and South America, Africa, and Asia. Invasive cervical cancer also disproportionately affects minority and medically underserved women in the United States. If treated appropriately, dysplasias and preinvasive cancers are rarely life threatening, but the cost and morbidity associated with their treatment is a significant public health problem.

Among the recent developments is our growing understanding of the central role played by the human papillomavirus in the development of most cervical cancers and of many vaginal and vulvar cancers. Confirmation of this relationship has stimulated major efforts to develop vaccines and targeted treatments that may one day reduce or eliminate the need for many of today's treatments. In the meantime, modern technology continues to provide more sensitive methods of detection, and clinicians are developing improved treatments that can reduce the cost and side effects of treatment for preinvasive disease. The past decade has also seen promising improvements in the diagnostic methods used to define sites of involvement. The recent results of five prospective randomized trials have established the role of concurrent chemotherapy and radiation therapy in the treatment of locoregionally advanced cervical cancer, thereby reducing the risk of recurrence by as much as 50 percent.

Not only are these changes of compelling interest to those of us who specialize in the treatment of these diseases, but they also may provide important models for the study and management of carcinomas arising in many other sites.

Patricia J. Eifel
Charles Levenback
July 2001

Dedication

Many thanks to our families for their love and support:

James Belli, Therese, Steven, Suzanne, John, and Anne

and

Ginny, Sam, and Ben Levenback.

Epidemiology

LYNDA ROMAN, MD
LAILA I. MUDERSPACH, MD

VULVAR CANCER

Demographics

Cancer of the vulva is the fourth most common gynecologic malignancy, accounting for 3 to 5 percent of gynecologic malignancies. In the year 2001, it is estimated that there will be 3,600 new cases reported and 800 deaths due to this disease in the United States.[1] The risk of developing vulvar cancer increases with age. The incidence rate of this disease from 1993 to 1997 was approximately 2 per 100,000 women per year; in women over the age of 75 years, the incidence is 13 per 100,000 women per year.[2] Though the vast majority of women who develop this disease are in the menopausal age range, there are several reports in the literature of young women (under 45 years) presenting with vulvar cancer.

Etiology

Vulvar Dystrophies

In the earlier portion of the 20th century, it was the general belief that vulvar cancers tended to arise from vulvar dystrophies. In a retrospective analysis published in 1930, Taussig[3] concluded that up to 50 percent of women with "leukoplakia" (which he defined as a whitening of the vulvar skin, often diffuse and accompanied by atrophy) go on to develop cancer of the vulva. He based this conclusion on the fact that over a given period of time, he had observed 40

women with "leukoplakia" who did not also have a vulvar cancer and approximately the same number of women with "leukoplakia" who also had a coexisting vulvar cancer. Subsequent studies have not supported this conclusion. Jeffcoate[4] reported a 4 to 5 percent risk of vulvar cancer developing in women with chronic vulvar dystrophy. Wallace[5] reported a 4 percent risk of vulvar cancer in women followed up for lichen sclerosus. McAdams and Kistner[6] reported a 10 percent risk of vulvar cancer in women followed up for atypical vulvar hyperplasia. Thus, despite the fact that vulvar dystrophies have been reported to be present in a large percentage of women at the time of diagnosis of vulvar cancer, the risk of developing vulvar cancer in a woman with a dystrophy is small. At this point, the exact nature of the relationship between vulvar dystrophy and vulvar cancer remains uncertain. While there appears to be an association between the two, the relationship may not be an etiologic one.

Human Papillomavirus

In 1972, Franklin and Rutledge[7] reported that 15 percent of their patients with preinvasive or invasive carcinoma of the vulva had either a history of or concomitant cervical neoplasia. They also noted an association between vulvar neoplasia and neoplasia of the anogenital skin, postulating that a venereal agent may play a role in the pathogenesis of the disease. Japaze and colleagues,[8] in a later publication, reported similar findings. In 1990, Brinton and colleagues[9] published a large case-control study of vulvar neoplasia. They found an independent association between vulvar neoplasia (in situ and invasive) and a history of genital warts, a history of abnormal Pap smears, and a history of smoking. On the basis of their findings, they concluded that vulvar neoplasia and cervical neoplasia may have a common etiology and suggested that human papillomavirus (HPV) (which at this point was established as a major etiologic factor in cervical neoplasia) be investigated as an etiologic agent in vulvar neoplasia.

Numerous studies have analyzed in situ and invasive vulvar carcinomas for the presence of HPV. The large majority (80 to 90%) of vulvar intraepithelial neoplasia (VIN) lesions are HPV positive.[10,11] HPV-16 is the most common type isolated. Invasive vulvar cancers are much less likely to be HPV positive than in situ lesions. Depending on the technique used and the age of the population studied, only 20 to 60 percent of invasive vulvar cancers are HPV positive.[11–14] The likelihood of being HPV positive is highest among women with vulvar cancer who have coexisting VIN, have multicentric lesions, are younger than age 70 years at the time of diagnosis, or have a history of cervical neoplasia or genital warts.[12] Certain histologic subtypes, such as basaloid, warty, or verrucous lesions, are HPV positive the vast majority of the time (85 to 95%), compared with typical or keratinizing squamous carcinomas, of which only 6 to 39 percent contain HPV deoxyribonucleic acid (DNA).[11,12] Although HPV has been isolated from vulvar cancers that have coexistant lichen sclerosus,[15] it is more common that when lichen sclerosus is present, HPV is not.[16]

Nonviral Infectious Diseases

A possible association among chronic vulvar granulomatous disease, syphilis, and cancer of the vulva was postulated on the basis of the frequency with which these diseases preceeded vulvar cancer in Jamaican women. Hay and Cole[17] reported that 66 percent of their Jamaican patients with vulvar cancer had a history of chronic granulomatous disease. Sengupta,[18] in a later publication, reported that 51 percent of Jamaican women in his study/practice with vulvar cancer had a history of either syphilis or chronic granulomatous vulvar disease. However, nei-

ther Brinton and colleagues[9] nor Mabuchi and colleagues[19] found a significant difference in the history of syphilis between study cases with vulvar neoplasia and their controls. It is likely that rather than having a direct etiologic role, these diseases identify women who have been sexually active and thus are more likely to have contracted HPV.

Other Factors

Numerous other factors, including reproductive, medical, menstrual, and occupational history, have been investigated as risk factors for the development of vulvar cancer. None have been shown to conclusively play a major role in the development of this disease. Histories of diabetes mellitus and hypertension are frequent in women with vulvar cancer, but this is most likely due to the usual advanced age of the affected individuals. Parity, type of contraceptive use, and menstrual history have not been found to be significant risk factors by multiple studies.[10,19,20] Mabuchi and colleagues[19] did report an increased risk of vulvar cancer in women who consume large amount of caffeine, those who work as household servants, or those who work in the garment industry. These specific factors have not been investigated thoroughly, so their exact association, if any, with vulvar cancer is unclear at this time.

Conclusion

It seems that there are two distinct subgroups of women who develop vulvar cancer (Table 1–1).[21] The first group tends to be older, has unifocal lesions, has no pre-existing history of vulvar dysplasia, and is more likely to have a history of vulvar dystrophy. Cancers in this group of women tend not to be HPV positive and may have a worse prognosis.[12] The women in the second group tend to be younger, frequently have a history of vulvar dysplasia or warts (as well as cervical neoplasia), and tend to have multifocal lesions. These women tend to be HPV positive and may have a better prognosis.[12] There are likely other factors, not yet elucidated, that play a role in the development of this disease. Unlike cervical cancer, in which the vast majority of cases are related to HPV infection, in a sizable

Table 1–1. DIFFERING CHARACTERISTICS OF VULVAR CANCER SUBGROUPS

	Group I	Group II
Age	Older (> 60 yr)	Younger (< 60 yr)
History of VIN/CIN	No	Yes
Coexisting VIN	No	Yes
History of vulvar dystrophy	Sometimes	No
Focality	Unifocal	Multifocal
HPV positivity	No	Yes

VIN = vulvar intraepithelial neoplasia; CIN = cervical intraepithelial neoplasia; HPV = human papillomavirus.

proportion of vulvar cancers, the etiology is not completely clear.

Vulvar Cancer in Young Women

While vulvar cancer is generally a disease of the postmenopausal years, there have been several reports in the literature describing the development of the disease in younger women. Choo[22] described 17 women below the age of 35 years who were diagnosed with invasive squamous carcinomas of the vulva. Eight of these women had disease invading < 5 mm into the stroma. Of these, 87.5 percent had VIN coexisting with the invasive cancer. In contrast, of the women with more deeply invasive vulvar cancers, only 22 percent had coexisting VIN. Of note, three women (33%) in this group had coexisting lichen sclerosus. Two of the 17 women were immunosuppressed. The rate of smoking in the study population was not reported. Roman and colleagues[23] reported 3 women, all under the age of 25 years, who were diagnosed with invasive squamous vulvar carcinomas. Two of the 3 patients (67%) had evidence of old lichen sclerosus, 1 (33%) had a history of vulvar condyloma, 2 (67%) had coexisting VIN, and 2 (67%) were smokers. Carter and colleagues[24] reported 27 patients with squamous vulvar cancer diagnosed under the age of 40 years. Eleven of the 27 (42%) had been treated in the past for lower genital tract neoplasia (thus suggesting HPV infection). Twenty of the 27 (80%) were smokers. Three (15%) had vulvar condyloma. Eight (40%) of the women were to some degree immunosuppressed as a result of autoimmune disease, history of renal transplantation, herpes zoster, chronic hepatitis, or pregnancy. Last, Messing and Gallup[25] reported 18 women diagnosed with squamous cancer of the vulva under the age of 45 years. Compared with older women (that is, women over the age of 45) with this disease, younger women were significantly more likely to have a history of condyloma and to smoke or be smokers.

Young women who develop vulvar cancer are similar to the overall population in regards to the prevalence of risk factors. HPV infection and immunosuppression may be more prevalent in the young patient with this disease. It is likely that gross or subtle alteration of the immune function may play a role in the development of this disease in the younger population.

VAGINAL CANCER

Demographics

Cancer of the vagina is a rare malignancy, accounting for only 2 to 3 percent of all gynecologic cancers. In the year 2001, it is estimated that 2,100 women will be diagnosed with this disease, and that 600 women will die from it.[1] The age-standardized incidence rate is approximately 1 per 100,000 women, based on data from the NCI SEER (National Cancer Institute Surveillance, Epidemiology, and End Results) program.[26]

Etiology

Given the rarity of vaginal cancer, little investigation into the etiology has been undertaken. Chronic vaginal irritation due to procidentia and the use of a pessary were mentioned as possible etiologic factors in early studies.[27,28] More recent papers have not found pessary use or prolapse to be especially common in women with vaginal carcinomas.[29,30] In contrast to cervical cancer, extensive study of the role of HPV in vaginal cancer has not been performed. However, there are various features of vaginal carcinoma that suggest a likely etiologic role for HPV. A significant percentage (38 to 56%) of women who develop vaginal carcinoma have had a previous hysterectomy, frequently for cervical neoplasia.[30,31] Also, vaginal carcinomas in situ will frequently be HPV positive.[32] Thus, while it is likely that HPV is an etiologic factor in the development of vaginal cancer, the magnitude of its association is unknown at this time.

Diethylstilbestrol

In 1971, Herbst and colleagues[33] published a landmark paper establishing the strong association between maternal diethylstilbestrol (DES) use during pregnancy and the later development of clear cell adenocarcinoma of the vagina in the female offspring who had been exposed in utero. At least two-thirds of all clear cell adenocarcinomas of the vagina are attributable to DES exposure while in utero. The mean age of diagnosis of vaginal clear cell carcinoma is 19 years. The approximate risk of developing vaginal adenocarcinoma in a woman exposed to DES in utero is 1:1,000, and the risk is highest if exposure was in the first trimester.[34] The greatest number of new cases of clear cell carcinoma of the vagina occurred in 1975 (32 cases);[35,36] since then, the number of cases has fallen. Use of DES was halted in 1971; thus, the number of new cases of clear cell carcinoma of the vagina is likely to continue to decrease with time.

Vaginal adenosis (presence of endocervical glandular tissue in the vagina) occurs in approximately one-third of women who have been exposed to DES in utero.[37,38] In most instances, squamous metaplasia occurs with time, and as the woman ages, the vagina assumes a normal appearance. Because the vast majority of women with clear cell vaginal carcinoma also have vaginal adenosis, a patient's risk for adenocarcinoma significantly diminishes once metaplasia has occurred.

CERVICAL CANCER

Demographics

Cancer of the cervix is the third most common gynecologic malignancy in the United States. Worldwide, however, cervical cancer is the leading gynecologic malignancy and is the second most common cancer in women following breast cancer. In the United States, in 2001, 12,900 new cases and 4,400 deaths are anticipated from cervical cancer.[37] The incidence rate for cervical cancer in 1997 for the US was 7.5 per 100,000. In developing countries, cervical cancer is the most commonly diagnosed and fatal cancer of women, with an estimated 500,000 new cases worldwide per year.[38] The areas with the highest incidence are Latin America (70 per 100,000), sub-Saharan Africa, and southern and southeastern Asia. The areas with the lowest incidence are Western Europe, North America, the Middle East, and China[39] (Figure 1–1).

The majority of women who develop cervical cancer are in their forties and fifties; however, more and more younger women are being affected. It is no longer uncommon to see women in their twenties or thirties diagnosed with cervical cancer.

The incidence of cervical cancer in the United States varies by race and socioeconomic status. Women belonging to the lowest socioeconomic groups have the highest incidence of cervical cancer due, at least in part, to inadequate screening. Although incidence rates are higher for African Americans and Hispanics than for Caucasians in the general population, the highest incidence is among poor Caucasian women in selected populations (Figure 1–2).

Etiology

Epidemiologic studies have looked at many possible explanations for the development of cervical cancer. Age at first intercourse, number of sexual partners, high parity, cigarette smoking, race, and low socioeconomic status have all been shown to be statistically associated with cervical cancer risk.[40–42] All these factors are linked to sexual behavior and most have not been shown to be independent risk factors. Some studies suggest that carcinogens from tobacco do reach the cervix, where they may act synergistically with HPV infection. Although socioeconomic status is statistically related to patterns of sexual activity, limited access to and use of Pap screening may also contribute to increased risk. It appears that the most important risk factor is the acquisition of HPV infection.[43]

The National Institutes of Health Consensus Statement on Cervical Cancer states that this cancer is "causally related to infection with the human papillomavirus."[44] In the past, other etiologies, such as herpes simplex virus (HSV) infection and other sexually transmitted diseases, were thought to be implicated for the development of cervical cancer. However, in 1974, zur Hausen suggested that HPVs were likely to be the sexually transmitted agents for squamous genital tract neoplasms.[45] Many studies since that time have shown that HPV is the precursor infection for 95 percent of cervical cancers.

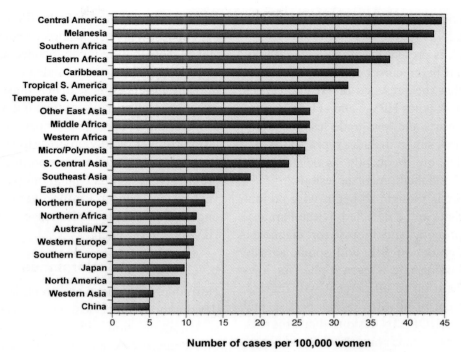

Number of cases per 100,000 women

Figure 1–1. Incidence of invasive cervical cancer in different regions of the world. (Reproduced with permission from Parkin DM, Pisani P, Ferlay J. Global cancer statistics. CA Cancer J Clin 1999;49:33–64.)

Human Papillomavirus

The papillomavirus is a small DNA virus that induces a range of proliferative lesions in most mammals, including humans. There are over 80 types of this virus, of which about 25 affect the genital tract. The HPV subtypes are classified into risk categories (low, intermediate, and high) on the basis of the strength of their association with high-grade and invasive lesions. These cancers are believed to develop from precursor, preinvasive lesions, which are called cervical intraepithelial neoplasias (CIN) or squamous intraepithelial lesions (SIL) of the cervix. The CIN is graded from 1 to 3 on the basis of the degree of disruption of the

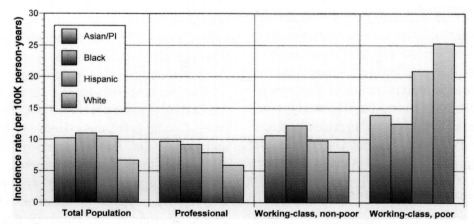

Figure 1–2. Age-adjusted cervical cancer incidence rates (per 100,000 person-years) by race/ethnicity and block-group socioeconomic position (from 1990 census figures) for women living in the San Francisco Bay Area between 1988 and 1992. (Reproduced with permission from Krieger N, Quesenberry C Jr, Peng T, et al. Social class, race/ethnicity, and incidence of breast, cervix, colon, lung, and prostate cancer among Asian, Black, Hispanic, and White residents of the San Francisco Bay Area, 1988–92 (United States). Cancer Causes Control 1999;10:525–37.)

epithelial differentiation. Cervical SIL is termed low (CIN1) or high (CIN2, 3).[46,47]

The HPV DNA is present in virtually all cases of cervical cancer and its precursor lesions. Two cohort studies indicate that the presence of HPV precedes disease.[48,49] Low-risk types HPV-6 and -11 are associated with genital warts and low-grade lesions (CIN1 or LSIL). A high-risk subset includes types 16, 18, 31, 33, and 51, which are frequently associated with anogenital cancers and their precursor lesions.[38,45,50–52]

Cervical cancer is thought to begin with premalignant changes that can be detected by the Pap test, followed by colposcopy and biopsy for diagnosis. One-third of all grades of SIL will spontaneously regress. The regression rate is even higher for low-grade lesions, where up to 60 percent will regress. However, 41 percent of all SIL lesions persist, and 25 percent progress. Of CIN lesions that progress, 10 percent progress to carcinoma in situ and 1 percent to invasive cancer. The majority (three-quarters) of all grades of SIL do not progress.[44,53–58]

Screening for Cervical Cancer

The Papanicolaou smear (Pap test) has been used to screen for cervical cancer since its implementation in the 1950s. It is generally accepted that screening has played a major role in the reduction of cervical cancer, where efforts are organized and access is not limited by socioeconomic status. Since initially developed, there have been several changes in the nomenclature and interpretation to clarify and make results more clinically relevant.[59] In addition, new techniques for collection and computer-assisted interpretation have been developed, which make Pap tests more sensitive and more accurate than ever before.[60] Triage schemes based on the cytologic interpretation of Pap smears that integrate HPV DNA testing have been suggested to identify women with equivocal Pap results and cervical neoplasia.[61] While this has not yet become the standard of care, it may become so in the next decade.

Human Immunodeficiency Virus

Since the 1980s, with the recognition of human immunodeficiency virus (HIV), much concern has existed about the rapid progression of CIN to cancer in this patient group. Cervical cancer was made an acquired immunodeficiency syndrome (AIDS) defin-

ing diagnosis in women with HIV infection. Initially, the Pap test was not considered reliable in this group, and all women were recommended to undergo routine colposcopy. This is confounded by the fact that HIV, in many instances, is sexually transmitted, as is HPV infection. However, after much initial fear about rapid progression, it appears that patients with precursor lesions do not rapidly progress to cervical cancer.[62,63] Regular screening with appropriate treatment for preinvasive lesions is vital in this patient group to prevent cervical cancer. Prospective studies are currently ongoing to elucidate the risk of cervical cancer in HIV-infected women.

Hormones

Hormonal influences are potential cofactors in the development of cervical cancer, as evidenced by the strong association with parity and some suggestion of increased risk with use of hormonal contraceptives.[64,65] However, this is complicated to deduce from confounding factors and warrants further investigation. The use of estrogen-progestin replacement therapy has not been shown to influence rates of cervical cancer.[66] Further information and research into this area are going to be important as the population in the United States ages.

Adenocarcinoma

Although squamous cell cervical cancer is more common, adenocarcinoma accounts for more than 10 percent of all cervical cancers. As with squamous lesions of the cervix, glandular lesions are also associated with HPV. The association is not as clear; however, HPV definitely has a role in the development of this type of cervical neoplasia.

The incidence of adenocarcinoma of the cervix is increasing in most developed countries, particularly among younger women. Between the early 1970s and mid-1980s, the incidence of adenocarcinoma has more than doubled among women under 35 years of age.[67,68] This does not appear to be due to a relative decrease in squamous carcinomas prevented by effective screening practices, but rather an absolute increase in adenocarcinoma and adenocarcinoma-in-situ in younger women. Some hypothesize that this increase may be due to increased oral contraceptive use, but there are confounding issues that need to be studied. Alternatively, it may be related to changes in the prevalence of HPV infection or to increased reporting of this histology.[69-71]

Conclusion

Current investigations in cervical cancer and its precursor lesions are focused not only on new and bettre screening and diagnostic tests but also on preventive strategies. Chemopreventive trials are underway, as are HPV vaccine trials; these will provide interesting information to guide future treatment of this disease.

REFERENCES

1. Greenlee RT, Hill-Harmon MB, Murray T, Thun M. Cancer statistics, 2001. CA Cancer J Clin 2001; 51:15-36.
2. National Cancer Institute. SEER Stat and SEER 1973-1998 Public-Use Data. NCI [online] 2001. http://seer.cancer.gov/ScientificSystems/SEERStat/ (accessed Jul 17, 2001).
3. Taussig FJ. Leukoplakia and cancer of the vulva. Arch Dermatol Syph 1948;57:431-45.
4. Jeffcoate TNA. Chronic vulval dystrophies. Am J Obstet Gynecol 1966;95:61-74.
5. Wallace HJ. Lichen sclerosus et atrophicus. Trans St. John's Hosp Dermatol Soc 1971;57:9-30.
6. McAdams AJ Jr, Kistner RW. The relationship of chronic vulvar disease, leukoplakia, and carcinoma in situ to carcinoma of the vulva. Cancer 1956;II:740-57.
7. Franklin EW, Rutledge FD. Epidemiology of epidermoid carcinoma of the vulva. Obstet Gynecol 1972; 39:165-72.
8. Japaze H, Garcia-Bunuel R, Woodruff JD. Primary vulvar neoplasia. Obstet Gynecol 1977;49:404-11.
9. Brinton LA, Nasca PC, Mallin K, et al. Case-control study of cancer of the vulva. Obstet Gynecol 1990; 75:859-66.
10. Ikenberg H, Gissman L, Gross G, Grussendorf-Conen EI. Human papillomavirus type-16-related DNA in genital Bowen's disease and bowenoid papulosis. Int J Cancer 1983;32:563-5.
11. Trimble CL, Hildesheim A, Brinton LA, et al. Heterogeneous etiology of squamous carcinoma of the vulvar. Obstet Gynecol 1996;87:59-64.
12. Monk BJ, Burger A, Lin F, et al. Prognostic significance of human papillomavirus DNA in vulvar carcinoma. Obstet Gynecol 1995;85:709-15.
13. Iwasawa A, Nieminen P, Lehtinen M, Paavonen J. Human papillomavirus in squamous cell carcinoma of the vulva by polymerase chain reaction. Obstet Gynecol 1997;89:81-4.
14. Carson LF, Twiggs LB, Okagaki T, et al. Human papillomavirus DNA in adenosquamous carcinoma and squamous cell carcinoma of the vulva. Obstet Gynecol 1988;72:63-7.
15. Ansink AC, Heintz APM. Epidemiology and etiology of squamous cell carcinoma of the vulva. Eur J Obstet Gynecol Reprod Biol 1993;48:111-5.
16. Neill SM. Lichen sclerosus, invasive squamous cell carcinoma, and human papillomavirus. Am J Obstet Gynecol 1990;162:1633-4.
17. Hay DM, Cole FM. Primary invasive carcinoma of the vulva in Jamaica. J Obstet Gynaecol Br Comm 1969;76:821-30.
18. Sengupta BS. Carcinoma of the vulva in Jamaican women. Acta Obstet Gynecol Scand 1981;60:537-44.
19. Mabuchi K, Bross DS, Kessler II. Epidemiology of cancer of the vulva: a case-control study. Cancer 1985;55:1843-8.
20. Newcomb PA, Weiss NS, Daling JR. Incidence of vulvar carcinoma of relation to menstrual, reproductive, and medical factors. J Natl Cancer Inst 1984;73:391-6.
21. Crum CP. Carcinoma of the vulva: epidemiology and pathogenesis. Obstet Gynecol 1992;79:448-54.
22. Choo YC. Invasive squamous carcinoma of the vulvar in young patients. Gynecol Oncol 1982;13:158-64.
23. Roman LD, Mitchell MF, Burke TW, Silva EG. Case report: unsuspected invasive squamous cell carcinoma of the vulva in young women. Gynecol Oncol 1991;41:182-5.
24. Carter J, Carlson J, Fowler J, et al. Invasive vulvar tumors in young women: a disease of the immunosuppressed? Gynecol Oncol 1993;51:307-10.
25. Messing MJ, Gallup DG. Carcinoma of the vulva in young women. Obstet Gynecol 1995;86:51-4.
26. Parkin DM, Whelan SL, Ferlay J, Young RL, editors. Cancer incidence in five continents. Vol VII. Lyon, France: IARC Scientific Publication; 1997. p. 686-9.
27. Rutledge F. Cancer of the vagina. Am J Obstet Gynecol 1967;97:635.
28. Way SJ. Carcinoma of the vagina. J Obstet Gynecol Br Emp 1948;55:739.
29. Herbst AL, Green TH, Ulfelder H. Primary carcinoma of the vagina. Am J Obstet Gynecol 1970;106:210-8.
30. Gallup DG, Talledo OE, Shah KJ, Hayes C. Invasive squamous cell carcinoma of the vagina: a 14-year study. Obstet Gynecol 1987;69:782-5.
31. Manetta A, Pinto JL, Larson JE, et al. Primary invasive carcinoma of the vagina. Obstet Gynecol 1988; 72:77-81.
32. Aho M, Vesterinen E, Meyer B, et al. Natural history of vaginal intraepithelial neoplasia. Cancer 1991;68: 195-7.
33. Herbst AL, Ulfelder H, Poskanzer DC. Adenocarcinoma of the vagina: association of maternal stilbestrol therapy with tumor appearance in young women. N Engl J Med 1971;284:878.
34. Herbst AL, Anderson S, Hubby MM, et al. Risk factors for the development of diethylstilbestrol-associated clear cell adenocarcinoma: a case-control study. Am J Obstet Gynecol 1986;154:814.
35. Herbst AL, Kurman RJ, Scully RE, Poskanzer DC. Clear cell adenocarcinoma of the genital tract in young females: registry report. N Engl J Med 1972;187:1259.

36. Herbst AL, Cole P, Norusis MJ, et al. Epidemiologic aspects of factors related to survival in 384 registry cases of clear cell adenocarcinoma of the vagina and cervix. Am J Obstet Gynecol 1979;135:876.
37. Landis SH, Murray T, Bilden S, Wingo PA. Cancer statistics 1998. Cancer 1998;48:6–29.
38. Pisani R, Parkin DM, Ferlay J. Estimates of the worldwide mortality from eighteen major cancers in 1985. Implications for prevention and projection of future burden. Int J Cancer 1993;55:891–903.
39. Herrero R, Brinton LA, Hartge P, et al. Determinants of the geographic variation of invasive cervical cancer in Costa Rica. Bull Pan Am Health Organ 1993;27:15–25.
40. Herrero R, Brinton LA, Reeves WC, et al. Sexual behavior, venereal diseases, hygiene practices, and invasive cervical cancer in a high-risk population. Cancer 1990;65:380–6.
41. Clarke EA, Morgan RW, Newman AM. Smoking as a risk factor in cancer of the cervix: additional evidence from a case-control study. Am J Epidemiol 1982;115:59–66.
42. Brinton LA, Hamman RF, Huggins GR, et al. Sexual and reproductive risk factors for invasive cervical cancer. J Natl Cancer Inst 1987;79:23–30.
43. Palefski JM, Holly EA. Molecular virology and epidemiology of human papillomavirus and cervical cancer. Cancer Epidemiol Biomarkers Prev 1995;4:415–28.
44. National Institutes of Health. Cervical cancer. NIH Consens Statement 1996;14:1–38.
45. zur Hausen H, Meinhof W, Scheiber W, Bornkamm GW. Attempts to detect virus-specific DNA in human tumors: I. Nuclear acid hybridizations with completmentary RNA of human wart virus. Int J Cancer 1974;13:650–6.
46. Schoell WMJ, Janicek MF, Mirhashemi R. Epidemiology and biology of cervical cancer. Semin Surg Oncol 1999;16:203–11.
47. Richart RM. A modified terminology for cervical intrapeithelial neoplasia. Obstet Gynecol 1990;75:131–2.
48. Remmink AJ, Walboomers JM, Helmerhorst TJ, et al. The presence of persistent high-risk HPV genotypes in dysplastic cervical lesions is associated with progressive disease: natural history up to 36 months. Int J Cancer 1995;61:306–11.
49. Liu T, Soong SJ, Alvarez RD, Butterworth CE Jr. A longitudinal analysis of human papillomavirus 16 infection, nutritional status, and cervical dysplasia progression. Cancer Epidemiol Biomarkers Prev 1995;4:373–80.
50. Wilczynski SP, Bergen S, Walker J, et al. Human papillomaviruses and cervical cancer: analysis of histopathologic features associated with different viral types. Hum Pathol 1988;19:697–704.
51. Matsukura M, Sugase M. Identification of genital human papillomaviruses in cervical biopsy specimens: segregation of specific virus types in specific clinicopathological lesions. Int J Cancer 1995;61:13–22.
52. Bosch FX, Manos MM, Munoz N, et al. Prevalence of human papillomavirus in cervical cancer: a world-wide perspective. International Biological Study of Cervical Cancer (IBSCC) Study Group. J Natl Cancer Inst 1995;87:796–802.
53. Nasiell K, Roger V, Nasiell M. Behavior of mild cervical dysplasia during long-term follow-up. Obstet Gynecol 1986;67:667–9.
54. Brewer CA, Wilczynski SP, Kurosaki T, et al. Colposcopic regression patterns in high-grade cervical intraepithelial neoplasia. Obstet Gynecol 1997;90:617–21.
55. McIndoe WA, McLean MR, Jones RW, Mullins PR. The invasive potential of carcinoma in situ of the cervix. Obstet Gynecol 1984;64:451–8.
56. Kolstad P, Klem V. Long-term followup of 1121 cases of carcinoma in situ. Obstet Gynecol 1976;48:125–9.
57. Richart RM, Barron BA. A follow-up study of patients with cervical dysplasia. Am J Obstet Gynecol 1969;105:386–93.
58. Benedet JL, Miller DM, Nickerson KG. Results of conservative management of cervical intraepithelial neoplasia. Obstet Gynecol 1992;79:105–10.
59. The 1988 Bethesda system for reporting cervical/vaginal cytologic diagnoses. NCI Workshop, December, 1988. J Reprod Med 1989;34:779–85.
60. Papillo JL, Zarka MA, St John TL. Evaluation of the ThinPrep Pap test in clinical practice. A seven-month, 16,314-case experiment in northern Vermont. Acta Cytol 1998;42:203–8.
61. Manos MM, Kinney WK, Hurley LB, et al. Identifying women with cervical neoplasia: using human papillomavirus DNA testing for equivocal Papanicolaou results. JAMA 1999;281:1605–10.
62. Korn AP, Autry M, DeRemer PA, Tan W. Sensitivity of the Papanicolaou smear in human immunodeficiency virus-infected women. 1994;83:401–4.
63. Adachi A, Fleming I, Burk RD, et al. Women with human immunodeficiency virus infection and abnormal Papanicolaou smears: a prospective study of colposcopy and clinical outcome. Obstet Gynecol 1993;81:372–7.
64. Eluf-Neto J, Booth M, Munoz N, et al. Human papillomavirus and invasive cervical cancer in Brazil. Br J Cancer 1994;69:114–9.
65. Bosch FX, Munoz N, de Sanjose S, et al. Risk factors for cervical cancer in Columbia and Spain. Int J Cancer 1992;52:750–8.
66. Persson I. Cancer risk in women receiving estrogen-progestin replacement therapy. Maturitas 1996;23 Suppl:S37–45.
67. Boffetta P, Parkin DM. Cancer in developing countries. Cancer 1994;44:81–90.
68. Hopkins MP, Morley GW. A comparison of adenocarcinoma and squamous cell carcinoma of the cervix. Obstet Gynecol 1991;77:912–7.
69. Herrero R. Epidemiology of cervical cancer. Monogr Natl Cancer Inst 1996;21:1–6.
70. Brinton LA, Reeves WC, Brenes MM, et al. Oral contraceptive use and risk of invasive cervical cancer. Int J Epidemiol 1990;19:4–11.
71. Ursin G, Peters RK, Henderson BE, et al. Oral contraceptive use and adenocarcinoma of cervix. Lancet 1994;344:1390–4.

2

Pathology

EVANTHIA KOSTOPOULOU, MD, DSC
JEFFREY T. KEATING, MD
CHRISTOPHER P. CRUM, MD

NEOPLASMS OF THE CERVIX

Anatomy

The uterus has three distinctive anatomic and functional regions: the cervix, the lower uterine segment, and the corpus. The cervix is further divided into the vaginal portio and the endocervix. The portio is visible to the eye on examination and is covered by a stratified nonkeratinizing squamous epithelium continuous with the vaginal vault. The squamous epithelium converges centrally. Just cephalad to the os is the endocervix, which is lined by columnar mucous-secreting epithelium that dips down into the underlying stroma to produce crypts (endocervical glands). The point at which the squamous and glandular epithelia meet is the squamocolumnar junction. The position of the junction is variable. Although its original position is at the cervical os, the endocervix is everted in virtually all adult women who have borne children, exposing the squamocolumnar junction to the naked eye. A combination of squamous maturation in the immature epithelium just proximal to the squamocolumnar junction and intrinsic squamous differentiation of subcolumnar reserve cells transforms this area into squamous epithelium and produces the *transformation zone* (Figures 2–1 and 2–2). During reproductive life, the squamocolumnar junction migrates cephalad on the leading edge of the transformation zone and may be invisible to the naked eye after menopause. It is in this transformation zone, including the squamocolumnar junction, where squamous cell carcinomas or precancerous lesions develop.[1] Glandular lesions have their origins here as well, implying that the interface of the squamous and columnar epithelia gives rise to stem cells capable of several (squamous, adenosquamous, adenoendocrine, neuroendocrine) lines of differentiation following infection by papillomaviruses.

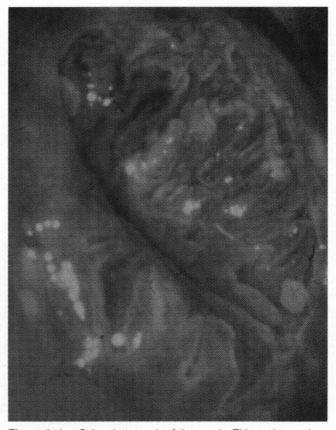

Figure 2–1. Colpophotograph of the cervix. This region evolves continually during reproductive life, and overgrowth of the columnar epithelium by squamous mucosa defines the "transformation zone." (H&E stain; ×40 original magnification) (Courtesy of Alex Ferenczy, MD.)

Benign Lesions of the Cervix

Endocervical Polyps

Endocervical polyps are relatively innocuous inflammatory tumors that occur in 2 to 5 percent of adult women. Perhaps the major significance of polyps lies in their production of irregular vaginal "spotting" or bleeding that arouses suspicion of more ominous lesions. Most polyps arise within the endocervical canal and vary from small and sessile to large 5-cm masses that may protrude through the cervical os. All are soft, almost mucoid, and are composed of a loose fibromyxomatous stroma harboring dilated, mucous-secreting endocervical glands and often accompanied by inflammation and squamous metaplasia. In almost all instances, simple curettage or surgical excision effects a cure.

Squamous Neoplasia

Fifty years ago, carcinoma of the cervix was the leading cause of cancer deaths in women in the United States, but the death rate has dropped remarkably to its present rank as the thirteenth source of cancer mortality, causing about 4,400 deaths annually. This reduced mortality is due, in part, to the high detection frequency of early cancers and precancerous conditions. Annually, there are an estimated 12,900 cases of new invasive cancers and 50,000 cases of advanced precancerous conditions.[2] Thus, well over

half of invasive cancers are cured by early detection and effective therapy, and many more precancerous lesions placing the patients at variable risk for subsequent cancer are eradicated by timely, appropriate treatment. Much credit for these dramatic gains belongs to the effectiveness of the Papanicolaou cytologic test (Pap smear test).

Epidemiologic data implicate a sexually transmitted agent, specifically on the basis of the risk factors for cervical cancer, which include (1) early age at first intercourse, (2) multiple sexual partners, and (3) a male partner with multiple previous sexual partners. Potential risk factors that remain poorly understood include oral contraceptive use, cigarette smoking, parity, family history, associated genital infections, and lack of circumcision in the male sexual partner.[3,4]

Evidence linking human papillomavirus (HPV) to cancer includes (1) HPV deoxyribonucleic acid (DNA) detected in approximately 90 percent of cervical cancers and precancerous lesions;[5] (2) specific HPV types being associated with cervical cancer (high risk) versus condylomata (low risk); low-risk types include types 6, 11, 42, and 44 and high-risk types 16, 18, 31, and 33;[6] (3) in vitro studies indicating that the high-risk HPV types have the capability to transform cells in culture, linked to specific viral oncogenes (E6 and E7 genes), which differ in sequence between the high-risk and low-risk HPV types; (4) the differing physical state of the virus in cancers, being covalently linked (integrated) with

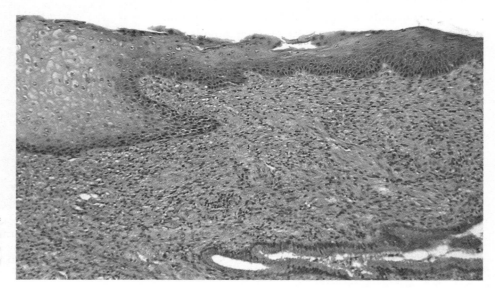

Figure 2–2. A photomicrograph of the cervical squamocolumnar junction illustrates the squamous mucosa in the transformation zone overlying glands (*bottom*).

the host genomic DNA, in contrast to free (episomal) viral DNA in condylomata and most precancerous lesions;[7] and (5) the E6 oncoprotein of HPV-16 and -18 (but not low-risk type 11) binds to the tumor suppressor gene *P53* and accelerates its proteolytic degradation.[7]

Because only a small percentage of women develop cervical cancer, other factors, including the immune and nutritional status of the individual and the status of the transformation zone, may influence who is vulnerable to HPV infections and who is more likely to develop a precancer capable of progressing to cancer.

Preinvasive Squamous Lesions (Cervical Intraepithelial Neoplasia)

The reason that Pap smear screening is so effective in preventing cervical cancer is that the majority of cancers are preceded by a precancerous lesion. This lesion may exist in the noninvasive stage for as long as 20 years and shed abnormal cells that can be detected on cytologic examination.[8] These precancerous changes should be viewed with the following in mind: (1) they represent a continuum of morphologic changes with relatively indistinct boundaries; (2) they will not invariably progress to cancer and may spontaneously regress, with the risk of persisting or progressing to cancer increasing with the severity of the precancerous change; and (3) they are associated with papillomaviruses, and "high-risk" HPV types are found in increasing frequency in the higher-grade precursors.[9]

Cervical precancers have been classified in a variety of ways. The oldest system is the dysplasia-carcinoma in situ system with mild dysplasia on one end and severe dysplasia/carcinoma in situ on the other. Another is the cervical intraepithelial neoplasia (CIN) classification, with mild dysplasias termed CIN grade 1 and carcinoma in situ lesions termed CIN3.[1] The Bethesda System for Reporting Cervical/Vaginal Cytologic Diagnoses categorizes squamous abnormalities as low-grade squamous intraepithelial lesion (LSIL), encompassing CIN1; high-grade squamous intraepithelial lesion (HSIL), encompassing CIN2 and CIN3; and squamous cell carcinoma.[10] An additional category, atypical squamous cells of undetermined significance (ASCUS), encompasses cellular abnormalities that qualitatively or quantitatively fall short of a definitive diagnosis of SIL.[10] In this chapter, they are referred to using a modification of the CIN terminology.[1,11]

Figure 2–3 depicts the spectrum of morphologic changes associated with cervical papillomavirus infection. At the low end are lesions that are indistinguishable histologically from condyloma acuminatum and may be either raised (acuminatum) or macular (flat condyloma) in appearance. These lesions may be multiple and often exhibit koilocytotic atypia (viral cytopathic effect), with few alterations in the other cells in the epithelium and fall within the range of CIN1 (see Figures 2–3A and B). These changes correlate strongly, but not invariably, with low- or intermediate-risk HPV. The next point in the spectrum consists of alterations in the replicating cell compartment (basal/parabasal cells), presumably signifying immortalization of these cells by high-risk HPV types (see Figure 2–3C). The atypical cells show changes in nucleocytoplasmic ratio; variation in nuclear size (anisokaryosis); loss of polarity; increased mitotic figures, including abnormal mitoses; and hyperchromasia. In other words, they take on some of the characteristics of malignant cells but still tend to manifest surface maturation. These lesions fall within the range of CIN2. These features have been associated with aneuploid cell populations and correlate strongly with high-risk HPV types, probably reflecting early changes associated with the viral oncogenes of these viruses. As the spectrum evolves, there is progressive loss of differentiation, with involvement of more and more layers of the epithelium, until it is totally replaced by immature atypical cells, exhibiting no surface differentiation (CIN3) (see Figure 2–3D). The cellular changes on Pap smear that correspond to this histologic spectrum are illustrated in Figure 2–4.

CIN almost always begins at the squamocolumnar junction in the transformation zone. The lowest-grade CIN lesions, including condylomata, most likely do not progress, whereas lesions containing greater degrees of cellular atypia are at greater risk. Roughly one-third and two-thirds of CIN1 and CIN2 lesions, respectively, persist or progress to high grade. It is important to realize that not all lesions begin as condylomata or as CIN1, and that they may enter at any point in the spectrum, depending on the associated HPV type and other host factors. The rates of progression are by no means uniform, and although HPV type is a potential predictor of lesion

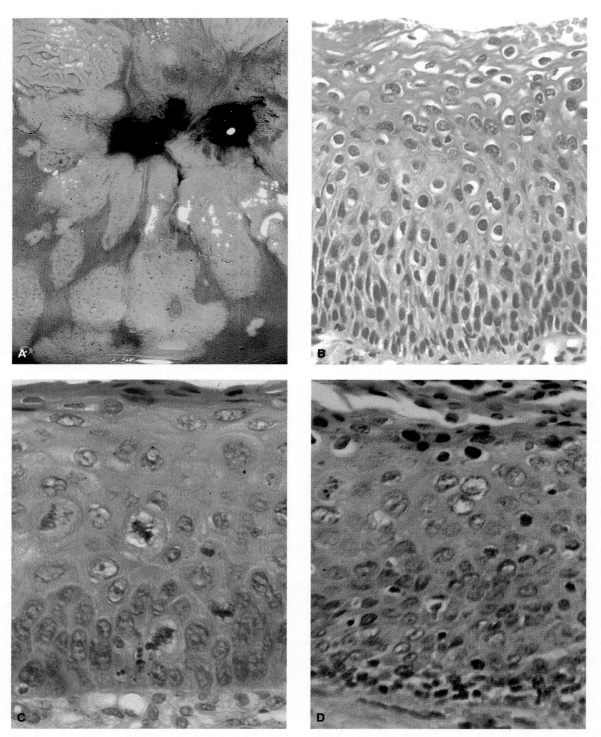

Figure 2–3. Cervical intraepithelial neoplasia. *A,* Colpophotograph illustrating a low-grade CIN in the transformation zone. Examples of CIN1, CIN2, and CIN3 are depicted in *B* to *D*, respectively (H&E stain; ×400 original magnification). (Courtesy of Richard Levine, MD.)

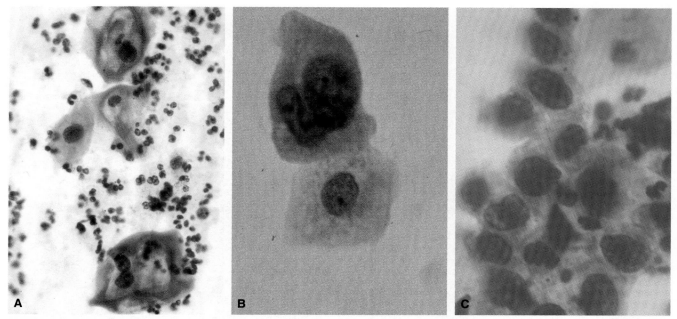

Figure 2–4. Cytologic changes associated with CIN, including *A*, CIN1 (×600 original magnification); *B*, CIN2 (×1000 original magnification); and *C*, CIN3 (×1000 original magnification). (H&E stain)

behavior, it is difficult to predict the outcome in an individual patient. These findings underscore that risk of cancer is conferred only in part by HPV type and depends not only on other carcinogens or genetic alterations that bring about the evolution of a precancer but also the cell types targeted for infection. Predictably, lesions that have completely evolved (CIN3) constitute the greatest risk. CIN3 is most frequently associated with invasive cancer when the latter is identified. Progression to invasive carcinoma, when it occurs, may develop in a few months to over 20 years.[12]

Microinvasive Carcinoma

Approximately 4 to 7 percent of CIN lesions have been associated with superficial invasion,[13,14] and a subset of invasive squamous cell carcinoma of the cervix is termed "microinvasive carcinoma" on the assumption that a portion of early invasive cancers can be treated conservatively by cone biopsy or simple hysterectomy. Tumors exceeding the criteria for microinvasion are managed with radical hysterectomy and pelvic lymph node dissection or radiation therapy. In recent years, the proportion of invasive cervical carcinoma, which invaded < 5 mm in depth

at diagnosis, has increased over 10-fold and currently is approximately 21 percent.[15,16]

For the pathologist, specific concerns must be addressed when determining if a cervical squamous cell carcinoma warrants designation as microinvasive. They include (1) identifying invasion, (2) distinguishing it from noninvasive mimics, (3) applying correctly the criteria for microinvasion, and (4) advising the gynecologist regarding management. It should be emphasized that the diagnosis of microinvasion can only be made on a specimen containing the entire lesion. The specimen must have uninvolved margins, and the pathologist must examine a sufficient number of sections, usually one for every 2 mm of cone thickness.

The criteria for microinvasive squamous cell carcinoma include the following: (1) a *desmoplastic response* in the adjacent stroma, (2) focal conspicuous *maturation* of the neoplastic epithelium with prominent nucleoli, (3) *blurring* of the epithelial stromal interface, and (4) *loss of polarity* of the nuclei at the epithelial stromal border, with absence of the pallisaded pattern characteristic of CIN (Figure 2–5). Three additional features include *scalloping* of the margins at the epithelial-stromal interface, the apparent *folding or duplication* of the neoplastic

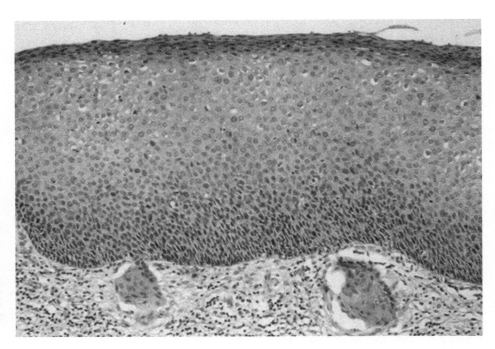

Figure 2–5. Microinvasive carcinoma of the cervix. This diagnosis requires invasion of < 3 mm and no evidence of capillary-lymphatic space invasion. (H&E stain; ×100 original magnification)

epithelium, and, less commonly, the appearance of *pseudoglands*. Scalloping refers to fine irregularities, which are not typically seen with gland (crypt) involvement or tangential sectioning through gland involvement. Duplication of epithelium refers to the presence of vascular structures within a sheet of neoplastic epithelial cells, producing an image of incompletely formed papillae. These features aid in recognizing invasion in the presence of an intense inflammatory response, which may obscure desmoplasia on the one hand and blur the epithelial-stromal interface on the other. Pseudoglands are defined as discrete circumscribed nests of invasive carcinoma, usually with central necrosis, that may mimic crypt involvement. In contrast to crypts, this form of invasive carcinoma does not exhibit glandular epithelium, is often composed of multiple circumscribed nests, often contains central necrosis, and may display a loss of polarity.[11]

Cone biopsy is necessary if (1) the lesion does not appear grossly invasive, clinically or colposcopically, and (2) if it is not clearly deeper than 3 mm in the original biopsy or does not exhibit capillary-lymphatic space invasion. Once the cone biopsy is performed, the measurement of depth of invasion should be made from the most superficial epithelial-stromal interface of the adjacent intraepithelial process. This is best accomplished using an ocular micrometer or a method of measurement that makes it possible to identify with certainty if the lesion has invaded to a depth of > 3 mm.

Three issues of potential concern when considering microinvasion are tumor depth, confluence of growth pattern, and capillary-lymphatic space invasion. Microinvasion has been defined variably depending on whether the definition was recommended by the International Federation of Gynecology and Obstetrics (FIGO) (5 mm) or the Society of Gynecologic Oncology (3 mm).[17,18] Depth of invasion and capillary lymphatic space invasion remain the most intensively studied parameters. The risk of pelvic lymph node metastases increases at between 1 and 5 mm and is estimated to be as high as 4.3 percent for lesions invading between 3.1 and 5.0 mm.[19,20] In a recent review by Ostor, the risk of lymph node metastases increased only slightly (from < 1 to 2%) as tumor depth increased from 1 to 5 mm.[21] On the basis of this estimate, Ostor questioned the premise that microinvasive carcinoma be defined by a 3 mm cut-off. However, a diagnosis of microinvasion (as defined by the therapeutic alternative of simple hysterectomy) in the United States requires that the carcinoma invade < 3 mm into the stroma, on the basis of recommendations of the Society of Gynecologic Oncology.[14]

Both confluent growth patterns and capillary-lymphatic space invasion correlate with depth of invasion,[18,20] but their independent value is less clear. Confluence has been defined as anastomosing tongues of epithelium with pushing borders, or a lesion front of > 1 mm.[14] Despite a report emphasizing the prognostic importance of confluent patterns of invasion, others have not found that confluence is an independent factor once the depth of invasion is controlled for.[19] In his review, Ostor noted an adverse outcome in < 3 percent of cases with this feature.[21]

The frequency of capillary-lymphatic space invasion (CLSI) has varied widely (Figure 2–6). van Nagell reported it in 33 of 177 cases (19%).[22] In a detailed study of 91 cases of microinvasive carcinoma, Oster reported CLSI in 22 (23%) on the basis of *Ulex europaeus* agglutinin I (UEAI) stains.[23]

These figures contrast with a high of 57 percent reported by Roche and Norris.[24] Its significance remains controversial. CLSI increases in frequency as a function of lesion depth, which increases the risk of lymph node metastases.[17,18,21] Whether CLSI is a critical prognostic factor in lesions of 3 mm in depth or less is unclear.[22] There are three components of this issue. The first is that the interpretation of CLSI is subjective. Inflammation and retraction artifacts may produce confusion in the interpretation of CLSI, and special stains for vascular endothelium may or may not be helpful. Displacement of neoplastic epithelium into vascular spaces during injection of anesthetic or biopsy may also mimic invasion.[25] Roche and Norris recommended that CLSI not be a parameter for determining therapy due to problems in its interpretation and significance.[24] In

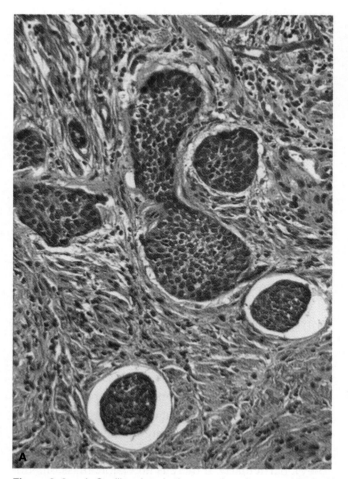
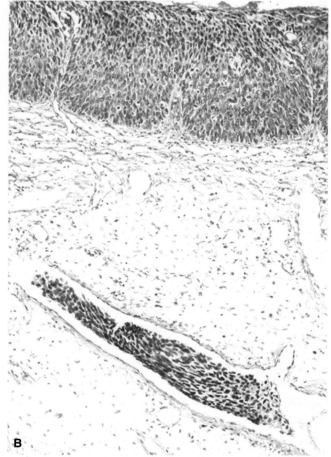

Figure 2–6. *A,* Capillary-lymphatic space invasion associated with a squamous carcinoma (×400 original magnification). *B,* Occasionally, biopsy or needle (anesthetic) artifact may introduce noninvasive (CIN) epithelium into vascular spaces, mimicking vascular invasion (×100 original magnification). (H&E stain) (Courtesy of David Genest, MD.)

fact, they recommended referring to this change as *capillary-like* space involvement. This may more accurately convey the uncertainty of the diagnosis; however, in our experience, the clinical response to this diagnosis is the same, irrespective of qualifiers. Hence, we either use the term "capillary-lymphatic space invasion" or issue a descriptive report if the diagnosis cannot be made with certainty. The second point is that the frequency of lymph node metastases with lesions < 3 mm and accompanied by CLSI has generally not been shown to be significantly greater than those lesions without vascular invasion. van Nagell and colleagues found that none of 17 patients with CLSI and invasion < 3 mm had lymph node metastases.[22] In a review of cases with < 5 mm of invasion, Roche and Norris also noted no relationship between CLSI and lymph node metastasis.[24]

In his recent review, Ostor noted that 6 of 12 (50%) tumors with lymph node metastases were associated with CLSI. Nevertheless, 192 of 1,036 (18%) cases with negative lymph nodes had CLSI. Similarly, 18 of 36 (50%) of invasive recurrences were associated with CLSI in the original tumor in contrast to 496 of 3,597 (14%) patients with no recurrence.[21] CLSI has been associated with an adverse prognosis in carcinomas exceeding 3 mm in depth in most,[20,22,26,27] if not all, reports. The implication from these multiple studies is that although CLSI is associated with cases having an adverse outcome, the vast majority of cases with CLSI do not present with histologically positive lymph nodes.

Many assumptions about managing CLSI are based on its relationship to histologically proven lymph node metastases. However, the third and infrequently discussed issue is that *there are no large studies following a series of microinvasive (< 3 mm) carcinomas with CLSI without lymphadenectomy.* This is not trivial, as it is conceivable that the removal of lymph nodes, even ostensibly negative ones, may influence prognosis. The 5-year survival of cases with pelvic lymph node involvement is approximately 50 percent, irrespective of the mode of management once the metastases are diagnosed.[28] This suggests that lymph node dissection may be therapeutic not only by removing microscopically visible metastases but, in some cases, by removing micrometastases not identified on pathologic exami-

nation as well. The degree to which such micrometastases are detected may depend heavily on the exactness with which the lymph nodes are processed.[29] If removal of even negative-appearing lymph nodes were to improve survival, the actual risk of metastatic disease in microinvasive lesions exhibiting CLSI cannot be determined without placing the patient at risk by deferring lymphadenectomy. Kolstad reported a frequency of CLSI at 13 percent for lesions < 3 mm. In that study, none of 50 cases of microinvasive (< 5 mm) carcinoma and CLSI treated by radical hysterectomy and lymph node dissection recurred. However, 4 of 8 treated by simple hysterectomy died of their disease, including those with lesions originally 2, 4, and 5 mm in depth.[30] These figures imply an increased risk of recurrence in patients who do not undergo lymphadenectomy but are not sufficient for determining the risk in women with lesions < 3 mm in depth. Moreover, it is not clear whether the increased risk conferred by CLSI can be reduced by lymphadenectomy. For example, one study found a relationship between CLSI and extrapelvic recurrences, while another found that a worse prognosis associated with CLSI was not influenced by lymph node dissection.[20,26]

Presently, the nomenclature committee of the Society of Gynecologic Oncology has not accepted the diagnosis of microinvasion if CLSI is present.[18] In standard practice, most oncologists will request that the presence of CLSI be reported, and they will usually opt for radical hysterectomy and pelvic lymphadenectomy if it is seen in a lesion < 3 mm in depth. For these reasons, over- and underinterpretation of CLSI must be avoided, as has been discussed above.

In our practice, we do not use the term "microinvasive carcinoma," opting to report such tumors as "superficially invasive squamous cell carcinomas." As summarized above, the criteria for "microinvasion" may vary slightly, and management may depend on multiple factors. When reviewing the biopsy, we report the largest dimensions of the lesion to aid the clinician in deciding the next step in management (ie, cone biopsy versus radical hysterectomy), particularly, if there is no visible mass on clinical examination. In cone biopsies, the following should be reported: (1) depth, (2) length of the entire lesion, (3) whether length span constitutes continuous tumor or is composed of multiple small foci, (4) the presence or absence of CLSI, (5) endocervical, ectocervical, and deep margins and distance (in mm) from invasive tumor to these margins, (6) intraepithelial disease and its relationship to the margins, and (7) clear-cut glandular differentiation, if present. The latter will generally preclude management of the lesion as microinvasive, if there is clear evidence of invasive adenocarcinoma.

Squamous Cell Carcinoma

Squamous cell carcinoma may occur at any age from the second decade of life to senility. The peak incidence is occurring at an increasingly younger age: 40 to 45 years for invasive cancer and about 30 years for high-grade precancers. This represents the combination of earlier onset of sexual activity (ie, earlier acquisition of HPV infection) and active Pap smear screening programs in the United States, which detect either cancers or precancerous lesions at an earlier point in life.

Histologically, about 95 percent of squamous cell carcinomas are composed of relatively *large cells*, either *keratinizing* (well-differentiated) or *nonkeratinizing* (moderately differentiated) patterns. A small subset (< 5%) are poorly differentiated small cell squamous carcinomas (Figure 2–7).[31]

With current methods of treatment, there is a 5-year survival rate of about 80 to 90 percent with stage I, 75 percent with stage II, 35 percent with stage III, and 10 to 15 percent with stage IV disease. Most patients with stage IV cancer die as a consequence of local extension of the tumor (eg, into and about the urinary bladder and ureters, leading to ureteral obstruction, pyelonephritis, and uremia) rather than of distant metastases.[32]

Variants of Squamous Carcinoma

Verrucous Carcinoma

These are very rare lesions.[33] The criteria for diagnosis are the same as in the vulva, and the diagnosis is one of exclusion. Verrucous carcinoma usually presents as a large sessile lesion resembling a condy-loma. Histologically, it consists of a lesion with both exophytic and endophytic growth patterns, lacking the more delicate architecture of condylomata and demonstrating columns of well-differentiated epithelium expanding the underlying stroma in lieu of crypt involvement. The pattern of invasion is blunt, with minimal nuclear atypia at the epithelial-stromal interface. An intense inflammatory infiltrate has been associated with verrucous carcinoma of the cervix but is, in itself, nonspecific. The differential diagnosis includes large exophytic condylomata with crypt involvement and well-differentiated squamous cell carcinoma. The latter usually exhibits finger-like or angulated invasive epithelial tongues. The presence of filiform papillary projections or marked nuclear atypia at the epithelial-stromal interface rules out verrucous carcinoma. Given the extreme rarity of this lesion, the diagnosis of verrucous carcinoma must be made with caution. Because verrucous carcinomas present grossly as large, sessile, wart-like growths, the diagnosis may be difficult without multiple biopsies or hysterectomy. Local excision is not usually possible, and extension into the adjacent pelvic tissues may occur. Very few reported cases are available to fully determine metastatic potential. None of 18 reported metastasized to lymph nodes, although the recurrence rates have been as high as 50 percent.[33]

Papillary Neoplasms

Papillary neoplasia of the cervix encompasses a broad spectrum of benign, potentially malignant, and clearly malignant lesions. In the benign category are conventional condylomata and immature variants thereof. The potentially malignant category includes any filiform papillary lesion with a transitional appearance to the epithelium, a high mitotic index, a flat component, or any morphologic features resembling a high-grade intraepithelial lesion (Figure 2–8). Papillary lesions have been described in the cervix, ranging from those resembling transitional cell papillomas to those diagnosed as papillary carcinoma in situ.[34,35] Although the former are not invariably associated with invasive cancer, a number of filiform cervical papillomas have been observed, in which deeper sampling disclosed invasive cancer. For this reason, any diagnosis of "transitional papilloma" should be made carefully and should be based on full excision of the lesion to rule out invasion. Papillary lesions containing marked squamous atypia (carcinoma in situ) may be associated with invasion and probably should be considered invasive until proven otherwise. The differential diagnosis, as with verrucous carcinoma, includes condylomata, although the latter usually do not exhibit delicate finger-like pro-

liferations. An occasional diagnostic problem is the presence of papillary immature metaplasia (immature condyloma), either overlying endocervical papillae or in association with condylomata.[36] In this case, the diagnosis of papillary neoplasia can be excluded by the bland nuclear appearance, very low mitotic index, and presence of endocervical columnar cells in the lesion more closely associated with metaplastic epithelium than a papillary neoplasm. Neverthe-

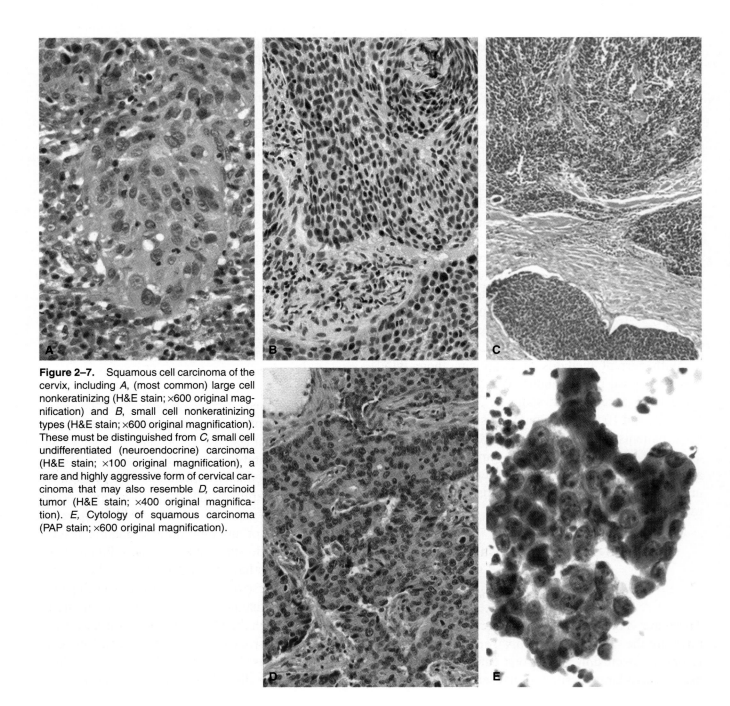

Figure 2–7. Squamous cell carcinoma of the cervix, including A, (most common) large cell nonkeratinizing (H&E stain; ×600 original magnification) and B, small cell nonkeratinizing types (H&E stain; ×600 original magnification). These must be distinguished from C, small cell undifferentiated (neuroendocrine) carcinoma (H&E stain; ×100 original magnification), a rare and highly aggressive form of cervical carcinoma that may also resemble D, carcinoid tumor (H&E stain; ×400 original magnification). E, Cytology of squamous carcinoma (PAP stain; ×600 original magnification).

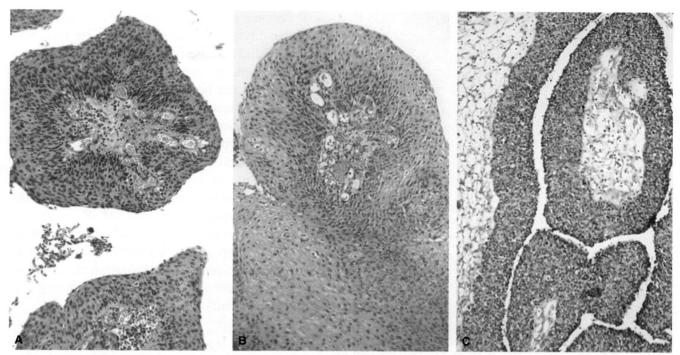

Figure 2–8. *A,* Papillary variant of squamous carcinoma. *B,* This may occasionally be confused with immature variants of condyloma but are usually easily distinguished by the lack of atypia and high mitotic index in the latter. *C,* Undifferentiated papillary carcinomas resembling high-grade transitional carcinoma are occasionally seen in the cervix. (H&E stain; ×200 original magnification)

less, papillary lesions resembling condyloma must be examined carefully, with particular attention to any areas that suggest a high-grade SIL or worse. If such areas exist in any large lesion, additional biopsies should be requested.

Spindle Cell (Sarcomatoid) Squamous Carcinoma

This is a rare form of squamous carcinoma demonstrating a mixture of both squamous and spindle cell features (Figure 2–9). The latter frequently emerges from the former, and while closely resembling a sarcoma, the spindle cell component usually stains positive for cytokeratin. Like all squamous carcinomas of the cervix, these tumors are associated with papillomaviruses.[37]

Glandular Neoplasia

Adenocarcinomas of the cervix comprise from 15 to 25 percent of cervical cancers in the United States. Like squamous carcinomas, papillomaviruses are associated with the common types, and additional risk factors include oral contraceptive use. Adenocar-cinomas are subdivided into two general categories: adenocarcinomas in situ and invasive carcinoma.

Adenocarcinoma in Situ

Adenocarcinoma in situ (ACIS) is a precursor to invasive carcinoma and is defined as an intraepithelial glandular neoplasm. ACIS occurs in women approximately 7 years younger than those with invasive adenocarcinoma (37 to 41 versus 44 to 54 years), often coexists with invasive disease, and is associated with HPV. Typically, ACIS involves the transformation zone and may be associated with a squamous precursor, usually CIN3, in up to 100 percent of cases. The principal morphologic features are crowded glands with stratified, enlarged, hyperchromatic nuclei and, invariably, mitotic activity (Figure 2–10). The distinction between ACIS and non-neoplastic glandular epithelium may at times be difficult, and some authors have coined terms such as "glandular dysplasia" or "glandular atypia" for these lesser changes. However, the relationship between these lesions and ACIS is questionable, due, in part, to imprecise histologic criteria and the

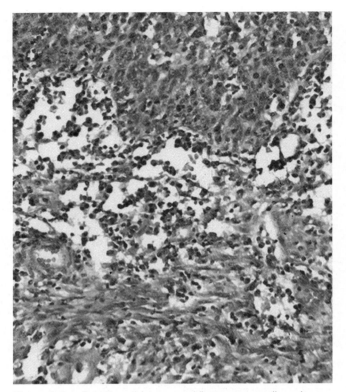

Figure 2–9. Spindle cell (sarcomatoid) squamous cell carcinoma. This variant of squamous cell carcinoma often exhibits a transition from squamous (*upper*) to sarcoma-like (*lower*) differentiation. (H&E stain; ×400 original magnification)

usual absence of HPV nucleic acids. Diagnoses of glandular "dysplasia" should always be met with scepticism and a request for further clarification.

Although the concept of "microinvasive" adenocarcinoma has not been universally accepted, recent studies suggest that lesions with invasion < 5 mm in depth behave similarly to so-called microinvasive squamous carcinomas and may be amenable to conservative therapy.[38] The current standard is to report the presence of any invasion, its depth, and the presence or absence of associated vascular space invasion.

Similar to squamous lesions, ACIS as well as adenocarcinomas may be detected by the Pap smear. However, the Pap smear has been less effective at reducing the incidence of adenocarcinoma, may be less sensitive, and is more prone to sampling and interpretation errors.[39]

Adenocarcinoma

Ten to 25 percent of cervical carcinomas constitute *adenocarcinomas, adenosquamous carcinomas, undifferentiated carcinomas*, or other rare histologic types (Figure 2–11). The adenocarcinomas presumably arise

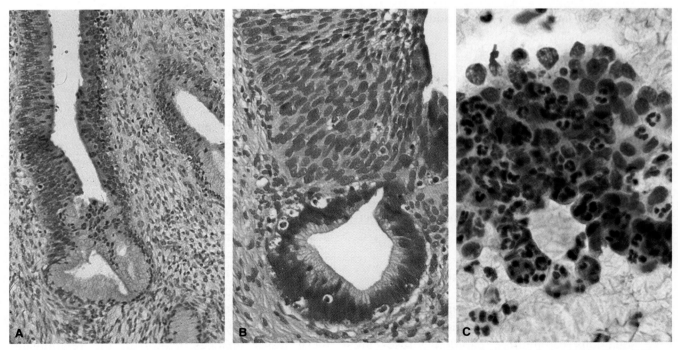

Figure 2–10. *A*, Adenocarcinoma in situ (*upper left*) arising in normal columnar epithelium (*bottom*) (×200 original magnification). *B*, These lesions often coexist with squamous carcinoma (*upper*) (×600 original magnification). *C*, The cytologic features may be difficult to distinguish from benign endocervical and endometrial cells (×600 original magnification). (H&E stain)

in the endocervical glands. They look grossly and behave clinically like the squamous cell lesions and may be associated with papillomaviruses but arise in a slightly older age group.[40] The adenosquamous carcinomas have mixed glandular and squamous patterns and are thought to arise from the reserve cells in the

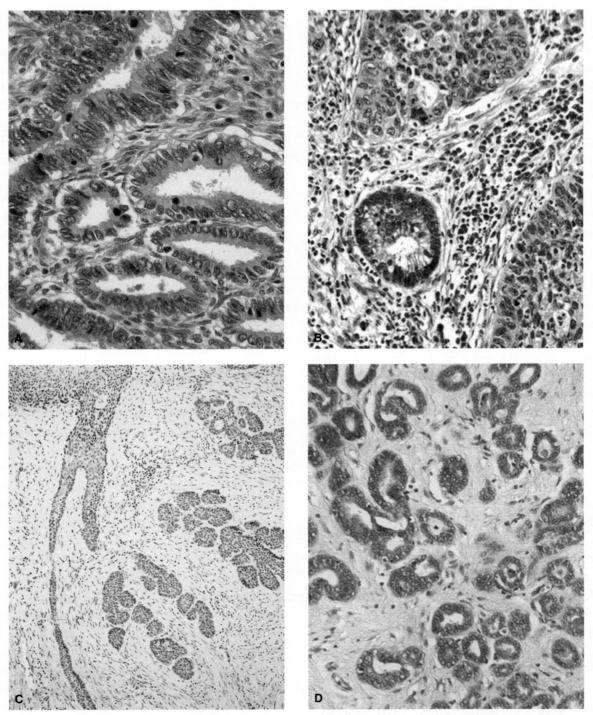

Figure 2–11. Variants of adenocarcinoma of the cervix, including *A*, conventional adenocarcinoma (×400 original magnification); *B*, adenosquamous carcinoma (×400 original magnification); *C*, adenoid basal carcinoma (×100 original magnification); and *D*, mesonephric neoplasia (×200 original magnification). The latter may range in appearance from very-well-differentiated (hyperplasia) to more poorly differentiated neoplasms (carcinoma). (H&E stain)

basal layers of the endocervical epithelium. They tend to have a less favorable prognosis than squamous cell carcinomas of similar stage. Clear cell adenocarcinomas of the cervix in diethylstilbestrol (DES)-exposed women are similar to those occurring in the vagina (described later). Additional rare variants of carcinoma include *adenoid basaloid carcinoma*. These lesions resemble basal cell carcinomas of the skin. They are rare in the cervix but have histologic features that distinguish them from conventional squamous cell or adenoid cystic carcinomas. The patients are older, and the tumors invade with minimal desmoplastic reaction. Finally, *glassy cell carcinomas* have been described, which are rare variants presumed to be derived from adenocarcinomas. *Mesonephric carcinomas*, like clear cell carcinomas, are a variant not associated with papillomaviruses, being derived from mesonephric rests in Gartner's duct.[39,40]

NEOPLASMS OF THE VAGINA

The vagina is a portion of the female genital tract that is remarkably free from primary disease. In the adult, inflammations often affect the vulva and perivulvar structures and spread to the cervix without significant involvement of the vagina. The major serious primary lesion of this structure is the uncommon primary carcinoma. The remaining entities can therefore be cited briefly.

Vaginal Intraepithelial Neoplasia

Vaginal intraepithelial neoplasia (VAIN) shares clinical features of both vulvar and cervical preinvasive disease. Like CIN, VAIN is characteristically associated with HPV, but like vulvar intraepithelial neoplasia (VIN), it occurs in an older age group. VAIN may follow routine hysterectomy (about one-third) for benign disease, but in our experience, most have a prior diagnosis of CIN or VIN. In some of these cases, VAIN is presumed to be a manifestation of multifocal disease attributed to HPV infection.

Squamous Cell Carcinoma of the Vagina

Primary carcinoma of the vagina is an extremely uncommon cancer (about 0.6 per 100,000 women yearly) accounting for about 1 percent of malignant neoplasms in the female genital tract, and of these, 95 percent are squamous cell carcinomas.[41] The greatest risk factor is a previous carcinoma of the cervix or vulva; from 1 to 2 percent of patients with an invasive cervical carcinoma eventually develop a vaginal squamous carcinoma. This has been attributed to the multicentric nature of squamous neoplasia in the lower genital tract (many are associated with papillomaviruses), inadequate removal of primary carcinomas, and the mutagenic effects of radiation therapy and possibly local extension/implantation from cervix to vagina. The peak age incidence is between 60 and 70 years, with 90 percent of patients over 50 years.

Most often, the tumor affects the upper-posterior vagina, particularly at the junction with the ectocervix. It begins typically as VAIN, progressing centrifugally to invade, by direct continuity, the cervix and perivaginal structures, such as the urethra, urinary bladder, and rectum. The lesions in the lower two-thirds of the vagina may metastasize to the inguinal nodes, while the upper lesions may involve the regional iliac nodes.[41]

Adenocarcinoma

Adenocarcinomas are rare but have received attention because of the increased frequency of clear cell adenocarcinomas in young women whose mothers had been treated with DES during pregnancy.[42] Fewer than 0.14 percent of such DES-exposed young women develop adenocarcinoma, and such tumors are usually discovered between the ages of 15 and 20 years.[43] The term "clear cell" is derived from the vacuolated, glycogen-containing cytoplasm (Figure 2–12).

Clear cell carcinomas are most often located on the anterior wall of the vagina, usually in the upper third, and vary in size from 0.2 to 10 cm in greatest diameter. These cancers can also arise in the cervix but typically arise in association with vaginal adenosis, a condition in which glandular columnar epithelium of the müllerian type either is situated beneath the vaginal squamous epithelium or replaces it.[44] Adenosis has been reported in 35 to 90 percent of the offspring of estrogen-treated mothers, but malignant transformation of this glandular mucosa occurs in

< 0.1 percent of cases.[43,45] Precisely why adenosis is prone to clear cell carcinoma (see above) is unknown.

NEOPLASMS OF THE VULVA

Benign Tumors and Tumor-Like Disorders

Papillary Hidradenoma

The vulva contains modified apocrine sweat glands and may contain tissue closely resembling breast tissue. One benign tumor arising in these tissues is the papillary hidradenoma, which is identical in appearance to intraductal papillomas of the breast. These tumors present as sharply circumscribed nodules, most commonly on the labia majora or interlabial folds, and may be confused with carcinoma because of a tendency to ulcerate. Histologically, it consists

of tubular ducts lined by a single or double layer of nonciliated columnar cells, with a subjacent layer of flattened myoepithelial cells. These myoepithelial elements are characteristic of benign sweat glands and sweat gland tumors (Figure 2–13).

Condyloma Acuminatum

The most common benign "tumor" of the vulva is condyloma acuminatum, a papillomavirus-induced squamous lesion, also called "venereal wart." Condyloma acuminata are sexually transmitted, predominate in women of reproductive age, and are frequently multiple, involving the perineal, vulvar, and perianal regions (Figure 2–14). Histologically, they consist of a combination of acanthosis (hyperplasia), hyperkeratosis, and parakeratosis. Nuclear atypia in the surface cells with perinuclear vacuolization (*koilocytosis*) is variable in vulvar lesions (Figure

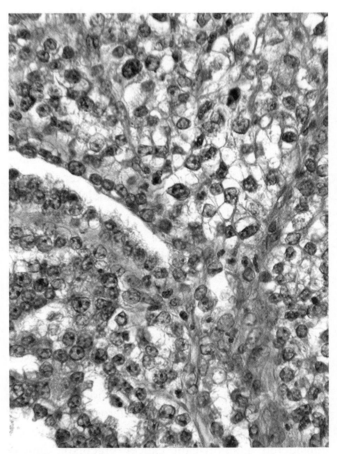

Figure 2–12. Clear cell carcinoma of the vagina. This is typically, but not invariably, associated with diethylstilbestrol exposure in utero. (H&E stain; ×400 original magnification)

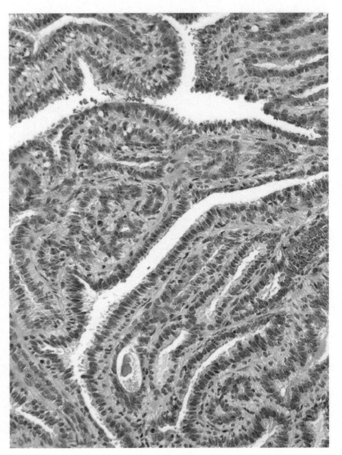

Figure 2–13. Hidradenoma of the vulva. This tumor exhibits a tubulopapillary morphology with a prominent reserve cell population. (H&E stain; ×200 original magnification)

2–15). Condylomata are caused by HPV, specifically types 6 and 11.[46] Except in immunosuppressed individuals, condyloma acuminata frequently regress spontaneously and are not considered to be precancerous lesions. They are, however, a marker for sexually transmitted disease.

Granular Cell Tumor

Granular cell tumor is a generally benign solitary circumscribed nonencapsulated tumor of presumed nerve sheath (Schwann cell) origin. The name stems from the characteristics of the tumor cells, which are polygonal in shape and contain a finely granular cytoplasm (Figure 2–16). The tumor involves the subcutaneous tissue but may elicit an impressive

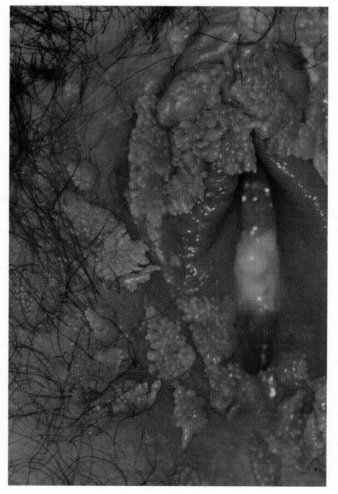

Figure 2–14. Multiple vulvar condylomata, manifesting as slightly elevated white patches on the labia minora. (Courtesy of Alex Ferenczy, MD.)

pseudoepitheliomatous hyperplasia of the overlying squamous mucosa. The latter may mimic squamous cell carcinoma and is a potential diagnostic pitfall.

Non-neoplastic Vulvar Lesions Associated with Vulvar Cancer

Lichen Sclerosus

Lichen sclerosus can occur anywhere on the body and leads to atrophy, fibrosis, and scarring. The skin becomes pale gray and parchment-like, the labia are atrophied, and the introitus is narrowed (Figure 2–17). Clinically, lichen sclerosus occurs in all age groups but is most common after menopause. Genetic as well as autoimmune and hormonal factors have been implicated in its pathogenesis.[47] At all ages, the disorder tends to be slowly developing, insidious, and progressive. It causes considerable discomfort and predisposes to acute infection but is usually of little systemic significance. Microscopically, lichen sclerosus is characterized by thinning of the epidermis, loss of cells at the stromal/epithelial interface, a zone of dense collagen, and an underlying band-like infiltrate of inflammatory cells (Figure 2–18). Lichen sclerosus is not considered a premalignant lesion per se, but it increases the risk of subsequent carcinoma slightly. A small but significant proportion of patients (about 1 to 4%) have been observed to develop carcinoma.[47] Recent studies suggest lichen sclerosus is a monoclonal process, with evidence of allelic loss.[48]

Squamous Hyperplasia (Lichen Simplex Chronicus)

Previously called "hyperplastic dystrophy," this lesion denotes hyperplasia of the vulvar squamous epithelium, frequently with hyperkeratosis. The epithelium is thickened and may show increased mitotic activity in both the basal and prickle cell layers with variable leukocytic infiltration of the dermis (Figure 2–19). Like lichen sclerosus, it is sometimes associated with carcinoma. It is not, however, considered a significant cancer precursor, unless there is coexisting epithelial atypia, in which case, it is classified as a precancerous lesion—VIN.[49]

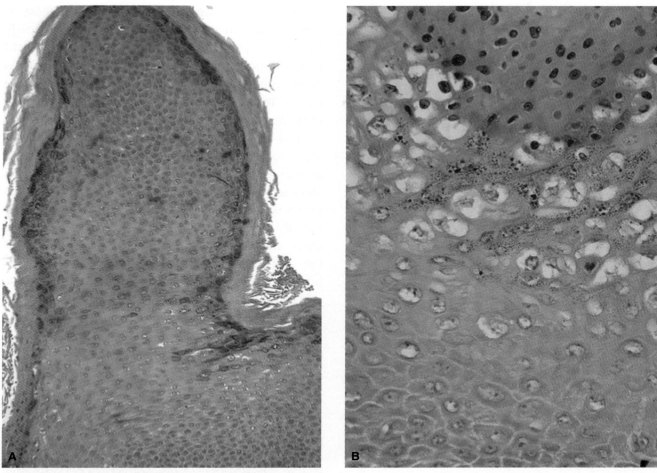

Figure 2–15. Microscopic pathology of condyloma, including *A*, prominent acanthosis and papillomatosis (×100 original magnification). *B*, Variable koilocytotic atypia (×400 original magnification). (H&E stain)

Vulvar Intraepithelial Neoplasia

There are three principal differences between the cervix and the vulva that influence the histopathology of the precursor lesions in these sites. First, the cervix is a transformation zone containing multipotential target cell populations. This leads to a multiplicity of phenotypes influenced by the maturational and differentiation characteristics of the target epithelium. Second, certain HPV types, specifically 6, 11, and 16, dominate the pathogenesis of vulvar lesions. In contrast, at least 30 different types are responsible for the cervix, where HPV types 6 and 11 are uncommon and many others, including not only 16 but 18, 31, 33, 35, and 39 are operative.[6] Combined with the differences in target epithelium, these multiple different infections conspire to produce a wide spectrum of morphology. Third, the pathogenesis of vulvar carcinoma is influenced by not only HPVs but other events in the mucosa. Nearly 60 percent of vulvar carcinomas derive from causes other than HPV.[43] Thus, the precursor spectrum is different, as will be discussed below.

Carcinoma of the vulva is an uncommon malignancy (approximately one-eighth as frequent as cervical cancer) representing about 4 percent of all genital cancers in the female; approximately two-thirds occur in women over age 60 years.[50] Eighty-five percent of these malignant tumors are squamous cell carcinomas, the remainder being basal cell carcinomas, melanomas, or adenocarcinomas. In terms of etiology, pathogenesis, and clinical presentation, vulvar squamous cell carcinomas may be divided into two general groups, as summarized in Table 2–1.

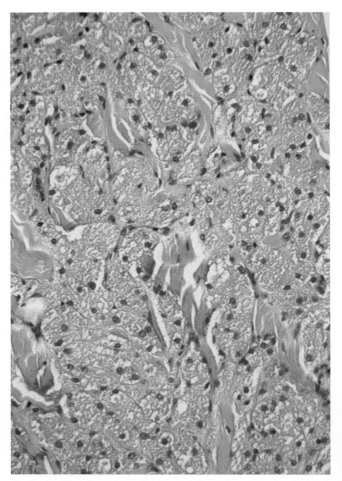

Figure 2–16. Granular cell tumor of the vulva, composed of uniform polyhedral cells with small nuclei and granular cytoplasm. (H&E stain; ×400 original magnification)

The first group is associated with papillomaviruses, may be multicentric, and frequently coexists with or is preceded by a defined precancerous change, termed "classic vulvar intraepithelial neoplasia," also known as carcinoma in situ or Bowen's disease.[43] VIN is characterized by nuclear atypia in the epithelial cells, increased mitoses, and lack of surface differentiation. These lesions usually present as white or pigmented plaques on the vulva; identical lesions are encountered in the male. VIN is appearing with increasing frequency in women under the age of 40 years. With or without associated invasive carcinoma, VIN is frequently multicentric, and from 10 to 30 percent are associated with another primary squamous neoplasm in the vagina or cervix. This association indicates a common etiologic agent. Indeed,

90 percent of cases of VIN and many associated cancers contain papillomavirus DNA, specifically types 16, 18, and other cancer-associated (high risk) types.[43] Spontaneous regression of VIN lesions has been reported; the risk of progression to invasive cancer increases in older (age over 45 years) or immunosuppressed women.[43]

The second group of squamous cell carcinomas are associated with vulvar inflammatory disorders, including squamous cell hyperplasia (lichen simplex chronicus) and lichen sclerosus. The etiology of this group of carcinomas is unclear, and they are infrequently associated with papillomaviruses. In some cases, the associated inflammatory conditions contain epithelial atypia (differentiated VIN), suggesting that precancerous changes can occur in these otherwise benign lesions and increase the risk of a subsequent cancer.[51] We have identified allelic loss in some of these lesions, suggesting that genetic damage may predate morphologic atypia.[48]

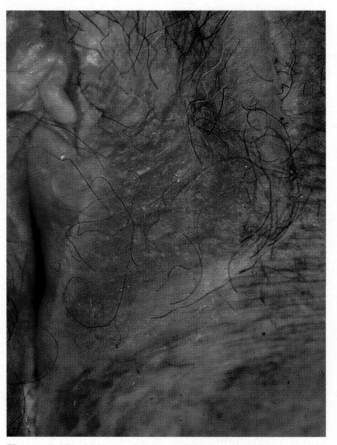

Figure 2–17. Lichen sclerosus, clinically presenting as white patches of thinned vulvar mucosa with atrophy of the labia.

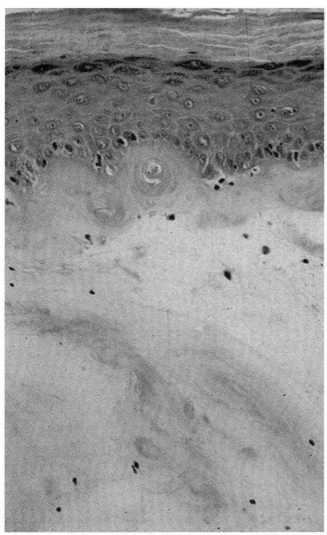

Figure 2–18. Lichen sclerosus. This is not considered a neoplasm, but is a risk factor for vulvar malignancy in approximately 4 percent of cases. Note the thinned epidermis and sclerotic stroma. (H&E stain; ×200 original magnification)

Classic Vulvar Intraepithelial Neoplasia

Classic VIN is morphologically identical to high-grade cervical intraepithelial lesions. They contain full- or near-full-thickness atypia, nuclear enlargement, multinucleation, abnormal mitoses, and apoptosis ("corps ronds") and are distinguished from condyloma by the presence of parabasal atypia, pigment in the epithelium, and markedly atypical parakeratosis (Figure 2–20). These lesions may resemble condyloma (warty) or carcinoma in situ (basaloid) in their differentiation. Most cases exhibit a spectrum of differentiation.[52]

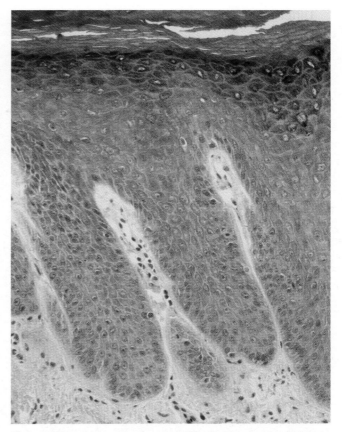

Figure 2–19. Lichen simplex chronicus. Previously termed "hyperplastic dystrophy," this entity is a manifestation of rubbing of the vulvar skin in response to nonspecific irritants. Like lichen sclerosus, lichen simplex chronicus is associated with vulvar cancer but is not considered a neoplastic lesion. (H&E stain; ×100 original magnification)

Table 2–1. CATEGORIES OF VULVAR SQUAMOUS NEOPLASIA

HPV-positive tumors
  Association with HPV exposure or history of STDs
  Slightly younger age group than HPV-negative tumors (average 7th decade)
  Tendency for multifocality or association with cervical neoplasia
  Share certain cytogenetic characteristics with cervical carcinomas
  Association with smoking
  Preceded by "classic VIN" (one-third of all vulvar cancers)
  Bowen's disease, CIS, bowenoid papulosis, bowenoid dysplasia

HPV-negative tumors
  Association with vulvar inflammatory diseases (lichen sclerosus, hyperplasia)
  Slightly older mean age (average 8th decade)
  Lower risk of other genital primary neoplasms
  Association with *P53* mutations/protein accumulation
  Typically associated with
  • no epithelial abnormality or lichen sclerosus/hyperplasia (one-third of all vulvar cancers)
  • lichen sclerosus/hyperplasia with atypia ("differentiated VIN") (one-third of all vulvar cancers)

HPV = human papillomavirus; STD = sexually transmitted disease; VIN = vulvar intraepithelial neoplasia; CIS = carcinoma in situ.

Differentiated Vulvar Intraepithelial Neoplasia

This is a poorly defined category of precursor lesions that often arise in association with either lichen sclerosus or lichen simplex chronicus. These lesions exhibit one or more of the following histologic features: prominent maturation/keratinization, nuclear atypia in the basal and parabasal keratinocytes, and abnormal keratinization, including dense cytoplasmic eosinophilia (Figure 2–21).[51,52]

Diagnostic Terminology and Implications

Practically speaking, because classic VIN lesions are identical to high-grade CIN, they are by default classified as either grade 2 (lesions with maturation,

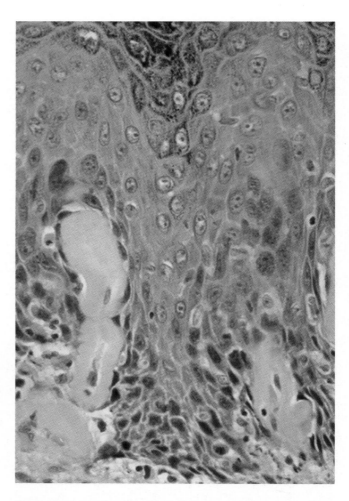

Figure 2–21. Differentiated VIN. This variant of VIN often arises in association with lichen sclerosus (as in this case) or hyperplasia. It is considered a cancer precursor and is usually not associated with papillomaviruses. (H&E stain; ×400 original magnification)

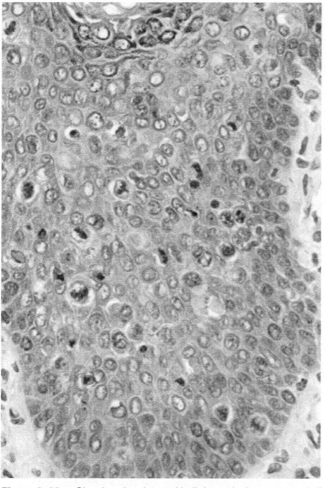

Figure 2–20. Classic vulvar intraepithelial neoplasia, composed of a full-thickness population of neoplastic keratinocytes. These lesions are strongly associated with papillomaviruses. (H&E stain; ×400 original magnification)

koilocytosis) or grade 3 (lesions with minimal maturation). The distinction of the two grades is of uncertain significance, and the options include either grading these lesions as VIN2 or VIN3 or simply classifying them as "VIN, classic type." For differentiated VIN, the recommended approach is to classify them as "VIN, differentiated type" and provide a comment that this lesion is often associated with lichen sclerosus and vulvar inflammatory diseases and has been associated with invasive carcinoma. Complete excision is advised for both classic and differentiated VIN, although the latter may be less easily demarcated in the presence of vulvar inflammatory disease and will require careful follow-up.

When should the term "VIN1" be used? In the cervix, CIN1 (LSIL) is generally defined as an exophytic or flat condyloma. In the vulva, we prefer to use the term "condyloma" to define "low-grade" vulvar intraepithelial lesions, so VIN1 is generally not used. We do not recommend VIN1 to define differentiated VIN lesions. Despite the sometimes subtle appearance of these differentiated VINs, their potential for progression may be significant, and the term "VIN1" is not recommended.

Invasive Squamous Cell Carcinoma

HPV-Associated Tumors

Vulvar carcinomas associated with HPV typically arise from a classic VIN and display cohesive growth patterns often architecturally resembling intraepithelial disease (intraepithelial-like) (Figure 2–22).[53,54] These patterns have been described as condyloma-like

or "warty" and "basaloid." Others are intermediate between the two. A smaller subset of HPV-associated carcinomas present as keratinizing tumors.

HPV-Negative Tumors

These are typically keratinizing squamous cell carcinomas showing small irregular tongues of invasive tumor with prominent basal cell atypia and maturation with keratinization (Figure 2–23). Some are extremely well differentiated, with blunt invasion patterns akin to verrucous carcinoma (Figure 2–24).[53,54]

It is important to emphasize that while cancer of the vulva appears to have two distinct pathways of development, some tumors share both characteristics. Reports of HPV-positive cases associated with lichen sclerosus exist and common risk factors to

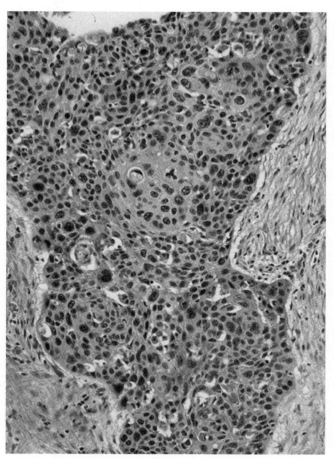

Figure 2–22. Vulvar cancer associated with human papillomaviruses. These tumors resemble their intraepithelial precursors and may vary from poorly differentiated (basaloid) carcinomas to well-differentiated tumors with warty features. (H&E stain; ×200 original magnification)

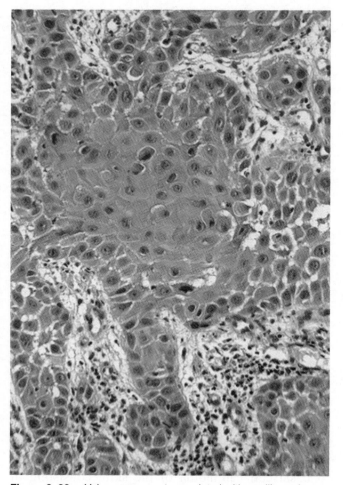

Figure 2–23. Vulvar cancer not associated with papillomaviruses. These tumors are typically keratinizing, as shown here. (H&E stain; ×400 original magnification)

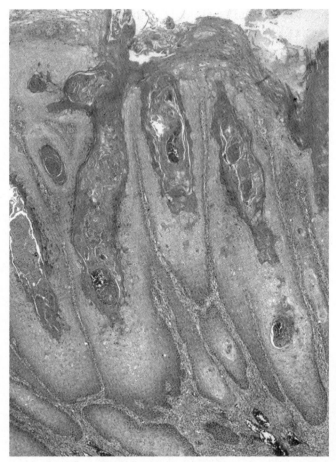

Figure 2–24. Verrucous carcinoma. This variant of nonmetastatic locally aggressive vulvar carcinoma is composed of broad, peg-like protrusions of extremely well-differentiated neoplastic epithelium. (H&E stain; ×40 original magnification)

both groups include older age, a lower incidence (about 7-fold) relative to cervical carcinoma, and similar cytogenetic abnormalities (Figure 2–25). This implies that common factors exist that may contribute to both categories of neoplasia and tempers the significance of HPV as a singular agent in the genesis of vulvar cancer in older women.[55]

Basal Cell Carcinoma of the Vulva

Basal cell carcinoma of the vulva is a rare locally aggressive variant of vulvar cancer that involves older women and should be distinguished for its low risk of metastatic spread. The morphology is similar to basal cell carcinoma of the skin, consisting of basaloid nests of tumor cells with a generally blunt pattern of infiltration (Figure 2–26).[56]

Adenoid Cystic Carcinoma of Bartholin's Gland

This is another rare tumor of the vulva ($< 0.5\%$), arising in Bartholin's gland and histologically identical to its namesake in the salivary gland. Like salivary gland tumors, adenoid cystic tumors of Bartholin's gland are characterized by a slow relentless local spread, a high risk of local recurrence, and late metastases to the lymph nodes and/or lungs (Figure 2–27).[57]

Extramammary Paget's Disease

This rare vulvar and sometimes perianal lesion is similar in presentation to Paget's disease of the breast. It manifests as a pruritic red, crusted, sharply demarcated, map-like area, occurring usually on the labia majora. The diagnostic microscopic feature of this lesion is the presence of large neoplastic cells

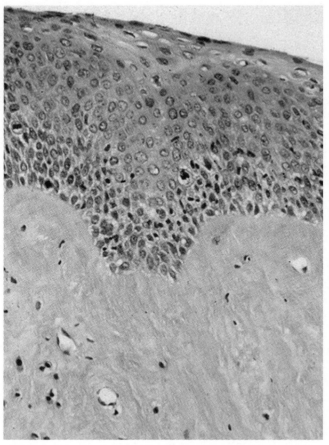

Figure 2–25. HPV-positive classic VIN arising in lichen sclerosus. This unusual combination coexisted with an adjacent invasive keratinizing carcinoma and illustrates the overlap between HPV-negative and -positive phenotypes. (H&E stain; ×200 original magnification)

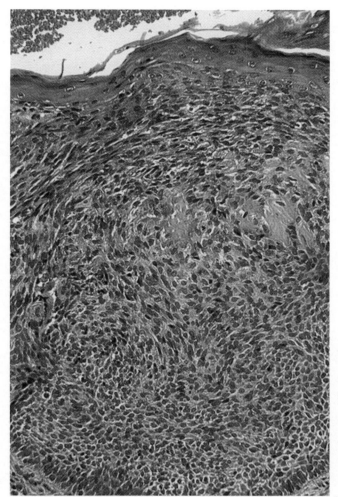

Figure 2–26. Basal cell carcinoma. This rare HPV-negative vulvar tumor is identical to the cutaneous version, with basaloid tumor nests arising in the lower portion of the squamous mucosa. (H&E stain; ×200 original magnification)

lying singly or in small clusters within the epidermis and its appendages. These cells are distinguished by a clear separation ("halo") from the surrounding epithelial cells and a finely granular cytoplasm containing periodic acid–Schiff (PAS)-, alcian blue-, or mucicarmine-positive mucopolysaccharides (Figure 2–28). Ultrastructurally, Paget's cells display apocrine, eccrine, and keratinocyte differentiation and presumably arise from primitive epithelial progenitor cells.[58]

In contrast to Paget's disease of the nipple, which almost invariably is associated with ductal carcinoma in situ (DCIS) in an underlying duct, vulvar lesions are most frequently confined to the epidermis of the skin and adjacent hair follicles and sweat glands. The prog-

nosis of Paget's disease is poor in uncommon cases with associated carcinoma, but intraepidermal Paget's disease may persist for many years, even decades, without the development of invasion. Because Paget's cells, however, often extend into skin appendages and may extend beyond the confines of the grossly visible lesion, they are prone to recurrence.

Malignant Melanoma

Malignant melanoma of the vulva/vagina is rare, accounting for approximately 1 to 10 percent of vulvar epithelial neoplasms and 2 to 3 percent of all melanomas. Vulvar melanomas are discovered as a change in a pre-existing pigmented lesion in a minority of cases and may occur on both the mucosa and skin of the vulva. They have also been reported in the

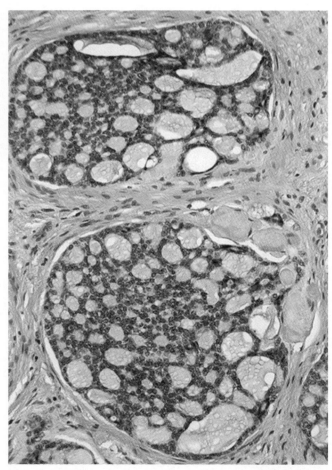

Figure 2–27. Adenoid cystic carcinoma of Bartholin's gland. This tumor is identical to its counterpart in the salivary gland, composed here of microcysts lined by thin layers of neoplastic cells and eosinophilic intraluminal material. (H&E stain; ×400 original magnification)

vagina, cervix, and uterus. Patterns include superficial spreading melanoma, nodular melanoma, and acral lentiginous melanomas (Figure 2–29). Prognosis of vulvar melanomas is determined by microstaging using a variant of the Clark level system as proposed by Chung. In this system, stages 1 to 5 designate lesions confined to the epidermis, invasive to < 1 mm, from 1 to 2 mm, beyond 2 mm, and finally, involving adipose tissue. Ten-year survivals are as follows: level 1–100 percent, 2–81 percent, 3–87 percent, 4–11 percent, and 5–33 percent.[59]

Because both melanoma and Paget's disease involve the squamous mucosa, the two may be confused histologically. Distinction of the two may be aided by special stains for mucicarmine (Paget's), S-100 (melanoma), and carcinoembryonic antigen (CEA) (Paget's).[60]

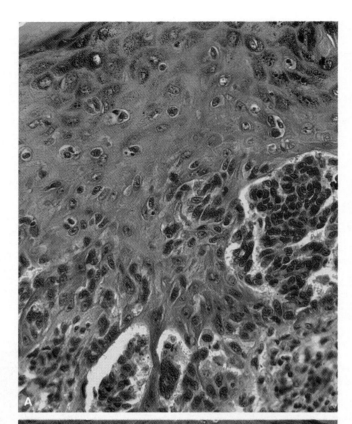

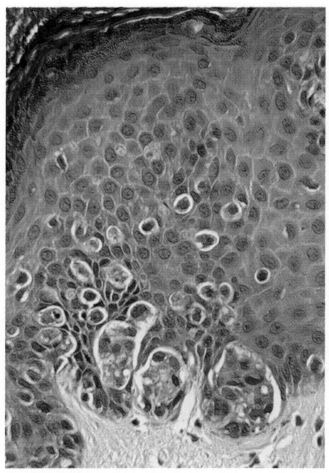

Figure 2–28. Paget's disease of the vulva is characterized by nests of neoplastic glandular cells in the epithelium, concentrating at the epithelial-stromal interface and extending into the upper epithelial layers. (H&E stain; ×400 original magnification)

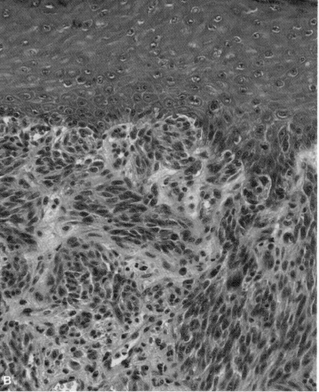

Figure 2–29. Melanoma of the vulva, including *A*, intraepithelial invasion similar to Paget's disease. *B*, Submucosal invasion is associated with very poor prognosis. (H&E stain; ×400 original magnification)

Soft Tissue Tumors

Mesenchymal neoplasms involving the vulva and lower genital tract may be divided into those that are not specific for this site, such as smooth muscle leiomyomas, granular cell tumors, hemangiomas, dermatofibromas, and others that are more specific for the lower genital tract, specifically the vulva, and include angiomyofibroblastoma, aggressive angio-myxoma, cellular angiofibroma, and fibroepithelial stromal polyps. The latter tumors appear to have their origin in a myofibroblastic cell.

Many vulvar soft tissue tumors present as solitary solid to cystic-appearing masses that may be confused with Bartholin's cysts. Histologic features are illustrated in Figure 2–30. *Fibroepithelial stromal* polyps are benign, can occur at any age, are common in the vagina, and may present during pregnancy (see Figure

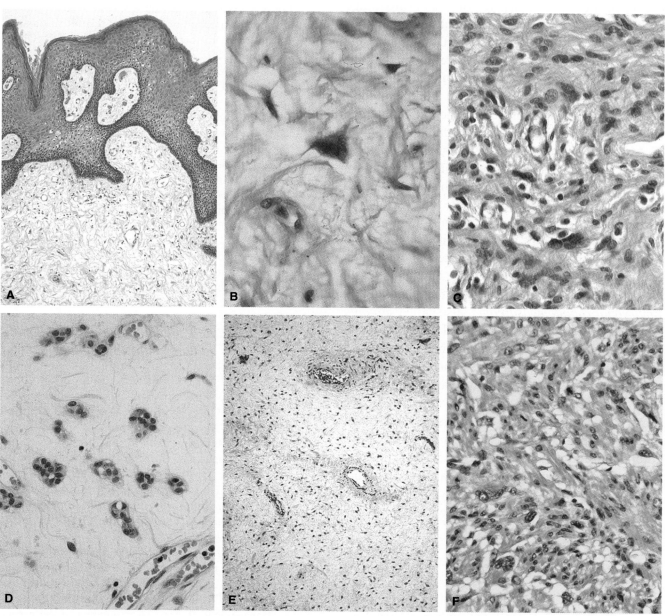

Figure 2–30. Soft tissue tumors of the lower genital tract, including *A,* (×100 original magnification) and *B,* (×400 original magnification) fibroepithelial stromal polyp; *C,* cellular angiofibroma (×400 original magnification); *D,* angiomyofibroblastoma (×400 original magnification); *E,* aggressive angiomyxoma (×200 original magnification); and *F,* leiomyosarcoma (×400 original magnification). (H&E stain) (Courtesy of Marisa R. Nucci, MD.)

2–30A). They have a fibrovascular core covered by keratinized squamous epithelium. A prominent feature is large stellate fibroblastic nuclei near the epidermal stromal junction (see Figure 2–30B).[61] *Cellular angiofibroma* is a benign, generally small tumor that occurs in middle-aged women and is usually well circumscribed and nonrecurring (see Figure 2–30C). The clinical impression is usually that of a Bartholin's gland or labial cyst.[62] *Angiomyofibroblastoma* (AMF) is another nonrecurring benign soft tissue tumor that occurs in the vulvovaginal region, has a broad age range, and may clinically resemble a lipoma or Bartholin's cyst (see Figure 2–30D).[63] *Aggressive angiomyxoma* is a locally aggressive tumor that differs from the above lesions by local infiltration and a tendency for recurrence (see Figure 2–30E).[64] Additional benign tumors of soft tissue origin include *rhabdomyomas* and, rarely, *mixed tumors.*

Malignant vulvovaginal soft tissue tumors include *leiomyosarcomas* (see Figure 2–30F) and *embryonal rhabdomyosarcomas*. The vulva is not a common site for smooth muscle tumors in the female genital tract, and smooth muscle tumors in this site have slightly different criteria for malignancy from those in the uterus. The most common features associated with recurrence are > 5 mitoses/10 hpf, tumors > 5 cm, and infiltrative margins.[65] *Embryonal rhabdomyosarcoma*, also called *sarcoma botryoides,* is an uncommon vaginal tumor most frequently found in infants and in children under the age of 5 years. The tumor consists predominantly of malignant embryonal rhabdomyoblasts and is thus a type of rhabdomyosarcoma.[66] Histologically, the tumor cells may have cross-striations akin to skeletal muscle. Like many soft tissue tumors in this site, embryonal rhabdomyosarcomas may be clinically mistaken for benign tumors, specifically inflammatory polyps. Conservative surgery, coupled with chemotherapy, appears to offer the best results in cases diagnosed sufficiently early.[67]

REFERENCES

1. Richart RM. Cervical intraepithelial neoplasia. In: Sommers SC, editor. Pathology annual. New York: Appleton-Century-Crofts; 1973. p. 301–28.

2. Greenlee RT, Hill-Harmon MB, Murray T, Thun M. Cancer statistics, 2001. CA Cancer J Clin 2001;51:15–36.

3. Koutsky LA, Holmes KK, Critchlow CW, et al. A cohort study of the risk of cervical intraepithelial neoplasia grade 2 or 3 in relation to papillomavirus infection. N Engl J Med 1992;327:1272–8.

4. Herrero R, Brinton LA, Reeves WC, et al. Sexual behavior, venereal diseases, hygiene practices and invasive cervical cancer in a high-risk population. Cancer 1990;65:380–6.

5. zur Hausen H, Schneider A. The role of human papilloma viruses in human urogenital cancer. In: Salzman N, Howley P, editors. The Papoviridae. New York: Plenum Press; 1987. p. 245–63.

6. Lorincz AT, Reid R, Jenson AB, et al. Human papillomavirus infection of the cervix: relative risk associations of 15 common anogenital types. Obstet Gynecol 1992;79:328–37.

7. Alani RM, Munger K. Human papillomaviruses and associated malignancies. J Clin Oncol 1998;16: 330–7.

8. Wright T, Kurman RJ, Ferenczy A. Precursors of cervical carcinoma. In: Kurman R, editor. Blaustein's pathology of the female genital tract. 4th ed. New York: Springer-Verlag; 1994. p. 229–77.

9. Crum CP, Mitao M, Levine P, Silverstein S. Cervical papillomaviruses segregate within morphologically distinct precancerous lesions. J Virol 1985;54: 675–81.

10. Kurman RJ, Solomon D. The Bethesda system for reporting cervical/vaginal cytologic diagnoses. New York: Springer-Verlag; 1994.

11. Crum CP, Cibas ES, Lee KR. Pathology of early cervical neoplasia. New York: Churchill Livingston; 1996.

12. Ostor AG. Natural history of cervical intraepithelial neoplasia: a critical review. Int J Gynecol Pathol 1993;12:186–92.

13. Boyes DA, Worth AJ, Fidler HK. The results of treatment of 4389 cases of preclinical squamous cell carcinoma. J Obset Gynecol Br Comm 1973;77:769.

14. Savage EW. Microinvasive carcinoma of the cervix. Am J Obstet Gynecol 1972;113:708.

15. Ng ABP, Reagan JW. Microinvasive carcinoma of the uterine cervix. Am J Clin Pathol 1969;52:511.

16. Robert ME, Fu YS. Squamous cell carcinoma of the uterine cervix: a review with emphasis on prognostic factors and unusual variants. Semin Diagn Pathol 1990;7:173.

17. Sedlis A, Sall S, Tsukada Y, et al. Microinvasive carcinoma of the uterine cervix: a clinicopathologic study. Am J Obstet Gynecol 1979;133:64.

18. Creasman WT, Fetter BF, Clarke-Pearson DL, et al. Management of stage IA carcinoma of the cervix. Am J Obstet Gynecol 1985;153:164.

19. Hasumi K, Sakamoto A, Sugano H. Microinvasive carcinoma of the uterine cervix. Cancer 1980;45:928.

20. van Nagell, Donaldson ES, Wood EG, Parker JC. The significance of vascular invasion and lymphocytic infiltration in invasive cervical cancer. Cancer 1978;41:228–34.

21. Ostor AG. Pandora's box or Ariadne's thread? Definition and prognostic significance of microinvasion in the uterine cervix. Pathol Annu 1995;30(2):103–36.

22. van Nagell JR, Greenwell N, Powell DF. Microinvasive carcinoma of the cervix. Am J Obstet Gynecol 1983;145:981.

23. Ostor AG. Studies on 200 cases of early squamous cell carcinoma of the cervix. Int J Gynecol Pathol 1993; 12;193–207.

24. Roche WD, Norris HJ. Microinvasive carcinoma of the cervix: the significance of lymphatic invasion and confluent patterns of growth. Cancer 1975;36:180.

25. McLachlin CM, Devine P, Muto M, Genest DR. Pseudoinvasion of vascular spaces: report of an artifact caused by cervical lidocaine injection prior to loop diathermy. Hum Pathol 1994;25:208–11.

26. Delgado G, Bundy BN, Fowler WC, et al. A prospective surgical pathological study of stage I squamous carcinoma of the cervix: a gynecologic oncology group study. Gynecol Oncol 1989;35:314–20.

27. Barber HRK, Sommers SC, Rotterdam H, Kwon T. Vascular invasion as a prognostic factor in stage IB cancer of the cervix. Obstet Gynecol 1977;52:343.

28. van Nagell JR, Higgins RV, Powell DE. Invasive cervical cancer. In: Knapp RC, Berkowitz RS, editors. Gynecologic oncology. 2nd ed. New York: McGraw-Hill; 1993. p. 192–222.

29. Girardi F, Pickel H, Winter R. Pelvic and parametrial lymph nodes in the quality control of the surgical treatment of cervical cancer. Gynecol Oncol 1993; 50:330–3.

30. Kolstad P. Follow-up study of 232 patients with stage IA1 and 411 patients with stage IA2 squamous cell carcinoma of the cervix (microinvasive carcinoma). Gynecol Oncol 1989;33:265–72.

31. Reagan JW, Wentz WB. Genesis of carcinoma of the uterine cervix. Clin Obstet Gynecol 1967;10:883.

32. Wright TC, Ferenczy A, Kurman RJ. Carcinoma and other tumors of the cervix. In: Kurman RJ, editor. Blaustein's pathology of the female genital tract. 4th ed. New York: Springer Verlag; 1994. p. 279–326.

33. Jennings RH, Barclay DL. Verrucous carcinoma of the cervix. Cancer 1972;30:430–4.

34. Randall ME, Andersen WA, Mills SE, et al. Papillary squamous cell carcinoma of the uterine cervix: a clinicopathology study of nine cases. Int J Gynecol Pathol 1986;5:1–10.

35. Qizilbash AH. Papillary squamous tumors of the uterine cervix: a clinical and pathologic study of 21 cases. Am J Clin Pathol 1974;61:508–20.

36. Trivijitsilp P, Mosher RE, Sheets EE, et al. Papillary immature metaplasia (immature condyloma) of the cervix: a clinicopathologic analysis and comparison with papillary squamous carcinoma. Hum Pathol 1998;29:641–8.

37. Steeper TA, Piscioli F, Rosai J. Squamous cell carcinoma with sarcoma-like stroma of the female genital tract: clinicopathology study of 4 cases. Cancer 1983;52:890.

38. Ostor A, Rome R, Quinn M. Microinvasive adenocarcinoma of the cervix: a clinicopathologic study of 77 women. Obstet Gynecol 1997;89(1):88–93.

39. Crum CP, Nuovo G, Lee KR. The cervix. In: Sternberg S, editor. Diagnostic surgical pathology. 3rd ed. Philadelphia: Lippincott Williams and Wilkins; 1999. p. 2155–202.

40. Norris HJ, Taylor HB. Polyps of the vagina: a benign lesion resembling sarcoma botryoides. Cancer 1966;19:227–32.

41. Hilborne LH, Fu YS. Intraepithelial, invasive and metastatic neoplasms of the vagina. Contemp Issues Surg Pathol 1987;9:181–208.

42. Herbst AL. Clear cell adenocarcinoma and the current status of DES-exposed females. Cancer 1981;48:484.

43. Crum CP. The female genital tract. In: Cotran R, Robbins SL, editors. Robbins pathologic basis of disease. 6th ed. Philadelphia: WB Saunders; 1999. p. 1040–5.

44. Scully RE, Welch WR. Pathology of the female genital tract after prenatal exposure to diethylstilbestrol. In: Herbst AL, Bern HA, editors. Developmental effects of diethylstilbestrol in pregnancy. New York: Thieme-Stratton; 1981. p. 26–45.

45. Vessey MP. Epidemiologic studies of the effects of diethylstilbestrol. IARC Sci Publ 1989;96:335–48.

46. Gissman L, Wolnik L, Ikenberg H, et al. Human papilloma virus type 6 and 11 DNA sequences in genital and laryngeal papillomas. Proc Natl Acad Sci U S A 1983;80:560.

47. Wilkinson EJ. Premalignant and malignant tumors of the vulva. In: Kurman R, editors. Blaustein's pathology of the female genital tract. 4th ed. New York: Springer-Verlag; 1994. p. 87–130.

48. Pinto A, Lin MC, Sun D, et al. Allelic imbalance in lichen sclerosus, hyperplasia and intraepithelial neoplasia of the vulva. Gynecol Oncol 2000;77:171–6.

49. Wilkinson EJ. Normal histology, and nomenclature of the vulva and malignant neoplasms, including VIN. Dermatol Clin 1992;10:283–96.

50. Zaino RJ. Carcinoma of the vulva, urethra, and Bartholin's glands. Contemp Issues Surg Pathol 1987;9:119.

51. Leibowitch M, Neill S, Pelisse M, Moyal-Baracco M. The epithelial changes associated with squamous cell carcinoma of the vulva: a review of the clinical, histological and viral findings in 78 women. Br J Obstet Gynaecol 1990;97:1135.

52. Crum CP. Vulvar intraepithelial neoplasia: histology and associated viral changes. Contemp Issues Surg Pathol 1987;9:119.

53. Andersen WA, Franquemont DW, Williams J, et al. Vulvar squamous cell carcinoma and papillomaviruses: two separate entities? Am J Obstet Gynecol 1991;165:329–36.

54. Kurman RJ, Toki T, Shiffman MH. Basaloid and warty carcinomas of the vulva: distinctive types of squamous cell carcinoma frequently associated with human papillomaviruses. Am J Surg Pathol 1993;17:133–45.

55. Haefner H, Tate J, McLachlin CM, Crum CP. Vulvar intraepithelial neoplasia: age, morphological phenotype, papillomavirus DNA and coexisting invasive carcinoma. Hum Pathol 1995;26:147–54.

56. Breen JL, Neubecker RD, Greenwald E, Gregori CA. Basal cell carcinoma of the vulva. Obstet Gynecol 1975;46:122.

57. Addison A, Parker RT. Adenoid cystic carcinoma of Bartholin's gland. Gynecol Oncol 1977;5:196.

58. Michael H, Roth LM. Paget's disease, skin appendage tumors, and cysts of the vulva. Contemp Issues Surg Pathol 1987;9:25.

59. Chung AF, Woodruff JM, Lewis JL Jr. Malignant melanoma of the vulva: a report of 44 cases. Obstet Gynecol 1975;45:6.

60. Reed W, Oppedal BR, Eeglarsen T. Immunohistochemistry is valuable in distinguishing Paget's disease, Bowen's, and superficial spreading melanoma. Histopathology 1990;16:583–8.

61. Ostor AG, Fortune DW, Riley CB. Fibroepithelial polyps with atypical stromal cells (pseudosarcoma botryoides) of vulva and vagina: a report of 13 cases. Int J Gynecol Pathol 1988;7:351–60.

62. Nucci MR, Granter SR, Fletcher CDM. Cellular angiofibroma: a benign neoplasm distinct from angiomyofibroblastoma and spindle cell lipoma. Am J Surg Pathol 1997;21:636–44.

63. Fletcher CDM, Tsang WYW, Fisher C, et al. Angiomyofibroblastoma of the vulva: a benign neoplasm distinct from aggressive angiomyxoma. Am J Surg Pathol 1992;16:373–82.

64. Steeper TA, Rosai J. Aggressive angiomyxoma of the female pelvis and perineum: report of nine cases of a distinctive type of gynecologic soft tissue neoplasm. Am J Surg Pathol 1983;7:463–75.

65. Newman PL, Fletcher CDM. Smooth muscle tumors of the external genitalia: clinicopathological analysis of a series. Histopathology 1991;18:523–9.

66. Copeland LJ, Gershenson DM, Saul PB, et al. Sarcoma botryoides of the female genital tract. Obstet Gynecol 1985;66:262.

67. Andrassy RJ, Hays DM, Raney RB, et al. Consevative surgical management of vaginal and vular pediatric rhabdomyosarcoma: a report from the International Rhabdomyosarcoma Study III. J Pediatr Surg 1995;30:1034.

3

Molecular Biology

JUDITH K. WOLF, MD

Over the past few decades, many advancements have been made in determining the molecular genetics of the development of cancer. This chapter will summarize the major disturbances in cellular function known, to date, to play a role in the development of cancers of the lower female genital tract. Oncogenes and tumor suppressor genes have been described in the different types of cancer, and their possible role in cancers of the female lower genital has been investigated.

For transformation to occur, tumor suppressor genes require homozygous loss of function by mutation, deletion, inactivation, or a combination of these events. The study of genetic abnormalities in cancers, in general, must include information about common chromosomal abnormalities, mutation and/or deletion of specific oncogenes and tumor suppressor genes, the role of angiogenesis and angiogenic factors, and the role of the bodies' own immune function.

Human papillomavirus (HPV) plays an important role in the development of cancers of the lower genital tract, and the genes of the virus interact with normal cellular genes. The effects of HPV-E6 and -E7 on important cell cycle genes are well documented. Because of the importance of HPV infection in the development of these cancers, the role of the body's immunity to the virus and these cancers are under study.

Cervical cancer remains a major worldwide health problem, especially in the developing countries. Because cervical cancer is a much more common cancer than either vulvar or vaginal cancer, the majority of research has focused in this area; however, much of the information known to date seems to apply to these tumors also. Specific information about these less common cancers, where available, is also included in this discussion.

Although the complete paradigm of the development of cervical cancer from the normal cervical epithelium is not yet known, continued study in this area will hopefully lead to the definition of the progression of molecular and immunologic abnormalities. The goal would be to use this information to help prevent and treat cervical cancer in the future. Preliminary trials of vaccines to HPV for the treatment of cervical cancer are already under way. The information gathered for cervical cancer could then possibly be further applied to the understanding of the less common vulvar and vaginal cancers.

ROLE OF HUMAN PAPILLOMAVIRUS

Understanding the biology of the HPV is important because the virus plays such an important role in cervical cancer. HPV consists of a double-stranded circular DNA genome, containing 7,800 to 7,900 base pairs, a nonenveloped virion, and an icosahedral capsid. The genome is organized into three regions: the early and late gene regions (protein encoding) and an upstream regulatory region (noncoding).

HPV belongs to the A genus of the Papovaviridae family. At least 77 different types of HPV have been characterized.[1] All are epitheliotropic and infect specific types of epithelia.[2] Twenty-three types are known to infect the anogenital area. Different types are associated with different types of lesions, with different oncogenic potential. HPV are generally categorized into non-oncogenic and oncogenic types, with a spectrum between these two. HPV types 6 and 11 are the two most common non-oncogenic types, found in women with condyloma.[3] Eighty percent of low-grade squamous intraepithelial lesions (SILs) have HPV deoxyribonucleic acid (DNA) identified. HPV types 6 and 11 were the predominant types found in early reports, but recently, many different types, including new, unrecognized types and multiple types are reported.[4] HPV DNA is found in up to 77 percent of high-grade SILs. Most high-grade lesions are associated with types 16 or 18, or a member of the 30s group.[5] HPV types 16, 18, and 31 are the types most commonly associated with invasive cervical cancer.[6] Up to 100 percent of vulvar intraepithelial neoplasias (VINs) are reported to be associated with HPV DNA, with HPV type 16, by far, being the commonest.[7,8] Types 18, 31, and 33 are also reported.[9,10] The association of HPV with low-grade VIN is less universal than with high-grade VIN, with positivity ranging from < 10 to > 90 percent.[8,11] In the case of invasive vulvar cancer, there appear to be two groups of patients. One group is of younger age, is associated with VIN, and has a high reported association with HPV infection. This group of patients has been reported to have up to 90 percent HPV positivity, again most commonly HPV-16 with 18, 31, and 33 being less common.[10,12,13] The other group is of older age and has a low incidence of HPV positivity. A basaloid or warty-type growth of the tumor is also more commonly associated with HPV infection.[10,12] As with cervical intraepithelial neoplasia (CIN) and VIN, vaginal intraepithelial neoplasia (VAIN) is associated with HPV DNA, most commonly type 16, in up to 85 percent of cases[14] and in 21 to 55 percent of invasive vaginal carcinoma cases reported.[15,16]

Knowledge of HPV and its interaction with the host genome helps in understanding the implications of this virus in the carcinogenesis of female lower genital tract cancers. As mentioned, there are three regions of the HPV genome (Figure 3–1). The upstream regulatory region (URR) contains overlapping binding sites for many different transcriptional activators and repressors, including activating protein-1 (AP-1), and nuclear factor-1 (NF-1).[17] This URR regulates transcription from the early and late regions, thus controlling the production of viral proteins and particles.

The early region is downstream of the URR and contains six open reading frames, E1 to E6. These encode for all the viral proteins, except for the viral capsid proteins, which come from the late region. Table 3–1 summarizes the major function of each of the proteins encoded by E1, E2, E4, E5, E6, and E7. The E6 and E7 proteins are of specific importance in cancer and will be discussed in more detail later.

The late region contains two open reading frames that encode for the viral capsid proteins. The L1 encodes for the major viral capsid protein, which is highly conserved between species. The L2 open reading frame encodes for the minor capsid protein and has more sequence variation between types. This has been used as an antigen for type-specific antibodies. When complete virions are being assembled, the L1 and L2 open reading frames are transcribed. This process is regulated by transcription factors that are produced only in the more differentiated epithelial cells in the upper layer of the infected epithelium.

As shown in Table 3–1, both the E6 and E7 protein products interact with important cellular genes. The E6 open reading frame encodes a protein of 150 amino acids, similar to the adenovirus E1B protein

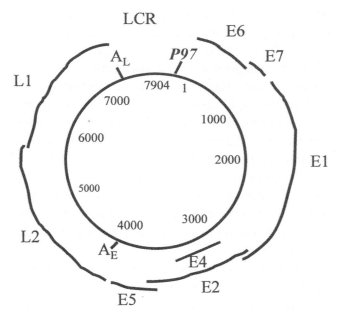

Figure 3–1. Genome map of HPV-16. Early genes are E1 to E7; late ones are L1 and L2. The long control region (LCR) contains replication and transcriptional control elements as well as the promoter *P97*.

and the large T antigen of the SV40 virus. The E6 protein is a zinc-binding protein.[18] The importance of HPV-E6 in cancer appears to be due to its effects on the cellular tumor suppressor gene, *P53*. Alterations in the *P53* gene, including deletion, insertion, and point mutation, are the most frequent genetic events in many different carcinomas, such as colon, breast, and lung carcinomas.[19–21] The *P53* gene negatively regulates the cell cycle and requires "loss of function" mutations for tumor formation.[22,23] The normal function of *P53* includes a transient increase in expression after DNA damage occurs, leading to cell cycle arrest in the G_1-phase. This arrest allows for repair of the DNA, or if repair is not possible, cells will undergo apoptosis (cell death). The *P53* gene acts through downstream regulators, such as P21,

leading to inhibition of cyclin-dependent kinases, and eventually blocks retinoblastoma (RB) phosphorylation preventing cell cycle progression.[24] It can lead to apoptosis through changes in levels of *BAX* and *BCL2* family members expression.[25] The SV40 large T antigen, adenovirus E1B protein, and the HPV-E6 protein all can complex with and inactivate *P53*. E6, however, also stimulates *P53* degradation through a selective ubiquitin-dependent proteolytic pathway.[26] The E6 proteins of high-oncogenic-risk types of HPV (HPV-16 and -18) have a higher affinity for *P53*, compared with the low-oncogenic-risk types (HPV-6 and -11).[27,28]

The E7 open reading frame encodes a 98-amino-acid phosphoprotein, which is similar to the adenovirus E1A protein and the SV40 large T antigen. It is a nuclear zinc-binding protein.[18] The importance of HPV-E7 in cancer appears to be due to its effects on the retinoblastoma gene product and its related proteins P107 and P130.[29] Proliferation of normal cells follows an orderly progression through the cell cycle under the influence of cyclins and cyclin-dependent kinases (CDKs). These interact, when the cell is released from a quiescent state, and phosphorylate such substrates as RB[30] (Figure 3–2). In its active form, hypophosphorylated RB is able to block cells in the G_1-phase of the cell cycle because it is

Table 3–1. FUNCTIONS OF THE PRODUCTS OF HPV EARLY REGION OPEN READING FRAMES

Early Region Open Reading Frame	Protein Function
E1	1. Two proteins required for extrachromosomal DNA replication and completion of viral life cycle 2. These work with E2 products
E2	1. Two proteins required for extrachromosomal DNA replication 2. These work with E1 products 3. Full-length protein acts as a transcriptional activator and binds to DNA in the URR to increase transcription of the early region 4. Smaller protein inhibits transcription of the early region
E4	1. Protein important for the maturation and replication of the virus 2. Expressed in later stages of infection when complete virions are being assembled
E5	1. Protein interacts with cell membrane receptors, such as EGF-R and PDGF-R 2. May stimulate cell proliferation in infected cells
E6	1. Protein critical for viral replication, host cell immortalization, and transformation 2. Binds to *P53* and stimulates *P53* degradation through ubiquitin-dependent proteolytic pathway
E7	1. Protein critical for viral replication, host cell immortalization, and transformation 2. Binds to RB protein and dissociates E2F-RB complex stimulating transcription of cellular genes

DNA = deoxyribonucleic acid; URR = upstream regulatory region; EGF-R = epidermal growth factor receptor; PDGF-R = platelet-derived growth factor receptor; RB = retinoblastoma; HPV = human papillomavirus.

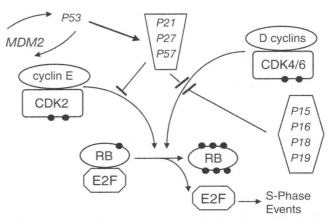

Figure 3–2. Regulators of G_1 progression. This shows a schematic of some of the interactions of *P53* and other cellular genes that have control of the cell cycle. Positive and negative feed back, as known, are indicated. *P53* and *MDM2* regulate each other. *P53* turns on *P21*, *P27*, or *P57*, which in turn, inhibit the cyclin-dependent kinases (CDKs) from phosphorylating the retinoblastoma (RB) gene product, thereby blocking the progression of the cell cycle. Through another pathway, *P15*, *P16*, *P18*, and *P19* can also block the CDK4 or -6 kinases from phosphorylating RB. Phosphorylated RB is released from E2F to allow progression to S-phase.

tightly bound to the transcription factors of the E2F family. When it is phosphorylated, the transcription factors are released and can activate genes responsible for progression to the S-phase.[31] The E7 protein also interacts with two of the CDK inhibitors, P21 and P27. These proteins would normally inhibit cellular proliferation.[32,33]

Both the RB and P53 proteins also interact with the double minute 2 ($MDM2$) gene. P53 acts as a transcriptional activator of $MDM2$, while $MDM2$ acts in an autoregulatory fashion as a negative feedback to P53.[34] $MDM2$ can also interact with Rb and restrain its action.[35] A recent report has found $MDM2$ overexpression in up to 35 percent of cervical tumors, although they did not correlate this with HPV infection.[36]

Although the complete relationship between HPV infection and cancer of the female lower genital tract is still unclear, recent advances in molecular biology have begun to elucidate the complex nature of interactions between this virus and cellular genes that may lead to carcinogenesis.

CHROMOSOMAL ABNORMALITIES

Although HPV obviously plays an important role in the development of these cancers, HPV alone is not sufficient to cause carcinogenesis. Chromosomal abnormalities, including loss of heterozygosity (LOH), have been studied fairly extensively in cervical cancer, and several reproducible abnormalities have been found. One of the most frequently reported areas of LOH in cervical cancer has been at chromosome 3p. As many as 70 percent of primary cervical cancers have been found to have LOH at this site, more specifically in the 3p14-25 regions.[37,38] LOH at this site has also been found in 30 to 57 percent of cervical cancer precursor lesions, suggesting that this may be an early event in carcinogenesis.[39,40] LOH at the 3p site has also been reported in up to 80 percent of vulvar cancer cases.[41,42] Several theories as to what genes might be disrupted in the area of chromosome 3 to cause carcinogenesis have been proposed. Larson and colleagues have suggested that the tumor suppressor gene $FHIT$ is located in this area (3p14.2) and may be disrupted.[37] Ohta and colleagues first identified the $FHIT$ gene as being lost in gastrointestinal tumors. It spans a fragile site (FRA3B), the renal cell

carcinoma–associated t(3;8) breakpoint, and a frequent site of HPV-16 integration.[43] LOH at this site, therefore, could potentially be important in cervical carcinogenesis. Although involvement of this tumor suppressor gene in cervical carcinogenesis would fit well with HPV's role, Chu and colleagues have found no aberration of $FHIT$ mRNA in cervical cancers with LOH at this site.[38] More recently, however, Holschneider and colleagues have reported loss of $FHIT$ expression in 57 percent of cervical tumors and 47 percent of adjacent CIN lesions. Furthermore, they have correlated the loss of $FHIT$ expression with smoking.[44] Therefore, this gene may, indeed, be important for at least a subgroup of patients with cervical cancer. Another candidate tumor suppressor gene located on the p arm of chromosome 3 is the β-catenin gene, at the 3P21.1 locus. β-Catenin is a structural mediator of the cytoskeletal actin filaments to cellular adhesion molecules, the cadherins.[45] Kersemaekers and colleagues found 41 percent LOH at this site in cervical cancers but no loss in the expression of β-catenin or of E-cadherin, to which it binds.[46] In summary, although LOH at 3p in cervical and vulvar cancers is a frequent event and the $FHIT$ gene in this region may be important for carcinogenesis in cervical cancer, other genes located in this region that may be responsible for carcinogenesis have yet to be identified.

Besides chromosome 3, nonrandom LOH has also been reported at chromosomes 6, 11, 13, 16, 17, and 19 in cervical cancer and 2, 5, 10, 11, 15, 17, 18, and 21 in vulvar cancer, although the significance of these losses has not been speculated on.[40–42,46] Also, microsatellite instability has been found in 14 to 30 percent of cervical cancers. Microsatellites appear to play a role in DNA repair, and abnormalities may lead to genetic instability.[39,46]

ROLE OF SPECIFIC ONCOGENES/TUMOR SUPPRESSOR GENES

Underlying all the discussion thus far is the idea that abnormalities in cellular genes, by either amplification/overexpression (oncogenes) or loss of function (tumor suppressor genes), are required for carcinogenesis, in general, and specifically in these cancers (Table 3–2). We have discussed abnormalities in the function of the $P53$ and RB tumor suppressor genes as a result of HPV infection. Up to 96 percent of invasive cervical carcinomas have been found to contain HPV-16 or -18 DNA, and in those few without evidence of HPV, *P53* mutations are often found.[47,48] As mentioned, there appear to be two subgroups of patients with vulvar cancer—those with HPV association and those without. Recently, several studies have found that *P53* mutations are common in vulvar cancers and are more likely to occur in those tumors without HPV infection. Ngan and colleagues reported *P53* mutation in 21 percent of vulvar cancers, but the mutation status was not related to HPV infection.[49] However, Flowers and colleagues reported allelic loss in the area of the *P53* gene in 20 percent of vulvar cancers overall and 62 percent of HPV-negative tumors, compared with 15 percent of HPV-positive ($p = .02$).[42] Kagie and colleagues also reported a significantly higher immunohistochemical positivity of nuclear staining for *P53* in HPV-negative (41 percent) versus HPV-positive (0 percent) vulvar tumors.[11] Finally, Lee and colleagues reported 44 percent of HPV-negative vulvar tumors with *P53* mutations but only 8 percent of HPV-positive tumors.[50] The combined results of these studies suggest that loss of *P53* function via HPV infection or mutation is important in the carcinogenesis of these tumors.

Other specific genetic abnormalities may also play an important role in carcinogenesis and the aggressiveness of cervical tumors, although, to date, the role of most of these genetic abnormalities in cervical cancer do not appear as important as does the role of HPV. The *CMYC* oncogene is expressed in almost all differentiated cell types. Its protein acts as a transcriptional regulator. The gene contains a transcriptional activation domain and a basic helix-loop-helix leucine zipper DNA-binding and dimerization domain. The *CMYC* gene is made up of three exons, two promoter sites, and two transcription-initiation sites. Transcription of *CMYC* normally increases after resting cells enter the G_1-phase. It acts as a heterodimer with MAX (a related protein), binds DNA in a sequence-specific way, and acts as a transcriptional activator for genes critical in the regulation of cell growth.[51] The *CMYC* gene also plays a role in apoptosis; by binding with MAX, it interacts with *P53*, *BAX*, and *BCLX*. It induces apoptosis in cells deprived of growth factors.[52] Amplification

of *CMYC* is the predominant route of activation in cervical cancer. Most studies report a 32 to 34 percent incidence of *CMYC* activation in cervical cancers. Amplification may be related to tumor size and nodal status or may be a risk factor for relapse.[53-55] A small study by Tate and colleagues suggests that *CMYC* mutations are not important in VINs.[56]

Another family of genes frequently mutated in cancers is the *RAS* family of genes. Three forms of *RAS, KRAS, HRAS,* and *NRAS,* encode for the 21-kDa proteins (P21), which are located on the inner plasma membrane and act as membrane-bound guanosine triphosphate (GTP)ases. Normally, *RAS* P21 hydrolyzes GTP, but the mutated *RAS* loses this ability and is activated.[57,58] Activation of *RAS* results in the induction of other cellular genes that lead to cellular proliferation.[59] Mutations have been reported in the *KRAS* and *HRAS* genes in cervical cancer at a rate of only 10 to 15 percent.[60] One report by Garzetti and colleagues found that increased *RAS* P21 expression correlated with risk of lymph node metastasis.[61] Tate and colleagues found no association between *RAS* mutations and vulvar cancers.[56]

Besides these transcription factors, amplification or overexpression of several different growth factor receptors (GF-Rs) have been implicated in carcinogenesis. Two, in particular, have been studied in gynecologic malignancies, including cervical cancer. These are the epidermal growth factor receptor (EGF-R), and

	Table 3–2. ONCOGENE/TUMOR SUPPRESSOR GENE ABNORMALITIES IN TUMORS OF THE LOWER GENITAL TRACT	
Gene	Association with Cervical Cancer	Association with Vulvar Cancer
P53	96% have HPV infection and decreased activity	44–62% HPV-negative tumors have mutation; 0–8% HPV-positive tumors have mutation
CMYC	32–34% amplification	NS
RAS	10–15% mutations	NS
EGF-R	> 50% overexpression or amplification	N/A
HER2/NEU	> 50 % slight overexpression	N/A
P21	90% overexpression	N/A
CDK4	69% overexpression	N/A
MDM2	35% overexpression	N/A
P27	65% decreased expression	N/A
BCL2	61–63% overexpression	N/A

NS = not significant; N/A = not available.

related *HER2/NEU*. The EGF-R is a 170-kDa transmembrane glycoprotein with an intracellular component. Its ligands are the EGF and transforming growth factor-alpha (TGF-α). Overexpression of the EGF-R is usually related to amplification of the gene, and overexpression seems to confer a growth advantage to cells. EGF-R is expressed not only in a large proportion of cervical carcinomas but also in normal and premalignant epithelia. Lakshmi and colleagues have suggested that in normal squamous epithelium, EGF-R expression is restricted to the basal and parabasal cell layers, whereas in premalignant and invasive lesions, the expression is more diffuse.[62]

The *HER2/NEU* gene also encodes for a transmembrane glycoprotein with 78 percent homology to the intracytoplasmic domain of the EGF-R. It is a 185-kDa glycoprotein with tyrosine kinase activity and several described possible ligands.[63] Both Lakshmi and colleagues and Berchuck and colleagues report a high percentage of cervical cancers (and squamous epithelium) to stain positive by immunohistochemistry for *HER2/NEU* expression, however, the staining is light and correlates with EGF-R expression.[62,64] Berchuck and colleagues did report one patient with stage IVb cervical cancer to have high intensity staining for *HER2/NEU*.[64] This little information, however, does not allow for the correlation of *HER2/NEU* or EGF-R expression and the prognosis of cervical cancer.

Besides *P53*, RB, and the oncogenes and GF-Rs already discussed, there are other tumor suppressor genes that seem to play a role in the carcinogenesis of some types of tumors and have been evaluated in cervical cancer. These include the CDKs, cyclins, *P16*, *P21*, *P27*, and *MDM2*, mentioned earlier when discussing the role of HPV and cervical cancer.

Skomedal and colleagues recently reported overexpression of *P21*, a G_1 cell cycle regulator downstream of *P53*, in 96 percent of cervical tumors, compared with normal cervical epithelium.[36] As mentioned earlier, HPV-E7 is known to interact with P21 and inhibit its normal cellular activity, which is to inhibit cyclin activities (see Figure 3–1). It is proposed that high levels of P21 may occur due to check-point adaptation after constant stimulation, altered binding to the CDK4/cyclin D1 complex, or mutations in the downstream P21 target.[65]

Skomedal and colleagues also looked at CDK4 expression and cyclin D1 expression and found overexpression of CDK4 in 69 percent of tumors, compared with normal cervical epithelium, while only 3 percent of tumors had overexpression of cyclin D1. Because of the action of HPV-E7 on RB in cervical cancer, cyclin D1 function may not be as important as in other types of cancer. Also, the overexpressed CDK4 is proposed to possibly bind with other D cyclins, D2 and/or D3.[36] As mentioned earlier, 35 percent of tumors had overexpression of the MDM2 protein.

Levels of P27, a cyclin dependent kinase inhibitor, were decreased in 65 percent of cervical tumors, compared with normal epithelium. Although this has been reported in other sites to correlate with a poorer prognosis, in the report by Skomedal and colleagues, no correlation with survival in cervical cancer was shown. In fact, in their report, there was no relationship between any of the cell cycle–associated proteins studied and histologic cell type, grade of differentiation, FIGO (International Federation of Gynecology and Obstetrics) stage, or relapse-free survival.[36]

Another CDK inhibitor, *P16*, has been found to be abnormal in many types of cancer. However, Kim and colleagues reported, in 1998, on 57 primary cervical tumors and found no deletions or mutations in this gene.[66]

Another important tumor suppressor gene is the apoptosis inhibitor *BCL2*. *BCL2* was first described in B-cell lymphomas with a t(14;18)(q32;q21) translocation.[67] Subsequently, it has been found to be expressed in lymphomas and epithelial tumors without this translocation. The *BCL2* gene product is a 25-kDa protein located at the outer mitochondrial membrane, in the nuclear envelope, plasma membrane, endoplasmic reticulum, and chromosomes.[68] Because it inhibits apoptosis, when *BCL2* is overexpressed, it extends cell survival. Overexpression of *BCL2* in a number of tumor types has been found to be associated with a less malignant phenotype. Two studies of *BCL2* expression and cervical cancer have found 61 to 63 percent of invasive cervical cancers to have *BCL2* overexpression, and in both studies, this correlated with increased overall survival, similar to reports in other tumor types.[69,70]

Although there are many other genetic abnormalities, known and unknown, involved in cancer development, only those studied thus far for their role in the development of cervical, vulvar, and vaginal cancers have been discussed here.

ROLE OF ANGIOGENESIS AND ANGIOGENIC FACTORS

Angiogenesis is essential for the growth of solid tumors. Hockel and colleagues have reported an association between tumor hypoxia and progression of cervical cancer, and this would seem to correlate with the angiogenic potential of the tumor.[71] However, any attempt to connect this finding with actual vessel counts or angiogenic factors has proven more difficult. Siracka and colleagues and Kohno and colleagues reported that high blood vessel density predicts improved survival with radiotherapy (Siracka) or intra-arterial chemotherapy (Kohno).[72,73] On the other hand, Bossi and colleagues and Rutgers and colleagues report no association between angiogenesis and stage of disease or prognosis.[74,75] Recently, Raleigh and colleagues tried to correlate both hypoxia and expression of vascular endothelial growth factor (VEGF) to prognosis in cervical cancer.[76] VEGF is a disulfide-bonded glycoprotein, whose transcription and expression are upregulated with hypoxia and appear to play an important role in the development and growth of tumors.[77] However, Raleigh and colleagues found no relationship between hypoxia and VEGF expression in cervical cancer.[76] In summary, it appears that hypoxia is important in the response of cervical tumors to treatment, but the actual role that angiogenic factors play in the development and progression of cervical tumors is not yet clear.

IMMUNOLOGY

Especially because of the apparent essential role of HPV in the development of cervical cancer, the importance of immune function in cervical cancer development is undergoing extensive study. Odunsi and Ganesan have written an elegant review of the role of human major histocompatibiltiy complex (MHC) and cervical cancer.[78] Both antibody and T-cell responses appear to be important in control of HPV infection and, therefore, cervical cancer. However, cell-mediated immune response seems to be more important in the control of the HPV infection. This is evident in that immunosuppressed patients

are more susceptible to HPV infections. However, not all who have HPV infections develop cervical cancer, and there seems to be an increased risk of progression to cancer in patients with HLA type DQB1*03.[78] One small study by Jochmus and colleagues found, in general, an increased expression of MHC class I molecules in VIN lesions that were HPV positive, compared with HPV-negative lesions.[79] Others have looked at the expression of cytokines to try to correlate the type of immune response in cervical cancer and preinvasive lesions in comparison with normal cervical tissue. The underlying premise has been that a Th1-type response to HPV infection is important for successful control of the virus, while a Th2-type response results in inadequate control of the infection (Table 3–3).[80] A Th1-type response augments cell-mediated immunity through production of cytokines, such as interleukin-2 (IL-2) and interferon-γ (IFN-γ). The Th2-type responses augment humoral immunity through cytokines, such as IL-4 and IL-10. Al-Saleh's report of decreased IL-2 levels and increased IL-4 levels in high-grade squamous intraepithelial lesions (HGSIL), compared with normal cervical tissue, supports this finding.[81] Hildesheim and colleagues also report decreased soluble IL2-receptor levels in patients with HGSIL.[82] Gianinni and colleagues found increased IL-10 in HGSIL lesions, compared with low-grade and normal cervical tissue.[83] All these findings support the Th1-type response being appropriate for HPV infections and a Th2-type response being detrimental in controlling the infection. Because of the important role of immune function in the development of cervical cancer, several studies of vaccines or other mechanisms to enhance the immune response to HPV infection are under way.

Table 3–3. Th1 AND Th2 IMMUNE RESPONSES AND HPV INFECTION	
Th1	Th2
Enhanced cell-mediated immunity	Enhanced humoral immunity
Increased IL-2	Increased IL-4
Increased interferon-γ	Increased IL-10
Adequate control of HPV infection	Inadequate control of HPV infection

IL = interleukin; HPV = human papillomavirus.

CONCLUSION

Although much is known about the genetics of cancers of the female lower genital tract, much, obviously, is yet to be known. As the relationship of HPV infection, other genetic defects, and immune function are further delineated, there is hope that a genetic paradigm for the development of cervical cancer will be more clearly defined. As the abnormalities leading to cervical cancer are better established, new therapies directed at correcting these may be developed.

As mentioned, in the area of immune function, several studies trying to find effective vaccination against HPV are under way or completed. One such study was by Borysiewicz and colleagues, reporting a phase I trial of a vaccinia virus containing HPV-16E6 and -19E6 to try to stimulate an immune response to the virus.[84] They found one patient who developed antibodies to HPV-18E7 and one for a short time who developed cytotoxic T cells against HPV-18. Another study of patients with refractory cervical or vaginal cancer by Stellar and colleagues found an HLA-A*0201–restricted HPV-16E7 lipopeptide vaccine capable of inducing epitope-specific CD8+ T-lymphocyte responses in 5 of 7 patients after two vaccinations.[85] Continued advanced studies of vaccines against HPV in the treatment of cervical cancer are ongoing.

Another possible treatment mechanism would be to try to correct the genetic abnormalities of the cancer cell. To this regard, Hamada and colleagues reported using an E1-deleted modified adenovirus containing cDNA for human $P53$ in cervical cancer cells in vitro.[86] Growth of both HPV-infected cell lines and those with no HPV, but with mutant $P53$, was inhibited with this $P53$-containing virus. Although not yet tested in human trials in cervical cancer, this virus is being tested in other sites and remains a possible new strategy for cervical cancer treatment.

REFERENCES

1. zur Hausen H. Papillomavirus infections—a major cause of human cancers. Biochim Biophys Acta 1996;1288:55–78.
2. Park TW, Fujiwara H, Wright TC. Molecular biology of cervical cancer and its precursors. Cancer Suppl 1995;76:1902–13.
3. Felix JF, Wright TC. Analysis of lower genital tract lesions clinically suspicious for condylomata using in situ hybridization and the polymerase chain reaction for the detection of human papillomavirus. Arch Pathol Lab Med 1994;118:39–43.
4. Bergeron C, Barrasso R, Beaudenon S, et al. Human papillomaviruses associated with cervical intraepithelial neoplasia: great diversity and distinct distribution in low- and high-grade lesions. Am J Surg Pathol 1992;19:641–740.
5. Genest DR, Stein L, Cibas E, et al. A binary (Bethesda) system for classifying cervical cancer precursors: criteria, reproducibility, and viral correlates. Hum Pathol 1993;24:730–6.
6. Lorincz AT, Reid R, Jenson AB, et al. Human papillomavirus infection of the cervix: relative risk associations of 15 common anogenital types. Obstet Gynecol 1992;79:328–37.
7. Van Beurden M, ten Kate FW, Tjong-A-Hung SP, et al. Human papillomavirus DNA in multcentric vulvar intraepithelial neoplasia. Int J Gynecol Pathol 1998; 17:12–6.
8. Kohlberger PD, Kirnbauer R, Bancher D, et al. Absence of $P53$ protein overexpression in precancerous lesions of the vulva. Cancer 1998;82:323–7.
9. Iwasawa A, Nieminen P, Lehtinen M, Paavonen J. Human papillomavirus in squamous cell carcinoma of the vulva by polymerase chain reaction. Obstet Gynecol 1997;89:81–4.
10. Hording U, Junge J, Daugaard S, et al. Vulvar squamous cell carcinoma and papillomaviruses: indications for two different etiologies. Gynecol Oncol 1994;52:241–6.
11. Kagie MJ, Kenter GG, Tollenaar RA, et al. P53 protein overexpression is common and independent of human papillomavirus infection in squamous cell carcinoma of the vulva. Cancer 1997;80:1228–33.
12. Trimble CL, Hildesheim A, Brinton LA, et al. Heterogeneous etiology of squamous carcinoma of the vulva. Obstet Gynecol 1996;87:59–64.
13. Monk BJ, Burger RA, Lin F, et al. Prognostic significance of human papillomavirus DNA in vulvar carcinoma. Obstet Gynecol 1995;85:709–15.
14. Minucci D, Cinel A, Insacco E, Oselladore M. Epidemiological aspects of vaginal intraepithelial neoplasia. Clin Exp Obstet Gynecol 1995;22:36–42.
15. Ikenberg H, Runge M, Goppinger A, Pfleiderer A. Human papillomavirus DNA in invasive carcinoma of the vagina. Obstet Gynecol 1990;76:432–8.
16. Ostrow RS, Manias DA, Clark BA, et al. The analysis of carcinomas of the vagina for human papillomavirus DNA. Int J Gynecol Pathol 1988;7:308–14.
17. Turek LP. The structure, function and regulation of papillomaviral genes in infection and cancer. Adv Viral Res 1994;44:305–56.
18. Barbosa MS, Lowry DR, Schiller JT. Papillomavirus polypeptides E6 and E7 are zinc-binding proteins. J Virol 1989;63:1404–7.
19. Rodrigues NR, Rowan A, Smith MEF, et al. $P53$ mutations in colorectal cancer. Proc Natl Acad Sci U S A 1990;7:7555–9.
20. Bartek J, Iggo R, Gannon J, Lane DP. Genetic and immunochemical analysis of mutant $P53$ in human breast cancer cell lines. Oncogene 1990;5:893–9.

21. Takahashi T, Suzuki H, Hida T, et al. The *P53* gene is very frequently mutated in small-cell lung cancer with a distinct nucleotide substitution pattern. Cancer Res 1992;52:734–6.

22. Hollstein M, Sidransky D, Vogelstein B, Harris CC. P53 mutations in human cancers. Science 1991;253: 49–53.

23. Levine AJ, Momand J, Finlay CA. The P53 tumor suppressor gene. Nature 1991;351:453–65.

24. El-Deiry WS, Harper JW, O'Connor PM, et al. *WAF1/CIP1* is induced in *P53*-mediated G_1 arrest and apoptosis. Cancer Res 1994;54:1169–74.

25. Miyashita T, Krajewski S, Krajewska M, et al. Immediate early upregulation of bax expression by P53 but not by TGFβ1: a paradigm for distinct apoptotic pathways. Oncogene 1994;9:1791–8.

26. Werness BA, Levine AJ, Howley PM. Association of human papillomavirus types 16 and 18 E6 proteins with P53. Science 1990;248:76–9.

27. Crook T, Tidy JA, Vousden KH. Degradation of P53 can be targeted by HPV E6 sequences distinct from those required for P53 binding and transactivation. Cell 1991;67:547–56.

28. Lechner MS, Laimins LA. Inhibition of P53 DNA binding by human papillomavirus E6 proteins. J Virol 1994;68:4262–73.

29. Vogelstein B, Kinzler K. The multistep nature of cancer. Trends Genet 1993;9:138–41.

30. Akiyama T, Ohuchi T, Sumida S, et al. Phosphorylation of the retinoblastoma protein by cdk2. Proc Natl Acad Sci U S A 1992;89:7900–4.

31. Weinberg RA. The retinoblastoma protein and cell cycle control. Cell 1995;81:323–30.

32. Jones DL, Alani RM, Munger K. The human papillomavirus E7 oncoprotein can uncouple cellular differentiation and proliferation in human keratinocytes by abrogating P21Cip1-mediated inhibition of cdk-2. Genes Dev 1997;11:2101–11.

33. Zerfass-Thome K, Zwerschke W, Mannhardt B, et al. Inactivation of the cdk inhibitor P27KIP1 by the human papillomavirus type 16 E7 oncoprotein. Oncogene 1996;13:2323–30.

34. Momand J, Zambetti GP, Olson DC, et al. The mdm-2 oncogene product forms a complex with the P53 protein and inhibits P53-mediated transactivation. Cell 1992;69:1237–45.

35. Xiao ZX, Chen J, Levine AJ, et al. Interaction between the retinoblastoma protein and the oncoprotein MDM2. Nature 1995;375:694–8.

36. Skomedal H, Kristensen GB, Lie AK, Holm R. Aberrant expression of the cell cycle associated proteins TP53, MDM2, P21, P27, cdk4, cyclin D1, RB and EGFR in cervical carcinomas. Gynecol Oncol 1999;73:223–8.

37. Larson AA, Kern S, Curtiss S, et al. High resolution analysis of chromosome 3p alterations in cervical cancer. Cancer Res 1997;57:4082–90.

38. Chu TY, Shen CY, Chiou YS, et al. HPV-associated cervical cancers show frequent allelic loss at 3p14 but no apparent aberration of *FHIT* mRNA. Int J Cancer 1998;75:199–204.

39. Wistuba II, Montellano FD, Milchgrub S, et al. Deletions of chromosome 3p are frequent and early events in the pathogenesis of uterine cervical carcinoma. Cancer Res 1997;57:3154–8.

40. Rader JS, Gerhard DS, O'Sullivan MJ, et al. Cervical intraepithelial neoplasia III shows frequent allelic loss in 3p and 6p. Genes Chromosomes Cancer 1998;22:57–65.

41. Pinto AP, Lin MC, Mutter GL, et al. Allelic loss in human papillomavirus-positive and -negative vulvar squamous cell carcinomas. Am J Pathol 1999;154: 1009–15.

42. Flowers LC, Wistuba II, Scurry J, et al. Genetic changes during the multistage pathogenesis of human papillomavirus positive and negative vulvar carcinomas. J Soc Gynecol Invest 1999;6:213–21.

43. Ohta M, Inoue H, Cotticelli MG, et al. The FHIT gene, spanning the chromosome 3p14.2 fragile site and renal-carcinoma-associated t(3;8) breakpoint, is abnormal in digestive-tract cancers. Cell 1996; 84:587–97.

44. Holschneider C, Baldwin RL, Epstein JS, et al. Lost fragile histidine triad (FHIT) gene expression may link cigarette smoking and cervical cancer. Proceedings of the Society of Gynecologic Oncologists 31st Annual Meeting; 2000 Feb 5–9; San Diego, CA. Chicago: SGO; 2000.

45. Jou SS, Stewart DB, Stappert J, et al. Genetic and biochemical dissection of protein linkages in the cadherin-catenin complex. Proc Natl Acad Sci U S A 1995;92:5067–71.

46. Kersemaekers AMF, Hermans J, Fleuren GJ, van de Vijver MJ. Loss of heterozygosity for defined regions on chromosomes 3, 11 and 17 in carcinomas of the uterine cervix. Br J Cancer 1998;77:192–200.

47. Kim JW, Cho YH, Lee CG, et al. Human papillomavirus infection and TP53 gene mutation in primary cervical carcinoma. Acta Oncol 1997;36:295–300.

48. Crook T, Wrede D, Tidy JA, et al. Clonal P53 mutation in primary cervical cancer: association with human-papillomavirus-negative tumors. Lancet 1992;339: 1070–3.

49. Ngan HY, Cheung AN, Liu SS, et al. Abnormal expression or mutation of TP53 and HPV in vulvar cancer. Eur J Cancer 1999;35:481–4.

50. Lee YY, Wilczynski SP, Chumakov A, et al. Carcinoma of the vulva: HPV and P53 mutations. Oncogene 1994;9:1655–9.

51. Vastrick I, Makela TP, Koskinen PJ, et al. Myc protein: partners and antagonists. Crit Rev Oncol 1994;5: 59–68.

52. Evan G, Harrington E, Fanidi A, et al. Integrated control of cell proliferation and cell death by the c-myc oncogene. Philos Trans R Soc Lond B Biol Sci 1994;345:269–75.

53. Riou G, Barrois M, Le MG, et al. C-myc proto-oncogene expression and prognosis in early carcinoma of the uterine cervix. Lancet 1987;1:761–3.

54. Bourhis J, Le MG, Barrois M, et al. Prognostic value of c-myc proto-oncogene overexpression in early invasive carcinoma of the cervix. J Clin Oncol 1990; 8:1789–96.

55. Baker VV, Hatch KD, Shingleton HM. Amplification of the c-myc proto-oncogene in cervical carcinoma. J Surg Oncol 1988;39:225–8.

56. Tate JE, Mutter GL, Prasad CJ, et al. Analysis of HPV-positive and -negative vulvar carcinomas for alterations in c-myc, Ha-, Ki- and N-ras genes. Gynecol Oncol 1994;53:78–83.

57. Kiaris H, Spandidos DA. Mutations of *ras* genes in human tumours (review). Int J Oncol 1995;7:413–21.

58. Teneriello MG, Ebina M, Linnoila RI, et al. P53 and K-ras gene mutations in epithelial ovarian neoplasms. Cancer Res 1993;53:3103–8.

59. Spandidos DA. The super-family of *ras* related genes. New York, London: Plenum Press; 1991. p. 311–38.

60. Dokianakis DN, Sourvinos G, Sakkas S, et al. Detection of HPV and *ras* gene mutations in cervical smears from female genital lesions. Oncol Rep 1998;5:1195–8.

61. Garzetti GG, Ciavattini A, Lucarini G, et al. *ras* P21 immunostaining in early stage squamous cervical carcinoma: relationship with lymph node involvement and 72 *kDa-metalloproteinase index*. Anticancer Res 1998;18:609–14.

62. Lakshmi S, Balaraman Nair M, Jayaprakash PG, et al. c-erbB-2 oncoprotein and epidermal growth factor receptor in cervical lesions. Pathobiology 1997;65:163–8.

63. Kay EW, Walsh CJB, Cassidy M, et al. c-erbB-2 immunostaining: problems with interpretation. J Clin Pathol 1994;47:816–22.

64. Berchuck A, Rodriguez G, Kamel A, et al. Expression of the epidermal growth factor receptor and *Her-2/neu* in normal and neoplastic cervix, vulva and vagina. Obstet Gynecol 1990;76:381–7.

65. Zhang H, Hannon GJ, Beach D. P21-containing cyclin kinases exist in both active and non-active states. Genes Dev 1994;8:1750–8.

66. Kim JW, Kim HS, Kim IK, et al. Transforming growth factor-β1 induces apoptosis through down-regulation of c-*myc* gene and overexpression of P27^{Kip1} protein in cervical carcinoma. Gynecol Oncol 1998;69:230–6.

67. Tusjimoto Y, Finger LR, Yunis J, et al. Cloning of the chromosome breakpoint of neoplastic B cells with the t(14;18) chromosome translocation. Science 1984;226:1097–9.

68. Krajewski S, Tanaka A, Takkayama S, et al. Investigation of the subcellular distribution of the *bcl-2* oncoprotein: residence in the nuclear envelope, endoplasmic reticulum, and outer mitochondrial membranes. Cancer Res 1993;53:4701–14.

69. Tjalma W, Weyler J, Goovaerts G, et al. Prognostic value of bcl-2 expression in patients with operable carcinoma of the cervix. J Clin Pathol 1997;50:33–6.

70. Tjalma W, DeCuyper E, Weyler J, et al. Expression of bcl-2 in invasive and in situ carcinoma of the uterine cervix. Am J Obstet Gynecol 1998;178:113–7.

71. Hockel M, Schlenger K, Aral B, et al. Association between tumor hypoxia and malignant progression in advanced cancer of the uterine cervix. Cancer Res 1996;56:4509–15.

72. Siracka E, Siracky J, Pappova N. Vascularization and radiocurability in cancer of the uterine cervix. A retrospective study. Neoplasma 1994;29:183–8.

73. Kohno Y, Iwanari O, Kitao M. Importance of histological vascular density in cervical cancer treated with intra-arterial chemotherapy. Cancer 1993;72:2394–400.

74. Bossi P, Viale G, Lee AKC, et al. Angiogenesis in colorectal tumors: microvessel quantitation in adenomas and carcinomas with clinicopathological correlations. Cancer Res 1995;55:5049–53.

75. Rutgers JL, Mattox TF, Vargas MP. Angiogenesis in uterine cervical squamous cell carcinoma. Int J Gynecol Pathol 1995;14:114–8.

76. Raleigh JA, Calkins-Adams DP, Rinker LH, et al. Hypoxia and vascular endothelial growth factor expression in human squamous cell carcinomas using pimonidazole as a hypoxia marker. Cancer Res 1998;58:3765–8.

77. Senger DR, Brown LF, Claffey KP, Dvorak HF. Vascular permeability factor, tumor angiogenesis and stroma generation. Invasion Metastasis 1994;14:385–94.

78. Odunsi KO, Ganesan TS. The roles of human major histocompatibility complex and human papillomavirus infection in cervical intraepithelial neoplasia and cervical cancer. Clin Oncol 1997;9:4–13.

79. Jochmus I, Durst M, Reid R, et al. Major histocompatibility complex and human papillomavirus type 16 E7 expression in high-grade vulvar lesions. Hum Pathol 1993;24:519–24.

80. Tsukui T, Hildesheim A, Schiffman MH, et al. IL-2 production by peripheral lymphocytes in response to human papillomavirus-derived peptides: correlation with cervical pathology. Cancer Res 1996;56:3967–74.

81. Al-Saleh W, Gianinni SL, Jacobs N, et al. Correlation of T-helper secretory differentiation and types of antigen-presenting cells in squamous intraepithelial lesions of the uterine cervix. J Pathol 1998;184:283–90.

82. Hildesheim A, Schiffman MH, Tsukui T, et al. Immune activation in cervical neoplasia: cross sectional association between plasma soluble interleukin 2 receptor levels and disease. Cancer Epidemiol Biomark Prev 1997;6:807–13.

83. Gianinni SL, Al-Saleh W, Piron H, et al. Cytokine expression in squamous intraepithelial lesions of the uterine cervix: implications for the generation of local immunosuppression. Clin Exp Immunol 1998;113:183–9.

84. Borysiewicz LK, Fiander A, Nimako M, et al. A recombinant vaccinia virus encoding human papillomavirus types 16 and 18, E6 and E7 proteins as immunotherapy for cervical cancer. Lancet 1996;347:1523–7.

85. Stellar MA, Gurski KJ, Murakami M, et al. Cell-mediated immunological responses in cervical and vaginal cancer patients immunized with a lipidated epitope of human papillomavirus type 16 E7. Clin Cancer Res 1998;4:2103–9.

86. Hamada K, Zhang WW, Alemany R, et al. Growth inhibition of human cervical cancer cells with the recombinant adenovirus P53 in vitro. Gynecol Oncol 1996;60:373–9.

4

Anatomy and Natural History

ROBERT L. COLEMAN, MD

Review of the normal female anatomic structures and comprehension of the natural history of the malignancies arising from them provide insight into disease staging, treatment intentions, and patterns of recurrence. In primary carcinomas of the vagina and uterine cervix, the degree of local spread assessed clinically is used to define the stage of disease. In all sites of female lower genital tract cancer, both surgical and nonsurgical treatment modalities are designed to address potential avenues of local and metastatic spread. In this chapter, a description of the normal lower genital tract anatomy will be provided along with an outline of the typical and variant patterns of cancer spread in these sites.

VULVA

Embryologically, the external female genitalia arise from undifferentiated tissues that comprise the genital tubercle, labioscrotal swellings, and urogenital folds.[1] In the absence of fetal androgens, further differentiation of these tissues forms the external female phenotype, which is distinguishable 12 weeks after fertilization. Ambiguity of this differentiation can result from the presence of exogenous or endogenous sex steroids during development; however, the null phenotype is female.

The vulva comprises the mons pubis, the clitoris, the labia majora and minora, the vestibule (urethral meatus and hymenal remnant), perineal body, the associated erectile tissues and muscles, and the supporting subcutaneous tissues (Figure 4–1). The vul-

var structures are situated atop the superficial perineal fascia, a caudal continuation of the abdominal Scarpa's layer. Support is given to the vulva through loose attachment to this fascia. The vulva is bounded by the anterior abdominal wall superiorly, the labial-crural folds laterally, and the anus posteriorly and is perforated by the distal vagina, urethra, and greater vestibular glands. In the adult female, the mons pubis is a hair-bearing, mounded fat pad that overlies the pubic symphysis. Distal continuation of the round ligaments and its fascial sheaths traverse the lateral mons before terminating into the labia majora. The clitoris is situated at the inferior aspect of the mons pubis and is supported by a suspensory ligament that lies beneath the anterior labia commissure (Figure 4–2). The labia majora are elongated bands of skin, connective tissue, and subcutaneous fat that bridge the vulva coming together at the posterior labial commissure. They are hair bearing in the adult and contain numerous sweat and sebaceous glands. Immediately medial to the labia majora are the labia minora. These thin, pigmented structures comprise mostly skin and fibrous tissue and contain little fat. They are non–hair bearing with scant sweat glands but do contain sebaceous glands. The labia minora commune posteriorly at the labial frenulum and divide just proximal to the clitoris anteriorly to form the prepuce and the frenulum of the clitoris. At the junction of the labia minora and vaginal vestibule is the duct opening for the greater vestibular (Bartholin's) gland.

The midline vulvar structures below the mons are the clitoris, the urethral meatus, the vaginal opening, and the perineal body. The clitoris is the most anterior and comprises erectile tissue and nerve endings that

Illustrations by Monique LeBlanc, Toronto, Ontario.

47

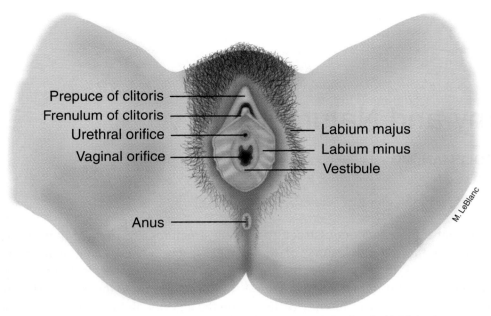

Labels on figure: Prepuce of clitoris, Frenulum of clitoris, Urethral orifice, Vaginal orifice, Labium majus, Labium minus, Vestibule, Anus, M. LeBlanc

Figure 4–1. The external female genitalia with the major anatomic landmarks highlighted.

are important in the sexual response. The terminal glans is generally visible between the prepuce and the frenulum. It is connected to the shaft, which is formed by the fusion of the corpora cavernosa. The shaft then divides into two crura, which are bounded on either side by the pubic rami and are supported by the inferior fascia of the urogenital diaphragm. The crura are covered by the ischiocavernosus muscle, which extends from the symphysis pubis to the ischial tuberosity. Most posteriorly lies the perineal body between the posterior fourchette and the anus. It overlies the central tendon of the perineum, which joins the superficial transverse perineal muscles and fascia. Vestiges of fetal labioscrotal fusion are represented by the perineal raphé.

The vascular supply to the vulva is derived principally from the terminal branches of the internal pudendal vessels and communicates with the superficial and deep external pudendal vessels through a rich anastamotic network (Figure 4–3). The internal pudendal arteries arise from the anterior division of the internal iliac artery and traverse behind the ischial spine to enter Alcock's canal on the obturator internus muscle. It courses adjacent to the ischiopubic ramus, providing vascular supply to the lateral and midline perineal structures, and terminates in the deep and dorsal arteries of the clitoris. Addi-

tional blood supply comes from the superficial and deep external pudendal vessels, which arise from the femoral artery.

Sensory and motor innervation of the vulva is provided by several nerves but is principally from the pudendal nerve. The pudendal nerve arises from the sacral plexus (the anterior rami of S2-S4), exits the pelvis through the greater sciatic foramen, between the piriformis and coccygeus muscles, and crosses beneath the ischial spine. From there, it travels to the vulva adjacent to the internal pudendal vessels in Alcock's canal and provides innervation to the lower vagina, labia, clitoris, perineal body, and their supporting structures. Additional innervation of the vulva comes from the illioinguinal nerve (L1), the genital branch of the genitofemoral nerve (L1-L2), and the perineal branches of the posterior femoral cutaneous nerve (S1-S3), which reach the mons pubis and upper labia through the external inguinal ring and round ligament and along the lateral ischiopubic ramus, respectively.

Lymphatic drainage of the vulva and lower third of the vagina goes primarily to the inguinal nodes (Figure 4–4). These node groups are situated in the subcutaneous tissue overlying the femoral triangle bounded by the inguinal ligament cephalad, the sartorius muscle inferiolaterally, and the adductor longus medially. Anatomically, the nodal group is divided into superficial and deep nodes on the basis of their location in reference to the fascia lata, the cribriform fascia over the fossa ovalis, and the femoral vessels (Figure 4–5). The superficial group primarily receives afferent channels from the vulvar tissues traversing the labia and the mons veneris. This group contains approximately 10 nodes, which lie in the subcutaneous tissue in or around the fossa ovalis and the saphenous vein and its tributaries.

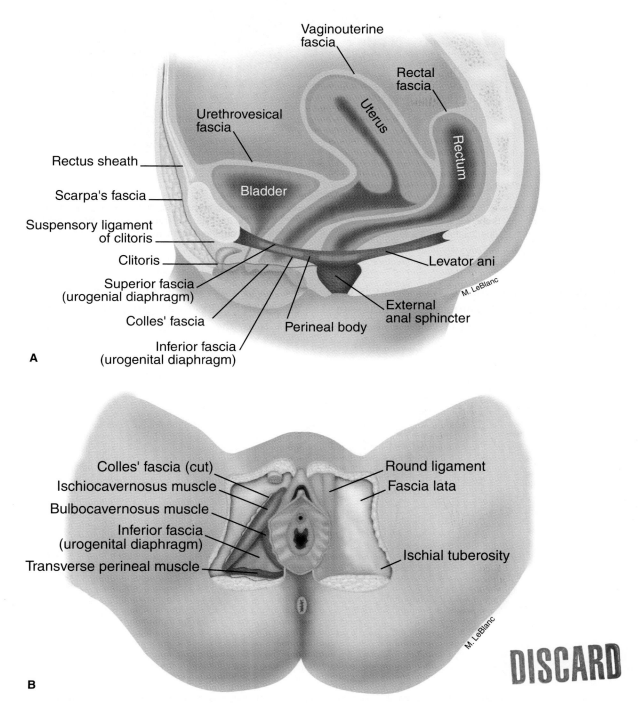

Figure 4–2. *A*, The lateral view of the vulva and lower abdomen demonstrates how the fascial and subcutaneous fat layers relate to one another. *B*, Skin and subcutaneous layers are removed, demonstrating the vulvar structures at the level of the fascia lata, Colles' fascia, and components of the urogenital diaphragm.

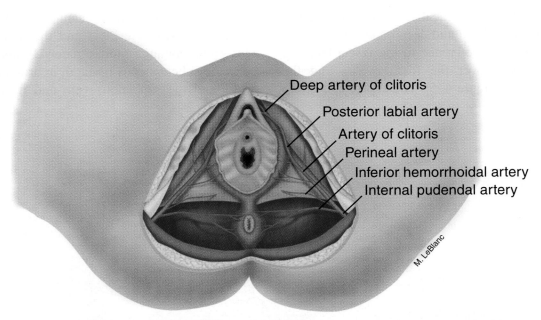

Figure 4–3. The vascular supply to the vulva is principally from the branches of the internal pudendal artery. Proximal branches supply the anus with terminal branches feeding the clitoral apparatus. Anastomoses are made with the superficial and deep external pudendal arteries arising from the femoral artery.

From this location, the efferent channels drain into the deep chain located along the femoral vein. There are approximately three to five deep nodes, the most cephalad being designated as Cloquet's node. Rarely, this node group receives drainage directly from the vulva through aberrant pathways or from

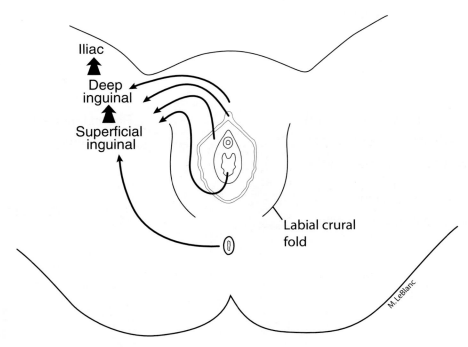

Figure 4–4. The general schema of lymphatic drainage is depicted. The superficial groin nodes receive most of the primary drainage of the vulva with subsequent drainage flowing into the deep nodes and ultimately under the inguinal ligament to the pelvic nodal vasculature. Alternative pathways are to the deep system or pelvic nodes directly, particularly from the clitoris.

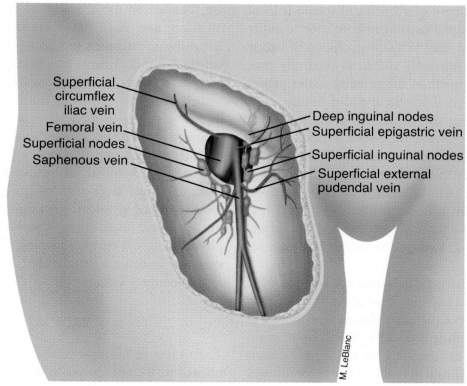

Superficial circumflex iliac vein
Femoral vein
Superficial nodes
Saphenous vein
Deep inguinal nodes
Superficial epigastric vein
Superficial inguinal nodes
Superficial external pudendal vein
M. LeBlanc

Figure 4–5. The anatomic relationship of the groin nodes to the femoral vasculature is demonstrated. The superficial nodal group contains approximately 7 to 10 nodes; the deep group contains approximately 3 to 5 nodes.

the clitoris (Cloquet's node).[2] Clinically important features of in vivo vulvar lymphatic drainage, first described by Parry-Jones, are that ipsilateral flow from the vulva does not cross the labial crural fold laterally, and that, in general, only midline structures (clitoris and perineum) have bilateral efferent drainage.[3] Direct communication of the clitoral lymphatics to the pelvis has been demonstrated, although this is clinically observed less often. Efferent drainage from the groin then passes under the inguinal ligament in the femoral canal to communicate with the external iliac and pelvic nodal chains.

Natural History and Patterns of Spread of Vulvar Cancer

Although many tumor cell types can arise within the vulva or its associated adnexal structures, the preponderance of primary carcinomas of the vulva are squamous cell carcinomas, which arise from the epithelium.[4] The most frequent sites of involvement are the labia minora, clitoris, fourchette, perineal body, and the medial labia majora.

The exact etiology of vulvar cancer is unknown and likely multifactorial. However, vulvar intraepithelial neoplasia (VIN) is found adjacent to these tumors in approximately 30 to 65 percent of cases.[5,6] Although the preponderance of VIN lesions never become invasive, as many as one-third of VIN1/2 lesions will persist, progress, or recur after a short remission, and approximately 20 percent of carcinoma in situ (CIS) lesions will harbor an invasive component.[7,8] The direct progression of VIN to cancer is difficult to document. In addition, the natural history of these lesions appears to have age-related factors. For instance, Basta and colleagues found that not only was CIS and stage I carcinoma increasing in frequency in women under age 45 years but also that this cohort was more likely to have multifocal disease (63% versus 32%).[7] In addition, the younger cohort was more likely to have lesions associated with human papillomavirus (HPV) infection (62% versus 18%).

The classic pattern of growth and spread is local extension and lymphovascular embolization to either regional or distant sites. With the exception of vulvar melanoma, the pattern of spread is relatively predictable. Local growth of the primary tumor generally occurs in a radial pattern and also invades deep into the underlying subcutaneous tissues. Objective measures of this growth have been standardized with the creation of the tumor, node, metastasis (TNM) staging system.[9] In this manner, tumor is described in reference to size (T1 $\leq$ 2 cm, T2 > 2 cm), involvement of the distal midline structures (T3: urethra, vagina, anus), and invasion of the midline organs (T4: bladder mucosa, upper urethra, rectal mucosa) or bony fixation.

Once invasion occurs, the tumor can spread via the dermal lymphatics to the regional nodes following the previously described pattern of flow. There appears to be a threshold with regard to the likelihood of groin metastatic disease, depending on the depth of invasion. Kelly and colleagues reported that the frequency of metastatic disease among 24 patients with $\leq$ 1 mm of invasion (measured as depth of deepest invasion from the most proximal adjacent rete peg) was 0 percent.[10] This observation has led to a subclassification of stage I disease, with the clinical implication being that the consideration of nodal dissection may safely be dismissed in these patients.[11]

Careful inspection of en bloc tumor resections and biopsies by Cherry and Glücks-mann demonstrated that tumor lymphatic emboli were present in only 19 percent of cases.[12] Clinically, recurrences in the retained skin bridges among patients undergoing separate incision removal of the primary lesion and the regional lymphatics are very uncommon. This observation would support the hypothesis that lymphatic metastases occur rapidly as a result of embolization and most often without interval deposition of viable tumor. Clinical experience of lymphatic metastatic disease would suggest that the descriptions of normal vulvar lymphatic drainage by Parry-Jones also hold for invasive disease.

Lymphatic metastases from lateralized lesions rarely involve the contralateral groin in the absence of ipsilateral metastatic disease, and spread from the midline lesions can be identified in either or both groins.[13] Treatment paradigms, as discussed later, are founded on these described principles of local invasion and potential metastatic spread sites. Recently, investigation has been pursued addressing whether tumor lymphatic drainage is a random process or if there is a particular node ("sentinel node") within a particular groin that may be at higher risk to receive the primary lymphatic drainage than others.[14] The node mapping procedure, performed by perilesional injection of blue dye and/or sulfur colloidal radionucleotide, identifies an average of one to two nodes per groin, which are then examined histologically (Figure 4–6). Immunohistochemical ultrastaging can be further accomplished with cytokeratin staining. The procedure is currently undergoing validation within the Gynecologic Oncology Group.

VAGINA

The vagina is a hollow pliable viscus structure that opens onto the vulva caudally and attaches to the uterine cervix cephalad. Embryologically, the vagina forms from the fusion of the distal paramesonephric ducts with the sinovaginal bulbs, which, by 18 weeks, undergo progressive evagination and subsequent canalization. The proximal one-third of the vagina forms in conjunction with the uterus, and the distal two-thirds of the vagina are separated from the urogenital sinus by the hymen. Failure of the fusion process leads to incomplete or complete vaginal septi. These may be oriented transversely or longitudinally, depending on where the fusion and canalization were incomplete. During development, the mesonephric duct disappears entirely; however, occasionally, vestiges of this structure line the vagina and can be responsible for cyst formation (Gartner's cyst).

The vagina is a potential space, typically about 7 to 10 cm in length, although great variation exists. The anterior wall is shorter than the posterior wall by about 3 cm because of the uterine cervix attachment. The upper or proximal vagina flares, giving rise to the fornices (Figure 4–7). In the prone position, the anteroposterior vaginal walls eventrate because of the urethra and urinary bladder and the rectum. The lateral vaginal sulci, together with this anatomic approximation, give the vagina an "H" appearance on cross-section. The lower vagina is

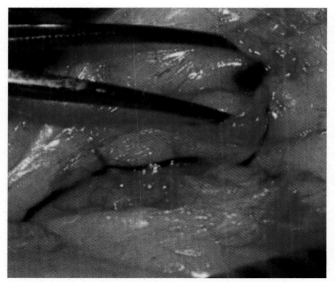
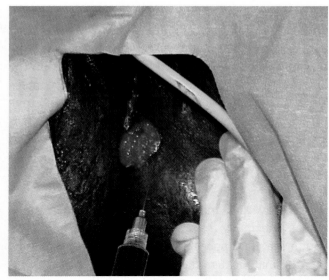

Figure 4–6. The lymphatic mapping procedure involves injection of blue dye at the soft tissue margin of the primary and identifies the sentinel node(s) by following the lymphatic channel in the subcutaneous tissue.

constricted as it passes through the urogenital hiatus in the levator ani. The vagina is angled at approximately 120° from the horizontal position by the anterior traction of the levators at the junction of the lower one-third and upper two-thirds of the vagina.

Like other hollow viscera, the vagina contains a mucosa, submucosa, muscularis, and adventitia but lacks a serosal surface (except at the pouch of Douglas). It is lined with nonkeratinizing, stratified squamous epithelium overlying a basement membrane containing many papillae. Generally, there are no glands per se in the vagina. Lubrication is predomi-

nantly achieved by mucous secretions of the cervix. The muscularis layer is arranged, most accurately, in a bihelical pattern but contains an inner circumferential layer and an outer longitudinal layer. This layer is attached to the adventia, a thin layer that is continuous with the endopelvic fascia in the pelvis. In this manner, it has muscular attachments to the levator ani and a deep transverse perineal body. The vagina is capable of dramatic alterations in size, particularly during parturition, but resulting tears in this adventitia and its attachments to the pelvic musculature along with nerve injury lead to prolapse.[15,16]

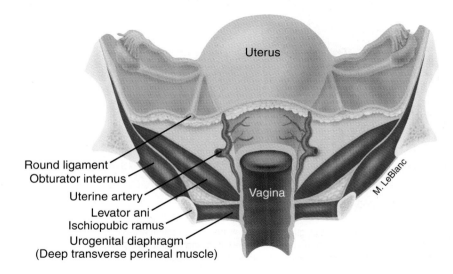

Round ligament
Obturator internus
Uterine artery
Levator ani
Ischiopubic ramus
Urogenital diaphragm
(Deep transverse perineal muscle)

Uterus

Vagina

M. LeBlanc

Figure 4–7. The vaginal anatomy and pelvic musculature are demonstrated in the axis of the vagina. The vascular supply from the uterine arteries is observed coursing through the lower cardinal ligament. The vaginal support is provided through attachment to the fascia of the levator ani and urogenital diaphragm.

The vascular supply to the vagina is rich and widely anastomotic (Figure 4–8). The proximal vagina is supplied by the descending branches of the uterine vessels. The vaginal artery, arising from the anterior division of the internal iliac artery, courses along the medial surface of the obturator internus muscle to supply the midvagina through an extensive branching network, both ascending and descending. The descending vessels supply the distal vagina, where they anastomose with the terminal (perineal) branches of the internal pudendal artery.

Sensory and motor innervation of the vagina comes principally from two regions. The major innervation to the upper-midvagina comes through the uterovaginal plexus. These sympathetic and parasympathetic nerve bundles originate with the sacral roots (S2-S4) and join the hypogastric plexus branches to the rectum, bladder, and uterus (Figure 4–9). They reach the vagina laterally and terminate throughout the vagina. The distal vagina also received somatic innervation from the terminal branches of the pudendal nerve, in particular, the perineal and labial branches.

The lymphatic vascular network of the vagina is fine and diffusely anastomotic. Early dye studies of the vagina demonstrated that the entire organ could be reached from a single injection site.[17] However, ultimately, this mucosal meshwork coalesces in the deeper layers of the submucosa and muscularis and forms coarser lateral channels, which, depending on location, find their way to the regional nodes (Figure 4–10). As has been outlined above, the distal or lower one-third of the vagina can drain to the femoral nodes through the vulvar tributaries. However, the majority of the vagina drains to the pelvic lateral sidewall. The exact destination of this flow is quite varied and is dependent on the axial and longitudinal points of reference. For instance, the midvaginal lateral lymphatic flow goes primarily to the inferior gluteal nodes, whereas the upper posterior, midline vaginal lymphatic flow drains into the superior rectal or presacral nodes. In general, the upper vaginal lymphatic flow mimics that of the uterine cervix, and the lower vaginal flow mimics that of the vulva; however, great variation exists. Nearly all pelvic nodes receive lymph flow from the vagina.

Natural History of Vaginal Cancer

Malignancy present within the vagina most commonly results from metastatic spread from other primary sites, particularly the cervix, endometrium, colon, ovary, and vulva.[18] Primary carcinoma of the

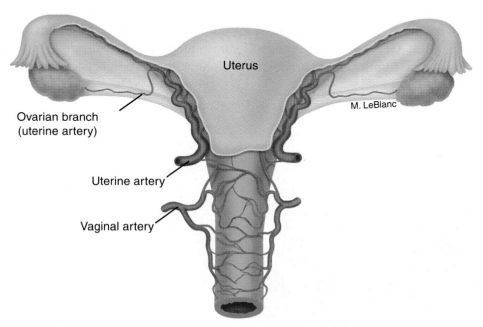

Figure 4–8. A detailed view of the vascular supply to the vagina is demonstrated. The vaginal artery arises from the anterior division of the internal iliac artery and supplies the length of the vagina. Anastomoses occur with the uterine artery cephalad and with the internal pudendal artery caudally.

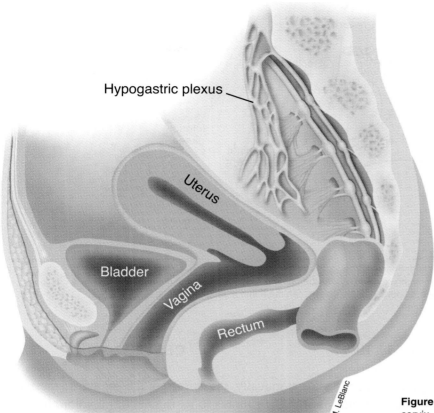

Hypogastric plexus

Uterus

Bladder

Vagina

Rectum

M. LeBlanc

Figure 4–9. Autonomic innervation of the vagina, cervix, uterus, and rectum comes from the hypogastric plexus arising in sacral roots (S2 to S4).

vagina is rare. Fu and Reagan found that just 58 of 355 (16%) vaginal tumors were primary to the vagina.[19] Lesions occur most frequently on the posterior vaginal wall and in the upper third of the vagina.[17] Since the vagina is typically devoid of glandular tissue, the principal histology of the primary vaginal cancer is squamous cell carcinoma.[20] However, notable exceptions exist, such as melanoma, sarcoma, and diethylstilbestrol (DES)-associated clear cell carcinoma, each of which have a different predilection for site of involvement.[21]

Vaginal tumors progress by local expansion. They may progress up or down the vagina to involve neighboring organs, although in general, such involvement usually redesignates the site of origin. For the most part, the vagina lacks anatomic barriers, and growth readily occurs into the underlying structures and organs. Since natural drainage of the vaginal lymphatics is to the pelvic wall, the paravaginal and parametric tissues are later involved

with progressive growth. Extension into the obturator fossa, uterosacral ligaments, and cardinal ligaments and invasion of the fascia of the obturator internus muscles are features of late disease. Clinical classification (staging) of disease is determined by and representative of this local expansion[9] (Figure 4–11). Not surprisingly, nodal involvement is frequent and stage related.[17] Treatment programs are currently designed to address local tumor control and the potential for nodal metastatic spread in this manner. Distant metastatic disease is identified in approximately 10 to 25 percent of patients and occurs as hematogenous dissemination.[21]

Although a preinvasive lesion has been described in the vagina (vaginal intraepithelial neoplasia [VAIN]) similar to that of the cervix, the rate of progression into invasive disease is unknown.[22,23] These lesions share clinicopathologic features with cervical intraepithelial neoplasia (CIN); they are frequently encountered as multifocal lesions in young,

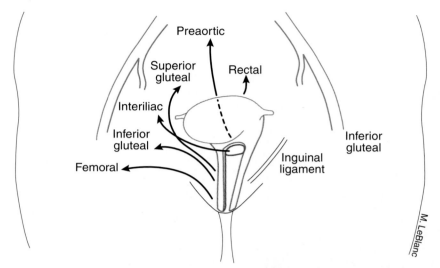

Figure 4–10. Lymphatic drainage of the vagina is dependent on location. Cephalad, the drainage approximates the cervix, draining into the pelvic nodes. Caudally, the groin nodes receive drainage. The central portion of the vagina can drain into a variety of pelvic locales.

sexually active women and are associated with HPV infection.[24] In addition, they often coexist with CIN. However, the low incidence of vaginal cancer, despite the prevalence of VAIN, likely stems from the lack of a transformation zone.

CERVIX

Anatomically, the cervix is the region of the uterus from the isthmus to its vaginal termination. It is variable in size with respect to the corpus, depending on

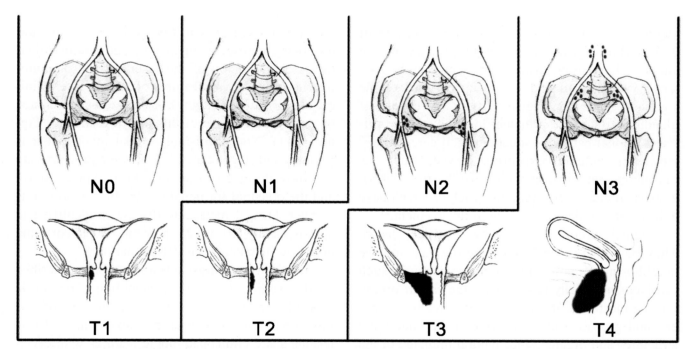

Figure 4–11. The International Federation of Gynecology and Obstetrics (FIGO) staging schema for carcinoma of the vagina. (Adapted from Perez CA, Grigsby PW, Mutch DG, et al. Gynecologic tumors. In: Rubin P, editor. Clinical oncology: a multidisciplinary approach for primary care physicians and students. 8th ed. Philadelphia: WB Saunders; 2001. [In press])

the age of the patient and other uterine and cervical factors, but in general, it ranges from 2 to 4 cm in length in the nulliparous woman. It is connected to the vagina through an oblique fibrous attachment, where approximately one-third of the anterior wall and about one-half of the posterior wall are exposed to the vagina (infravaginal cervix)[25] (Figure 4–12). The vaginal portion or exocervix is convex in shape. Centrally located within the exocervix is the external cervical os. This opening to the uterus is variable in size, depending on age and history of parturition. Proximal to the external os is the elliptical endocervical canal, which terminates at the internal cervical os. Here, the cervix joins the uterine isthmus. Anteroposteriorly, the supravaginal cervix is covered by the parietal peritoneum. The cervix comprises fibrous, elastic, and smooth muscular tissues. It is more fibrous than the corpus, with smooth muscle comprising just 15 percent in the body of the cervix, primarily at the endocervix. It is lined by columnar and squamous epithelium. The endocervix is lined by a single layer of mucin-producing columnar epithelium, which also lines the many endocervical glands. In this respect, the mucin-producing apparatus is not truly glandular but rather a complex infolding of the mucosal surface. The distal extent of this mucosa joins stratified, nonkeratinizing squamous epithelium on or near the exocervix. The location of this abrupt transformation is variable and undergoes continuous change during the reproductive years, responding to the lower vaginal pH after puberty. In this process, the columnar epithelium undergoes metaplastic change to the more resilient squamous epithelium. It is in this transformation zone that most preinvasive and invasive lesions arise. Distally, the ectocervical tissue is continuous with the vaginal epithelium.

The paired uterosacral and cardinal ligaments primarily support the cervix and uterus. The uterosacral ligaments attach at the base of the uterus and run in the rectouterine peritoneal folds to the sacrum. The cardinal ligaments are thickened bands of fibrous tissue in continuation with the endopelvic fascia that extend to the lateral pelvic sidewall (Figure 4–13). Within these bands also run the nerves and vessels to the cervix and pelvic viscera. The principal arterial supply to the cervix comes from the descending branches of the uterine artery, which reaches the cervix at the upper margin of the cardinal ligaments and anastomoses with the ascending vaginal arterial branches. The venous drainage parallels the arterial supply. Innervation of the cervix is from the pelvic autonomic system arising in the sacral roots (S2-S4) and traveling through the superior, middle, and inferior hypogastric plexuses, predominately to the endocervix and peripheral deep exocervix. This innervation pathway explains the relative insensitivity to pain in the upper vaginal vault and exocervix.

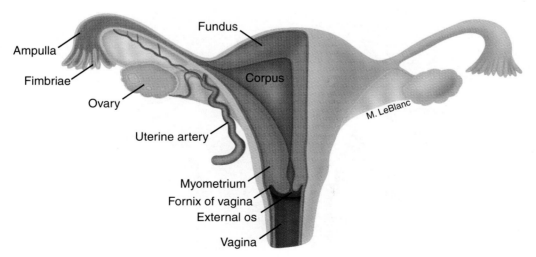

Figure 4–12. The relationship between the cervix and the upper vagina is demonstrated. The cervix normally protrudes into the vagina, more so posteriorly. The vascular supply reaches the cervix through the cardinal ligament.

The regular and repetitive form of the mucosal and stromal lymphatic capillaries makes the efferent drainage of the cervix less ambiguous, compared with those of the vagina and uterine corpus. The anastomosing meshwork courses from the lattice in the mucosa to more organized channels within the stroma, eventually forming three dominant trunks: lateral, posterior, and anterior[26] (Figure 4–14). The lateral trunk is composed of three branches (upper, middle, and lower), which drain into a variety of pelvic and parametrial locations. The upper branch primarily drains into the upper interiliac nodal bundle and is considered by some to be the dominant pathway of the cervix. The middle and lower branches drain to the parametrial, obturator, inferior, and superior gluteal and external iliac node groups. The posterior collecting trunks run most often with the uterosacral ligaments and drain into lymph nodes in the superior rectal, presacral, and subaortic chains. A second pathway follows the course of the ureter, sometimes draining into small ureteric nodes but also draining into the common iliac and paraortic nodes (Figure 4–15). The anterior collecting trunk is the least developed pathway and was initially disputed. However, lymphatic drainage from the anterior cervix has been described along the undersurface of the bladder, traversing laterally to the obliterated umbilical vessels and entering the distal external iliac nodal group, separate from the lymphatics of the bladder.

Natural History of Cervical Cancer

Most cancers arising in the uterine cervix are carcinomas of its epithelium. The predominant histology is squamous; however, an increased proportion of adenocarcinoma has recently been observed.[27] These malignancies are believed to develop, in most cases, from a preinvasive lesion (CIS), over a number of years. The preinvasive lesion to endocervical adenocarcinoma is less well defined.[28] However, longitudinal studies of untreated patients with squamous CIS

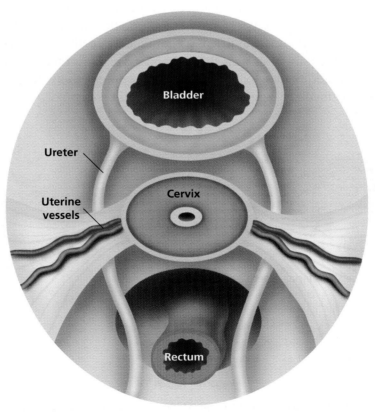

Figure 4–13. Supportive tissues to the cervix are from the cardinal and uterosacral ligaments, which blend with the fascia of the pelvic diaphragm.

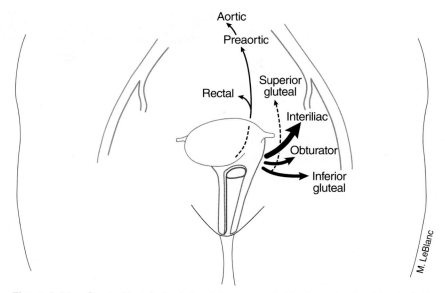

Figure 4–14. Cervical lymphatic drainage is represented by three dominant trunks (anterior, lateral, and posterior).

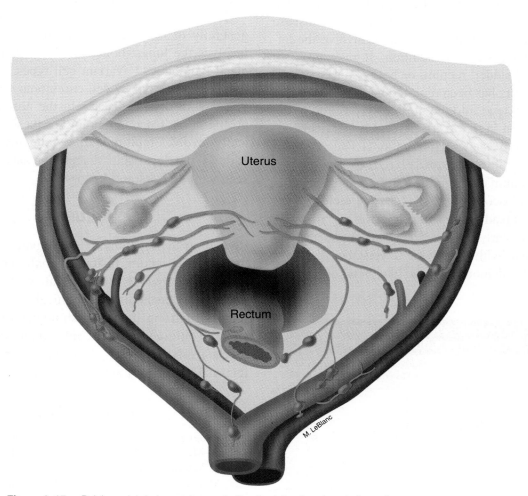

Figure 4–15. Pelvic nodal drainage demonstrating the lateral and posterior pathways.

have documented progression into invasive disease in a significant number of cases if followed up long enough.[29–35] Table 4–1 outlines the studies of CIS that have been reported demonstrating this finding.

HPV infection is present in most cases and has been identified in over 95 percent of cervical cancers.[36] The molecular events driving CIS to invade and, therefore, establish the diagnosis of cancer are not well known. However, recent information suggests that the viral load, in addition to the presence of HPV, places patients at increased risk for subsequent cancer development.[37] Most certainly, it is a result of the accumulation of genetic errors, such as altered expression of the *FHIT* gene and the interaction of HPV DNA with the host genome.[38–40] The natural history of growth is believed to progress through a state of microscopic invasion into the stroma and radial growth on the surface. Ultimately, a mass is formed, which, in general, first grows locally to invade the deeper stroma and, later, the paracervical and parametrial tissues. If left untreated, the disease will expand through these tissues to involve the lateral pelvic sidewall. In addition, it may grow to involve the bladder, rectum, or both. Cancer arising from the cervix has been reported in 10 to 30 percent of cases to extend into the uterine corpus and to the uterine adnexa in 0.5 to 1.6 percent.[41] Cervical cancer is currently staged (International Federation of Gynecology and Obstetrics [FIGO]) by findings on physical examination, limited radiographic evaluation, and endoscopy of the bladder and rectum.[9]

Lateral spread is the rule; however, as many as 17 percent of early-stage cervical cancer patients will be identified with lymphatic metastatic disease.[42] Table 4–2[43–45] demonstrates the likelihood of metastatic disease and the distribution of these metastases among patients with early-stage disease. The pelvic nodes, as a group, are most commonly involved. It is very uncommon to find isolated paraortic lymphatic disease in the absence of metastatic pelvic disease.[46] However, which node group is at greatest risk is variable and dependent on tumor size and location. At present, lymphatic mapping of cervical cancer with blue dye and lymphoscintigraphy is undergoing evaluation.

Hematogenous spread of disease is a finding generally of late presentation and most commonly involves the lungs, bone, intrabdominal viscera, or distal lymphatics.[47] Variant cell types, such as neuroendocrine or glassy cell carcinoma, may be associated with distant disease in the absence of local proliferation. Current therapy for these variants typically involves multimodality strategies designed to address the local and distant metastatic potential seen with their natural history.[48]

CONCLUSION

Review of the anatomy of the female lower genital tract and the natural history of malignancies occurring there provides the clinician with a reference point to understanding the clinical presentation and intent of current treatment strategies for individual sites. Continued efforts into understanding the mechanisms by which these malignancies exhibit their natural history are paramount.

REFERENCES

1. Langman J. Urogenital system. In: Langman J, editor. Medical embryology. Baltimore, MD: Williams & Wilkins; 1981. p. 255–9.
2. Merrill J, Ropss N. Cancer of the vulva. Cancer 1961; 14:13–6.

Table 4–2. LIKELIHOOD OF LYMPHATIC METASTASES IN EARLY-STAGE CERVICAL CANCER

Stage	% Involved
Ia1	0.15
Ia2	1.13
Ib1	16
Ib2	32
IIa	25
IIb	43

Adapted from Sakuragi N, et al;[46] Carlson V, et al;[47] Chang TC, et al.[48]

Table 4–1. PROGRESSION OF SQUAMOUS CIS TO CANCER WITHOUT TREATMENT

Author	N	Median Follow-Up (mo)	Invasive Disease (%)
Peterson[35]	127	108	33
Koss[33]	67	39	13
Clemmesen[32]	67	99	40
Kottmeier[34]	31	144	80
Saito[29]	45	26	58
Luthra[31]	43	24	32
Holowaty[30]	507	4–24	1.4

CIS = carcinoma in situ.

3. Parry-Jones E. Lymphatics of the vulva. J Obstet Gynecol Br Emp 1963;70:751.

4. Wilkinson E. Premalignant and malignant tumors of the vulva. In: Kurman RJ, editor. Blaustein's pathology of the female genital tract. New York: Springer-Verlag; 1994. p. 87–129.

5. Gomez Rueda N, Garcia A, Vighi S, et al. Epithelial alterations adjacent to invasive squamous carcinoma of the vulva. J Reprod Med 1994;39(7):526–30.

6. Dvoretsky PM, Bonfiglio TA, Helmkamp BF, et al. The pathology of superficially invasive, thin vulvar squamous cell carcinoma. Int J Gynecol Pathol 1984;3(4):331–42.

7. Basta A, Adamek K, Pitynski K. Intraepithelial neoplasia and early stage vulvar cancer. Epidemiological, clinical and virological observations. Eur J Gynaecol Oncol 1999;20(2):111–4.

8. Modesitt SC, Waters AB, Walton L, et al. Vulvar intraepithelial neoplasia III: occult cancer and the impact of margin status on recurrence [see comments]. Obstet Gynecol 1998;92(6):962–6.

9. AJCC. Cancer staging manual. 5th ed. Atlanta: Lippincott-Raven; 1997.

10. Kelley JLD, Burke TW, Tornos C, et al. Minimally invasive vulvar carcinoma: an indication for conservative surgical therapy. Gynecol Oncol 1992;44(3):240–4.

11. International Federation of Gynecology and Obstetrics. Modifications in the staging for stage I vulvar and stage I cervical cancer. Report of the FIGO Committee on Gynecologic Oncology. Int J Gynaecol Obstet 1995;50(2):215–6.

12. Cherry C, Glücks-mann A. Lymphatic embolism and lymph node metastasis in cancer of vulva and of uterine cervix. Cancer 1955;8:564.

13. Sedlis A, Homesley H, Bundy BN, et al. Positive groin lymph nodes in superficial squamous cell vulvar cancer. A Gynecologic Oncology Group Study. Am J Obstet Gynecol 1987;156(5):1159–64.

14. Levenback C, Burke TW, Gerhenson DM, et al. Intraoperative lymphatic mapping for vulvar cancer. Obstet Gynecol 1994;84(2):163–7.

15. van Dongen L. The anatomy of genital prolapse. S Afr Med J 1981;60(9):357–9.

16. Allen RE, Hosker GL, Smith AR, Warrell DW. Pelvic floor damage and childbirth: a neurophysiological study [see comments]. Br J Obstet Gynaecol 1990;97(9):770–9.

17. Plentl A, Friedman E. Lymphatic system of the female genitalia. Philadelphia: W. B. Saunders Company; 1971. p. 51–6.

18. Hilborn L, Fu Y. Intraepithelial, invasive and metastatic neoplasms of the vagina. In: Wilkinson E, editor. Pathology of the vulva and vagina. New York: Churchill Livingston; 1987. p. 184.

19. Fu YS, Reagan JW, Bennington JL. Pathology of the uterine cervix, vagina, and vulva. Philadelphia: W.B. Saunders; 1989. p. 336–79.

20. Herbst AL, Green TH Jr, Ulfelder H. Primary carcinoma of the vagina. An analysis of 68 cases. Am J Obstet Gynecol 1970;106(2):210–8.

21. Creasman WT, Phillips JL, Menck HR. The National Cancer Data Base report on cancer of the vagina. Cancer 1998;83(5):1033–40.

22. Brinton LA, Nasca PC, Mallin K, et al. Case-control study of in situ and invasive carcinoma of the vagina. Gynecol Oncol 1990;38(1):49–54.

23. Eddy GL, Singh KP, Gansler TS. Superficially invasive carcinoma of the vagina following treatment for cervical cancer: a report of six cases. Gynecol Oncol 1990;36(3):376–9.

24. Lenehan PM, Meffe F, Lickrish GM. Vaginal intraepithelial neoplasia; biologic aspects and management. Obstet Gynecol 1986;68(3):333–7.

25. Ferenczy A, Wright T. Anatomy and histology of the cervix. In: Kurman R, editor. Blaustein's pathology of the female genital tract. New York: Springer-Verlag; 1994. p. 185–201.

26. Plentl A, Friedman E. Lymphatic system of the female genitalia. Philadelphia: W.B. Saunders; 1971. p. 75–84.

27. Zaino RJ. Glandular lesions of the uterine cervix. Mod Pathol 2000;13(3):261–74.

28. Nicklin JL, Perrin LC, Crandon AJ, Ward BG. Microinvasive adenocarcinoma of the cervix. Aust N Z J Obstet Gynaecol 1999;39(4):411–3.

29. Saito J, Fukuda T, Hoshiai H, Noda K. High-risk types of human papillomavirus associated with the progression of cervical dysplasia to carcinoma. J Obstet Gynaecol Res 1999;25(4):281–6.

30. Holowaty P, Miller AB, Rohan T, To T. Natural history of dysplasia of the uterine cervix [see comments]. J Natl Cancer Inst 1999;91(3):252–8.

31. Luthra UK, Prabhakar AK, Seth P, et al. Natural history of precancerous and early cancerous lesions of the uterine cervix. Acta Cytol 1987;31(3):226–34.

32. Clemmesen J, Poulsen H. Report of the Ministry of the Interior. Copenhagen: Ministry of the Interior; 1971.

33. Koss L, Stewart F, Foote F. Some histological aspects of behavior of epidermoid carcinoma in situ and related lesions of the uterine cervix. Cancer 1963; 16:1160.

34. Kottmeier H. Evolution et traitment des epitheliomas. Rev Fr Gynecol Obstet 1961;56:821.

35. Peterson O. Spontaneous course of cervical pre-cancerous conditions. Am J Obstet Gynecol 1956;72: 1063–7.

36. Walboomers JM, Jacobs MV, Manos MM, et al. Human papillomavirus is a necessary cause of invasive cervical cancer worldwide [see comments]. J Pathol 1999;189(2):12–9.

37. Josefsson A, Magnusson P, Ylitalo N, et al. Viral load of human papilloma virus 16 as a determinant for development of cervical carcinoma in situ: a nested case-control study. Lancet 2000;355:2189–93.

38. Park TW, Fujiwara H, Wright TC. Molecular biology of cervical cancer and its precursors. Cancer 1995;76(10 Suppl):1902–13.

39. Muller CY, O'Boyle JD, Fong KM, et al. Abnormalities of fragile histidine triad genomic and complementary DNAs in cervical cancer: association with human papillomavirus type [see comments]. J Natl Cancer Inst 1998;90(6):433–9.

40. Wistuba II, Montellano FD, Milchgrub S, et al. Deletions of chromosome 3p are frequent and early events in the pathogenesis of uterine cervical carcinoma. Cancer Res 1997;57(15):3154–8.

41. Sutton GP, Bundy BN, Delgado G, et al. Ovarian metastases in stage IB carcinoma of the cervix: a Gynecologic Oncology Group study [see comments]. Am J Obstet Gynecol 1992;166(1 Pt 1):50–3.

42. Hopkins MP, Morley GW. Stage IB squamous cell cancer of the cervix: clinicopathologic features related to survival. Am J Obstet Gynecol 1991;164(6 Pt 1): 1520–9.

43. Ueki M, Okamoto Y, Misake O, et al. Conservative therapy for microinvasive carcinoma of the uterine cervix. Gynecol Oncol 1994;53(1):109–13.

44. Delgado G, Bundy BN, Fowler WC Jr, et al. A prospective surgical pathological study of stage I squamous carcinoma of the cervix: a Gynecologic Oncology Group Study. Gynecol Oncol 1989;35(3):314–20.

45. Lagasse LD, Creasman WT, Shingleton HM, et al. Results and complications of operative staging in cervical cancer: experience of the Gynecologic Oncology Group. Gynecol Oncol 1980;9(1):90–8.

46. Sakuragi N, Satoh C, Takeda N, et al. Incidence and distribution pattern of pelvic and paraaortic lymph node metastasis in patients with stages IB, IIA, and IIB cervical carcinoma treated with radical hysterectomy. Cancer 1999;85(7):1547–54.

47. Carlson V, Delclos L, Fletcher G. Distant metastases in squamous cell carcinoma of the uterine cervix. Radiology 1967;88:961–5.

48. Chang TC, Lai CH, Hong JH, et al. Randomized trial of neoadjuvant cisplatin, vincristine, bleomycin, and radical hysterectomy versus radiation therapy for bulky stage IB and IIA cervical cancer. J Clin Oncol 2000;18(8):1740–7.

5

Diagnostic Imaging

SILVIA D. CHANG, MD
HEDVIG HRICAK, MD, PhD

In the last 20 years, technical advances in cross-sectional imaging modalities, such as ultrasonography, computed tomography (CT), and magnetic resonance imaging (MRI) have resulted in dramatic changes in the imaging evaluation of female lower genital tract cancers. By improving clinicians' ability to define the location and extent of tumors, these techniques have facilitated treatment planning. However, knowledge of the advantages and limitations of each imaging modality is necessary to optimize patients' evaluations and to streamline the approach to their clinical management.

The past 10 years have seen a marked decline in the use of conventional imaging techniques, such as lymphangiography (LAG), intravenous pyelography (IVP), and barium enema, for evaluation of female lower genital tract cancers. For the most part, conventional studies have been replaced by cross-sectional imaging, which provides more detailed information about the extent of disease. However, in some cases, conventional imaging is still important.

Although the imaging modalities that are used routinely to assess gynecologic tumors provide only anatomic information, newer studies (eg, MR spectroscopic imaging [MRSI] and positron emission tomography [PET]) can add metabolic and functional information. These methods are already being used to assess brain, prostate, and other cancers and may soon become part of the routine evaluation of female lower genital tract cancers.

CONVENTIONAL IMAGING MODALITIES

Radiography

Traditionally, conventional radiographic evaluation of female lower genital tract cancers included chest radiography, barium enema, and IVP. *Chest radiography* is still used frequently in the work-up of gynecologic malignancies. Lung metastases usually manifest as parenchymal nodules with or without cavitation; less commonly, mediastinal lymphadenopathy may be seen in patients with advanced disease.

Double-contrast *barium enema* can be used to assess rectal or colonic involvement. Radiographic features of tumor invasion include fixation or tethering of the bowel wall, irregular serrations, mucosal ulceration, or fistula formation.[1,2] Although barium enema was once obtained routinely to evaluate gynecologic cancer patients, it has largely been replaced by sigmoidoscopy and colonoscopy, studies that permit direct visualization and biopsy of the bowel wall. The low positive yield of barium enema also contributed to the decline in its use.[3-5] Barium enema is most useful in the evaluation of advanced disease; even then, it is often replaced by CT.[6,7]

The *IVP* can be used to identify obstruction of the urinary tract by tumor. A delayed or persistent nephrogram, hydronephrosis, or hydroureter may be signs of involvement. Extrinsic compression of the ureter by tumor can also be identified. However, the low positive yield and the increased use of cross-sectional imaging have contributed to a reduction in the use of the IVP.[8,9]

Lymphangiography

Lymphangiography was once considered to be the best study to assess nodal disease. This technique requires catheterization of a small lymphatic vessel in the foot, usually between the first and second toes, and slow injection of an oil-based contrast agent. With serial imaging, the course of the contrast media is followed cephalad, through the pelvic and para-aortic nodes and into the thoracic duct and left supraclavicular (Virchow) nodes. Radiographic features of lymph node involvement include enlarged nodes, distortion of nodal architecture, and lymphatic obstruction. The reported positive predictive value for lymphangiography in detecting nodal metastases ranges from 14 to 80 percent.[10–12]

A Gynecologic Oncology Group study in 1990 compared the sensitivity and specificity of LAG, CT, and ultrasonography (US) with the results of lymphadenectomy. The sensitivity of LAG was 79 percent and the specificity 73 percent; the sensitivities of CT and US were 34 percent and 19 percent, respectively, and their specificities were 96 percent and 99 percent, respectively.[13] The low sensitivity of CT that was reported in this study may reflect the relatively large size threshold (1.5 cm) used to define abnormal lymph nodes; other investigators have used a threshold of 1 cm.[14,15] For evaluation of pelvic lymph nodes, one disadvantage of LAG is that it does not visualize the presacral and obturator lymph nodes. Today, the number of centers where LAG is routinely performed has declined, and the procedure is being replaced with cross-sectional imaging techniques that are less invasive, identify lymph node involvement with comparable accuracy,[14–16] and evaluate extranodal structures.[16]

CROSS-SECTIONAL IMAGING MODALITIES

Ultrasonography

Ultrasonography is widely available, is relatively inexpensive, and provides multiplanar images without using ionizing radiation. However, the image quality is operator dependent and can be degraded by body habitus and bowel gas. Although US is used extensively to assess ovarian and endometrial abnormalities, it is less often used to assess cancers of the cervix, vagina, or vulva.

Technique

For transabdominal US, the bladder must be full to provide an acoustic window for assessment of the underlying pelvic structures. A 3- to 5-MHz transducer is used routinely. An empty bladder is preferred for transvaginal US, and because the tissues being examined are very close, a 5- to 7.5-MHz transducer can be used to obtain better spatial resolution. Hysterosonography, which involves the instillation of fluid (sterile saline) into the endometrial cavity through a small (5- to 7F) catheter, is sometimes used to assess endometrial abnormalities.[17,18] Transrectal US, performed with a 5-MHz transducer, is used to examine the cervix.[19] Vascularity may be assessed with Doppler interrogation.

Normal Ultrasonographic Appearance

In women of childbearing years, the normal ultrasonographic appearance of the *uterus* (Figure 5–1) varies, depending on the stage of the menstrual cycle. In general, the endometrium is seen as a hyperechoic line. The thickness of the endometrium ranges from 3 to 5 mm during the proliferative phase of the menstrual cycle and 6 to 12 mm during the secretory phase. In postmenopausal women who are not taking hormone replacement therapy, the endometrium is < 5 mm thick. The myometrium is homogeneous and of medium echogenicity. The cervical stroma is isoechoic to the myometrium, but its mucosa is hyperechoic (see Figure 5–1). The mucosa of the *vagina* is also hyperechoic, and the vaginal wall demonstrates medium echogenicity. The superior parametrium, which contains the uterine artery and venous plexus, is hypoechoic; the inferior parametrium contains fibrillar connective tissue, which makes them hyperechoic.[19] The *ovaries* have a relatively hyperechoic center surrounded by anechoic follicular cysts (Figure 5–2). The ovaries become atrophic in postmenopausal women and may not be visualized on US.

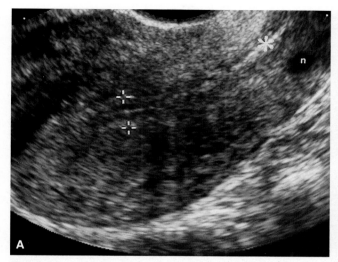
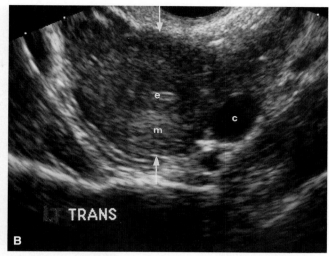

Figure 5–1.   Normal ultrasound of the uterus and cervix. *A*, Sagittal and *B*, transverse endovaginal ultrasound images. The endometrium is demonstrated as a thin echogenic line (e) with the thickness denoted by calipers (+). The endocervical canal is also echogenic (*). *Arrows* = uterus; m = myometrium; c = follicular cyst in left ovary; n = nabothian cyst in the cervix.

Computed Tomography

Computed tomography is the study most frequently used to evaluate the local and distant extent of gynecologic malignancies and to assess the presence of residual or recurrent disease.

Technique

Helical (spiral) CT, which allows rapid scanning, can provide a range of temporal resolution from different phases of intravenous contrast. Contrast-enhanced images help to delineate the vascular structures, ureters, and bladder. Delayed images may also be used to demonstrate the ureters and bladder. To achieve the best imaging results, the small bowel and colon should be opacified with contrast. Advances in the technology of CT scanning continue to be made. These include multidetector CTs (which permit faster imaging), improved thin-section imaging, improved CT angiography, and image reconstruction.

Normal CT Anatomy

The *uterus* is seen as a triangular or ovoid soft-tissue structure posterior to the bladder. The normal *cervix* appears as a rounded soft-tissue structure at the inferior aspect of the uterus (Figure 5–3). On early postcontrast scans, the endometrium demonstrates decreased attenuation adjacent to the higher-

attenuation myometrium (see Figure 5–3). The axial plane of CT images compromises the evaluation of endometrial thickness; sagittal plane images, provided by US or MRI (see Figure 5–1), are needed to assess this. On CT, the normal *vagina* is seen as a rectangular soft-tissue structure inferior to the cervix (Figure 5–4). In menarchal females the *ovaries* are usually posterolateral to the uterine corpus (see Figure 5–3). Characteristically, the CT depiction of the ovaries includes low-attenuation structures representing follicular cysts. In postmenopausal women, the ovaries may not be identifiable on CT.

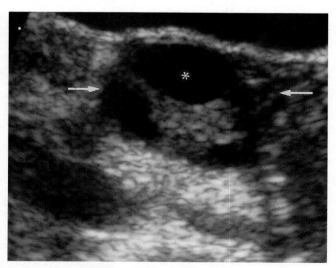

Figure 5–2.   Transabdominal ultrasound image of a normal ovary (*arrows*) containing follicular cysts. * = dominant follicular cyst.

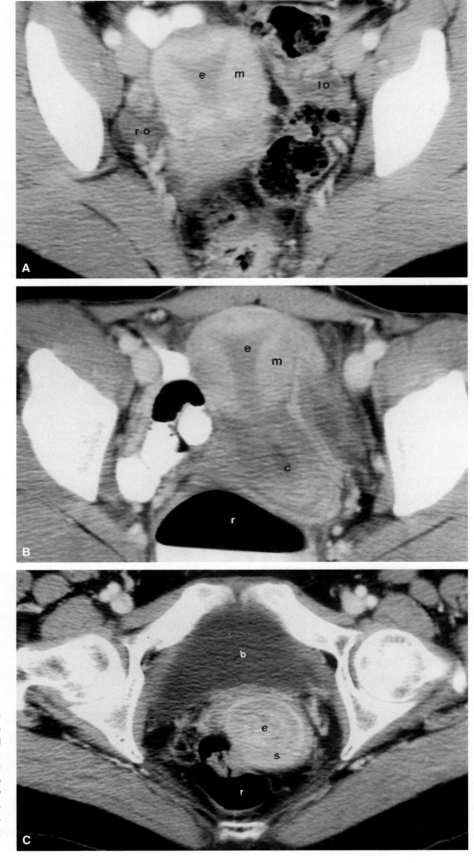

Figure 5–3. Normal CT anatomy. Intravenous contrast-enhanced scans. *A*, The endometrium (e) is hypodense, compared with the myometrium (m). The ovaries (lo, ro) are hypodense structures posterolateral to the uterus. *B*, The cervix (c) is the inferior aspect of the uterus. *C*, On early enhanced scans, the mucosa of the endocervix (e) enhances earlier than the surrounding stroma (s). b = bladder; r = rectum.

Magnetic Resonance Imaging

Magnetic resonance imaging provides excellent soft-tissue contrast and multiplanar capability without using ionizing radiation. The intravenous gadolinium chelates used to enhance contrast in MR images are also less nephrotoxic than the iodinated agents used for CT. Disadvantages of MRI include its high cost, limited availability, and restrictions in its use for patients with certain implanted devices. Claustrophobia can be a problem for some patients but can usually be overcome with sedation.

Technique

To achieve the best results, movement artifact must be minimized. Having patients fast for 4 to 6 hours before the study reduces bowel motion. If there are no medical contraindications, an antiperistaltic agent (ie, glucagon, 1 mg intravenously [IV] or intramuscularly [IM]) also can be administered just before the examination. Respiratory compensation is used to minimize breathing artifact. A superficial surface coil is preferable to a generalized body coil because it provides a higher signal-to-noise ratio and better spatial resolution.

Both T1- and T2-weighted sequences are needed to evaluate the female pelvis. T1-weighted images provide excellent contrast between fat and soft tissue and are best to assess lymphadenopathy. T1-weighted sequences are also used to characterize soft tissues. Both hemorrhagic and fat-containing lesions demonstrate high signal intensity on T1-weighted images. A fat-saturation sequence can be used to differentiate

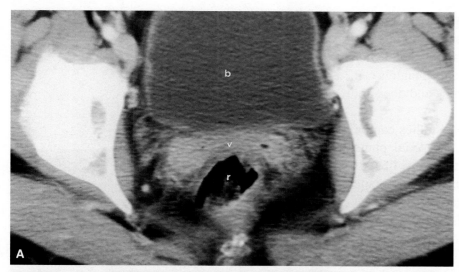

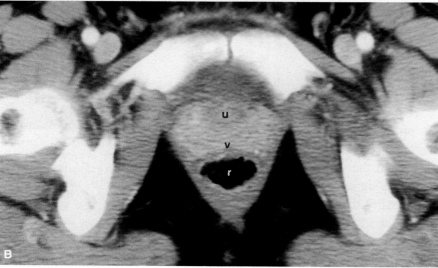

Figure 5–4. Intravenous contrast-enhanced CT scans of the normal vagina. *A,* Axial image of the upper third of the vagina (v) (vaginal fornices). *B,* Axial image of the middle third of the vagina (v). b = bladder; u = urethra; r = rectum.

between the two; with this technique, a fat-containing lesion appears dark (fat saturated), and a hemorrhagic lesion has high signal intensity.

The T2-weighted sequences most effectively demonstrate the zonal anatomy of the uterus, ovaries, and pathologic conditions. Conventional spin echo T2-weighted imaging now has been replaced by fast spin echo (FSE) T2-weighted techniques, which require less imaging time and therefore reduce motion artifacts.[20–23] Recently, breath-hold single-shot FSE pulse sequences have been developed to further decrease imaging time and artifacts.[20,24] Whether these pulse sequence methods will replace the FSE T2-weighted sequences has yet to be determined.

Intravenous contrast enhancement with gadolinium chelates (0.1 mmol/kg), may be useful to characterize the extent of neoplastic lesions and to assess vascular anatomy. Gadolinium chelates are safe in patients who have allergies to iodinated contrast media or renal impairment. However, the routine use of gadolinium to assess the cervix and vagina is not recommended. Gradient-recalled echo imaging can also be used to assess vascular patency and does not require intravenous access.

With multiplanar capability, MRI studies can be tailored to specific clinical problems. Axial plane images are acquired routinely. Sagittal plane images aid the evaluation of the uterus, and coronal plane images may be used to assess the ovaries. An oblique plane perpendicular to the long axis of the cervix is useful for staging cervical carcinomas.

Normal MRI Appearance

The normal zonal anatomy of the *uterus* is best depicted on T2-weighted images (Figure 5–5). The thickness of the endometrium varies with a patient's age and with the phase of her menstrual cycle, measuring up to 3 mm during the proliferative phase and up to 7 mm during the secretory phase. The endometrium is < 3 mm thick in postmenopausal women who are not on hormone replacement therapy. The endometrium demonstrates high signal intensity; an adjacent band of low signal intensity, the junctional zone, is the innermost aspect of the myometrium. The peripheral myometrium displays intermediate signal intensity. On gadolinium contrast-

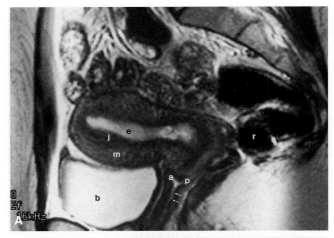

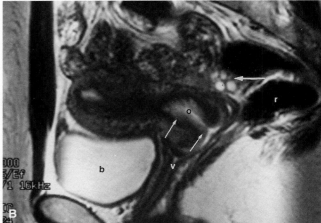

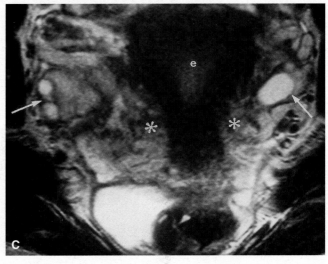

Figure 5–5. Normal MR anatomy. *A,* Sagittal and *B,* coronal T2-weighted sequences. *A,* The endometrium (e) is hyperintense relative to the intermediate intensity myometrium (m) and the low-intensity junctional zone (j). The endocervical canal is hyperintense (o) to the adjacent cervical stroma (*midsize arrows*). *C,* The ovaries are well-demonstrated containing high-signal-intensity follicular cysts (*large arrows*). The parametrium (*) is seen as soft tissue of varying signal intensity lateral to the uterus and cervix. a = anterior; p = posterior fornices of the vagina (v); *small arrows* = high signal intensity of the vaginal mucosa; r = rectum.

enhanced T1-weighted images, the endometrium and myometrium are enhanced, while the junctional zone remains low in signal intensity.

The zonal anatomy of the *cervix* is demonstrated best on T2-weighted sequences (see Figure 5–5). The mucosa of the endocervix is seen as a central stripe of high signal intensity that is surrounded by low-signal-intensity stroma. The peripheral cervical tissue demonstrates intermediate signal intensity, similar to the myometrium. On gadolinium contrast-enhanced T1-weighted images, the inner mucosal epithelium and the peracervical tissue are enhanced more than the inner cervical stroma.

The *parametrium*, the connective soft tissue that is adjacent and lateral to the uterus and not covered by peritoneum, is vascular and contains many efferent lymphatics (see Figure 5–5). The uterine arteries and the distal ureters pass through the lateral parametrial tissues. The parametrium demonstrates intermediate signal intensity on T1-weighted images and varying degrees of high signal intensity on T2-weighted images.

On T2-weighted images, the *vagina* usually demonstrates a central stripe of high signal intensity, representing the mucosa, surrounded by the intermediate signal intensity of the vaginal wall (Figure 5–6). However, the appearance of the vagina varies with hormonal influences. The high-signal-intensity stripe may be thin or absent in premenarchal girls and in postmenopausal women who are not on hormone replacement therapy. The vaginal mucosa is enhanced following the administration of intravenous gadolinium. The *vulva* demonstrates low to intermediate signal intensity on both T1- and T2-weighted sequences.

On T2-weighted images, the *ovaries* can be recognized by the presence of high-signal-intensity follicular cysts (see Figure 5–5). On T1-weighted images, the ovaries are intermediate in signal intensity. Although the ovarian tissue is enhanced with contrast, follicular cysts are not, facilitating detection of the ovaries with MRI. In women of reproductive age, normal ovaries can be identified by MRI in 87 to 97 percent of cases.

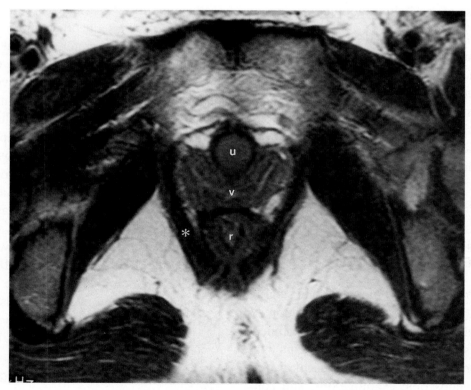

Figure 5–6. Normal axial T2-weighted MR image of the vagina. The mucosa of the vagina (v) is seen as a high-signal-intensity stripe surrounded by an intermediate-signal-intensity wall. u = urethra; r = rectum; * = levator ani muscle.

Functional and Metabolic Imaging

Positron Emission Tomography

Positron emission tomography is an increasingly important modality in the field of oncologic imaging. PET detects biochemical changes, which often precede the anatomic changes depicted with CT or MRI.[25] At present, the agent most commonly used for PET scanning is the glucose analogue, 2-fluoro-2-deoxy-D-glucose (FDG).[26] Metabolically active cells accumulate FDG, which then becomes trapped within the cells. Neoplastic cells undergo a higher rate of glycolysis and, therefore, use more FDG than normal tissue. The magnitude of this effect correlates with the degree of malignancy.[27,28] Today, the availability of PET scanning is limited by the high cost of installation and operation and by the cost of producing the necessary radionuclides on a cyclotron or particle accelerator. At present, the spatial resolution of PET is inferior to CT or MRI. However, image fusion techniques that overlay PET images onto cross-sectional images are being developed to overcome this limitation.

Magnetic Resonance Spectroscopic Imaging

Three-dimensional-MRSI (3D-MRSI) provides metabolic information and can be directly correlated with the structural anatomy displayed on MRI scans.[29–34] The 3D-MRSI information can be obtained from an additional sequence during the standard MRI examination, using the same hardware and magnet strength. Levels and ratios of metabolites can be measured to determine whether the tissue is normal or abnormal. Combined MRI and 3D-MRSI are currently being used in the assessment of prostate cancer.[35,36]

IMAGING EVALUATION OF CERVICAL CANCER

Radiographic imaging is used in the clinical staging system defined by the International Federation of Gynecology and Obstetrics (FIGO). This clinical staging system is used to classify most patients with cervical carcinoma and is based on physical examination, biopsy, endoscopic examinations, and conventional radiographic imaging with chest radiography, barium enema, and IVP.[37–39] As discussed earlier, chest radiography is the only one of these studies still in common use for the evaluation of gynecologic malignancies in the United States.

Despite its widespread use, the value of the FIGO staging system is limited by its tendency to under- or overestimate the extent of disease. For patients with FIGO stage Ib disease, the inaccuracy rate ranges between 17 and 32 percent; for those with more advanced disease, the rate may be as high as 67 percent.[40–45] Also, the FIGO system does not address important prognostic factors, such as the presence of lymph node involvement or the depth of stromal invasion. The prognostic value of the FIGO cervical staging system was improved somewhat in 1996 by subdividing the stage I category according to tumor size ($\leq$ 4 cm or > 4 cm). Although surgical staging provides more accurate information about regional metastasis, it is not suitable for every patient with cervical cancer and, in many cases, may increase the morbidity from subsequent radiation therapy.

Lymph Node Evaluation

Lymph node status is the single most important prognostic factor in cervical carcinoma. Lymphatic spread occurs in a sequential pattern, extending from the parametrial, obturator, internal iliac, external iliac, and lateral sacral nodes, and to the common iliac chain and para-aortic nodes. Involvement of the mediastinal and/or supraclavicular nodes can occur with extensive disease. Common iliac involvement carries a worse prognosis than does pelvic nodal disease.[46] As discussed earlier, LAG was at one time the primary modality used to assess metastatic lymph node involvement. In a recent meta-analysis of studies used to evaluate lymph node metastases from cervical cancer, the positive predictive value was 14 to 80 percent with LAG, 61 percent with CT, and 66 percent with MRI.[15] Since CT and MRI provide additional information about tumor size and stage, they are usually preferred over LAG. Also, because it is rarely used today, few clinicians now have the expertise needed to perform and interpret LAGs.

Cross-Sectional Imaging

Although cross-sectional imaging cannot be used to alter the FIGO stage, the advantages of CT and MRI have led to a dramatic increase in their use in the evaluation of patients with cervical cancer. Between 1978 and 1988, Montana and colleagues[8] reported a decrease in the use of IVP (86 down to 42 percent), barium enema (58 down to 32 percent) and lymphangiography (18 down to 14 percent). In the same 10-year period, the use of CT increased from 6 to 70 percent. Cross-sectional imaging is a valuable and increasingly cost-effective supplement to clinical examination.

Ultrasonography

To date, US, both transvaginal (TVUS) and transrectal (TRUS), has had only a limited role in the early detection of cervical cancer and in the evaluation of the extent of disease. However, recent investigations using an intracervical US probe show promise in the detection of early cancers.[47] The ultrasonographic appearance of cervical carcinoma (Figure 5–7) is characterized by an enlarged cervix, an ill-defined hypo- or isoechoic mass, and, occasionally, a hyperechoic mass which may represent hemorrhage or air within the tumor. Obstruction of the endocervical canal by tumor can cause hydrometra, hematometra, or pyometra.

The US assessment of disease extent is limited by poor contrast resolution, even with the higher spatial resolution probes used for TVUS or TRUS.[19,48] Uterine or adnexal pathology can be difficult to differentiate from paracervical infiltration by tumor. Disease extension beyond the cervix is suggested by specific US findings:

- An irregular cervical margin, encasement of vessels, or a reduction in the normal hyperechogenicity of the parametrial fat suggests *parametrial invasion*.[19,49]
- A soft-tissue mass or thickened parametrial strands that extend to the muscular pelvic side wall or encase the iliac vessels suggest *pelvic wall involvement*.[19,49]
- Hydronephrosis or hydroureter suggests obstruction of the ureter by tumor.
- A mass invading the bladder or bladder immobility suggests *bladder involvement*.

Although the accuracy of TRUS has been reported to be as high as 83 percent,[19] these results have not been confirmed, and US is usually not recommend for the staging of cervical cancer.

Computed Tomography

The overall accuracy of CT in predicting the pathologic stage of cervical cancers ranges between 55 and 88 percent. Although its accuracy may be better in patients with more advanced disease (clinical stages IIa to IV), its primary drawback is a high rate of false-positive findings suggesting parametrial extension. Intravaginal extension is assessed more accurately by physical examination.[50] However, CT has largely replaced IVP for the evaluation of urinary obstruction because it also provides information about local and regional disease extent.

On CT scans, cervical carcinomas may appear as hypodense areas that enhance less than normal cervical stroma after administration of contrast (Figure 5–8). The endometrial cavity may be enlarged by fluid if the endocervix is obstructed. Specific CT criteria for assessing the extent of cervical carcinomas include the following:

- If the tumor has not extended beyond the cervix, the cervix may be enlarged but it maintains smooth, well-defined outer margins. The periureteral fat planes are intact without parametrial stranding or a parametrial soft-tissue mass.
- Parametrial invasion is suggested by an irregular cervical margin, prominent parametrial soft-tissue stranding, a parametrial mass, or loss of the periureteral fat plane (see Figure 5–8). Parametrial stranding is a nonspecific finding that may represent parametritis. Loss of the periureteral fat plane is a more reliable sign of parametrial invasion, but it is usually a late finding associated with gross parametrial invasion.
- Pelvic sidewall invasion may appear as irregular soft-tissue stranding that extends to the piriformis or obturator internus muscles. Findings of a soft-tissue mass that extends to within 3 mm of the pelvic side wall, obliterates fat planes, or encases the iliac vessels also suggests pelvic wall fixation. Hydronephrosis and pelvic lymphadenopathy are frequently seen in patients with stage IIIb disease.

- Bladder or rectal invasion may obliterate the perivesical or perirectal fat planes, or cause thickening, nodularity, or serration of the bladder or rectal wall. Invasion of these structures may also be seen as an intraluminal mass or fistula (Figure 5–9).[50,51]

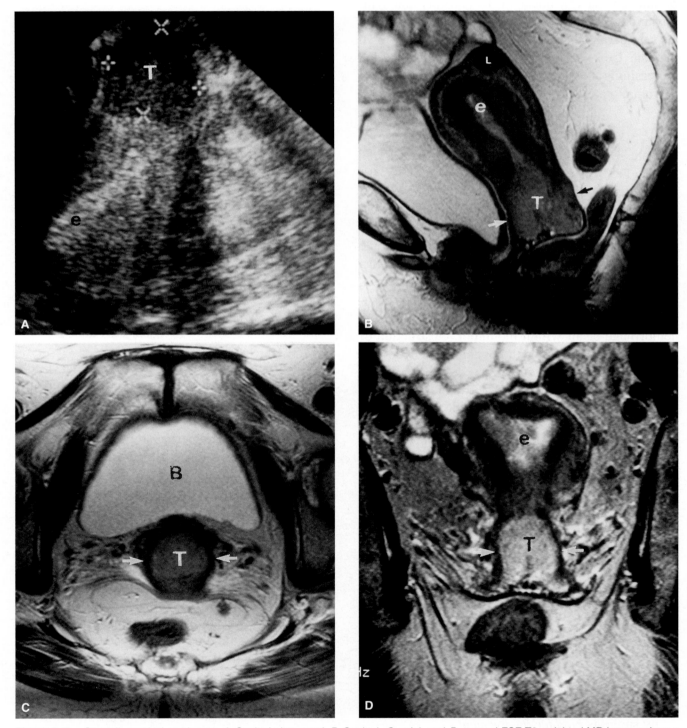

Figure 5–7.   Stage Ib cervical carcinoma. *A*, Sagittal ultrasound. *B*, Sagittal, *C*, axial, and *D*, coronal FSE T2-weighted MR images show a mass (T) arising from and enlarging the cervix. The mass (T) is hypoechoic on ultrasound (*demarcated by calipers*) and is of intermediate to high signal intensity on the MR T2-weighted sequence. The lesion is confined to the cervix as indicated by the intact low-signal peripheral fibrous stroma (*arrows*). e = endometrrum; L = leiomyoma; B = bladder.

The CT assessment of lymph node involvement is based on nodal size. However, lymph nodes may be enlarged by inflammatory or reactive processes as well as by tumor. Also, normal-sized lymph nodes may contain metastatic deposits that are not detected by CT. When a nodal size of > 1 cm in the short axis is used as the criterion for calling a lymph node abnormal, CT has a high specificity (92 percent) but a low sensitivity (44 percent) for tumor involvement.[15,52–55]

The overall accuracy of CT for the detection of pelvic lymph node metastases ranges from 70 to 85 percent.[15,16,56] CT-guided percutaneous biopsy can be used to further evaluate suspicious lymph nodes. PET may also be useful but is not widely available.

Overall, CT is most useful in the evaluation of more advanced disease (stages IIb to IV) and in the detection and biopsy of lymph node metastases. Tumor size and parametrial invasion are not assessed reliably by CT.

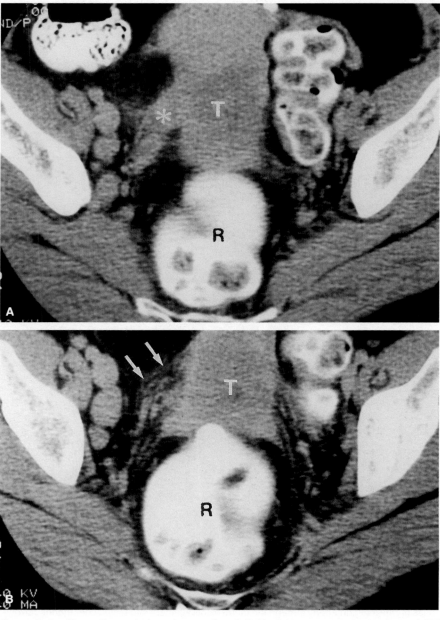

Figure 5–8. Stage IIb cervical carcinoma. *A* and *B*, Nonintravenous contrast-enhanced CT scans show an irregular hypodense cervical mass (T). Right parametrial invasion is demonstrated by a prominent soft-tissue mass (*) and stranding of the parametrial fat (*arrows*). R = rectum.

Magnetic Resonance Imaging

The superior soft-tissue contrast that is obtained with MRI makes it a better study than CT or US for the assessment of tumor size and extent. On T2-weighted sequences, the intensity of cervical cancer is usually greater than that of normal stroma. Neoplasms may not be seen on T1-weighted images because their intensity is similar to that of normal stroma.

Contrast may be used to differentiate viable tumor from debris and areas of necrosis but has not been shown to improve the overall accuracy of MRI.[57-60] However, studies suggest that dynamic contrast imaging may be used to predict the prognosis of patients undergoing radiation therapy or chemotherapy.[61,62] With dynamic contrast imaging, cervical cancers have earlier enhancement than non-neoplastic tissues.

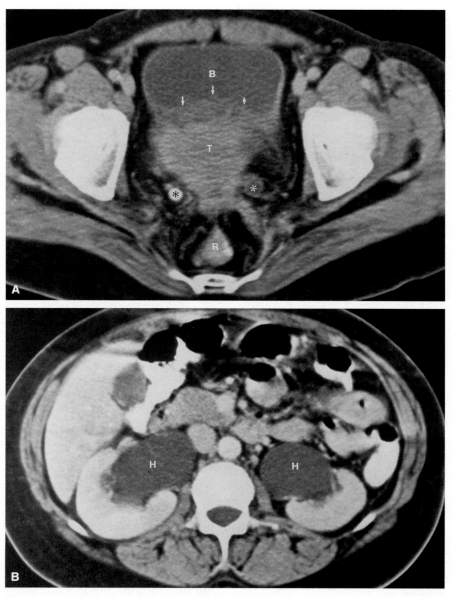

Figure 5–9. Stage IVa cervical carcinoma. Oral and intravenous contrast-enhanced CT scans of the *A*, pelvis (delayed image) and *B*, the midabdomen show a large irregular cervical mass (T) invading anteriorly through the uterovesical ligament into the bladder trigone (*arrows*) resulting in bilateral hydronephrosis (H) and hydroureter (*). The right side is relatively less obstructed as the ureter (black *) contains contrast on the delayed image and the kidney has a denser nephrogram.

In up to 93 percent of cases, the MRI assessment of tumor size is within 0.5 cm of measurements taken from surgical specimens.[52,63–65] MRI also provides an accurate assessment of the depth of cervical stromal invasion.[66] Both factors are important predictors of prognosis.

To summarize, MRI criteria for assessing the extent of cervical carcinomas are as follows:

- A tumor that is confined to the cervix is indicated by a high-signal-intensity lesion that is surrounded by normal cervical stroma (Figure 5–10).[14,67–69]

- Vaginal invasion is suggested by disruption of the low-signal-intensity vaginal wall.[14,70]

- Parametrial invasion is associated with an irregular cervical margin, obliterated parametrial fat planes, parametrial stranding, parametrial enlargement, or disruption of the low-signal-intensity peripheral stroma by high-signal-intensity tumor (Figures 5–11 to 5–13).[14,67–69]

- Pelvic side wall involvement is suggested when the tumor extends beyond the lateral margins of the cardinal ligaments and when the signal intensity of the pelvic musculature is increased on T2-weighted sequences.[14]

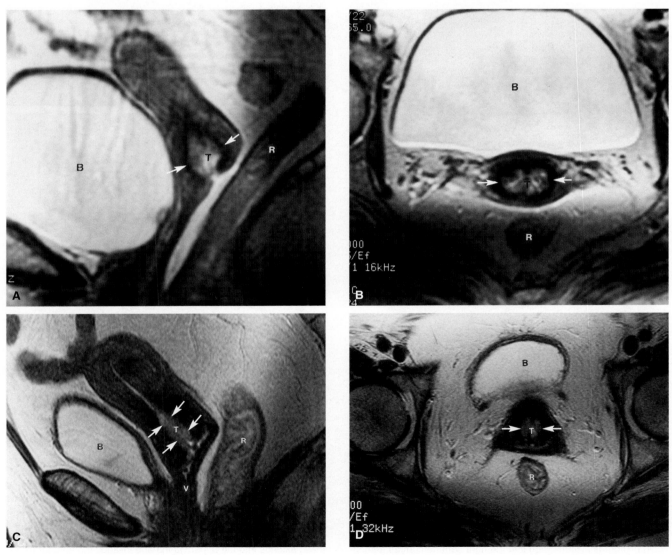

Figure 5–10. Cervical carcinoma stage Ib. *A*, Sagittal and *B*, axial FSE T2-weighted MR images of one patient. *C*, Sagittal and *D*, axial FSE T2-weighted MR images in another patient show a hyperintense mass (T) within the endocervical canal. There is an intact ring of dark cervical stroma (*arrows*) surrounding the endocervical lesion without evidence of deep stromal invasion.

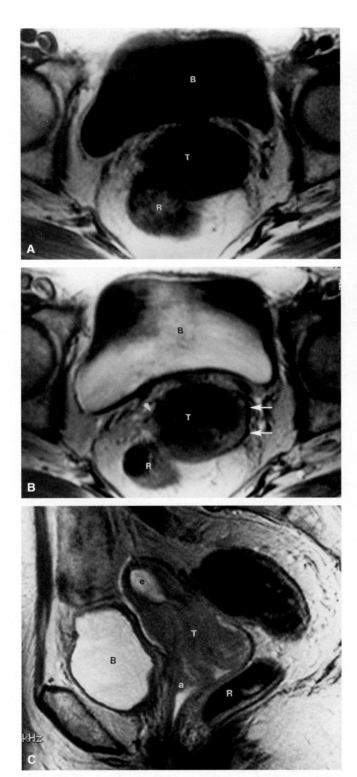

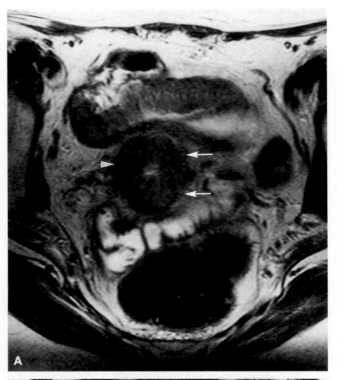

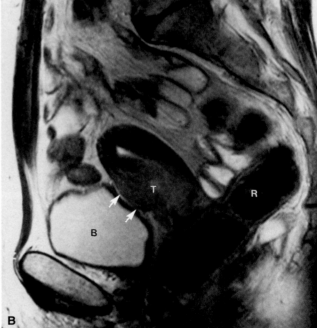

Figure 5–11. Cervical carcinoma stage IIb. *A*, Axial T1-weighted without gadolinium, *B*, with gadolinium, and *C*, sagittal FSE T2-weighted MR images show a large cervical mass extending into the lower uterine segment and invading the anterior fornix (a) of the vagina. There is also invasion into the right parametrium as demonstrated by irregular cervical contours and loss of the normal low-signal peripheral stroma (*arrowhead*). *Arrows* = normal peripheral fibrous stroma; e = endometrium; B = bladder; R = rectum.

Figure 5–12. Cervical carcinoma stage IIb. *A*, Sagittal and *B*, axial FSE T2-weighted MR images show a mass (T) centered in the endo-cervix that extends across the internal os and into the lower uterine segment. There is full-thickness stromal invasion of the cervix and deep myometrial invasion into the lower uterine segment. Anteriorly, there is also invasion into the uterovesicular ligament (*arrows*), but no invasion into the muscular bladder wall is evident. Inferiorly, the mass extends into the upper vagina and invades the anterior fornix. *B*, Axial image shows left parametrial invasion with loss of the low-signal peripheral stroma (*small arrows*). *Arrowhead* = intact normal peripheral fibrous stroma; B = bladder; R = rectum.

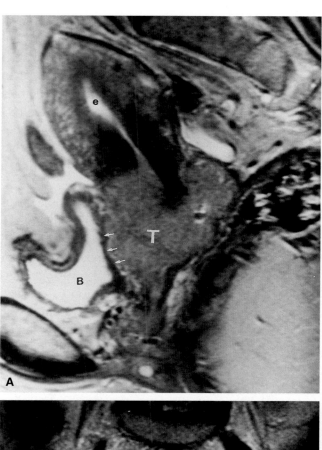

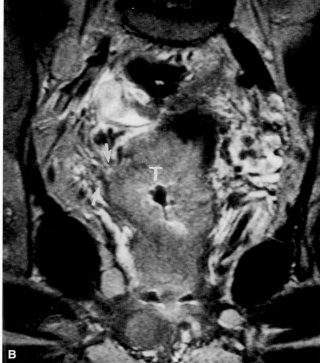

Figure 5–13. Cervical carcinoma stage IIb. *A*, Sagittal and *B*, coronal FSE T2-weighted MR images show a cervical mass extending into the lower uterine segment and anteriorly invading the ureterovesical ligament contacting the normal-signal-intensity bladder wall (*small arrows*) with no definite mucosal invasion. Right parametrial invasion (*large arrows*) is demonstrated on the coronal images. e = endometrium; B = bladder.

- Bladder and rectal invasions are demonstrated by increased signal intensity in the normally low-signal-intensity bladder or rectal wall on T2-weighted and contrast-enhanced T1-weighted sequences (Figures 5–14 and 5–15).

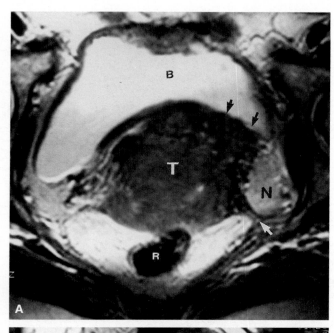

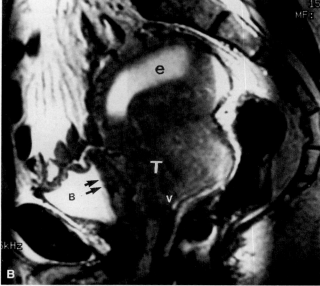

Figure 5–14. Cervical carcinoma stage IVa. *A*, Axial and *B*, sagittal FSE T2-weighted MR images show a large, heterogeneous-signal-intensity cervical mass causing endocervical obstruction with an enlarged fluid-filled endometrium (e). There is invasion into the vagina (v) and to the left pelvic side wall (*white arrow*). Anteriorly, there is invasion into the bladder wall demonstrated as areas of increased signal intensity and irregularity of the bladder wall (*black arrows*). Left obturator lymphadenopathy is also present (N). B = bladder; R = rectum.

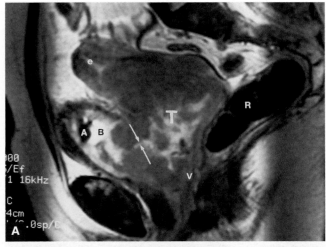

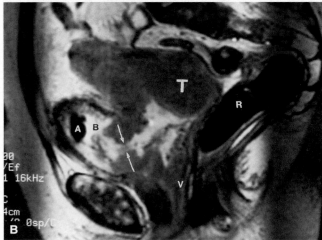

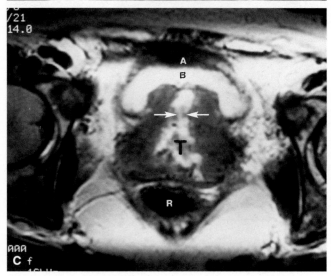

Figure 5–15. Cervical carcinoma stage IVa. *A* and *B*, Sagittal and *C*, axial FSE T2-weighted MR images show a large necrotic cervical mass extending into the lower uterine segment and vagina (v) with full-thickness stromal involvement and bilateral parametrial invasion. There is direct bladder invasion at the level of the trigone with fistula formation (*arrows*) and air (A) in the bladder (B). The tumor abuts the rectum (R) without definite mucosal invasion. e = endometrium.

For patients with cervical cancer, a precise assessment of the extent of disease is critical because it determines the choice of treatment. MRI appears to provide more accurate information than more traditional methods. For example, MRI detects parametrial invasion with an accuracy of between 87 and 94 percent. The accuracy of examination under anesthesia has been reported to be between 75 and 82 percent,[66] suggesting that MRI may provide a better guide for clinical decisions.

For assessing lymph node involvement, the accuracy of MRI (72 to 93 percent) is similar to that of CT (Figure 5–16).[15,67,69,71–73] MRI is superior to clinical examination, US, or CT in the evaluation of tumor location, tumor size, depth of stromal invasion, vaginal extension, and parametrial extension of cervical cancer. When compared with surgical findings, the overall accuracy of MRI staging is between 76 and 89 percent, and thus superior to clinical examination, US, or CT.[14,57,67,69,71,74] Furthermore, studies suggest that MRI is a cost-effective method of evaluating cervical cancers.[75] The cost-effectiveness of other imaging modalities, such as CT, has not yet been determined. We recommend MRI as the initial imaging modality for patients with tumors that are clinically assessed to be > 2 cm in diameter and for those with tumors that cannot be accurately assessed on clinical examination because they are endocervical or infiltrative.[70,75,76]

Positron Emission Tomography

Positron emission tomography is a new and rapidly expanding modality in oncologic imaging. Early reports on the utility of FDG-PET in the imaging of cervical carcinoma are encouraging in the evaluation of both local and distant diseases. A study in 32 patients has shown radioisotope uptake in 91 percent of cervical tumors. Compared with surgical staging, FDG-PET had a sensitivity of 72 percent and a specificity of 92 percent for detecting para-aortic lymphadenopathy.

IMAGING EVALUATION OF VAGINAL AND VULVAR CARCINOMAS

Vaginal and vulvar carcinomas are usually diagnosed by physical examination and biopsy. Cross-

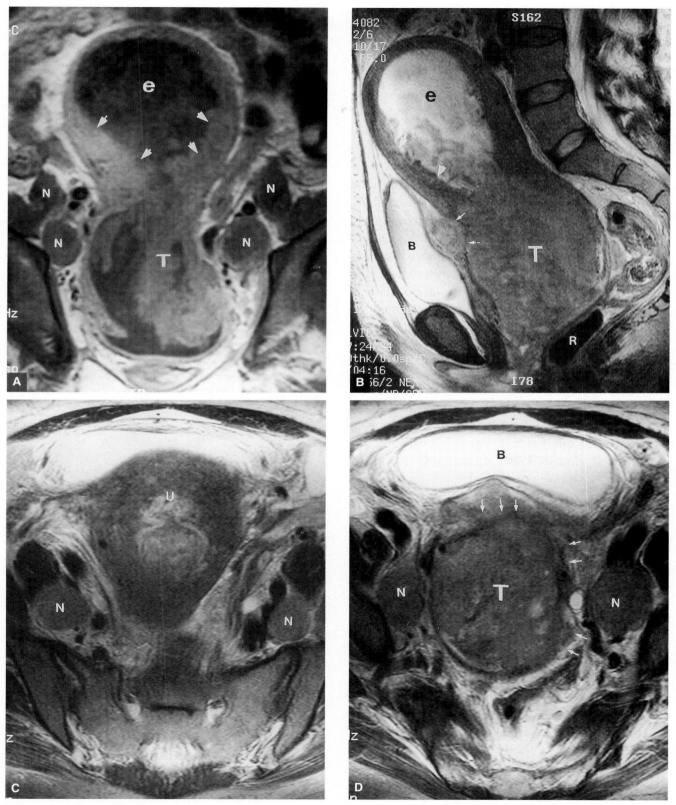

Figure 5–16. Cervical carcinoma (stage IIb) with endocervical obstruction and lymphadenopathy. *A,* Coronal T1-weighted image with gadolinium. *B,* Sagittal and *C* and *D,* axial T2-weighted images show a large necrotic cervical mass (T) causing endocervical obstruction (e) and invading the lower segment and body of the uterus (*arrowheads*). There is parametrial invasion (*arrows*) and bilateral internal iliac lymphadenopathy (N). U = uterus; B = bladder.

sectional imaging, however, can make a valuable contribution to patient evaluation.

Vaginal Carcinoma

The MRI examination, which offers excellent soft-tissue contrast, allows assessment of the extent of the tumor as well as staging. US and CT are limited in the assessment of early localized disease by inferior (compared with MRI) soft-tissue contrast resolution. For tumors that involve the upper third of the vagina, when clinical examination is suboptimal, MRI may help to accurately clarify the site of origin in the vagina or cervix.

On T2-weighted images, vaginal cancer is seen as an intermediate- to high-signal-intensity mass. On T1-weighted images, the tumor is intermediate in signal intensity and may not be visualized. Alteration of the vaginal contour may be the only indication of disease on these sequences.[69] MRI criteria for evaluating vaginal carcinomas include the following:

- When tumor is confined to the vaginal wall, the normal low signal intensity of the wall may be preserved, or the superficial tumors may appear as areas of intermediate signal intensity on T2-weighted images. The surrounding fat plane remains intact (Figure 5–17).[75]
- Involvement of the paravaginal tissues appears as a medium to high signal extension of the vaginal mass into paravaginal tissues with an indistinct fat-tumor interface (Figure 5–18).[75]
- Tumor extension to the pelvic side wall is indicated by increased signal in the muscles of the pelvic floor (levator ani, obturator internus, or piriformis) on T2-weighted sequences.[69]
- Bladder or rectal involvement may appear as direct tumor invasion or as increased signal within the bladder or rectal wall on T2-weighted sequences. Vaginal cancer may present with a vesicovaginal fistula, which can often be demonstrated on MRI particularly with a gadolinium contrast–enhanced study.

The MRI evaluation of vaginal cancer can facilitate treatment planning by clarifying the initial extent of disease. MRI can assess the initial tumor size and extent of disease, providing important prognostic information.

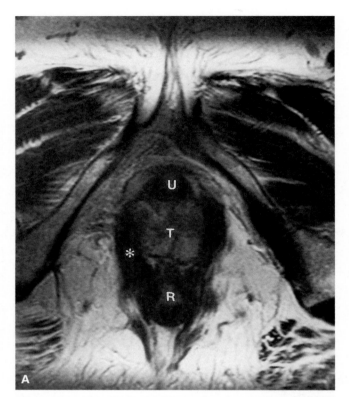

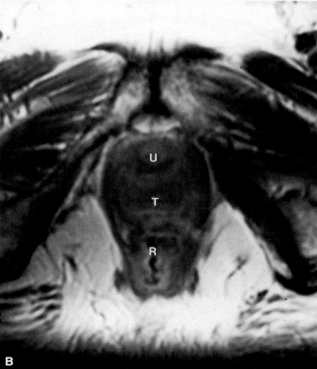

Figure 5–17. Vaginal carcinoma stage I. *A*, Axial T2-weighted and *B*, T1- weighted sequence with gadolinium MR images show a 2.7 x 2.6 cm mass (T) arising from the lower third of the vagina. The mass demonstrates high signal intensity on the T2-weighted sequence and minimal contrast enhancement. The mass abuts the urethra (U), rectum (R), and levator ani muscle (*), with no definite invasion into these structures.

As with cervical cancer, CT or MRI can be used to evaluate lymph node metastases. The pattern of lymphatic involvement depends on the location of the tumor. Tumors in the vaginal vault spread to the obturator and hypogastric nodes. Tumors arising from the posterior wall spread to the superior and inferior gluteal nodes. Tumors originating from the lower third of the vagina spread to the vulva and to the pelvic and/or inguinofemoral nodes. Suspicious nodes can be biopsied under CT guidance.

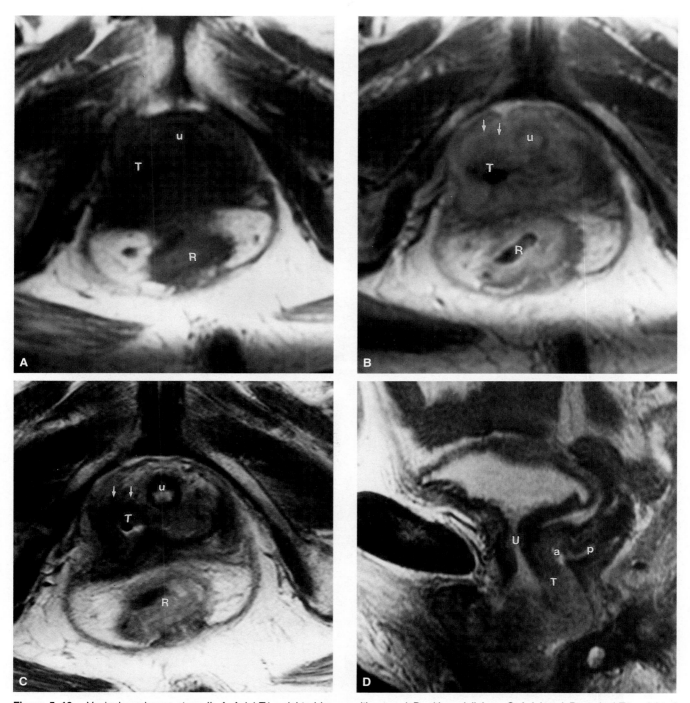

Figure 5–18. Vaginal carcinoma stage II. *A*, Axial T1-weighted image without and *B*, with gadolinium. *C*, Axial and *D*, sagittal T2-weighted images show a mass (T) arising from the middle third of the vagina. The mass is predominantly on the right and demonstrates contrast enhancement. There is invasion of the mass into the right and anterior paravaginal tissues (*arrows*) with loss of the fat-tumor interface. a = anterior fornix; p = posterior fornix; u = urethra; R = rectum.

Vulvar Carcinoma

Although the FIGO currently recommends a surgical system for staging vulvar carcinomas, CT and MRI may be very helpful in the clinical evaluation of vulvar cancers, particularly to detect abnormal lymph nodes.

Vulvar cancer may be seen on T2-weighted sequences as an increased-signal-intensity mass (Figure 5–19). On T1-weighted sequences, vulvar carci-

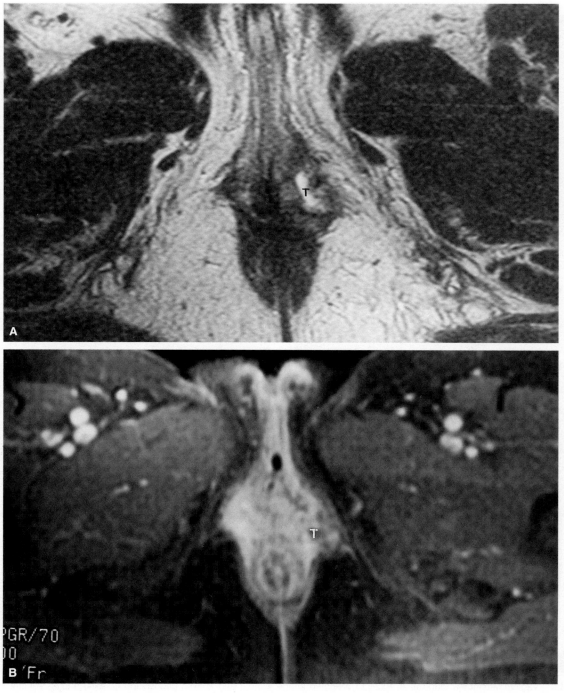

Figure 5–19.   Vulvar carcinoma stage I. *A*, Axial T2-weighted and *B*, axial T1-weighted image with gadolinium and fat suppression. The small left vulvar mass (T) demonstrates high signal intensity on T2-weighted image and heterogeneous enhancement. There is no invasion into the adjacent structures.

noma usually has an intermediate signal intensity.[75] There may be associated lymphadenopathy (Figure 5–20). Invasion of the lower urethra, vagina, or anus may be seen as intermediate to high signal intensity extending into these structures. Invasion of the upper urethra, bladder, and/or the rectal mucosa and pelvic bony structures may also be seen as areas of intermediate to high signal intensity within these structures (Figure 5–21). The excellent soft-tissue resolution of MRI may aid in the assessment of additional prog-

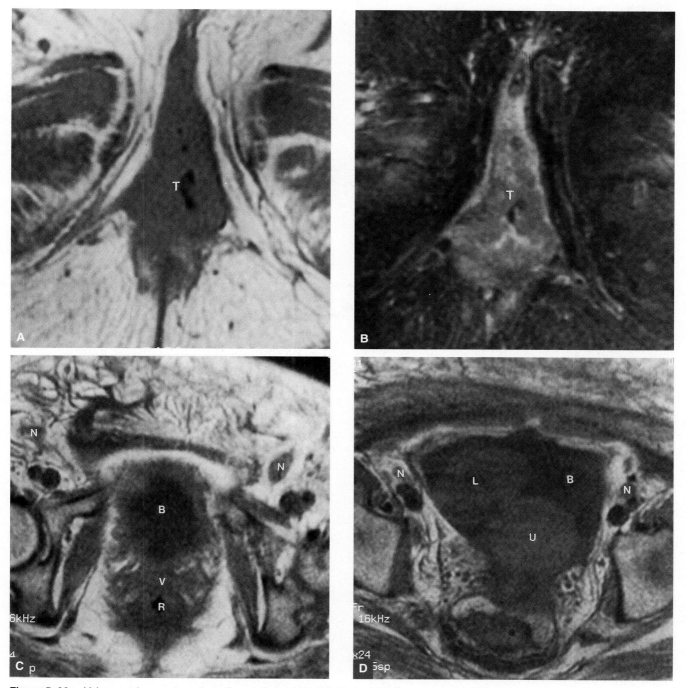

Figure 5–20. Vulvar carcinoma stage II. *A, C,* and *D,* Axial T1-weighted and *B,* fat suppression T2-weighted MR images show a large, diffuse irregular vulvar mass (T), demonstrated as intermediate signal intensity on T1-weighted images and high signal intensity on T2-weighted images. Associated inguinal and pelvic lymphadenopathy (N) is also present. V = vagina; U = uterus; L = exophytic subserosal leiomyoma; B = bladder; R = rectum.

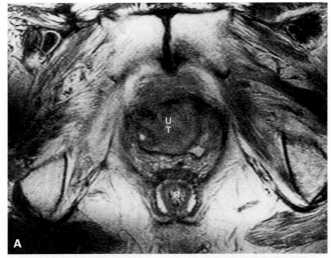

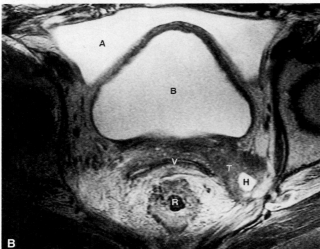

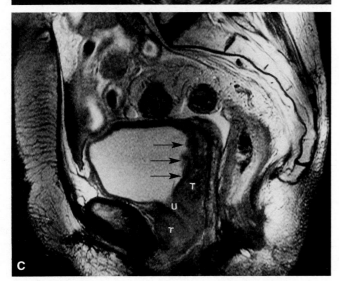

Figure 5–21. Vulvar carcinoma stage IVa. *A* and *B*, Axial and *C*, sagittal T2-weighted MR images show a mass (T) invading the urethra (U) and the vagina (V), including the left paravaginal tissues resulting in left hydroureter (H). The sagittal image demonstrates invasion of the bladder resulting in irregularity of the bladder wall (*arrows*).

nostic indicators, such as lesion size, lesion type (exophytic or infiltrating), and clitoral involvement.

Enlarged lymph nodes, particularly in the deep inguinal and pelvic regions, may be difficult to detect on physical examination but are well visualized with CT or MRI. CT- or US-guided biopsy can be performed if the presence of metastases would influence clinical decisions.

SUMMARY

The imaging evaluation of cervical, vaginal, and vulvar cancers has changed dramatically in the last two decades. Technical improvements and the greater availability of cross-sectional imaging methods, such as US, CT, and MRI, have increased their use; in the United States, these studies have almost completely replaced more conventional imaging techniques. US is of limited value in the staging of gynecologic malignancies. CT has the advantages of wide availability and quick imaging time. It is most useful for staging more advanced disease and in the detection and biopsy of suspected lymph nodes and metastases. MRI provides excellent soft-tissue contrast without ionizing radiation and has rapidly gained acceptance as the most accurate imaging modality for assessing local disease extent.

Future improvements in the imaging evaluation of gynecologic cancers will probably focus on functional imaging. The ability of functional imaging to detect early local and distant diseases, coupled with anatomic imaging will continue to play an increasing role in the diagnostic evaluation and development of successful treatment plans for women with these diseases.

REFERENCES

1. Gedgaudas-McClees RK. Gastrointestinal complication of gynecologic diseases. In: Gore RM, Levine MS, Laufer I, editors. Textbook of gastrointestinal radiology. Philadelphia: W.B. Saunders; 1993. p. 2564.
2. Gedgaudas RK, Kelvin FM, Thompson WM, Rice PP. The value of the preoperative barium-enema examination in the assessment of pelvic masses. Radiology 1983;146:609–13.
3. Griffin TW, Parker RG, Taylor WJ. An evaluation of procedures used in staging carcinoma of the cervix. AJR Am J Roentgenol 1976;127:825.

4. Pearl ML, Griffen T, Valea FA, Chalas E. The utility of pretreatment barium enema in women with endometrial carcinoma. Gynecol Oncol 1997;64: 442–5.

5. Schmitz MJ, Nahhas WA, Clark MA, Brown M. Stage Ib carcinoma of the cervix: are all staging tests and procedures necessary? Eur J Gynaecol Oncol 1994;15:199–204.

6. Shingleton HM, Fowler WC Jr, Koch GG. Pretreatment evaluation in cervical cancer. Am J Obstet Gynecol 1971;110:385–9.

7. Lindell LK, Anderson B. Routine pretreatment evaluation of patients with gynecologic cancer. Obstet Gynecol 1987;69:242–6.

8. Montana GS, Hanlon AL, Brickner TJ, et al. Carcinoma of the cervix: patterns of studies: review of 1978, 1983, and 1988-1989 surveys. Int J Radiat Oncol Biol Phys 1995;32:1481–6.

9. Van Nagell JR, Sprague AD, Roddick JW. The effect of intravenous pyelography and cystoscopy on the staging of cervical cancer. Gynecol Oncol 1975;3:87–91.

10. Kajanoja P, Raisanen I, Lehtovirta P. Wertheim radical hysterectomy. Surgical complications, accuracy of clinical staging and value of lymphangiography in cervical carcinoma. Ann Chir Gynaecol 1985;74: 94–7.

11. La Fianza A, Dore R, DiGiulio G, et al. Lymph node metastasis of carcinoma of the cervix uteri. Role of lymphangiography and computerized tomography. Radiol Med 1990;80:486–91.

12. Volterrani F, Sigurta D, Gardani G, et al. Clinical value of lymphography in cervical cancer. Radiol Med 1980;66:611–4.

13. Heller PB, Malfetano JH, Bundy BN, et al. Clinical-pathologic study of stage IIB, III and IVA carcinoma of the cervix: extended diagnostic evaluation of paraaortic node metastasis—a Gynecologic Oncology group study. Gynecol Oncol 1990;38:425–30.

14. Hricak H, Lacey CG, Sandles LG, et al. Invasive cervical carcinoma: comparison of MR imaging and surgical findings. Radiology 1988;166:623–31.

15. Kim SH, Choi BI, Han JK, et al. Preoperative staging of uterine cervical carcinoma: comparison of CT and MRI in 99 patients. J Comput Assist Tomogr 1993;17:633–40.

16. Scheidler J, Hricak H, Yu KK, et al. Radiological evaluation of lymph nodes in patients with cervical cancer: meta-analysis. JAMA 1997;278(13):1096–111.

17. Cullinan JA, Fleischer AC, Kepple DM, Arnold AL. Sonohysterography: a technique for endometrial evaluation. Radiographics 1995;15:501–14.

18. Lev-Toaff AS. Sonohysterography: evaluation of endometrial and myometrial abnormalities. Semin Roentogenol 1996;31:288.

19. Innocenti P, Pulli F, Savino L, et al. Staging of cervical cancer: reliability of transrectal US. Radiology 1992;185:201–5.

20. Ascher SM. MR imaging of the female pelvis: the time has come. Radiographics 1998;18:931–45.

21. Gryspeerdt S, Van Hoe L, Bosmans H, et al. T_2-weighted MR imaging of the uterus: comparison of optimized fast spin-echo and HASTE sequences with conventional fast spin-echo sequences. AJR Am J Roentgenol 1998;171:211–5.

22. Niitsu M, Tanaka YO, Anno I, Itai Y. Multishot echo-planar MR imaging of the female pelvis: comparison with fast spin-echo MR imaging in an initial clinical trial. AJR Am J Roentgenol 1997;168:651–5.

23. Smith RC, Reinhold C, McCauley TR, et al. Multicoil high-resolution fast spin echo MR imaging of the female pelvis. Radiology 1992;184:671–5.

24. Ascher SM, O'Malley J, Semelka RC, et al. T_2-weighted MRI of the uterus: fast spin echo vs. breath-hold fast spin echo. J Magn Reson Imaging 1999;9:384–90.

25. Wahl RL, Siegel BA. Positron emission tomography imaging in cancer staging and therapy assessment: basic principles and clinical applications. In: Perry MC, editor. ASCO Educational Book. Alexandria (VA): American Society of Clinical Oncology; 1999. p. 604–13.

26. Som P, Atkins HL, Bandopadhyay D, et al. A fluorinated glucose analog, 2-fluoro-2-deoxy-D-glucose (F-18): nontoxic tacer for rapid tumor detection. J Nucl Med 1980;21:670–5.

27. Warburg OH. On the origin of cancer cells. Science 1956;123:309–14.

28. Warburg OH. The metabolism of tumors. New York, NY: Richard B. Smith; 1931.

29. Barker PB, Glickson JD, Bryan RN. In vivo magnetic resonance spectroscopy of human brain tumors. Top Magn Reson Imaging 1993;5:32–45.

30. Brown TR, Kincaid BM, Ugurbil K. NMR chemical shift imaging in three dimensions. Proc Natl Acad Sci U S A 1982;79:3523–6.

31. Brown TR. Practical applications of chemical shift imaging. NMR Biomed 1992;5:238–43.

32. Maudsley AA, Hilal SK, Simon HE, Wittekoek S. In vivo MR spectroscopic imaging with P-31: work in progress. Radiology 1984;153:745–50.

33. Vigneron D, Nelson S, Kurhanewicz J. Proton chemical shift imaging of cancer. In: Hricak H, Higgin CB, Helms CA, editors. Magnetic resonance imaging of the body. New York, NY: Raven; 1996. p. 205–20.

34. Kurhanewicz J, Vigneron DB, Hricak H, et al. Three-dimensional H-1 MR spectroscopic imaging of the in situ human prostate with high (0.24–0.7 cm^3) spatial resolution. Radiology 1996;198(3):795–805.

35. Scheidler J, Hricak H, Vigneron DB, et al. Prostate cancer: localization with three-dimensional proton MR

spectroscopic imaging—clinico-pathologic study. Radiology 1999;213:473–80.

36. Yu KK, Scheidler J, Hricak H, et al. Prostate cancer: prediction of extracapsular extension by endorectal MR imaging and three-dimensional proton MR spectroscopic imaging. Radiology 1999;213:481–8.

37. Morrow CP, Curtin JP. Tumors of the cervix. In: Morrow CP, Curtin JP, editors. Synopsis of gynecologic oncology. 5th ed. New York: Churchill Livingston; 1998. p. 107–49.

38. Creasman WT. New gynecologic cancer staging. Gynecol Oncol 1995;58:157–8.

39. Rubin SC, Hoskins WJ. Cervical cancer and preinvasive neoplasia. Philadelphia: W.B. Saunders; 1996. p. 2564.

40. Martimbeau PW, Kjorstad KE, Iversen T. Stage IB carcinoma of the cervix, the Norwegian Radium Hospital: II. Results when pelvic lymph nodes are involved. Obstet Gynecol 1982;60:215–8.

41. Delgado G, Bundy B, Zaino R, et al. Prospective surgical pathological study of disease-free interval in patients with stage Ib squamous cell carcinoma of the cervix: a gynecologic oncology group study. Gynecol Oncol 1990;38:352–7.

42. Van Nagell JR, Roddick JW, Lowin DM. The staging of cervical cancer: inevitable discrepancies between clincial staging and pathologic findings. Am J Obstet Gynecol 1971;110:973–7.

43. Dargent D, Frobert JL, Beau G. V factor (tumor volume) and T factor (FIGO classification) in the assessment of cervix cancer prognosis: the risk of lymph node spread. Gynecol Oncol 1985;22:15–22.

44. Chung CK, Nahhas WA, Zaino R, et al. Histologic grade and lymph node metastasis in squamous cell carcinoma of the cervix. Gynecol Oncol 1981;12:348–54.

45. Zander J, Baltzer J, Lohe KJ, et al. Carcinoma of the cervix: and attempt to individualize treatment. Am J Obstet Gynecol 1981;139:752–9.

46. Kikuchi A, Okai T, Kobayashi K, et al. Intracervical US with a high-frequency miniature probe: a method for diagnosing early invasive cervical cancer. Radiology 1996;198:411–3.

47. Lagasse LD, Creasman WT, Shingleton HM, et al. Results and complications of operative staging in cervical cancer: experience of the gynecologic oncology group. Gynecol Oncol 1980;9:90–8.

48. Gitch G, Deutinger J, Rheinthaller A, et al. Cervical cancer: the diagnostic value of rectosonography for the judgement of parametrial invasion in regard to inflammatory stromal reaction. Br J Obstet Gynaecol 1993;100:696–7.

49. Carter JR, Carson LF, Twiggs LB. Gynecologic oncology. In: Nyberg DA, Hill LM, Bohm-Velez M, Mendelson E, editors. Transvaginal ultrasound. St. Louis: Mosby; 1992. p. 241.

50. Walsh JW, Goplerud DR. Prospective comparison between clinical and CT staging in primary cervical carcinoma. AJR Am J Roentgenol 1981;137: 997–1003.

51. Kilcheski TS, Arger PH, Mulhern CB Jr, et al. Role of computed tomography in the presurgical evaluation of carcinoma of the cervix. J Comput Assist Tomogr 1981;5:378–83.

52. Subak LL, Hricak H, Powell CB, et al. Cervical carcinoma: computed tomography and magnetic resonance imaging for preoperative staging. Obstet Gynecol 1995;86:43–50.

53. Newton WA, Robers WS, Marden DE, et al. Value of computed axial tomography in cervical cancer. Oncology 1987;44:124–7.

54. Matsukuma K, Tsukamoto N, Matsuyama T, et al. Preoperative CT study of lymph nodes in cervical cancer—its correlation with histologic findings. Gynecol Oncol 1989;33:168–71.

55. Camilien L, Gorden D, Fruchter RG, et al. Predictive value of computerized tomography in the presurgical evaluation of primary carcinoma of the cervix. Gynecol Oncol 1988;30:209–15.

56. Lee JKT, Willms AB, Semelka RC. Pelvis. In: Lee JKT, Sagel SS, Stanley RJ, Heiken JP, editors. Computed body tomography with MRI correlation. 3rd ed. Philadelphia: Lippincott-Raven; 1998. p. 1209–74.

57. Hawighorst H, Schoenberg SO, Knapstein PG, et al. Staging of invasive cervical carcinoma and of pelvic lymph nodes by high resolution MRI with a phased-array coil in comparison with pathological findings. J Comput Assist Tomogr 1998;22:75–81.

58. Hricak H, Hamm B, Semelka RC, et al. Carcinoma of the uterus: use of gadopentetate dimeglumine in MR imaging. Radiology 1991;181:95–106.

59. Scheidler J, Heuck AF, Steinborn M, et al. Parametrial invasion in cervical carcinoma: evaluation of detection at MR imaging with fat suppression. Radiology 1998;206:125–9.

60. Sironi S, De Cobelli F, Scarfone G, et al. Carcinoma of the cervix: value of plain and gadolinium-enhanced MR imaging in assessing degree of invasiveness. Radiology 1993;188:797–801.

61. Mayr NA, Yuh WTC, Magnotta VA, et al. Tumor perfusion studies using fast magnetic resonance imaging technique in advanced cervical cancer—a new noninvasive predictive assay. Int J Radiat Oncol Biol Phys 1996;36:623–33.

62. Griebel J, Mayr NA, de Vries, A, et al. Assessment of tumor microcirculation: a new role of dynamic contrast MR imaging. J Magn Reson Imaging 1997;7: 111–9.

63. Lien HH, Blomlie V, Iversen T, et al. Clinical stage I carcinoma of the cervix: value of MR imaging in

determining invasion into the parametrium. Acta Radiol 1993;34:130–2.

64. Yu KK, Hricak H, Subak LL, et al. Preoperative staging of cervical cancer with MR imaging: comparison of body versus phased array coil. Radiology 1995;197:321.

65. Burghardt E, et al. Magnetic resonance imaging in cervical cancer: a basis for objective classification. Gynecol Oncol 1989;33:61–7.

66. McCarthy S, Hricak H. The uterus and vagina. In: Higgins CB, Hricak H, Helms CA. editors. Magnetic resonance imaging of the body. Philadelphia: Lippicott-Raven; 1997. p. 801–5.

67. Kim SH, Choi BI, Lee HP, et al. Uterine cervical carcinoma: comparison of CT and MR findings. Radiology 1990;175:45–51.

68. Sironi S, Belloni C, Taccagni GL, Del Maschio A. Carcinoma of the cervix: value of MR in detecting parametrial involvement. AJR Am J Roentgenol 1991;156:753–6.

69. Togashi K, Nishimura D, Sagoh T, et al. Carcinoma of the cervix: staging with MR imaging. Radiology 1989;171:245–51.

70. Chang YCF, Hricak H, Thurnher S, Lacey CG. Vagina: evaluation with MR imaging, Part II. neoplasms. Radiology 1988;169:175–9.

71. Kim MJ, Chung JJ, Lee YH, et al. Comparison of the use of the transrectal surface coil and the pelvic phased-array coil in MR imaging for preoperative evaluation of uterine cervical carcinoma. AJR Am J Roentgenol 1997;168:1215–21.

72. Hricak H, Yu KK. Radiology in invasive cervical cancer. AJR Am J Roentgenol 1996;167:1101–8.

73. Kim SH, Kim SC, Choi BI, Han MC. Uterine cervical carcinoma: evaluation of pelvic lymph node metastasis with MR imaging. Radiology 1994;190:807–11.

74. Yu KK, Hricak H, Subak LL, et al. Preoperative staging of cervical carcinoma: phased array coil fast spin-echo versus body coil spin-echo T_2-weighted MR imaging. AJR Am J Roentgenol 1998;171:707–11.

75. Hricak H, Powell B, Yu KK, et al. Invasive cervical carcinoma: role of MR imaging in pretreatment work-up—cost minimization and diagnostic efficacy analysis. Radiology 1996;198:403–9.

76. Carrington B, Hricak H. The uterus and vagina. In: Hricak H, Carrington BM, editors. MRI of the pelvis: a text atlas. London: Appleton & Lange; 1991. p. 93–184.

6

Screening for Neoplasms

ADNAN R. MUNKARAH, MD

Cervical cancer continues to be a leading cause of cancer-related death among women worldwide, with approximately 500,000 cases diagnosed annually. Eighty percent of these cancers occur in the developing countries. In the developed world, cervical cancer is relatively uncommon, ranking 10th behind more common cancers, such as cancers of the breast, lung, colon, rectum, and prostate.[1] Cancers of the vulva and vagina are uncommon and represent 4 to 7 percent of all gynecologic malignancies.

The concept that invasive cervical cancer develops from precursor dysplastic lesions was first introduced in the early 20th century. In the 1960s, on the basis of clinical studies and supporting laboratory data, Richart proposed that the dysplastic lesions were preinvasive lesions that preceded the development of invasive cancer in the cervix; he also suggested that those lesions formed a biologic continuum that he called cervical intraepithelial lesions (CIN).[2] The concept of similar precursor lesions was quickly applied to those of the vulva and vagina. The terms vulvar intaepithelial lesions (VIN) and vaginal intraepithelial lesions (VAIN) were used to refer to these preinvasive diseases. However, unlike the cervix, where most carcinomas are associated with a dysplastic (CIN) lesion, only a third of invasive vulvar cancers have a coexisting VIN lesion.[3] A number of molecular and pathologic studies have confirmed the presence of a strong association between human papillomavirus (HPV) and neoplastic lesions of the lower genital tract.

The presence of a preinvasive stage that can be diagnosed and treated makes cancers of the lower genital tract, especially the cervix, ideal diseases for screening and prevention. Cytologic screening with the Pap test has been the standard of care around the world. Recent developments in molecular and computer technology have generated a number of new tests designed to improve the accuracy of detecting cervical cancer.[4,5] In this chapter, we will discuss these new technologies and their present applications.

CYTOLOGIC SCREENING: THE PAP TEST

In 1924, George Papanicolaou, an investigator interested in the endocrinology of the menstrual cycle, made an accidental observation that cancer cells derived from the uterine cervix may be detected in vaginal smears. In the past four decades, the wide use of the Pap test for cervical cancer screening in the developed world has led to a significant reduction in the incidence of invasive cervical cancer as well as mortality from the disease.[6–13] In fact, the cervical cancer incidence rate has dropped by 70 to 90 percent in highly screened populations. In the developing countries, the limited access to screening programs continues to be a major contributor to the high mortality rates associated with cervical cancer. It is estimated that approximately 50 percent of women in the developed world have had at least one Pap test during a 5-year period, and 85 percent have had at least one Pap test during their lifetime. In contrast, only 5 percent of women in the developing countries have had one screening in 5 years.

In 1987, the American Cancer Society approved new guidelines for the detection of cervical cancer in asymptomatic women. It recommended that all women who are or who have been sexually active or have reached age 18 years should have an annual physical examination and Pap test. After three or more consecutive normal examinations, Pap testing may be performed less frequently at the discretion of the physician.[14] Other health professional organizations, including the National Cancer Institute (NCI), the American College of Obstetricians and Gynecologists (ACOG), the American Medical Association, the American Medical Women's Association, the American Nursing Association, and the American Academy of Family Practice, have adopted identical recommendations (Table 6–1). Despite minor variations in the suggested screening interval, the importance of repetitive population-based screening has been emphasized by everyone.[15,16] The degree of protection against cervical cancer is proportional to the number of screenings a woman has during her lifetime. When women are screened at 1- to 2-year intervals, the incidence of cervical cancer is reduced by 93 percent; the reduction in cervical cancer incidence is 91 percent for 3-year-interval screening and 83 percent for 5-year intervals.[17]

Recently, there has been a rising concern regarding the false-negative rate of cervical cytology. False-negative smears may be due to errors in sampling, interpretation, or follow-up and management. Sampling errors may be overcome by adequate training of personnel performing the smear, avoiding vaginal douches and digital examination prior to collection of the specimen, use of a moistened Ayers spatula and cytobrush, and immediate fixation of the specimen. Errors in the interpretation of Pap smears have been attributed to a variety of factors, including the quality of the smear as well as human error due to lack of training or fatigue. Approximately 50 million Pap tests are performed annually in the United States; of those, around 8 percent are abnormal. Pap smears are usually read by cytotechnologists and any abnormal results confirmed by pathologists. It is estimated that each slide contains from 50,000 to 300,000 cells, and that it takes a technologist at least 5 minutes to screen a slide.[18] An individual technologist is expected to read no more than 90 smears in a 7.5-hour day. In reality, screening that many smears a day can be attained only by a few technologists; 50 cases per day is a more reasonable limit. In 1987, a report in the *Wall Street Journal* claimed that some medical laboratories were more concerned with financial profit than quality and were processing huge numbers of Pap smears with little quality control. In an attempt to help monitor the performance of individual cytotechnologists, the federal government enacted the Clinical Laboratory Improvement Act. It limited the number of smears that could be read by any technologist in a given day and required that 10 percent of all Pap smears be reread for quality assurance.

The "diagnostic chaos" and confusing terminology that existed in cervical cytology reporting led the National Cancer Institute to convene a number of multidisciplinary workshops and to develop a new reporting system. The classification that was developed was designated the 1988 Bethesda System for Reporting Cervical/Vaginal Cytologic Diagnoses.[19] The new system eliminated the old numerical Pap class designation, required an evaluation of specimen adequacy, and used new terms that can be correlated with the histologic findings (Table 6–2).

Table 6–1. FREQUENCY OF PAP SMEAR TESTING: ACOG RECOMMENDATIONS

Initial Screening
Smears should be obtained from all women by age 18 years and from sexually active women regardless of age.

Frequency
High-risk patients: Screening should be done annually.
Low-risk patients: After two successive negative annual smears, the interval of screening is arbitrary and should be based on the informed decision of the patient and physician. The risk of an abnormality occurring within 3 to 5 years is minimal.

DES Exposed Patients
Screening should begin at menarche, at age 14 years, or at the onset of symptoms. Subsequent Pap smears should be done at 6- to 12-month intervals.

Following Hysterectomy
Vaginal cytology is recommended at minimum intervals of 3 to 5 years.

Following Therapy for Preinvasive Disease of the Cervix
Screening should be done at approximately 2-year intervals.

Following Therapy for Invasive Cervical Malignancy
Screening is customarily performed at 3-month intervals for 2 years and every 6 months thereafter.

ACOG = American College of Obstetricians and Gynecologists; DES = diethylstilbestrol.

In the United States, two groups of the population continue to suffer from a disproportionately higher cervical cancer–related death: the low-income underserved women and the elderly.[20] It is estimated that 40 percent of deaths from cervical cancer occur in women aged 65 years or more. This death rate has been unchanged in the past two decades.[21] Underscreening is felt to be the main contributor to the high cancer-related mortality rates in this subpopulation. In order to solve this problem, current efforts are focusing on improving access to medical care and public education regarding the importance of screening.

There are no widely accepted guidelines for screening women who have had a hysterectomy.[22] Women with a previous hysterectomy may be divided into three groups: (1) those who have had a total hysterectomy for benign disease, (2) those who had supracervical hysterectomy for benign disease, and (3) patients with a previous history of an abnormal Pap smear. Women who have undergone total hysterectomy for benign diseases are at low risk for vaginal dysplasia or cancer. Recommendations for screening in this group have varied from no further screening to once-every-10-years screening.[23,24] Women with a history of benign gynecologic disease and an intact cervix should continue screening as per the guidelines for the general population. Women with a previous history of an abnormal Pap smear are at increased risk for vaginal neoplastic lesions. These women should continue with regular surveillance, with annual Pap smear testing initially. After three consecutive normal tests, the frequency of such surveillance could be reduced to once every 3 to 5 years.

COLPOSCOPY AND CERVICOGRAPHY

Hinselmann first introduced colposcopy in 1920 as a screening method for cervical cancer. At present, it is widely used for the evaluation of abnormal Pap smears. The colposcope is a binocular microscope that is connected to a light source and attached to a mobile arm or pole. The objectives' focal length ranges from 200 to 300 mm, and the images are enlarged 6 to 16 times. The colposcope may include accessories. A tilting mechanism facilitates the examination. Still and video photography allows examina-

Table 6–2. THE BETHESDA SYSTEM FOR REPORTING CERVICAL/VAGINAL CYTOLOGIC DIAGNOSES

Format of the Report
 a. A statement on adequacy of the specimen for evaluation
 b. A general categorization that may be used to assist with clerical triage (optimal)
 c. The descriptive diagnosis

Adequacy of the Specimen
 Satisfactory for evaluation
 Satisfactory for evaluation but limited by. . . (specify reason)
 Unsatisfactory for evaluation . . . (specify reason)

General Categorization (Optional)
 Within normal limits
 Benign cellular changes: see descriptive diagnoses
 Epithelial cell abnormality: see descriptive diagnoses

Descriptive Diagnoses
 Benign cellular changes
  Infection
   – *Trichomonas vaginalis*
   – Fungal organisms morphologically consistent with *Candida* spp
   – Predominance of coccobacilli consistent with shift in vaginal flora
   – Bacteria morphologically consistent with *Actinomyces* spp
   – Cellular changes associated with herpes simplex virus
   – Other
 Reactive changes
  Reactive cellular changes associated with:
   – Inflammation (includes typical repair)
   – Atrophy with inflammation ("atrophic vaginitis")
   – Radiation
   – Intrauterine contraceptive device (IUD)
   – Other

Epithelial Cell Abnormalities
 Squamous cell
  • Atypical squamous cells of undetermined significance: qualify*
  • Low-grade squamous intraepithelial lesion encompassing:
   – HPV†
   – Mild dysplasia/CIN1
  • High-grade squamous intraepithelial lesion encompassing:
   – Moderate and severe dysplasia
   – CIS/CIN2 and CIN3
  • Squamous cell carcinoma
 Glandular cell
  • Endometrial cells, cytologically benign, in a postmenopausal woman
  • Atypical glandular cells of undetermined significance: qualify*
  • Endocervical adenocarcinoma
  • Endometrial adenocarcinoma
  • Extrauterine adenocarcinoma
  • Adenocarcinoma, not otherwise specified (NOS)
  • Other malignant neoplasms: specify
  • Hormonal evaluation (applied to vaginal smears only)
  • Hormonal pattern compatible with age and history
  • Hormonal pattern incompatible with age and history: specify
  • Hormonal evaluation not possible due to: specify

CIN = cervical intraepithelial lesion; CIS = carcinoma in situ.
*Atypical squamous or glandular cells of undetermined significance should be further qualified as to whether a reactive or a premalignant/malignant process is favored.
†Cellular changes of human papillomavirus (HPV)—previously termed koilocytosis atypia, or condylomatous atypia—are included in the category of low-grade squamous intraepithelial lesion.

tions to be reviewed and discussed with other professionals. A green filter absorbs red light and highlights the abnormal vascular patterns. In order to visualize the abnormal areas, acetic acid (3 to 5 percent) is usually applied for 2 to 3 minutes prior to examining the cervix and vagina and for 5 minutes prior to vulvar examination (Figure 6–1).

It has been proposed that the use of colposcopy as a primary screening tool might reduce the false-negative rate of cytologic screening with the Pap test.[25–27] However, studies have shown only a slight increase in detection of cervical lesions when colposcopy was added to the cytologic screening program.[26] There are significant limitations to the use of colposcopy as a screening tool: (1) its low specificity with a high false-positive rate can result in overtreatment of a large number of patients; (2) the invisibility of the squamocolumnar junction in some women leads to unsatisfactory evaluations; and (3) experienced colposcopists are needed to perform adequate examinations, and there is significant interobserver variability. Some have proposed that the low specificity and positive predictive rate of colposcopic examination may be improved by directed biopsies.[28]

Cervicography was introduced by Adolph Stafl in 1981.[29] Using specialized equipment, high quality colposcopic-type photographs are taken by paraprofessional personnel and later interpreted by experts in the field.[30] Many studies have reported that cervicography has a higher sensitivity but lower specificity than cytologic examination for all grades of cervical dysplasias.[31,32] The positive predictive value of cervicography ranges between 19 and 46 percent.

In the developing countries, the cost and availability of a screening test or special equipment are significant limitations. A recent study evaluated the role of direct visualization of the cervix after application of acetic acid as an alternative to cytology for the detection of premalignant lesions of the cervix.[33] The sensitivity of that method to detect high-grade dysplasia was 64 percent, which is a lower rate than that achieved with cytologic screening.

AUTOMATED CYTOLOGIC TESTS

The AutoPap® (Neopath, Inc., Redmond, WA)[34–36] and Papnet® (Neuromedical Systems Inc., Suffern, NY)[37]

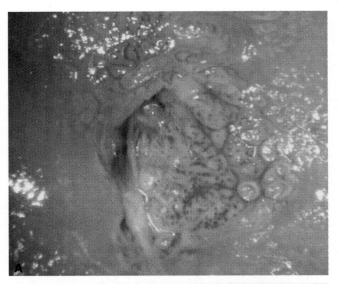
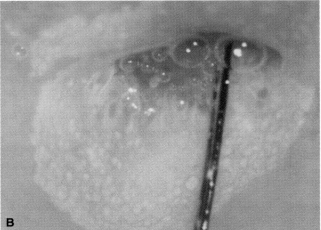
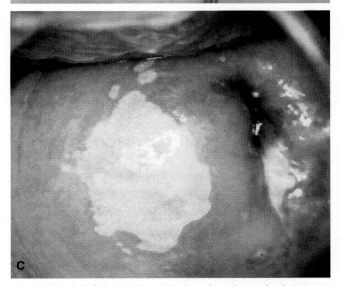

Figure 6–1. *A,* Colposcopic evaluation of carcinoma in situ: coarse punctation and mosaicism. *B,* Colposcopic evaluation of cervical dysplasia: mosaicism. *C,* Colposcopic evaluation of cervical dysplasia: acetowhite discoloration and mosaicism. (Specimen was stained with acetic acid for two minutes.)

are two cytologic screening systems that combine automated cytology and computerized analysis to reduce human error in screening. Both systems have been approved by the Food and Drug Administration (FDA) to rescreen the previously manually screened Pap smears in order to identify false-negative smear results. Recently, the AutoPap system was approved by the FDA for primary screening.

The AutoPap system was initially devised as a quality control rescreener that reviews all normal and satisfactory smears and assigns them a quality-control score based on certain cytologic parameters. The slides with the highest quality-control scores are then rescreened manually. When compared with 100 percent manual rescreening, the AutoPap system was found to be only half as sensitive in detecting false-negative smears.[38] Since 100 percent manual rescreening is neither realistic nor physically feasible, the Laboratory Improvement Act mandated 10 percent manual rescreening. The advantage of the AutoPap system is that it allows a 100 percent rescreening of smears thus resulting in a fivefold improved detection in false-negative smears, compared with the 10 percent random manual review that is presently applied.[39]

The new AutoPap primary screening system is geared for use in initial screening of conventionally prepared Pap smear slides. It consists of two main components: the workstation (computer, monitor, keyboard, mouse, modem, and printer) and the instrument (slide processor). Slides are labeled with a barcode label, mounted on a tray, and then automatically moved, scanned, and analyzed under the microscope. The system algorithms are programmed to detect evidence of morphologic changes associated with epithelial abnormalities, specimen adequacy, benign cellular changes, and infection. Each processed slide is classified as "No Further Review," "Review," or "QC Review." Up to 25 percent of slides are classified as "No Further Review" and require no manual screening. The slides classified as "Review" contain the abnormal and unsatisfactory slides and require manual screening. The system also classifies at least 15 percent of all the successfully processed slides as "QC Review." Those slides have the highest likelihood of being abnormal and are eligible for rescreening. The AutoPap primary screening system thus removes 25 percent of adequate and normal smears from the cytotechnologist's workload. According to the company, the system is not intended to replace laboratory slide review processes for "high-risk" slides. The definition of high-risk cases consists of one or more of the following: physician-designated high-risk patients; prior abnormal gynecologic history; postmenopausal or abnormal vaginal bleeding; diethylstilbestrol (DES) patients; previous breast cancer or history of malignancy; previous tissue or Pap test diagnosis of HPV, dysplasia, or human immunodeficiency (HIV) infection; multiple sex partners; visible lesion; early onset of sexual activity; and smoking. A recent study showed that primary screening with AutoPap maintained a high sensitivity (96%) while reducing the workload by eliminating 30 percent of adequate and normal smears.[40,41]

The PapNet scans the slides and records on tape digitalized images of 128 of the most abnormal fields found on the slide. The exact location of the abnormal cells (X and Y coordinates) on the actual slide is also recorded. The images are reviewed by the cytotechnologist who will identify the test as "Negative" (indicating the absence of abnormality) or "Review" (indicating that a true cytologic abnormality exists). Images labeled as "Review" will be referred to the microscopist for final evaluation and diagnosis. The initial experience with PapNet testing suggested that it would be valuable in quality control and would result in a significant reduction in the rate of false-negative smears in an "efficient and timely manner."[42] PapNet testing is supposed to be seven to eight times more sensitive than 100 percent manual rescreening in detecting missed abnormalities.[43] Studies which evaluated PapNet as a primary screening technique found a higher detection rate for carcinoma in situ and invasive cervical cancer.[44]

If applied with the present screening recommendations, these new technologies will significantly increase the cost of cervical screening. However, they will become cost effective when incorporated into infrequent screening every 3 to 4 years.[45]

FLUID-BASED CYTOLOGY

Fluid-based cytology is geared toward optimizing the collection and preparation of cervical cells prior to their examination. In 1996, the FDA approved the ThinPrep 2000® System (Cytic Corporation, Boston, Massachusetts) for cervical cancer screening. With this system, the specimen is obtained from the cervix in the usual manner using a cervical broom, spatula, or cytobrush. The collection device is then rinsed into a vial containing an alcohol-based solution (Figure 6–2). The vial is then placed in the ThinPrep processor, which prepares the slides through three steps: dispersion, filtration, and transfer of the cells to a slide (Figure 6–3).

The advantage of this technique is that it removes mucus and red blood cells from the specimen and improves the fixation of cellular structure. In addition, the cells displayed represent a more uniform sample of the specimen collected (Figure 6–4). However, it is felt that these differences in preparation may lead to certain changes that result in overdiagnosis of cervical abnormalities.[46] Therefore, cytotechnologists need to be trained to read ThinPrep

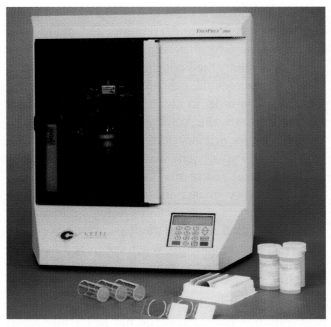

Figure 6–3. ThinPrep 2000® processor.

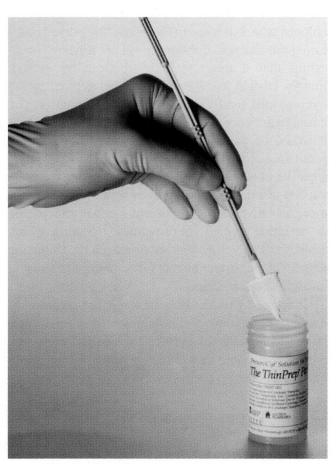

Figure 6–2. ThinPrep® specimen collection kit.

slides. Multiple studies have shown that, compared with conventional cytologic methods, ThinPrep was significantly more sensitive in detecting cervical dysplasia.[47–49] In patients in whom biopsies were used to confirm cervical abnormalities, ThinPrep increased the true positive predictive rate of screening by 9.4 to 20.9 percent.[50] Earlier reports raised the concern that glandular abnormalities may be more difficult to assess on ThinPrep.[51,52] However, a recent study has shown that the ThinPrep test has a higher sensitivity and specificity for glandular lesions.[53]

HUMAN PAPILLOMAVIRUS TESTING

In the past 20 years, there has been a large body of evidence showing an association between HPV infection and cancers of the lower genital tract.[54–57] Out of more than 80 HPV genotypes that have been identified, 15 to 20 infect organs of the female lower genital tract. Depending on the severity of neoplastic changes that they induce, these HPV types have been subdivided into a high-risk group, usually detected in high-grade dysplastic lesions and invasive cancers, and a low-risk group, usually seen in lower-grade lesions and subclinical infections (Table 6–3). The association between HPV infection and cervical pathology stimulated the interest to use

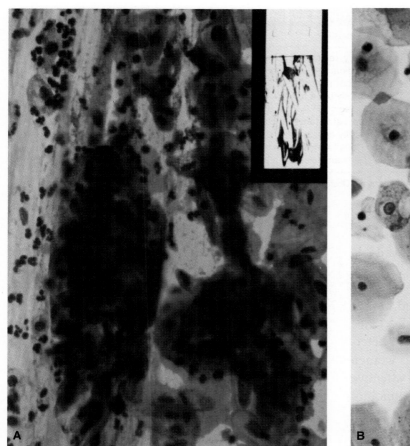
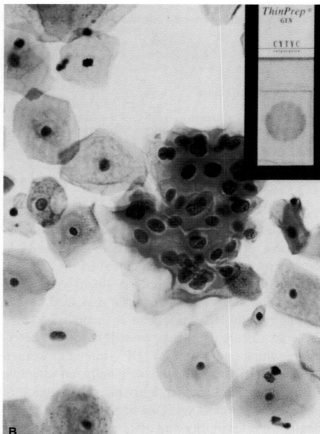

Figure 6–4. Differences between Pap slides. *A*, Conventionally prepared Pap smear. *B*, ThinPrep® smear.

HPV detection as an adjunct screening method to cytologic evaluation.[30,58–60]

A variety of HPV testing methods have been explored (Table 6–4).[5] Most of those, including the widely used ViraPap® and ViraType® (Digene Diagnostics, Inc., Silver Spring, Maryland), have been found to be of limited clinical use because of problems with sensitivity and positive predictive value.[61–63] In 1992, Rothrode reported a novel non-isotopic technique for HPV detection—the hybrid capture technique.[63] The hybrid capture kit presently on the market has a higher sensitivity than the previously used methods and detects five low-risk and nine high-risk HPV types. In addition, it can measure the amount of viral DNA in the sample. Many studies have shown that HPV infection is a self-limited infection that usually lasts 1 to 2 years. Persistent long-term infection with a high "viral load" of specific HPV genotypes is necessary, but not sufficient, for cervical carcinogenesis.[56,64–68]

There are few limitations to the routine use of HPV testing as a screening test in the general population. First, the prevalence of HPV infection is dependent on age and sexual activity. In women with normal cytologic smears, HPV infection rates are < 5 percent in women older than 55 years, compared with 10 to 15 percent in younger women.[69] Since HPV infection is frequently transient, a decision to treat every woman with confirmed HPV infection will lead to unnecessary treatment in a large number of women. On the other hand, when used to screen a high-risk population, HPV testing may have a high positive predictive value for cervical neoplasia.[70] Second, the natural history of HPV infection is not completely understood. Potentially oncogenic HPV-

Table 6–3. HPV TYPES	
Low risk	6, 11, 42, 43, 44
High risk	16, 18, 31, 33, 35, 39, 45, 51, 52, 56, 58

HPV = human papillomavirus.

Table 6–4. COMPARISON OF VARIOUS METHODS AVAILABLE FOR DETECTION OF HPV

Method	Sensitivity	Specificity	Comment
Cytology	Low	Low	Easy, relatively inexpensive, but subjective, insensitive, and nonspecific
Dot blot	Moderate	Moderate	Radioactive, commercially available as ViraPap, ViraType, HPV Profile; labor intensive
Filter in situ hybridization	Low	Low	Rarely used today
In situ hybridization	Moderate	Moderate	Detects HPV in paraffin-embedded tissue
Southern blot hybridization	High	High	Gold standard, but cumbersome; not feasible for large-scale clinical use
Hybrid capture	High	High	Newly approved for commercial use; nonradioactive, easier to use, and less expensive than dot blot
Polymerase chain reaction	Very high	High	Uses amplification and so is prone to contamination errors (false positives)

Adapted from Spitzer M. Cervical screening adjuncts: recent advances. Am J Obstet Gynecol 1998;179:544–56.
HPV = human papillomavirus.

type infections are found in women with low-grade, equivocal, or normal smears.[71] There is no available data as to the optimal management of these cases. Current research is geared to identify specific genetic and molecular factors that may lead to progression from HPV infection to neoplasia. Once these factors are identified, we will be able to determine which subgroup of HPV-infected women would benefit from treatment. Finally, an effective HPV treatment, whether antiviral or immunobiologic, does not exist yet. Ongoing studies are investigating the feasibility and efficacy of various vaccines for the treatment as well as the prevention of HPV infection.

One potential role for HPV DNA testing is to sort women with atypical or low-grade smears into two groups: one group of women who are at high risk for progression into more severe lesions and thus need treatment or close follow-up, and the second group with very low risk of progression. In 1996, the NCI initiated a large multi-institutional study to establish the optimal management of mildly abnormal Pap smears. Women whose Pap smears reveal atypical squamous cells of undetermined significance (ASCUS) or a low-grade squamous intraepithelial lesion (LSIL) are randomized to one of three arms.[72,73] In the first arm, the women will undergo HPV testing; women with low-risk HPV type and normal cervicogram will be followed up expectantly with cytologic testing; women with high-risk HPV type will undergo immediate colposcopy. Those women randomized to the second arm will undergo immediate colposcopy, and those in the third arm will be followed up with cytologic screening. Hopefully, the results of this large prospective randomized trial will help determine the role of HPV testing in the management of women with ASCUS or LSIL Pap smears.

The high enrollment and follow-up rates in the study have been encouraging. Early available data reveal that a very high percentage of women (82.9%) with an LSIL diagnosis from Pap smears are positive for HPV DNA by Hybrid Capture II (HC II) assay. As a result, it looks like there will be limited potential for HPV testing to direct decisions about the clinical management of women with LSIL. On the other hand, testing for high risk HPV DNA might be helpful in women with ASCUS. Preliminary analysis shows that HC II has greater sensitivity to detect severe dysplasia, or more severe lesions, than a single additional cytologic test indicating ASCUS or above. Its specificity, on the other hand, was comparable to repeat cytology. Future analyses and longer follow-up will hopefully help us determine the exact role of HPV testing in the screening of cervical neoplasia.

CONCLUSION

The Pap test has been one of the most successful cancer screening procedures in medicine. Efforts should continue to educate women about the importance of screening and to improve access to the underscreened population.[74–78] Advances in technology and a better understanding of the biology of cervical neoplasia have led to the development of new tests to improve the detection of precancerous lesions of the cervix. Further studies are needed to investigate new strategies for cervical cancer screening using these new techniques. Outcome data are needed to determine the cost of those new strategies and their impact on cervical cancer prevention and mortality.[79]

REFERENCES

1. Noller KL. Incidence and demographic trends in cervical neoplasia. Am J Obstet Gynecol 1996;175:1088–90.
2. Mitchell MF. Premalignant disorders of the lower genital tract. Gynecologic oncology. In: Ransom SB, Dombrowski MP, McNeeley SG, et al., editors. Practical strategies in obstetrics and gynecology. Philadelphia, PA: WB Saunders Co.; 2000. p. 439–48.
3. Buscema J, Stern J, Woodruff JD. The significance of the histological alterations adjacent to invasive vulvar carcinoma. Am J Obstet Gynecol 1987;156:212.
4. Richart RM. Screening. The next century. Cancer 1995;76:1919–27.
5. Spitzer M. Cervical screening adjuncts: recent advances. Am J Obstet Gynecol 1998;179:544–56.
6. Brinton LA, Fraumeni JF Jr. Epidemiology of uterine cervical cancer. J Chron Dis 1986;39:1051–65.
7. Fidler HK, Boyes DA, Nichols TM, Worth AJ. Cervical cytology in the control of cancer of the cervix. Mod Med 1970;25(12):9–15.
8. Christopherson WM, Parker JE, Mendez WM, Lundin FE Jr. Cervix cancer death rates and mass cytologic screening. Cancer 1970;26:808–11.
9. Johannesson G, Geirsson G, Day N. The effect of mass screening in Iceland, 1965–74, on the incidence and mortality of cervical carcinoma. Int J Cancer 1978;21:418–25.
10. Nieburgs HE, Stergus I, Stephenson EM, Harbin BL. Mass screening of the total female population of a county for cervical carcinoma. JAMA 1957;164:1546–51.
11. Hakama M. Mass screening for cervical cancer in Finland. In: Miller AB, editor. Screening in cancer. Geneva, Switzerland: International Union Against Cancer; 1978.
12. Chamberlain J. Reasons that some screening programs fail to control cervical cancer. In: Hakama M, Miller AB, Day NE, editors. Screening for cancer of the uterine cervix. Lyon, France: International Agency for Research on Cancer; 1986.
13. Miller AB, Knight J, Narod S. The natural history of cancer of the cervix and the implications for screening policy. In: Miller AB, Chamberlain J, Day NE, et al., editors. Cancer screening. New York, NY: Cambridge University Press; 1991. p. 141–52.
14. Fink DJ. Change in American Cancer Society check-up guidelines for detection of cervical cancer. CA Cancer J Clin 1988;38:127–8.
15. Blomfield PI, Lancashire RJ, Woodman CBJ. Can women at risk of cervical abnormality be identified? Br J Obstet Gynaecol 1988;105:486–92.
16. Gram IT, Macaluso M, Stalsberg H. Incidence of cervical intraepithelial neoplasia grade III, and cancer of the cervix uteri following a negative Pap smear in an opportunistic screening. Acta Obstet Gynecol Scand 1998;77:228–32.
17. World Health Organization. Control of cancer of the cervix uteri. Bull World Health Organ 1986;64:607–18.
18. Koss LG. The Papanicolaou test for cervical cancer detection. JAMA 1989;261:737–43.
19. National Cancer Institute Workshop. The 1988 Bethesda system for reporting cervical/vaginal cytological diagnoses. JAMA 1989;262:931–4.
20. Lawson HW, Lee NC, Thames SF, et al. Cervical cancer screening among low-income women: results of a national screening program, 1991–1995. Obstet Gynecol 1998;92:745–52.
21. NIH Consensus Statement. Cervical Cancer 1996;14(1):1–38.
22. Eaker ED, Vierkant RA, Konitzer KA, Remington PL. Cervical cancer screening among women with and without hysterectomies. Obstet Gynecol 1998;91:551–5.
23. McIntosh DG. Pap smear screening after hysterectomy. Compr Ther 1998;24:14–8.
24. Piscitelli J, Bastian L, Wilkes A, Simel D. Cytologic screening after hysterectomy for benign disease. Am J Obstet Gynecol 1995;173:424–32.
25. Guerra B, DeSimone P, Gabrielli S, et al. Combined cytology and colposcopy to screen for cervical cancer in pregnancy. J Reprod Med 1998;43:647–53.
26. Olatunbosun OA, Okonofua FE, Ayangade SO. Screening for cervical neoplasia in an African population: simultaneous use of cytology and colposcopy. Obstet Gynecol Surv 1992;47:497.
27. Pete I, Toth V, Bosze P. The value of colposcopy in screening cervical carcinoma. Eur J Gynaecol Oncol 1998;19:120–2.
28. Hopman EH, Kenemans P, Helmerhorst THM. Positive predictive rate of colposcopic examination of the cervix uteri: an overview of literature. Obstet Gynecol Surv 1998;53:97–106.
29. Stafl A. Cervicography: a new method for cervical cancer detection. Am J Obstet Gynecol 1981;139:815–25.
30. Reid R, Greenberg MD, Lorincz A, et al. Should cervical cytologic testing can be augmented by cervicography or human papillomavirus deoxyribonucleic acid detection? Am J Obstet Gynecol 1991;164:1461–71.
31. Szarewski A, Cuzick J, Edwards R, et al. The use of cervicography in a primary screening service. Br J Obstet Gynaecol 1991;98:313–7.
32. Tawa K, Forsythe A, Cove K, et al. A comparison of the Papanicolaou smear and the cervigram: sensitivity, specificity, and cost analysis. Obstet Gynecol 1988;71:229–35.
33. Megevand E, Denny L, Dehaeck K, et al. Acetic acid

visualization of the cervix: an alternative to cytologic screening. Obstet Gynecol 1996;88:383–6.

34. AutoPap 300 QC Automatic Pap Smear Screener System. Package Insert. Redmond, WA: NeoPath; 1996.

35. Bartels PH, Wied GL. Automated screening for cervical cancer: diagnostic decision procedures. Acta Cytol 1997;41:6–10.

36. Patten SF Jr. Development of an automated Papanicolaou smear screening system. Cancer 1997;81(6):332–6.

37. PapNet Testing System. Package insert. Suffern, NY: Neuromedical Systems; 1996.

38. Hematology and Pathology Devices Panel of the Medical Devices Advisory Committee to the FDA. Transcript of proceedings. Washington, D.C.: U.S. Department of Health and Human Services; 1995.

39. Colgan TJ, Patten SF, Lee JSJ. A clinical trial of the AutoPap 300 QC system for quality control of cervicovaginal cytology in the clinical laboratory. Acta Cytol 1995;39:1191–8.

40. Lee JSJ, Wilhelm P, Kuan L, et al. AutoPap system performance in screening for low prevalence and small cell abnormalities. Acta Cytol 1997;41:56–64.

41. AutoPap® Primary Screening. Product insert. Redmond, WA: Neopath; 1998.

42. Koss LG, Lin E, Schreiber K, et al. Evaluation of the Papnet™ cytologic screening system for quality control of cervical smears. Am J Clin Pathol 1994;101:220–9.

43. Mango LJ, Vanente PT. Neural network-assisted analysis and microscopic rescreening in presumed negative cervical cytologic smears. A comparison. Acta Cytol 1998;42:227–32.

44. Boon ME, Kok LP, Beck S. Histologic validation of neural network-assisted cervical screening comparison with the conventional procedure. Cell Vision 1995;2:23–7.

45. Brown AD, Garber AM. Cost-effectiveness of 3 methods to enhance the sensitivity of Papanicolaou testing. JAMA 1999;281:347–53.

46. Hutchinson ML, Cassin CM, Ball HG. The efficacy of an automated preparation device for cervical cytology. Am J Clin Pathol 1991;96:300–5.

47. Sheets EE, Constantine NM, Dinisco S, et al. Colposcopically directed biopsies provide a basis for comparing the accuracy of ThinPrep and Papanicolaou smears. J Gynecol Technol 1995;1:27–34.

48. Diaz-Rosario LA, Kabawat SE. Performance of a fluid-based, thin-layer Papanicolaou smear method in the clinical setting of an independent laboratory and an outpatient screening population in New England. Arch Pathol Lab Med 1999;123:817–21.

49. Carpenter AB, Davey DD. ThinPrep® Pap test™. Performance and biopsy follow-up in a university hospital. Cancer Cytopathol 1999;87:105–12.

50. Sherman ME, Mendoza M, Lee KR, et al. Performance of liquid-based, thin-layer cervical cytology: correlation with reference diagnoses and human papillomavirus testing. Mod Pathol 1998;11(9):837–43.

51. Wilbur DC. False negatives in focused rescreening of Papanicolaou smears. Arch Pathol Lab Med 1997;121:273–6.

52. Wilbur DC, Dubeshter B, Angel C, Atkinson KM. Use of thin layer preparations for gynecologic smears, practical considerations. Acta Cytol 1995;39:837–8.

53. Ashfaq R, Gibbons D, Vela C, et al. ThinPrep Pap test. Accuracy for glandular disease. Acta Cytol 1999; 43:81–5.

54. Konno R, Sato S, Yajima A. Progression of squamous cell carcinoma of the uterine cervix from cervical intraepithelial neoplasia infected with human papillomavirus: a retrospective follow-up study by in situ hybridization and polymerase chair reaction. Int J Gynecol Pathol 1992;11:105–12.

55. Schiffman MH, Bauer HM, Hoover RN, et al. Epidemiologic evidence showing that human papillomavirus infection causes most cervical intraepithelial neoplasia. J Natl Cancer Inst 1993;85: 958–64.

56. Cuzick J, Terry G, Ho L, et al. Type-specific human papillomavirus DNA in abnormal smears as a predictor of high grade cervical intraepithelial neoplasia. Br J Cancer 1994;69:167–71.

57. Syrjanen K, Mantyjarvi R, Vayrynen M, et al. Evolution of human papillomavirus infections in the uterine cervix during a long-term prospective follow-up. Appl Pathol 1987;5:121–35.

58. Cuzick J, Szarewski A, Terry G, et al. Human papillomavirus testing in primary cervical screening. Lancet 1995;345:1533–6.

59. Herrington CS, Evans MF, Hallam NF, et al. HPV status in the prediction of high grade CIN in patients with persistent low grade cervical cytological abnormalities. Br J Cancer 1995;71:206–9.

60. Johnson K. Periodic health examination, 1995 update 1. Screening for human papillomavirus infection in asymptomatic women. Can Med Assoc J 1995;152: 483–93.

61. Lorincz A. Detection of HPV infection by nucleic acid hybridization. Obstet Gynecol Clin North Am 1987; 14:451–69.

62. Meijer CJ, van den Brule AJ, Snijders PJ, et al. Detection of human papillomavirus in cervical scrapes by the polymerase chain reaction in relation to cytology: possible implications for cervical cancer screening. IARC Sci Publ 1992;119:271–81.

63. Rothrode RS. Hybrid capture system: an innovative nonisotopic method for human papillomavirus detection. Eur Clin Lab 1992;10:12.

64. Moscicki AB, Palefsky J, Smith G, et al. Variability of human papillomavirus DNA testing in a longitudi-

nal cohort of young women. Obstet Gynecol 1993;82:578–85.

65. Cox JT, Lorincz AT, Schiffman MH, et al. Human papillomavirus testing by Hybrid Capture appears to be useful in triaging women with a cytologic diagnosis of atypical squamous cells of undetermined significance. Am J Obstet Gynecol 1995;172:946–54.

66. Cuzick J, Terry G, Ho L, et al. Human papillomavirus type 16 DNA in cervical smears as predictor of high grade cervical intraepithelial neoplasia. Lancet 1992;339:959–60.

67. Koutsky LA, Holmes KK, Critchlow CW, et al. A cohort study of the risk of cervical intraepithelial neoplasia grade 2 or 3 in relation to papillomavirus infection. N Engl J Med 1992;327:1272–8.

68. Schneider A, Kirchhoff T, Meinhardt G, Gissmann L. Repeated evaluation of human papillomavirus 16 status in cervical swabs of young women with a history of normal Papanicolaou smears. Obstet Gynecol 1992;79:683–8.

69. de Villiers EM, Wagner D, Schneider A, et al. Human papillomavirus infections in women with and without abnormal cervical cytology. Lancet 1987;2: 703–6.

70. Schiffman M, Herrero R, Hildesheim A, et al. HPV DNA testing in cervical cancer screening. Results from women in a high-risk province of Costa Rica. JAMA 2000;283:87–93.

71. Herrington CS, Evans MF, Hallam NF, et al. HPV testing in patients with low grade cervical cytological abnormalities: a follow-up study. J Clin Pathol 1996;49:493–6.

72. The Atypical Squamous Cells of Undetermined Significance/Low-Grade Squamous Intraepithelial Lesions Triage Study (ALTS) Group. Human papillomavirus testing for triage of women with cytologic evidence of low-grade squamous intraepithelial lesions: baseline data from a randomized trial. J Nat Cancer Inst 2000;92:397–402.

73. Solomon D, Schiffman M, Tarone R. Comparison of three management strategies for patients with atypical squamous cells of undetermined significance: basline results from a randomized trial. J Nat Cancer Inst 2001;4:293–99.

74. Greimel ER, Gappmayer-Locker E, Girardi FL, Huber HP. Increasing women's knowledge and satisfaction with cervical cancer screening. J Psychosom Obstet Gynecol 1997;18:273–9.

75. Anderson LM, May DS. Has the use of cervical, breast, and colorectal cancer screening increased in the United States? Am J Public Health 1995;85:840–2.

76. Austin RM, McLendon WW. The Papanicolaou smear. Medicine's most successful cancer screening procedure is threatened [editorial]. JAMA 1997;277:754–5.

77. Baldauf J-J, Dreyfus M, Ritter J, et al. Screening histories of incidence cases of cervical cancer and high grade SIL. A comparison. Acta Cytol 1997;41:1431–8.

78. Wells BL, Horm JW. Targeting the underserved for breast and cervical cancer screening: the utility of ecological analysis using the National Health Interview Survey. Am J Public Health 1998;88:1484–9.

79. Grohs DH. Impact of automated technology on the cervical cytologic smear. A comparison of cost. Acta Cytol 1998;42:165–70.

7

Treatment of Squamous Intraepithelial Lesions

MOLLY A. BREWER, DVM, MD, MS

Diagnosis and treatment of lower genital tract squamous intraepithelial lesions (SILs) have undergone numerous changes over the last 25 years. Prior to the Pap test, diagnosis most often occurred when large cancers of the cervix and vagina were observed incidentally because no screening tests existed. Although the incidence of cervical cancer has significantly decreased over the last 40 years because of the use of the Pap test for screening, cervical cancer remains the second most common malignancy of women worldwide, accounting for 15 percent of all cancers diagnosed in women.[1] It is a major health problem, particularly in countries where access to preventive health care is limited. Although vulvar and vaginal cancers are less prevalent, they also constitute a health problem for women, particularly older women who are not sexually active and do not have regular gynecologic examinations. The SILs are thought to be precursors for these cancers. Treatment is ideally done prior to the development of cancer, yet controversies continue to exist regarding the management of these preneoplastic lesions. There is, as yet, no reliable way of differentiating lesions that will regress, lesions that will persist without regression, and lesions that will progress to higher-grade dysplasia and ultimately to cancer.

DIAGNOSIS

Abnormal Pap Test Results

The Pap smear may exhibit cells from the entire reproductive tract, depending on the hormonal status of the woman. Abnormal smears can result from abnormalities of the ectocervix, endocervix, vagina, vulva, distal urethra, endometrium, and even the fallopian tube and ovary if the tubes are patent. So, while an abnormal Pap smear most likely represents an abnormality of the uterine cervix, an abnormal smear in the presence of a normal ectocervical and endocervical examination and sampling requires investigation of the remaining components of the genital tract. In addition, one of the more difficult areas of microscopy is interpretation of the cytology smear, since no underlying stroma is present to use as a point of reference.[1] Therefore, high-grade SIL may closely resemble carcinoma on the Pap smear and must be carefully differentiated from cancer.

Patients who present with abnormal Pap smear results can be placed into two groups, those at high risk and those at low risk. The level of risk is determined by the patient's history of abnormal Pap smears in one of two ways. The first determination of risk is from the current Pap smear. The low-risk group includes low-grade SIL (LGSIL) favoring human papillomavirus (HPV) infection, LGSIL favoring dysplasia, abnormal squamous cells of uncertain significance (ASCUS), and atypical glandular cells of undetermined significance (AGUS) favoring reactive changes among its differential diagnoses.[2,3] The high-risk group includes high-grade SIL (HGSIL), AGUS favoring dysplasia, squamous cell carcinoma, and adenocarcinoma among its differential diagnoses. The second determination of risk lies in the patient's history of abnormal Pap smears. A patient with a first abnormal smear after having yearly normal Pap smears is placed in the low-risk group unless her current Pap result includes a high-risk lesion. Patients who have had multiple abnormal Pap smears, those who have been treated for sexually transmitted diseases, those who do not have a yearly gynecologic examination, those who have not followed treatment recommendations in the past, and those with human immunodeficiency virus (HIV) are considered to be in a higher risk-group.[4]

Approximately 25 percent of HPV lesions regress, 55 percent persist, and 20 percent progress.[5–8] Patients in the low-risk category with HPV/LGSIL, ASCUS, or AGUS (reactive) can receive follow-up care in the form of Pap smear tests every 6 months. By 9 months, 78 percent of patients with cervical intraepithelial neoplasia grade 1 (CIN1) or LGSIL will have disease regression, and 7 percent will have disease progression.[9,10] In contrast, moderate dysplasia, now classified as HGSIL, will show a regression rate of 54 percent and a progression rate of 30 percent.[11] Patients in the high-risk category, by virtue of diagnosis or history, should receive treatment.

Atypical Glandular Cells of Undetermined Significance

A smear showing AGUS represents a condition that is problematic in terms of work-up and treatment. The diagnosis of AGUS on a Pap smear requires further work-up because a substantial number of patients will have a clinically significant lesion either of the cervix or of the endometrium. Twenty-five percent of the patients in the study by Kim and colleagues had clinically significant lesions: 18 percent of the lesions involved the cervix and included LGSIL, HGSIL, glandular dysplasia, adenocarcinoma in situ (ACIS), microinvasive adenocarcinoma, and invasive adenocarcinoma. Interestingly, 7 percent of the lesions were endometrial and included hyperplasia, adenocarcinoma, malignant mixed mesodermal (müllerian) tumor (MMMT), and metastatic adenocarcinoma.[12] Other studies have shown clinically significant lesions occurring in as many as 50 percent of the patients.[13] However, 25 percent of these cases were squamous metaplasia or chronic inflammation, which is of questionable significance.

Treatment of a patient whose Pap smear shows AGUS should include colposcopy, colposcopically directed biopsies, if an abnormality is seen, endocervical curettage (ECC), and endometrial biopsy. The cytopathologist can help differentiate between AGUS suggestive of neoplasia or AGUS suggestive of reaction. Although there is no clear consensus regarding management, patients with consistently abnormal smears, particularly those suggestive of dysplasia, may benefit from more invasive procedures because of the concern for endocervical or endometrial adenocarcinoma. Prior history of dysplasia confers an increased risk for abnormal pathology being found during subsequent follow-up care, with only 60 percent of these patients having normal cytology on follow-up versus 82 percent normal cytology in women who have no prior history of dysplasia.[14] Therefore, a prior history of abnormalities may help guide the clinician in the extent of the work-up and follow-up care of patients with AGUS.

Abnormal Squamous Cells of Uncertain Significance

Modification of the Bethesda system has helped guide clinicians in the management of ASCUS. In the initial classification (the Bethesda system), the issue of inadequate specimens was addressed by requiring a commentary that the smear was adequate for interpretation, less than optimal, or unsatisfactory with an explanation for the last two categories. The descriptive diagnoses listed were of infection (with a description of type), reactive or reparative changes, epithelial cell abnormalities, and nonepithelial malignant neoplasms.[15] If there were epithelial abnormalities, the new system distinguished between squamous and glandular components and had several descriptions for the abnormalities, including ASCUS or AGUS, LGSIL, favoring HPV or CIN, or HGSIL. In 1991, after 3 years of experience with the Bethesda system, the classification was modified to clarify the necessity for further work-up.[16–18] Infection and reparative/reactive changes were reclassified into the new category of benign cellular changes. The atypical category for both squamous and glandular cells was retained but was qualified by a description of the process, that is, whether a reactive or neoplastic process is favored.[19] ASCUS has received attention because of the fear of an underlying cancer, although the majority of ASCUS smears reflect either a reparative process or a low-grade lesion. However, 38 percent of high-grade lesions are first seen as ASCUS on a Pap smear.[20] ASCUS favoring SIL has a high correlation with the histopathologic changes of HGSIL.[21] Other studies have shown that the number of Pap smears with ASCUS is higher than warranted and is under scrutiny using neural networks.[22] A third study showed that the risk of having or developing HGSIL following ASCUS on Pap smear is only 9 percent, and the probability of cancer developing if HGSIL is untreated is only 1 percent or less,[23] suggesting that immediate referral for colposcopy and biopsies may be overtreatment and unacceptably expensive. Alanen and colleagues showed that 70 percent of women with LGSIL and ASCUS later have Pap smears showing normal cytology and so are spared the costs of colposcopy. However, they found that only 30 percent of women returned for follow-up care, which is why some clinicians advocate immediate treatment, even for ASCUS.[24] Other studies show higher rates of HGSIL and cancers,[25,26] but these studies were done prior to the changes made in the Pap smear classifications. A cost-effectiveness model by Raab and colleagues showed that a repeat Pap smear in 1 year is the most cost-effective strategy for women with ASCUS.[27] Postmenopausal women have a lower rate of ASCUS and a lower rate of underlying dysplasia.[28] Although ASCUS is worrisome because it may indicate an underlying HGSIL or cancer, the rates are low enough that repeat screening in 6 months to 1 year may well be efficacious and cost effective. Care for these patients needs better standardization so that physicians do not overtreat or overdiagnose women with abnormal Pap smears because of fear of litigation.[29]

Colposcopy

Colposcopy has become the standard of care for the work-up that follows an abnormal Pap smear. When Pap smear results are abnormal, it has been standard for a woman to undergo colposcopy, which is the examination of the cervix using magnification after application of acetic acid to accentuate dysplastic areas. The cervix, vagina, and vulva should all be examined, as these are the three most probable sites for dysplasia to occur. Patients who are at high risk are usually referred for colposcopy after their first abnormal Pap smear. This practice has been costly for many women whose disease will never progress to cancer or even to high-grade dysplasia. The shortage of experienced colposcopists and the clinician's fear of missing a cancer causes these women to be referred to a specialist. LGSIL or CIN1 is usually seen colposcopically as small foci of abnormality.[29,30] HGSIL or CIN2/3 differs in appearance colposcopically from CIN1 and HPV infection by the increased thickness of the acetowhite epithelium, the presence of punctation, and the presence of abnormal vessels. Invasive cancer may mimic CIN3 on colposcopy if the cancer is small, while a larger cancer may have exophytic areas. It is difficult to distinguish carcinoma in situ (CIS) from microinvasive or invasive carcinoma. As a result, invasion may be missed frequently on colposcopy.[31–33] At the other end of the spectrum, HPV is typically confused with low-grade dysplasia on colposcopy and is often overtreated with either the loop electrical excision procedure (LEEP) or multiple biopsies. In a retrospective review, 24 patients (0.06% of the population studied) developed invasive carcinoma within 14 months of conservative treatment for undiagnosed microinvasive disease.[30] This was largely attributable to failure to colposcopically diagnose or biopsy the affected area at the time of the original diagnosis. Retrospective review of the Pap smears showed malignant cells on three slides that were not documented by biopsy.[30]

In prospective studies, colposcopy had a sensitivity of 69 to 95 percent and a specificity of 67 to 93 percent for diagnosing CIN.[10,11,31,32] There were variable results in the diagnosis of invasive disease; sensitivity ranged from 0 to 78 percent in the colposcopic diagnosis of carcinoma. In these prospective studies, three diagnoses of microinvasion or invasion were made at the time of colposcopy despite negative biopsy results.[33] The total number of invasive carcinomas was small. A larger retrospective study described 10 to 15 percent incorrect diagnoses of microinvasive carcinoma.[33] Changes caused by HPV are frequently confused with CIN on colposcopy, especially by inexperienced colposcopists,[34–36] which often results in overtreatment.

Endocervical Curettage

Although some clinicians believe an ECC is not necessary if the colposcopy is adequate,[37] in one large retrospective study, it was found that ECC was the one test that consistently found an abnormality in patients with invasive cancers.[37–40] Although ECC results did not identify carcinoma, finding the abnormality was the impetus for further diagnostic procedures that identified the invasive component. Although ECC is painful for the patient and represents a superficial biopsy that does not sample the underlying stroma, it is still considered a worthwhile diagnostic procedure.

Inadequate colposcopy, especially in older women, may be associated with a significant number of endocervical abnormalities, including microinvasion and invasion, that would be identified from the ECC results.[38] A positive ECC finding is usually associated with abnormalities within the endocervical canal and warrants further diagnostic procedures, such as cold knife conization (CKC) of the cervix or LEEP conization.[41,42] There is enough evidence that a positive ECC has a high probability of representing an invasive or microinvasive cancer, and that ECC should be done with every colposcopy in the evaluation of an abnormal Pap smear.[41,42]

TREATMENT OF PATIENTS WITH ABNORMAL PAP SMEARS

Observation

The natural history of CIN is variable and depends primarily on the HPV type involved. There has been reluctance to observe CIN without treatment because of the fear that dysplasia would progress to cancer. Many women have received multiple procedures in an attempt to eradicate the virus and any LGSIL present, resulting in a costly treatment with variable morbidity. CIN1 will completely regress over 1 to 3 years in up to 62 percent of patients.[2,10] A decision analytic model evaluated the management of mild cervical dysplasia[43] and found that expectant management of low-grade dysplasia ultimately led to more invasive procedures, but such an approach was preferred over immediate cryotherapy for low-grade dysplasia because more patients

"recovered" from the dysplasia without intervention than if immediate cryotherapy was done. Observation is now thought to be appropriate for patients with low-risk LGSIL, ASCUS (favoring reactive), or AGUS (favoring reactive), as long as the work-up results are negative.

Interventions

Multiple modalities have been used over the years to treat CIN. Laser ablation and cryotherapy have been used for the treatment of mild dysplasia and CKC or laser conization for the treatment of severe dysplasia.[44–46]

Cryotherapy

Cryotherapy has the lowest complication rate of all the ablative therapies and the equipment is the least costly. Richart prospectively evaluated 2,839 women receiving cryotherapy for CIN1 to -3 and found a very low incidence of recurrence of dysplasia over 14 years (0.41 to 0.44%).[46,47] However, in patients with HGSIL, failure rates of cryotherapy range from 10 to 40 percent, depending on the size of the lesion.[48] Another study involving 336 patients receiving either cryotherapy or laser ablation, showed a higher rate of treatment failure for cryotherapy (25% versus 7.7%) than for laser ablation in CIN3/CIS, suggesting that cryotherapy may be less efficacious than laser ablation in high-grade dysplasia.[49] A large proportion of LGSIL and HPV lesions will regress without cryotherapy treatment. However, cryotherapy has been well tested and proven to be a good way to remove persistent low-risk lesions; it remains one of the least invasive methods of treating dysplasia (Figures 7–1 to 7–8).

Laser Conization or Ablation

Laser conization became popular with the increased use of the laser as an ablative and surgical tool. Laser conization has no advantage in comparison with CKC, is technically more difficult, and requires more costly equipment. For these reasons, this technique is not frequently used. Laser ablation is still used by some, but its primary use remains ablation of vaginal and/or vulvar intraepithelial neoplasms.

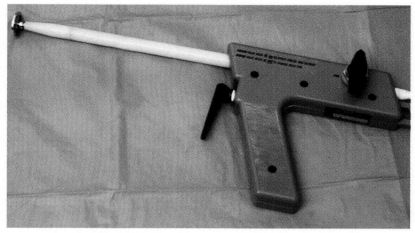

Figure 7–1. Cryotherapy machine.

Laser vaporization has not been found to eradicate subclinical HPV of the lower genital tract and causes significant short-term tissue damage.[50] However, in a prospective trial comparing cryotherapy and laser treatment involving 200 patients, there were comparable failure rates (7% and 11%, respectively), with the morbidity from laser treatment being greater.[51] A larger study showed a lower fail-

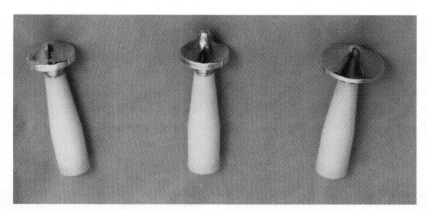

Figure 7–2. Cryotherapy probe.

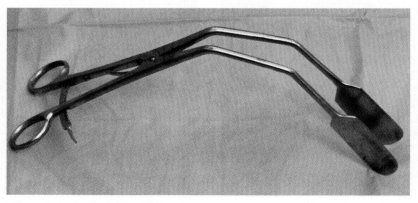

Figure 7–3. Vaginal sidewall retractor.

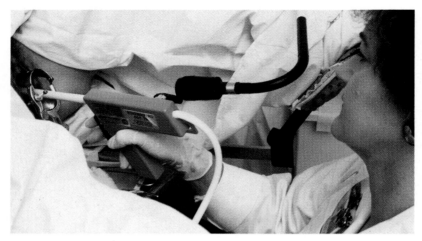

Figure 7–4. Application of cryotherapy.

ure rate with laser treatment, depending on the extent of involvement of the cervix. The rate was 1.6 percent when only one cervical quadrant was involved, but 26 percent with three or four quadrants involved.[52] The cost of laser equipment is so much higher than that of the other modalities that there are few advantages of laser conization over cryotherapy.

Cold Knife Conization

Cold knife conization is used for both diagnostic and therapeutic purposes. Part of the efficacy of CKC in treating CIN may be due to the elimination of HPV by removal of susceptible cells.[53] The technique pro-

vides an excellent pathology specimen and may reveal invasion where none was suspected.[54–56] Post-CKC hysterectomy has shown that there is residual disease in 42 to 82 percent of patients whose surgical specimens had margins positive for disease, and 18 to 23 percent of patients with negative margins on the surgical specimens.[55–57] Some studies have concluded that post-conization cervical cytology is more useful than the status of cone margins as a predictor of recurrent or persistent disease, although other studies have concluded the opposite.[55,56,58] Women whose specimens have positive margins may be followed up conservatively and thus avoid further surgery.[59,60]

Figure 7–5. Cryotherapy probe in place.

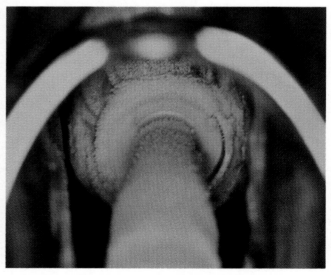

Figure 7–6. Cryotherapy probe in place with ice ball.

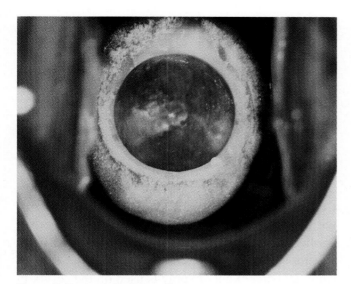

Figure 7–7. Ice ball after cryotherapy.

In some institutions, CKC specimens can be evaluated by frozen section prior to hysterectomy. Advantages of this approach include avoiding the need for two procedures, planning a surgical treatment with greater accuracy, and avoiding the delay associated with a two-step procedure. The diagnosis of invasive disease can be made using frozen sections, with excellent sensitivity and specificity of 89 percent and 100 percent, respectively.[61,62] However, this technique is limited to institutions with experience with frozen cones and is not widely available because many pathologists are reluctant to use a frozen cone biopsy to guide treatment because of the potential of missing an invasive lesion.

Complications of CKC are well known; they include hemorrhage, pelvic cellulitis, cervical stenosis, and incompetent cervix.[45] In addition, CKC requires general anesthesia, which adds significantly to the cost of the procedure.

Loop Electrosurgical Excision Procedure

There has been a change in treatment patterns in the last few years as the new LEEP technique has become more popular (see below). As data have accumulated, it is evident that this technique has complications that are similar to, but not the same as, those of CKC: infection, bleeding, burns to the vagina, cervical stenosis, cervical incompetence, and recurrence of dysplasia. Bleeding usually occurs between 5 and

10 days after the procedure as the eschar sloughs off the cervix. Bleeding can usually be controlled with Monsel's solution. Stenosis is rare (occurring in 1% of patients) and is seen primarily in the nulliparous, perimenopausal, or the postmenopausal patient. If stenosis occurs, dilation of the cervix should first be tried. If this does not allow sampling of the cervix, a repeat LEEP of the stenotic os can be done, followed by dilation and hormones for the menopausal patient.[63] Cervical incompetence is usually only a complication of multiple procedures.

Because general anesthesia is not required for LEEP, it is possible to perform colposcopy, biopsies, and LEEP in the same clinical visit. This "see-and-treat" protocol has become increasingly popular because it is convenient and cost effective. However, 14 to 40 percent of the specimens are found to be negative with this approach. Such results are attributable to thermal injury, incomplete tissue sampling, or false-positive cytology results.[64,65] Even if colposcopy was done at the initial visit, there was still an overtreatment (LEEP with negative specimen) rate of 39 percent in one population.[66] While the see-and-treat approach may eliminate compliance problems and reduce the risk of missing an invasive cancer, it is also associated with excessive loss of cervical tissue and overtreatment,[66] particularly of low-grade lesions. A decision analysis evaluating immediate treatment with LEEP, compared with colposcopy, showed that LEEP for patients with HGSIL

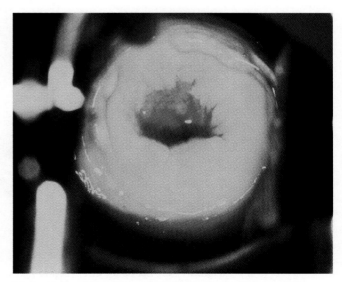

Figure 7–8. Appearance of cervix after ice ball has melted.

on Pap smears was less expensive than colposcopy followed by LEEP because 87 percent of these women eventually required treatment.[67] Patients whose Pap smears done elsewhere revealed CIN2 or -3 probably benefit from the see-and-treat strategy, but colposcopy may or may not be necessary. Because of the possibility of overtreatment, the see-and-treat protocol is not recommended for younger patients or those with cytologic evidence of CIN1; these patients benefit from having their biopsy results reviewed before treatment. A 1998 study of 604 cone biopsies showed that if the lesions were low-grade on preoperative work-up, only 21 percent showed high-grade dysplasia on a subsequent cone, while 74 percent of those showing high-grade dysplasia preoperatively showed high-grade dysplasia in the cone specimen.[68]

The majority of patients with CIN2 or -3 treated with LEEP are disease free after 6 months of follow-up care.[66] In addition, pregnancy outcomes following LEEP are generally good. A 1995 study evaluated 574 women after LEEP and found an incidence of 8.5 pregnancies per 100 woman years, in comparison with 7.4 per 100 woman years in women with CIN who did not receive LEEP; these pregnancy outcomes were comparable.[69]

A 1997 paper comparing CKC, laser conization, and LEEP showed fewer complications with LEEP, as well as a decrease in operating time. Evaluation of surgical margins was equally possible with LEEP and CKC. The laser cone procedure showed the highest rate of complications. The only drawbacks for the LEEP procedure were the slightly shorter cone depth and a slightly higher risk of lesion recurrence.[70] In conclusion, LEEP compares favorably with CKC[71] and is more cost effective without the anesthetic costs and operating room costs associated with CKC.

The LEEP Technique

Colposcopy is done prior to LEEP to fully visualize the lesion with acetic acid. Lugol's solution is then applied to the cervix, and the nonstaining areas and squamocolumnar junction are visualized. Benzocaine 20 percent gel or spray is used on the cervix in preparation for the lidocaine injection. The cervix is then injected with 10 to 20 mL of 2 percent lidocaine with epinephrine (1:50,000 or 1:100,000). This technique provides excellent analgesia. Using a Potocky needle (Figures 7–9 and 7–10), which is more rigid than a spinal needle, the cervix is injected at the 12, 3, 6, and 9 o'clock positions. Occasionally, after the injection of lidocaine, some patients experience a rapid heartbeat that may last for 2 to 3 minutes.

For LEEP, the Cabot system is favored, using the monopolar output and a blend of coagulation and cut. A 2×0.8 cm loop is used for the ectocervical specimen at a power of 7 watts for the average, multiparous, premenopausal patient (see Figure 7–10). However, with a small or low-grade lesion or in a

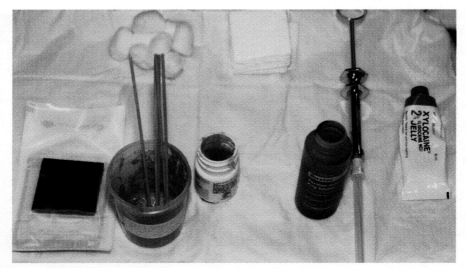

Figure 7–9. Set-up for LEEP (*left to right*): cautery pad, Monsel's solution, Hurricane jelly, iodine, Potocky needle, and lidocaine jelly.

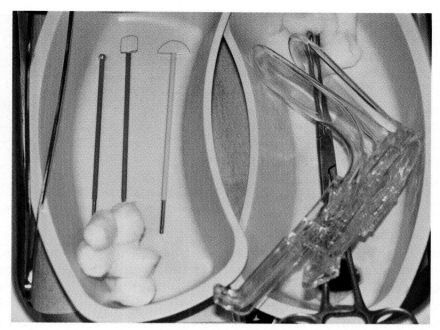

Figure 7–10. Instruments needed (*left to right*): loop for ectocervical/endocervical and cautery ball, plastic speculum, forceps, and ring forceps.

nulliparous or postmenopausal patient in whom a conservative LEEP is indicated, a 15×10 mm or 15×8 mm loop is used for the ectocervical specimen. The cervix should remain moist throughout the procedure. Starting at the 6 or 12 o'clock position, the ectocervical specimen is removed in an anterior-to-posterior direction or vice versa (Figure 7–11), rather than laterally, to avoid lateral vaginal wall damage. The electrode must be activated before actually touching the cervix to avoid introduction of cautery artifacts in the specimen and to avoid cautery damage to the cervical os. The loop is pushed perpendicular to the surface of the cervix to a depth of 8 mm at the os, which is approximately

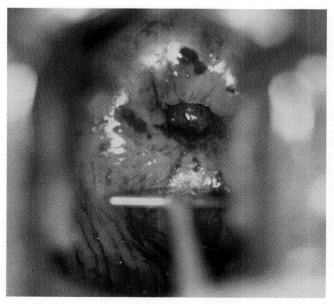

Figure 7–11. Ectocervical LEEP specimen as loop is going through tissue.

Figure 7–12. Ectocervical LEEP specimen.

up to the crossbar of the electrode, and an oblong specimen that is thinner on the edges and thicker in the middle is removed (Figures 7–12 and 7–13). The specimen is marked at the 12 o'clock position (usually with a stitch), and the margins are inked according to the recommendations of the pathology department (Figures 7–14 and 7–15). If the loop stalls at any time, the pressure is released, the power stopped, and the procedure restarted at the area that would have originally been the exit site.

If the procedure is a LEEP cone, a 1×1 cm loop is used, the power is reduced to 5 watts, and either *one or two more specimens* are removed (see Figures 7–15 and 7–18). The direction of the endocervical canal is ascertained by inserting the end of a cotton tip applicator or uterine sound to assure central placement of the specimen. It should be emphasized that the loop should never be advanced too slowly, as cautery artifact will be introduced into the specimen, and the margins will not be interpretable. Nor should the loop be advanced too rapidly, as the steam envelope that precedes the loop will not excise the tissue. To avoid stenosis, the external os is fulgurated for hemostasis, but the internal os is not (Figures 7–16 and 7–17).

Treatment of Adenocarcinoma in Situ

There has been increasing interest in the management of ACIS as women postpone having children

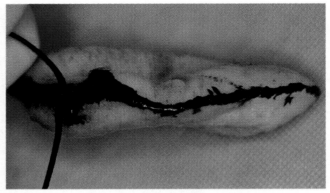

Figure 7–14. Inking margins of ectocervical specimen.

and opt for conservative management of the disease. Treatment of ACIS has traditionally been extrafascial hysterectomy because of the concern about disease in the endocervical canal. Skip lesions in which glands with CIS are found adjacent to normal glands have been described. Three recent retrospective studies have shown that even with disease-negative margins on the cone specimen and a negative ECC, there may be residual disease higher in the endocervical canal or in the endometrium: this may consist of ACIS or invasive adenocarcinoma.[72–74] CKC or LEEP specimens with negative margins and negative ECC are associated with a 30 to 50 percent risk of residual disease in the canal or endometrium and a 10 to 15 percent risk of invasive carcinoma.[75] Patients with positive margins and/or positive ECC have a 75 to 80 percent probability of residual disease.[76] These patients should have a repeat cone biopsy (LEEP or CKC) and an endometrial biopsy because they have been found to have an unaccept-

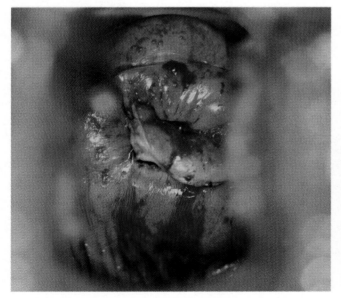

Figure 7–13. Ectocervical LEEP specimen after cautery.

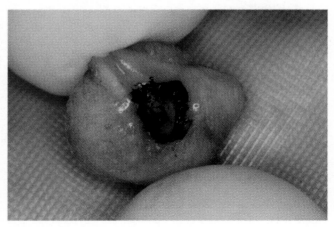

Figure 7–15. LEEP endocervical specimen.

ably high rate (10 to 20%) of invasive adenocarcinoma. Although these estimates for an invasive component may be erroneously high, they are ominous nevertheless. Patients who wish to preserve their fertility must be carefully counseled that they will need meticulous follow-up care and must have Pap smear tests using the cytobrush, ECC, and endometrial biopsies every 3 months for the first 2 years following their initial diagnosis if they have negative margins on cone CKC or LEEP cone.[75] There is preliminary evidence that LEEP may be superior to CKC if done carefully enough to avoid cautery artifacts, although one study concluded that LEEP was inferior to CKC because the rate of disease-positive surgical margins with LEEP was 50 percent, whereas it was only 33 percent with CKC. These authors concluded that LEEP was inferior to CKC because there was a higher percentage of recurrent disease in the LEEP group.[76] These conclusions, however, were based on small numbers. A LEEP cone and two endocervical specimens can provide tissue samples from the entire endocervical canal. This may provide a better pathologic specimen with less disruption of the endocervical canal because a thinner specimen may be obtained (unpublished data).

Failure of Diagnosis and/or Treatment

Progression of dysplasia to carcinoma following treatment is considered a treatment failure. As discussed earlier, the most important predictive factor for progression, regardless of treatment, is HPV type. Types 16, 18, 31, and 33 are associated with a significantly higher rate of progression than are the nononcogenic HPV types.[77] Infrequent or suboptimal Pap smears are another risk factor for progression. Among 20 patients in whom CIN3 or invasive carcinoma developed following three normal Pap smears, over half of them had a smear that was obscured by inflammation or had at least a 2-year interval from their last Pap smear test.[78] After CKC for preinvasive disease, invasive cancer may develop in 1.4 percent of women 1 to 16 years later. In one study, disease developed in 25 percent of patients; carcinoma deep in the cervical stroma was inaccessible to a second CKC and presumably had been buried as a result of the prior cone procedure.[79]

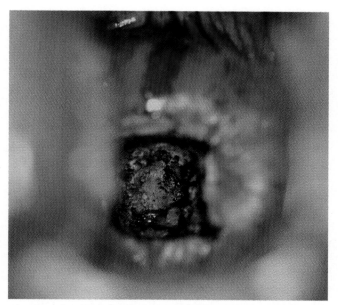

Figure 7–16. Cavity left after LEEP and cautery.

Inadequate biopsy specimens have been a problem in evaluating risk of progression. HPV, CIN1, CIN2, and CIS often coexist in the cervix. If the biopsy was taken from an area with CIS, then a true sample of the worst area of disease or abnormality has been taken, and the diagnosis of progression from CIS to invasive cancer is accurate. However, if

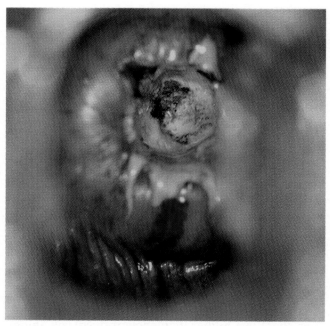

Figure 7–17. Cavity left after LEEP, cautery, and Monsel's solution applied.

the biopsy sample was not taken from the most severe lesion, and subsequent biopsy samples show progression from low-grade dysplasia to high-grade dysplasia or carcinoma, then what is called progression may actually be a failure to diagnose the most severe lesion.[80]

As has been stated earlier, colposcopy has a high rate of diagnostic inaccuracy in cases of carcinoma, and colposcopically directed biopsies may miss the area of invasion, particularly if the colposcopist is inexperienced. Colposcopy by an inexperienced practitioner increases the risk that progression of dysplasia to invasive cancer will occur.[81] According to Webb, "Colposcopic triage of the abnormal Pap smear is increasingly undertaken by gynecologists who have only modest colposcopic experience. Ideally, colposcopy should only be performed by an expert colposcopist."[81] Error rates due to inexperience in colposcopic diagnosis of microinvasive and occult carcinoma range from 10 to 15 percent.[81,82] This is of particular concern today, as more physicians with minimal colposcopic experience are performing colposcopy with directed biopsy. These practitioners lack the colposcopic expertise to determine the areas most suggestive of disease and may not follow recommended treatment protocols. The most common cause of treatment failure is deviation from protocol and use of ablative treatment without adequate pathologic evaluation to rule out invasive cancer.[30]

Treatment of Patients with HIV and Abnormal Cervical Cytology

Women with HIV or acquired immunodeficiency syndrome (AIDS) should be treated as patients at high risk for rapid progression of CIN to cervical cancer.[83,84] Some studies demonstrate that the rates of CIN are inversely proportional to CD4 counts in HIV-positive women.[85] When cervical cancer is diagnosed in HIV-positive women, they usually have a more advanced stage of disease and have a poorer prognosis for cure of their cancer than do their non–HIV-infected counterparts. This later diagnosis may be due, in part, to socioeconomic factors and lack of compliance or access to health care.[86] However, there is a higher incidence of dysplasia among HIV-positive women who present with abnormal

Pap smears. They are more likely to have recurrent disease following treatment, and they are more likely to have disease progress to cancer, if untreated; therefore, aggressive treatment, including yearly colposcopy and biopsy, may be more appropriate in this population.[84]

New Concepts in Diagnosis and Prevention

Fluorescence Spectroscopy

A very promising new technique that has superior sensitivity and specificity to Pap smear testing and colposcopy has been developed by the University of Texas M.D. Anderson Cancer Center and University of Texas Optics Division, under the direction of Drs. Michele Follen and Rebecca Richards-Kortum. Fluorescence spectroscopy is completely noninvasive and involves white light at different wavelengths being applied to the surface of the cervix. This light excites the natural fluorophores within the tissue, resulting in tissue emission of fluorescence of different wavelengths depending on the intrinsic fluorescence of the tissue, the scattering within the tissue, and the biochemical composition of the tissue. It is a near real-time measurement that is fully automated and does not require the expertise needed for colposcopy. The higher the grade of the dysplasia, the more absorption and the less emitted fluorescence there is; therefore, there is a lower signal from the tissue.[87–92] Preliminary data and cost analysis of this technique show that fluorescence spectroscopy of the cervix has a higher sensitivity than the Pap smear test and a higher specificity than colposcopy in differentiating SIL from the normal cervix and LGSIL from HGSIL. Fluorescence spectroscopy combined with the see-and-treat approach was as efficacious and more cost effective than colposcopy alone. Spectroscopically directed biopsy is significantly less expensive than colposcopy with LEEP. Thus, this technique holds promise in the future for more accurately assessing treatment recommendations.

Chemoprevention

Chemoprevention may be the most efficacious treatment for cervical dysplasia in the next 20 years, and it is currently the topic of aggressive research. Chemoprevention is defined as the administration of a medication intended to prevent cancer in a healthy person. There are multiple studies linking diets low in vitamin A to an increased risk of all epithelial cancers. Laboratory data have shown that retinoids can induce apoptosis in dysplastic cervical cells, suggesting that these compounds may be active in cell cycle control.[93] Women with HGSIL and colposcopically evident lesions are the target population for chemopreventive activity because they have a higher risk of persistent disease or progression to cancer. α-Difluoromethylornithine (DFMO) and retinoids (vitamin A derivatives) are two drugs currently receiving attention in the United States and China.[94,95] Other studies showed that vitamin C and β-carotene did not increase the regression of low-grade dysplasia.[96] An excellent case-control study from Japan showed that high serum levels of α-carotene were associated with an odds ratio of 0.16 of developing cervical dysplasia,[97] even when controlling for HPV status. This suggested that α-carotene might be involved in the prevention of cervical dysplasia. Retinol levels have also been associated with a decreased incidence of cervical dysplasia. These are all compounds closely associated with vitamin A and retinoids. It is doubtful that the population with LGSIL warrants chemoprevention because the rate of regression without intervention is high.

Conclusion

Cervical dysplasia has been treated aggressively in the past because of the fear that it would progress to invasive cancer. However, in the next 10 to 20 years, we anticipate advances in our ability to predict which women are at high risk for development of invasive carcinoma, and we hope to have fluorescence spectroscopy available to identify those women who would benefit from the see-and-treat protocol. Better HPV testing may prove helpful in determining which patients with ASCUS need immediate colposcopy and which patients may be followed expectantly with follow-up Pap smear tests. Such testing also may be helpful in determining which low-grade lesions will progress to HGSIL or cancer.[98] There is widespread interest in developing an HPV vaccine to treat dysplasia prior to its progression to cancer; this could be used in all women at high risk and would have the potential to change our approach to the management of cervical dysplasia. Women at high risk for either disease recurrence or progression may have the option to choose an HPV vaccine, chemopreventive agent tailored to their unique situation and risk factors, or both, in lieu of the more invasive procedures described in this section, resulting in more efficacious, less costly, and less morbid treatment for cervical dysplasia.

Figure 7–18. LEEP cone specimen; ectocervix and endocervix specimen.

VULVAR INTRAEPITHELIAL NEOPLASIA

Although it is much less prevalent than CIN, the overall incidence of vulvar intraepithelial neoplasia (VIN) in younger women has increased. Most studies do not have a large cohort of women because of the rarity of this condition, so information on the best treatment for this disease is limited. However, as with CIN, treatment has become less aggressive because these lesions do not progress to cancer as commonly as had been thought in the past. VIN is related to HPV infection, as is true of CIN, but there is little evidence to suggest that VIN3 uniformly progresses to invasive disease.[99] A few series report regression of low-grade lesions.[100]

VIN frequently presents with symptoms of raised areas on the vulva and vulvar pruritus, pain, or burning.[99] More than 30 percent of women are symptomatic on presentation. An abnormality seen on the vulva should prompt complete colposcopic examination of the vulva, vagina, and cervix along with the perianal area. Biopsies should be done on all suspicious areas. There is a known link between HPV infection,[101,102] multiple sexual partners, cigarette smoking, immunosuppression, history of prior cervical dysplasia, and the incidence and recurrence rate of VIN.[103] Multicentricity of lesions is associated with multifocal mutations,[104] suggesting that these lesions may independently progress to cancer.

Treatment of VIN is less controversial. Colposcopic examinations are sufficient for most women with VIN1 or low-grade dysplasia as long as the lesions do not change. High-grade or VIN2/3 should be excised or treated with laser ablation; laser ablation is only appropriate if invasion has been excluded.[99] Older women or women with colposcopic features suggestive of invasion should undergo wide local excision so that the pathology specimen can be closely evaluated. Younger women with multifocal disease can be followed up expectantly if lesions are low grade; they may have laser ablation if lesions are high grade because less scarring occurs with ablative procedures than with excision. Skinning vulvectomy with skin grafting may be an option for an older patient with multifocal disease, in whom the risk of invasion is greater and the concern for cosmetic appearance may be less. However, a retrospective review of 21 women who underwent skinning vulvectomy for presumed multifocal disease showed that actually only 3 of the 21 patients had multifocal disease in the final pathology specimen. Thus, 18 patients underwent a more morbid procedure when it was not warranted.[105] In a prospective trial of 36 patients with CIS of the vulva who received follow-up care for 2 to 23 years, 4 had recurrent CIS after undergoing local excision. Four patients were managed with biopsy and observation, and in all 4, CIS progressed to cancer, suggesting that observation of CIS may not be an aggressive enough treatment for this population. However, this study was biased because 50 percent of the population had a prior history of lower genital tract malignancy, and in 4 of 5 cases of carcinoma, there was a history of prior radiation: both these factors increase the risk of malignancy.[106]

Younger patients with multifocal high-grade VIN are better suited to undergo laser ablation, as long as multiple biopsy samples show that the disease is limited to the basement membrane. The risk of occult cancer may be as high as 23 percent in excised specimens,[107] without any influence of patients' age on the incidence. Other studies showing risk rates of 18 percent[108] and 20 percent,[109] confirm these findings. Laser treatment has been shown to eradicate the lesions in 94 percent of patients,[110] although long-term follow-up data for recurrence rates after laser ablation are scanty.

Wide local excision is an alternative for older patients, patients with areas suspicious for invasion, or patients at high risk for malignancy. Both procedures require general anesthesia and are associated with moderate discomfort postoperatively. Surgical samples with disease-positive margins have been shown to indicate higher recurrence rates,[106,107] but the numbers in these series are too small to be conclusive. A newer technique that is being used with some success and avoids the need for general anesthesia is LEEP for excisional biopsy of the vulva. This can be done under local anesthesia, with only a superficial area of vulvar skin removed. There are no long-term or large studies of this technique, but it is a treatment option for single lesions. Alternatively, sharp excision can be done under local anesthesia in the clinic, again avoiding general anesthesia.

In conclusion, VIN, which was once thought to be a disease exclusively of older women, has become more prevalent in the younger population. It is often multifocal and thus amenable to laser ablation, if invasion can be definitively excluded. For the older woman whose risk of invasion may be higher or for the younger woman in whom invasion is suspected, wide local excision is the standard treatment because it is both diagnostic and potentially curative.

VAGINAL INTRAEPITHELIAL NEOPLASIA

Vaginal intraepithelial neoplasia (VAIN) is a fairly recent diagnosis and was first reported in 1952. The condition is rarer than VIN and CIN and is closely associated with both HPV and a history of cervical dysplasia. The upper third of the vagina is most often involved, and the clinician is alerted to do a full colposcopic examination of the vagina on the basis of an abnormal Pap smear. VAIN is known to occur after therapy for cervical carcinoma.[111]

As with VIN, there are fewer treatments available and, thus, less controversy over methodologies. An abnormal Pap smear necessitates colposcopy of the vagina. Lesions are recognized as raised white areas that are clearly visible under the microscope with the application of acetic acid. Biopsy of these areas is mandatory to grade the severity of the dysplasia and exclude invasion. As in VIN, follow-up care for low-grade dysplasia may consist of Pap smear testing and colposcopy, while high-grade lesions can be treated by laser ablation, wide local excision, or topical 5-fluorouracil (5-FU). The treatments are approximately equal in efficacy.[111–113]

As with VIN, the treatment should be tailored to the individual patient. An older woman with a large area of disease and suspected invasive disease is best treated with local excision. Upper vaginectomy, although technically more difficult than a CKC or LEEP, allows excision of the affected area and provides a biopsy specimen that can be carefully examined for invasion if a large part of the upper vagina is involved. Shortening of the vagina may occur, particularly if the patient had prior radiation. Cheng and colleagues[111] evaluated 40 patients who had wide local excision en bloc (upper vaginectomy) for VAIN. These patients were hospitalized for an average of 2 days rather than receiving outpatient treatment. Twenty-eight percent of the patients had complications, which were more numerous in the irradiated group of patients and included serious injuries, such as vesicovaginal fistula, vault necrosis with erosion into the prudendal artery, and cystotomy. Five of 40 patients had invasive disease that was missed colposcopically, underscoring the need for pathologic diagnosis rather than ablative treatment. Thus, wide local excision needs to be done by a surgeon with experience operating on patients who have had radiotherapy.[111] Sixty-six percent of patients were disease free 44 months later, emphasizing the efficacy of this procedure.

An alternative to wide excision is topical 5-FU. Twenty-seven patients were treated with 5-FU for VAIN. Biopsy samples of the worst areas were taken colposcopically. Twenty-five of the patients with VAIN responded with resolution of their dysplasia, and 3 patients had recurrent disease between 3 and 11 months later.[112] Although complications were not reported in this series, a known complication of 5-FU is vaginal ulceration, which can be severe. Other studies have shown similar responses with similar recurrence rates.[114–117]

Laser ablation is another acceptable method of treating VAIN. The disadvantage of this technique is the inability to get a biopsy specimen, so careful colposcopy and biopsy of the worst area are imperative. In a series of 15 patients, all but one were treated with the laser in the office without general anesthesia. Nine of 15 patients had no evidence of disease for more than 1 year.[113] Townsend and colleagues had similar success with 92 percent of their patients experiencing resolution of VAIN after the initial treatment. However, almost 25 percent later required further treatment.[110] The critical element in determining the success of treatment in these women was the size of the lesion.[113] The limitations of laser ablation in the treatment of VAIN are the cost of the equipment and the multifocal nature of VAIN; the folds in the upper vagina are difficult to access. The advantages of laser treatment are avoidance of scarring and retention of normal sexual function.

VAGINAL ADENOSIS

The connection between diethylstilbestrol (DES) exposure and vaginal adenosis (the presence of glandular epithelium in the vagina) and vaginal clear cell carcinoma was made in the early 1970s. The glandular cells may be similar in appearance to those of the endocervix or may resemble the epithelial cells of the endometrium and fallopian tubes.[118] Adenosis may be present in the fetus or neonate,[118] rather than developing at puberty as was hypothesized; adenocarcinoma, should it arise, usually does so by age 40 years. However, there is a twofold to fourfold increase in CIS of the cervix and vagina in women whose mothers received DES during pregnancy,[119] suggesting that these women should receive diligent follow-up care consisting of Pap smear tests and colposcopy of the vagina to ensure that if dysplasia develops, it will be discovered quickly.

SUMMARY

Squamous intraepithelial lesions of the lower genital tract, particularly of the cervix, affect a widespread population, and the cost of follow-up care for these patients is high. Such care is necessary because predicting cancer development accurately is not yet possible. However, new information on ASCUS and LGSIL reassures the physician that most of these women will subsequently have normal smears; so diagnostic work-ups and treatment can be less expensive and less invasive, while adequate surveillance is maintained. Fluorescence spectroscopy, the new modality for evaluation of the cervix, holds great promise for guiding the physician to appropriate, cost-effective treatments. New emphasis on chemoprevention holds equally great promise for women with cervical dysplasia, and both early diagnosis with spectroscopy and treatment of dysplasia to prevent the progression to cancer are within our grasp. The development of vaccines against HPV also holds promise for decreasing the risk of progression by stimulation of the immune system. Twenty years from now, we can anticipate significantly different treatments for these diseases.

REFERENCES

1. Koss LG. The Papanicolaou test for cervical cancer detection. JAMA 1989;261:737–43.
2. Nasiell K, Roger V, Nasiell M. Behavior of mild cervical dysplasia during long-term follow-up. Obstet Gynecol 1986;67:665.
3. Nasiell K, Nasiell M, Vaclavinkova V. Behavior of moderate cervical dysplasia during long-term follow-up. Obstet Gynecol 1983;61:609–14.
4. Wingo PA, Tong T, Bolden S. Cancer statistics, 1995. CA Cancer J Clin 1995;45:8–30.
5. Richart RM, Doyle GB, Ramsay GC. Colpomicroscopic studies of the distribution of dysplasia and carcinoma in situ on the exposed portion of the human uterine cervix. Cancer 1965;18:950.
6. Syrjanen K, Hakama M, Saarikoski S, et al. Prevalence, incidence and estimated life-time risk of cervical human papillomavirus infections in a non-selected Finnish female population. Sex Transm Dis 1990;17:15–9.
7. Lorincz AT, Reid R, Jenson AB, et al. Human papillomavirus infection of the cervix: relative risk associations of 15 common anogenital types. Obstet Gynecol 1992;79:328–37.
8. Bollen LJM, Tjon-A-Hung SP, van der Velden J, et al. Prediction of recurrent and residual cervical dysplasia by human papillomavirus detection among patients with abnormal cytology. Gynecol Oncol 1999;72:199–201.
9. Kurman RJ, Malkasian GD, Sedlis A, Solomon D. From Papanicolaou to Bethesda: the rationale for a new cervical cytologic classification. Obstet Gynecol 1991;77:779–81.
10. Edebiri AA. The relative significance of colposcopic descriptive appearances in the diagnosis of cervical intraepithelial neoplasia. Int J Gynaecol Obstet 1990;33:23–9.
11. Benedet JL, Boyes DA, Nichols TM, Millner A. Colposcopic evaluation of patients with abnormal cervical cytology. Br J Obstet Gynaecol 1976;83:177–82.
12. Kim TJ, Kim HS, Park CT, et al. Clinical evaluation of follow-up methods and results of atypical glandular cells of undetermined significance (AGUS) detected on cervicovaginal Pap smears. Gynecol Oncol 1999;73;292–8.
13. Goff BA, Atanasoff P, Brown E, et al. Endocervical glandular atypia in Papanicolaou smears. Obstet Gynecol 1992;79:101–4.
14. Raab SS, Bishop NS, Zaleski MS. Effect of cervical disease history on outcomes of women who have a Pap diagnosis of atypical glandular cells of undetermined significance. Gynecol Oncol 1999;74:460–4.
15. Lundberg GD. The 1988 Bethesda system for reporting cervical/vaginal cytological diagnoses. JAMA 1989;262(7):931–4.
16. Herbst AL. The Bethesda system for cervical/vaginal cytologic diagnosis: a note of caution. Obstet Gynecol 1990;76:449–50.
17. Bottles K, Reiter RC, Steiner AL, et al. Problems encountered with the Bethesda system: the University of Iowa experience. Obstet Gynecol 1991;78:410–4.
18. Isacson C, Kurman RJ. The Bethesda system: a new

classification for managing Pap smears. Contemp Obstet Gynecol 1995:67–74.

19. Widra EA, Dookhan D, Jordan A, et al. Evaluation of the atypical cytologic smear. J Reprod Med 1994; 39:682–4.

20. Kinney WK, Manos MM, Hurley LB, Ransley JE. Where's the high-grade cervical neoplasia? The importance of minimally abnormal Papanicolaou diagnoses. Obstet Gynecol 1998;91:973–6.

21. Sherman ME, Tabbara SO, Scott DR, et al. "ASCUS, rule out HSIL": cytologic features, histologic correlates, and human papillomavirus detection. Mod Pathol 1999;12(4):335–43.

22. Kok MR, Habers MA, Schreiner-Kok PG, Boon ME. New paradigm for ASCUS diagnosis using neural networks. Diagn Cytopathol 1998;19:361–6.

23. Raab SS, Bishop NS, Zaleski MS. Long-term outcome and relative risk in women with atypical squamous cells of undetermined significance. Am J Clin Pathol 1999;112:57–62.

24. Alanen KW, Elit LM, Molinaro PA, McLachlin CM. Assessment of cytologic follow-up as the recommended management for patients with atypical squamous cells of undetermined significance of low grade squamous intraepithelial lesions. Cancer Cytopathol 1998;84:5–10.

25. Davis GL, Hernandez E, Davis JL, Miyazawa K. Atypical squamous cells in Papanicolaou smears. Obstet Gynecol 1987;69:43–6.

26. Sandmire HF, Austin SD, Bechtel RC. Experience with 40,000 Papanicolaou smears. Obstet Gynecol 1976;48:56.

27. Raab SS, Steiner AL, Hornberger J. The cost effectiveness of treating women with a cervical vaginal smear diagnosis of atypical squamous cells of undetermined significance. Am J Obstet Gynecol 1998;179:411–20.

28. Rader AE, Rose PG, Rodriguez M, et al. Atypical squamous cells of undetermined significance in women over 55. Acta Cytol 1999;43:357–62.

29. Horowitz IR. Improving the cost-effective evaluation and management of atypical squamous cells of undetermined significance and low grade squamous intraepithelial lesions. Cancer Cytopathol 1998;84:1–4.

30. Stafl A, Wilbanks GD. An international terminology of colposcopy: report of the nomenclature committee of the International Federation of Cervical Pathology and Colposcopy. Obstet Gynecol 1991;77:313–4.

31. Shumsky AG, Stuart GCE, Nation J. Carcinoma of the cervix following conservative management of cervical intraepithelial neoplasia. Gynecol Oncol 1994;53:50–4.

32. Javaheri G, Fejgin MD. Diagnostic value of colposcopy in the investigation of cervical neoplasia. Am J Obstet Gynecol 1980;137:588–94.

33. Benedet JL, Anderson GH, Boyes DA. Colposcopic accuracy in the diagnosis of microinvasive and occult invasive carcinoma of the cervix. Obstet Gynecol 1985;65;557–62.

34. zur Hausen H, de Villiers EM. Human papillomaviruses. Annu Rev Microbiol 1994;48:427–47.

35. zur Hausen H. Papillomaviruses in human genital cancer. Med Oncol 1987;4:187–92.

36. Koutsky LA, Galloway DA, Holmes KK. Epidemiology of genital human papillomavirus infection. Epidemiol Rev 1988;10:122–63.

37. Swan RW. Evaluation of colposcopic accuracy without endocervical curettage. Obstet Gynecol 1979;53(6): 680–4.

38. Dinh TA, Dinh TV, Hannigan EV, et al. Necessity for endocervical curettage in elderly women undergoing colposcopy. J Reprod Med 1989;34:621.

39. Krebs HB, Wheelock JB, Hurt WG. Positive endocervical curettage in patients with satisfactory and unsatisfactory colposcopy: clinical implications. Obstet Gynecol 1987;69:601–5.

40. Urguyo R, Rome RM, Nelson HJ Jr. Some observations on the value of endocervical curettage performed as an integral part of colposcopic examination of patients with abnormal cervical cytology. Am J Obstet Gynecol 1977;128:787.

41. Drescher CW, Peters WA III, Roberts JA. Contribution of endocervical curettage in evaluating abnormal cervical cytology. Obstet Gynecol 1983;62:343.

42. El-Dabh A, Rogers RE, Davis TE, Sutton GP. The role of endocervical curettage in satisfactory colposcopy. Obstet Gynecol 1989;74:159–63.

43. Hamm RM, Loemker V, Reilly KL, et al. A clinical decision analysis of cryotherapy compared with expectant management for cervical dysplasia. J Fam Pract 1998;47:93–201.

44. Ahlgren M, Ingemarsson I, Lindberg LG, Nordqvist RB. Conization as treatment of carcinoma in situ of the uterine cervix. Obstet Gynecol 1975;46:135–40.

45. Villasanta U, Durkan JP. Indications and complications of cold conization of the cervix. Obstet Gynecol 1966;27:717–23.

46. Richart RM, Townsend DE. Outpatient therapy of cervical intraepithelial neoplasia with cryotherapy or CO_2 laser. In: Osofsky HJ, editor. Advances in clinical obstetrics and gynecology. Vol. 1. Baltimore, MD: Williams & Wilkins; 1982. p. 235–46.

47. Richart RM, Townsend DE, Crisp W, et al. An analysis of "long-term" follow-up results in patients with cervical intraepithelial neoplasia treated by cryotherapy. Am J Obstet Gynecol 1980;137:823–6.

48. Ferenczy A. Management of patients with high grade squamous intraepithelial lesions. Cancer 1995;76: 1928–33.

49. Wright VC, Davies EM. The conservative management of cervical intraepithelial neoplasia: the use of cryosurgery and the carbon dioxide laser. Br J Obstet Gynaecol 1981;88:663–8.

50. Riva JM, Sedlacek TV, Cunnane ME, Mangan CE. Extended carbon dioxide laser vaporization in treatment for subclinical papillomavirus infection of the lower genital tract. Obstet Gynecol 1989;73:25.

51. Townsend DE, Richart RM. Cryotherapy and carbon dioxide laser management of cervical intraepithelial neoplasia: a controlled comparison. Obstet Gynecol 1983;61:75–8.

52. Higgins RV, van Nagell JR, Donaldson ES, et al. The efficacy of laser therapy in the treatment of cervical intraepithelial neoplasia. Gynecol Oncol 1990; 36:79–81.

53. Elfgren K, Bistoletti P, Dillner L, et al. Conization for cervical intraepithelial neoplasia is followed by disappearance of human papillomavirus deoxyribonucleic acid and a decline in serum and cervical mucus antibodies against human papillomavirus antigens. Am J Obstet Gynecol 1996;174:937–42.

54. Killackey MA, Jones WB, Lewis JL Jr. Diagnostic conization of the cervix: review of 460 consecutive cases. Obstet Gynecol 1986;67:766.

55. Buxton EJ, Luesley DM, Wade-Evans T, Jordan JA. Residual disease after cone biopsy completeness of excision and follow-up cytology as predictive factors. Obstet Gynecol 1987;70:529–32.

56. Paterson-Brown S, Chappatte OA, Clark SK, et al. The significance of cone biopsy resection margins. Gynecol Oncol 1992;46:182–5.

57. Phelps JY III, Ward JA, Szigetti J II, et al. Cervical cone margins as a predictor for residual dysplasia in post-cone hysterectomy specimens. Obstet Gynecol 1994;84:128–30.

58. Abdul-Karim FW, Nunez C. Cervical intraepithelial neoplasia after conization: a study of 522 consecutive cervical cones. Obstet Gynecol 1985;65:77–81.

59. Monk A, Pushkin SF, Nelson AL, Gunning JE. Conservative management of options for patients with dysplasia involving endocervical margins of cervical cone biopsy specimens. Am J Obstet Gynecol 1996;174:1695–700.

60. Lapaquette TK, Dinh TV, Hannigan EV, et al. Management of patients with positive margins after cervical conization. Obstet Gynecol 1993;82:440–3.

61. Neiger R, Bailey SA, Wall AM III, et al. Evaluating cervical cone biopsy specimens with frozen sections at hysterectomy. J Reprod Med 1991;36:103–7.

62. Hoffman MS, Collins E, Roberts WS, et al. Cervical conization with frozen section before planned hysterectomy. Obstet Gynecol 1993;82:394–8.

63. Curtis M. The use of the loop electrosurgical excision procedure (LEEP) in relieving stenosis of the external cervical os. J Gynecol Surg 1996;12(3):201–3.

64. Ferenczy A, Choukroun D, Arseneau J. Loop electrosurgical excision procedure for squamous intraepithelial lesions of the cervix: advantages and potential pitfalls. Obstet Gynecol 1996;87:332–7.

65. Alvarez RD, Helm CW, Edwards RP, et al. Prospective randomized trial of LLETZ versus laser ablation in patients with cervical intraepithelial neoplasia. Gynecol Oncol 1994;52:175–9.

66. Brady JL, Fish ANJ, Woolas RP, et al. Large loop diathermy of the transformation zone: is 'see and treat' an acceptable option for the management of women with abnormal cervical smears? J Obstet Gynecol 1994;14:44–9.

67. Roland PY, Naumann RW, Alvarez RD, et al. A decision analysis of practice patterns used in evaluating and treating abnormal Pap smears. Gynecol Oncol 1995;59:75–80.

68. Spitzer M, Chernys AE, Shifrin A, Ryskin M. Indications for cone biopsy: pathologic correlation. Am J Obstet Gynecol 1998;178:74–9.

69. Ferenczy A, Choukroun D, Falcone T, Fanco E. The effect of cervical loop electrosurgical excision on subsequent pregnancy outcome: North American experience. Am J Obstet Gynecol 1995;172:1246–50.

70. Linares AC, Storment J, Rhodes-Morris H, et al. A comparison of three cone biopsy techniques for evaluation and treatment of squamous intraepithelial lesions. J Gynecol Tech 1997;3:151–6.

71. Duggan BD, Felix JC, Muderspach LI, et al. Cold-knife conization versus conization by the loop electrosurgical excision procedure: a randomized, prospective study. Am J Obstet Gynecol 1999;180:276–82.

72. Denehy TR, Gregori CA, Breen JL. Endocervical curettage, cone margins, and residual adenocarcinoma in situ of the cervix. Obstet Gynecol 1997;90:1–6.

73. Wolf JK, Levenback C, Malpica A, et al. Adenocarcinoma in situ of the cervix: significance of cone biopsy margins. Obstet Gynecol 1996;88:82–6.

74. Poynor EA, Barakat RR, Hoskins WJ. Management and follow-up of patients with adenocarcinoma in situ of the uterine cervix. Gynecol Oncol 1995;57:158–64.

75. Muntz HG, Bell DA, Lage JM, et al. Adenocarcinoma in situ of the uterine cervix. Obstet Gynecol 1992; 80:935–9.

76. Widrich T, Kennedy AW, Myers TM, et al. Adenocarcinoma in situ of the uterine cervix: management and outcome. Gynecol Oncol 1996;61:304–8.

77. Wright TC, Richart RM. Role of human papillomavirus in the pathogenesis of genital tract warts and cancer. Gynecol Oncol 1990;37:151–64.

78. Sherman ME, Kelly D. High-grade squamous intraepithelial lesions and invasive carcinoma following the report of three negative Papanicolaou smears: screening failures or rapid progression? Mod Pathol 1992;5:337.

79. Brown JV, Peters WA, Corwin DJ. Invasive carcinoma after cone biopsy for cervical intraepithelial neoplasia. Gynecol Oncol 1991;40:25–8.

80. Ostor AG. Natural history of cervical intraepithelial

neoplasia: a critical review. Int J Gynecol Pathol 1993;12:186–92.

81. Webb MJ. Invasive cancer following conservative therapy for previous cervical intraepithelial neoplasia. Colposc Gynecol Laser Surg 1985;1:245.

82. Richart RM, Crum CP, Townsend DE. Workup of the patient with an abnormal Papanicolaou smear. Gynecol Oncol 1981;12:S265–76.

83. Rellihan MA, Dooley DP, Burke TW, et al. Rapidly progressing cervical cancer in a patient with human immunodeficiency virus infection. Gynecol Oncol 1990;36:435–8.

84. Schwartz LB, Carcangiu ML, Bradham L, Schwartz PE. Rapidly progressive squamous cell carcinoma of the cervix coexisting with human immunodeficiency virus infection: clinical opinion. Gynecol Oncol 1991;41:255–8.

85. Bernardes J. The adequacy of cytology and colposcopy in diagnosing cervical neoplasia in HIV-seropositive women. Gynecol Oncol 1994;55:133–7.

86. Maiman M, Fruchter RG, Guy L, et al. Human immunodeficiency virus infection and invasive cervical carcinoma. Cancer 1993;71:402–6.

87. Ramanujam N, Mitchell MF, Mahadevan A, et al. Development of a multivariate statistical algorithm to analyze human cervical tissue fluorescence spectra acquired in vivo. Lasers Surg Med 1996;19:46–62.

88. Mahadevan A, Michell MF, Silva E, et al. Study of the fluorescence properties of normal and neoplastic human cervical tissues. Lasers Surg Med 1993;13:647–55.

89. Ramanujam N, Mitchell MF, Mahadevan A, et al. Fluorescence spectroscopy: a diagnostic tool for cervical intraepithelial neoplasia (CIN). Gynecol Oncol 1994;52:31–8.

90. Ramanujam N, Mitchell MF, Mahadevan A, et al. In vivo diagnosis of cervical intraepithelial neoplasia (CIN) using 337 nm laser induced fluorescence. Proc Natl Acad Sci U S A 1994;91:10193–7.

91. Ramanujam N, Mahadevan A, Mitchell MF, et al. Fluorescence spectroscopy of the cervix. Clin Consult Obstet Gynecol 1994;6(1):62–9.

92. Ramanujam N, Mitchell MF, Mahadevan A, et al. Spectroscopic diagnosis of cervical squamous intraepithelial neoplasia in vivo using laser induced fluorescence spectra at multiple excitation wavelengths. Lasers Surg Med 1996;19(1):63–74.

93. Oridate N, Suzuki S, Higuchi M, et al. Involvement of reactive oxygen species in N-(4hydroxyphenyl) Retinamide-induced apoptosis in cervical carcinoma cells. J Natl Cancer Inst 1997;89(16):1191–8.

94. Mitchell MF, Tortolero-Luna G, Lee JJ, et al. Phase I dose de-escalation trial of α-difluoromethylornithine in patients with grade 3 cervical intraepithelial neoplasia. Clin Cancer Res 1998;4:303–10.

95. Rui H. Research and development of cancer chemopreventive agents in China. J Cell Biochem Suppl 1997;27:7–11.

96. Mackerras D, Irwig L, Simpson JM, et al. Randomized double-blind trial of beta-carotene and vitamin C in women with minor cervical abnormalities. Br J Cancer 1999;79(9/10):1448–53.

97. Nagata C, Shimizu H, Yoshikawa H, et al. Serum carotenoids and vitamins and risk of cervical dysplasia from a case-control study in Japan. Br J Cancer 1999;81(7):1234–7.

98. Montz FJ, Monk BJ, Fowler JM, Nguyen L. Natural history of the minimally abnormal Papanicolaou smear. Obstet Gynecol 1992;80:385–8.

99. Campion MJ, Hacker NF. Vulvar intraepithelial neoplasia and carcinoma. Semin Cutan Med Surg 1998;17(3):205–12.

100. Barbero M, Micheletti L, Preti M, et al. Biologic behavior of vulvar intraepithelial neoplasia. J Reprod Med 1993;38(2):108–12.

101. Kagie MJ, Kenter GG, Zomerdijk-Nooijen Y, et al. Human papillomavirus infection in squamous cell carcinoma of the vulva, in various synchronous epithelial changes and in normal vulvar skin. Gynecol Oncol 1997;67:178–83.

102. Flowers LC, Wistuba II, Scurry J, et al. Genetic changes during the multistage pathogenesis of human papillomavirus positive and negative vulvar carcinomas. J Soc Gynecol Invest 1999;6:213–21.

103. Sturgeon SR, Brinton LA, Devesa SS, Kurman RJ. In situ and invasive vulvar cancer incidence trends (1973 to 1987). Am J Obstet Gynecol 1992;166:1482–5.

104. Wilkinson EJ, Friedrich EG, Fu YS. Multicentric nature of vulvar carcinoma in situ. Obstet Gynecol 1981;58:69.

105. Ayhan A, Tuncer ZS, Dogan L, et al. Skinning vulvectomy for the treatment of vulvar intraepithelial neoplasia 2-3: a study of 21 cases. Eur J Gynaecol Oncol 1998;5:508–10.

106. Jones RW, McLean MR. Carcinoma in situ of the vulva: a review of 31 treated and five untreated cases. Obstet Gynecol 1986;68:499–503.

107. Modesitt SC, Waters AB, Walton L, et al. Vulvar intraepithelial neoplasia III: occult cancer and the impact of margin status on recurrence. Obstet Gynecol 1998;92:962–6.

108. Chafe W, Richards A, Morgan L, Wilkinson E. Unrecognized invasive carcinoma in vulvar intraepithelial neoplasia (VIN). Gynecol Oncol 1988;31:154–62.

109. Husseinzaddeh N, Recinto C. Frequency of invasive cancer in surgically excised vulvar lesions with intraepithelial neoplasia (VIN 3). Gynecol Oncol 1999;73:119–20.

110. Townsend DE, Levine RU, Richart RM, et al. Management of vulvar intraepithelial neoplasia by carbon dioxide laser. Obstet Gynecol 1982;60:49.

111. Cheng D, Ng TY, Ngan HYS, Wong LC. Wide local excision (WLE) for vaginal intraepithelial neoplasia (VAIN). Acta Obstet Gynecol Scand 1999;78: 648–52.

112. Caglar H, Hertzog RW, Hreshchyshyn MW. Topical 5-fluorouracil treatment of vaginal intraepithelial neoplasia. Obstet Gynecol 1981;58:580–3.

113. Capen CV, Masterson BJ, Magrina JF, Calkins JW. Laser therapy of vaginal intraepithelial neoplasia. Am J Obstet Gynecol 1982;142:973.

114. Daly JW, Ellis GF. Treatment of vaginal dysplasia and carcinoma in situ with topical 5-fluorouracil. Obstet Gynecol 1979;54:163.

115. Woodruff JD, Parmley TH, Julian CG. Topical 5-fluorouracil in the treatment of vaginal carcinoma-in-situ. Gynecol Oncol 1975;3:124.

116. Ballon SC, Roberts JA, Lagasse LD. Topical 5-fluorouracil in the treatment of intraepithelial neoplasia of the vagina. Obstet Gynecol 1997;54:163.

117. Petrilli ES, Townsend DE, Morrow CP, Nakao CY. Vaginal intraepithelial neoplasia: biologic aspects and treatment with topical 5-fluorouracil and the carbon dioxide laser. Am J Obstet Gynecol 1980; 138:321.

118. Kurman RJ, Scully RE. The incidence and histogenesis of vaginal adenosis. Hum Pathol 1974;5(3): 265–76.

119. Robboy SJ, Noller KL, O'Brien P, et al. Increased incidence of cervical and vaginal dysplasia in 3,980 diethylstilbestrol-exposed young women. JAMA 1984;252:2979–83.

8

Invasive Carcinoma of the Cervix

PATRICIA J. EIFEL, MD

Today, surgery, radiation therapy, and chemotherapy play critical roles in the curative management of patients with invasive carcinoma of the cervix. As will be discussed in subsequent chapters, these modalities have been effectively combined in many ways to improve treatment results for selected patients.

Because distant metastasis tends to occur relatively late in the course of cervical cancer, accurate initial assessment of the extent of local and regional disease is particularly important in the planning of surgical treatment and radiation therapy. Although high cure rates can be achieved with carefully selected treatment, inappropriate initial treatment is usually difficult to salvage; when cure is still possible, it is usually achieved at the expense of significant additional side effects and cost. For this reason, too, then, it is particularly important that clinicians carefully assess the distribution of a patient's initial disease, They must also understand the natural history of cervical cancer so that they can predict the likelihood of undetected microscopic disease in local and regional sites.

Because accurate local treatment is so important, it may seem as though every patient should have the benefit of any diagnostic tool that could possibly add to the pretreatment assessment. Computed tomography (CT), magnetic resonance imaging (MRI), lymphangiography, positron emission tomography (PET), ultrasonography, surgical staging, and many other studies provide unique information in at least some cases. However, the cost of obtaining all these studies is usually prohibitive, and in the medically underserved societies that experience most of the world's cases of invasive cervical cancer, these studies may be entirely unavailable.

In this chapter, a practical approach to patient evaluation, disease staging, and selection of treatment for patients with cervical cancer will be suggested, with the understanding that new methods are constantly becoming available and may have important influences on future management. The advantages and limitations of the international staging system that has generally been used to classify patients and report results of treatment will also be discussed. Finally, to provide a background for the individual chapters on surgical, radiotherapeutic, and chemotherapeutic management, some of the issues and controversies relating to the selection of treatment for individual patients will be outlined.

INITIAL EVALUATION

History

Every patient with cervical cancer should be carefully interviewed to obtain a history of her present illness and any other medical problems. Cervical cancer tends to affect women of limited financial means; in many cases, the symptoms of advanced cancer lead to the patient's first direct contact with the medical community. Undiagnosed diabetes, hypertension, and thyroid disease are common and should be evaluated and treated promptly. Previous surgical procedures, pelvic infections, medical illnesses, and other conditions may influence the patient's tolerance of treatment and her risk of complications. Any medications being used by the patient should be carefully inventoried. The interview should include specific questioning about the use of herbal or "natural" remedies, many of which can interfere with conventional treatment. A history of alcohol or drug abuse may affect compliance and the effectiveness of treatments for cancer-related pain.

A detailed social history is particularly important. Factors that might interfere with the patient's treatment must be identified early. Cervical cancer frequently affects young women who are responsible for small children. Patients are usually poor and may have limited family support, and in the United States, minorities are disproportionately affected. Any cultural, educational, and language differences between the patient and her physician can interfere with effective communication. These factors can leave the patient feeling lost, frightened, and overwhelmed by responsibilities that conflict with her ability to make regular appointments for evaluation and treatment. Every effort should be made to fully inform the patient about the demands of treatment before treatment begins. This way she can plan accordingly and arrange for help before treatment is compromised by social circumstances beyond her control.

Physical Examination

Each patient should have a thorough physical examination, including a detailed pelvic examination. Although modern radiographic studies provide remarkable anatomic detail, these should not be used as a substitute for skillful examination of the pelvis, which is a quick, inexpensive study that provides a great deal of information that can guide subsequent work-up. The patient should be examined by clinicians responsible for the delivery of radiation therapy, surgery, or chemotherapy, and the results should be documented immediately in a tumor diagram (Figure 8–1). Pelvic examination should include the following:

1. *Careful inspection of the external genitalia, vagina, and cervix.* Particular care should be taken to examine all the mucosal surfaces of the vagina, rotating the speculum to visualize areas that might be obscured by the speculum blades. If a histologic diagnosis has not yet been made, a biopsy should be performed. If the lesion is not visible to the naked eye, colposcopy may be helpful.

2. *Digital vaginal examination* (Figure 8–2). Any irregularities of the vaginal mucosa should be noted. Digital examination is often more sensitive than visual inspection or radiographic study for detecting small vaginal lesions or extension from cervical cancer to the vaginal fornix (Figure 8–3). The size and configuration of exophytic cervical lesions should also be noted. However, to minimize bleeding, the examination should be done gently, with as little trauma to the tumor as possible.

3. *Bimanual examination.* The size and shape of the uterus should be assessed by balloting it between the vagina and suprapubis (Figure 8–4). The position (anteverted, axial, or retroverted), flexion (anteflexed or retroflexed), size, and mobility of the uterus, as well as any nodularity, should be noted. These factors may be of particular importance in planning subsequent intracavitary radiation therapy. The adnexa should be carefully examined for any masses or tenderness. Pelvic, particularly adnexal, tenderness may indicate the presence of pelvic inflammatory disease and should be investigated carefully.

4. *Rectovaginal examination.* The parametria and pelvic wall should be evaluated with the index finger in the vagina and the middle finger in the anus (Figure 8–5). The examining fingers are used to palpate the paracervical ligaments and the pelvic wall. The size of the cervix is also best evaluated during this part of the examination by comparing its diameter with the width of the pelvis (usually about 12 cm at the level of the cervix). Paracervical nodularity, fixation, and distortion of the normal anatomy should be noted. If the uterus is severely retroflexed, the fundus can usually be palpated on rectal examination.

Endoscopic Studies

Cystoscopy and proctoscopy are accepted by the International Federation of Gynecology and Obstetrics (FIGO) as staging studies.[1] However, the yield is extremely low for patients with early cervical can-

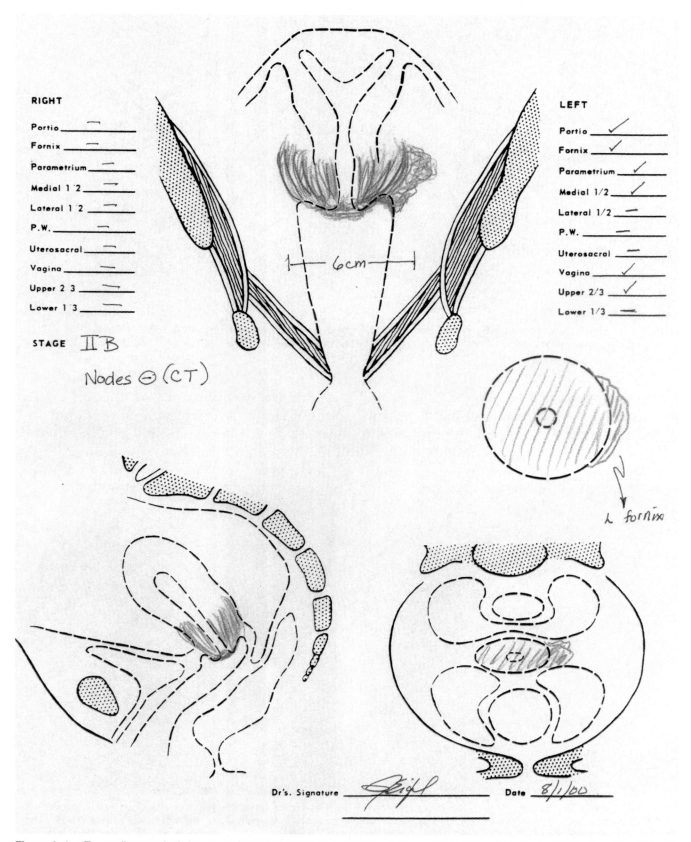

RIGHT

Portio _____
Fornix _____
Parametrium _____
Medial 1/2 _____
Lateral 1/2 _____
P.W. _____
Uterosacral _____
Vagina _____
Upper 2/3 _____
Lower 1/3 _____

STAGE IIB

Nodes ⊖ (CT)

LEFT

Portio ____✓____
Fornix ____✓____
Parametrium ____✓____
Medial 1/2 ____✓____
Lateral 1/2 _____
P.W. _____
Uterosacral _____
Vagina ____✓____
Upper 2/3 ____✓____
Lower 1/3 _____

6cm

L fornix

Dr's. Signature _____ Date 8/1/00

Figure 8–1. Tumor diagram depicting an endocervical tumor invading the left parametrium and vaginal fornix (FIGO stage IIb). Palpable tumor is indicated in blue and visible tumor in red.

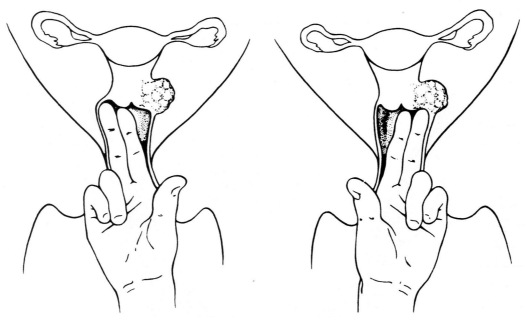

Figure 8–2. Digital vaginal examination. (Reproduced with permission from del Regato JA, Spjut HJ. Female genital organs/cervix. In: Ackerman LV, del Regato JA, editors. Cancer. 5th ed. St. Louis: Mosby, 1977.)

cer. Cystoscopy should be performed in patients who have extensive disease involving the anterior vaginal wall, symptoms suggesting fistula, or other urinary tract symptoms. MRI or CT images suggesting bladder involvement must be confirmed with cystoscopy and biopsy (Table 8–1). The rectum is

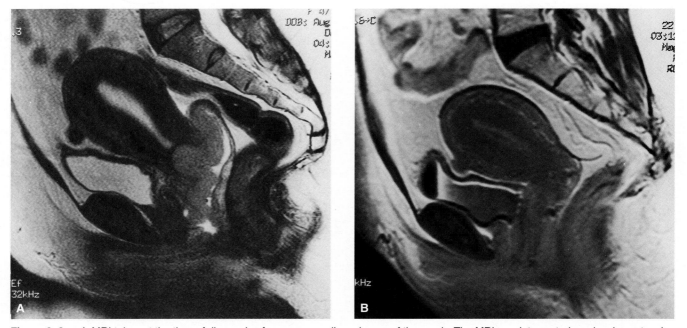

Figure 8–3. *A*, MRI taken at the time of diagnosis of squamous cell carcinoma of the cervix. The MRI was interpreted as showing extensive anterior vaginal involvement. However, on physical examination, it was apparent that the patient had a very large extensive exophytic cancer that protruded almost to the introitus but did not grossly involve the vagina. In this case, clinical examination may have been more accurate—in retrospect, the vagina was probably pushed down by the tumor and folded up behind the bladder. *B*, Repeat MRI after 45 Gy of external beam irradiation with concurrent chemotherapy. The tumor is markedly smaller, and there is no evidence of vaginal involvement.

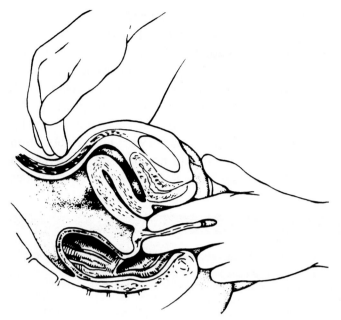

Figure 8–4. Bimanual examination. (Reproduced with permission from Greenhill JP. Office gynecology. 9th ed. Chicago: Year Book, 1971.)

involved in fewer than 1 percent of cases, but proctoscopy should be performed if the patient has rectal bleeding or other symptoms or findings that suggest rectal involvement.

Laboratory Studies

In all patients with cervical cancer, a complete blood count and measurement of serum electrolytes, blood urea nitrogen, and creatinine levels should be performed at diagnosis. Additional studies may be required, depending on the patient's symptoms and any concurrent illnesses.

Some investigators have reported that the serum concentration of squamous cell carcinoma antigen correlates with the stage and size of squamous cervical carcinomas and with the presence of lymph node metastases; however, investigators disagree about the independent predictive value of this antigen.[2–5] Histologic features that have been investigated for their predictive power, with variable results, include deoxyribonucleic (DNA) ploidy or S-phase[6,7] and human papillomavirus (HPV) subtype.[8–10] However, these studies are not yet considered to be part of the routine evaluation of patients with cervical cancer.

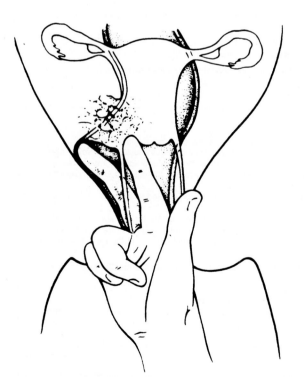

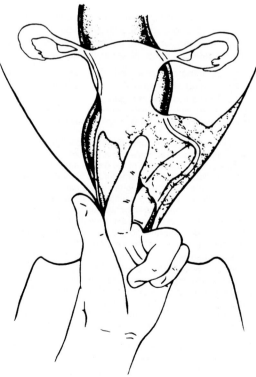

Figure 8–5. Rectovaginal examination. (Reproduced with permission from del Regato JA, Spjut HJ. Female genital organs/cervix. In: Ackerman LV, del Regato JA, editors. Cancer. 5th ed. St. Louis: Mosby, 1977.)

Radiographic Evaluation of Local and Regional Disease

The advantages and disadvantages of various radiographic studies in the evaluation of cervical cancer are discussed in detail in Chapter 7. Only intravenous pyelography (IVP) and radiographic examinations of the chest and bones can be used to determine the FIGO stage (see Table 8–1). However, these studies provide little or no information about the possible involvement of regional lymph nodes. In modern medical practice, unless the patient has very early disease (stage Ia or Ib1), additional studies are nearly always obtained to evaluate the pelvic and para-aortic nodes.

Most clinicians obtain a contrast-enhanced CT scan of the abdomen and pelvis.[11] In practice, the renal information obtained from this study is usually substituted for conventional IVP. Other information from the CT scan should not be used to increase a patient's stage (see Table 8–1). However, lymph nodes

Table 8–1. THE FIGO STAGING SYSTEM FOR CERVICAL CANCER (1994)

Stage

0   Carcinoma in situ, intraepithelial carcinoma; *cases of stage 0 should not be included in any therapeutic statistics for invasive carcinoma.*

I   The carcinoma is strictly confined to the cervix (*extension to the corpus should be disregarded*).
-    Ia   Invasive cancer identified only microscopically. All gross lesions, even with superficial invasion, are stage Ib cancers. Invasion is limited to measured stromal invasion with a maximum depth of 5 mm and no wider than 7 mm. (*The depth of invasion should not be more than 5 mm taken from the base of the epithelium, either surface or glandular, from which it originates. Vascular space involvement, either venous or lymphatic, should not alter the staging.*)
  -     Ia1   Measured invasion of stroma no greater than 3 mm in depth and no wider than 7 mm.
  -     Ia2   Measured invasion of stroma greater than 3 mm and no greater than 5 mm in depth and no wider than 7 mm.
-    Ib   Clinical lesions confined to the cervix or preclinical lesions greater than Ia.
  -     Ib1   Clinical lesions no greater than 4 cm in size.
  -     Ib2   Clinical lesions greater than 4 cm in size.

II   The carcinoma extends beyond the cervix, but has not extended to the pelvic wall; the carcinoma involves the vagina, but not as far as the lower third.
-    IIa   No obvious parametrial involvement.
-    IIb   Obvious parametrial involvement.

III   The carcinoma has extended to the pelvic wall; on rectal examination there is no cancer-free space between the tumor and the pelvic wall; the tumor involves the lower third of the vagina; all cases with hydronephrosis or nonfunctioning kidney should be included unless they are known to be due to other causes.
-    IIIa   No extension to the pelvic wall, but involvement of the lower third of the vagina.
-    IIIb   Extension to the pelvic wall or hydronephrosis or nonfunctioning kidney.

IV   The carcinoma has extended beyond the true pelvis or has clinically involved the mucosa of the bladder or rectum.
-    IVa   Spread of the growth to adjacent organs.
-    IVb   Spread to distant organs.

FIGO = International Federation of Gynecology and Obstetrics.

Notes

Stage 0 comprises those cases with full-thickness involvement of the epithelium with atypical cells but with no signs of invasion into the stroma.

   As a rule, it is impossible to estimate clinically whether a cancer of the cervix has extended to the corpus. Extension to the corpus should, therefore, be disregarded.

A patient with a growth fixed to the pelvic wall by a short and indurated but not nodular parametrium should be allotted to stage IIb. It is impossible, at clinical examination, to decide whether a smooth and indurated parametrium is truly cancerous or only inflammatory. Therefore, the case should be placed in stage III only if the parametrium is nodular to the pelvic wall or if the growth itself extends to the pelvic wall.

The presence of hydronephrosis or nonfunctioning kidney due to stenosis of the ureter by cancer permits a case to be allotted to stage III, even if, according to the other findings, the case should be allotted to stage I or stage II.

The presence of bullous edema, as such, should not permit a case to be allotted to stage IV. Ridges and furrows into the bladder wall should be interpreted as signs of submucosal involvement of the bladder if they remain fixed to the growth at palposcopy (ie, examination from the vagina or the rectum during cystoscopy). A finding of malignant cells in cytologic washings from the urinary bladder requires further examination and biopsy from the wall of the bladder.

Rules for Clinical Staging

The staging should be based on careful clinical examination and should be performed before any definitive therapy. It is desirable that the examination be performed by an experienced examiner under anesthesia.

The clinical stage must under no circumstances be changed on the basis of subsequent findings.

When it is doubtful to which stage a particular case should be allotted, the case must be referred to the earlier stage.

For staging purposes the following examination methods are permitted: palpation, inspection, colposcopy, endocervical curettage, hysteroscopy, cystoscopy, proctoscopy, intravenous urography, and radiographic examination of the lungs and skeleton. Suspected bladder or rectal involvement should be confirmed by biopsy and histologic evidence.

Findings by examinations, such as lymphangiography, arteriography, venography, laparoscopy, and so on, are of value for the planning of therapy, but because these are not yet generally available and also because the interpretation of results is variable, the findings of such studies should not be the basis for changing the clinical staging.

Infrequently, it happens that hysterectomy is carried out in the presence of unsuspected extensive invasive cervical carcinoma. Such cases cannot be clinically staged or included in therapeutic statistics, but it is desirable that they be reported separately.

Only if the rules for clinical staging are strictly observed will it be possible to compare results among clinics and by differing modes of therapy.

that are more than 1 to 1.5 cm in diameter are suspicious for tumor involvement and should be biopsied. Unfortunately, microscopic metastases are not readily detected with CT, and the inflammation frequently associated with advanced disease may cause nodes that do not have metastases to be enlarged.

The sensitivity of MRI for the detection of regional metastases is similar to that of CT. However, MRI provides more detailed images of the cervix and paracervical tissues (see Chapter 7). Sagittal views are particularly helpful for determining the morphology of the tumor and the position of the uterus. MRI also yields a more objective assessment of tumor diameter than does pelvic examination. However, in medically underserved communities, particularly in the developing nations, the cost of MRI may outweigh the benefit.

Lymphangiography is more sensitive than CT for assessment of the aortic nodes[12] but does not visualize internal iliac or presacral nodes and is difficult to perform. PET and other studies discussed in Chapter 7 may be more sensitive than more standard radiographic studies, but remain investigational.

Role of Surgical Staging

Today, surgical evaluation continues to be the most sensitive method of evaluating whether regional lymph nodes contain metastases. However, surgical staging is invasive and expensive and delays treatment of the patient's primary lesion. In the past, transperitoneal lymphadenectomy followed by radiation therapy was associated with a high incidence of severe, even fatal, complications. However, the risk appears to be much less when lymphadenectomy is performed using a retroperitoneal approach.[13] Staging may also be performed laparoscopically; this approach is associated with a shorter postoperative recovery time and probably less late radiation morbidity than open transperitoneal staging.[14]

Because patients with grossly involved pelvic nodes have the highest risk of occult para-aortic metastases, we usually recommend retroperitoneal lymph node sampling for patients with radiographic evidence of pelvic lymph nodes larger than 1.5 cm, if they have no medical contraindication to the operation. These patients also may benefit from removal

of the grossly enlarged nodes, which may be difficult to control with radiation alone.[15,16]

The sensitivity of surgical lymph node evaluation depends on the number of nodes removed and the surgical pathologist's treatment of the specimen. If lymphangiography is performed preoperatively, intraoperative abdominal radiography may be performed to confirm that the abnormal nodes have been removed.[17] Intraoperative lymphatic mapping may someday improve the accuracy of surgical staging of cervical cancer but remains highly investigational at this time.[18]

Evaluation of Possible Distant Metastases

Anaplastic small cell carcinomas of the cervix are very aggressive and usually warrant an extensive work-up for distant disease, including CT of the chest and brain. Otherwise, distant (extranodal) metastases are rarely present at initial diagnosis of cervical cancer. A chest radiograph is usually obtained to evaluate the lungs. CT or MRI is performed primarily to evaluate the pelvis and paraaortic nodes but also to visualize the liver and peritoneal cavity. Bone metastases are very rare at presentation; a radiographic examination or bone scan is indicated only if the patient has symptoms. Patients who have very extensive aortic metastasis should have CT of the chest to rule out mediastinal or supraclavicular adenopathy before curative treatment is initiated.

FIGO STAGING OF CERVICAL CANCER

The 1994 revision of the FIGO staging system[19] is currently accepted internationally as the staging system for cervical cancer. As a predictor of prognosis, guide for management, and method of reporting results, the staging system is seriously flawed. Each stage group includes patients with a range of identifiable features that predict widely different prognoses (Figures 8–6 to 8–9). Many of the system's deficiencies are dictated by the need to have a system that can be implemented internationally under a variety of socioeconomic conditions and can be applied equally well to patients who are treated initially with surgery, radiation, or chemotherapy. These two requirements have led FIGO to limit the

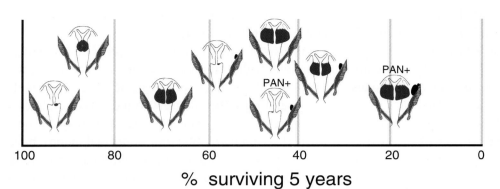

% surviving 5 years

Figure 8–6. Approximate survival rates of eight cervical cancers of varying sizes and extent of regional spread. According to the FIGO staging system, all these tumors fall into the Ib category. (Reproduced with permission from Eifel PJ. Problems with the clinical staging of carcinoma of the cervix. Semin Radiat Oncol 1994;4:1–8.)

diagnostic studies on which staging is based; only findings that can be documented before any surgery has been performed are taken into consideration in determining the FIGO stage. Although the reasons for excluding CT, MRI, and other modern diagnostic tests have been primarily socioeconomic, there is also another factor that influenced this decision: the absence of a sensitive, widely accepted method of evaluating the regional lymph nodes has made it difficult to design a staging system that would address lymph node metastasis in a consistent fashion.

In 1994, FIGO modified the staging system to divide the 1b category according to tumor size.

Although clinical assessment of tumor size is subjective, this division of the Ib category improved the predictive value of the staging system. Patients with stage Ib1 disease are generally accepted to be good candidates for treatment with surgery alone or radiation therapy alone, while those with stage Ib2 disease are usually poor candidates for treatment with surgery alone.

Also in 1994, FIGO clarified its definition of microinvasive (stage Ia) disease. Although this improved on the formerly vague description of the Ia categories, FIGO's many changes to the stage I categories[19–25] (Table 8–2) have made it difficult to deter-

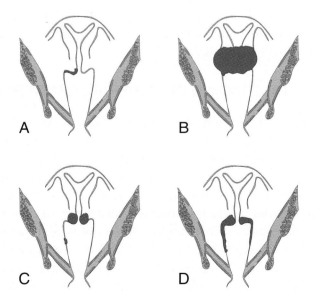

Figure 8–7. Four possible tumor presentations classified as FIGO stage IIa. *A* and *B,* Vaginal involvment may be minimal or *D,* quite extensive. *C,* Although the vagina is usually involved by tumor extending directly from the cervix, there may also be skip metastases to the vagina. However, if tumor is involving the distal one-third of the vagina, it is classified as stage IIIa.

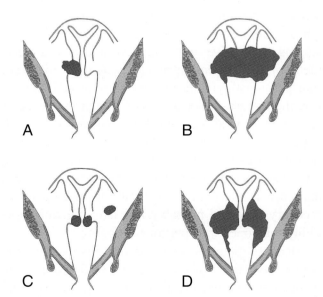

Figure 8–8. Four possible tumor presentations classified as FIGO stage IIb. Although all are clinically estimated to involve the parametrium, tumors range from *A,* relatively small to *B* and *D,* very large. Although the parametrium is usually involved directly, separate parametrial nodules occasionally raise the stage of a tumor to IIb (*C*). These may represent metastases to parametrial lymph nodes.

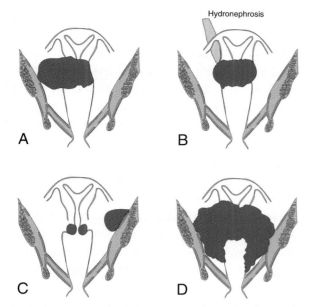

Figure 8–9. Four possible tumor presentations classified as FIGO stage IIIb. *A, C,* and *D,* Tumors may be classified as stage IIIb because of tumor fixation to the pelvic wall or *B,* because the tumor is obstructing a ureter. Although the tumor usually extends directly to the pelvic wall or merges with pelvic lymph nodes, occasionally, relatively small primary tumors are classified as IIIb because of palpable pelvic lymphadenopathy. Patients with such tumors have a particularly poor prognosis.

mine the composition of treatment groups in studies that use the FIGO staging system. Also, in the absence of an internationally accepted definition of microinvasion, the Society of Gynecologic Oncologists devised its own definition, which continues to be widely used in the United States, although it differs from the FIGO definition of microinvasion.

Despite its limitations, the FIGO staging system is the only consistent language that can currently be used to compare results among institutions. It should always be applied strictly according to the rules defined by FIGO. However, investigators should always be encouraged to provide more detailed information about the diagnostic tests and methods used to select patients for their studies. Only consistent staging and detailed description of methods will improve clinicians' ability to determine the generalizability of studies to their own patients.

TREATMENT SELECTION

In Chapters 9, 10, and 17, the indications for and expected outcomes of surgery, radiation therapy, and chemotherapy are discussed in detail. Although consensus has been achieved on some details of treatment selection, many areas of controversy remain. To introduce the chapters that will address specific treatments, some of the issues and controversies regarding treatment selection for patients with different presentations of cervical carcinoma will be summarized here.

Stage Ib1

Conventional wisdom suggests that for stage Ib1 disease, radiation therapy and surgery are equally effective treatments with somewhat different side effects. However, almost all comparisons of surgery and radiation therapy for stage Ib1 disease have been retrospective, and results of these retrospective comparisons are biased because young women with small, node-negative tumors tend to be preferentially selected for surgical treatment. Only one study has prospectively compared initial surgery versus initial radiation therapy.[26] In that study, survival rates were similar with the two treatments. However, nearly half the patients treated with surgery for stage Ib1 disease had adjuvant pelvic irradiation, contributing to a higher rate of major complications in that treatment arm.

Table 8–2. EVOLUTION OF THE CLASSIFICATION OF CERVICAL CANCERS CONFINED TO THE CERVIX

1929[20]	In the first international staging system (accepted by the League of Nations Health Organization), stage I is defined as "cancer strictly confined to cervix (not otherwise specified)"
1937[20]	Cancers invading the uterine corpus are moved into the stage II category
1950[21]	Cancers invading the uterine corpus are moved back into stage I
	For the first time, preinvasive disease is assigned a special category (stage 0)
1962[22]	Tumors with "early stromal invasion" are placed in a new category (stage Ia) and other tumors confined to the cervix are classified as "Ib"
1972[23]	Stage Ia is divided into stage Ia1 ("early stromal invasion") and stage Ia2 ("occult cancer")
1974[24]	"Occult cancer" is moved to a special subcategory of stage Ib (stage Ib$_{occult}$)
1985[25]	"Stage Ib$_{occult}$" is eliminated as a subcategory of stage Ib
1994[19]	Current definitions of stages Ia and Ib are adopted (see Table 8–1)

Most investigators agree that patients with stage Ib1 disease with more than one positive lymph node require postoperative radiation therapy, which is now usually combined with concurrent chemotherapy.[27] A recent randomized trial[28] demonstrated a significantly better recurrence-free survival rate when patients with negative nodes and high-risk local (cervical) findings had postoperative radiation therapy, but in their preliminary analysis, the authors did not compare overall survival rates for the surgery-only and surgery-plus-radiation groups. Also, the possible role of concurrent chemotherapy is untested in this group of patients.

Stage Ib2, IIa, (IIb)

Within the past 5 to 10 years, investigators have recommended various combinations of radiation therapy, chemotherapy, and surgery for treatment of stage Ib2, IIa, and IIb cervical cancer. Those combinations are as follows:

1. *Radiation therapy.* Although randomized trials suggest that most patients with stage Ib2, IIa, and IIb disease benefit from radiation therapy with concurrent chemotherapy, the studies could not define subsets of patients who might be equally effectively treated with radiation alone.

2. *Neoadjuvant chemotherapy followed by radiation therapy.* Negative results of at least seven randomized trials have caused most clinicians to abandon the use of neoadjuvant chemotherapy followed by radiation therapy in patients with stage Ib2, IIa, or IIb disease (see Chapter 17).

3. *Radiation therapy followed by adjuvant simple hysterectomy.* Although a randomized trial including patients with bulky stage Ib disease apparently failed to demonstrate a survival advantage for radiation therapy followed by adjuvant simple hysterectomy, compared with radiation therapy alone,[29] final results of the trial have not been published. Adjuvant hysterectomy is still commonly performed for patients with bulky stage Ib, IIa, and occasionally IIb cancers, particularly if there is bulky endocervical disease.[11]

4. *Radical hysterectomy (with or without postoperative radiation therapy).* Although many clinicians restrict the use of initial surgical treatment to patients with stage Ib1 tumors, others advocate much broader indications for radical hysterectomy (see Chapter 9). The Italian randomized trial[26] also compared radical hysterectomy with radiation therapy for patients with stage Ib2 disease. Although survival rates for the two arms were similar, more than 80 percent of surgically treated patients who had tumors larger than 4 cm required postoperative irradiation. Also, the radiation therapy used in this study has been criticized because of the low dose, protracted treatment, and lack of concurrent chemotherapy.

5. *Extended-field radiation therapy (including the para-aortic nodes).* A prospective randomized trial first published in 1990[30] and updated in 1995[31] demonstrated a better overall survival rate when prophylactic extended-field irradiation was added to standard locoregional pelvic irradiation in patients with stage I/II disease. Although Radiation Therapy Oncology Group trial 90-01[32] demonstrated better survival rates with pelvic irradiation and concurrent chemotherapy than with extended-field irradiation alone, the role of prophylactic aortic irradiation remains controversial.

6. *Neoadjuvant chemotherapy followed by radical hysterectomy (with or without radiation therapy).* A prospective trial comparing radical hysterectomy and postoperative radiation therapy with or without neoadjuvant chemotherapy in patients with stage Ib2 disease indicated that outcome was better with the trimodality treatment.[33] However, this approach has not been compared with concurrent chemoradiation.

7. *Concurrent chemoradiation.* Results of two trials that included patients with stage Ib2 and IIa disease[32,34] and other trials that included patients with more advanced disease[35,36] have caused many clinicians to prefer concurrent chemoradiation to the other available treatment choices, but many of the other approaches discussed above are still being studied actively.

Stages IIb to IVa

Patients with advanced lesions (stages IIb to IVa) are usually treated with radiation therapy and concurrent chemotherapy. However, the optimal drug regimen, the optimal radiation therapy technique, and the role of surgery in selected cases continue to be subjects of controversy.

CONCLUSION

Significant advances have been made in the diagnostic work-up, staging, and treatment of patients with cervical cancer. However, treatment is becoming increasingly complicated and expensive. Although improvements in treatment are needed, particularly for patients with the most advanced stages of disease, additional studies are also needed to more clearly define which patients are most likely to benefit from multimodality treatment and to further assess the impact of the choice of therapy on treatment-related complications and quality of life.

REFERENCES

1. Benedet J, Odicino F, Maisonneuve P, et al. Carcinoma of the cervix uteri. J Epidemiol Biostat 1998;3:5–34.
2. Bolger BS, Dabbas M, Lopes A, Monaghan JM. Prognostic value of preoperative squamous cell carcinoma antigen level in patients surgically treated for cervical carcinoma. Gynecol Oncol 1997;65:309–13.
3. Duk JM, Groenier KH, de Bruijn HWA, et al. Pretreatment serum squamous cell carcinoma antigen: a newly identified prognostic factor in early-stage cervical carcinoma. J Clin Oncol 1996;14:111–8.
4. Hong JH, Tsai CS, Chang JT, et al. The prognostic significance of pre- and posttreatment SCC levels in patients with squamous cell carcinoma of the cervix treated by radiotherapy. Int J Radiat Oncol Biol Phys 1998;41:823–30.
5. Massuger LF, Koper NP, Thomas CM, et al. Improvement of clinical staging in cervical cancer with serum squamous cell carcinoma antigen and CA 125 determinations. Gynecol Oncol 1997;64:473–6.
6. Gasinska A, Urbanski K, Jakubowicz J, et al. Tumour cell kinetics as a prognostic factor in squamous cell carcinoma of the cervix treated with radiotherapy. Radiother Oncol 1999;50:77–84.
7. Kristensen GB, Kaern J, Abeler VM, et al. No prognostic impact of flow-cytometric measured DNA ploidy and S-phase fraction in cancer of the uterine cervix: a prospective study of 465 patients. Gynecol Oncol 1995;57:79–85.
8. Lombard I, Vincent-Salomon A, Validire P, et al. Human papillomavirus genotype as a major determinant of the course of cervical cancer. J Clin Oncol 1998;16:2613–9.
9. Burger RA, Monk BJ, Kurosaki T, et al. Human papillomavirus type 18: association with poor prognosis in early stage cervical cancer [see comments]. J Natl Cancer Inst 1996;88:1361–8.
10. Duggan MA, McGregor SE, Benoit JL, et al. The human papillomavirus status of invasive cervical adenocarcinoma: a clinicopathological and outcome analysis. Hum Pathol 1995;26:319–25.
11. Eifel PJ, Moughan J, Owen JB, et al. Patterns of radiotherapy practice for patients with squamous carcinoma of the uterine cervix. A Patterns of Care study. Int J Radiat Oncol Biol Phys 1999;43:351–8.
12. Heller PB, Malfetano JH, Bundy BN, et al. Clinical-pathologic study of stage IIB, III, and IVA carcinoma of the cervix: extended diagnostic evaluation for paraaortic node metastasis—a Gynecologic Oncology Group study. Gynecol Oncol 1990;38:425–30.
13. Weiser EB, Bundy BN, Hoskins WJ, et al. Extraperitoneal versus transperitoneal selective paraaortic lymphadenectomy in the pretreatment surgical staging of advanced cervical carcinoma (a Gynecologic Oncology Group study). Gynecol Oncol 1989;33:283–9.
14. Possover M, Krause N, Plaul K, et al. Laparoscopic para-aortic and pelvic lymphadenectomy: experience with 150 patients and review of the literature. Gynecol Oncol 1998;71:19–28.
15. Hacker NF, Wain GV, Nicklin JL. Resection of bulky positive lymph nodes in patients with cervical carcinoma. Int J Gynecol Cancer 1995;5:250–6.
16. Potish RA, Downey GO, Adcock LL, et al. The role of surgical debulking in cancer of the uterine cervix. Int J Radiat Oncol Biol Phys 1989;17:979–84.
17. Coleman RL, Burke TW, Morris M, et al. Intra-operative radiographs to confirm the adequacy of lymph node resection in patients with suspicious lymphangiograms. Gynecol Oncol 1994;51:362–7.
18. Medl M, Peters-Engl C, Schutz P, et al. First report of lymphatic mapping with isosulfan blue dye and sentinel node biopsy in cervical cancer. Anticancer Res 2000;20:1133–4.
19. International Federation of Gynecology and Obstetrics. Staging announcement. FIGO staging of gynecologic cancers; cervical and vulva. Int J Gynecol Cancer 1995;5:319.
20. League of Nations Health Organization. Inquiry into the results of radiotherapy in cancer of the uterus. Atlas illustrating the division of cancer of the uterine cervix into four stages according to the anatomo-clinical extent of the growth. Stockholm, Sweden: Kungl. Boktryckeriet P. A. Norstedt & Söner; 1938.
21. World Health Organization, et al. Annual report on the results of radiotherapy in carcinoma of the uterine cervix. Vol. 6. Stockholm, Sweden: World Health Organization; 1951.

22. International Federation of Gynecology and Obstetrics. Classification and staging of malignant tumors in the female pelvis. Acta Obstet Gynecol Scand 1971; 50:1–12.

23. International Federation of Gynecology and Obstetrics. Annual report on the results of treatment in carcinoma of the uterus, vagina, and ovary. Vol. 15. Stockholm, Sweden: Kungl. Boktryckeriet P.A. Norstedt & Söner; 1973.

24. Pettersson F, Björkholm E. Staging and reporting of cervical carcinoma. Semin Oncol 1982;9:287–98.

25. International Federation of Gynecology and Obstetrics. Staging Announcement: FIGO Cancer Committee. Gynecol Oncol 1986;25:383–5.

26. Landoni F, Maneo A, Colombo A, et al. Randomised study of radical surgery versus radiotherapy for stage Ib–IIa cervical cancer. Lancet 1997;350:535–40.

27. Whitney CW, Sause W, Bundy BN, et al. A randomized comparison of fluorouracil plus cisplatin versus hydroxyurea as an adjunct to radiation therapy in stages IIB–IVA carcinoma of the cervix with negative para-aortic lymph nodes: a Gynecologic Oncology Group and Southwest Oncology Group study. J Clin Oncol 1999;17:1339–48.

28. Sedlis A, Bundy BN, Rotman MZ, et al. A randomized trial of pelvic radiation therapy versus no further therapy in selected patients with stage IB carcinoma of the cervix after radical hysterectomy and pelvic lymphadenectomy: a Gynecologic Oncology Group study. Gynecol Oncol 1999;73:177–83.

29. Keys H, Bundy B, Stehman F, et al. Adjuvant hysterectomy after radiation therapy reduces detection of local recurrence in "bulky" stage IB cervical cancer without improving survival: results of a prospective randomized GOG trial. Cancer J Sci Am 1997;3:117.

30. Rotman M, Choi K, Guze C, et al. Prophylactic irradiation of the para-aortic lymph node chain in stage 2B and bulky stage IB carcinoma of the cervix, initial treatment results of RTOG 7920. Int J Radiat Oncol Biol Phys 1990;19:513–21.

31. Rotman M, Pajak M, Choi K, et al. Prophylactic extended-field irradiation of para-aortic lymph nodes in stages IIB and bulky IB and IIA cervical carcinomas. Ten-year treatment results of RTOG 79-20. JAMA 1995;274:387–93.

32. Morris M, Eifel PJ, Lu J, et al. Pelvic radiation with concurrent chemotherapy compared with pelvic and paraaortic radiation for high-risk cervical cancer. N Engl J Med 1999;340:1137–43.

33. Sardi JE, Giaroli A, Sananes C, et al. Long-term follow-up of the first randomized trial using neoadjuvant chemotherapy in stage Ib squamous carcinoma of the cervix: the final results. Gynecol Oncol 1997;67:61–9.

34. Keys HM, Bundy BN, Stehman FB, et al. Cisplatin, radiation, and adjuvant hysterectomy for bulky stage IB cervical carcinoma. N Engl J Med 1999; 340:1154–61.

35. Peters WA III, Liu PY, Barrett RJ II, et al. Concurrent chemotherapy and pelvic radiation therapy compared with pelvic radiation therapy alone as adjuvant therapy after radical surgery in high-risk early-stage cancer of the cervix. J Clin Oncol 2000;18:1606–13.

36. Rose PG, Bundy BN, Watkins J, et al. Concurrent cisplatin-based chemotherapy and radiotherapy for locally advanced cervical cancer. N Engl J Med 1999;340:1144–53.

Surgical Treatment of Invasive Cervical Cancer

THOMAS W. BURKE, MD

KAREN LU, MD

The success of surgical therapy for cancer is typically dependent on disease that is confined to the site of origin being resected with a clear margin of normal uninvolved tissue. When disease spreads to adjacent soft tissue, abutting organs, or regional lymph nodes, the curative potential of surgical resection is greatly diminished. Cancers of the cervix are assigned to stage I by the International Federation of Gynecologists and Obstetricians (FIGO) system when their growth is confined to the cervix.[1] However, the stage I group encompasses a wide range of tumor sizes. Substage Ia is used to describe early tumors that are not clinically obvious (Figure 9–1). Women with these lesions are most often diagnosed

by colposcopic examination and directed biopsy performed to evaluate the cervix following an abnormal Pap smear. Cancers with minimal invasion of the underlying stroma (< 3 mm) are considered microinvasive and further categorized as stage Ia1 lesions (Figure 9–2). The slightly larger microcarcinomas demonstrate stromal invasion between 3 and 5 mm but do not have lateral spread greater than 7 mm (Figure 9–3). The accurate diagnosis of stage Ia cervical cancer requires a well-evaluated cone biopsy specimen with clear margins because tumor measurements cannot be made on a punch biopsy that does not include the entire lesion.[2,3] Clinically evident cancers that remain confined to the cervix

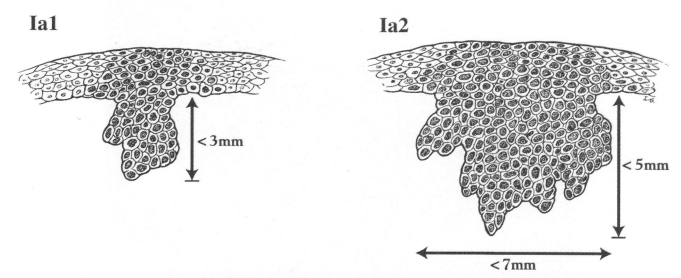

Figure 9–1. Stage Ia cervical cancers include those tumors that demonstrate early invasion of the underlying stroma. Stage Ia1 lesions are characterized by microscopic invasion to less than 3 mm in depth from the overlying epithelium. The slightly larger stage Ia2 tumors are microcarcinomas that invade to 3 to 5 mm in depth and have lateral spread that measures less than 7 mm. Because stage Ia tumors are defined by measured microscopic limits, complete resection by conization is required to determine correct assignment to these substages.

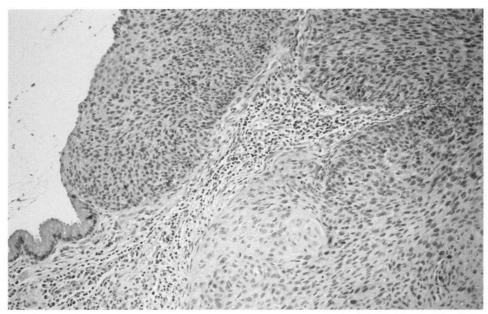

Figure 9–2. This photomicrograph illustrates minimal invasion of the cervical stroma to the right. Total depth of invasion was less than 1 mm (stage Ia1). The squamocolumnar junction can be seen at the left. (H&E stain)

are defined as stage Ib tumors (Figure 9–4). Stage Ib is subdivided on the basis of clinical measurement of cervix diameter into stage Ib1 (diameter < 4 cm) and stage Ib2 (diameter > 4 cm).

Most American centers offer surgical therapy only to women with stage I cancers. Although some reports have described excellent long-term survival rates in selected groups of surgically treated stage II cases, our experience has shown that primary irradiation—and more recently, chemoradiation—provide better local control and survival than does surgical treatment for these women.[4] Extensive review of our

Figure 9–3. Invasive carcinoma extends 4 mm into the stroma of this specimen. Lateral spread measures 6 mm. Such microcarcinomas are assigned to substage Ia2. (H&E stain)

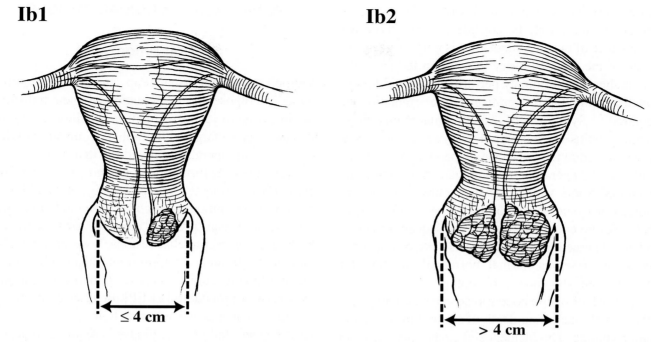

Ib1 **Ib2**

$\leq$ 4 cm | > 4 cm

Figure 9–4. Stage Ib cervical cancers that are grossly evident but limited to the cervix. Substage assignment is based on the clinical measurement of cervical diameter during routine pelvic examination. When the cervical diameter is 4 cm or less, the tumor is categorized as stage Ib1. If the cervical diameter exceeds 4 cm, the tumor is categorized as stage Ib2.

stage I cases also suggests that improved results can be obtained with irradiation (and presumably chemoradiation) than with surgery in women with stage Ib2 cancers.[5] Consequently, we consider surgical therapy an option for patients with stage Ia1, Ia2, and Ib1 tumors only. Our goal is to select cases for surgical treatment that are likely to be curatively treated without additional therapy. It is preferable to avoid the combination of radical operation followed by pelvic irradiation because the morbidity of combined treatment is excessive.[6]

All women who are considered candidates for surgical therapy should be evaluated for potential operative risks. Fortunately, most women who develop cervical cancer are premenopausal and without major comorbid medical conditions. Those with significant cardiac, pulmonary, or renal dysfunction as well as those with extreme obesity can often be treated more safely with irradiation than with surgery. For all other cases, we provide our patients with a detailed description of both forms of therapy, including a discussion of potential complications, and allow them to choose the modality that they prefer. Possible advantages to surgical therapy

include a shorter treatment course, the ability to retain natural ovarian function, and less interference with vaginal function. Ultimately, the selection of a specific therapeutic approach should be tailored to the inherent risk factors of the patient's cancer, treatment preferences, and likelihood of long-term cure.

Once a decision for operative therapy has been made, several surgical issues must be considered: (1) How aggressive should the resection be? (2) What is the plan for the adnexal structures? and (3) Is the risk of lymph node spread high enough to warrant lymphadenectomy as a component of the operation? The extent of the resection is matched to the tumor size or volume. Realistically, this correlates directly with substage and is discussed in detail in subsequent sections. A decision to preserve one or both ovaries should be reserved for premenopausal women because there would seem to be no benefit to conserving the adnexae in those in whom hormone production has ceased. Some have suggested that because the risk of occult metastases to the ovaries is greater in women with adenocarcinomas of the cervix, ovarian conservation should not be considered in such tumors. However, the data are too limited to allow objective evaluation of this issue. Ovarian conservation should only be considered when the gross appearance of one or both ovaries is normal. Transposition of the retained ovary to a site in the paracolic gutter should be routinely performed to avoid loss of function should postoperative pelvic irradiation be required.[7–9] Symptoms of ovulation may mimic those of appendicitis when the right ovary is so placed. We, therefore, routinely perform appendectomy at the time of the operation to eliminate this diagnostic dilemma. Some women develop chronic pain syndromes or cystic degeneration of the retained ovary that is severe enough to warrant subsequent resection in 5 to 10 percent of cases. Nevertheless, ovarian conservation preserves normal hormonal function for most women who choose this option.

The risk of lymph node spread can be directly correlated with increasing depth of stromal invasion and tumor volume. The incidence of nodal metastases in women with stage Ia1 cancers is consistently less than 1 percent.[10–14] No lymphatic dissection is recommended in these cases. Lymph node metastases have been observed in 3 to 5 percent of women with stage Ia2 lesions.[12,15] We routinely perform pelvic lymphadenectomy in these cases, but others do not. Stage Ib1 cancers have a 5 to 15 percent incidence of nodal spread.[16–19] All patients in this category receive pelvic lymphadenectomy as part of their surgical therapy.

Because lymphatic metastases tend to follow a stepwise progression from pelvic to common iliac to para-aortic lymph nodes, upper-level lymphadenectomy is usually not performed. Women without pelvic lymph node involvement almost never have metastases that skip to higher nodal groups. Patients with clinically obvious metastatic nodal disease are best treated with chemoradiation. When gross adenopathy is encountered at operation, an attempt to remove gross disease should be considered to enhance the ability of irradiation to control regional disease, but the primary surgical procedure should be aborted. Consequently, pelvic lymphadenectomy is routinely paired with radical hysterectomy to provide prognostic and therapeutic benefits for women with stage Ia2 and Ib1 cancers that have no gross nodal involvement. This strategy is designed to limit the use of postoperative adjuvant irradiation to only those cases with microscopic nodal or margin disease.

NONRADICAL SURGICAL OPTIONS

Conization

Women with abnormal Pap smears commonly undergo colposcopic examination of their transformation zone to identify small or subclinical lesions that can then be targeted for biopsy. Conization of the cervix is an operative procedure that removes or destroys the transformation zone and can be considered either diagnostic, therapeutic, or both. Although destructive techniques (such as laser ablation and cryotherapy) can provide effective treatment for high-grade intraepithelial lesions,[20] we prefer techniques that provide an appropriate histologic specimen (cold knife conization [CKC], loop electrosurgical excision procedure [LEEP], or laser conization) for pathologic analysis when early invasion is identified or suspected.[21] Cone biopsy is required to accurately diagnose stages Ia1 and Ia2 cervical cancers because specific measurements of microscopic invasion must be made. The technique for performing CKC is illustrated in Figure 9–5. The biopsy should provide for complete excision of the cervical lesion along with a margin of microscopically normal mucosa.[22] Conization is typically performed as an outpatient procedure. Endocervical curettings from above the biospy site are usually obtained along with the biopsy specimen in an effort to detect extension of the disease into the endocervical canal. Immediate

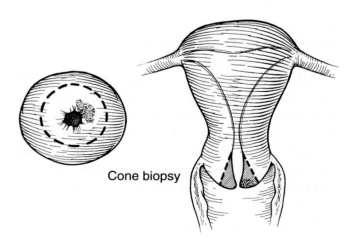

Cone biopsy

Figure 9–5. Cone biopsy is designed to completely remove the squamocolumnar junction and the lower portion of the endocervical canal in women with very small cervical cancers. The surgical specimen should include the entire lesion, as this permits measurement of both depth of invasion and extent of lateral spread.

complications are uncommon and consist of bleeding or adjacent organ injury. Late complications, such as infection, cervical stenosis, and incompetent cervix, are also rare.

Conization as the sole treatment of early cervical cancers is a relatively recent concept. While removal of the uterus should be considered the standard therapy for women with invasive lesions of the cervix, conization has been offered to some who have very limited risk of lymph node spread and who have a strong desire to maintain fertility.[23-27] Current experience with this approach is not extensive (Table 9-1). Despite the increasing popularity of "conization only" therapy, patients must be cautioned that long-term follow-up data on women whose cancer has been managed in this way is lacking.

Nevertheless, several reasonable guidelines can be suggested to minimize the risk for undetected nodal disease and recurrence. These guidelines can be used to select a subset of low-risk cases for whom this option can be considered. Our recommendations would be to limit therapeutic conization to those with squamous lesions that (1) invade less than 3 mm, (2) have no lymph-vascular invasion, and (3) have uninvolved resection margins. Patients whose lesions do not meet these eligibility requirements should be advised to have more definitive surgical procedures. There is very little current information on which to base a recommendation regarding the use of conization as treatment for women with nonsquamous cervical cancers.[28] Patients who elect conization therapy must be willing to be monitored closely for the development of residual or recurrent cervical neoplasia. Frequent Pap smears, supplemented by the liberal use of colposcopy and biopsy, should be obtained in every patient whose cancer is managed in this manner.

Patients who select conization as therapy must be apprised of the known fertility risks of the procedure. These include cervical stenosis from postoperative scarring within the endocervical canal, inadequate cervical mucus that inhibits sperm transport and prevents fertilization, and an incompetent cervix that predisposes the patient to premature cervical dilatation and delivery should a pregnancy occur. The reported pregnancy experiences of women treated by conization are very limited. For the series abstracted in Table 9-1, there were 13 term deliveries and two cases of premature delivery as a result of an incompetent cervix.

Extrafascial Hysterectomy

The traditional approach to hysterectomy involves removal of the uterus by detaching the adnexal structures and round ligaments superiorly, followed by serial application of surgical clamps immediately adjacent to the uterine wall (Figure 9-6). Inferiorly, complete removal of the uterus and cervix requires mobilization of the bladder and entry into the upper vagina. This extrafascial technique permits removal of the intact uterine fundus and cervix, leaving the parametrial soft tissues or a portion of the upper vagina. Hysterectomy can be accomplished through an abdominal incision, transvaginally, or

Table 9-1. REPORTS OF WOMEN WITH EARLY CERVICAL CANCER TREATED BY CONIZATION ALONE						
Report (Year)	Criteria	Patients	Recurrence CIN	Recurrence SCC	Term Pregnancies	Follow-Up Years
Kolstad (1989)[23]	Squamous < 5 mm invasion	41	—	4	NS	3–17
Morris (1993)[24]	Squamous < 3 mm invasion no LVSI	14	1	0	3	2
Ostor (1994)[25]	Squamous < 3 mm invasion	23	0	1	NS	15
Tseng (1997)[26]	Squamous < 3 mm invasion no LVSI	12	1	0	4	6.7
Anderson (1997)[27]	Squamous < 3 mm invasion no LVSI	41	1*	0	6	5–12

CIN = cervical intraepithelial neoplasia; SCC = squamous cell carcinoma; LVSI = lymph-vascular space invasion; NS = not stated.
*Adenocarcinoma in situ.

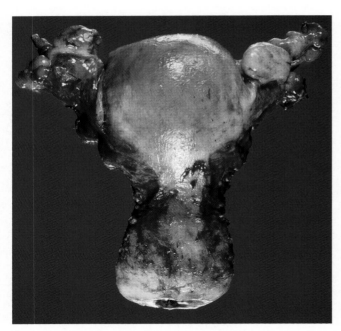

Figure 9–6. This surgical specimen of the uterus with attached tubes and ovaries was obtained by extrafascial hysterectomy. Note the absence of parametrial soft tissue and upper vagina.

using a combination of laparoscopic and transvaginal techniques.

Simple extrafascial hysterectomy should be considered the standard definitive treatment option for women with stage Ia1 cervical cancers.[23,25,29–33] The risk of lymph node spread is so low in this substage that routine surgical removal or evaluation of the pelvic lymph nodes is not recommended. Retention of one or both ovaries should be considered for hormonal production in women below the age of 45 years. Hysterectomy provides curative treatment for virtually

all women with microscopic invasion (Table 9–2). Because squamous neoplasia can develop in the vagina or vulva of women with a history of cervical neoplasia, those treated for early cervical cancer should be followed with regular examinations and Pap smears, even if the cervix has been removed.

There is some controversy regarding the most appropriate surgical procedure for the treatment of women with stage Ia2 cancers. Although some data suggest that these lesions can be effectively resected with extrafascial hysterectomy,[23,30] many American gynecologic oncologists limit this operation to women with Ia1 tumors. They prefer the traditional radical or modified radical hysterectomy with pelvic lymphadenectomy for the treatment of stage Ia2 cases. A higher rate of vaginal recurrence and an incidence of lymph node metastases of 3 to 5 percent are often cited as reasons for a more aggressive surgical approach. Clearly, radical resection of the uterus provides a wider margin of normal tissue (Figure 9–7). Identification and resection of occult nodal metastases certainly provide useful therapeutic and prognostic information for the small number of Ia2 patients who have them. An equally compelling argument can be made that this risk is still so low that routine lymphadenectomy is not warranted. Excellent outcomes and long-term survivals have been reported for either treatment approach. This remains an area of debate, pending the development of additional clinical data. Nevertheless, there is relatively uniform consensus that conization-only therapy should not be offered to women with stage Ia2 disease.

RADICAL SURGICAL OPTIONS

Radical surgery refers to the extended removal of tumor along with an adequate margin of uninvolved tissue. It is performed with the intent to achieve a definitive cure. The pattern of growth of cervical cancer (initially confined to the cervix, then spreading in a predictable, stepwise manner by direct extension) makes radical surgery a useful option in the treatment of cervical cancer. In appropriately selected patients, radical surgery results in excellent long-term outcome with minimal surgical morbidity. In addition, radical surgery has the additional benefit of pathologic confirmation of the extent of disease.

Table 9–2. OUTCOMES FOR WOMEN WITH STAGE Ia CERVICAL CANCER TREATED BY EXTRAFASCIAL HYSTERECTOMY			
Report (Year)	Patients (Stage)	Recurrence*	Deaths
Seski (1977)[29]	17 (Ia1)	0	0
Lohe (1978)[30]	157 (Ia1)	—	0
	52 (Ia2)	1	1
van Nagell (1983)[31]	93 (Ia1)	1	1
Creasman (1985)[32]	24 (Ia1)	0	0
	3 (Ia2)	0	0
Kolstad (1989)[23]	57 (Ia1)	5†	0
	81 (Ia2)		
Ostor (1994)[25]	81 (Ia1)	5†	0
	20 (Ia2)		

*Includes preinvasive and invasive recurrences.
†Data not separated by substage.

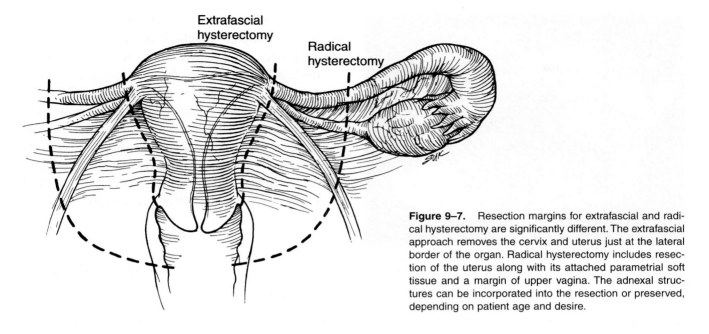

Extrafascial hysterectomy

Radical hysterectomy

Figure 9–7. Resection margins for extrafascial and radical hysterectomy are significantly different. The extrafascial approach removes the cervix and uterus just at the lateral border of the organ. Radical hysterectomy includes resection of the uterus along with its attached parametrial soft tissue and a margin of upper vagina. The adnexal structures can be incorporated into the resection or preserved, depending on patient age and desire.

Radical Hysterectomy

Radical hysterectomy involves the en bloc removal of the uterus, cervix, parametrial tissues, and upper vagina (Figure 9–8). In the early 20th century, Wertheim of Vienna described the radical hysterectomy for the treatment of cervical cancer. In the 1940s, Meigs of the United States championed the procedure, to which he added a pelvic lymphadenectomy. Today, radical hysterectomy with pelvic lymphadenectomy is the standard treatment in the management of stage Ia2 and Ib and sometimes IIa cervical cancers. Although primary radiation therapy has been shown to produce overall survival rates comparable with those produced by radical hysterectomy in women with early-stage cervical cancer,[34,35] a patterns-of-care study by the American College of Surgeons found that most clinicians in the United States favor primary surgical therapy.[36] Purported advantages of primary surgical treatment include pathologic confirmation of the extent of disease, shorter treatment time, preservation of ovarian function, if desired, and avoidance of radiation-induced vaginal stenosis.

Description

The tissues adjacent to the uterus and cervix contain the primary lymphatic channels that are the earliest repositories for tumor that has moved beyond the cervix. In order to remove the central tumor as well as obtain a wide margin, a radical hysterectomy involves resection of the uterus, cervix, upper vagina, and adjacent parametrial tissue (Figure 9–9). Using margins of resection as the basis, Piver and

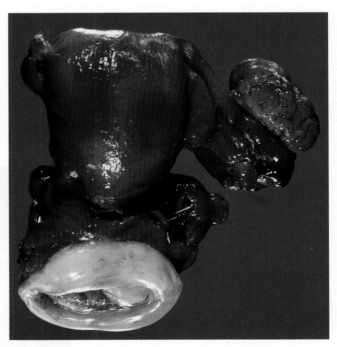

Figure 9–8. The parametrial and upper vaginal resection margins are readily evident in this radical hysterectomy specimen from a woman with stage Ib1 squamous cell carcinoma. The right tube and ovary have been preserved for hormonal function.

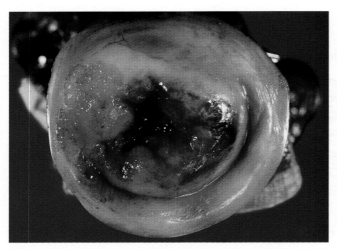

Figure 9–9. Another view of the specimen shown in Figure 9–8 shows the small but grossly identifiable central ulcerative lesion.

colleagues described five classes of hysterectomy.[37] The classic radical hysterectomy used today for stage Ib cervical cancer has also been termed a type III hysterectomy. In the type III hysterectomy, the lateral ligamentous uterine attachments are severed at or near the pelvic wall, the uterosacral ligaments are transected near their base, and the upper-third of the vagina is removed[37] (Figure 9–10).

Pelvic lymphadenectomy is performed routinely at the time of radical hysterectomy and provides valuable prognostic information. The dissection removes the nodal groups that primarily drain the cervix: the obturator and the external, internal, and common iliac nodes. Some clinicians will also perform a para-aortic lymph node dissection. Though rare, there have been reports of patients having tumor in the para-aortic

nodes without evidence of disease in the pelvic nodes.[38] In general, lymphatic metastases in cervical cancer proceed in a stepwise and predictable fashion.

Radical hysterectomy for cervical cancer does not require removal of the ovaries and fallopian tubes, since metastases to these organs are uncommon. In patients who choose ovarian conservation, the ovaries can be transposed to a position midway up the lateral paracolic gutters. Transposition preserves hormonal and reproductive functions, even if postoperative pelvic radiation is required.

Criteria

Criteria for selecting patients who are appropriate candidates for radical hysterectomy include factors involving the patient's suitability for major surgery as well as tumor characteristics, including tumor volume and lymphatic involvement (Figures 9–11 and 9–12). Studies of prognostic features of early-stage cervical cancers have consistently emphasized the association between increasing tumor size and increasing risk of lymph node spread, increasing chance for recurrence, and decreasing survival rate. While overall survival of patients with stage Ib cervical cancer is 80 to 90 percent, survival rates fall to 40 to 70 percent in patients with high-risk factors, including cervical diameters larger than 4 cm, lymph node metastases, parametrial involvement, and positive surgical margins. When making the decision to treat a patient with newly diagnosed early-stage cervical cancer, clinicians should consider that those women known to have high-risk fac-

Figure 9–10. This bisected radical hysterectomy specimen clearly shows a gross lesion protruding from the cervical os and extending into the endocervical canal.

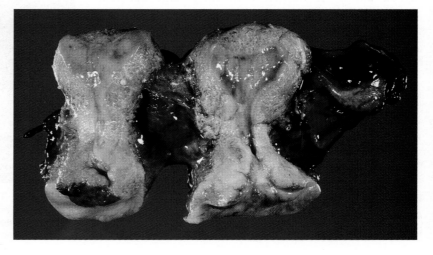

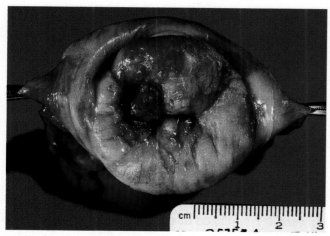

Figure 9–11. A small 1-cm cancer can be seen at the 9 o'clock position in this radical resection specimen. The tumor was grossly evident at the time of pelvic examination, although the cervical diameter was only 3 cm. The diagnosis was confirmed by biopsy done as an outpatient procedure.

tors may benefit from upfront combined radiation therapy and chemotherapy. Multiple studies have found that morbidity increases in patients who receive both radical surgery and radiation therapy.[35]

Patient factors play a significant role in the selection of primary radical surgery or radiation therapy in the treatment of women with early-stage cervical cancer. The ability to preserve ovarian function, in terms of both hormones and reproductive capability, is important to young women facing the treatment decision. The risk of vaginal stenosis secondary to radiation therapy may influence women to choose radical hysterectomy. Finally, the surgeon must also determine whether a patient is a candidate for radical surgery. Women with significant medical problems, including obesity, may be better suited for primary radiation therapy.

Morbidity

Advances in anesthesia, availability of blood products, use of broad-spectrum antibiotics, and specialized surgical training have made radical hysterectomy a significantly less morbid procedure than when first reported by Wertheim. More serious complications, including ureterovaginal fistula and vesicovaginal fistula are rare (1 to 2% and < 1%, respectively). Bladder dystonia occurs postoperatively but, in the majority of patients, resolves within a few weeks.

Outcome

Reported 5-year survival rates for women with stage Ib cervical cancer treated with radical hysterectomy and pelvic lymphadenectomy are approximately 80 to 90 percent[16,17,39–43] (Table 9–3). Women with small tumors who have negative nodes and clear margins have the most favorable prognosis, with survival rates upwards of 90 percent.

As stated previously, patients noted to have positive surgical margins and tumor present in the lymph nodes are at highest risk for recurrence and poor outcome. In a large, prospective study, Delgado and colleagues reported that patients with negative lymph nodes had a 3-year disease-free interval rate of 85.6 percent.[43] In patients found to have positive lymph nodes, survival decreases to 50 to 74 percent.[10,17,42] Within this subgroup, an increasing number of positive lymph nodes and extended involvement in the common iliac chain decrease survival rates. A recent report by Peters and colleagues demonstrates that in women with positive lymph nodes, positive surgical margins, or tumor present in the endometrium, postoperative radiation therapy and platinum-based chemotherapy improve survival.[44]

In women with negative lymph nodes or negative surgical margins, the risk of disease recurrence is 3 to 5 percent. However, because this subgroup

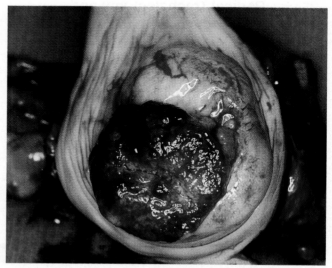

Figure 9–12. The growth pattern of this 3-cm tumor is largely exophytic and involves only a single quadrant of the cervix. The cervical diameter was about 3.5 cm. This specimen also provides a good illustration of the typical vaginal resection margin obtained during radical hysterectomy.

Table 9–3. OUTCOME OF WOMEN TREATED BY RADICAL HYSTERECTOMY

Report (Year)	Criteria	Patients	Recurrence (%)	Survival (%)	Follow-Up
Chung (1980)[40]	Ib/2a	98	17	85	NS
Burke (1987)[16]	Ib	275	11.3	NS	NS
Larsen (1988)[41]	Ib	249	11	94	48 months
Fuller (1989)[42]	Ib/2a	431	20	81.7	NS
Delgado (1990)[43]	Ib	645	17	86	NS
Alvarez (1991)[39]	Ib	401	NS	85	3.9 years
Landoni (1997)[35]	Ib/2a	172	25	83	87 months

NS = not significant.

accounts for 50 percent of treatment failures, a number of studies have attempted to identify more subtle prognostic factors associated with radical hysterectomy failure. Some of the criteria that have been studied include lymph-vascular space invasion, depth of invasion, degree of differentiation, and histologic subtype. Smiley and colleagues evaluated 95 patients who had negative lymph nodes and clear resection margins after radical hysterectomy.[19] They found that differentiation was the only feature useful in identifying patients at risk for recurrence. Whether postoperative radiation therapy and chemotherapy will benefit this subgroup of women is unknown. Unfortunately, no clear factor or combination of factors has consistently been reported that might identify which low-risk patients will suffer a recurrence after radical hysterectomy.

Radical Trachelectomy and Laparoscopic Lymphadenectomy

Recently, a number of groups have presented their series of patients with early-stage cervical cancer who were treated with radical vaginal trachelectomy in an effort to preserve the uterus and child-bearing capability[45–47] (Table 9–4). This technique involves a laparoscopic pelvic lymphadenectomy, followed by vaginal resection of the cervix, the upper 1 to 2 cm of the vaginal cuff, and the medial portions of the cardinal and uterosacral ligaments. The cervix is transected at the lower uterine segment, and a prophylactic cerclage is placed at the time of surgery. Covens and colleagues reported a series of 32 patients who underwent radical vaginal trachelectomy and compared them with a matched control group who had undergone radical hysterectomy. He found a similar recurrence rate in the two groups (3 to 5%).[46] Dargent and colleagues reported a recurrence rate of 4 percent with a median follow-up of 52 months.[47]

In Covens' study, among 13 women who attempted conception, there were 3 term births (by scheduled cesarian section) and 2 spontaneous first trimester abortions. Dargent and colleagues reported 25 pregnancies in 18 patients, 5 of whom had been pregnant at the time laparoscopic radical hysterectomy was performed. There were 13 deliveries by cesarian section, with an average gestational period of 36 weeks. There were also 6 second trimester losses. In Roy and Plante's series, 4 patients delivered at 39, 38, 34, and 25 weeks' gestation.[45]

Recurrence, survival, and pregnancy outcome of patients who undergo radical vaginal trachelectomy and laparoscopic pelvic lymphadenectomy will take more years to determine. A critical issue will be to determine which subgroup of patients with early cervical cancer can safely undergo this procedure. Both Roy and Covens recommend that the procedure be limited to patients with a tumor not exceeding 2 cm. As more gynecologic oncologists adopt the procedure, prospective trials may be possible.

Table 9–4. REPORTS OF WOMEN WITH EARLY CERVICAL CANCER TREATED BY RADICAL TRACHELECTOMY

Report (Year)	Criteria	Patients	Recurrence	Live Births	Follow-Up
Roy (1998)[45]	Stage Ia1-IIa	30	1	4	25 months
Covens (1999)[46]	Stage Ib < 2 cm	32	1	3	23.5 months
Dargent (2000)[47]	Stage Ia1-IIb	47	2	13	52 months

Radical Parametrectomy

Women who are unexpectedly found to have cervical cancer after undergoing a simple hysterectomy may require additional therapy. In most of these cases, pelvic radiation is given. Alternatively, radical parametrectomy can be considered[48,49] (Table 9–5). Radical parametrectomy involves removal of the parametrial tissue and the upper vagina. In addition, bilateral pelvic lymphadenectomy is performed at the time of surgery. Advantages of radical parametrectomy with

Table 9–5. OUTCOMES FOR WOMEN UNDERGOING RADICAL PARAMETRECTOMY				
Report (Year)	Patients	Patients With Disease At Operation*	Recurrence	Deaths
Orr (1986)[49]	23	6	1	1
Chapman (1992)[48]	17	2	2	1

*Nodal or parametrial disease.

bilateral pelvic lymphadenectomy include the ability to surgically evaluate the extent of disease and obviate the need for radiation therapy if the parametria and pelvic nodes are free of disease. Contraindications to the surgery include parametrial or uterosacral ligament involvement, extensive vaginal involvement, and involvement of the rectum or bladder. Patients who are found at the time of radical parametrectomy to have metastatic disease in multiple lymph nodes, parametrial involvement, or positive surgical margins should undergo postoperative radiation therapy with concurrent chemotherapy with cisplatin and 5-fluorouracil.

Both radical parametrectomy and radical trachelectomy are currently being evaluated in selected patients only. Neither of these operations should be considered to be standard of care.

CONCLUSION

Over the last quarter century, our increased understanding of the natural history of cervical cancer has allowed us to refine our surgical techniques to improve cure rates while decreasing surgical morbidity. In women with small cervical tumors and no evidence of lymphatic spread, primary surgical therapy is curative and associated with excellent long-term

outcome, a rapid treatment course, and minimal risk. Extent of surgery is tailored to tumor size such that microscopic tumors are now treated with simple hysterectomy or, in selected patients, with CKC. Morbidity from radical hysterectomy has been dramatically reduced, and options now exist for fertility and hormonal preservation. Recent advances, such as laparoscopic radical hysterectomy and radical trachelectomy, aim to decrease operative morbidity while not compromising overall cure rates. As our operative techniques evolve and our understanding of cervical cancer increases, we will continue to improve long-term outcomes for women with cervical cancer.

REFERENCES

1. Creaseman WT. New gynecologic cancer staging. Gynecol Oncol 1995;58:157.
2. Burghardt E, Holzer E. Diagnosis and treatment of microinvasive carcinoma of the cervix uteri. Obstet Gynecol 1977;49:641–53.
3. Lohe KJ. Early squamous cell carcinoma of the uterine cervix. I. Definition and histology. Obstet Gynecol 1978;6:10–30.
4. Morris M, Eifel PJ, Lu JD, et al. Pelvic radiation with chemotherapy compared with pelvic and para-aortic radiation for high-risk cervical cancer. N Engl J Med 1999;340:1137.
5. Eifel PJ, Morris M, Wharton JT, Oswald MJ. The influence of tumor size and morphology on the outcome of patients with FIGO stage IB squamous cell carcinoma of the uterine cervix. Int J Radiat Oncol Biol Phys 1994;29:9.
6. Sedlis A, Bundy BN, Rotman MZ, et al. A randomized trial of pelvic radiation therapy versus no further therapy in selected patients with stage IB carcinoma of the cervix after radical hysterectomy and pelvic lymphadenectomy: a Gynecologic Oncology Group study. Gynecol Oncol 1999;73:177–83.
7. Webb GA. The role of ovarian conservation in the treatment of carcinoma of the cervix with radical surgery. Am J Obstet Gynecol 1975;122:476.
8. Anderson B, LaPolla J, Truner D, et al. Ovarian transposition in cervical cancer. Gynecol Oncol 1993;49:206.
9. Parker M, Bosscher J, Barnhill D, Park R. Ovarian management during radical hysterectomy in the premenopausal patient. Obstet Gynecol 1993;82:187.
10. Sedlis A, Sall S, Tsukada Y, et al. Microinvasive carcinoma of the uterine cervix: a clinical-pathologic study. Am J Obstet Gynecol 1979;133:64.
11. Simon NL, Gore H, Shingleton HM, et al. Study of superficially invasive carcinoma of the cervix. Obstet Gynecol 1986;68:19.

12. DePriest PD, van Nagell JR, Powell DE. Microinvasive cervical cancer. Clin Obstet Gynecol 1990;33: 846–51.

13. Copeland LJ, Silva EG, Gershenson DM, et al. Superficially invasive squamous cell carcinoma of the cervix. Gynecol Oncol 1992;45:307.

14. Benson WL, Norris HJ. A critical review of the frequency of lymph node metastasis and death from microinvasive carcinoma of the cervix. Obstet Gynecol 1977;49:632–8.

15. Creasman WT, Zaino RJ, Francis J, et al. Early invasive carcinoma of the cervix (3–5 mm invasive). Risk factors and prognosis. A Gynecologic Oncology Group study. Am J Obstet Gynecol 1998;178:62–5.

16. Burke TW, Hoskins WJ, Heller PB, et al. Prognostic factors associated with radical hysterectomy failure. Gynecol Oncol 1987;26:153–9.

17. Alvarez RD, Soong SJ, Kinney WK, et al. Identification of prognostic factors and risk groups in patients found to have nodal metastasis at the time of radical hysterectomy for early-stage squamous carcinoma of the cervix. Gynecol Oncol 1989;35:130–5.

18. Delgado G, Bundy BN, Fowler WC Jr, et al. A prospective surgical pathological study of stage I squamous carcinoma of the cervix: a Gynecologic Oncology Group study. Gynecol Oncol 1989;35:314–20.

19. Smiley LM, Burke TW, Silva EG, et al. Prognostic factors in stage IB squamous cervical cancer patients with low risk for recurrence. Obstet Gynecol 1991;77:271–5.

20. Mitchell MF, Tortolero-Luna G, Cook E, et al. A randomized clinical trial of cryotherapy, laser vaporization, and loop electrosurgical excision for treatment of squamous intraepithelial lesions of the cervix. Obstet Gynecol 1998;92:737–44.

21. Kennedy AW, Belinson JL, Wirth S, Taylor J. The role of the loop electrosurgical excision procedure in the diagnosis and management of early invasive cervical cancer. Int J Gynecol Cancer 1995;5:117–20.

22. Roman LD, Felix JC, Muderspach LI, et al. Risk of residual invasive disease in women with microinvasive squamous cancer in a conization specimen. Obstet Gynecol 1997;90:759–64.

23. Kolstad P. Followup study of 232 patients with stage IAI and 411 patients with stage IA2 squamous cell carcinoma of the cervix (microinvasive carcinoma). Gynecol Oncol 1989;33:265–72.

24. Morris M, Mitchell MF, Silva EG, et al. Cervical conization as definitive therapy for early invasive squamous carcinoma of the cervix. Gynecol Oncol 1993;51:193–6.

25. Ostor AG, Rome RM. Micro-invasive squamous cell carcinoma of the cervix: a clinico-pathologic study of 200 cases with long-term follow-up. Int J Gynecol Cancer 1994;4:257–64.

26. Tseng CJ, Horng SG, Soong YK, et al. Conservative conisation for microinvasive carcinoma of the cervix. Am J Obstet Gynecol 1997;176:1009–10.

27. Andersen ES, Nielsen K, Pedersen B. Combination laser conization as treatment of microinvasive carcinoma of the uterine cervix. Eur J Gynaecol Oncol 1997;XIX:352–5.

28. Schorge JO, Lee KR, Sheets EE. Prospective management of stage IA_1 cervical adenocarcinoma by conization alone to preserve fertility: a preliminary report. Gynecol Oncol 2000;78:217–20.

29. Seski JC, Abell MR, Morley GW. Microinvasive squamous carcinoma of the cervix. Definition, histologic analysis, late results of treatment. Obstet Gynecol 1977;50:410–4.

30. Lohe KJ, Burghardt E, Hillemanns HG, et al. Early squamous cell carcinoma of the uterine cervix: II. Clinical results of a co-operative study in the management of 419 patients with early stromal invasion and microcarcinoma. Gynecol Oncol 1978;6:31–50.

31. van Nagell JR, Greenwell N, Powell DF, et al. Microinvasive carcinoma of the cervix. Am J Obstet Gynecol 1983;145:981–91.

32. Creasman WT, Fetter BF, Clarke-Pearson DL, et al. Management of stage IA carcinoma of the cervix. Am J Obstet Gynecol 1985;153:164–72.

33. Sevin B-U, Nadji M, Averette HE, et al. Microinvasive carcinoma of the cervix. Cancer 1992;70:2121–8.

34. Hopkins MP, Morley GW. Radical hysterectomy versus radiation therapy for stage Ib squamous cell carcinoma of the cervix. Cancer 1991;68:272–7.

35. Landoni F, Maneo A, Colombo A, et al. Randomised study of radical surgery versus radiotherapy for stage Ib-2a cervical cancer. Lancet 1997;350: 535–40.

36. Shingleton HM, Jones WB, Russell A, et al. Hysterectomy in invasive cervical cancer: a national patterns of care study of the American College of Surgeons. J Am Coll Surg 1996;183:393–400.

37. Piver MS, Rutledge FN, Smith JP. Five classes of extended hysterectomy for women with cervical cancer. Obstet Gynecol 1974;44:265–72.

38. Christopherson WA, Buchsbaum HJ. The influence of pretreatment celiotomy and para-aortic lymphadenectomy on the management of advanced stage squamous cell carcinoma of the cervix. Eur J Gynaecol Oncol 1987;8:90–8.

39. Alvarez RD, Potter ME, Soong SJ, et al. Rationale for using pathologic tumor dimensions and nodal status to subclassify surgically treated stage IB cervical cancer patients. Gynecol Oncol 1991;43:108–12.

40. Chung CK, Nahhas WA, Stryker JA, et al. Analysis of factors contributing to treatment failures in stages IB and IIA carcinoma of the cervix. Am J Obstet Gynecol 1980;138:550–60.

41. Larson DM, Copeland LJ, Stringer A, et al. Recurrent cervical carcinoma after radical hysterectomy. Gynecol Oncol 1988;30:381–7.

42. Fuller AF, Elliott N, Kosloff C, et al. Determinants of increased risk for recurrence in patients undergoing radical hysterectomy for stage IB and IIA carcinoma of the cervix. Gynecol Oncol 1989;33:34.

43. Delgado G, Bundy B, Zaino R, et al. Prospective surgical-pathological study of disease-free interval patients with stage IB squamous cell carcinoma of the cervix: a Gynecologic Oncology Group study. Gynecol Oncol 1990;38:352–7.

44. Peters WA, Liu PY, Barrett RJ, et al. Concurrent chemotherapy and pelvic radiation therapy compared with pelvic radiation therapy alone as adjuvant therapy after radical surgery in high-risk early-stage cancer of the cervix. J Clin Oncol 2000;18:1606–13.

45. Roy M, Plante M. Pregnancies after radical vaginal trachelectomy for early-stage cervical cancer. Am J Obstet Gynecol 1998;179:1491.

46. Covens A, Shaw P, Murphy J, et al. Is radical trachelectomy a safe alternative to radical hysterectomy for patients with stage IIA-B carcinoma of the cervix? Cancer 1999;86:2273–9.

47. Dargent D, Martin X, Sacchetoni A, Mathevet P. Laparoscopic vaginal radical trachelectomy: a treatment to preserve the fertility of cervical carcinoma patients. Cancer 2000;88:1877–82.

48. Chapman JA, Mannel RS, DiSaia PJ, et al. Surgical treatment of unexpected invasive cervical cancer found at total hysterectomy. Obstet Gynecol 1992;80: 931–4.

49. Orr JW Jr, Ball GC, Soong SJ, et al. Surgical treatment of women found to have invasive cervix cancer at the time of total hysterectomy. Obstet Gynecol 1986;68:353–6.

10

Radiation Therapy for Invasive Cervical Cancer

ANUJA JHINGRAN, MD
PATRICIA J. EIFEL, MD

Radiation therapy plays a major role in the management of gynecologic malignancies. Among cervical cancer patients, it is the primary treatment for those having advanced disease.[1,2] It yields cure rates equal to those of radical surgery for early tumors,[3,4] and reduces the risk of local recurrence after surgery in those having high-risk features.[5,6] Radiation techniques in both external beam and in brachytherapy are very important in achieving excellent local control and cure rates without increasing complications. Recently published randomized clinical trials demonstrated a significant improvement in pelvic disease control and survival when concurrent chemotherapy was added to radiation therapy in patients having locally advanced cervical cancer.[7–11] These results have led to one of the most significant changes in the standard treatment of cervical cancer in decades.

In this chapter, results of radical radiation therapy for cervical cancer as well as the technical aspects of radiation therapy will be discussed.

TREATMENT

Microinvasive Carcinoma (Stage Ia)

Carcinoma in situ (CIS) and microinvasive cancer are usually treated using surgery, but patients having severe medical problems or other contraindications to surgical treatment can receive radical radiation therapy. Specifically, Grigsby and Perez[12] reported a 10-year progression-free survival rate of 100 percent in 21 patients having CIS and 34 patients having microinvasive carcinoma treated using irradiation alone. These patients can usually receive brachytherapy alone. Hamberger and colleagues[13] reported that all patients having stage Ia disease and 89 of 93 (96 percent) patients having small stage Ib disease (< 1 cervical quadrant involved) were disease-free 5 years after treatment using intracavitary irradiation alone. However, for most patients having greater than 3 to 5 mm invasion, the risk of lymph node metastasis is sufficient to justify administering external-beam radiation therapy.

Stage Ib and IIa Carcinoma

Early stage Ib cervical carcinomas can be treated equally effectively using combined external-beam irradiation and brachytherapy or radical hysterectomy and bilateral pelvic lymphadenectomy. Both treatment modalities destroy malignant cells in the cervix, paracervical tissues, and regional lymph nodes. The overall survival rate in patients having stage Ib cervical cancer treated using surgery or radiation therapy usually ranges from 80 to 90 percent, suggesting that the two treatments are equally effective (Figure 10–1).[4,14–30] However, biases introduced through patient selection, variations in the definition of stage Ia disease, and variable indications for postoperative radiation therapy or adjuvant hysterectomy confound comparisons of the efficacy of radiation therapy with that of surgery.

The only prospective trial comparing radical surgery with radiation therapy alone was reported in 1997 by Landoni and colleagues.[31] In this study,

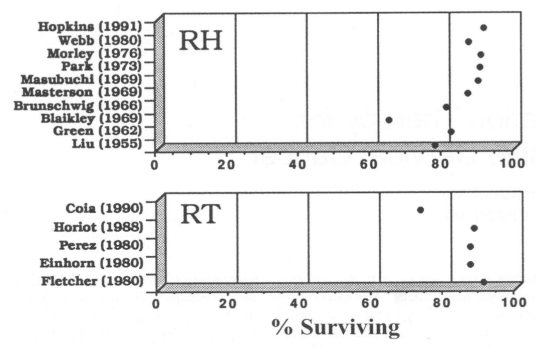

Figure 10–1. Survival rates of patients with FIGO stage I disease treated with radiation therapy (RT) or radical hysterectomy (RH).

patients having stage Ib or IIa disease were randomized between radical hysterectomy and radiation therapy. Patients having high-risk factors after surgery received postoperative radiation therapy. At a median follow-up of 87 months, the 5-year actuarial disease-free survival rate of patients in the surgery and radiation therapy groups was 80 percent and 82 percent, respectively, in those having tumors that were 4 cm in diameter or smaller and 63 percent and 57 percent, respectively, in those having larger tumors. The authors reported a significantly higher rate of complications in the patients who underwent initial surgery; they attributed this finding to the frequent use of combined modality treatment in this group.

For patients having stage Ib1 squamous carcinomas, the choice of treatment is based primarily on patient preference, anesthetic and surgical risks, physician preference, and understanding of the nature and incidence of complications of radiation therapy and hysterectomy. The overall rate of major complications of surgery is similar to that of radiation therapy, although urinary tract complications tend to be more common after surgical treatment, and bowel complications are more common after radiation therapy. In general, surgery is often chosen for younger patients to preserve ovarian function and hopefully reduce vaginal shortening, while radiation therapy is selected for older postmenopausal women to avoid the morbidity of a major surgical procedure.

Radical Radiation Therapy

Radical radiation therapy achieves excellent survival and pelvic disease control rates in patients having stage Ib cervical cancers. For example, Eifel and colleagues[4] reported a 5-year disease-specific survival rate of 90 percent in 701 patients who received irradiation alone for stage Ib1 squamous tumors less than 4 cm in diameter. The disease-specific survival rate was 86 percent and 67 percent, respectively, in patients having tumors measuring 4 to 4.9 cm and greater than or equal to 5 cm (Figure 10–2). Perez and colleagues[26] and Lowrey and colleagues[15] reported similarly excellent disease-control rates in patients having stage Ib tumors treated using radiation therapy. In addition, the survival rate in patients having International Federation of Gynecology and Obstetrics (FIGO) stage IIa disease treated using irradiation ranged from 70 to 85 percent and was strongly correlated with tumor size.[15,26,32] For

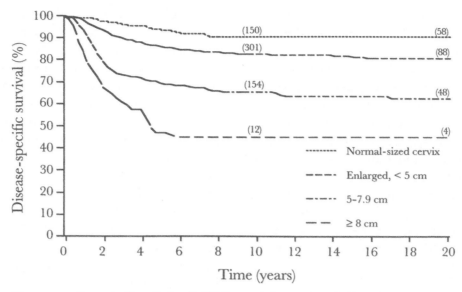

Figure 10–2. Disease-specific survival in patients with FIGO stage I disease treated with radiation therapy by cervical tumor diameter. Numbers in parentheses represent the number of patients remaining at risk at 10 or 20 years. (Reproduced with permission from Eifel PJ, Morris M, Wharton JT, Oswald MJ. The influence of tumor size and morphology on the outcome of patients with FIGO stage IB squamous cell carcinoma of the uterine cervix. Int J Radiat Oncol Biol Phys 1994;29:9–16.)

patients having bulky tumors, recent studies suggested that results may be improved further with concurrent administration of chemotherapy.[10,11]

Cervical cancer patients usually receive a combination of external-beam irradiation to the pelvis and brachytherapy. Each component is very critical in the treatment of cervical cancer, and clinicians should be able to balance the components in different ways for each patient. Even small tumors that involve multiple quadrants of the cervix require delivering at least 80 to 85 Gy to point A through a combination of external-beam irradiation and brachytherapy. With these small tumors, there is still a risk of nodal spread, and care must be taken to adequately cover the obturator, external iliac, low common iliac, and presacral nodes in the external-beam field.

Irradiation Followed by Hysterectomy

In 1969, Durrance and colleagues[33] reported that most central recurrences occur in patients having bulky ($\geq$ 6 cm in diameter) endocervical tumors and recommended adjuvant hysterectomy for these patients, if there was no palpable parametrial disease following initial external-beam irradiation. Many groups subsequently adopted this policy as their standard treatment of bulky stage Ib tumors of the cervix. However, a 1992 update from the same institution suggested that the differences observed in earlier reports may have resulted from a tendency to select patients having massive tumors (8 cm in diameter) or clinically positive nodes for treatment using irradiation alone. When these patients were excluded, the pelvic disease control rates using the two approaches were similar.[34] Since that time, several studies have shown that with adequate radiation doses (> 80 Gy to point A), adjuvant hysterectomy does not add to pelvic disease control and/or survival in patients having bulky Ib disease.[4,35,36]

Additionally, in 1991, the Gynecologic Oncology Group (GOG) completed a prospective randomized trial of irradiation with or without extrafascial hysterectomy in patients having stage Ib tumors that were 4 cm or more in diameter. Preliminary analysis demonstrated no significant improvement in the survival rate of patients who had an adjuvant hysterectomy.[37] In fact, the complication rate of combined therapy may be higher, particularly if radical hysterectomy is performed after high-dose radiation therapy.[34,36,38] Specifically, Mendenhall and colleagues[36] reported an 18 percent rate of major complications at 6 years for patients who underwent adjuvant hysterectomy, compared with 7 percent for patients who received irradiation alone ($p = .027$).

The addition of concurrent chemotherapy may further reduce the margin of improvement using adjuvant hysterectomy.[10]

Therefore, there is no clear evidence that adjuvant hysterectomy improves the outcome in patients having bulky stage Ib or IIa tumors, though many clinicians continue to recommend combined treatment.[39] When combined treatment is planned, the dose of intracavitary irradiation is usually reduced by 15 to 25 percent. Also, a type I extrafascial hysterectomy is usually performed, which removes the cervix, adjacent tissues, and a small cuff of the upper vagina in a plane outside the pubocervical fascia. This procedure involves minimal disturbance of the bladder and ureters.

Postoperative Radiation Therapy

In a review of the results of several surgical series, 72 percent of the recurrences following radical hysterectomy for cervical carcinoma only involved the pelvis, while 42 percent were in the pelvis alone.[40] Despite numerous published reports addressing the issue of postoperative radiation therapy in this group of patients, its role is still being defined. Patients having positive or close surgical margins definitely need to undergo postoperative radiation therapy to achieve local control. Many investigators have reported a decrease in pelvic recurrences after postoperative radiation therapy in patients having high-risk factors, such as extensive cervical involvement, positive lymph nodes, lymph-vascular space invasion, and adenocarcinoma. Many studies[5] (Table 10–1) have demonstrated that the incidence of pelvic relapse can be decreased by radiation therapy, but the influence on survival has been difficult to determine.

The GOG recently reported the results of a randomized prospective trial that looked at postoperative radiation therapy in patients having intermediate-risk factors.[6] Two hundred and seventy-seven patients having negative pelvic nodes and local high-risk factors, such as greater than one-third stromal invasion, lymphatic space involvement, or a clinical tumor diameter of at least 4 cm, were randomized to postoperative irradiation or observation. Overall, there was a 47 percent reduction in the risk of recurrence with adjuvant radiation therapy ($p = .008$). Unfortu-

nately, this was only a preliminary analysis that had a very short follow-up for a significance level to be assigned to the overall survival comparison. However, there were 18 deaths (13 percent) in the radiation therapy arm versus 30 (21 percent) in the radical hysterectomy–only arm.

The overall risk of major complications (particularly small-bowel obstruction) is probably increased in patients who receive postoperative pelvic irradiation, but inconsistencies in the methods of analysis and the small number of patients in most series make it very difficult to analyze this information.[31,40–46] In particular, Bandy and colleagues[47] reported that patients who received irradiation after hysterectomy had more long-term problems, specifically, bladder contraction and instability, than did those who underwent surgery alone.

Stage IIb, III, and IVa Tumors

Radiation therapy is the primary local treatment for most patients having locoregional advanced cervical carcinoma. Five-year survival rates of 65 to 75 percent, 35 to 50 percent, and 15 to 20 percent have been reported in patients who received radiation therapy alone for stage IIb, IIIb, and IV tumors, respectively.[1,15,26,32,48,49] In a French Cooperative Group study of 1,875 patients who received radiation therapy according to Fletcher's guidelines, Barillot and colleagues[32] (Figure 10–3) reported a 5-year survival rate of 70 percent, 45 percent, and

Table 10–1. RECURRENCE SITES IN 193 PATIENTS TREATED WITH RADICAL HYSTERECTOMY (WITH OR WITHOUT RADIATION THERAPY)

Site	RT (%)	No RT (%)
Pelvis	10.6	18.5
C	6.4	5.5
PW	4.2	13.0
DM	18.4	6.2
Both	8.1	14.4
Unknown	4.2	–
Total	38.3 (18/47)	39 (57/146)

Reproduced with permission from Morrow CP. Is pelvic radiation beneficial in the postoperative management of stage IB squamous cell carcinoma of the cervix with pelvic node metastases treated by radical hysterectomy and pelvic lymphadenectomy. Gynecol Oncol 1980;10:105–10.
RT = radiation therapy; C = central; PW = pelvic wall; DM = distant metastasis.

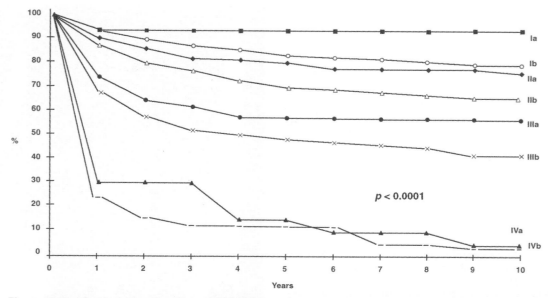

Figure 10–3. Survival rates of patients with all FIGO stages treated with definitive radiation therapy according to Fletcher's guidelines. (Reproduced with permission from Barillot I, Horiot JC, Pigneux J, et al. Carcinoma of the intact uterine cervix treated with radiotherapy alone: a French cooperataive study: update and multivariage analysis of prognostic factors. Int J Radiat Oncol Biol Phys 1997;38:969–78.)

10 percent in patients having stage IIb, IIIb, and IVa tumors, respectively.

The success of radiation therapy depends on a careful balance between external-beam radiation therapy and brachytherapy, optimizing the dose to tumor and normal tissue, and the overall duration of treatment. The addition of concurrent chemotherapy to radiation therapy consisting of cisplatin-containing regimens may further improve local control and survival.[7,8,10] Several reports recently have shown that magnetic resonance imaging (MRI) at the end of external-beam radiation is useful in determining the extent of regression and response to radiation therapy, and the response may be predictive for local control[50–52] (Figures 10–4 and 10–5). This may be helpful in the future in identifying patients who may benefit from additional therapy, such as surgery or chemotherapy, after definitive therapy.

TECHNICAL ASPECTS OF RADIOTHERAPEUTIC MANAGEMENT

Traditionally, the treatment of cervical cancer using irradiation involves some combination of external-beam and intracavitary irradiation, whether at a low- or high-dose rate. The goal of treatment is to balance these two elements in a way that optimizes the ratio of tumor control to treatment complications.

External-Beam Radiation Therapy

External-beam radiation therapy is used to (1) shrink bulky endocervical tumors to bring them within a higher-dose portion of the intracavitary radiation therapy (ICRT) dose distribution, (2) improve tumor geometry by shrinking exocervical tumors that may distort anatomy and prevent optimal brachytherapy, and (3) sterilize disease (paracentral and nodal) that receives an inadequate dose using ICRT. Therefore, patients having locally advanced disease or bulky tumors usually receive external-beam radiation therapy first, followed by ICRT. These patients should be examined weekly for tumor response to determine the best time to begin intracavitary treatments. Some practitioners prefer to maximize the brachytherapy component of treatment by performing the first ICRT course as soon as the tumor has responded sufficiently to permit an acceptable intracavitary placement (with very bulky tumors, this may still require 40+ Gy). Pelvic irradiation is subsequently delivered using a central block. This technique delivers a higher total paracentral dose but relies greatly on the complex match between the

Figure 10–4. *A*, Pretreatment sagittal MRI of a patient with IIIb squamous cell carcinoma of the cervix. The small arrow shows a large fibroid and the large arrow points to the tumor. *B*, Same patient, sagittal MRI after 4,500 cGy and concurrent chemotherapy consisting of weekly cisplatin. Patient had a good response. Again, the small arrows point to fibroids in the uterus. *C*, Same patient, sagittal MRI three weeks after completion of treatment including external-beam radiation, two intracavitary implants, and concurrent chemotherapy. Shows further response of the tumor. Again, the small arrows point to fibroids in the uterus.

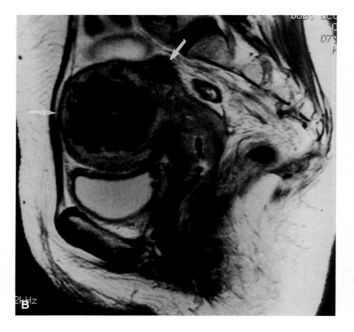

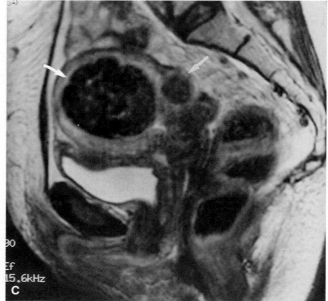

brachytherapy dose distribution and the border of the central shield. This may result in overdoses to medial structures, such as the ureters[53] or underdoses to posterior uterosacral disease.[54] Some practitioners prefer to give an initial dose of 40 to 45 Gy to the whole pelvis, which provides a homogeneous distribution to the entire region at risk for micro-

scopic disease and allows somewhat more shrinkage of the central disease prior to brachytherapy. Both approaches have been used for several decades and, when optimally applied, appear to provide excellent tumor control and acceptable complication rates. However, administering external-beam doses of more than 40 to 50 Gy to the central pelvis tends to

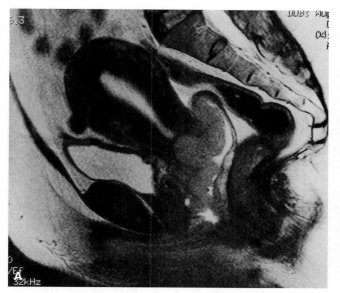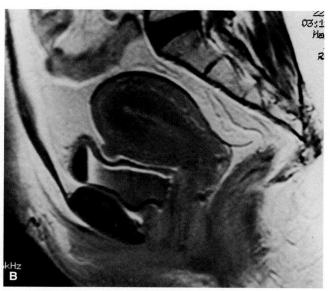

Figure 10–5. *A,* Pretreatment sagittal MRI of a patient with stage Ib2 disease. The tumor was exophytic coming down the vagina but not involving the vagina, as can be seen with this MRI. Therefore, it was staged as Ib2 and not IIIa. *B,* Same patient after 4,500 cGy and concurrent chemotherapy consisting of cisplatin and 5-fluorouracil. Sagittal MRI shows response of the tumor.

compromise the dose deliverable to the paracentral tissues and increase the risk of late complications.[1] There is a very steep increase in the complication rate when the external-beam contribution to the central pelvis exceeds 50 Gy according to the experience at The University of Texas M.D. Anderson Cancer Center[1] (Figure 10–6).

Carcinoma in situ and stage Ia1 disease respond well to ICRT alone. Additionally, some patients having FIGO stage Ia2 disease may also receive ICRT alone, particularly if they have relative contraindications to external-beam irradiation. However, for most patients having greater than 3- to 5-mm invasion, the risk of lymph node metastasis is sufficient to justify external-beam irradiation.

Many physicians prescribe a 1- to 2-week break between external-beam irradiation and the first intracavitary treatment to allow for tumor regression. However, such breaks should be discouraged, and every effort should be made to complete the entire treatment in less than 7 to 8 weeks. In our institution, the first intracavitary treatment is almost always performed within 1 week of the completion of external-beam irradiation (usually within 1 to 4 days). To minimize the duration of treatment of pelvic-wall disease, boosts are delivered during the 1-week break between the two intracavitary treatments. However, the favorable results

documented in reports of large single-institution studies have been based on policies that dictate a relatively short overall treatment duration (< 8 weeks),[55] and several studies of patients having locally advanced cervical cancer have suggested that longer treatment courses are associated with decreased pelvic disease control and survival rates.[56–60]

Technique

High-energy photons (15 to 18 MV) are generally preferred for pelvic treatment because they spare superficial tissues that are unlikely to have tumor involvement. With these high-energy photons, the whole pelvis may be treated using either a four-field (anterior, posterior, and right and left lateral) technique or a two-field (anterior and posterior) technique (Figure 10–7). However, when only 4- to 6-MV photons are available, the four-field technique minimizes the dose administered to subcutaneous tissues and usually permits some shielding of the anterior small bowel and the posteroinferior rectum. Some physicians prefer the four-field technique for all patients and report that the rectum and bladder as well as the bowel are spared more (Figure 10–8). However, if a lateral field is used, one must be careful not to shield potential sites of disease. In particu-

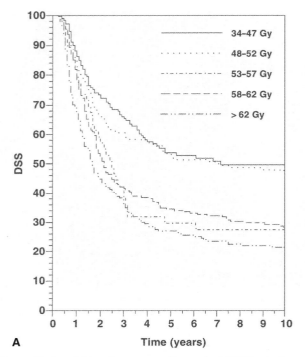

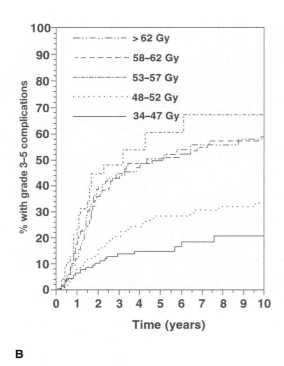

A

B

Figure 10–6. *A*, The disease-specific survival (DSS) rate for patients who completed treatment that was given with curative intent according to the dose of external-beam therapy given to the central pelvis. *B*, The rate of major complications (grades 3 to 5) for patients who completed treatment that was given with curative intent according to the dose of external-beam therapy given to the central pelvis. (Reproduced with permission from Logsdon MD, Eifel PJ. FIGO IIIB squamous cell carcinoma of the cervix: an analysis of prognostic factors emphasizing the balance between external beam and intracavitary radiation therapy. Int J Radiat Oncol Biol Phys 1999;43:763–75.)

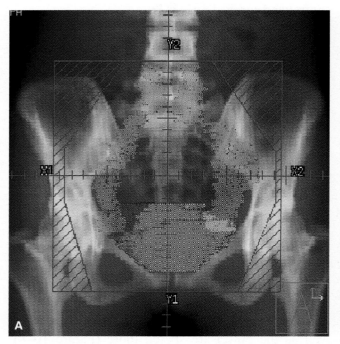

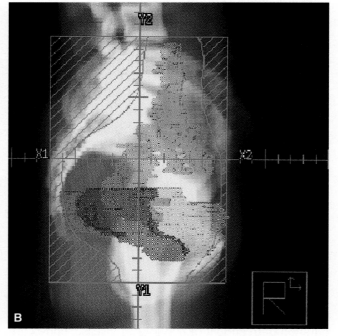

Figure 10–7. *A*, Typical anterior field used in the treatment of cervical cancer. *B*, Typical lateral field used in the treatment of cervical cancer. Care must be taken not to shield the cervical disease, particularly with posterior shielding on the lateral fields. The cervix with margin is in red, rectum is blue, bladder is yellow, and the nodes are shown in aquamarine.

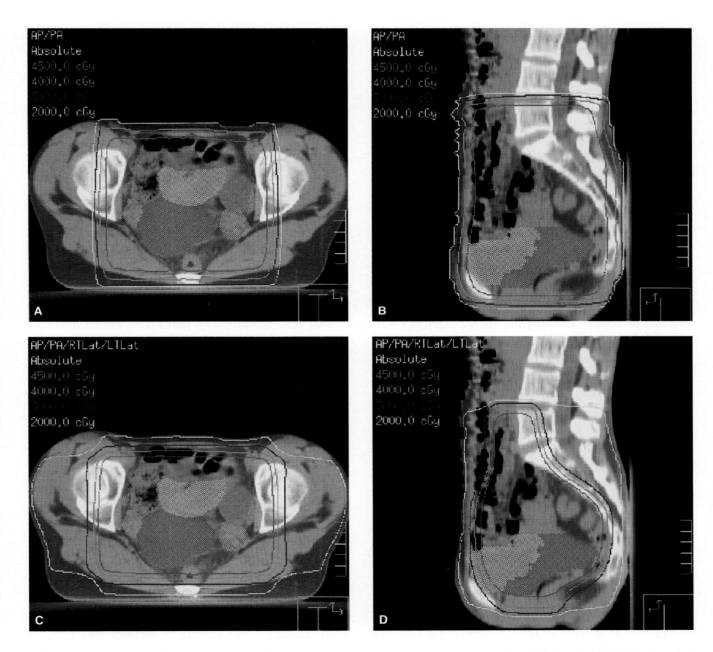

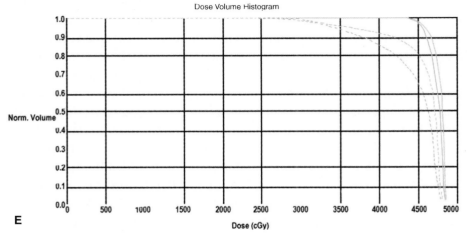

Figure 10–8. *A* and *B*, This shows the dose distribution to the pelvis and tumor using the two-field technique (anterior/posterior [AP/PA]) versus *C* and *D*, four-field (AP/PA and lateral fields). *E*, Dose-volume histogram comparing the dose to the rectum and bladder when using AP/PA versus four-field. The AP/PA is shown in solid lines, and the four-field is shown with dash lines. The rectum is sky-blue and the bladder is light orange.

lar, in the past, the "standard" anterior and posterior borders of the lateral fields were placed in a way that shielded regions at risk for microscopic regional disease in the presacral and external iliac nodes and presacral and cardinal ligaments. Also, the borders sometimes underestimated the posterior extent of central cervical disease in patients having bulky tumors.[61-63] As seen in Figure 10–8, if the patient is thin or the tumor is bulky, one does not spare very much of the normal tissues using the four-field technique but can take the risk of sparing the tumor.

The most inferior extent of disease can be determined by placing radiopaque seeds in the cervix or at the lowest extent of vaginal disease. We generally place the lower border of the field midpubis or 4 cm below the lowest vaginal disease indicated by the radiopaque seed. The upper border is placed at L4 to L5, unless the para-aortic nodes are deemed to be at risk, while the lateral borders of the anterior and posterior fields are placed at least 1 cm lateral to the pelvic margins (see Figure 10–7). Lymphangiograms are helpful in tailoring blocks, particularly at the anterior border of lateral fields. Also, MRI and computed tomography (CT) scans can improve clinicians' understanding of uterine position and thus help them design anterior and posterior borders. In fact, some investigators have argued that these scans should be obtained routinely for patients having bulky disease to avoid errors in the lateral-field design.[64] However, when all these factors are considered, differences in the volume treated using the four-field or high-energy two-field technique may be small (see Figure 10–8). For this reason, some clinicians prefer to use the simpler technique for patients having bulky tumors.

A course of 40 Gy delivered to the whole pelvis and two 48-hour intracavitary systems (40 to 45 Gy to point A) usually deliver 52 to 56 Gy to the pelvic wall. When the patient has grossly involved nodes on a lymphangiogram or CT scan, extracapsular extension or unresected nodal disease, or palpable pelvic-wall disease remaining after the 40-Gy dose is delivered, a boost up to 60 to 62 Gy should be given to these high-risk regions (including the ICRT contribution). Nodal boosts are designed to include the nodes with a margin of 1 to 2 cm while taking care not to overlap with the intracavitary system.

Intensity-modulated radiation therapy may be used to boost doses to large pelvic nodes (up to approximately 70 Gy) to a very tightly defined volume (Figures 10–9 and 10–10).

Role of Para-aortic Irradiation

Numerous small series of patients having documented para-aortic node involvement have demonstrated that some patients have a long-term disease-free survival duration.[65-73] Patients having microscopic involvement have a better survival duration than those having gross involvement do, but even 10 to 15 percent of patients having gross lymphadenopathy have disease that appears to be curable using aggressive management. Specifically, a 1991 study by Cunningham and colleagues[65] reported a 48 percent 5-year survival rate in patients who had para-aortic node involvement discovered on exploration for radical hysterectomy that was subsequently aborted. This experience with patients who had small, radiocontrollable primary disease demonstrates that patients having para-aortic node metastases can often have a cure if their primary disease can be sterilized.

Two randomized prospective trials have addressed the role of prophylactic para-aortic irradiation in patients not having known para-aortic node involvement.[74,75] One of these studies was the one conducted by the Radiation Therapy Oncology Group in which 367 patients having primary stage IIb or stage Ib or IIa tumors greater than 4 cm in diameter were randomly assigned to receive either standard pelvic radiation therapy or extended-field radiation therapy before brachytherapy.[75] No consistent method was used to evaluate the para-aortic nodes in this study. Among the 337 evaluable patients, the absolute survival rate was significantly better in those who received therapy using extended fields than in those treated using standard pelvic radiation therapy (67 percent versus 55 percent at 5 years; $p = .02$). There was not a significant difference in disease-free survival ($p = .56$).

Both studies described above revealed an increased rate of enteric complications in patients who received therapy using extended fields. A variety of techniques have been used to treat extended fields to try to decrease the amount of bowel in the field. One such technique is to treat a single field encom-

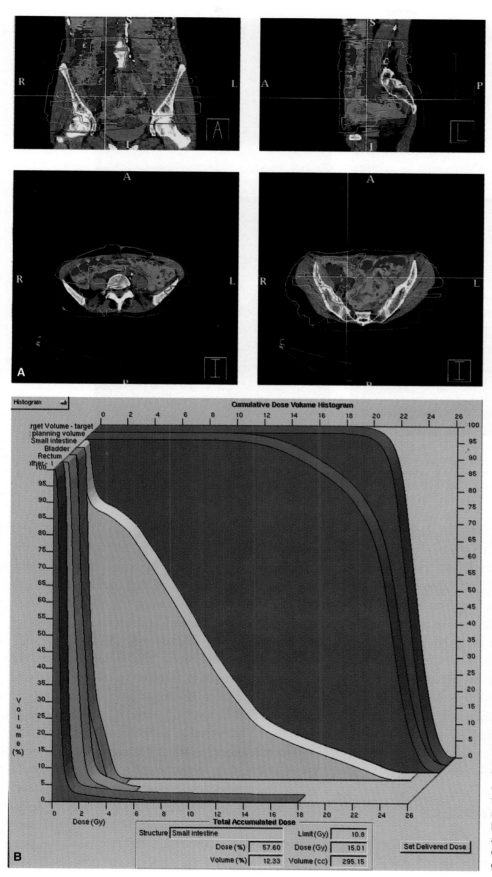

Figure 10–9. *A*, Plan showing a node boost using intensity-modulated radiation therapy (IMRT) in a patient who already received 4,500 cGy with external-beam irradiation and will receive two brachytherapy treatments. Twenty Gy was given to the node while minimizing dose to normal tissue. The blue is the node or the target volume, green is the small bowel. The pink line is the 20 Gy isodose line, and the green line is the 15 Gy line. *B*, Dose volume histogram showing the dose to different structures on the plan of the patient receiving nodal boost. Blue is the target volume or the nodal volume, yellow is the small intestine, pink is the bladder, green is the rectum, and purple is other structures. As can be seen, the node is getting 20 Gy, but 50 percent of the small intestine is only getting 10 Gy and only 16 percent of the small intestine is getting 16 Gy. The bladder and rectum, which will also get a dose from the brachytherapy procedure, are being limited to 50 percent, getting 2 Gy.

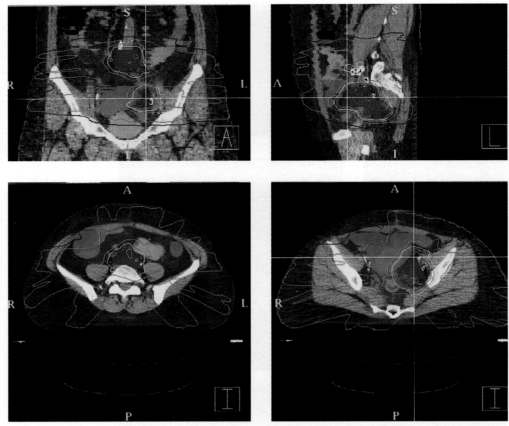

Figure 10–10. Plan with intesity-modulated radiation therapy (IMRT) for a patient who had a cut-through hysterectomy with residual parametrial disease and nodal disease. She initially received 4,500 cGy to an extended field, and then received further therapy to the residual disease using IMRT. The parametrial disease was taken to a total dose of 69 Gy, and the para-aortic node was taken to a total dose of 66 Gy. Pink isodose line is 24 Gy, yellow isodose line is 19 Gy, and the light blue line is 5 Gy.

passing the pelvis and para-aortic nodes with 18-MV photons using anterior-posterior fields or the four-field technique. The width of the "chimney" portion of the lateral field should not be less than 5 cm. However, the use of three-dimensional conformal radiation therapy for the para-aortic nodes may reduce the dose delivered to normal tissues even further (Figure 10–11), thus reducing enteric complications. However, conformal treatment of the pelvis should be done with caution because once the primary site, paracervical tissues, and various sites of primary and secondary regional drainage are considered, the target volume encompasses most of the pelvis.

Brachytherapy Technique

The importance of ICRT in the treatment of cervical cancer should not be underestimated. Although external-beam radiation therapy plays a critical role in sterilizing pelvic wall disease and improving tumor geometry, too much reliance on external-beam radiation therapy will compromise the chance for central disease control and increase the risk of complications.[1] In a previous study, Fletcher[76] described three conditions that should be met for successful intracavitary therapy: (1) the geometry of the radioactive sources must prevent underdosed regions on and around the cervix, (2) an adequate dose must be delivered to the paracervical areas, and (3) mucosal tolerance must be respected. Although some clinicians have proposed a number of variations of the low-dose-rate intracavitary brachytherapy techniques practised at The University of Texas M.D. Anderson Cancer Center, Fletcher's conditions continue to dictate the character, intensity, and timing of brachytherapy for cervical cancer.

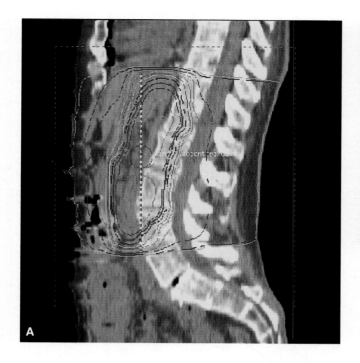

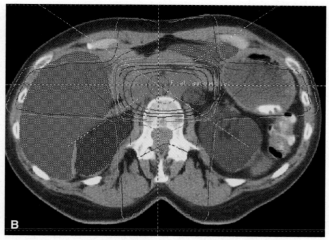

Figure 10–11. Patient receiving three-dimensional conforming therapy to the para-aortic nodes to a total dose of 45 Gy using six-field technique. *A,* Lateral view of plan. *B,* Transverse slice of the treatment field. This technique spares the small bowel. The red line is the 45 Gy line, orange line is the 30 Gy, and the dark green line is the 25 Gy isodose line.

Brachytherapy is usually delivered using afterloading applicators that are placed in the uterine cavity and vagina. Though a variety of different intracavitary applicators have been used, the most popular ones in the United States are variations of the Fletcher-Suit-Delclos low-dose-rate system.[39,77–80] In this system, the intrauterine tandem and vaginal applicators are carefully positioned, usually with the patient under anesthesia, to provide an optimal relationship between the system and the adjacent tumor and normal tissues. The tandem should be placed midway between the bladder and the sacrum (ideally about one-third of the way from the S1 and S2 vertebrae to the tip of the pubis) (Figure 10–12). Also, the ovoids should be separated by 0.5 to 1 cm, admitting the flange (on the tandem) in the space between (see Figure 10–12). To optimize the ratio of the dose at depth to the vaginal mucosal dose, the largest ovoids that will fit comfortably should be used. In addition, the axis of the tandem should be centered between the ovoids on the anterior view and usually should bisect them on the lateral view (see Figure 10–12). Vaginal packing is used to hold the tandem and colpostats in place and to maximize the distance between the sources and the bladder and rectum (Figure 10–13). Furthermore, radiographs should always be taken in the operating room at the time of the insertion, and

the system should be repositioned and repacked if it is suboptimal (Figures 10–14 and 10–15). Ultrasonography in the operating room may be helpful in determining the position of the tandem in the uterine cavity as well as where it is in relation to the bladder and the rectum (Figure 10–16). Encapsulated radioactive sources are then inserted into the applicators after the patient has returned to her hospital bed, reducing the exposure of clinical personnel to the sources during applicator placement. Finally, although ^{226}Ra (radium-226) was used in most patients before the 1980s, it has gradually been replaced by ^{137}Cs (cesium-137), which has a similar dose distribution and avoids the radiation protection problems caused by the radon gas byproduct of radium decay.

Dose

Ideal placement of the uterine tandem and vaginal ovoids produces a pear-shaped distribution, delivering a high-radiation dose to the cervix and paracervical tissues and a reduced dose to the rectum and bladder. However, the treatment dose has been specified in a number of ways, making it very difficult to compare experiences. Therefore, there is no inherently correct way to specify the extremely inhomogeneous dose distribution delivered using an intra-

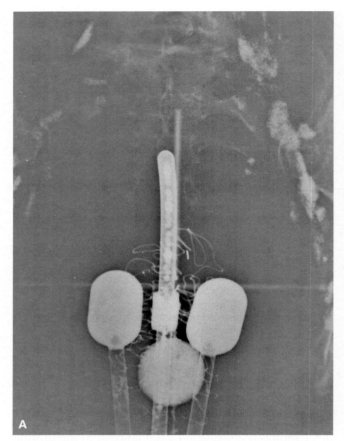

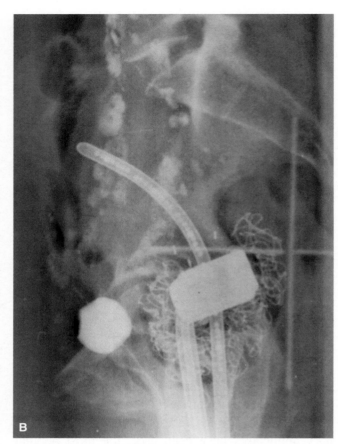

Figure 10–12. *A,* Anterior (AP) and *B,* lateral radiographs of tandem and colpostat insertion. Radiopaque seeds are placed into the cervix. Anteriorly and posteriorly, packing is used to keep the system in place and to displace the rectum and bladder away from the system.

cavitary system. In the United States, the paracentral doses are most frequently expressed at a single point (point A). Point A is placed 2 cm lateral and 2 cm superior to the external cervical os in the central plane of the intracavitary system. This measurement bears no consistent relationship with the tumor or target volume but lies approximately at the crossing of the ureter and uterine artery.

In 1985, the International Commission on Radiation Units and Measurements (ICRU) recommended in the ICRU Report 38 that reference points like point A not be used because "such points are located in a region where the dose gradient is high and any inaccuracy in the determination of distance results in large uncertainties in the absorbed doses evaluated at these points."[81] Instead, it recommended the use of total reference air kerma expressed in uGy at 1 m, as an alternative to milligram-hours, which allows for the use of various radionuclides.[81] The ICRU also defined reference points for estimating the dose deliv-

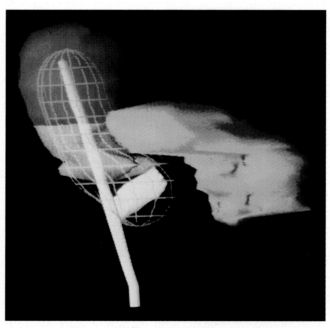

Figure 10–13. Digital view of a lateral film showing how the rectum can fall on top of the colpostats next to the tandem, increasing the dose to the rectum.

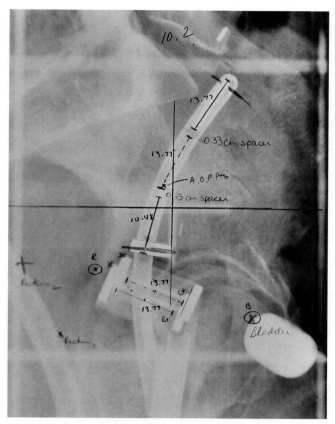

Figure 10–14. Although the rectal and bladder doses in this insertion were within limits, on close inspection, it is obvious that the tandem is not in the uterus.

ered to the bladder and rectum (Figure 10–17). These points have been widely, though not universally, accepted. Although normal tissue reference points provide useful information about the dose delivered to a portion of normal tissue, several studies have demonstrated that they consistently underestimate the maximum dose delivered to those tissues.[82–84]

Other units of measure, such as milligram-hours or mgRaEq-hours, are proportional to the dose of radiation at relatively distant points from the system; therefore, they give a sense of the dose delivered to the whole pelvis. Whichever system of dose specification is used, however, emphasis should always be placed on optimizing the relationship between the intracavitary applicators and the cervical tumor and other pelvic tissues. Source strengths and positions should be carefully chosen to provide optimal tumor coverage without exceeding normal tissue tolerance. Also, an effort should always be made to deliver at least 85 Gy (using low-dose-rate brachytherapy) to

point A in patients having bulky central disease. If the intracavitary placement has been optimized, this can usually be accomplished without exceeding a dose of 75 Gy delivered to the bladder reference point or 70 Gy delivered to the rectal reference point, doses that are usually associated with an acceptably low risk of major complications.[85,86] In addition, the dose delivered to the surface of the lateral wall of the apical vagina should not usually exceed 130 to 140 Gy.[87]

Dose Rate

In the past, clinicians have regarded the radiobiologic advantages of low-dose-rate intracavitary treatment (usually delivery of 40 to 60 cGy/h to point A) (Figure 10–18) as major factors contributing to the success of cervical cancer treatment. These low-dose rates permit repair of sublethal cellular injury, preferentially spare normal tissues, and optimize the therapeutic ration. In an effort to reduce the hospitalization stay of 3 to 4 days needed to deliver an appropriate dose in low-dose-rate irradiation, some investigators have explored the use of intermediate-dose-rate brachytherapy (80 to 100 cGy/h). However, in a randomized trial, this increase in dose rate led to an increase in complication rates, even after compensatory dose reductions.[88]

During the past two decades, computer technology has made it possible to deliver brachytherapy at very-high-dose rates (< 100 cGy/min) using a high-activity ^{60}Co (Cobalt-60) or ^{192}Ir (iridium-192) source and remote afterloading. High-dose-rate intracavitary therapy is now being used for radical treatment of cervical cancer by a number of groups, including several in Japan, Canada, and Europe and, more recently, some in the United States.[89–97] Clinicians have found this approach attractive because it does not require hospitalization and may be more convenient for the patient and the physician. However, unless it is heavily fractionated, high-dose-rate brachytherapy loses the radiobiologic advantages of low-dose-rate treatment, potentially narrowing the therapeutic window for a complication-free cure.[98,99] Additionally, advocates of high-dose-rate treatment disagree about the number of fractions and the total dose that should be delivered. Published reports have suggested that survival rates produced by high-dose-rate treatment are roughly similar to those

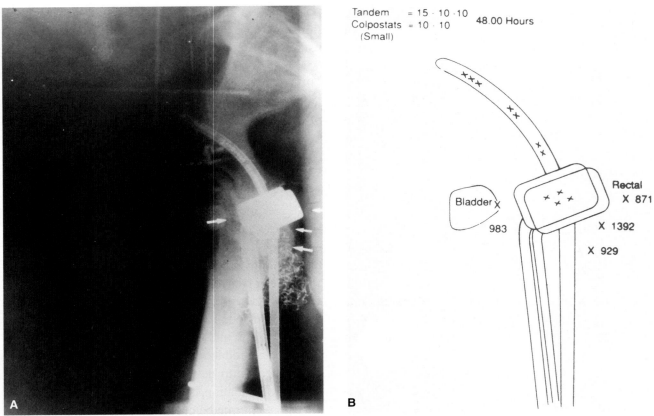

Figure 10–15. *A*, Lateral radiograph taken in the operating room of a patient who had a tandem and colpostats placement. As can be seen in this radiograph, the posterior packing is not adequate, allowing the rectum to slip in behind the colpostats. *B*, Same patient, showing rectal and bladder doses that would be delivered if the patient were treated without repacking the system. The loading of the tandem and colpostats are typical for the treatment of cervical cancer. This figure demonstrates the importance of adequate posterior packing.

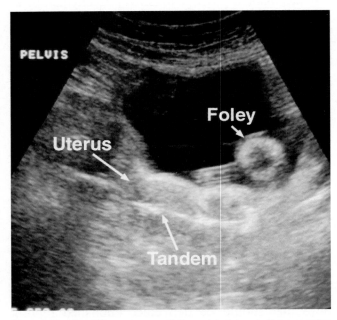

Figure 10–16. Ultrasonogram of the pelvis taken in the operating room showing the tandem in the uterus, and its position in regard to the bladder and the rectum.

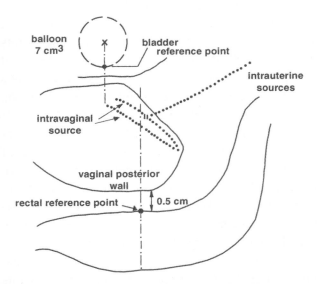

Figure 10–17. Point definitions for bladder and rectum reference points from ICRU #38. (Reproduced with permission from International Commission on Radiation Units and Measurements. Dose and volume specification for reporting intracavitary therapy in gynecology. Vol. 38. Bethesda, MD: International Commission on Radiation Units and Meaurements; 1985. p. 1–23.)

achieved using traditional low-dose-rate treatment, but these reports are difficult to compare because of the same potential problems of selection bias that confound other nonrandomized comparisons.[95,99] Also, many of the retrospective reviews provided incomplete descriptions of tumor and treatment detail.[95] Two purported randomized trials[94,96] also have been criticized for methodologic flaws. The use of high-dose-rate brachytherapy for cervical cancer continues to be a source of controversy.

Interstitial Brachytherapy

Several groups have advocated the use of interstitial perineal template brachytherapy in patients whose poor anatomy or bulky tumor may compromise the quality of intracavitary treatment. These implants are usually placed transperineally, guided by a Lucite template that encourages parallel placement of hollow needles that penetrate the cervix and paracervical spaces; the needles are usually loaded using ^{192}Ir. Advocates describe the relatively homogeneous dose, the ease of inserting implants in patients whose uterus is difficult to probe, and the ability to place sources directly into the parametrium as the advantages of using this method. Although the early reports were enthusiastic in describing these theoretic advantages and high initial local control rates, they had a very small number of patients and too short a follow-up to provide significant long-term survival rates.[100-104]

In 1986, Syed and colleagues[104] reported a projected 5-year survival rate of 53 percent in 26 patients having stage IIIb disease. Prior to that, Martinez and colleagues[103] reported an 83 percent local control rate in 37 patients having stage IIb-IIIb disease treated at Stanford University and the Mayo Clinic. However, the survival results from two more recent reports were disappointing. In a review of the combined experience of Stanford University and the Joint Center,[105] the 3-year disease-free survival rate in patients having stages IIb and IIIb disease was 36 percent and 18 percent, respectively, while the local control rate was 22 percent and 44 percent, respectively. Also, in patients having local control, the rate of complications requiring surgical intervention was high. A report of the Irvine experience

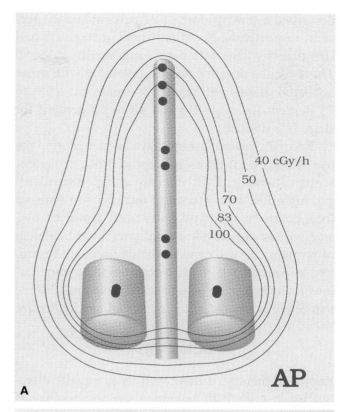

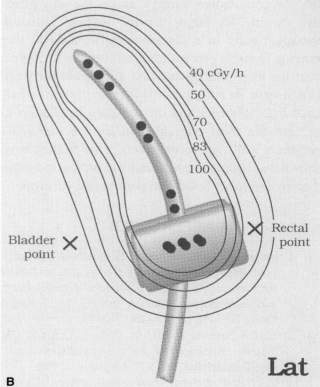

Figure 10–18. Typical dose distribution of a tandem and colpostats loaded with cesium. The loading of the tandem is 15, 10, 10 mgRaEq of cesium and the loading of the colpostats are 10 and 10 mgRaEq of cesium. *A*, Anterior view. *B*, Lateral view.

described a survival rate of 21 percent and 29 percent, respectively, in patients having stage IIb and IIIb disease, also with high complication rates.[106] These results do not compare favorably with those achieved using intracavitary treatment (65 to 75 percent for stage IIb and 40 to 50 percent for stage IIIb disease).

Recently, several groups have been exploring the use of transrectal ultrasonographic, MRI, or laparoscopic guidance,[107–109] interstitial hyperthermia,[110] and high-dose-rate interstitial therapy[111] to improve local control and complication rates. However, outside an investigational setting, interstitial treatment of primary cervical cancers should probably be limited to patients who cannot accommodate intrauterine brachytherapy or who have distal vaginal disease that requires a boost using interstitial brachytherapy.

SUMMARY

Radiation therapy, if done well, is as equally effective against small Ib squamous cell carcinomas of the cervix as radical surgery, and is the only effective therapy for larger tumors. Radical radiation therapy results in a disease-specific survival rate ranging from 90 percent for small tumors to 50 percent for stage IIIb disease and 20 percent for stage IVa disease. In addition, it is very important to balance external-beam and intracavitary irradiation to achieve the most optimal plan for the individual patient. Finally, in recent years, five studies have shown that adding chemotherapy to radical radiation therapy improves both local control and survival.

REFERENCES

1. Logsdon MD, Eifel PJ. Figo IIIB squamous cell carcinoma of the cervix: an analysis of prognostic factors emphasizing the balance between external beam and intracavitary radiation therapy. Int J Radiat Oncol Biol Phys 1999;43(4):763–75.
2. Perez CA. Uterine cervix. In: Perez CA, Brady LW, editors. Principles and practice of radiation oncology. Philadelphia, PA: J. B. Lippincott; 1992.
3. Eifel PJ. Radiotherapy versus radical surgery for gynecologic neoplasms: carcinomas of the cervix and vulva. Front Radiat Ther Oncol 1993;27:130–42.
4. Eifel PJ, Morris M, Wharton JT, Oswald MJ. The influence of tumor size and morphology on the outcome of patients with FIGO stage IB squamous cell carcinoma of the uterine cervix. Int J Radiat Oncol Biol Phys 1994;29:9–16.
5. Morrow CP. Is pelvic radiation beneficial in the postoperative management of Stage IB squamous cell carcinoma of the cervix with pelvic node metastases treated by radical hysterectomy and pelvic lymphadenectomy? Gynecol Oncol 1980;10:105–10.
6. Sedlis A, Bundy BN, Rotman MZ, et al. A randomized trial of pelvic radiation therapy versus no further therapy in selected patients with stage IB carcinoma of the cervix after radical hysterectomy and pelvic lymphadenectomy: a Gynecologic Oncology Group Study. Gynecol Oncol 1999;73(2):177–83.
7. Rose PG, Bundy BN, Watkins J, et al. Concurrent cisplatin-based chemotherapy and radiotherapy for locally advanced cervical cancer. N Engl J Med 1999;340:1144–53.
8. Whitney CW, Sause W, Bundy BN, et al. A randomized comparison of fluorouracil plus cisplatin versus hydroxyurea as an adjunct to radiation therapy in stages IIB–IVA carcinoma of the cervix with negative para-aortic lymph nodes: a Gynecologic Oncology Group and Southwest Oncology Group study. J Clin Oncol 1999;17:1339–48.
9. Peters WAI, Liu PY, Barrett R, et al. Cisplatin, 5-fluorouracil plus radiation therapy are superior to radiation therapy as adjunctive therapy in high-risk, early-stage carcinoma of the cervix after radical hysterectomy and pelvic lymphadenectomy. Report of a Phase III Intergroup Study. Gynecol Oncol 1999;72:443.
10. Morris M, Eifel PJ, Lu J, et al. Pelvic radiation with concurrent chemotherapy compared with pelvic and paraaortic radiation for high-risk cervical cancer. N Engl J Med 1999;340:1137–43.
11. Keys HM, Bundy BN, Stehman FB, et al. Cisplatin, radiation, and adjuvant hysterectomy for bulky stage IB cervical carcinoma. N Engl J Med 1999;340:1154–61.
12. Grigsby PW, Perez CA. Radiotherapy alone for medically inoperable carcinoma of the cervix: stage IA and carcinoma in situ. Int J Radiat Oncol Biol Phys 1991;21:375–8.
13. Hamberger AD, Fletcher GH, Wharton JT. Results of treatment of early stage I carcinoma of the uterine cervix with intracavitary radium alone. Cancer 1978;41:980–5.
14. Boyce J, Fruchter R, Nicastri A, et al. Prognostic factors in stage I carcinoma of the cervix. Gynecol Oncol 1981;12:154–65.
15. Lowrey GC, Mendenhall WM, Million RR. Stage IB or IIA-B carcinoma of the intact uterine cervix treated with irradiation: a multivariate analysis. Int J Radiat Oncol Biol Phys 1992;24:205–10.
16. Horiot JC, Pigneux J, Pourquier H, et al. Radiotherapy

alone in carcinoma of the intact uterine cervix according to G. H. Fletcher guidelines: a French cooperative study of 1383 cases. Int J Radiat Oncol Biol Phys 1988;14:605–11.

17. Liu W, Meigs JV. Radical hysterectomy and pelvic lymphadenectomy. A review of 473 cases including 244 for primary invasive carcinoma of the cervix. Am J Obstet Gynecol 1955;69:1–32.

18. Hoskins WJ, Ford J, Lutz M, Averette H. Radical hysterectomy and pelvic lymphadenectomy for the management of early invasive cancer of the cervix. Gynecol Oncol 1976;4:278–90.

19. Volterrani F, Feltre L, Sigurta D, et al. Radiotherapy versus surgery in the treatment of cervix stage Ib cancer. Int J Radiat Oncol Biol Phys 1983;9:1781–4.

20. Inoue T. Prognostic significance of the depth of invasion relating to nodal metastases, parametrial extension, and cell types. A study of 628 cases with stage IB, IIa, and IIB cervical cancer. Cancer 1984;54:3035–42.

21. Kenter GG, Ansink AC, Heintz APM, et al. Carcinoma of the uterine cervix stage I and IIa: results of surgical treatment: complications, recurrence, and survival. Eur J Surg Oncol 1989;15:55–60.

22. Hopkins MP, Morley GW. Radical hysterectomy versus radiation therapy for stage IB squamous cell cancer of the cervix. Cancer 1991;68:272–7.

23. Burghardt E, Hofmann HMH, Ebner F, Haas J. Results of surgical treatment of 1028 cervical cancers studied with volumetry. Cancer 1992;70:648–55.

24. Montana GS, Fowler WC, Varia MA, et al. Analysis of results of radiation therapy for stage IB carcinoma of the cervix. Cancer 1987;60:2195–200.

25. Coia L, Won M, Lanciano R, et al. The Patterns of Care Outcome Study for cancer of the uterine cervix. Results of the second national practice survey. Cancer 1990;66:2451–6.

26. Perez CA, Grigsby PW, Nene SM, et al. Effect of tumor size on the prognosis of carcinoma of the uterine cervix treated with irradiation alone. Cancer 1992;69:2796–806.

27. Piver MS, Chung WS. Prognostic significance of cervical lesion size and pelvic node metastases in cervical carcinoma. Obstet Gynecol 1975;46:507–10.

28. Fuller AF, Elliott N, Kosloff C, et al. Determinants of increased risk for recurrence in patients undergoing radical hysterectomy for stage IB and IIa carcinoma of the cervix. Gynecol Oncol 1989;33:34–9.

29. Lee YN, Wang KL, Lin MH, et al. Radical hysterectomy with pelvic lymph node dissection for treatment of cervical cancer: a clinical review of 954 cases. Gynecol Oncol 1989;32:135–42.

30. Alvarez RD, Potter ME, Soong SJ, et al. Rationale for using pathologic tumor dimensions and nodal status to subclassify surgically treated stage IB cervical cancer patients. Gynecol Oncol 1991;43:108–12.

31. Landoni F, Maneo A, Colombo A, et al. Randomised study of radical surgery versus radiotherapy for stage Ib–IIa cervical cancer. Lancet 1997;350:535–40.

32. Barillot I, Horiot JC, Pigneux J, et al. Carcinoma of the intact uterine cervix treated with radiotherapy alone: a French cooperative study: update and multivariate analysis of prognostic factors. Int J Radiat Oncol Biol Phys 1997;38:969–78.

33. Durrance FY, Fletcher GH, Rutledge FN. Analysis of central recurrent disease in stages I and II squamous cell carcinomas of the cervix on intact uterus. AJR Am J Roentgenol 1969;106:831–8.

34. Thoms WW, Eifel PJ, Smith TL, et al. Bulky endocervical carcinomas: a 23-year experience. Int J Radiat Oncol Biol Phys 1992;23:491–9.

35. Perez CA, Kao MS. Radiation therapy alone or combined with surgery in the treatment of barrel-shaped carcinoma of the uterine cervix (stages IB, IIA, IIB). Int J Radiat Oncol Biol Phys 1985;11:1903–9.

36. Mendenhall WM, McCarty PJ, Morgan LS, et al. Stage IB-IIa-B carcinoma of the intact uterine cervix greater than or equal to 6 cm in diameter: is adjuvant extrafascial hysterectomy beneficial? Int J Radiat Oncol Biol Phys 1991;21:899–904.

37. Keys H, Bundy B, Stehman F, et al. Adjuvant hysterectomy after radiation therapy reduces detection of local recurrence in "bulky" stage IB cervical cancer without improving survival: results of a prospective randomized GOG trial. Cancer J Sci Am 1997;3:117.

38. Rotman M, John MJ, Moon SH, et al. Limitations of adjunctive surgery in carcinoma of the cervix. Int J Radiat Oncol Biol Phys 1979;5:327–32.

39. Eifel PJ, Moughan J, Owen JB, et al. Patterns of radiotherapy practice for patients with squamous carcinoma of the uterine cervix. A Patterns of Care Study. Int J Radiat Oncol Biol Phys 1999;43:351–8.

40. Thomas GM, Dembo AJ. Is there a role for adjuvant pelvic radiotherapy after radical hysterectomy in early stage cervical cancer? Int J Gynecol Cancer 1991;1:1–8.

41. Bloss JD, Berman ML, Mukhererjee J, et al. Bulky stage IB cervical carcinoma managed by primary radical hysterectomy followed by tailored radiotherapy. Gynecol Oncol 1992;47:21–7.

42. Soisson AP, Soper JT, Clarke-Pearson DL, et al. Adjuvant radiotherapy following radical hysterectomy for patients with stage IB and IIa cervical cancer. Gynecol Oncol 1990;37:390–5.

43. Barter JF, Soong SJ, Shingleton HM, et al. Complications of combined radical hysterectomy—postoperative radiation therapy in women with early stage cervical cancer. Gynecol Oncol 1989;32:292–6.

44. Fiorca JV, Roberts WS, Greenberg H, et al. Morbidity and survival patterns in patients after radical hysterectomy and postoperative adjuvant pelvic radiotherapy. Gynecol Oncol 1990;36:343–7.

45. Montz FJ, Holschneider CH, Solh S, et al. Small bowel obstruction following radical hysterectomy: risk factors, incidence and operative findings. Gynecol Oncol 1994;53:114–20.

46. Snijders-Keilholz A, Hellebrekers BW, Zwinderman AH, et al. Adjuvant radiotherapy following radical hysterectomy for patients with early-stage cervical carcinoma (1984–1996). Radiother Oncol 1999; 51(2):161–7.

47. Bandy LC, Clarke-Pearson DL, Soper JT, et al. Long-term effects on bladder function following radical hysterectomy with and without postoperative radiation. Gynecol Oncol 1987;26:160–8.

48. Lanciano RM, Martz K, Coia LR, Hanks GE. Tumor and treatment factors improving outcome in stage III-B cervix cancer. Int J Radiat Oncol Biol Phys 1991;20:95–100.

49. Benedet J, Odicino F, Maisonneuve P, et al. Carcinoma of the cervix uteri. J Epidemiol Biostat 1998;3:5–34.

50. Mayr NA, Yuh WT, Zheng J, et al. Prediction of tumor control in patients with cervical cancer: analysis of combined volume and dynamic enhancement pattern by MR imaging. AJR Am J Roentgenol 1998;170(1):177–82.

51. Mayr NA, Yuh WT, Zheng J, et al. Tumor size evaluated by pelvic examination compared with 3-D quantitative analysis in the prediction of outcome for cervical cancer. Int J Radiat Oncol Biol Phys 1997; 39(2):395–404.

52. Hatano K, Sekiya Y, Araki H, et al. Evaluation of the therapeutic effect of radiotherapy on cervical cancer using magnetic resonance imaging. Int J Radiat Oncol Biol Phys 1999;45(3):639–44.

53. McIntyre JF, Eifel PJ, Levenback C, Oswald MJ. Ureteral stricture as a late complication of radiotherapy for stage IB carcinoma of the uterine cervix. Cancer 1995;75(3):836–43.

54. Chao KS, Williamson JF, Grigsby PW, Perez CA. Uterosacral space involvement in locally advanced carcinoma of the uterine cervix. Int J Radiat Oncol Biol Phys 1998;40(2):397–403.

55. Eifel PJ, Thames HD. Has the influence of treatment duration on local control of carcinoma of the cervix been defined? [editorial; comment]. Int J Radiat Oncol Biol Phys 1995;32(5):1527–9.

56. Fyles AW, Pintilie M, Kirkbride P, et al. Prognostic factors in patients with cervix cancer treated by radiation therapy: results of a multiple regression analysis. Radiother Oncol 1995;35(2):107–17.

57. Girinsky T, Rey A, Roche B, et al. Overall treatment time in advanced cervical carcinomas: a critical parameter in treatment outcome. Int J Radiat Oncol Biol Phys 1993;27(5):1051–6.

58. Lanciano RM, Pajak TF, Martz K, Hanks GE. The influence of treatment time on outcome for squa-mous cell cancer of the uterine cervix treated with radiation: a patterns-of-care study. Int J Radiat Oncol Biol Phys 1993;25(3):391–7.

59. Perez CA, Grigsby PW, Castro-Vita H, Lockett MA. Carcinoma of the uterine cervix. I. Impact of prolongation of overall treatment time and timing of brachytherapy on outcome of radiation therapy [see comments]. Int J Radiat Oncol Biol Phys 1995; 32(5):1275–88.

60. Petereit DG, Sarkaria JN, Chappell R, et al. The adverse effect of treatment prolongation in cervical carcinoma [see comments]. Int J Radiat Oncol Biol Phys 1995;32(5):1301–7.

61. Thomas L, Chacon B, Kind M, et al. Magnetic resonance imaging in the treatment planning of radiation therapy in carcinoma of the cervix treated with the four-field pelvic technique. Int J Radiat Oncol Biol Phys 1997;37(4):827–32.

62. Kim RY, McGinnis LS, Spencer SA, et al. Conventional four-field pelvic radiotherapy technique without CT treatment planning in cancer of the cervix: potential geographic miss. Radiother Oncol 1994;30(2):140–5.

63. Greer BE, Koh WJ, Figge DC, et al. Gynecologic radiotherapy fields defined by intraoperative measurements. Gynecol Oncol 1990;38(3):421–4.

64. Russell AH. Contemporary radiation treatment planning for patients with cancer of the uterine cervix. Semin Oncol 1994;21(1):30–41.

65. Cunningham MJ, Dunton CJ, Corn B, et al. Extended-field radiation therapy in early-stage cervical carcinoma: survival and complications. Gynecol Oncol 1991;43(1):51–4.

66. Podczaski E, Stryker JA, Kaminski P, et al. Extended-field radiation therapy for carcinoma of the cervix. Cancer 1990;66(2):251–8.

67. Tewfik HH, Buchsbaum HJ, Latourette HB, et al. Para-aortic lymph node irradiation in carcinoma of the cervix after exploratory laparotomy and biopsy-proven positive aortic nodes. Int J Radiat Oncol Biol Phys 1982;8(1):13–8.

68. Komaki R, Mattingly RF, Hoffman RG, et al. Irradiation of para-aortic lymph node metastases from carcinoma of the cervix or endometrium. Preliminary results. Radiology 1983;147(1):245–8.

69. Rubin SC, Brookland R, Mikuta JJ, et al. Para-aortic nodal metastases in early cervical carcinoma: long-term survival following extended-field radiotherapy. Gynecol Oncol 1984;18(2):213–7.

70. Brookland RK, Rubin S, Danoff BF. Extended field irradiation in the treatment of patients with cervical carcinoma involving biopsy proven para-aortic nodes. Int J Radiat Oncol Biol Phys 1984;10(10):1875–9.

71. Piver MS, Barlow JJ, Krishnamsetty R. Five-year survival (with no evidence of disease) in patients with

biopsy-confirmed aortic node metastasis from cervical carcinoma. Am J Obstet Gynecol 1981; 139(5):575–8.

72. Buchsbaum HJ. Extrapelvic lymph node metastases in cervical carcinoma. Am J Obstet Gynecol 1979; 133(7):814–24.

73. Berman ML, Keys H, Creasman W, et al. Survival and patterns of recurrence in cervical cancer metastatic to periaortic lymph nodes (a Gynecologic Oncology Group study). Gynecol Oncol 1984;19(1):8–16.

74. Haie C, Pejovic MH, Gerbaulet A, et al. Is prophylactic para-aortic irradiation worthwhile in the treatment of advanced cervical carcinoma? Results of a controlled clinical trial of the EORTC radiotherapy group. Radiother Oncol 1988;11(2):101–12.

75. Rotman M, Pajak TF, Choi K, et al. Prophylactic extended-field irradiation of para-aortic lymph nodes in stages IIB and bulky IB and IIa cervical carcinomas. Ten-year treatment results of RTOG 79-20 [see comments]. JAMA 1995;274(5):387–93.

76. Fletcher GH. Female pelvis. In: Textbook of radiotherapy. 3rd edition. Fletcher GH, editor. Philadelphia, PA: Lea & Febiger; 1980.

77. Fletcher GH. Female pelvis. In: Textbook of radiotherapy. Philadelphia, PA: Lea & Febiger; 1966. p. 434–503.

78. Delclos L, Fletcher GH, Sampiere V, Grant WHI. Can the Fletcher gamma ray colpostat system be extrapolated to other systems? Cancer 1978;41:970–9.

79. Delclos L, Fletcher GH, Moore EB, Sampiere VA. Minicolpostats, dome cylinders, other additions and improvements of the Fletcher-Suit afterloadable system: indications and limitations of their use. Int J Radiat Oncol Biol Phys 1980;6:1195–206.

80. Delclos L. Gynecologic cancers: pelvic examination and treatment planning. In: Levitt S, Tapley N, editors. Technological basis of radiation therapy: practical clinical applications. Philadelphia, PA: Lea & Febiger; 1984. p. 193–227.

81. International Commission on Radiation Units and Measurements. Dose and volume specification for reporting intracavitary therapy in gynecology. Vol. 38. Bethesda, MD: International Commission on Radiation Units and Measurements; 1985. p. 1–23.

82. Kapp KS, Stuecklschweiger GF, Kapp DS, Hackl AG. Dosimetry of intracavitary placements for uterine and cervical carcinoma: results of orthogonal film, TLD, and CT-assisted techniques. Radiother Oncol 1992;24(3):137–46.

83. Ling CC, Schell MC, Working KR, et al. CT-assisted assessment of bladder and rectum dose in gynecological implants. Int J Radiat Oncol Biol Phys 1987;13:1577–82.

84. Schoeppel SL, LaVigne ML, Martel MK, et al. Three-dimensional treatment planning of intracavitary gynecologic implants: analysis of ten cases and

85. Roeske JC, Mundt AJ, Halpern H, et al. Late rectal sequelae following definitive radiation therapy for carcinoma of the uterine cervix: a dosimetric analysis. Int J Radiat Oncol Biol Phys 1997;37(2):351–8.

86. Perez CA, Grigsby PW, Lockett MA, et al. Radiation therapy morbidity in carcinoma of the uterine cervix: dosimetric and clinical correlation. Int J Radiat Oncol Biol Phys 1999;44(4):855–66.

87. Eifel PJ, Morris M, Delclos L, Wharton JT. Radiation therapy for cervical carcinoma. In: Dilts PVJ, Sciarra JJ, editors. Gynecology and obstetrics. Philadelphia, PA: J. B. Lippincott Co.; 1993. p. 1–25.

88. Haie-Meder C, Kramar A, Lambin P, et al. Analysis of complications in a prospective randomized trial comparing two brachytherapy low dose rates in cervical carcinoma. Int J Radiat Oncol Biol Phys 1994;29:1195–7.

89. Akine Y, Arimoto H, Ogino T, et al. High-dose-rate intracavitary irradiation in the treatment of carcinoma of the uterine cervix: early experience with 84 patients. Int J Radiat Oncol Biol Phys 1988;14:893–8.

90. Ito H, Kumagaya H, Shigematsu N, et al. High dose rate intracavitary brachytherapy for recurrent cervical cancer of the vaginal stump following hysterectomy. Int J Radiat Oncol Biol Phys 1991;20:927–32.

91. Kapp KS, Stuecklschweiger GF, Kapp DS, et al. Prognostic factors in patients with carcinoma of the uterine cervix treated with external beam irradiation and IR-192 high-dose-rate brachytherapy. Int J Radiat Oncol Biol Phys 1998;42(3):531–40.

92. Newman H, James K, Smith C. Treatment of cancer of the cervix with a high-dose-rate afterloading machine (the Cathetron). Int J Radiat Oncol Biol Phys 1983;9:931–7.

93. Orton CG, Seyedsadr M, Somnay A. Comparison of high and low dose rate remote afterloading for cervix cancer and the importance of fractionation. Int J Radiat Oncol Biol Phys 1991;21:1425–4.

94. Patel FD, Sharma SC, Neigi PS, et al. Low dose rate vs. high dose rate brachytherapy in the treatment of carcinoma of the uterine cervix: a clinical trial. Int J Radiat Oncol Biol Phys 1993;28:335–41.

95. Petereit DG, Pearcey R. Literature analysis of high dose rate brachytherapy fractionation schedules in the treatment of cervical cancer: is there an optimal fractionation schedule? Int J Radiat Oncol Biol Phys 1999;43(2):359–66.

96. Shigematsu Y, Nishiyama K, Masaki N, et al. Treatment of carcinoma of the uterine cervix by remotely controlled afterloading intracavitary radiotherapy with high-dose rate: a comparative study with a low-dose rate system. Int J Radiat Oncol Biol Phys 1983;9:351–6.

97. Stitt JA, Fowler JF, Thomadsen BR, et al. High dose rate intracavitary brachytherapy for carcinoma of the cervix: the Madison system: I. Clinical and radiobiological considerations. Int J Radiat Oncol Biol Phys 1992;24:383–6.

98. Scalliet P, Gerbaulet A, Dubray B. HDR versus LDR gynecological brachytherapy revisited. Radiother Oncol 1993;28:118–26.

99. Eifel PJ. High dose-rate brachytherapy for carcinoma of the cervix: high tech or high risk? Int J Radiat Oncol Biol Phys 1992;24:383–6.

100. Aristizabal SA, Woolfitt B, Valencia A, et al. Interstitial parametrial implants in carcinoma of the cervix stage II-B. Int J Radiat Oncol Biol Phys 1987;13:445–50.

101. Fontanesi J, Dylewski G, Photopulos G, et al. Impact of dose on local control and development of complications in patients with advanced gynecological malignancies treated by interstitial template boost technique. Endocuriether Hyperther Oncol 1993;9:115–9.

102. Gaddis O, Morrow CP, Klement V, et al. Treatment of cervical carcinoma employing a template for transperienal interstitial Ir^{192} brachytherapy. Int J Radiat Oncol Biol Phys 1983;9:819–27.

103. Martinez A, Edmundson GK, Cox RS, et al. Combination of external beam irradiation and multiple-site perineal applicator (MUPIT) for treatment of locally advanced or recurrent prostatic, anorectal, and gynecologic malignancies. Int J Radiat Oncol Biol Phys 1985;11:391–8.

104. Syed AMN, Puthwala AA, Neblett D, et al. Transperineal interstitial-intracavitary "Syed-Neblett" applicator in the treatment of carcinoma of the uterine cervix. Endocuriether Hyperther Oncol 1986;2: 1–13.

105. Hughes-Davies L, Silver B, Kapp D. Parametrial interstitial brachytherapy for advanced or recurrent pelvic malignancy: the Harvard/Stanford experience. Gynecol Oncol 1995;58:24–7.

106. Monk BJ, Tewari K, Burger RA, et al. A comparison of intracavitary versus interstitial irradiation in the treatment of cervical cancer. Gynecol Oncol 1997; 67:241–7.

107. Stock RG, Chan K, Terk M, et al. A new technique for performing Syed-Neblett template interstitial implants for gynecologic malignancies using transrectal-ultrasound guidance. Int J Radiat Oncol Biol Phys 1997;37(4):819–25.

108. Recio FO, Piver MS, Hempling RE, et al. Laparoscopic-assisted application of interstitial brachytherapy for locally advanced cervical carcinoma: results of a pilot study. Int J Radiat Oncol Biol Phys 1998;40(2):411–4.

109. Erickson B, Gillin MT. Interstitial implantation of gynecologic malignancies. J Surg Oncol 1997;66(4): 285–95.

110. Gupta AK, Vicini FA, Frazier AJ, et al. Iridium-192 transperineal interstitial brachytherapy for locally advanced or recurrent gynecological malignancies. Int J Radiat Oncol Biol Phys 1999;43(5):1055–60.

111. Demanes DJ, Rodriguez RR, Bendre DD, Ewing TL. High dose rate transperineal interstitial brachytherapy for cervical cancer: high pelvic control and low complication rates. Int J Radiat Oncol Biol Phys 1999;45(1):105–12.

11

Radical Management of Recurrent Cervical Cancer

WUI-JIN KOH, MD
PAMELA J. PALEY, MD
NATHAN D. COMSIA, BA
BENJAMIN GREER, MD

Following primary management for cervical cancer, a small proportion of patients will present with loco-regional failure for whom salvage therapy may be contemplated. The management of these patients with recurrent cervical cancer presents a difficult therapeutic challenge. Multiple factors, including prior therapy, site and extent of relapse, and the feasibility of different re-treatment modalities and techniques, need to be evaluated in each individual case.

Although there are anecdotal cases of long-term survival in patients treated with various approaches for limited extrapelvic metastases,[1] the scarcity of such experiences precludes development of generalized treatment algorithms. Chemotherapy alone for metastatic disease is considered palliative in nature. Therefore, for the purposes of the ensuing discussion, radical treatment of recurrent cervical cancer, delivered with curative intent, is available solely for patients with isolated pelvic relapse.

RISK OF PELVIC FAILURE FOLLOWING PRIMARY THERAPY

While overall recurrences after initial surgery or radiotherapy for cervical cancer are not uncommon, particularly in higher-stage tumors, the incidence of isolated relapse confined to the pelvis is infrequent. Recent advances in radiologic technology, including high-resolution spiral computed tomography (CT), magnetic resonance imaging (MRI), and positron emission tomography (PET), allow clinicians to evaluate candidates for potential radical salvage with increasing precision. Without these modern imaging tools, previous reports documenting patterns of failures have undoubtedly underestimated the true distant metastatic component of relapse. Nevertheless, the results discussed below provide an estimate of the scope of pelvic recurrence following initial therapy for cervical cancer.

Improvements in radiation therapy techniques and an emphasis on the integral role of brachytherapy have led to better pelvic control for cervical cancer patients undergoing primary radiotherapy.[2,3] Perez and colleagues reviewed 1,499 cases of cervical cancer (stages Ia to IVa) treated with definitive irradiation. With a median at-risk follow-up interval of 11 years, a total of 570 patients (38%) relapsed. Pelvic failure occurred in 345 patients (23%), but isolated pelvic recurrence, without distant metastases, presented in only 140 cases (9%). The majority of patients with pelvic relapse, thus, had an associated component of distant failure.[4] A previous analysis by this group of investigators noted that the rate of distant metastases was significantly influenced by failure to achieve pelvic control.[5] In a separate large single-institution experience, Logsdon and Eifel evaluated the outcome in 907 patients with stage IIIb cervical cancers who completed curative-intent radiotherapy. The 5-year disease-specific survival rate was 39 percent, with an overall documented pelvic recurrence rate of 22 percent, one-quarter of whom also had an extrapelvic component of failure. The overall rate of documented distant metastases was 28 percent.[6] The large series reported by Perez and colleagues and Logsdon and Eifel underscore the fact that with appropriate radiotherapy, the incidence of isolated pelvic recurrence following definitive radiation for cervical cancer, even in locally advanced disease, is low.

Surgery is often chosen as primary therapy for patients with early-stage invasive cervical cancer. Of the pathologic risk features associated with recurrence, the single most consistently identified adverse prognostic factor is lymph node involvement. A recent review by Koh and colleagues analyzed patients from seven reported series who underwent radical hysterectomy and lymphadenectomy alone for node-positive cervical cancer. They noted a 34 percent risk of pelvic relapse, with about 25 percent of these harboring a component of synchronous distant failure also.[7] Patients without lymph node metastases may also be at risk for failure, on the basis of varying combinations of tumor size, depth of cervical stromal penetration, and lymph-vascular space involvement. The Gynecologic Oncology Group reported a pelvis-confined failure rate of 19 percent in node-negative patients with primary tumor risk factors who underwent surgery alone.[8] While previously controversial, the role of adjuvant postoperative pelvic radiation therapy in patients with high-risk early-stage cervical cancer is currently supported by results from two large randomized clinical trials,[8,9] in which pelvic failures were substantially reduced. Hence, with appropriate inclusion of adjuvant therapy, isolated pelvic relapse following radical hysterectomy is uncommon.[7–9]

PROGNOSTIC FACTORS IN RECURRENT CERVICAL CANCER

Various clinicopathologic features have been associated with adverse outcomes in patients with pelvis-confined recurrent cervical cancer and are listed in Table 11–1. The relatively small number of patients reported in most series and the heterogeneity of clinical and treatment parameters have precluded detailed statistical analysis of these prognostic fac-

tors, and explain the variable predictive value of such by different investigators.

Two clinical features commonly correlated with the probability of salvage success are location (central versus side wall involvement) and size of the recurring pelvic tumor.[10] These are often interdependent variables. Many reports have noted that patients with side wall or parametrial tumor involvement have a substantially poorer prognosis than those whose recurrences are confined to the cervix or vagina.[1,3,11–16] Likewise, the bulk of the recurrent tumor has prognostic implications, with larger lesions faring worse than smaller ones, although the "threshhold" size for analysis is arbitrary and varies from one series to another.[3,14,16–20] It is intriguing to note that while Potter and colleagues reported an adverse impact of pelvic side wall involvement in their series of patients with recurrent cervical cancer, the influence of disease location on survival was lost when analysis was limited to previously unirradiated patients who underwent radical salvage irradiation.[13] This observation underscores the difficulty of addressing pelvic side wall disease in previously irradiated patients but has implications for possible therapeutic advances discussed later.

The presence of nodal disease in conjunction with pelvic relapse portends a dismal outcome.[3,16,19,21,22] Some investigators have also noted that even lymph node metastases retrospectively documented at primary diagnosis limit successful salvage for recurrence.[1,12]

A short interval between primary therapy and relapse has been correlated with poorer prognosis in some reports, compared with patients with a more protracted time to failure,[11,16,22,23] and is likely reflective of underlying aggressive tumor biology. However, this observation has not been confirmed by others.[12,15,19] Other potential unfavorable clinical

Table 11–1. ADVERSE PROGNOSTIC FACTORS IN PATIENTS WITH PELVIS-CONFINED RECURRENT CERVICAL CANCER

Location of recurrence within pelvis—side wall versus central
Large tumor volume
Nodal involvement
Early relapse following initial treatment
Adenocarcinoma histology
Higher FIGO stage at initial diagnosis

FIGO = International Federation of Gynecology and Obstetrics.

variables include nonsquamous histologies, in particular adenocarcinomas,[1,15,22] and an initial higher International Federation of Gynecology and Obstetrics (FIGO) stage at primary diagnosis.[16,23] The prognostic influence of symptomatic versus asymptomatic pelvic failures remains undetermined.[11,12]

RESTAGING AND WORK-UP

For patients who present with pelvic failure, careful work-up to rule out extrapelvic metastases is crucial. Following biopsy confirmation of recurrence, minimum additional restaging should include CT of the pelvis, abdomen, and chest. Further tests, such as a bone scan or MRI, are obtained on the basis of symptomatology or other equivocal findings. PET is a new and promising imaging modality that reportedly has greater sensitivity and specificity than CT for the detection of retroperitoneal metastases in primary advanced cervical cancer.[24] While not yet studied extensively in recurrent cervical cancer, experiences with PET in other recurrent malignancies suggest that it would be a useful restaging tool. In addition to metastatic work-up, a thorough medical evaluation of each patient is required to determine the feasibility of salvage therapy.

The ability to detect smaller metastatic deposits with the increased use of contemporary imaging technology admittedly would result in a "functional stage shift" of patients with apparent pelvis-confined failure, rendering outcome comparisons with historic series problematic. Nevertheless, these advances will clearly lead to better selection of patients who can ultimately benefit from radical salvage of recurrent cervical cancer.

RADICAL SALVAGE OPTIONS

The most important determinant of therapy options is whether the patient has received prior pelvic radiotherapy. In general, surgery forms the cornerstone of salvage for previously irradiated patients, while several radiation options can be considered and optimized in previously unirradiated individuals. In all cases, treatment has to be individualized to the specific clinical parameters of each patient.

Previously Irradiated Patients

Given the role of radiation as primary therapy for initial advanced cervical cancers, as well as adjuvant treatment following radical hysterectomy in high-risk early-stage tumors, it is not surprising that the majority of patients with recurrent pelvic disease will have been previously irradiated. For most of these patients, an attempt at curative salvage requires radical surgery.

Radical Hysterectomy

In rare, carefully selected patients initially treated with primary radiation, radical hysterectomy for salvage may be a feasible alternative to exenterative surgery. Rubin and colleagues reported on 21 patients who underwent radical hysterectomy for cervical cancer failing in the central pelvis following previous radiotherapy. They noted a 62 percent survival rate at a median follow-up of 73 months. Of 11 patients with recurrent tumors ≤ 2 cm in size, none experienced a second recurrence, while 7 of 10 with disease > 2 cm subsequently relapsed again. Morbidity was high, and the authors concluded that radical hysterectomy as salvage following prior radiation therapy should be undertaken only by experienced surgeons and limited to patients with initial early-stage tumors who present with central recurrences ≤ 2 cm in size.[18] Terada and Morley described 14 patients who underwent radical hysterectomy for recurrent tumor following previous pelvic irradiation. The 5-year disease-free survival rate from attempted salvage was 27 percent. However, when six cases with nodal disease at the time of surgery, all of whom died of ensuing relapses, were excluded, the 5-year survival rate for the remaining patients was 54 percent. Major complications requiring subsequent surgical intervention occurred in 29 percent of patients. The investigators suggested that there might be a limited role for radical hysterectomy as surgical salvage in patients with central pelvic relapse following previous irradiation.[19] Coleman and colleagues reported 50 patients who underwent radical hysterectomy for persistent or recurrent cervical cancer after primary irradiation. The 5- and 10-year actuarial survival rates were 72 percent and 60 percent, respectively. Factors at the time of radical hysterectomy associated with a favorable outcome included tumor size < 2 cm, lesion confined to the cervix, histologically negative lymph nodes, and a normal preoperative intravenous pyelogram. Severe complications were noted in 64 percent of patients and were permanent in 42 percent of cases. It was concluded that radical hysterectomy was an alternative to exenteration in patients with small, centrally recurrent cervical cancer, but that its use required highly selective application.[3]

Pelvic Exenteration

In most previously irradiated cervical cancer patients who develop a central pelvic recurrence, the only potentially curative option is pelvic exenteration. This procedure, which originally entailed en bloc resection of all pelvic viscera, was first described by Brunschwig in 1948, who noted that no specific patient selection was exercised except that all known disease be confined to the pelvis.[25] With accumulated technical and clinical experience, Barber subsequently described the preoperative criteria and intraoperative findings that should be considered in evaluating patients for this radical approach.[26] Augmented by observations from more recent reports, these guidelines have remained the basis for appropriate selection of patients for exenteration.

A recent review of pelvic exenteration for recurrent cervical cancer has recently been published by Paley and Greer.[27] Obviously, patients considered candidates for exenteration must undergo thorough staging to exclude extrapelvic disease. Preoperatively, the presence of disease fixation to the pelvic side wall is felt by many to be a contraindication to proceeding, as clear surgical margins cannot be typically obtained. The clinical triad of unilateral leg edema, ureteral obstruction, and sciatic-nerve distribution pain in a patient with known tumor recurrence strongly suggests unresectable side wall disease. However, in previously irradiated patients, physical examination alone may be inadequate to assess for side wall involvement due to confounding fibrosis; an examination under anesthesia, with multiple biopsies of the suspected parametria/side wall regions, may be prudent before surgical feasibility is ruled out. Intraoperatively, findings that are considered contraindications to exenteration include peritoneal cavity contamination and side wall involve-

ment detected at exploration. Although the presence of positive pelvic nodes is clearly associated with a poorer prognosis, there is some debate as to whether this factor represents a clear contraindication to completion of an exenteration. While some have reported dismal outcomes following exenteration in node-positive cases, it has been suggested by other investigators that this surgery still confers curative potential in patients with a limited number of nodes harboring only microscopic disease.[21,22,26-30]

Despite careful preoperative evaluation and staging, approximately 30 to 50 percent of patients explored for exenteration will have the procedure aborted.[22,31] The most common intraoperative reasons identified for abandoning planned salvage exenteration include peritoneal disease, nodal metastases, and parametrial/pelvic side wall fixation.[31] Improvements in radiologic imaging, as discussed earlier, may lead to a decrease in aborted procedures, sparing patients the physical and emotional trauma of failed surgery. The use of laparoscopy to confirm eligibility for pelvic exenteration preceding a more extensive laparotomy has also been proposed.[32]

For patients with recurrent cervical cancer in whom pelvic exenteration is completed, 5-year overall survival rates approximating 50 percent are achieved.[21,22,28,30,33-35] In patients with relatively favorable prognostic features, such as those with small centralized recurrences, negative nodes, and a longer interval between initial therapy and relapse, 70 percent or more may be successfully salvaged by pelvic exenteration.[22,30,35]

Historically, the use of pelvic exenteration as salvage for recurrent cervical cancer in previously irradiated patients has been tempered by technical challenges, as well as patient and physician acceptance of what was perceived as an ultra-radical procedure. As originally descibed by Brunschwig,[25] the surgery included complete excision of all pelvic viscera, with resultant colostomy, urinary diversion, and loss of the vagina. Early reports of postsurgical mortality (20% or higher) and morbidity were very high.[21,26,36] With advancements in surgical methods, perioperative and postoperative management, more careful patient selection, and tailoring of the extent of exenteration, substantial improvements in outcome have been realized. More recent institutional experiences note a postoperative mortality rate of 5 percent or less,[22,30,35,37] with an attendant decrease in morbidity as well.[2,22,27,38] Functional compromise in patients has been further reduced by new surgical reconstructive techniques that allow low colorectal reanastomosis, continent urinary diversion, and neovagina creation.[2,27,37–39] Figures 11–1 and 11–2 illustrate exenteration specimens from salvage surgeries of different extents, as tailored to the location and size of disease. While pelvic exenteration remains a technically challenging procedure, advances in surgical management may prompt re-evaluation of the indications and acceptability of its role as salvage for recurrent cervical cancer.

Intraoperative Radiation Therapy as an Adjunct to Exenteration

Proximity or fixation of tumor to the pelvic side wall is an adverse finding in previously irradiated patients with recurrent cervical cancer. Patients with microscopically close or positive margins have dismal survival rates following exenteration,[21,28,30] leading many to abandon attempted surgical salvage for patients with intraoperatively detected side wall involvement.[31]

In an effort to extend the potential curative role of radical resection in patients with recurrent cervical cancer, when there is a significant noncentral tumor component, various institutions have investigated the feasibility of tightly focused radiation applied during surgery to address residual side wall disease. Several approaches have been used. In common, these techniques seek to deliver a high dose to the surgical bed in question, while physically displacing critical surrounding normal tissues from the field of radiation.

Stelzer and colleagues reported on 22 patients with recurrent cervical cancer who received intraoperative radiation therapy (IORT) in conjunction with radical surgery. The IORT was used to address gross residual side wall disease in 12 patients, and micro-

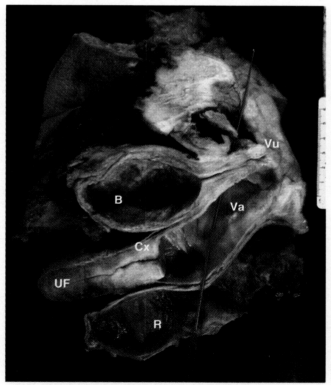

Figure 11–1. Surgical specimen from a patient who underwent extended pelvic exenteration with vulvectomy. Recurrent tumor involved the previously irradiated cervix and extended distally along the anterior vaginal wall. The probe denotes the position of a fistulous tract. B = bladder; Cx = cervix; R = rectum; UF = uterine fundus; Va = vagina; Vu = vulva.

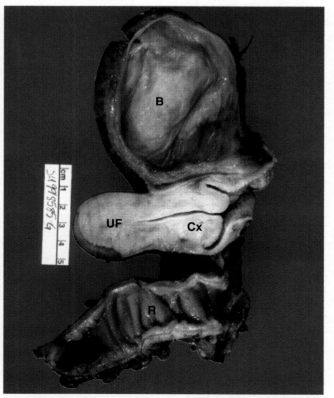

Figure 11–2. Surgical specimen from a previously irradiated patient who underwent supralevator pelvic exenteration for recurrent disease confined to the cervix. A low rectal reanastomosis and neovagina creation was successfully performed. B = bladder; Cx = cervix; R = rectum; UF = uterine fundus.

scopically positive or close surgical margins in the remaining 10 patients. The 5-year disease-specific survival and local control rates were 43 percent and 48 percent, respectively. While there was a trend toward better results in patients with only microscopic residual disease, it is noteworthy that a few cures were apparently obtained in patients with gross residual disease after maximal surgical debulking and IORT.[40] Illustrations from a typical case in which IORT was used are provided in Figures 11–3 to 11–6. Garton and colleagues analyzed 39 patients with recurrent or locally advanced gynecologic cancers who underwent IORT following maximal tumor resection. Twenty-three patients had microscopically positive margins, while 16 had gross residual disease. The 5-year local control rate was 67 percent, with a corresponding disease-free survival rate of 41 percent.[41]

A different technique for addressing residual pelvic side wall disease in recurrent gynecologic malignancies has been described by Hockel and colleagues. This approach involved placement of afterloading brachytherapy catheters onto the residual tumor or surgical bed at the pelvic wall following surgical debulking and was called combined operative and radiotherapeutic treatment (CORT). The investigators have recently updated their results in 48 patients treated with CORT, noting a 5-year overall survival rate of 44 percent.[42] These investigators have postulated that the ability to perform CORT and sterilize residual disease may overcome the adverse prognosis previously associated with pelvic side wall involvement.[20]

Figure 11–4. Placement of Lucite cone for delivery of IORT using electrons after maximal surgical debulking. The tumor bed area covered is determined by the selected cone diameter, while the depth of tissue irradiated is influenced by the chosen electron energy.

The application of IORT or CORT may eventually allow the expansion of selection criteria for candidates for exenteration, but this requires further evaluation. Additionally, their use in previously irradiated patients is not without adverse consequences. In particular, peripheral neuropathy, which may be debilitating, has been recognized as a significant potential complication.[40,43]

Radical Reirradiation

Concerns regarding radiation complications have limited attempts at radical reirradiation of patients

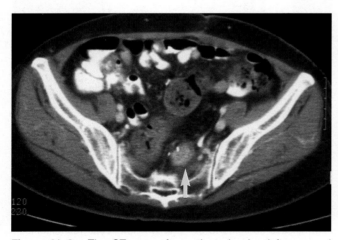

Figure 11–3. The CT scan of a patient showing left presacral tumor recurrence (*arrow*).

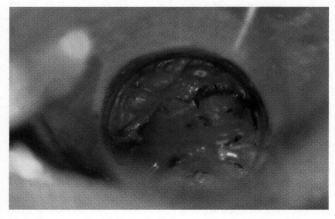

Figure 11–5. Direct view of the surgical bed on the pelvic wall, through the lumen of the IORT cone. The cone physically displaces uninvolved viscera away from the field of irradiation.

Figure 11–6. The IORT cone docked to the linear accelerator.

with recurrent cervical cancer. However, in rare instances, previously irradiated patients with pelvis-confined relapses for whom surgery is not an option may be salvaged by a second course of radiotherapy. Radical reirradiation has to be implemented with extreme caution, balancing the desire to achieve sufficient tumoricidal doses with the realization that radiation dose effect on normal tissues is cumulative. Doses to some adjacent normal tissues will unavoidably exceed generally accepted tolerance levels. The volume chosen for reirradiation, and the techniques used to minimize normal tissue exposure are, therefore, critical. Earlier reports of reirradiation using low-energy external-beam radiotherapy provided disappointingly low survival and high complication rates.[44,45] More recent experiences have provided encouraging results in selectively reirradiated patients with small central recurrences, in whom the use of brachytherapy was emphasized. Despite these advances, a higher complication rate than that seen with primary radiation is to be expected, and patients have to be appropriately counseled prior to embarking on salvage reirradiation.[44–47]

Previously Unirradiated Patients

This select population is limited to early-stage cervical cancer patients treated with primary surgery alone who subsequently relapse. Historically, salvage radiation has been used as front-line therapy for localized pelvic recurrences after radical hysterectomy. A recent literature review by Lanciano noted disease-free survival rates ranging from 20 to 50 percent following radiotherapy for locoregional

failures. More favorable outcomes were reported in patients with small-volume disease and a central pelvic relapse location, possibly resulting from greater incorporation of brachytherapy, and hence better tumor dosing, compared with cases with side wall involvement.[10]

Radiotherapy

Larson and colleagues in an analysis of patients with recurrent cervical cancer following radical hysterectomy, identified 15 cases with isolated pelvic or vulvar relapses who were treated with salvage radiotherapy. Doses of up to 70 Gy, mostly delivered via a shrinking-field external-beam technique, were used. Eight of 15 patients (53%) remained free of disease at a median follow-up interval of 4 years.[12]

Potter and colleagues reported on 28 patients with pelvis-confined recurrent cervical cancer after radical hysterectomy who underwent salvage radiation therapy. Most patients received external-beam radiotherapy alone, to a median dose of 59.4 Gy. Persistent tumor control was noted in 10 patients (36%), with a projected 5-year disease-free survival rate in excess of 30 percent. The authors concluded that radiation therapy remains the treatment of choice in previously unirradiated patients who develop isolated pelvic relapses following initial radical hysterectomy.[13]

Jobsen and colleagues described the use of radical radiotherapy in 18 patients with locoregional recurrent cervical cancer after primary surgery. The patients typically underwent external-beam irradiation alone to doses ranging from 40 to 60 Gy. The authors reported initial clinical complete responses in 16 of 18 patients (88%), with a 5-year disease-free survival rate of 39 percent.[48]

Virostek and colleagues analyzed 30 patients with postsurgical pelvic recurrence of cervical cancer. Using variable combinations of external-beam radiation and/or brachytherapy, persistent local tumor control was obtained in 11 patients (37%) after a median follow-up period exceeding 9 years. While not statistically significant due to the small patient numbers, the study suggested that increased radiation doses, facilitated by the addition of brachytherapy, led to better local control probability.[14]

Ijaz and colleagues evaluated 43 patients with isolated locoregional failures after radical hysterectomy who received radiotherapy with curative intent. Radiation therapy was individualized and followed approaches similar to those used for the management of primary vaginal cancers, using external-beam radiation with selective intracavitary or interstitial brachytherapy boost. The 5-year overall survival rate was 39 percent. For 16 patients with recurrent tumors limited to the vagina or paravaginal tissues and no pelvic side wall involvement, the survival rate was 69 percent. The authors concluded that patients with isolated central pelvic recurrence of cervical cancer after radical hysterectomy had a notably good curative opportunity with radical radiotherapy. They also suggested that while patients with pelvic side wall relapses had poorer outcomes, there was sufficient salvage potential to justify an aggressive treatment approach.[15]

Clearly, radiotherapy has curative potential in patients with pelvis-confined recurrent cervical cancer following initial surgery. A consistent theme in the previously discussed series is that salvage radiation is most effective in cases with small, central pelvic relapses. Therefore, close surveillance of patients after radical hysterectomy, especially for those with pathologic risk factors who do not receive adjuvant therapy, is important to identify early and salvageable recurrences.

Chemotherapy and Radiation

The therapeutic benefit of concurrent chemotherapy and radiation has recently been emphasized in the primary management of advanced cervical cancer.[49] By extrapolation, it is tempting to infer that chemoradiation may provide a therapeutic advantage to patients with locally recurrent cervical cancer. This combined modality approach has been evaluated by several investigators, with intriguing results. Thomas and colleagues[50] reported on 40 patients with isolated recurrent cervical cancer following primary surgery who were treated with salvage concurrent chemotherapy and radiation. While the treatment algorithm evolved over time, all patients received 5-fluorouracil. The typical radiation dose was 52.8 Gy, delivered at 1.6 Gy fractions, twice daily during chemotherapy infusion and once daily otherwise. The study included many cases with very high-risk features—31 patients (78%) had some component of pelvic side wall disease, and more than one-third had nodal involvement. A complete response to therapy was noted in 58 percent of patients, and at a median at-risk follow-up interval of 57 months, 18 patients (45%) remained alive without evidence of disease. It was noted that sustained complete remissions and apparent cures were achieved in patients with pelvic side wall or even common iliac node involvement and in those with rapid recurrences after initial surgery. Perhaps the most provocative finding was that on multivariate analysis of potential prognostic factors, only the number of 5-fluorouracil courses administered was predictive of ultimate pelvic control and survival.[50]

Two other experiences using concurrent chemotherapy and radiotherapy for recurrent cervical cancer have been published. Maneo and colleagues described 35 patients treated with external radiation and three cycles of 5-fluorouracil and carboplatin, the first two cycles given concurrently with radiotherapy. The actuarial 2-year and 3-year survival rates were 44 percent and 25 percent, respectively. However, when 7 patients with a para-aortic component of relapse were excluded from analysis, the 2-year relapse-free survival rate improved to 57 percent.[16] As part of a large retrospective analysis of 177 recurrent cervical cancer cases after primary radical hysterectomy, Wang and colleagues evaluated 45 patients with extravaginal tumor involvement who were irradiated with curative intent. Within the limits of a nonrandomized comparison, it was noted that patients receiving concurrent chemoradiation fared better than did those undergoing radiotherapy alone.[1]

The role of concurrent chemoradiation in recurrent cervical cancer has not been definitively established and probably never will be through randomized trials, given the rarity and heterogeneity of these cases. However, in patients without contraindications to chemotherapy, combined modality chemoradiation may be a reasonable consideration, given the acknowledged overall poor prognosis in this population.

Brachytherapy

Brachytherapy is a crucial component of radiotherapy when used in the primary management of cervical cancer. It permits central dose intensification that is unachievable with external-beam radiation alone. Given the absence of the uterus, the use of brachytherapy in recurrent cervical cancer after radical hysterectomy has to be highly customized, on the basis of the location and size of the tumor. Furthermore, altered pelvic anatomy following primary surgery and the potential presence of small bowel adhesions to the vaginal apex require special consideration. Nevertheless, selective application of brachytherapy allows delivery of higher tumoricidal radiation doses, which may translate into improved salvage in patients with pelvic recurrences.[51–53] For most cases of recurrent cervical cancer in previously unirradiated patients, brachytherapy should be combined with external-beam radiation to provide optimal coverage of the volume at risk.

The integration of brachytherapy for salvage of recurrent cervical cancer varies from case to case. Intracavitary vaginal brachytherapy is typically less demanding technically, but its use is limited to patients with thin lesions confined to the vagina or to the superficial paravaginal tissues. In many patients, the extent and location of recurrent disease would necessitate an interstitial approach to achieve adequate tumor coverage.[51] Several investigators have suggested techniques that may assist in optimizing localization of intersitial brachytherapy. Monk and colleagues reported on the feasibility of laparotomy to guide interstitial needle placement in patients with pelvic tumor recurrences. The rationale for this treatment approach included the ability to accurately determine size and extent of recurrent disease, remove bowel and bladder adhesions to the tumor, allow insertion of the interstitial catheters under direct visual guidance, and form an omental pedicle graft to displace normal structures away from the irradiated tumor.[54] In some patients, location of recurrence relative to the bony pelvis precludes satisfactory placement of the interstitial needles through the transperineal approach. Paley and colleagues have described a new technique using an open retropubic dissection to guide and accommodate interstitial brachytherapy in patients with bulky recurrences involving the anterior vagina, thereby overcoming pubic arch interference to implantation (Figures 11–7 and 11–8).[55]

Surgery

In patients with cervical cancer undergoing primary radiotherapy, it has been suggested that extraperi-

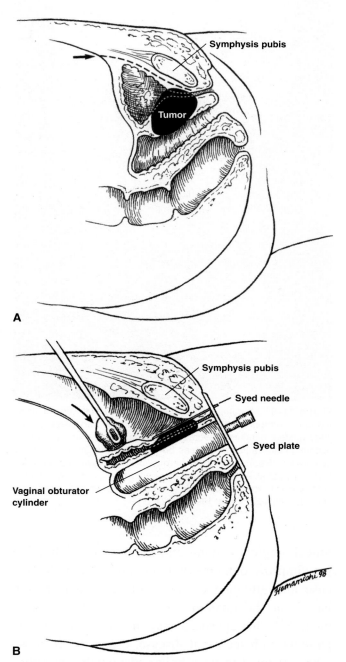

Figure 11–7. *A,* Sagittal view of an anterior vaginal tumor extending into the retropubic space, showing potential pubic arch interference with standard transperineal interstitial brachytherapy. The arrow and hashed line indicate the plane of dissection for tumor exposure and mobilization. *B,* With development of the space of Retzius, optimal interstitial needle placement is facilitated. (Reproduced with permission from Paley PJ, Koh WJ, Stelzer KS, et al. A new technique for performing Syed template interstitial implants for anterior vaginal tumors using an open retropubic approach. Gynecol Oncol 1999; 73:121–5.)

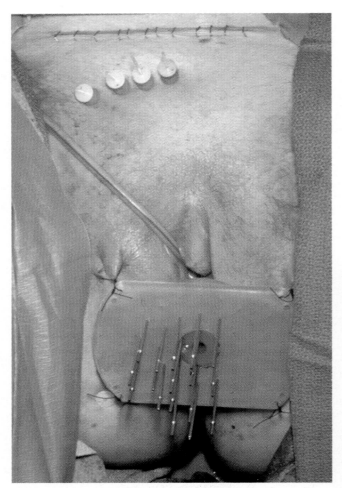

Figure 11–8. A completed afterloading interstitial implant using the open retropubic approach. In addition to the transperineal template-guided needles, several flexible catheters were placed to accommodate radiation sources behind the curvature of the pubic symphysis. (Reproduced with permission from Paley PJ, Koh WJ, Stelzer KS, et al. A new technique for performing Syed template interstitial implants for anterior vaginal tumors using an open retropubic approach. Gynecol Oncol 1999;73:121–5.)

toneal surgical staging and lymph node debulking may improve outcome by removing gross nodal disease and allowing optimal radiation field design based on the anatomic extent of nodal involvement.[56,57] This approach may also be applicable in patients with recurrent disease, especially in those who are noted to have bulky adenopathy on radiologic imaging.

While previously unirradiated patients with central failures may be technical candidates for radical surgical salvage, including possible pelvic exenteration, extirpative surgery should generally be reserved for cases that have failed radiation therapy.

Clinical Case Illustration

The synthesis of concepts discussed above is presented in the following actual case scenario and is illustrated in Figures 11–9 to 11–13. The patient is a 65-year-old woman who had undergone radical hysterectomy 7 years earlier for a stage Ib cervical cancer, without further adjuvant therapy. She was doing well until she presented with vaginal bleeding and was found to have an extensive local relapse involving essentially the entire vagina and extending to the left pelvic side wall. Biopsy confirmed recurrent squamous cell cancer. The CT

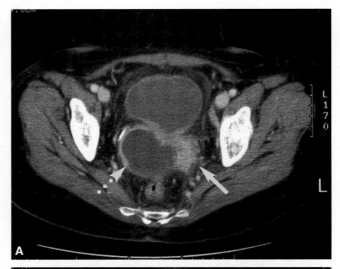

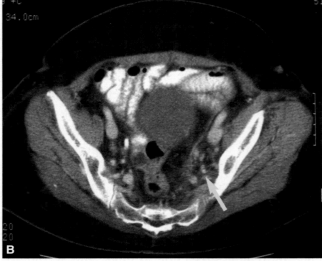

Figure 11–9. CT scans of a patient with recurrent cervical cancer following initial radical hysterectomy. *A,* The tumor was noted to involve essentially the whole vagina, with extension to the left pelvic side wall, and contained both solid (*solid arrow*) and cystic (*dotted arrow*) components. *B,* Additionally, a cluster of nodes in the left obturator region was identified (*arrow*).

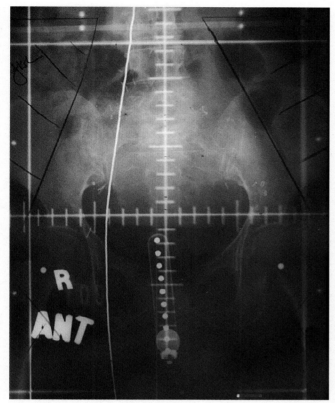

Figure 11–10. Initial anterior whole-pelvis external-beam radiation field used. The patient was treated with a four-field technique. Vaginal and rectal markers were used during simulation to assist in treatment set-up.

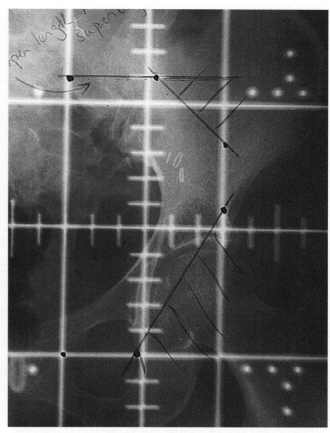

Figure 11–11. Anterior external boost field covering a limited left paravaginal/pelvic side wall volume.

scan noted mixed solid and cystic components of the recurrence (see Figure 11–9A), and a cluster of left pelvic lymph nodes (see Figure 11–9B). She underwent retroperitoneal lymph node dissection, with debulking of multiple (at least nine) replaced and matted nodes in the left obturator region. The patient received external-beam whole-pelvis radiotherapy to 45 Gy (see Figure 11–10), with concurrent weekly cisplatin chemotherapy. Subsequent tailored boosts included an additional 10 Gy external radiation delivered to a limited left paravaginal/pelvic side wall volume (see Figure 11–11), as well as separate intracavitary (see Figure 11–12) and interstitial (see Figure 11–13) brachytherapy insertions. The patient had a complete tumor response and remains alive without evidence of disease at 1.5 years following salvage therapy. This clinical example highlights the potential benefit of customization of care in patients with recurrent cervical cancer.

FUTURE DIRECTIONS

Advancements in the primary management of cervical cancer, including concurrent chemoradiation, an

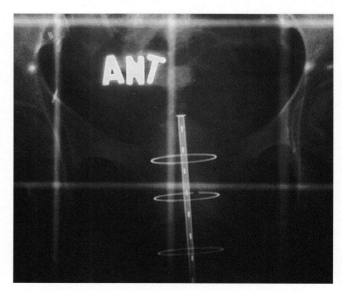

Figure 11–12. Intracavitary vaginal brachytherapy.

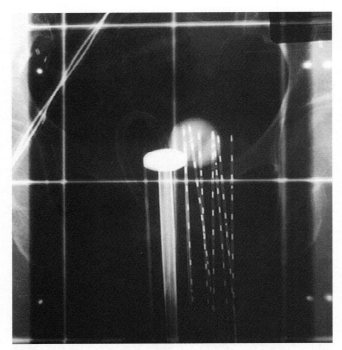

Figure 11–13.   Interstitial brachytherapy insertion as final boost.

emphasis on brachytherapy integration, better radiation field design and treatment planning, and appropriate selection of postsurgical adjuvant therapy, have fortuitously reduced the incidence of pelvic recurrences. Nevertheless, there will remain a small subset of patients with pelvis-confined relapses, in whom radical salvage management is needed.

Further improvements in the treatment of patients with recurrent cervical cancer are expected from several fronts. Increased use of contemporary imaging studies will lead to better selection of patients who can benefit from radical local treatment modalities. Continued progress in operative techniques, reconstructive methods, and postoperative care will further reduce the mortality, morbidity, and functional impairment in patients undergoing salvage surgery. Developments in radiation oncology, such as three-dimensional conformation applications, stereotactic approaches, and intensity-modulated radiotherapy, allow better radiation coverage of tumor, while sparing adjacent normal structures. These advancements in radiation technology may be exploited to optimize dose delivery to tumors involving the pelvic side wall or in selected cases of radical reirradiation. Finally, given the high rate of distant metastases in relapsing patients, the

identification and incorporation of active systemic agents into the management of recurrent cervical cancer are eagerly anticipated.

REFERENCES

1. Wang CJ, Lai CH, Huang HJ, et al. Recurrent cervical carcinoma after primary radical surgery. Am J Obstet Gynecol 1999;181:518–24.
2. Hogan WM, Boente MP. The role of surgery in the management of recurrent gynecologic cancer. Semin Oncol 1993;20:462–72.
3. Coleman RL, Keeney ED, Freedman RS, et al. Radical hysterectomy for recurrent carcinoma of the uterine cervix after radiotherapy. Gynecol Oncol 1994;55:29–35.
4. Perez CA, Grigsby PW, Chao KSC, et al. Tumor size, irradiation dose, and long-term outcome of carcinoma of uterine cervix. Int J Radiat Oncol Biol Phys 1998;41:307–17.
5. Fagundes H, Perez CA, Grigsby PW, Lockett MA. Distant metastases after irradiation alone in carcinoma of the uterine cervix. Int J Radiat Oncol Biol Phys 1992;24:197–204.
6. Logsdon MD, Eifel PJ. FIGO IIIB squamous cell carcinoma of the cervix: an analysis of prognostic factors emphasizing the balance between external beam and intracavitary radiation therapy. Int J Radiat Oncol Biol Phys 1999;43:763–75.
7. Koh WJ, Panwala K, Greer BE. Adjuvant therapy for high-risk, early stage cervical cancer. Semin Radiat Oncol 2000;10:51–60.
8. Sedlis A, Bundy BN, Rotman MZ, et al. A randomized trial of pelvic radiation therapy versus no further therapy in selected patients with stage IB carcinoma of the cervix after radical hysterectomy and pelvic lymphadenectomy: a Gynecologic Oncology Group study. Gynecol Oncol 1999;73:177–83.
9. Peters WA III, Liu PY, Barrett RJ II, et al. Concurrent chemotherapy and pelvic radiation therapy compared with pelvic radiation therapy alone as adjuvant therapy after radical surgery in high-risk early-stage cancer of the cervix. J Clin Oncol 2000;18:1606–13.
10. Lanciano R. Radiotherapy for the treatment of locally recurrent cervical cancer. Monogr Natl Cancer Inst 1996;21:113–5.
11. Krebs HB, Helmkamp BF, Sevin BU, et al. Recurrent cancer of the cervix following radical hysterectomy and pelvic node dissection. Obstet Gynecol 1982;59:422–7.
12. Larson DM, Copeland LJ, Stringer CA, et al. Recurrent cervical carcinoma after radical hysterectomy. Gynecol Oncol 1988;30:381–7.
13. Potter ME, Alvarez RD, Gay FL, et al. Optimal therapy

for pelvic recurrence after radical hysterectomy for early-stage cervical cancer. Gynecol Oncol 1990; 37:74–7.

14. Virostek LJ, Kim RY, Spencer SA, et al. Postsurgical recurrent carcinoma of the cervix: reassessment and results of radiation therapy options. Radiology 1996;201:559–63.

15. Ijaz T, Eifel PJ, Burke T, Oswald MJ. Radiation therapy of pelvic recurrence after radical hysterectomy for cervical carcinoma. Gynecol Oncol 1998;70:241–6.

16. Maneo A, Landoni F, Cormio G, et al. Concurrent carboplatin/5-fluorouracil and radiotherapy for recurrent cervical carcinoma. Ann Oncol 1999;10:803–7.

17. Shingleton HM, Gore H, Soong SJ, et al. Tumor recurrence and survival in stage IB cancer of the cervix. Am J Clin Oncol 1983;6:265–72.

18. Rubin SC, Hoskins WJ, Lewis JL Jr. Radical hysterectomy for recurrent cervical cancer following radiation therapy. Gynecol Oncol 1987;27:316–24.

19. Terada K, Morley GW. Radical hysterectomy as surgical salvage therapy for gynecologic malignancy. Obstet Gynecol 1987;70:913–5.

20. Hockel M, Baussmann E, Mitze M, Knapstein PG. Are pelvic side-wall recurrences of cervical cancer biologically different from central relapses? Cancer 1994;74:648–55.

21. Rutledge FN, Smith JP, Wharton JT, O'Quinn AG. Pelvic exenteration: analysis of 296 patients. Am J Obstet Gynecol 1977;129:881–92.

22. Morley GW, Hopkins MP, Lindenauer SM, Roberts JA. Pelvic exenteration, University of Michigan: 100 patients at 5 years. Obstet Gynecol 1989;74:934–43.

23. Sommers GM, Grigsby PW, Perez CA, et al. Outcome of recurrent cervical carcinoma following definitive irradiation. Gynecol Oncol 1989;35:150–5.

24. Rose PG, Adler LP, Rodriguez M, et al. Positron emission tomography for evaluating para-aortic nodal metastasis in locally advanced cervical cancer before surgical staging: a surgicopathologic study. J Clin Oncol 1999;17:41–5.

25. Brunschwig A. Complete excision of pelvic viscera for advanced carcinoma: a one-stage abdominoperineal operation with end colostomy and bilateral ureteral implantation into the colon above the colostomy. Cancer 1948;1:177–83.

26. Barber HRK. Relative prognostic significance of preoperative and operative findings in pelvic exenteration. Surg Clin North Am 1969;49:431–47.

27. Paley PJ, Greer BE. Surgical therapy for recurrent cervical cancer: pelvic exenteration. In: Gershenson DM, DeCherney A, Curry S, Brubaker L, editors. Operative gynecology. 2nd ed. New York, NY: W.B. Saunders Company; 2001. p. 325–34.

28. Averette HE, Lichtinger M, Sevin BU, Girtanner RE. Pelvic exenteration: a 15-year experience in a general metropolitan hospital. Am J Obstet Gynecol 1984;150:179–84.

29. Stanhope CR, Symmonds RE. Palliative exenteration—what, when, and why? Am J Obstet Gynecol 1985;152:12–6.

30. Shingleton HM, Soong SJ, Gelder MS, et al. Clinical and histopathologic factors predicting recurrence and survival after pelvic exenteration for cancer of the cervix. Obstet Gynecol 1989;73:1027–34.

31. Miller B, Morris M, Rutledge F, et al. Aborted exenterative procedures in recurrent cervical cancer. Gynecol Oncol 1993;50:94–9.

32. Plante M, Roy M. The use of operative laparoscopy in determining eligibility for pelvic exenteration in patients with recurrent cervical cancer. Gynecol Oncol 1995;59:401–4.

33. Stanhope CR, Webb MJ, Podratz KC. Pelvic exenteration for recurrent cervical cancer. Clin Obstet Gynecol 1990;33:897–909.

34. Crozier M, Morris M, Levenback C, et al. Pelvic exenteration for adenocarcinoma of the uterine cervix. Gynecol Oncol 1995;58:74–8.

35. Magrina JF, Stanhope CR, Weaver AL. Pelvic exenterations: supralevator, infralevator, and with vulvectomy. Gynecol Oncol 1997;64:130–5.

36. Brunschwig A, Daniel WW. Pelvic exenteration operations. Ann Surg 1960;151:571–6.

37. Penalver MA, Barreau G, Sevin BU, Averette HE. Surgery for the treatment of locally recurrent disease. Monogr Natl Cancer Inst 1996;21:117–22.

38. Estape R, Angioli R. Surgical management of advanced and recurrent cervical cancer. Semin Surg Oncol 1999;16:236–41.

39. Hatch KD, Gelder MS, Soong SJ, et al. Pelvic exenteration with low rectal anastomosis: survival, complications, and prognostic factors. Gynecol Oncol 1990;38:462–7.

40. Stelzer KJ, Koh WJ, Greer BE, et al. The use of intraoperative radiation therapy in radical salvage for recurrent cervical cancer: outcome and toxicity. Am J Obstet Gynecol 1995;172:1881–8.

41. Garton GR, Gunderson LL, Webb MJ, et al. Intraoperative radiation therapy in gynecologic cancer: update of the experience at a single institution. Int J Radiat Oncol Biol Phys 1997;37:839–43.

42. Hockel M, Sclenger K, Hamm H, et al. Five-year experience with combined operative and radiotherapeutic treatment of recurrent gynecologic tumors infiltrating the pelvic wall. Cancer 1996;77:1918–33.

43. Hu KS, Harrison LB. Results and complications of surgery combined with intra-operative radiation therapy for the treatment of locally advanced or recurrent cancers in the pelvis. Semin Surg Oncol 2000;18:269–78.

44. Russell AH, Koh WJ, Markette K, et al. Radical reirra-

diation for recurrent or second primary carcinoma of the female reproductive tract. Gynecol Oncol 1987;27:226–32.

45. Randall ME, Evans L, Greven KM, et al. Interstitial reirradiation for recurrent gynecologic malignancies: results and analysis of prognostic factors. Gynecol Oncol 1993;48:23–31.

46. Nori D, Hilaris BS, Kim HS, et al. Interstitial irradiation in recurrent gynecological cancer. Int J Radiat Oncol Biol Phys 1981;7:1513–7.

47. Xiang-E W, Shu-mo C, Ya-qin D, Ke W. Treatment of late recurrent vaginal malignancy after initial radiotherapy for carcinoma of the cervix: an analysis of 73 cases. Gynecol Oncol 1998;69:125–9.

48. Jobsen JJ, Leer JW, Cleton FJ, Hermans J. Treatment of locoregional recurrence of carcinoma of the cervix by radiotherapy after primary surgery. Gynecol Oncol 1989;33:368–71.

49. Thomas GM. Improved treatment for cervical cancer—concurrent chemotherapy and radiotherapy. N Engl J Med 1999;340:1198–200.

50. Thomas GM, Dembo AJ, Myhr T, et al. Long-term results of concurrent radiation and chemotherapy for carcinoma of the cervix recurrent after surgery. Int J Gynecol Cancer 1993;3:193–8.

51. Rush S, Lovecchio J, Gal D, et al. Comprehensive management including interstitial brachytherapy for locally advanced or recurrent gynecologic malignancies. Gynecol Oncol 1992;46:322–5.

52. Bellotti JE, Kagan AR, Wollin M, Olch A. Application of the ICRU report 38 reference volume concept to the radiotherapeutic management of recurrent endometrial and cervical carcinoma. Radiother Oncol 1993;26:254–9.

53. Greven KM. Interstitial radiation for recurrent cervix or endometrial cancer in the suburethral region. Int J Radiat Oncol Biol Phys 1998;41:831–4.

54. Monk BJ, Walker JL, Tewari K, et al. Open interstitial brachytherapy for the treatment of local-regional recurrences of uterine corpus and cervix cancer after primary surgery. Gynecol Oncol 1994;52:222–8.

55. Paley PJ, Koh WJ, Stelzer KS, et al. A new technique for performing Syed template interstitial implants for anterior vaginal tumors using an open retropubic approach. Gynecol Oncol 1999;73:121–5.

56. Cosin JA, Fowler JM, Chen MD, et al. Pretreatment surgical staging of patients with cervical carcinoma: the case for lymph node debulking. Cancer 1998;82:2241–8.

57. Goff BA, Muntz HG, Paley PJ, et al. Impact of surgical staging in women with locally advanced cervical cancer. Gynecol Oncol 1999;74:436–42.

12

Management of Vaginal Cancer

HIGINIA R. CARDENES, MD
KATHERINE Y. LOOK, MD
MARCUS E. RANDALL, MD

Primary vaginal cancer is a rare entity accounting for only 1 to 2 percent of all female genital neoplasias. Invasive carcinomas account for 70 to 75 percent of the carcinoma cases, whereas in situ carcinomas account for 25 to 30 percent. The most common histologies are squamous cell carcinoma, ranging from 74 to 86 percent, and adenocarcinoma making up to 13 to 15 percent of most series.[1-4] Nearly 50 percent of patients with carcinoma in situ (CIS) or invasive carcinoma of the vagina have undergone prior hysterectomy.[4-7] Ten to 50 percent of patients with vaginal cancer have previously been treated with surgery or radiotherapy (RT) for CIS or invasive carcinoma of the cervix.[3-14]

The majority (57 to 83%) of vaginal primaries occur in the upper third of the vault or at the apex, most commonly in the posterior wall; the lower third of the vagina may be involved in as many as 31 percent of patients.[3-6] Lesions confined to the middle third are uncommon. Location of the vaginal carcinoma is an important consideration in planning therapy and determining prognosis.

The two commonly used staging systems for carcinoma of the vagina are the International Federation of Gynecology and Obstetrics (FIGO) (Table 12–1) and the American Joint Commission on Cancer (AJCC) TNM (tumor-node-metastasis) classifications.[15] According to FIGO guidelines, patients with tumor involvement of the cervix or vulva should be classified as primary cervical or vulvar cancers, respectively.

A metastatic work-up, including routine laboratory work (complete blood count [CBC] with differential and platelets, liver and renal function tests) and chest radiography, should be obtained in all patients. Cystoscopy and proctoscopy should be performed on patients with symptoms or clinical findings suspicious for bladder or rectal infiltration, respectively. Pelvic computed tomography (CT) and/or magnetic resonance imaging (MRI) scans are often performed to evaluate inguinofemoral and/or pelvic lymph nodes, as well as the extent of local disease. Patients with vaginal melanoma or sarcoma should have CT scans of the chest, abdomen, and pelvis as part of the work-up.

SQUAMOUS CELL CARCINOMA OF THE VAGINA

General Considerations

Due to the rarity of vaginal carcinoma, data concerning the natural history, prognostic factors, and treatment derive from small retrospective studies. In most patients, the primary treatment modality is RT as reported by the Society of Gynecologic Oncologists in its practice guidelines published in 1998.[1] RT provides excellent tumor control in early and superficial lesions with satisfactory functional results. This makes it imperative that RT techniques yielding optimal tumor control and functional results are used. Furthermore, most patients are elderly, and a radical surgical approach is often not feasible, even in patients with early-stage disease.

Patients who have a history of previous hysterectomy most often have tumors that are limited to the upper one-third of the vagina.[4,13] Some of these may be candidates for treatment with partial upper vaginectomy. In contrast, among patients with an intact uterus, only 25 to 30 percent of vaginal cancers are limited to the upper vagina, partly because cancers that have spread to involve the cervix are often classified as cervical cancers.

It has been suggested that some patients with early-stage vaginal cancers can be treated successfully with surgery alone. However, few studies directly compare treatments with radiation and surgery. For all but the earliest stages of the disease, curative surgical resection requires a radical approach, with urinary and fecal diversion to secure adequate margins. Local excision and partial and complete vaginectomy have given way to a more individualized approach that takes into consideration the patient's age, the extent of the lesion, and whether it is localized or multicentric. In younger patients with early-stage disease, treatment may also depend on the patient's desire to preserve a functional vagina.[4]

Radiotherapy Techniques

External-beam radiation therapy (EBRT) and brachytherapy are both used to treat carcinomas of the vagina. Brachytherapy can be performed with intracavitary (ICB) or interstitial (ITB) techniques.

External-Beam Radiotherapy

External-beam radiation therapy is advisable for patients with deeply infiltrating or poorly differentiated stage I lesions and for all patients with stage II to IVa disease. The treatment is generally delivered using opposed anterior and posterior fields (AP/PA) (Figure 12–1A). The pelvis receives between 20 and 45 Gy, depending on the stage of the disease, followed, in some cases, by bilateral pelvic side wall boosts to 45 to 55 Gy. High energy photons (> 10 MV) are usually preferred. Treatment portals cover at least the true pelvis with a 1.5 to 2 cm margin beyond the pelvic rim; superiorly, the field extends to either L4-L5 or L5-S1, to cover the pelvic lymph nodes up to the common iliacs, and extends distally to include the entire vagina. Lateral fields, if used, should extend anteriorly to adequately include the external iliac nodes, anterior to the pubic symphysis, and at least to the junction of S2-S3 posteriorly (Figure 12–1B).

For tumors that involve the middle and lower vagina with clinically negative groins, the bilateral

Table 12–1. VAGINAL CANCER STAGING SYSTEMS: FIGO AND TNM			
	TNM	FIGO	DEFINITION
Primary Tumor (T)	Tx		Primary tumor cannot be assessed
	T0		No evidence of primary tumor
	Tis	0	Carcinoma in situ
	T1	I	Tumor confined to the vagina
	T2	II	Tumor invades paravaginal tissues but not to pelvic wall
	T3	III	Tumor extends to pelvic wall
	T4*	IVa	Tumor invades mucosa of the bladder or rectum and/or extends beyond the true pelvis
		IVb	Distant metastasis
Regional Lymph Nodes (N)	Nx		Regional lymph nodes cannot be assessed
	N0		No regional lymph node metastasis
Upper two-thirds of vagina	N1		Pelvic nodes metastasis
Lower one-third of vagina	N1		Unilateral inguinal node metastasis
	N2		Bilateral inguinal node metastasis
Distant Metastasis (M)	Mx		Presence of distant metastasis cannot be assessed
	M0		No distant metastasis
	M1		Distant metastasis
Staging Grouping	St 0		Tis N0 M0
	St I		T1 N0 M0
	St II		T2 N0 M0
	St III		T1 N1 M0
			T2 N1 M0
			T3 N0 M0
			T3 N1 M0
	St IVa		T1 N2 M0
			T2 N2 M0
			T3 N2 M0
			T4, Any N, M0
	St IVb		Any T, Any N, M1

FIGO = International Federation of Gynecology and Obstetrics; TNM = tumor-node-metastasis; St = stage.
*Note that the presence of bullous edema is not sufficient evidence to classify a tumor as T4. If the mucosa is not involved, the tumor is stage III.

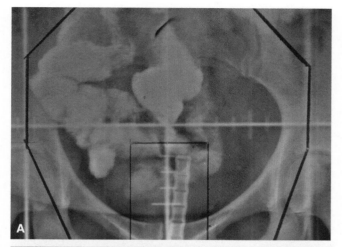

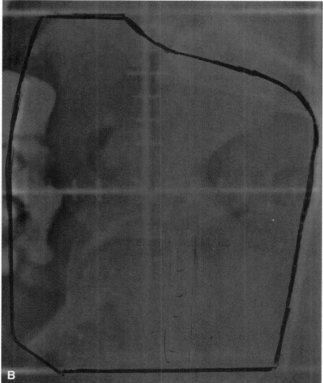

Figure 12–1. *A,* Pelvic AP/PA field, including the central block added after the first intracavitary implant at 2,000 cGy, whole pelvis dose, for the treatment of early-stage vaginal cancer involving the vaginal vault without clinical involvement of the inguinofemoral nodes. *B,* Lateral field.

inguinofemoral lymph node regions should be treated electively with 45 to 50 Gy. This requires a modification of the standard portals (Figure 12–2). Planning CT is recommended to adequately determine the depth of the inguinofemoral nodes. A number of techniques have been used to treat the pelvis and inguinal nodes without overtreating the femoral

heads. Dittmer and Randall[16] described one approach, in which the inguinal nodes are boosted with an anterior photon field using asymmetric collimator jaws. An advantage of this technique is its simplicity (a single isocenter is used, and no partial transmission block is needed) (Figure 12–3). If the inguinal nodes are clinically involved, they may be boosted using small electron or photon fields. For patients with positive pelvic nodes, a boost to the areas of gross nodal disease, as defined by CT, should be given, using small high-energy photon fields to deliver a total dose of between 60 and 65Gy.

Low-Dose-Rate Intracavitary Brachytherapy

Carcinoma in situ and some small T1 lesions, < 0.5 cm thick, can be treated adequately with ICB alone. Low-dose-rate (LDR)-ICB is performed using Burnett, Bloedorn, Delclos,[17] or MIRALVA[18] vaginal applicators loaded with cesium-137 sources. Delclos afterloading vaginal cylinders have a central hollow metallic tube, in which the sources are placed; plastic rings of varying diameter (2.5 to 4.5 cm) are inserted over the cylinder (Figure 12–4). The largest diameter that can comfortably be accommodated by the patient should be used to improve the ratio of mucosa-to-tumor dose and to eliminate vaginal rugations. The vulva is usually sutured closed during the implant, to secure the applicators.

Thin (< 0.5 cm) apical vaginal lesions can be treated using vaginal colpostats or, if the uterus is in place, with an intrauterine tandem and colpostats. A minimum dose of 65 to 70 Gy (including external-beam irradiation) is usually prescribed at a depth of 0.5 cm from the mucosal surface (Figure 12–5). Treatment is usually delivered over 2 to 3 days at a rate of 50 to 80 cGy/h to exploit the radiobiologic advantages of low-dose-rate irradiation. If indicated, the remainder of the vagina can be treated (usually to a total dose of 50 to 60 Gy to the vaginal surface) with a second application using vaginal cylinders. After the applicators are placed, radiographs should be obtained, with radiopaque markers in the vaginal apex and at the introitus to confirm the adequacy of the applicator placement and to assist treatment planning. To minimize the risk of vulvar complications, sources should not be allowed to protrude beyond the introitus. The use of LDR remote-control afterloading technology reduces radiation exposure to hospital personnel and permits optimization of the isodose distribution. A number of intracavitary applicator systems have been designed specifically to treat the vagina. One of these, designed by Perez and colleagues,[18,19] incorporates into the vaginal applicator, two ovoid sources and a central tandem to treat the vagina (alone or in combination with the uterine cervix) (Figure 12–6).

High-Dose-Rate Intracavitary Brachytherapy

Computer technology and remote afterloading have made it possible to deliver brachytherapy treatments at

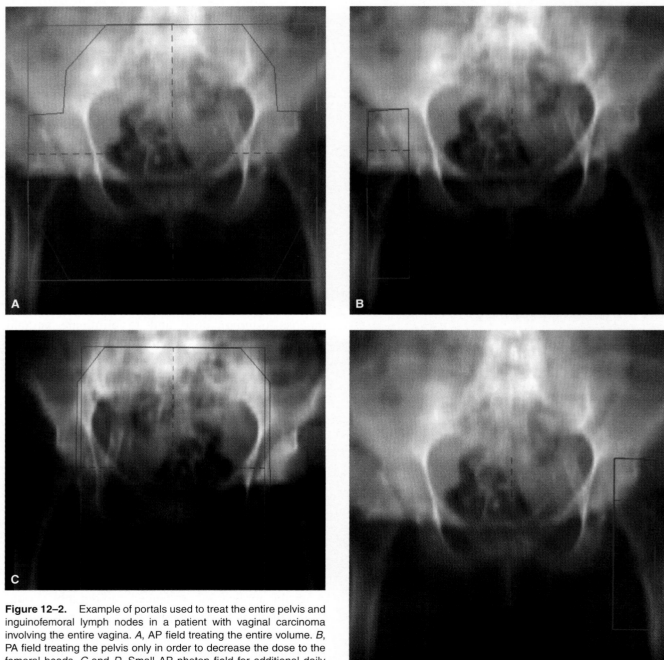

Figure 12–2. Example of portals used to treat the entire pelvis and inguinofemoral lymph nodes in a patient with vaginal carcinoma involving the entire vagina. *A*, AP field treating the entire volume. *B*, PA field treating the pelvis only in order to decrease the dose to the femoral heads. *C* and *D*, Small AP photon field for additional daily boost to the inguinofemoral nodes.

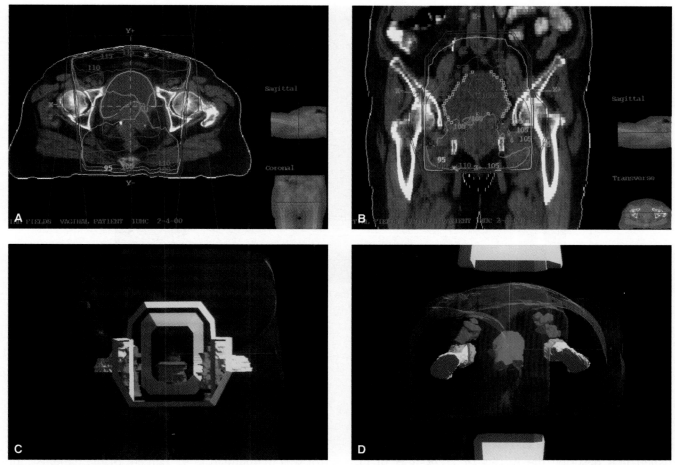

Figure 12–3.   *A*, Axial and *B*, coronal isodose distribution for the treatment of locally advanced carcinoma of the vagina. *C*, "Beams-eye-view" of target volumes and *D*, isodose distribution.

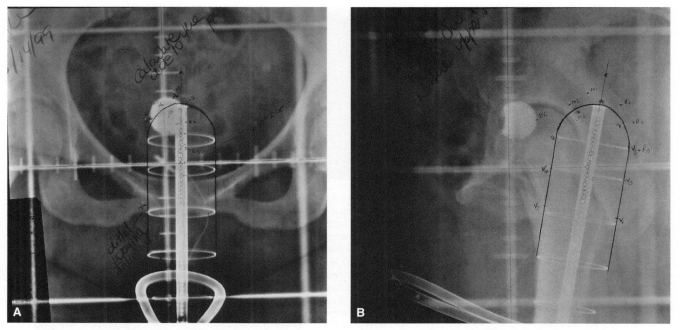

Figure 12–4.   *A*, AP and *B*, lateral films showing 4-cm Delclos vaginal cylinders in the treatment of early-stage vaginal cancer.

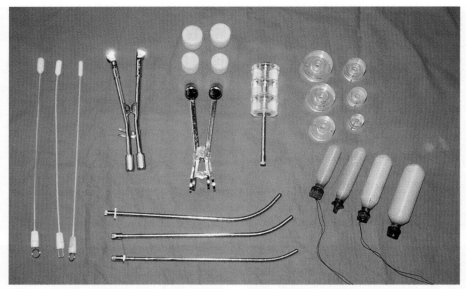

Figure 12–5.   Applicators commonly used in the treatment of gynecologic malignancies, including intrauterine tandem and vaginal ovoids.

very-high-dose rates. High-dose-rate (HDR)-ICB has typically been performed with a train of multiple cobalt-60 pellets (4-Ci source activity) or with a single traveling 10-Ci iridium-192 source (Micro-Selectron HDR, Nucletron). The applicators are similar to those used to deliver LDR-ICB. Few reports have been published that describe the results of HDR-ICB in the treatment of primary carcinomas of the vagina.[13,20]

The reports that are available include few patients and have short follow-up. Nanavati and colleagues[20] described 13 patients with primary vaginal cancers who were treated using EBRT (45 Gy) and HDR-ICB (20 to 28 Gy, three to four fractions, calculated at 0.5 cm from the surface of the applicator). Local control was maintained in 92 percent of the patients, but the median follow-up was only 2.6 years (range 0.7 to

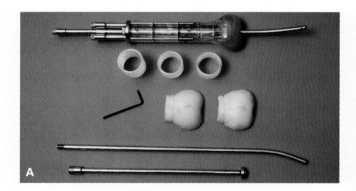

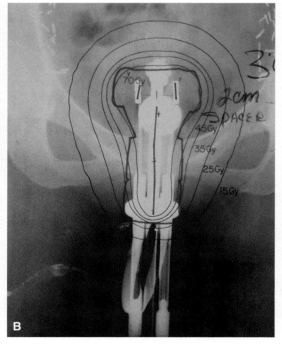

Figure 12–6.   *A,* MIRALVA applicator with plastic sleeves to increase the diameter of the vaginal cylinder, afterloading tandem, and plastic caps of different sizes to increase diameter of vaginal cuff portion of the applicator. (Reproduced with permission from Perez CA, Slessinger ED, Grigsby PW. Design of an afterloading vaginal applicator (MIRALVA). Int J Radiat Oncol Biol Phys 1990;18: 1503–8.) *B,* Corresponds to the coronal, sagittal, and axial isodose distributions for the applicator loaded with cesium-137 radioactive sources. (Reproduced with permission from Slessinger ED, Perez CA, Grigsby PW, Williamson JF. Dosimetry and dose specification for a new gynecological brachytherapy applicator. Int J Radiat Oncol Biol Phys 1992;22:1117–24.)

5.2 years). Although the authors initially treated patients with a dose of 21 Gy in three fractions, they changed their prescription to 20 Gy in four equal fractions to reduce the risk of complications. Although they did not report severe, acute or chronic intestinal or bladder toxicity, moderate to severe vaginal stenosis occurred in 46 percent of the patients. The authors recognized that follow-up may have been too short to accurately estimate the risk of late toxicity.

Many aspects of the use of HDR-ICB remain unknown or poorly understood. Specifically, the ideal fractionation schedule, total dose, and methods of dose specification, optimization, and calculation are unknown. Also the relative radiobiologic effects of HDR and LDR,[21,22] and the best ways of combining HDR with EBRT and/or LDR-ICB are incompletely understood. In the authors' opinion, until further data are available with longer follow-up and a better understanding of the physical and radiobiologic principles involved in the HDR-ICB is reached, this should not be routinely used in the management of primary vaginal carcinoma. We strongly encourage the continued use of LDR-ICB, given its excellent results and extensively documented long-term outcome.

Interstitial Brachytherapy

Interstitial brachytherapy is an important component in the treatment of more advanced primary vaginal carcinomas, typically in combination with EBRT or ICB. The first step in treatment planning is to define the tumor volume, using clinical, radiologic, or operative findings. Second, the type of implant (permanent or temporary) must be selected, and its size and geometry (eg, single plane, double plane) should be estimated considering the tumor's size, location, and the extent and proximity of normal structures. The principal advantages of temporary implants are readily controlled distribution of the radioactive sources and easier modification of the dose distribution; the main advantages of a permanent seed implant include relative safety/simplicity, easy applicability, cost-effectiveness, and ability to be performed with local anesthesia. As a general rule, temporary implants are more commonly used in the curative treatment of larger gynecologic malignancies; permanent implants may be used to treat smaller tumors or recurrent disease.

The number and strength of the radioactive sources and their intended distribution within the target volume are determined preoperatively, using available guidelines, such as nomograms, tables, and computer-assisted optimization techniques. Following this, it is necessary to specify an approximate dose rate to the target volume, which requires careful localization of the sources and computer calculation of the three-dimensional radiation dose distribution. Finally, a dose prescription, based on the treatment volume, tumor sensitivity, dose rate, prior treatments, and tolerance of normal surrounding tissues, is required.[23]

When performing an interstitial procedure, freehand implants or template systems can be employed. Different templates have been designed to assist in preplanning and to guide and secure the position of the needles in the target volume. All rely on pelvic examination to help guide the location and depth of needle placement. A popular commercially available template is the Syed-Neblett device (Alpha Omega Services, Bellflower, CA) (Figure 12–7A).[24] The modified Syed-Neblett[25] applicator consists of a perineal template, vaginal obturator, and 17-gauge hollow guides of various lengths, making it possible to combine interstitial and intracavitary sources (Figures 12–7B and 12–8). A similar afterloading applicator, the "MUPIT" (Martinez Universal Perineal Interstitial Template) (Figure 12–9) was developed by Martinez and colleagues.[26] The major advantage of these systems is greater control of the placement of the sources relative to the tumor volume and critical structures because of the fixed geometry of the template and cylinders. In addition, improved dose-rate distributions can be obtained using computer-assisted optimization of the source placement and strength during the planning and loading phase.

The inaccuracies of pelvic examination and the close proximity of the rectum and bladder to the target volume can contribute to a risk of either underdosing the target volume or causing bladder and rectal morbidity. Recently, techniques have been developed to decrease potential morbidity. Newer techniques that may improve the accuracy of target localization and needle placement include transrectal

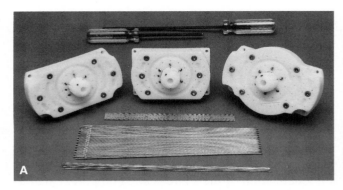

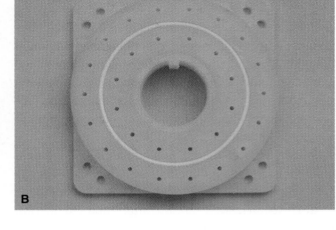

Figure 12–7.   *A*, Syed-Neblett (Reproduced with permission from Syed AMN, Puthawala AA, Neblett D, et al. Trasperineal interstitial-intracavitary "Syed-Neblett" applicator in the treatment of carcinoma of the uterine cervix. Endocuriether Hypertherm Oncol 1986; 2:1–13.) and *B*, modified templates (Reproduced with permission from Disain PJ, Syed N, Puthwala AA. Malignant neoplasia of the upper vagina. Endocuriether Hypertherm Oncol 1990;6:251–6).

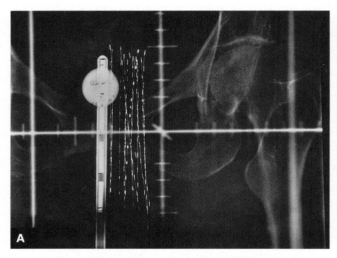

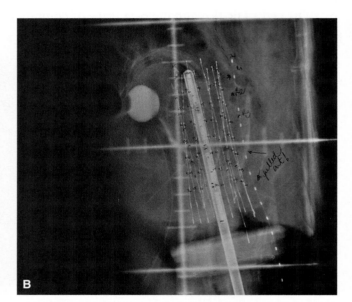

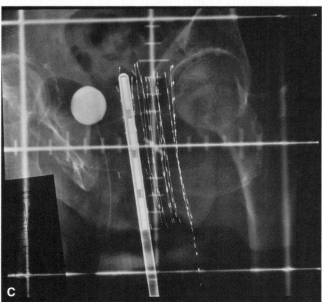

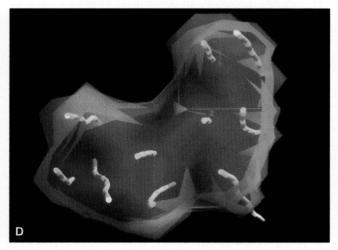

Figure 12–8.   *A*, AP, *B*, lateral, and *C*, oblique radiographs of an interstitial and intracavitary implant in carcinoma of the vagina using the modified Syed-Neblett template. *D*, Three-dimensional isodose distribution.

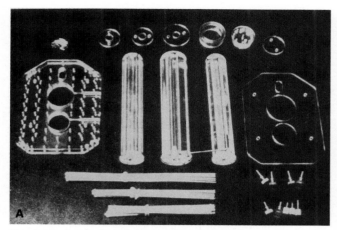 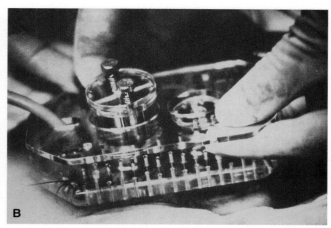

Figure 12–9. *A,* Multiple-site perineal applicator (MUPIT) containing acrylic predrilled template and cover plate, acrylic cylinders, obturator screws, and stainless steel needles. *B,* MUPIT sutured to patient's perineum. The cover plate is screwed to the template to keep the needles and radioactive material in place. (Reproduced with permission from Martinez A, Cox RS, Edmudson GK. A mutiple-site perineal applicator (MUPIT) for treatment of prostatic, anorectal and gynecologic malignancies. Int J Radiat Oncol Biol Phys 1984;10:297–305.)

ultrasonography (TRUS)-, CT-, or MRI-based treatment planning, and laparotomy- or laparoscopic-guided needle placement.[27–29] Laparoscopy is a shorter and less invasive procedure than laparotomy (Figure 12–10). The real-time TRUS-guided Syed-Neblett template implantation technique was reported by Stock and colleagues,[29] providing an interactive noninvasive technique that allows for highly accurate needle placement.

Management Options and Outcomes

Stage I

The results of several reviews of treatment using different treatment approaches for stage I vaginal cancer are summarized in Table 12–2.[1–9,12,30–36] For patients with small stage I lesions limited to the upper third of the vagina, primary surgery or RT may be appropriate therapy. Several institutions have reported excellent results after radical surgery in highly selected cases, with survival rates ranging from 75 to 100 percent.[1–5,32] Patients in whom surgery may be the preferred option include those with lesions at the apex, in which a partial vaginectomy or extension of a radical hysterectomy with upper vaginectomy can provide adequate margins, and those with very superficial lesions, which may be removed with wide local excision. Surgical treatment of lesions that involve the lower third of the vagina may be approached with

radical vulvovaginectomy and inguinal node dissection though some may require exenteration.[2,3,5] (As radiation therapy has improved, primary exenteration

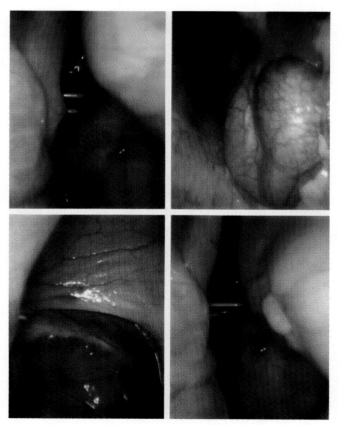

Figure 12–10. Laparoscopically guided interstitial brachytherapy implant allows displacement of bowel during the procedure and correct placement of the needles, avoiding their protrusion into the peritoneal cavity.

Table 12–2. STAGE I VAGINAL CANCER: TREATMENT APPROACH AND RESULTS

Treatment Modality Author	No. Patients	Survival	DFS
Irradiation ± Surgery			
Ali[35]	13	5 yr 100%	
Andersen[7]	12	5 yr 58.3%	
Chyle[8]	59		10 yr 76%
Creasman[1] (NCDB)	169	5 yr 73%	
		79% S+RT (47)	
		63% RT (122)	
Davis[2]	19	5 yr	
		100% S+RT (5)	
		65% RT (14)	
Kirkbride[9]	40	5 yr 72%	
Kucera[34]	16	5 yr 81.3%	
Lee[30]	17		5 yr 94%
Perez[31]	59		10 yr 80%
Prempree[36]	6		5 yr 83%
Reddy[33]	15	5 yr 78%	
Spirtos[12]	18	5 yr 94%	
Stock[4]	8		5 yr
			100% S+RT (6)
			80% RT (2)
Urbanski[14]	33	5 yr 73%	
Radical Surgery			
Ball[5]	19	5 yr 76%	5 yr 84%
Creasman[1] (NCDB)	76	5 yr 90%	
Davis[2]	25		LCR 85%
Gallup[6]	3		LCR 100%
Peters[32]	12	5 yr 75%	
Rubin[3]	5		LCR 80%
Stock[4]	15		5 yr 56%

DFS = disease-free survival; LCR = local control rate; S = surgery; RT = radiation therapy; NCDB = National Cancer Data Base.

has fallen out of favor for such lesions.) If tumor is found to be involving or close to the surgical margins, adjuvant RT may also be needed.

For most patients who have stage I disease involving the middle third of the vagina, the treatment of choice is RT, using brachytherapy with or without EBRT. If the lesion is very small, wide local excision can be considered. For most patients with distal vaginal lesions, RT is also the treatment of choice because a surgical approach would require resection of the vulva or sphincters. Most authors emphasize that brachytherapy alone, using afterloading vaginal cylinders, is adequate for superficial stage I patients achieving 95 to 100 percent local-control rates. Mucosal doses of 80 to 120 Gy are typically delivered, depending on the diameter of the cylinders, when prescribing 65 to 70 Gy at a depth of 0.5 cm beyond the vaginal surface.[37] For lesions thicker than 0.5 cm, at the time of implantation, it is advisable to combine ICB and ITB (single- or double-plane implant). This should enhance the probability of tumor control without exposing the entire mucosa of the vagina to high doses of RT (proximal and distal vaginal mucosal doses should be limited to 140 Gy and 100 Gy, respectively.

There are no well-established criteria regarding the use of EBRT in patients with stage I disease.[8,11,14,38] Perez and colleagues[11,31] did not find a significant correlation between the technique of irradiation used and the probability of local or pelvic recurrence, probably because the treatment technique varied according to tumor-related factors. There is general consensus that EBRT (20 to 50 Gy) is advisable for larger, more infiltrating or poorly differentiated tumors that may have a higher risk of lymph node metastasis.[8]

Stage II

In 1973, Perez and colleagues[39] proposed that FIGO stage II vaginal cancer should be subdivided into stage IIa (infiltration of subvaginal tissues without extension to parametrium) and stage IIb (infiltration of the parametrium without extension to pelvic side walls). However, most authors do not use this classification, and there is limited published data to support it.[10,12,36]

Patients with stage II disease are uniformly treated with EBRT followed by ICB and/or ITB. Perez and colleagues[31] showed that in stage IIa, the local tumor control was 70 percent (37 of 53) in patients receiving brachytherapy combined with EBRT, compared with 40 percent (4 of 10) in patients treated with either brachytherapy or EBRT alone. In stage IIb, the locoregional control was also superior with combined EBRT and brachytherapy (61% versus 50%, respectively).

Generally, 40 to 50 Gy is delivered to the whole pelvis to treat the primary and regional lymphatics. An additional boost of 30 to 35 Gy is given with brachytherapy. Patients with lesions limited to the upper third of the vagina can be treated with an intrauterine tandem and vaginal ovoids or cylinders. In patients with parametrial infiltration, a boost with EBRT and/or an interstitial implant is advisable to deliver a minimum tumor dose of

Table 12–3. STAGE II VAGINAL CANCER: TREATMENT APPROACH AND RESULTS

Treatment Modality Author	No. Patients	Survival	DFS
Irradiation ± Surgery			
Ali[35]	11 (proximal)	5yr 91%	
	10 (distal)	5 yr 20%	
Andersen[7]	7	5 yr 43%	
Chyle[8]	104		10 yr 69%
Creasman (NCDB)[1]	175	5 yr 58%	
		58% S+RT (39)	
		57% RT (136)	
Davis[2]	18	5 yr 53%	
		69% S+RT (9)	
		50% RT (9)	
Gallup[6]	12		5 yr 50%
Kirkbride[9]	38	5 yr 70%	
Kucera[34]	23	5 yr 43.5%	
Lee[30]	IIa 6		5 yr CSS 80%
	IIb 10		5 yr CSS 39%
Perez[31]	IIa 63		10 yr 55%
	IIb 34		10 yr 35%
Prempree[36]	IIa 20		5 yr 65%
	IIb 11		5 yr 64%
Reddy[33]	22	5 yr 71%	
Spirtos[12]	5	5 yr 80%	
Stock[13]	27	5 yr 48%	
Stock[4]	35		69% S+RT (10)
			31% RT (25)
Urbanski[14]	37	5 yr 54%	
Radical Surgery			
Ball[5]	8	5 yr 37%	LCR 63%
Creasman (NCDB)[1]	34	5 yr 70%	
Davis[2]	27	5 yr 49%	
Peters[32]	St I+II 12		LCR 75%
Rubin[3]	3		LCR 33%
Stock[4]	23		5 yr 68%

DFS = disease-free survival; CSS = cause-specific survival; LCR = local control rate; NCDB = National Cancer Data Base; S = surgery; RT = radiation therapy; St = stage.

70 to 75 Gy, with 55 to 60 Gy to the pelvic side wall. The results of several series by different treatment modalities, including radical surgery, in highly selected stage II patients are presented in Table 12–3.[1–9,12,13,15,30–36]

Despite careful selection of patients in most surgical series,[2,3,5] survival rates usually compare unfavorably with those of patients treated with radiation. A possible exception is the experience reported by Stock and colleagues.[4] In this series, the apparent superiority of surgical treatment for stage II patients may have been due to selection bias because those treated with RT alone were more likely to have had stage IIb disease with extensive paracolpal involvement, while those offered surgical treatment tended to have less advanced disease.

Stage III

Generally, these patients receive 45 to 50 Gy EBRT to the pelvis and, in some cases, an additional parametrial dose with midline shielding to deliver up to 60 Gy to the pelvic side walls. Ideally, interstitial brachytherapy boost is performed, if technically feasible, to deliver a minimum tumor dose of 70 to 75 Gy. In patients with an intact uterus, it is possible to combine intracavitary and interstitial techniques in order to improve dosimetry and safety. Templates such as the MUPIT[26] or Syed-Neblett[24,25] can be used in an effort to improve dose distribution. If brachytherapy is not feasible, a shrinking-field technique can be used, with fields defined using the three-dimensional treatment planning capabilities, when available (Figure 12–11).

The overall cure rate for patients with stage III disease is 30 to 50 percent. Table 12–4 shows the treatment results with different therapeutic modalities, including four series that reported the use of primary surgery in highly selected patients with advanced disease,[1–4,7–9,12–14,30–35] However, each of these series reported a far greater number of patients with similar stage disease treated with RT, which represents the preferred approach in contemporary practice.[3–6]

Stage IV

Stage IVa includes patients with rectal or bladder mucosa involvement. Patients with positive inguinal nodes may also be classified as having stage IV disease. Although some patients with stage IVa disease are curable, many patients are treated palliatively with EBRT only. Curative-intent RT might involve only high-dose EBRT using a shrinking-field technique, with a boost to gross positive inguinal nodes to 60 to 65 Gy. Pelvic exenteration can also be curative in highly selected stage IV patients with small-volume central disease. The results of different treatment approaches in stage IV vaginal cancer are very disappointing with local control rates of 25 to 30 percent and long-term survival of < 5 percent.[4–9,12,14,30–33]

Patterns of Failure

Of patients who have a recurrence, at least 85 percent will have locoregional failure, usually confined to the pelvis and vagina.[4,8,31,34] The rate of locoregional recurrence in stage I is approximately 10 to 20 percent, versus 30 to 40 percent in stage II. The pelvic control rate for patients with stage III (pelvic

wall fixation) and stage IV disease is relatively low, and about 50 to 70 percent of the patients have recurrence or persistence in spite of well-designed RT. Median time to recurrence is 6 to 12 months. Tumor recurrence is associated with a dismal prognosis with only a few long-term survivors after salvage therapy. Failure in distant sites alone or associated with locoregional failure does occur in about 25 to 40 percent of patients with locally advanced tumors (Table 12–5).[2,4,7–9,12–14,30,31,33–35]

Salvage Therapy

Patients with recurrent or new primary vaginal cancer after definitive RT have few treatment options. Salvage therapy has been predominantly radical surgery for local and regional failures after primary RT and chemotherapy for distant disease. A number of investigators have reported anecdotal experiences with exenteration for patients with recurrent vaginal cancer.[2,4,12–14,35] Reirradiation of small vaginal or pelvic recurrences using primarily interstitial techniques has been attempted with some success.[40,41] Permanent radioactive seed implants (eg,

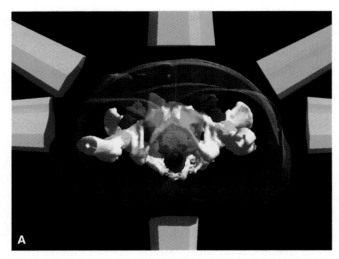

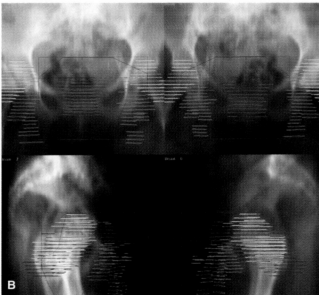

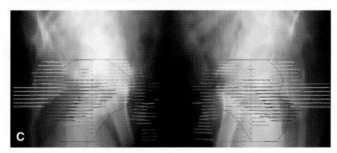

Figure 12–11. Three-dimensional treatment planning allows the use of conformal therapy in those patients with advanced vaginal carcinoma not amenable for interstitial implant boost. *A*, Three-dimensional view of beams arrangement. *B* and *C*, Digital reconstructed radiographs of the boost fields.

Table 12–4. STAGE III VAGINAL CANCER: TREATMENT APPROACH AND RESULTS			
Treatment Modality Author	No. Patients	Survival	DFS
Irradiation ± Surgery			
Ali[35]	St III-Iv 6	5 yr 22%	
Andersen[7]	6		5 yr 50%
Chyle[8]	55		10 yr 47%
Creasman[1] (NCDB)	St III-IV 180	5 yr 36% 60% S+RT (36) 35% RT (144)	
Kirkbride[9]	42	5 yr 53%	
Kucera[34]	46	5 yr 35%	
Lee[30]	10		5 yr CSS 79%
Perez[31]	20		10 yr 38%
Reddy[33]	6	5 yr 0%	
Spirtos[12]	10	5 yr 50%	
Stock[13]	10	5 yr 40%	
Stock[4]	9		5 yr 0%
Urbanski[14]	40	5 yr 22.5%	
Radical Surgery			
Ball[5]	2		LCR 50%
Creasman[1] (NCDB)	St III-IV 21	5 yr 47%	
Rubin[3]	2		LCR 50%

DFS = disease-free survival; CSS = cause-specific survival; LCR = local control rate; St = stage; NCDB = National Cancer Data Base; S = surgery; RT = radiation therapy.

Table 12–5. SITES OF RECURRENCE

Author	No. Patients	No. Recurrence	Locoregional Recurrence	Distant Recurrence	Local + Distant
Ali[35]	40	13 (32.5%)	13		
Andersen[7]	26	13 (50%)	10	2	1
Chyle[8]	301	106 (35%)*	64	32	10
Davis[2]	89	26 (29%)			
		St I 10/44 (23%)	St I 8/44 (18%)	St I 2/44 (5%)	Not shown
		St II 16/45 (36%)	St II 7/45 (16%)	St II 9/45 (20%)	
Kirkbride[9]	153	64 (42%)	49	11	4
Kucera[34]	110	27 (24.5%)	23	4	
Lee[30]	59	21 (36%)	10 (17%)	6 (10%)	5 (8%)
Perez[31]	212	St 0 1/20 (5%)	St 0 1 (5%)	0	0
		St I 13/59 (22%)	St I 5 (8%)	St I 5 (8%)	St I 3 (5%)
		St IIa 30/64 (47%)	St IIa 11 (17%)	St IIa 8 (13%)	St IIa 11 (17%)
		St IIb 24/34 (71%)	St IIb 5 (15%)	St IIb 9 (26%)	St IIb 10 (29%)
		St III 11/20 (55%)	St III 1 (5%)	St III 4 (20%)	St III 6 (30%)
		St IVa 11/15 (73%)	St IVa 4 (27%)	0	St IVa 7 (47%)
		TOTAL: 90/212 (42%)	27 (13%)	26 (12%)	37 (17%)
Reddy[33]	45	15 (33%)	12	2	1
Spirtos[12]	38	12 (32%)	5	3	4
Stock[13]	49	30 (61%)	29	1	0
Stock[4]	100	46	Not shown	Not shown	Not shown
Urbanski[14]	125	66 (53%)	51	10	5

St = stage.

*Grouping local, pelvic, and inguinal nodes as "pelvic failures" revealed that 80 patients (27%) sustained such failure. Actuarial 10-year local, pelvic, and inguinal node recurrence rates were 26%, 9%, and 4%, respectively.

gold-198) may provide long-lasting tumor control for elderly or medically debilitated patients who have small vaginal recurrences after definitive RT[41] (Figure 12–12).

Role of Chemotherapy and Irradiation

Although advanced stages of vaginal cancer may be treated effectively with RT alone, there remains room for improvement. Agents such as 5-fluorouracil (5-FU), mitomycin, and cisplatin have shown promise when combined with RT, with complete response rates as high as 60 to 85 percent,[42–44] but long-term results of such combined treatment have been variable. Further investigation is needed to determine the efficacy of concurrent chemoradiotherapy and to define the most effective chemotherapy agents and schedule. Recently published data on locally advanced cervical cancer have showed an advantage in locoregional control, overall survival, and disease-free survival, for patients receiving concurrent cisplatin-based chemotherapy and RT.[45–47] On the basis of these data, consideration should be given to a similar approach in patients with advanced vaginal cancer.

Prognostic Factors

Disease-Related Factors

Stage of the disease is probably the most significant prognostic factor in terms of ultimate outcome.[8–11,30–32,38,48,49] The average 5-year survival rate for patients with carcinoma of the vagina, all stages, treated with RT alone ranges from 35 to 65 percent.

Size was found to be a prognostic factor for local control by Chyle and colleagues.[8] Lesions measuring < 5 cm in maximum diameter had a 20 percent 10-year local recurrence rate, compared with 40 percent for those lesions > 5 cm. Similarly in the Princess Margaret Hospital (PMH) experience, tumors > 4 cm in diameter fared significantly worse than did smaller lesions.[9] In the Perez and colleagues' series,[31] stage was an important predictor of pelvic tumor control and 5-year disease-free survival (DFS), but the size of the tumor in stage I patients was not a significant prognostic factor. However, in stage IIa disease, lower pelvic tumor control and survival were noted with tumors > 4 cm. In stages IIb-III, tumor size was not a significant prognostic factor, probably related to the difficulty in assessing size and the fact

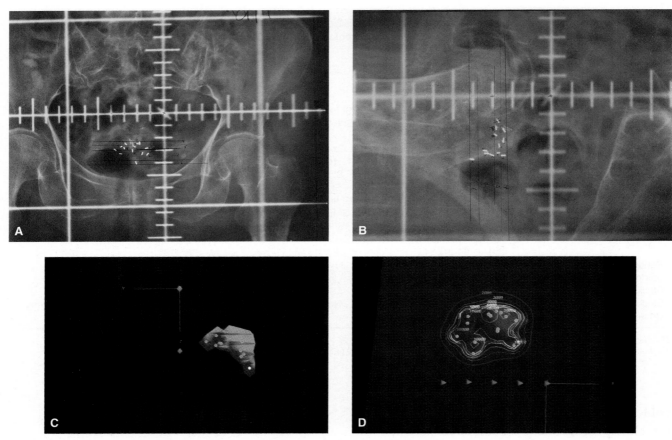

Figure 12–12.   *A*, AP view of an interstitial iodine-125 implant in a patient with recurrent carcinoma of the vagina in the apex. *B*, Lateral radiograph. *C* and *D*, Three-dimensional reconstruction of the isodose distribution.

that higher doses of RT were delivered for larger tumors. Similar results have been reported by Stock and colleagues.[4]

Age was a significant prognostic factor in Urbanski and colleagues' series,[14] with 5-year survival of 63.2 percent for patients below the age of 60 years, compared with 25 percent for those over 60 years of age ($p < .001$). Similar findings were reported by Eddy and colleagues.[48] No statistical significance of age to survival was found in the series of Dixit and colleagues[49] and Perez and colleagues.[31]

Ali and colleagues[35] analyzed the outcome of 40 patients with carcinoma of the vagina on the basis of the location of the tumor (proximal versus distal vagina). They showed that patients with cancer involving the proximal half had better survival (81%) than those with tumors in the distal half of the vagina (41%), presumably because of the higher radiation tolerance of the upper vagina, allowing higher RT doses (median doses for the proximal and

distal groups were 78 Gy and 70 Gy, respectively). These findings have been confirmed in other large series as well.[14,34] Chyle and colleagues[8] reported 10-year recurrence rates of 15 percent, 29 percent, and 35 percent for patients with lesions involving the upper third, mid-lower third, and the entire vagina, respectively. In addition, they found that lesions of the posterior wall of the vagina had a worse prognosis than those involving other vaginal walls (10-year recurrence rates of 32% and 19%, respectively). This probably reflected the greater difficulty of performing adequate brachytherapy procedures in this location.

The histologic grade has been found of prognostic significance in several series,[9,14,34] with well- and moderately differentiated tumors having significantly better survival rates than poorly differentiated lesions. However, no significant difference in survival was found by histology (squamous versus adenocarcinoma) among the patients with invasive tumors.

Treatment-Related Factors

It is important to recognize that analysis of RT doses and techniques[8,9,30,31,33–35] and their impact on local/pelvic tumor control is fraught with difficulty because the available data are obtained retrospectively and not by prospective randomized or dose-escalation studies. On the other hand, clinical experience suggests that higher doses of RT, should be prescribed for more advanced stages of disease, whenever possible. The combination of EBRT and brachytherapy with minimum tumor doses of 70 to 75 Gy has been associated with better tumor control and survival than lower-dose treatment.[7–10,12,13,31,34] Perez and colleagues[11,31] reported increased tumor control in patients with stages IIa to IVa with EBRT and brachytherapy, compared with patients receiving brachytherapy alone. In patients with stage I disease, no correlation was found between the technique of RT used and the incidence of local or pelvic recurrences. These authors also suggested that doses in the range of 70 to 75 Gy to the primary tumor volume and 55 to 65 Gy to the medial parametria are needed to optimize tumor and pelvic control.

Patients with distal vaginal involvement may have occult inguinal node involvement. In the series reported by Perez and colleagues[31] of patients who did not have groin irradiation, inguinal recurrence was observed in 3 of 29 whose tumors were in the distal third and in 1 of 20 whose tumors involved the entire length of the vagina. In contrast, there were no inguinal recurrences seen in 100 patients whose tumors were confined to the upper two-thirds of the vagina. Of 7 patients who had palpable inguinal lymph nodes that were treated with doses in the range of 60 Gy, only 1 developed a nodal recurrence. The authors recommended that elective RT of the inguinal lymph nodes should be carried out only in patients whose tumors involved the lower third of the vagina.

Lee and colleagues[30] identified overall treatment time as the most significant treatment factor predicting pelvic tumor control in 65 patients with carcinomas of the vagina treated with definitive RT. If the entire course of RT, including EBRT and brachytherapy was completed within 9 weeks, pelvic tumor control was 97 percent, in contrast to only 57 percent when treatment time extended beyond 9 weeks ($p < .01$). Perez and colleagues[31] did not find a significant impact of prolongation of treatment time on pelvic tumor control, but these authors did advocate completion of treatment within 7 to 9 weeks.

Treatment Complications and Management

The anatomic location of the vagina places the lower gastrointestinal and genitourinary tracts at greatest risk for complications. Most authors comment on the nature of the complications encountered in their series, but little information is typically given regarding prevention or manangement.[3–6,32] Furthermore, different authors have different criteria for classifying a complication as serious.

As an immediate response to high-dose RT, there is a loss of most or all of the vaginal epithelium, especially in areas in proximity to the brachytherapy sources. Clinically, the severity of the acute effects (eg, edema, erythema, moist desquamation, and confluent mucositis with or without ulceration) varies in intensity and duration depending on patient age, hormonal status, tumor size, stage, irradiation dose, and personal hygiene. These effects usually resolve within 2 to 3 months after completion of therapy. In the same patients, there is progressive vascular damage with subsequent ulcer formation and mucosal necrosis, which may require 4 to 8 months for healing. Chemotherapy concurrently with RT enhances the acute mucosal response to both EBRT and brachytherapy. The effect of chemotherapy on the incidence of late complications, if any, is unclear.

Over time, most patients will develop some degree of vaginal atrophy, fibrosis, and stenosis; telangiectasis is commonly seen in the vagina. Vagina narrowing, shortening, paravaginal fibrosis, and loss of elasticity, in addition to reduced lubrication, often result in dyspareunia. More severe complications include necrosis with ulceration that can progress to fistula formation (eg, rectovaginal, vesicovaginal, urethrovaginal).

Treatment options for acute radiation vaginitis include vaginal douching with a 1:10 mixture of hydrogen peroxide and water. This should continue for 2 to 3 months or until the mucosal reactions have subsided. Patients are then advised to continue douching once or twice a week for several months. Regular vaginal dilation is widely recommended as a way for patients to maintain vaginal health and good sexual function, despite the knowledge that the compliance rate with this recommendation is low. The lack of resolution of vaginal ulceration or necrosis after several months of adequate therapy must be appropriately evaluated taking into consideration the possibility of a recurrent tumor. The use of topical estrogens following the completion of RT appears to stimulate epithelial regeneration more than systemic estrogens. Some patients with severe radiation sequelae, such as fistula formation, will respond to conservative treatment with antibiotics and periodic débridement of necrotic tissue. Others will require urinary or fecal diversion with the possibility of delayed reanastomosis. Occasionally, repair of the fistula may be attempted by employing a myocutaneous graft in which the skin, subcutaneous fat, and muscle are mobilized using a neurovascular pedicle to maintain the blood supply to the pedicled graft or by excision of the necrotic tissue with re-establishment of organ continuity (such as in the treatment of high rectovaginal fistula).

The radiation tolerance limits of the entire vagina are ill-defined given the variety of techniques used to treat vaginal cancers. Rubin and Casarett[50] suggested that the tolerance of the vaginal mucosa (tumor dose [TD] 5/5: 5% necrosis in 5 years) was around 90 Gy for ulceration and more than 100 Gy for fistula formation. This tolerance limit has been specified as a direct summation of dosage given by LDR-ICB and EBRT. Within the LDR range, whether a correction for brachytherapy dose rate is necessary remains controversial. Hintz and colleagues[51] showed that the distal vagina has a lower RT tolerance than has the upper vagina. The authors did not observe any cases of vaginal necrosis even after doses of 140 Gy to the upper vaginal mucosa. They recommended keeping the total dose to the distal vagina at < 98 Gy and adjusting the dose delivered with brachytherapy according to the total dose delivered with EBRT. It was also observed that the posterior wall of the vagina was more prone to RT injury than the anterior or lateral walls, and that the dose should be kept below 80 Gy to minimize the risk of rectovaginal fistula. The threshold dose for a vesicovaginal fistula was found to be approximately 150 Gy.

It is likely that improvements in modern practice, such as advancements in surgical and postsurgical care, use of more sophisticated RT planning and treatment delivery, and more accurate brachytherapy techniques, have lessened the complication rates.

CLEAR CELL CARCINOMA OF THE VAGINA

Since Herbst and colleagues' first report[52] of several adenocarcinomas arising in the vagina of adolescent females after in utero exposure to diethylstilbestrol (DES), there have been several reports limited to DES-related vaginal clear cell adenocarcinomas (CCA).[53–58] In 1979, Herbst and colleagues[53] reported 142 cases of stage I CCA of the vagina. An 8.1 percent risk of recurrence was seen after radical surgery (N = 117) with an 87 percent survival. There was a 36 percent risk of recurrence after RT for stage I lesions; however, the authors acknowledged that, in general, RT was reserved for large stage I lesions that involved more of the vault and were less amenable to surgical resection.

Senekjian and colleagues[55] reported a series of 219 stage I CCA cases with a 92 percent overall 5-year survival rate in 176 patients receiving radical surgery, identical to 43 who had undergone local therapy (limited surgery, RT, or a combination of both). However, the local control rate was inferior in those treated with local therapy; specifically, the vaginectomy and local excision patients had 27 percent local failure, whereas the patients who received local RT had only 6 percent local failure, comparing well with the 16 percent rate seen after conventional radical surgical therapy. Of the 17 treated with local excision alone, 7 (45%) developed local recurrences. The authors advocated a combination of wide local excision and extraperitoneal node dissection followed by local RT for patients desirous of fertility preservation. Senekjian and colleagues[56] also reviewed the experience with 76 stage II CCA cases. The overall 5-year survival rate was 87 percent, 85 percent, and 80 percent for patients treated with primary RT, surgery, and a combination of both, respectively. The authors concluded that most patients with stage II vaginal CCA should be treated with combination EBRT and brachytherapy; however, small, easily resectable lesions might be approached with surgery, if the lesion arises in the upper vagina, given the advantage of better preservation of coital and ovarian functions. In their opinion, exenterative procedures should be reserved for patients who have failed primary RT.[57]

MELANOMA OF THE VAGINA

Vaginal melanoma is an exceedingly rare entity, accounting for 2 to 3 percent of all primary tumors of the vagina and approximately 0.5 percent of all malignant melanomas in females. The number of patients with vaginal melanoma is too small to permit prospective controlled trials. Authors have reported small series with generally disappointing results, irrespective of the treatment modality.[58–65] Because of the reputation of melanoma as a radioresistant tumor, it is not surprising that radical surgery has been considered the treatment of choice in operable patients. However, limited data that validate its efficacy are available.

Reid and colleagues[64] reported 15 patients with vaginal melanomas and pooled data including 115 patients reported in the literature. No differences in survival, recurrence rate, or DFS were noted among the four treatment strategies of surgery only, RT only, surgery plus RT, and chemotherapy plus surgery or RT. Similar results were reported by Buchanan and colleagues[59] and Levitan and colleagues.[63]

Recent retrospective data suggest that vaginal melanoma is reasonably radioresponsive and possibly radiocurable.[62,66] In Petru and colleagues' series[66] of 14 patients, the three long-term survivors received either primary RT after biopsy only or adjuvantly after local excision. In Irvin and colleagues' series,[62] all patients treated with wide local excision or brachytherapy alone had local recurrences, whereas those patients treated with radical surgical resection or with wide local excision followed by high-dose per fraction EBRT maintained locoregional control until death.

Given that the high incidence of distant metastasis remains a major factor limiting curability, a more conservative treatment approach might be more reasonable in selected patients. Wide local excision with 1- to 2-cm margins should be the surgical treatment of choice for most primary vaginal melanomas, since radical surgery has failed to improve long-term survival. The role of adjuvant RT is unclear, but it appears to improve survival in some series.

SARCOMAS OF THE VAGINA

Sarcomas represent 2 to 3 percent of all gynecologic malignancies, and only 10 percent occur outside the uterus.[1] Leiomyosarcomas represent 50 to 65 percent of vaginal sarcomas. Less common mesenchymal tumors of the vagina include malignant mixed müllerian tumor (MMMT, carcinosarcoma), endometrial stromal sarcoma, and angiosarcoma. Embryonal rhabdomyosarcoma/sarcoma botryoides is a rare pediatric tumor. Prior pelvic RT is a risk factor, particularly for mixed mesodermal tumors and vaginal angiosarcomas. Unfortunately, most vaginal sarcomas are diagnosed at an advanced stage. Histopathologic grade appears to be the most important predictor of outcome.[67]

Vaginal MMMTs occur more commonly in postmenopausal women. In approximately half the cases, there is a history of prior pelvic RT.[68,69] Despite surgery and adjuvant RT, patients usually do poorly, with a high incidence of local and distant recurrences. The treatment of choice is surgical resection followed by EBRT and ICB, in an attempt to decrease the local recurrence rate. Most vaginal leiomyosarcomas arise from the posterior wall of the vagina. Radical surgical resection, such as posterior pelvic exenteration,[1,70] offers the best chance for cure.

The roles of adjuvant chemotherapy and RT in vaginal sarcomas have not been clearly defined, primarily due to limited data. Adjuvant RT seems indicated in patients with high-grade tumors and locally recurrent low-grade sarcomas. According to Peters and colleagues,[69] pelvic failure is the most common pattern, and the only site of failure in 50 percent of patients with recurring disease. Extrapolating data for uterine sarcomas from the Gynecologic Oncology Group,[71] patients with localized MMMTs would be appropriately treated with pelvic exenteration or more limited surgical resection followed by postoperative RT, unless the patient has received prior pelvic RT.

Table 12–6[72–81] summarizes the progress achieved in patients with vaginal rhabdomyosarcoma (RMS). An early review, prior to the era of modern RT and multiagent CT, reported that although 70 percent of patients with RMS confined to the vagina were cured with exenteration, only 36 percent survived if there was extravaginal involvement.[72–74] Exenterations

Table 12–6. VAGINAL RHABDOMYOSARCOMA: TREATMENT RESULTS

Author	No. Pts	Survival	Comments
Extirpative/Exenterative Era			
Copeland[72]	10	70%	6 had CT (VAC), 5 of them had exenterations
Grosfeld[73]	3	66%	All had exenterations+RT+CT
Hilgers[74]	21	70%: vagina only	5 had RT–60% survival
		36%: extravaginal extent	9 had CT–33% survival
Modern Era			
Andrassy[75]	24	85%	17 NED
			Only 7 required vaginectomy
			4 had RT after CT
Flamant[76]	11	100%	8 had CT first
			All had brachytherapy
			Only 1 had hysterectomy
			All had maintenance CT (VAC alt. VAD)
Friedman[77]	8	87%	6 had RHV
			1 had exenteration
			1 had hysterectomy+colon resection+colostomy
Hays[78]	24	95%	
Kilman[79]	9	75%	Prior to CMT 0% survival
Kumar[80]	3	100%	None required exenteration
Piver[81]	3	100%	One required exenteration

RT = radiation therapy; CT = chemotherapy; RHV = radical hysterectomy and vaginectomy; CMT = combined modality therapy; NED = no evidence of disease; NS = not stated; VAD = vincristine, actinomycin D, doxorubicin; VAC = vincristine, actinomycin D, cyclophosphamide.

undertaken in very young girls significantly compromised their quality of life. Several series suggest that responses to combination chemotherapy with or without RT may permit less radical resections.[77,79–81] These observations have been confirmed by cooperative groups using multimodality therapies that preserve anatomy and function.[75,76,78]

REFERENCES

1. Creasman WT, Phillips JL, Menck HR. The National Cancer Data Base report on cancer of the vagina. Cancer 1998;83:1033–40.
2. Davis KP, Stanhope CR, Garton GR, et al. Invasive vaginal carcinoma: analysis of early stage disease. Gynecol Oncol 1991;42:131–6.
3. Rubin SC, Young J, Mikuta JJ. Squamous carcinoma of the vagina: treatment, complications and long-term follow-up. Gynecol Oncol 1985;20:346–53.
4. Stock RG, Chen ASJ, Seski J. A 30-year experience in the management of primary carcinoma of the vagina: analysis of prognostic factors and treatment modalities. Gynecol Oncol 1995;56:45–52.
5. Ball H, Berman M. Management of primary vaginal carcinoma. Gynecol Oncol 1982;14:154–63.
6. Gallup DG, Talledo OE, Shah KJ, Hayes C. Invasive squamous cell carcinoma of the vagina. A 14-year study. Obstet Gynecol 1987;69:782–5.
7. Andersen ES. Primary carcinoma of the vagina. Gynecol Oncol 1989;33:317–20.
8. Chyle V, Zagars GK, Wheeler JA, et al. Definitive radiotherapy for carcinoma of the vagina. Int J Radiat Oncol Biol Phys 1996;35:891–905.
9. Kirkbride P, Fyles A, Rawlings GA, et al. Carcinoma of the vagina—experience at the Princess Margaret Hospital (1974–1989). Gynecol Oncol 1995;56:435–43.
10. Leung S, Sexton M. Radical radiation therapy for carcinoma of the vagina—impact of treatment modalities on outcome. Peter MacCallum Cancer Institute experience 1970–1990. Int J Radiat Oncol Biol Phys 1993;25:413–8.
11. Perez CA, Camel HM, Galakatos AE, et al. Definitive irradiation in carcinoma of the vagina: long-term evaluation and results. Int J Radiat Oncol Biol Phys 1988;15:1283–90.
12. Spirtos NM, Doshi BP, Kapp DS, Teng N. Radiation therapy for primary squamous cell carcinoma of the vagina: Stanford University experience. Gynecol Oncol 1989;35:20–6.
13. Stock RG, Mychalczak B, Asmstrong JG, et al. The importance of the brachytherapy technique in the management of primary carcinoma of the vagina. Int J Radiat Oncol Biol Phys 1992;24:747–53.
14. Urbanski K, Kojs Z, Reinfuss M, Fabisiak W. Primary invasive vaginal carcinoma treated with radiotherapy: analysis of prognostic factors. Gynecol Oncol 1996;60:16–21.
15. Sobin LH, Wittekind CH, editors, for International Union Against Cancer (UICC). TNM classification of malignant tumors. 5th ed. New York: John Wiley & Sons, Inc.; 1997.
16. Dittmer PH, Randall ME. A technique for inguinal node boost using photon fields defined by asymmetric collimator jaws. Radiother Oncol 2001;59:61–4.

17. Delclos L, Fletcher GH, Moore EB, et al. Minicol-postats, dome cylinders, other additions and improvements of the Fletsher-Suit afterloadable system: indications and limitations of their use. Int J Radiat Oncol Biol Phys 1980;6:1195–206.

18. Perez CA, Slessinger ED, Grigsby PW. Design of an afterloading vaginal applicator (MIRALVA). Int J Radiat Oncol Biol Phys 1990;18:1503–8.

19. Slessinger ED, Perez CA, Grigsby PW, Williamson JF. Dosimetry and dose specification for a new gynecological brachytherapy applicator. Int J Radiat Oncol Biol Phys 1992;22:1117–24.

20. Nanavati PJ, Fanning J, Hilgers RD, et al. High-dose brachytherapy in primary stage I and II vaginal cancer. Gynecol Oncol 1993;51:67–71.

21. Gore E, Gillin MT, Albano K, Erikson B. Comparison of high dose-rate and low dose-rate dose distributions for vaginal cylinders. Int J Radiat Oncol Biol Phys 1995;31:165–70.

22. Li Z, Liu C, Palta JR. Optimized dose distribution of a high dose rate vaginal cylinder. Int J Radiat Oncol Biol Phys 1998;41:239–44.

23. Hilaris BS, Nori D, Anderson LL. Brachytherapy treatment planning. Front Radiat Ther Oncol 1987;21: 94–106.

24. Syed AMN, Puthawala AA, Neblett D, et al. Transperineal interstitial-intracavitary "Syed-Neblett" applicator in the treatment of carcinoma of the uterine cervix. Endocuriether/Hypertherm Oncol 1986;2: 1–13.

25. Disaia PJ, Syed N, Puthwala AA. Malignant neoplasia of the upper vagina. Endocuriether/Hypertherm Oncol 1990;6:251–6.

26. Martinez A, Cox RS, Edmudson GK. A mutiple-site perineal applicator (MUPIT) for treatment of prostatic, anorectal and gynecologic malignancies. Int J Radiat Oncol Biol Phys 1984;10:297–305.

27. Corn BW, Lanciano RM, Rosenblum N, et al. Improved treatment planning for the Syed-Neblett template using endorectal-coil magnetic resonance and intra-operative (laparotomy/laparoscopy) guidance: a new integrated technique for hysterectomized women with vaginal tumors. Gynecol Oncol 1995;56:255–61.

28. Childers JM, Surwit EA. Current status of operative laparoscopy in gynecologic malignancies. Oncology 1993;7:47–57.

29. Stock RG, Chen K, Terk M, et al. A new technique for performing Syed-Neblett template interstitial implants for gynecological malignancies using transrectal-ultrasound guidance. Int J Radiat Oncol Biol Phys 1997;37:819–25.

30. Lee WR, Marcus RB Jr, Sombeck MD, et al. Radiotherapy alone for carcinoma of the vagina: the importance of overall treatment time. Int J Radiat Oncol Biol Phys 1994;29:983–8.

31. Perez C, Grigsby P, Garipagaoglu M, et al. Factors affecting long-term outcome of irradiation in carcinoma of the vagina. Int J Radiat Oncol Biol Phys 1999;44:37–45.

32. Peters WA, Kumar NB, Morley GW. Carcinoma of the vagina. Factors influencing treatment outcome. Cancer 1985;55:892–7.

33. Reddy S, Saxena VS, Reddy S, et al. Results of radiotherapeutic management of primary carcinoma of the vagina. Int J Radiat Oncol Biol Phys 1991;21: 1041–4.

34. Kucera H, Vavra N. Radiation management of primary carcinoma of the vagina: clinical and histopathological variables associated with survival. Gynecol Oncol 1991;40:12–6.

35. Ali M, Huang D, Goplerud D, et al. Radiation alone for carcinoma of the vagina. Variation in response related to the location of the primary tumor. Cancer 1996;77:1934–9.

36. Prempree T, Amommam R. Radiation therapy of primary carcinoma of the vagina. Acta Radiol Oncol 1985;24:51–6.

37. Perez CA, Korba A, Sharma S. Dosimetric considerations in irradiation of carcinoma of the vagina. Int J Radiat Oncol Biol Phys 1977;2:639–49.

38. MacNaught R, Symonds RP, Hole D, Watson ER. Improved control of primary vaginal tumors by combined external beam and interstitial brachytherapy. Clin Radiol 1986;37:29–32.

39. Perez CA, Arneson AN, Galakatos A. Radiation therapy in carcinoma of the vagina. Cancer 1973;31:36–44.

40. Gupta AK, Vicini FA, Frazier AJ, et al. Iridium-192 transperineal interstitial brachytherapy for locally advanced or recurrent gynecological malignancies. Int J Radiat Oncol Biol Phys 1999;43:1055–60.

41. Randall ME, Evans L, Greven K, et al. Interstitial re-irradiation for recurrent gynecologic malignancies: results and analysis of prognostic factors. Gynecol Oncol 1993;48:23–31.

42. Thigpen JT, Blessing JA, Homesley HD, et al. Phase II trial of cisplatin in advanced or recurrent carcinoma of the vagina: a Gynecologic Oncology Group Study. Gynecol Oncol 1986;23:101–4.

43. Evans LS, Kersh CR, Constable WC, Taylor PT. Concomitant 5-fluorouracil, mitomycin-C and radiotherapy for advanced gynecological malignancies. Int J Radiat Oncol Biol Phys 1988;15:901–6.

44. Roberts W, Hoffman M, Kavanagh J, et al. Further experience with radiation therapy and concomitant intravenous chemotherapy in advanced carcinoma of the lower female genital tract. Gynecol Oncol 1991;43:233–6.

45. Morris M, Eifel PJ, Lu J, et al. Pelvic irradiation with concurrent chemotherapy compared with pelvic and para-aortic radiation for the high-risk cervical cancer. N Engl J Med 1999;340:1137–43.

46. Rose PG, Bundy BN, Watkins EB, et al. Concurrent cisplatin-based radiotherapy and chemotherapy for locally advanced cervical cancer. N Engl J Med 1999;340:1144–53.

47. Whitney CW, Sause W, Bundy BN, et al. Randomized comparison of fluorouracil plus cisplatin versus hydroxyurea as an adjunct to radiation therapy in stage IIB-IVA carcinoma of the cervix with negative para-aortic lymph nodes: a Gynecologic Oncology

Group and Southest Oncology Group Study. J Clin Oncol 1999;17:1339–48.

48. Eddy GL, Marks RD, Miller MC, Underwood PB. Primary invasive vaginal carcinoma. Am J Obstet Gynecol 1991;165:292–8.

49. Dixit S, Singhal S, Baboo HA. Squamous cell carcinoma of the vagina. A review of 70 cases. Gynecol Oncol 1993;48:80–7.

50. Rubin P, Casarett GW. The female genital tract. In: Rubin P, Casarett GW, editors. Clinical radiation pathology. Philadelphia: W.B. Saunders; 1986. p. 396–402.

51. Hintz BL, Kagan AR, Gilbert HA, et al. Radiation tolerance of the vaginal mucosa. Int J Radiat Oncol Biol Phys 1980;6:711–6.

52. Herbst A, Uldelfer H, Poskanzer D. Adenocarcinoma of the vagina: association of maternal stilbestrol therapy with tumor appearance in young women. N Engl J Med 1971;284:878–81.

53. Herbst AL, Norusis MJ, Rosenow PJ, et al. An analysis of 346 cases of clear cell adenocarcinoma of the vagina and cervix with emphasis on recurrence and survival. Gynecol Oncol 1979;7:111–22.

54. Herbst AL, Anderson D. Clear cell adenocarcinoma of the vagina and cervix secondary to intrauterine exposure to diethylstilbestrol. Semin Surg Oncol 1990;6:343–6.

55. Senekjian EK, Frey KW, Anderson D, Herbst AL. Local therapy in stage I clear cell adenocarcinoma of the vagina. Cancer 1987;60:1319–24.

56. Senekjian EK. Frey KW, Stone C, Herbst AL. An evaluation of stage II vaginal clear cell adenocarcinoma according to substages. Gynecol Oncol 1988;31:56–64.

57. Senekjian EK, Frey K, Herbst AL. Pelvic exenteration in clear cell adenocarcinoma of the vagina and cervix. Gynecol Oncol 1989;34:413–6.

58. Bonner JA, Perez-Tamayo C, Reid GC, et al. The management of vaginal melanoma. Cancer 1988;62:2066–72.

59. Buchanan D, Schlaerth J, Kuroaki T. Primary vaginal melanoma: thirteen-year disease free survival after wide local excision and review of recent literature. Am J Obstet Gynecol 1998;178:1177–84.

60. Chung AF, Casey MJ, Flannery JT, et al. Malignant melanoma of the vagina—report of 19 cases. Obstet Gynecol 1980;55:720–7.

61. Geisler J, Look K, Moore D, Sutton G. Pelvic exenteration for malignant melanomas of the vagina or urethra with over 3 mm of invasion. Gynecol Oncol 1995;59:338–41.

62. Irvin W, Bliss S, Rice L, et al. Case report. Malignant melanoma of the vagina and locoregional control: radical surgery revisited. Gynecol Oncol 1998;71:476–80.

63. Levitan Z, Gordon AN, Kaplan AL, Kaufman RH. Primary malignant melanoma of the vagina: report of four cases and review of the literature. Gynecol Oncol 1989;33:85–90.

64. Reid G, Schmidt R, Roberts J, et al. Primary melanoma of the vagina: a clinicopathologic analysis. Obstet Gynecol 1989;74:190–9.

65. Van Nostrand K, Lucci J, Schell M, et al. Primary vaginal melanoma: improved survival with radical pelvic surgery. Gynecol Oncol 1994;55:234–7.

66. Petru E, Nagele F, Czerwenka K, et al. Primary malignant melanoma of the vagina: long-term remission following radiation therapy. Gynecol Oncol 1998;70:23–6.

67. Curtin JP, Saigo P, Slucher B, et al. Soft-tissue sarcoma of the vagina and vulva: a clinicopathologic study. Obstet Gynecol 1995;86:269–72.

68. Neesham D, Kerdemelidis P, Scurry J. Case report. Primary malignant mixed mullerian tumor of the vagina. Gynecol Oncol 1998;70:303–7.

69. Peters WA, Kumar NB, Andersen WA, Morley GW. Primary sarcoma of the adult vagina: a clinicopathologic study. Obstet Gynecol 1985;65:699–704.

70. Hachi H, Ottmany A, Bougtab A, et al. Leiomyosarcoma of the vagina: a rare case. Bull Cancer 1997;84:215–7.

71. Hornback N, Omura G, Major F. Observations on the use of adjuvant radiation therapy in patients with stage I and II uterine sarcoma. Int J Radiat Oncol Biol Phys 1986;12:2127–30.

72. Copeland LJ, Gershenson DM, Saul PB, et al. Sarcoma botryoides of the female genital tract. Obstet Gynecol 1985;66:262–6.

73. Grosfeld JL, Smith JP, Clatworthy HW. Pelvic rhabdomyosarcoma in infants and children. J Urol 1972;107:673–5.

74. Hilgers RD. Pelvic exenteration for vaginal embryonal rhabdomyosarcoma: a review. Obstet Gynecol 1975;45:175–80.

75. Andrassy R, Hays D, Raney R, et al. Conservative surgical management of vaginal and vulvar pediatric rhabdomyosarcoma: a report from the IRS III. J Pediatr Surg 1995;30:1034–7.

76. Flamant F, Gerbaulet A, Nihol-Fekete C, et al. Long-term sequelae of conservative treatment by surgery, brachytherapy and chemotherapy for vulvar and vaginal rhabdmyosarcoma in children. J Clin Oncol 1990;8:1847–53.

77. Friedman M, Peretz BA, Nissenbaum M, Paldi E. Modern treatment of vaginal embryonal rhabdomyosarcoma. Obstet Gynecol Surv 1986;41:614–8.

78. Hays DM, Shimada H, Raney RB Jr, et al. Sarcomas of the vagina and uterus: the Intergroup Rhabdomyosarcoma Study. J Pediatr Surg 1985;20:718–24.

79. Kilman JW, Clatworthy HW, Newton WA, Grosfeld JL. Reasonable surgery for rhabdomyosarcoma. A study of 67 cases. Ann Surg 1973;178:346–51.

80. Kumar A, Wrenn E, Fleming I, et al. Combined therapy to prevent complete pelvic exenteration for rhabdomyosarcoma of the vagina or uterus. Cancer 1976;37:118–22.

81. Piver M, Barlow J, Wang J. Combined radical surgery, radiation therapy, and chemotherapy in infants with vulvovaginal embryonal rhabdomyosarcoma. Obstet Gynecol 1973;42:522.

13

Surgery for Vulvar Cancer

CHARLES LEVENBACK, MD

At the start of the 20th century, vulvar cancer was considered a fatal disease leading to a particularly gruesome death.[1] Death resulted from sepsis caused by the tumor's erosion of the bladder, anus, and symphysis pubis. The tumor itself was considered radioresistant, and all surgical procedures for treating it were inadequate. In addition, the social norms of the time were often a barrier to requesting gynecologic evaluation. Nevertheless, women who were otherwise doomed to a slow and painful death were being cured by radical vulvectomy with en bloc resection of the groin, pelvic, and even para-aortic nodes.[2,3] Though the procedure was mutilating and morbid, its curative potential ultimately led to anatomic studies that improved the understanding of the surgical anatomy of the vulva. Later, as social inhibitions about the discussion of gynecologic illness began to disappear and women became more willing to seek gynecologic evaluation, it became possible to detect tumors earlier and at much smaller sizes. This made it possible to reduce the radicality of the surgery for vulvar cancer, by all measures, while improving outcomes. Consequently, the classic use of radical vulvectomy and bilateral inguinal femoral lymphadenectomy to treat vulvar cancer is now obsolete.

EPIDEMIOLOGY

Vulvar carcinoma and its precursors are uncommon. The incidence of vulvar intraepithelial neoplasia is about 2.1 per 100,000[4] and is increasing particularly among women under 35 years of age. This increase of vulvar intraepithelial neoplasia (VIN) in younger women is presumed to be related to the increase in human papillomavirus (HPV) infection in this age group. Vulvar cancer accounts for 1 percent of all cancers in women and less than 5 percent of all female genital cancers. In 2001, 3,600 new cases of vulvar cancer are expected in the United States, compared with 12,900 cases of cervical cancer and over 190,000 cases of breast cancer.[5] The incidence of vulvar cancer does not appear to be strongly associated with either age or geography, but some studies have suggested that the disease is more common in patients of lower socioeconomic status.[6,7] The relationship between economic status and other factors, such as hygiene, access to health care, and lifestyle, and its effect on vulvar cancer incidence is difficult to measure.

PATHOGENESIS

Past theories of the pathogenesis of vulvar cancer have frequently included the chronic inflammation and irritation associated with preinvasive disease, vulvar dystrophy, and invasive disease. One theory, in particular, proposed a connection between vulvar cancer and the vulva's direct contact with various substances, much like the proven connection between scrotal cancer and contact with coal dust in chimney sweeps.

Current thinking, however, has focused on the role of HPV infection and the resulting genetic alterations in the pathogenesis of vulvar cancer. The HPV-E6 protein binds to the wild-type tumor suppressor $P53$ gene, resulting in tumor suppressor malfunction. Several authors[8–10] have gone so far as to suggest two different etiologies for vulvar cancer. The first is based on studies of a group of younger women who had "warty" VINs associated with invasive disease and a high prevalence of HPV infection. This group had epidemiologic features usually associated with cervical cancer (eg, early first intercourse, multiple sexual partners, history of cervical dysplasia, and history of smoking). The second etiology is based on studies of another group of patients who were older and had a low prevalence of HPV infection but none of the epidemiologic risk factors just described. From a surgical point of view, however, the treatment for these two groups did not differ.

SCREENING AND PREVENTION

Currently, there are no screening guidelines for vulvar cancer endorsed by any major medical organizations. Vulvar cancer or its precursors may be detected early by primary care physicians, physician assistants, advance practice nurses, and midwives who perform vulvar examinations and biopsies of suspicious lesions. It may be detected early by women who perform regular vulvar self-examination and report any new findings promptly to a health-care provider. Women over 70 years, who have a history of HPV infection or who smoke are especially at risk for vulvar cancers. Occasionally, smokers, unmoved by the risk of heart and lung disease, become motivated to stop smoking when they learn that their smoking behavior is linked to their gynecologic health.

CLINICAL PRESENTATION

Patients with vulvar carcinoma frequently complain of burning, pruritus, and/or a lump or growth on the vulva. The carcinoma may be fungating and largely exophytic or invasive. Most patients have some bleeding, although it is usually minor, unless the tumor is very large. Pain is usually present but not prominent.

Vulvar carcinoma may be mistaken for a number of other entities. Prominent vaginal papulosis, flat condyloma, and various forms of chronic inflammatory changes have all been mistaken for cancer. Conversely, carcinomas have sometimes been treated with a variety of local antifungal, antibiotic, and steroid creams by clinicians who thought they were treating a benign condition. Such mistaken diagnoses underscore the importance of performing a vulvar biopsy before initiating treatment of a vulvar lesion (Figure 13–1).

DIAGNOSTIC EVALUATION

A histologic tissue diagnosis of invasive disease is necessary before proceeding with treatment. This is most easily obtained with a punch biopsy (see Figure 13–1). In some patients, distinguishing carcinoma in situ from invasive disease will not be straightforward and will require multiple punch biopsies or, occasionally, a wide local excision.

Physical examination should focus on determining the features of the primary tumor and the status of the inguinal lymph nodes. The inguinal lymph nodes are best evaluated with the patient in a supine position because palpable nodes are common; physical examination is an extremely poor predictor of node status. However, a single, enlarged, firm node is suspicious. Fine-needle aspiration may determine the status of such a node with minimal discomfort and side effects.

The vulva is examined with the patient in the lithotomy position. Special care should be taken to determine the dimensions of the tumor and the distance from the major midline structures, including the clitoris, urethral meatus, and anus (Figure 13–2). A digital rectal examination is mandatory in patients to both accurately assess the extent of the primary tumor and rule out a rare coexisting squamous carcinoma of the anus. An annotated drawing is very useful for documenting these findings.

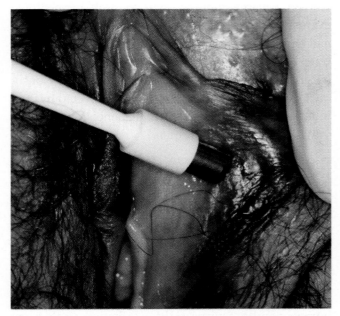

Figure 13–1. All suspicious vulvar lesions should be biopsied. This can be performed with local anesthesia in the outpatient setting.

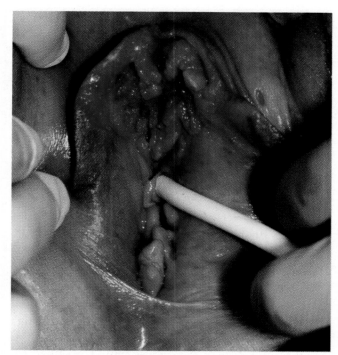

Figure 13–2. Vulvar cancers should be carefully described with an annotated drawing in the medical record. This lesion involves the clitoris and is a few millimeters from the urethral meatus.

The vulvar examination can be difficult in an obese patient with a painful lesion. Topical anesthetic jelly, which can serve as a lubricant, is helpful in such patients. In rare cases, an examination must be done under anesthesia.

A patient with a lesion limited to the vulva and with normal inguinal lymph nodes does not require further testing besides routine preoperative assessment including a chest radiograph. Patients with grossly suspicious inguinal nodes should undergo computed tomography (CT) of the abdomen and pelvis to rule out metastases to the pelvic lymphatic basin. CT should also be performed in patients whose tumor extends to the vagina or anus, since lymph nodes can drain directly from the vagina and anus to the pelvis. Cystoscopy and flexible sigmoidoscopy should be considered, where appropriate. Magnetic resonance imaging (MRI) might be helpful in determining the extent of soft-tissue involvement in patients with locally advanced disease.

STAGING

Early studies of patients with vulvar cancer were confounded by the lack of a common staging system. The International Federation of Gynecology and Obstetrics (FIGO) responded by adopting a clinical staging system that proved inadequate because of the inability of physical examination to correctly determine the status of the groin nodes. In 1988, following numerous reports of the inaccuracy of clinical assessment of inguinal lymph nodes with this system, FIGO introduced a revised system for staging vulvar cancer surgically.[11]

This new system was used by the Gynecologic Oncology Group (GOG) to analyze outcome in over 500 patients with vulvar cancer.[12] The staging system discriminated the risk of death from vulvar cancer extremely well, thus confirming its usefulness. The GOG also noted that within the stage III category, there was a wide variation in survival on the basis of tumor size and node involvement. These findings underscore the fact that clinicians must look beyond simple staging in planning treatment for patients with advanced disease.

Several efforts have been made to describe the microinvasive stage of vulvar carcinoma along the lines used to describe microinvasive cervical cancer. Patients with microinvasive cervical cancer (ie, invasion to < 3 mm and no lymphatic space involvement) have little or no risk of lymph node metastasis and do not require radical hysterectomy or pelvic lymphadenectomy. Wharton and colleagues[13] proposed that vulvar cancers invading to less than 5 mm and therefore not requiring groin dissection pose a minimal risk of nodal metastasis. This theory was disproven by other authors who documented nodal metastasis in patients with < 5-mm deep tumors[14–16] and death in patients with 3-mm deep tumors who were treated by local resection only.[17] Now, it is widely agreed that the only patients who do not require groin dissection are those with tumors invading less that 1 mm.

PROGNOSTIC FACTORS

The most powerful prognostic factor in patients with vulvar cancer is lymph node status. This was first established in a 1984 GOG study of 588 patients, who underwent radical vulvectomy and inguinal femoral lymphadenectomy for vulvar cancer. The 5-year survival for the node-negative group was 90.9 percent versus 57.2 percent for the node-positive group

(Table 13–1). In addition, survival was inversely related to the number of positive lymph nodes.

There are several predictors of nodal metastases. One of them, depth of invasion, has been widely studied. Although the risk of nodal metastases increases with depth of invasion, investigators have found that nodal metastases can occur with invasion just over 1 mm (Table 13–2). Surgical assessment of the inguinal nodes is, therefore, recommended for all patients with tumors deeper than 1 mm as measured from the nearest rete peg. Three other predictors—tumor size, grade, and lymphatic space involvement—were exhaustively studied on behalf of the GOG by Sedlis and colleagues,[18] who found that increases in these parameters predicted nodal metastases (Tables 13–3 to 13–5).

The extent of lymph node involvement is another important predictor of survival. Increasing size of the metastases and extranodal spread are important risk factors for recurrence and death.[19–21]

In addition, S-phase fraction, overexpression of *HER-2/NEU* protein product, and *P53* status[22] have all been found to be associated with increased risk of nodal metastases. However, these predictors are not routinely used in triaging patients to surgical evaluation or treatment because the assays for them are not routinely available.

PREOPERATIVE PREPARATION

Before surgery, the patient should give her informed consent. All risks of the surgery, including its impact on sexual function, and alternatives to surgery should be discussed. No assumptions based on age

Table 13–2. NODAL STATUS VERSUS DEPTH OF INVASION IN T1 SQUAMOUS CELL CARCINOMA OF THE VULVA

Depth of Invasion (mm)	No. Patients	No. Patients with Positive Nodes	(%)
< 1	163	0	(0)
1.1–2	145	11	(7.7)
2.1–3	131	11	(8.3)
3.1–5	101	27	(26.7)
> 5	38	13	(34.2)
All depths	578	62	(10.7)

Adapted from Hacker NF. Current treatment of small vulvar cancers. Oncology 1990;4:21–8.

should be made about a patient's sexuality. A simple straightforward question about sexual activity is appropriate.

For most patients with vulvar cancer, preoperative assessment is simple: a complete blood count and chest radiography in otherwise healthy patients with a small lesion. Liver and renal laboratory studies and an electrocardiogram (ECG) should be performed in older patients. Perioperative antibiotics should be routinely administered and intermittent compression devices applied to reduce the risk of thrombosis and embolisms. Oral antibiotics should be continued as long as the groin drains are in place.

PRINCIPLES OF VULVAR RESECTION

Separate Incisions

Modern surgical management of vulvar cancer calls for separate vulvar and groin procedures. Classic radical vulvectomy included resection of all the skin and fat of the vulva so that all the lymphatic channels would be removed (Figure 13–3). This was thought to

Table 13–1. FREQUENCY OF VULVAR CANCER AND RELATIVE 5-YEAR SURVIVAL BY GROIN NODE STATUS

Node Status	No. Patients	(%)	5-Year Survival (%)
Negative	385	(65.5)	90.9
Positive	203	(34.5)	57.2
1–2 nodes	125	(62.5)	75.2
3–4 nodes	40	(20)	36.1
5–6 nodes	19	(9.5)	24.0
≥ 7 nodes	16	(8)	0
Total	588	(100)	

Adapted from Homesley HD, Bundy BN, Sedlis A, et al. Assessment of current International Federation of Gynecology and Obstetrics staging of vulvar carcincoma relative to prognoctic factors for survival (a Gynecologic Oncology Group study). Am J Obstet Gynecol 1991;164:997–1004.

Table 13–3. CLINICAL TUMOR SIZE AND LYMPH NODE STATUS IN VULVAR CANCER

Tumor Size (cm)	No. Patients with Positive Nodes	(%)
< 1	6/45	(13.3)
1.1–2	12/83	(14.5)
2.1–3	20/81	(24.7)
3.1–4	10/28	(35.7)
> 4	7/30	(23.3)

Adapted from Sedlis A, Homesley H, Bundy BN, et al. Positive groin lymph nodes in superficial squamous cell vulvar cancer. A Gynecologic Oncology Group study. Am J Obstet Gynecol 1987;156:1159–64.

Table 13–4. CONVENTIONAL HISTOLOGIC GRADE AND LYMPH NODE STATUS IN VULVAR CANCER

Grade	No. Patients with Positive Nodes	(%)
1	18/118	(15.3)
2	25/123	(20.3)
3	14/31	(45.2)

Adapted from Sedlis A, Homesley H, Bundy BN, et al. Positive groin lymph nodes in superficial squamous cell vulvar cancer. A Gynecologic Oncology Group study. Am J Obstet Gynecol 1987;156:1159–64.

be a vital step in reducing local recurrence. Early efforts to reduce the morbidity of radical vulvectomy included separate groin and vulvar incisions (Figure 13–4).[23] Recurrences in the skin bridge have been described, though very infrequently, because lymph nodes in transit between the groin and vulva have not been described.[24] At least two small case-control studies could detect no difference in recurrence or survival between matched pairs treated with en bloc versus separate-incision techniques,[25,26] though Helm and colleagues found that operative time and blood loss were significantly reduced in the separate-incision group.[26] In another comparative trial, the incidence of wound breakdown was significantly lower in the separate-incision group (64% versus 38%), while the incidence of wound infection, lymphocyst formation, and wound cellulitis was similar.[27]

Pelvic Node Dissection

Pelvic lymph node dissection is no longer considered part of the routine surgical management of vulvar cancer. In some large series, the only patients with positive pelvic nodes had three or more positive groin nodes.[15] Even more importantly, GOG protocol 37 demonstrated survival advantage for patients with positive inguinal nodes treated with pelvic radiation versus pelvic lymphadenectomy.[28] There remains

Table 13–5. CAPILLARY-SPACE INVOLVEMENT AND LYMPH NODE STATUS IN VULVAR CANCER

Involvement Status	No. Patients with Positive Nodes	(%)
No tumor present	44/252	(17.5)
Tumor present	13/20	(65.0)

Adapted from Sedlis A, Homesley H, Bundy BN, et al. Positive groin lymph nodes in superficial squamous cell vulvar cancer. A Gynecologic Oncology Group study. Am J Obstet Gynecol 1987;156:1159–64.

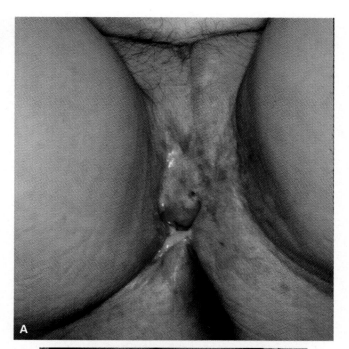

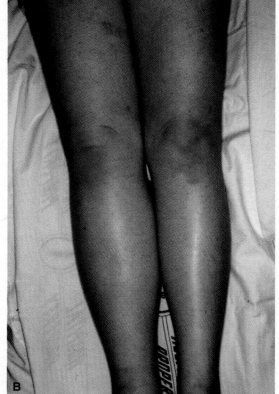

Figure 13–3. *A*, Radical vulvectomy has been largely abandoned because of its mutilating effects. This patient was treated with a radical vulvectomy and bilateral inguinal femoral lymph adenectomy for a right Bartholin's gland carcinoma. She suffered a local recurrence and was treated with radiotherapy and chemotherapy. She has ureteral and vaginal stenosis; however, she does void spontaneously. She is not sexually active. *B*, Chronic lymphedema in the same patient. Lymphedema occurs most commonly in patients receiving combination therapy, usually surgery and radiotherapy.

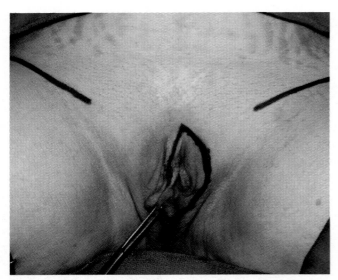

Figure 13–4. Separate vulvar and groin incisions improve healing without compromising survival.

only one category of patients for whom pelvic node dissection is appropriate: patients with grossly involved pelvic nodes imaged by preoperative CT. Radiation alone is unlikely to control disease in these patients, and tumor reduction should be considered.

Surgical Margins

Primary surgical treatment of vulvar cancer is best suited to situations in which the entire lesion can be removed with adequate margins. Adequate surgical margins range from 1 cm (acceptable) to 2 cm (ideal). A margin of < 1 cm significantly increases the risk of local recurrence.[29] Interestingly, the incidence of local recurrence is about the same in patients treated with radical vulvectomy versus radical local excision. A wide margin (eg, 10 cm) in one location does not compensate for an inadequate margin in another.

Adequate margins can be especially difficult to obtain in patients with midline tumors. The amount of subcutaneous fat in the perineum is usually small and a 2-cm margin, which does not involve the anal sphincter, can be problematic. The clitoris and distal urethra can be removed to obtain adequate margins; however, these types of resections will affect sexual and urinary functions.

In most situations, margins should not be compromised for fear of the inability to close the defect.

There are several techniques for wound closure that are relatively simple and safe to perform (see below). If adequate margins can be achieved only by exenteration, chemoradiation should be strongly considered. Primary exenterative surgery at this time is discouraged, given chemoradiation's dramatic organ-sparing potential.

In summary, the goal of primary surgical treatment is removal of the primary tumor with adequate margins while preserving bladder, anal, rectal, and sexual functions as completely as possible. However, the surgical approach can and should be individualized to take into account the anatomy and preferences of the patient.

Clitoral Margins

Lesions close to the clitoris in a sexually active patient can be problematic. In this situation, a 1-cm margin must suffice at times in order to preserve sexual function. Although there are no data on sexual function following radiotherapy to preserve the clitoris, consultation with a radiation oncologist about nonsurgical options is appropriate in selected patients.

Urethral Margins

Lesions close to the urethral meatus can also be problematic. With detailed history taking, physical examination, and cystometric data, Reid and colleagues[30] exhaustively studied the pre- and postoperative bladder function in patients treated for invasive vulvar cancer. Fifteen patients underwent radical vulvectomy, including 4 who underwent partial urethral resection or hemivulvectomy. The most common subjective complaint was spraying of urine (57% of cases). Six patients, including the 4 who had urethral resection, and 2 patients whose resection came within 1 cm of the urethral meatus, developed a change in continence (total, stress, or urge). Reid and colleagues[30] concluded that incontinence was more a result of urethral resection than radical vulvectomy, but that it was unlikely that all patients treated with urethral resection would become incontinent. The decision to remove a portion of the urethra should not be taken lightly, and appropriate preoperative counseling is imperative.

Anal Margins

Like clitoral and urethral lesions, lesions close to the anus and rectum can be a surgical challenge, too. Lateral margins around such lesions are usually not a problem; however, the anal sphincter or rectum may be too close to allow an adequately deep margin. Several options should be considered, depending on the area of rectum or anus involved. If the area of compromised margin is more than 1 to 2 cm, then chemoradiation and sparing of the anal sphincter should be considered. In selected patients with very limited involvement of the rectum or anus, a local resection that preserves organ function is possible. Remmenga and colleagues[31] reported on a small series of patients treated in this manner along with a protective colostomy. Two-thirds of patients in the series had their colostomies successfully reversed 6 months after the initial resection. This author has successfully performed similar procedures without a protective colostomy.

Techniques for Vulvar Resection

Once adequate anesthesia is established, the patient is placed in adjustable stirrups. In this way, the groin can be dissected while the patient lies relatively flat, and then the legs are raised to better expose the vulva for resection of the primary tumor. Allen stir-

rups or their equivalent are superior to candy-cane stirrups for this purpose (Figures 13–5 to 13–7).

In the operating room, adequate margins can be ensured by actually measuring and drawing the margins on the patient's skin following induction of anesthesia (see Figure 13–6). In most cases, the incision is carried down to the deep perineal fascia to ensure an adequately deep margin; however, in patients with very superficial lesions, this is probably not necessary (see Figure 13–7). The shape of the excision is frequently irregular. The labium, mons, vagina, and part of the buttocks can be mobilized to permit tension-free closure. If tension-free closure is not possible, as is commonly the case

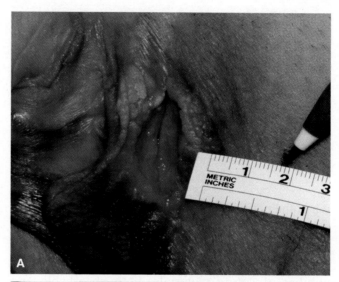

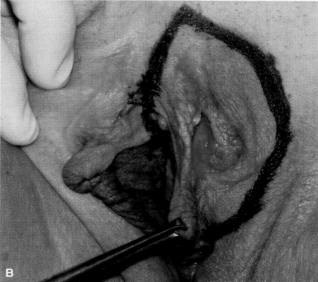

Figure 13–6. *A* and *B*, Drawing 2-cm margins around a labial tumor.

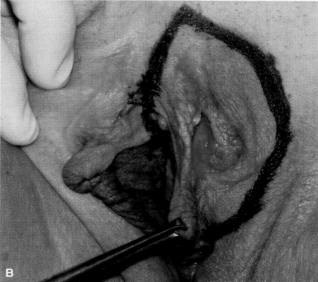

Figure 13–5. Adjustable Allen stirrups are ideal for the triple-incision approach. Following groin dissection, the legs can be raised to make the vulvar resection easier.

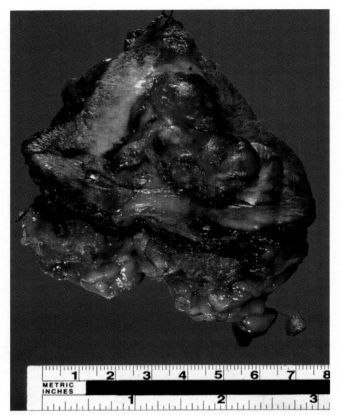

Figure 13–7. Surgical specimen with adequate margins, both lateral and deep.

removed), categorically (by the name of the operation), and visually (by one of three line drawings provided in the survey form). Analysis of the responses showed a very good correlation between the description of the procedure and the drawings but considerable variation in the names given to the procedures.[32]

The nomenclature for the anatomic landmarks for groin dissection is also ambiguous. The cribriform fascia, which is considered a vital landmark, is really not a fascia at all but a thickening of connective tissue covering the fossa ovalis. Micheletti and colleagues[33] have proposed renaming this structure "cribriform lamina," to distinguish it from the true fascial structures of the femoral triangle. They have also provided a complete glossary of terms related to surgical treatment for vulvar cancer.

Surgical Anatomy of the Groin

As described by Micheletti and colleagues, the surgical anatomy of the groin contains three nodal subgroups: (1) the superficial inguinal nodes (or superficial inguinal upper group), which are caudad to the inguinal ligament and oriented horizontally. These nodes lie above the femoral fascia and cribriform lamina; (2) the superficial femoral nodes (or superficial inguinal lower group or superficial subinguinal nodes), which are oriented vertically along the terminus of the saphenous vein as it enters the fossa ovalis; and (3) the deep femoral nodes (or deep inguinal group), which usually number only 1 to 3 and lie medial to the femoral vein.[34]

The goal of groin dissection in patients with vulvar cancer is to remove the target nodes and minimize the morbidity of doing so. Most authors agree that metastases to femoral nodes occur infrequently in the absence of metastases to the two superficial nodal groups. Yet, the treatment failure rate following superficial inguinal lymphadenectomy in the groin is 5 to 6 percent.[35–37] This compares with the groin treatment failure rate of less than 1 percent among the 385 patients on the GOG protocol 37 who had negative inguinal femoral lymphadenectomies. For this reason, inguinal femoral lymphadenectomy remains the procedure of choice for many gynecologic oncologists.

when the perineum is involved or the tumor is large, one of the plastic procedures should be considered. The wound is closed with a deep layer of absorbable sutures to reduce tension on the skin closure. A number of suture materials, both absorbable and nonabsorbable, can be used on the skin. Simple interrupted sutures usually suffice; however, vertical mattress sutures are useful, if the tension on the wound is more than the optimal level.

PRINCIPLES OF GROIN DISSECTION

Problems with Nomenclature

No other procedure in gynecologic oncology is surrounded with as much confusion as groin dissection for invasive vulvar cancer. This was illustrated in a 1995 survey of 50 gynecologic oncologists who were asked to describe the groin procedure they performed for early vulvar cancer in three ways: descriptively (by the nodes

Prevention of Lymphedema

It is widely understood that full groin dissection combined with groin irradiation for the treatment of vulvar cancer will result in lymphedema (see Figure 13–3B). Therefore, gynecologic oncologists have developed alternative strategies to avoid using this combination: limited surgery to remove grossly involved nodes alone or radical dissection with no postoperative treatment.

The measurement of lymphedema is totally subjective. In the literature on vulvar cancer, there are no standard methods for measuring lymphedema or comparing lymphedema following different procedures. Nevertheless, it appears that over the years, several innovations have helped reduce the severity of lymphedema associated with vulvar cancer treatment. The first innovation has come in the extent of groin dissection. Classic inguinal femoral groin dissection included removing parts of the femoral fascia and all the fat around the femoral artery and vein. Closure required a sartorius transposition to cover the vessels and disruption of all the lymphatics of the groin. The current thinking, which is based largely on the anatomic studies described above, is that the femoral fascia and the femoral artery can be left undisturbed. This preserves some of the lymphatic channels from the leg that traverse the groin to the pelvis.

Other innovations have come in equipment and treatment of infections. Widespread use of closed suction drains, calf compression devices, and perioperative antibiotics has probably helped reduce the incidence of lymphedema. Maintaining flow of lymph in the legs probably helps with long-term outcome. Prevention of infection helps keep lymphatics patent and makes secondary procedures unnecessary.

Techniques for Groin Dissection

The groin incision is best made 1 to 2 cm below and parallel to the inguinal ligament. The incision must extend medially enough to allow access to the medial portion of the femoral triangle, which means approaching close to or even entering the mons. Few nodes are found in the most lateral portion of the femoral triangle; therefore, the incision should

extend only 4 to 5 cm lateral to the femoral vessels. Because the size of the incision is also a function of the patient's habitus, there is no universal formula for deciding on the length of the groin incision.

The skin incision is carried to the level of Camper's fascia. Camper's fascia is another misnamed landmark of the groin: it is not really fascia at all but a thickening of connective tissue. Yet, it is a valuable landmark because skin flaps can be raised once it is reached. These flaps should allow access to the femoral triangle and all the target nodes without having to go beyond the node-bearing areas. Care should be taken on two accounts: first, the larger the area undermined, the more space is available for the formation of lymphocysts. Second, thinning out the skin flaps may increase the risk of wound breakdown.

Once the skin flaps are raised, node dissection starts laterally and then moves in a circular fashion until the fossa ovalis is reached. The femoral fascia is left intact as the node-bearing fat is lifted up. In the obese patient, the inguinal ligament is the easiest landmark to identify first. The saphenous vein can be ligated; however, it is easy to preserve and may help reduce the risk of wound complications. Like Camper's fascia, the fossa ovalis is little more than a thickening of connective tissue in some patients and so is not easy to identify until after the nodes are removed. The cribriform lamina is best identified where the saphenous vein joins the femoral vein. At this point, the superficial inguinal nodes are completely mobilized. The fossa ovalis is entered, and the superficial femoral nodes resting on the pectineus muscle are mobilized with the rest of the specimen. This leaves the femoral vessels still encased in fat. If desired, the one to three medial femoral nodes can be removed at this time, thus exposing the femoral vein but not the femoral artery (Figure 13–8).

SENTINEL NODE IDENTIFICATION AND LYMPHATIC MAPPING

An innovative approach to lymph node assessment in patients with vulvar cancer is lymphatic mapping and sentinel lymph node identification. This strategy is being widely employed in the treatments for other diseases, notably breast cancer and cutaneous melanoma, to identify patients with nodal metastases

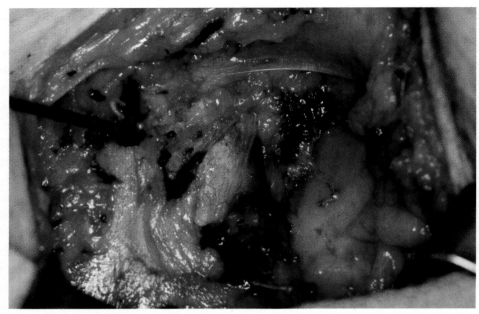

Figure 13–8. Right groin dissection following removal of superficial inguinal and medial femoral nodes. The pointer is at the edge of the fossa ovalis, and the femoral vein is visible in the middle of the picture.

without performing a complete regional lymphadenectomy. The concept is that a single lymphatic channel draining the tumor will deliver metastases to a lymph node designated as the sentinel node (Figure 13–9). This sentinel node can be identified by a variety of mapping techniques including preoperative lymphoscintigraphy, intraoperative lymphoscintigraphy, intraoperative intradermal injection of a vital blue dye, or a combination of these methods. If the concept is validated in a disease site, complete lymphadenectomy can be replaced by sentinel node dissection. The result is a corresponding reduction in morbidity, especially lymphedema, whose treatment is woefully inadequate.

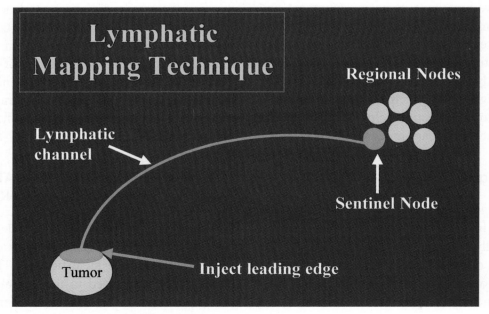

Figure 13–9. The sentinel node concept.

Lymphoscintigraphy—whether preoperative or intraoperative—requires peritumoral injection of a weak radionuclide (usually a technetium-labeled sulfur microcolloid). This is followed by scanning with a gamma counter in the preoperative setting or a hand-held probe in the operating room. Preoperative lymphoscintigraphy is of special value when a tumor has ambiguous drainage patterns (eg, periumbilical melanoma). In patients with vulvar cancer, preoperative lymphoscintigraphy may prove valuable in determining if there is unilateral or bilateral drainage from a lesion close to the midline. In one series, preoperative lymphoscintigraphy revealed unilateral lymphatic drainage in 21 percent of patients with midline lesions.[38]

Identifying the sentinel node offers pathologists an opportunity to perform targeted in-depth analyses, such as step-sectioning and immunohistochemistry. Though it is not feasible to apply this technology to analysis in all 9 to 13 nodes of the groin, one or two sentinel nodes can reasonably be step-sectioned and stained with special markers.

In several large series of patients with breast cancer or cutaneous melanoma, identification of the sentinel node by various techniques led to correct predictions of the tumor status of the entire lymphatic basin.[39,40] This concept has now been investigated in

patients with vulvar cancer. In a series of 52 patients at The University of Texas M.D. Anderson Cancer Center, the sentinel node was successfully identified in around 95 percent of selected cases using blue dye alone, once surgeons mastered the technique.[41,42] There have been no false-negative identifications of sentinel nodes in the series. Conversely, in a multi-institutional trial of 50 patients in the Netherlands,[43] the sentinel node was identified in only 56 percent of cases using blue dye alone. There have been two false-negative identifications of sentinel nodes. Several small series combining blue dye injection and lymphoscintigraphy have reported a high rate of sentinel node identification.[44,45]

Blue dye mapping studies have led to important in vivo findings regarding the lymphatic anatomy of the groin, which, in turn, have practical surgical applications. In patients with labial tumors, the sentinel node is frequently found in Micheletti's superficial inguinal nodal upper group just below the inguinal ligament. Such a sentinel node and its afferent lymphatic channel are easy to identify near the level of Camper's fascia (Figure 13–10). In patients with midline lesions, the sentinel node is frequently found in the superficial inguinal lower group, that is, in the medial femoral triangle just above the pectineus muscle. In these

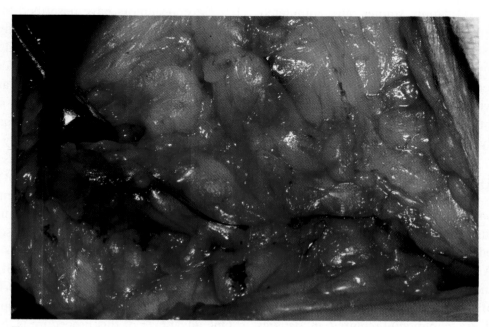

Figure 13–10. Afferent lymphatic channel and sentinel node in a patient with a labial primary lesion.

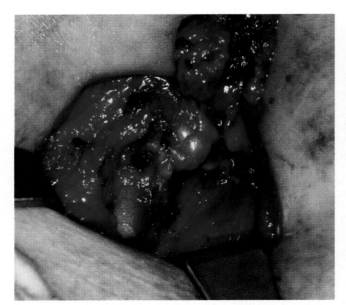

Figure 13–11.   Afferent lymphatic channel and sentinel node in a patient with a clitoral primary lesion. The pubic tubercle is marked. Note the sentinel node was medial to the femoral vein that is visible.

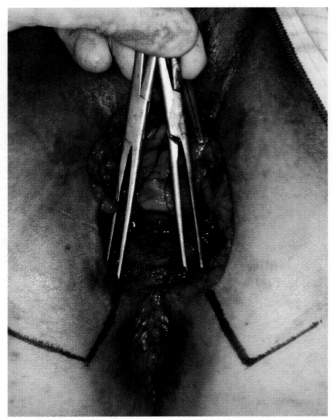

Figure 13–12.   Rhomboid flaps under construction to fill a large perineal defect.

cases, the afferent lymphatic channel may enter the sentinel node from below and, therefore, will not be seen until after the sentinel node is found (Figure 13–11).

Lymphatic mapping in patients with vulvar cancer is still under development. However, it will very likely change the way vulvar cancer patients are cared for, just as it has in other types of cancer patients. Until validation studies are completed, groin dissection will remain the gold standard. Despite this, sentinel node biopsy alone may be appropriate for patients who are medically infirm. In addition, the sentinel node mapping may benefit the patient even when a full lymphadenectomy is performed by identifying the sentinel node for extended histologic analysis.

TECHNIQUES FOR PLASTIC SURGERY

A number of plastic surgery techniques can be used to cover a defect that cannot be closed primarily. Rhomboid flap procedures are particularly reliable and easy to perform.[46] A rhomboid flap derives its blood supply from the underlying subcutaneous tissue and can cover an area of about 4×4 cm. Bilateral flaps can be developed and are commonly required in patients with perineal lesions. The simplicity, speed, and low

morbidity of the rhomboid flap procedure make it ideal, when applicable (Figure 13–12).

Several authors have described the use of short gracilis myocutaneous flaps for vulvar or vaginal reconstruction.[47–49] These flaps, only 8 to 12 cm long, are smaller than the classically described flaps. In this case, the flap is mapped out and then developed along the medial thigh. The skin paddle is sutured to the fascia to prevent shearing off of the skin and fat. The vascular bundle may be ligated and cut without compromising the flap, as the blood supply from the underlying muscle is not disturbed. The flap is then fitted into place and secured. The most common complication is loss of some or all of the skin of the graft; necrosis of the muscle is rare.

Another flap option is the mons pubis pedicle flap.[50] This flap takes advantage of the excellent blood supply from both the superficial external pudendal artery and the superficial epigastric artery. One advantage of this procedure is that it mobilizes hair-bearing skin to the vulva. The published experience with this flap is smaller than that with the gracilis flap. Another procedure, which is gaining wider use among gynecologic oncologists, is the transverse rectus abdominus myocutaneous (TRAM) flap procedure. The TRAM flap is especially useful when there is a large defect to cover.[51]

REFERENCES

1. Way S. Malignant disease of the female genital tract. Philadelphia: The Blakiston Co.; 1951. p. 27–8.
2. Taussig FJ. Cancer of the vulva: an analysis of 155 cases. Am J Obstet Gynecol 1940;40:764.
3. Twombly G. The technique of radical vulvectomy for carcinoma of the vulva. Cancer 1953;3:516–30.
4. Sturgeon S, Brinton L, Devesa S, Kurman R. *In situ* and invasive vulvar cancer incidence trends (1973–1987). Am J Obstet Gynecol 1992;166:1482–5.
5. Greenlee RT, Hill-Harmon MB, Murray T, Thun M. Cancer statistics 2001. Ca Cancer J Clin 2001;51: 15–37.
6. Parazzini F, La Vecchia C, Garcia S, et al. Determinants of invasive vulvar cancer risk: an Italian case-control study. Gynecol Oncol 1993;48:50–5.
7. Franklin E, Rutledge F. Epidemiology of epidermoid carcinoma of the vulva. Obstet Gynecol 1972;29: 165–72.
8. Trimble C, Hildesheim A, Brinton L, et al. Heterogeneous etiology of squamous carcinoma of the vulva. Obstet Gynecol 1996;87:59–64.
9. Hording U, Junge J, Daugaard S, et al. Vulval squamous cell carcinomas and papillomavirus: indications for two different aetiologies. Gynecol Oncol 1994;52:241–4.
10. Andersen WA, Franquemont DW, Williams H, et al. Vulvar squamous cell carcinoma and papillomaviruses: two separate entities. Am J Obstet Gynecol 1991;165:329–36.
11. FIGO Stages—1988 Revision. Gynecol Oncol 1987; 35:125–7.
12. Homesley HD, Bundy BN, Sedlis A, et al. Assessment of current International Federation of Gynecology and Obstetrics staging of vulvar carcinoma relative to prognostic factors for survival (a Gynecologic Oncology Group study). Am J Obstet Gynecol 1991;164:997–1004.
13. Wharton J, Gallager S, Rutledge F. Microinvasive carcinoma of the vulva. Am J Obstet Gynecol 1974; 118:159–62.
14. Parker R, Duncan I, Rampone J, Creasman W. Operative management of early invasive epidermoid carcinoma of the vulva. Am J Obstet Gynecol 1975;123:349–55.
15. Hacker N, Berek J, Lagasse L, et al. Management of regional lymph nodes and their prognostic influence in vulvar cancer. Obstet Gynecol 1983;61:408–12.

16. DiPaola G, Gomez-Rueda N, Arrigil L. Relevance of microinvasion in carcinoma of the vulva. Obstet Gynecol 1975;45:647–9.
17. Report of the ISSVD Task Force. Microinvasive cancer of the vulva. J Reprod Med 1984;29:454–6.
18. Sedlis A, Homesley H, Bundy BN, et al. Positive groin lymph nodes in superficial squamous cell vulvar cancer. A Gynecologic Oncology Group study. Am J Obstet Gynecol 1987;156:1159–64.
19. van der Velden J, Lindert ACM, Lammes FB, et al. Extracapsular growth of lymph node metastases in squamous cell carcinoma of the vulva. The impact on recurrence and survival. Cancer 1995;75:2885–90.
20. Paladini D, Cross P, Lopes A, Monaghan J. Prognostic significance of lymph node variables in squamous cell carcinoma of the vulva. Cancer 1994;74:2491–6.
21. Origoni M, Sideri M, Garsia S, et al. Prognostic value of pathological patterns of lymph node positivity in squamous cell carcinoma of the vulva stage III and IVA FIGO. Gynecol Oncol 1992;45:313–6.
22. Gordinier ME, Steinhoff MM, Hogan JW, et al. S-phase fraction, *p53*, and *HER-2/neu* status as predictors of nodal metastasis in early vulvar cancer. Gynecol Oncol 1997;67:200–2.
23. Hacker NF, Leuchter RS, Berek JS, et al. Radical vulvectomy and bilateral inguinal lymphadenectomy through separate groin incisions. Obstet Gynecol 1981;58:574–9.
24. Christopherson W, Buchsbaum HJ, Voet R, Lifschitz S. Radical vulvectomy and bilateral groin lymphadenectomy utilizing separate groin incisions: report of a case with recurrence in the intervening skin bridge. Gynecol Oncol 1985;21:247–51.
25. Siller BS, Alvarez RD, Conner WD, et al. T2/3 vulvar cancer: a case-control study of triple incision versus en bloc radical vulvectomy and inguinal lymphadenectomy. Gynecol Oncol 1995;57:335–9.
26. Helm CW, Hatch K, Austin JM, et al. A matched comparison of single and triple incision techniques for the surgical treatment of carcinoma of the vulva. Gynecol Oncol 1992;46:150–6.
27. Hopkins MP, Reid GC, Morley GW. Radical vulvectomy. The decision for the incision. Cancer 1993; 72:799–803.
28. Homesley HD, Bundy BN, Sedlis A, Adcock L. Radiation therapy versus pelvic node resection for carcinoma of the vulva with positive groin nodes. Obstet Gynecol 1986;68:733–40.
29. Heaps JM, Fu YS, Montz FJ, et al. Surgical-pathologic variables predictive of local recurrence in squamous cell carcinoma of the vulva. Gynecol Oncol 1990; 38:309–14.
30. Reid GC, DeLancey JOL, Hopkins MP, et al. Urinary incontinence following radical vulvectomy. Obstet Gynecol 1990;75:852–8.

31. Remmenga S, Barnhill D, Nash J, et al. Radical vulvectomy with partial rectal resection and temporary colostomy as primary therapy for selected patients with vulvar carcinoma. Obstet Gynecol 1991; 77:577–9.

32. Levenback C, Burke TW, Morris M, et al. Potential applications of intraoperative lymphatic mapping in vulvar cancer. Gynecol Oncol 1995;59:216–20.

33. Micheletti L, Levi AC, Bogliatto F. Anatomosurgical implications derived from an embryological study of the scarpa's triangle with particular reference to groin lymphadenectomy. Gynecol Oncol 1998;70:358–64.

34. Borgno G, Micheletti L, Barbero M, et al. Topographic distribution of groin lymph nodes. J Reprod Med 1990;35:1127–9.

35. Berman ML, Soper JT, Creasman WT, et al. Conservative surgical management of superficially invasive stage I vulvar carcinoma. Gynecol Oncol 1989; 35:352–7.

36. Burke TW, Stringer CA, Gershenson DM, et al. Radical wide excision and selective inguinal node dissection for squamous cell carcinoma of the vulva. Gynecol Oncol 1990;38:328–32.

37. Stehman FB, Bundy BN, Dvoretsky PM, Creasman WT. Early stage I carcinoma of the vulva treated with ipsilateral superficial inguinal lymphadenectomy and modified radical hemivulvectomy: a prospective study of the Gynecologic Oncology Group. Obstet Gynecol 1992;79:490–7.

38. Van der Zee A, De Hullu J, Verheijen R, et al. Sentinel lymph node (SLN) detection in early stage squamous cell cancer of the vulva. 31st Annual Meeting. San Diego, CA: Society of Gynecologic Oncologists; 2000.

39. Gershenwald JE, Colome MI, Lee JE, et al. Patterns of recurrence following a negative sentinel lymph node biopsy in 243 patients with stage I or II melanoma. J Clin Oncol 1998;16:2253–60.

40. Krag D, Weaver D, Ashikaga T, et al. The sentinel node in breast cancer. N Engl J Med 1998;339:941–6.

41. Levenback C, Burke TW, Gershenson DM, et al. Intraoperative lymphatic mapping for vulvar cancer. Obstet Gynecol 1994;84:163–7.

42. Levenback C. Intraoperative lymphatic mapping of the vulva with blue dye. 31st Annual Meeting. San Diego, CA: Society of Gynecologic Oncologists; 2000.

43. Ansink AC, Sie-Go DM, van der Velden J, et al. Identification of sentinel lymph nodes in vulvar carcinoma patients with the aid of a patent blue V injection: a multicenter study. Cancer 1999;86:652–6.

44. Terada KY, Coel MN, Ko P, Wong JH. Combined use of intraoperative lymphatic mapping and lymphoscintigraphy in the management of squamous cell cancer of the vulva. Gynecol Oncol 1998;70:65–9.

45. de Hullu JA, Doting E, Piers DA, et al. Sentinel lymph node identification with technetium-99m-labeled nanocolloid in squamous cell cancer of the vulva. J Nucl Med 1998;39:1381–5.

46. Burke TW, Morris M, Levenback C, et al. Closure of complex vulvar defects using local rhomboid flaps. Obstet Gynecol 1994;84:1043–7.

47. Burke TW, Levenback C, Coleman RL, et al. Surgical therapy of T1 and T2 vulvar carcinoma: further experience with radical wide excision and selective inguinal lymphadenectomy. Gynecol Oncol 1995; 57:215–20.

48. Chen SH, Hentz VR, Wei FC, Chen YR. Short gracilis myocutaneous flaps for vulvoperineal and inguinal reconstruction. Plast Reconstr Surg 1995;95:372–7.

49. Soper JT, Larson D, Hunter VJ, et al. Short gracilis myocutaneous flaps for vulvovaginal reconstruction after radical pelvic surgery. Obstet Gynecol 1989;74:823–7.

50. Potkul RK, Barnes WA, Barter JF, et al. Vulvar reconstruction using a mons pubis pedicle flap. Gynecol Oncol 1994;55:21–4.

51. Patsner B, Hetzler P. Post-radical vulvectomy reconstruction using the inferiorly based transverse rectus abdominis (TRAM) flap: a preliminary experience. Gynecol Oncol 1994;55:78–81.

14

Radiation Therapy for Vulvar Cancer

ANTHONY H. RUSSELL, MD

First proposed and initially carried out in cadavers by the French pathologist Basset in 1912, en-bloc radical vulvectomy in continuity with bilateral inguinofemoral lymphadenectomy had become the standard of operative therapy for primary cancer of the vulva by the middle of the 20th century.[1] This comprehensive approach succeeded in more than doubling cure rates previously obtained by more limited surgery.[2-5] Patients with metastatic involvement of groin nodes might additionally be treated by pelvic lymphadenectomy and, in some instances, extension of the surgical dissection to encompass the para-aortic nodes. Selected patients with locally extensive disease were treated with anterior, posterior, or total pelvic exenteration, with cure rates exceeding 50 percent when the regional nodes were found to be free of metastatic involvement.[6]

As early as 1918, radiotherapy had been proposed as a potential alternative to surgery.[7] However, patients relegated to treatment by radiation usually comprised individuals whose disease extended beyond the boundaries of surgical feasibility[8] and others deemed too frail for rigorous surgical intervention. Radiotherapy was administered (in hindsight) using suboptimal dose/fractionation schedules as well as primitive techniques.[9-12] Patients cured by radiotherapy would sometimes trade the symptomatic burden of uncontrolled vulvar malignancy for debilitating late effects caused by the application of high-dose radiation to the vulva and perineum.[11,12]

The last quarter of the 20th century witnessed a series of remarkable transformations in the management of this disease. Possibly as a consequence of changing mores and diminished social stigma tied to female lower genital tract malignancies, the extent of vulvar cancer at the time of diagnosis has been steadily diminishing. This trend can be seen by comparing surgical patients treated with radical vulvectomy in the 1940s and 1950s to more recent surgical experience. The percentage of patients with groin node metastases has fallen from 50 to 60 percent near the middle of the 20th century to 35 percent or less in more recent times. Modifications in the surgical approach to vulvar cancer have been stimulated by the desire to reduce chronic morbidities associated with radical extirpative surgery in young, sexually active patients diagnosed with disease of limited extent. The evolution of combined modality therapy for patients with vulvar cancer has paralleled successful efforts to preserve structure, function, and cosmesis in the treatment of patients with primary cancers of the head and neck, breast, rectum, and sarcomas of the extremities.

Following radical groin and pelvic node dissection, lower extremity swelling may be transient and of limited severity. But some patients will develop permanent, massive, and disabling lymphedema.[13,14] Radical vulvar surgery can result in pelvic relaxation, organ prolapse, and urinary incontinence in some patients, particularly when removal of the distal urethra or a portion of the lower vagina is required. Significant stenosis of the vaginal introitus can occur. Fecal incontinence may result when surgical therapy requires resection of a portion of the anal sphincter.[15] Removal of the vulva and venereal fat has the functional consequence of shortening effective vaginal depth and removing a protective cushion from the pubic arch, contributing to dyspareunia in many surgically treated patients. Major alterations in body image, decreased capacity for sexual arousal because of removal of the clitoris, and reduced coital activity consequent to pain during intercourse may result in feelings of guilt, worthlessness, depression, and anxiety.[16,17]

For selected individuals, conservative excision of a small primary cancer coupled with limited groin dissection, can achieve equivalent cancer control compared with more extensive surgery, with less mutilation and less functional loss.[18-20] Planned in coordination with conservative surgery, preoperative or postoperative radiation (alone or with concurrent chemotherapy) permits salvage of patients with extensive primary cancers, who might otherwise require exenterative procedures for cure, and has made possible clitoral preservation in others.[21-38] Chemoradiation can convert most patients with unresectable groin node metastases to operative candidates who may enjoy prolonged disease-free survival following resection of residual palpable nodal tissue.[39] Synchronous chemotherapy and concurrent radiation (chemoradiation) have allowed curative, nonsurgical management of some patients with massive, unresectable primary disease.[34,35,40-45] Chemoradiation, by employing reduced total radiation dose and reduced dose per fraction, may accomplish equivalent or better tumor control with less chronic injury than a higher radiation dose given alone. By integrating radiation into a comprehensive initial treatment strategy, a menu of sensible and effective therapeutic options becomes possible. Management may be responsibly tailored to initial disease extent, defined clinical and histopathologic factors, comorbidities, and the hierarchy of personal concerns expressed by an individual patient. The multiple contexts in which radiation is currently employed in the curative management of patients with vulvar cancer are listed in Table 14–1.

ANATOMIC, HISTOPATHOLOGIC, AND PHYSIOLOGIC FACTORS

The vulva is composed of the mons veneris, labia majora, labia minora, clitoris, and the vulvar vestibule, which harbors the urethral meatus and is bounded by the vaginal introitus. The labia, limited laterally by the labiocrural folds, are the female ana-

logue of the male scrotum and are pigmented and covered by hair lateral to the crests of the labia majora. Like scrotal skin, the skin of the vulva will atrophy with topical application of estrogen and will hypertrophy in response to topical application of testosterone, facts of potential importance in assisting patients with chronic radiotherapy-induced changes in the vulvar skin and vaginal mucosa. The paired, mucus-secreting Bartholin's glands lie deep to the posterior labia majora and drain by a simple duct to the vulvar vestibule between the hymenal membrane and the medial borders of the labia minora. Coursing posteromedially, the labia minora taper and join in a fold called the posterior fourchette. Anteriorly, the labia minora taper, then split to envelop the clitoris, fusing in front of the clitoris to form the prepuce or clitoral hood and behind the clitoris to form the frenulum. The clitoris, an erectile organ analagous to the penis in the male, is composed of the glans and a body consisting of two corpora cavernosa that diverge into the two crura, which lie attached to the undersurface of the pubic rami. The arterial supply is from the pudendal arteries, which are branches of the hypogastric arteries.

Table 14–1. INDICATIONS FOR RADIATION THERAPY* IN THE CURATIVE MANAGEMENT OF PATIENTS WITH CARCINOMA OF THE VULVA

1. Salvage therapy for local or regional recurrence after initial surgical therapy.
2. Adjuvant postoperative therapy for patients with metastasis to groin nodes, inadequate surgical margins, or other histopathologic factors predictive for local or regional recurrence.
3. Preoperative therapy to enable conservative surgical resection in patients with cancers that would ordinarily require functionally, psychologically, or cosmetically destructive procedures, if treated with radical surgery as the initial intervention.
4. Preoperative therapy for patients with initially unresectable, fixed, or ulcerated groin nodes.
5. Definitive treatment for patients with extensive primary cancers that have grown beyond the confines of surgical resectability.
6. Definitive therapy for patients who are judged medically inoperable.
7. Alternative therapy for patients with extensive vulvar cancers that would conventionally require exenterative procedures to attempt surgical cure despite preoperative doses of radiation.
8. Elective therapy of inguinofemoral nodes as an alternative to radical lymph node dissection in patients with locally extensive vulvar cancers but clinically and radiographically negative groin nodes.

---

*Radiation therapy alone or with synchronous administration of radiopotentiating cytotoxic chemotherapy (chemoradiation).

Innervation is from branches of the third and fourth sacral nerves through the pudendal nerve.

Sequential metastatic contamination of regional lymph nodes by carcinoma of the vulva is the somewhat predictable consequence of the lymphatic anatomy of the normal vulva.[46-48] The lymphatics of the vulva (Figure 14–1) consist of a veil of fine endothelium-lined spaces that encompass the entire labia minora, fourchette, prepuce, and distal vagina below the hymenal membrane. These vessels coalesce anteriorly, forming larger trunks that run lateral to the clitoris to the mons veneris, acquiring tributaries from the lymphatics of the labia majora that run in a paral-

lel fashion anteriorly from the perineal body. The vulvar lymphatics run through the vulva and do not cross the labiocrural fold. The lymphatics of the perineum course lateral to the labiocrural fold, traversing the superficial tissues of the upper medial thigh. The 1969 International Federation of Obstetrics and Gynecology (FIGO) staging system (Table 14–2) classified cancers that extended onto the perineum as stage III. The 1988 and 1992 American Joint Committee of Cancer (AJCC) classifications (Table 14–3) do not consider involvement of perineal skin a criterion for upstaging from T2 to T3 or from stage II to stage III. However, this distinction does influence the

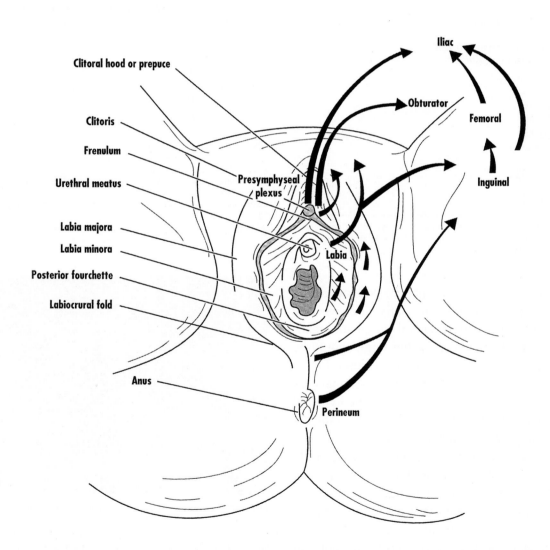

Figure 14–1. Anatomy and lymphatic drainage of the vulva and perineum. Lymphatic channels from the posterior vulva run anterior through the labia, and then laterally to the groin nodes. Lymphatic channels from the perineum and tissue lateral to the labiocrural fold traverse the upper medial thigh.

Table 14–2. AJCC TNM CLASSIFICATION AND FIGO 1969 STAGE GROUPING

T	Primary tumor
Tis	Preinvasive carcinoma (carcinoma in situ)
T1	Tumor confined to the vulva, 2 cm or less in greatest dimension
T2	Tumor confined to the vulva, more than 2 cm in greatest dimension
T3	Tumor of any size with adjacent spread to the urethra and/or vagina and/or perineum and/or anus
T4	Tumor of any size invading any of the following: the upper urethral mucosa, the bladder mucosa, the rectal mucosa, or tumor fixed to the bone
N	Regional lymph nodes
N0	No nodes palpable
N1	Nodes palpable in either groin, not enlarged, and mobile (not clinically suspicious of neoplasm)
N2	Nodes palpable in one or both groins, enlarged, firm, and mobile (clinically suspicious of neoplasm)
N3	Fixed or ulcerated nodes
M	Distant metastases
M0	No clinical metastases
M1a	Palpable pelvic lymph nodes
M1b	Other distant metastases
FIGO STAGE	
0	Tis
I	T1N0,1M0
	T2N0,1M0
III	T1,2N2M0
	T3N0,1,2M0
IV	TxN3M0
	T4N0,1,2M0
	TxNxM1a
	TxNxM1b

X = any T or N category; AJCC = American Joint Committee of Cancer; TNM = tumor-node-metastasis; FIGO = International Federation of Gynecology and Obstetrics.

Table 14–3. AJCC TNM CLASSIFICATION 1992 AND FIGO 1988 STAGE GROUPING

T	Primary tumor
Tis	Carcinoma in situ (preinvasive carcinoma)
T1	Tumor confined to the vulva and perineum* 2 cm or less in greatest dimension
T2	Tumor confined to the vulva and perineum* more than 2 cm in greatest dimension
T3	Tumor of any size with adjacent spread to the lower urethra and/or vagina and/or anus
T4	Tumor of any size invading any of the following: the upper urethral mucosa, the bladder mucosa, the rectal mucosa, or tumor fixed to the bone
N	Regional lymph nodes†
N0	No nodal metastases
N1	Unilateral regional lymph node metastasis
N2	Bilateral regional lymph node metastasis
M	Distant metastasis
M0	No evidence of distant metastasis
M1	Any distant metastasis including pelvic lymph nodes
FIGO STAGE	
0	Tis
I	T1N0M0
II	T2N0M0
III	T3N0M0
	T1,2,3N1M0
IVa	T1,2,3N2M0
	T4NxM0
IVb	TxNxM1

X = any T or N category; AJCC = American Joint Committee of Cancer; TNM = tumor-node-metastasis; FIGO = International Federation of Gynecology and Obstetrics.
*Note that lesions extending onto the perineum were previously classified as T3.
†Note that assessment of inguinofemoral nodes is histopathologic.

design of radiation ports. In a patient with advanced vulvar cancer extending laterally across the labiocrural fold, these more lateral lymphatic channels in the skin of the upper medial thigh should be included in the radiation target volume (Figure 14–2). Similarly, extension of an advanced vulvovaginal cancer along the vaginal barrel proximal to the hymenal ring requires attention to the direct pelvic lymphatic flow of the middle and upper vagina. At the mons veneris, the vulvar lymphatic trunks deviate laterally to the primary regional nodes in the groin. Studies of the localization of radiolabeled tracer in regional lymph nodes after focal injection of discrete sites in the vulva and on the perineum reveal that the lymphatic drainage of the perineum, clitoris, and anterior labia minora is often bilateral, whereas the lymph flow from well-lateralized sites in the vulva is pre-

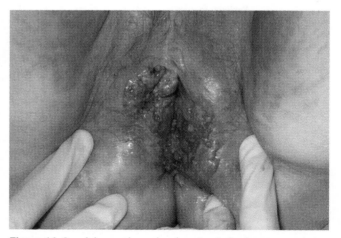

Figure 14–2. Advanced, previously untreated vulvar cancer crossing the labiocrural fold. Note the diffuse dermal lymphatic permeation (peau d'orange) extending to the skin of the upper thighs. Very wide skin margins must be used in designing a radiation target volume. (Reproduced with permission from Russell AH. Vulva. In: Leibel SA, Phillips TL, editors. Textbook of radiation oncology. Philadelphia: W.B. Saunders; 1998.)

dominantly to the ipsilateral groin.[48] Discrete (2-cm diameter or less), well-lateralized primary cancers limited to the vulva and not approaching midline structures will rarely manifest any spread to contralateral groin nodes in the absence of spread to ipsilateral nodes.[19,20,49-52] From the superficial inguinal nodes, lymphatic drainage is through the cribriform lamina to the femoral nodes, with subsequent tertiary flow under the inguinal ligaments to the external iliac nodes. Although direct lymphatic channels from the clitoris to the deep pelvic nodes have been described, three surgical series of patients with clitoral involvement by primary cancers of the vulva have failed to find evidence of pelvic node metastasis in the absence of groin metastasis.[53-55] Similarly, direct lymphatic channels from the clitoris and anterior vulva to the femoral nodes exist, and though occasional patients with metastatic spread to the deep femoral nodes without inguinal node metastasis have been reported,[50,56-58] this is a rare event when the inguinal nodes have been fully dissected and histologically examined. Metastatic spread to pelvic nodes will be found in approximately 15 to 25 percent of patients with histologically verified groin node metastasis, but very rarely without prior contamination of the inguinal or femoral nodes.[13,59-67] On the basis of bipedal lymphangiography, inguinal nodes are seen not to lie lateral to the medial 80 percent of the inguinal ligament and not to lie medial to the pubic tubercle.[68] On the basis of dissection of cadavers, the deep femoral nodes are seen to be one to four in number and located at the fossa ovalis medial to the femoral vein[69] and, thus, can often be irradiated without inclusion of most of the neck of the femur in the radiation ports. Depending on patient size, the depth of the inguinal nodes can be quite variable and difficult to accurately estimate by palpation.[70-72] The depth of the femoral nodes should be measured by computed tomography (CT). Radiation dose should be prescribed to the depth of the femoral artery as it passes beneath the inguinal ligament. Failure to measure the depth accurately can result in delivery of an inadequate dose to the deep nodes, particularly, if all or a portion of the treatment is administered using electron beam.[73,74]

More than 85 percent of invasive vulvar malignancies are epidermoid carcinomas[46,75] leading to the common practice of using the terms squamous carci-

noma of the vulva and vulvar carcinoma synonymously. Because of distinctive histopathology and characteristic clinical behaviors, it is important to recognize verrucous carcinoma[76-79] and the so-called "spray" pattern carcinomas[80,81] as variants of squamous carcinoma with somewhat different clinical manifestations and different implications for radiotherapeutic intervention. The verrucous variant of squamous cancer is characterized by minimal nuclear anaplasia, infrequent mitotic figures, exuberant hyperkeratosis and parakeratosis, and reactive inflammation consisting of plasma cells, mononuclear cells, and polymorphonuclear leukocytes. Often, this cancer is associated with condyloma acuminata.[79] Generally large, pearly gray to white in color, and with gross morphology similar to a cauliflower (Figure 14–3), these cancers characteristically invade with a sharply circumscribed pushing margin (Figure 14–4). While locally destructive, this cancer will rarely metastasize to regional lymph nodes or distantly[77-79] but will often recur at the margin of surgical resection. Radiation therapy has generally been considered ineffective and possibly dangerous. Transformation of the verrucous lesions to a more anaplastic histology following unsuccessful radiation treatment has been attributed to

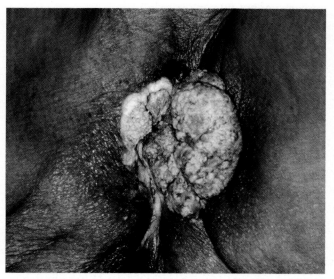

Figure 14–3. Locally recurrent verrucous cancer following radical vulvectomy. Warty, exophytic, cauliflower morphology is characteristic. This patient had persistent local disease despite salvage chemoradiation consisting of 54 Gy in 30 fractions with twice-daily fractionation over 7 weeks with three cycles of synchronous 5-fluorouracil and cisplatin. (Reproduced with permission from Russell AH. Vulva. In: Leibel SA, Phillips TL, editors. Textbook of radiation oncology. Philadelphia: W.B. Saunders; 1998.)

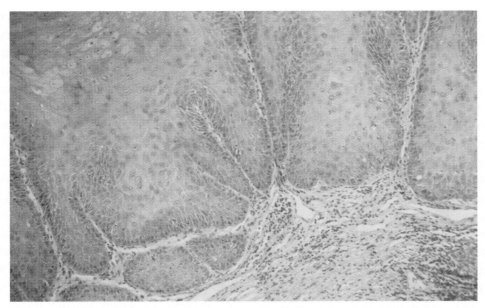

Figure 14–4. Color photomicrograph of verrucous cancer. Tumor is characterized by a broad, bulbous, pushing interface with surrounding stroma. (H&E stain) (Reproduced with permission from Russell AH. Vulva. In: Leibel SA, Phillips TL, editors. Textbook of radiation oncology. Philadelphia: W.B. Saunders; 1998.)

radiation mutagenesis or accelerated repopulation, although the evidence for this is anecdotal. However, reports of any favorable outcomes after radiation are infrequent.[78] It would seem sensible to limit the use of radiation to circumstances where potentially curative surgery cannot be performed.

The so-called "spray pattern" carcinoma refers to epidermoid cancer characterized by a discontiguous, erratic invasive border with early, and often extensive, lymphatic permeation (Figure 14–5). This variant of squamous cancer is associated with a high probability of marginal recurrence or "skip" lesions following surgery, despite negative histologic margins that might ordinarily be considered fully adequate. Finding this histopathologic variant in a surgical specimen should prompt consideration of adjuvant postoperative radiation. If radiation is employed as whole or a component of therapy, the irradiated target volume should include a more extensive skin area because of the tendency of this histologic variant to recur as regional satellite lesions within dermal lymphatics.

RADIATION AS SALVAGE THERAPY

Although cancer of the vulva can disseminate hematogenously, this is uncommon and rarely seen as the solitary manifestation of failure. Approximately 80 percent of patients who fail surgical therapy will have recurrences in the residual vulva, on the perineum, at the vaginal margin, in the groin or upper thighs, or in the pelvis, and less than 20 percent will have distant recurrences[20,82–87] (Table 14–4). Following surgery, those with central, limited volume recurrence in the residual vulva, at the vaginal introitus, or on the perineum can be successfully salvaged with secondary surgery, radiation, or combined modality therapy.[82,86–91] A disease-free interval of 2 or more years and lack of involvement of regional nodes at the time of initial treatment portend a favorable outcome with salvage therapy,[86] although overall 2-year actuarial survival following local relapse may be as little as 22 to 25 percent.[91,92] Regional relapse in the groin or in pelvic nodes is much less likely to be cured, regardless of the combination of modalities employed.[82,86–89,91]

In circumstances where the anticipated salvage surgical margin will be less than that of the original surgery, when recurrent neoplasm approaches or involves functionally important midline structures (urethra, anus, vagina, clitoris), when the pattern of recurrence is multifocal, or when the recurrent disease appears to be proliferating rapidly, it is prudent

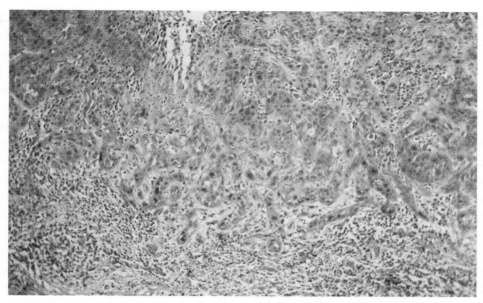

Figure 14–5. Color photomicrograph of infiltrative or "spray" pattern of epidermoid vulvar cancer. Nests of cells along the advancing margin are discontiguous and may be widely separate from the main tumor mass, reminiscent of a painting by Jackson Pollack or a starry sky by Van Gogh. (H&E stain) (Reproduced with permission from Russell AH. Vulva. In: Leibel SA, Phillips TL, editors. Textbook of radiation oncology. Philadelphia: W.B. Saunders; 1998.)

to plan for delivery of radiation as at least a component of the salvage strategy. When a combined approach employing surgery and radiation is planned, it is usually wise to commence with radiation. Despite a reputation for the slow, even indolent growth of vulvar cancer, the majority of patients will develop clinical recurrences within 2 years of initial therapy,[86] and recurrent disease may grow rapidly. Residual occult cancer after salvage surgery may proliferate as rapidly as the wound matures, with the disheartening appearance of cancer regrowth within granulation tissue that is inadequately healed to permit initiation of radiation.

Radiation alone, in doses ranging from 63 to 72 Gy, employing progressive volume reductions or partial treatment with brachytherapy, will often be successful in controlling small-volume central recurrence. Preoperative radiation, ranging in dose from 45 to 54 Gy, followed by local excision may be less damaging to normal tissues than a large perineal volume carried to a high radiation dose in the absence of surgery. Those with recurrence in the lymphatics in the groin or in the pelvic nodes are rarely salvaged, justifying consideration of innovative, multimodality treatment strategies.

RADIOTHERAPY AS SURGICAL ADJUVANT

Given the observation that the large majority of failures of surgical therapy for cancer of the vulva are locoregional, it is sensible to consider locoregional adjuvant therapy for patients determined to be at high risk for recurrence.

For almost 50 years, en bloc radical vulvectomy and bilateral regional lymphadenectomy (inguinofemoral ± pelvic) was the benchmark surgical standard of care in the United States for patients with operable carcinoma of the vulva. Understanding the results of primary surgical therapy is the foundation for understanding the treatment innovations of the

Table 14–4. PATTERN OF RECURRENCE* IN 267 PATIENTS FAILING REGIONAL THERAPY† FOR CARCINOMA OF THE VULVA			
Vulva/Perineum	Groin	Pelvis	Distant
162 (60.7%)	62 (23.2%)	42 (15.7%)	51 (19.1%)

Adapted from Hacker NF, et al;[20] Podratz KC, et al;[82] Malfetano J, et al;[83] Cavanagh D, et al;[84] Bryson SCP, et al;[85] Tilmans AS, et al;[86] Piura B, et al.[87]
*Due to some patients manifesting recurrence at more than one site, the total recurrences exceed 267 and the total of the percentages exceeds 100 percent.
†The majority of patients underwent radical surgery. Adjunctive radiation was administered in some, and a small number were treated with radiation alone.

past quarter century. Much of the classic surgical literature analyzes outcomes using the 1969 FIGO staging system, which employed clinical evaluation of both the primary tumor and groin nodes (see Table 14–2). In 1988, FIGO adopted modifications to this staging system, resulting in a hybrid, clinicopathologic staging system (see Table 14–3) that incorporated the results of histologic assessment of regional nodes. This revision explicitly acknowledged the pivotal prognostic importance of nodal status and implicitly recognized the inaccuracies of assessment of the regional lymph nodes by palpation. Approximately 20 percent of patients with clinically uninvolved groin nodes (1969 FIGO N0,1) will have histologic evidence of groin metastasis if the nodes are radically dissected.[4,59,60,62,64,93] Conversely, enlarged, palpably suspicious nodes, including matted nodes tethered to overlying skin, may be the consequence of injury or infection in the lower extremities, prior venereal infection, or a reaction to necrosis or infection of the primary cancer. Approximately 22 percent of patients with clinically suspicious groin nodes (1969 FIGO N2,3) will show no histologic evidence of nodal spread if the groin nodes are dissected and studied pathologically[4,59,60,62,64,93] (Table 14–5). If a

Table 14–5. ASSESSMENT OF INGUINOFEMORAL NODES

	Histologically (–)	Histologically (+)
CLINICALLY (–) 1969 FIGO N0,1 (N = 451 patients)	363 (80.5%)	88 (19.5%)
CLINICALLY (+) 1969 FIGO N2,3 (N = 243 patients)	53 (21.8%)	190 (78.2%)

Adapted from Way S;[4] Morley GW;[59] Iversen T, et al;[60] Rutledge F, et al;[62] Morris JM;[64] Goplerud DR, Keettel WC.[93]

treatment decision is contingent on the histopathologic status of the groin nodes, fine-needle aspiration or excisional biopsy prior to treatment is sensible.

The prognosis of surgically treated cancer of the vulva is directly related to the presence or absence of regional node metastasis, the extent of lymph node infestation, and the anatomic level of nodal involvement. Five-year disease-free survival probability is approximately 95 percent for patients with T1,2N0 tumors treated surgically[59,94] decreasing to approximately 70 percent for patients with stage T3N0.[59] Metastasis to a single node is less ominous than involvement of multiple nodes.[52,95] Patients with unilateral node metastasis fare better than those with bilateral spread.[94] Five-year survival is approximately 75 percent with metastasis to one or two nodes, approximately 36 percent with the finding of three or four involved nodes, and 24 percent with five or six nodes.[96] Metastatic involvement of pelvic (iliac) nodes is ominous, but approximately 20 percent of patients with pelvic node metastasis can be cured by locoregional therapies (surgery, radiation, or combined therapy).[13,53,59,62,63,66,97] When metastatic disease is present in multiple groin nodes, pelvic lymphadenectomy will detect disease in 15 percent to 25 percent of patients[13,59–67] but rarely when only one groin node is microscopically contaminated.[53,95] Appraisal of the risk and anatomic level of lymph node spread is an essential part of determining target volume, dose, and technique for any course of radiation-based therapy, whether in the salvage, adjuvant, or definitive context.

The most reliable indicator predictive of local recurrence is the width of the surgical margin[98] (Table 14–6). An 8-mm margin in fixed tissue, corresponding to a clinical margin of approximately 1 cm in vivo, is a useful guide in planning conservative surgery for patients with primary tumors that encroach on functionally important structures, such as the anus, urethra, distal vagina, and clitoris, and is a useful parameter to identify patients who may be at risk for local recurrence in the residual vulva, distal vagina, or the perineum. Additional factors predictive for local failure include extensive lymphvascular space invasion and an infiltrative growth pattern. The presence of any of these factors warrants consideration of local adjuvant radiation.

In a retrospective study of 62 surgical patients with positive or close margins (< 8 mm) from Magee Women's Hospital of the University of Pittsburgh,

Table 14–6. CORRELATION OF SURGICAL MARGIN WITH LOCAL RECURRENCE FOLLOWING SURGICAL THERAPY OF VULVAR CANCER

	Surgical Margin < 8 mm (N = 44)	Surgical Margin ≥ 8 mm (N = 91)
Local recurrence	21/44 (48%)	0/91

Adapted from Heaps JM, Fu YS, Montz FJ, et al. Surgical-pathologic variables predictive of local recurrence in squamous cell carcinoma of the vulva. Gynecol Oncol 1990;38:309–14.

31 patients underwent adjuvant local radiotherapy, and 31 patients were observed without further therapy. The local failure rate was 58 percent in patients observed, comparing unfavorably with a rate of 16 percent in irradiated patients.[92]

The presence of groin node metastasis is predictive of pelvic node metastasis as well as locoregional recurrence, and verification of groin node metastasis was historically used to select patients for extended lymph node dissections above the inguinal ligament. In 1977, the Gynecologic Oncology Group (GOG) commenced a randomized trial comparing pelvic lymphadenectomy with radiotherapy directed to the bilateral groins and pelvic nodes (but not including the tumor bed or perineum) for surgically treated vulvar cancer patients found to have groin node metastasis. Because of significant relapse-free survival differences between the treatment arms at 2 years (Figure 14–6), the study was closed to patient accrual in 1984. A total of 114 eligible patients were randomized, of whom 40 had only one positive groin node. Fifteen of 53 patients undergoing pelvic lymphadenectomy had spread to the pelvic nodes (28.3%), of whom 9 (60%) had died of cancer within 1 year of study entry. The survival advantage for radiation at 2 years (68% survival for radiation, 54% for pelvic node dissection) was statistically limited to patients with metastases in two or more groin nodes (63% survival for radiation, 37% for pelvic node dissection). The benefit of radiation was attributed to a decrease in groin recurrence among the irradiated patients (5.1%), compared with those patients treated with surgery alone (23.6%). Lymphedema was observed in 19 percent of patients irradiated after surgery, compared with 11 percent of patients treated with surgery alone. Of the 44 patients who failed, only 11 patients relapsed with a component of "distant" disease (a number that includes 3 patients who had recurrences in the thigh, para-aortic nodes, or abdominal skin), whereas 75 percent of patients failed with locoregional disease alone (vulvar area, perineum, groin, or pelvis). Eleven patients had recurrences in the unirradiated vulvar area (25%), of whom 10 had no other apparent sites of failure. Consequent to this study, elective pelvic lymphadenectomy is rarely performed, and regional adjuvant radiation has become the standard of additional care for patients

with metastasis to two or more groin nodes.[61] Many patients who have spread to the regional nodes have additional adverse prognostic factors predictive of local relapse. Inclusion of the primary tumor bed and perineum in the treatment volume should be given serious consideration when postoperative radiation is administered, as this may further improve relapse-free survival by preventing local recurrence.[92,99]

PREOPERATIVE RADIATION THERAPY

Under circumstances where the clinical extent of either the primary disease or regional node involvement would indicate postoperative irradiation, it is reasonable to consider preoperative irradiation if this has the potential to reduce the scope of surgery and to, thus, conserve normal tissue structure and function. Preoperative radiotherapy may convert the unresectable cancer to an operable status.[21-26] An anticipated clinical margin of 1 cm or less from structures that will not be removed surgically is a useful guide for selecting patients for preoperative irradiation. Tumors that encroach on the anal sphincter, abut the pubic arch, or involve more than the distal urethra should be considered for preoperative therapy. Patients with tumors that approach the clitoris, invade the clitoral hood or frenulum, or extend more than minimally past the vaginal introitus

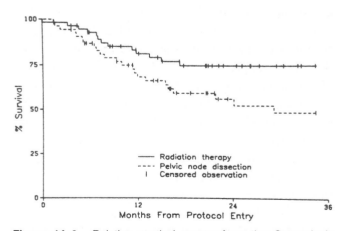

Figure 14–6. Relative survival curves from the Gynecologic Oncology Group study of adjuvant radiation versus pelvic node dissection for patients with established groin node metastasis after radical vulvectomy and groin dissection. Relative survival differences are statistically different at 2 years ($p = .004$). (Reproduced with permission from Homesly HD, Bundy BN, Sedlis A, Adcock L. Radiation therapy versus pelvic node resection for carcinoma of the vulva with positive groin nodes. Obstet Gynecol 1986;68:733–40.)

should be considered for preoperative therapy if preservation of vaginal and clitoral function is desired. Patients with extensive groin node metastases (matted, fixed, or ulcerated) should also be considered candidates for preoperative radiotherapy.

Moderate-dose (36 to 54 Gy) preoperative irradiation, followed by excision of residual palpable abnormalities, has resulted in surgical specimens with no evidence of persistent primary cancer in 50 percent of cases.[23–25] Studies from Milan, Italy, employing preoperative chemoradiation using a radiation dose of 54 Gy with synchronous 5-fluorouracil and mitomycin-C followed by surgery, including groin dissection, have demonstrated eradication of gross and microscopic cancer in as many as 55 percent of patients with inguinal nodes previously confirmed by biopsy to harbor metastatic disease.[36,37] The GOG used preoperative chemoradiation (47.6 Gy and two cycles of concomitant 5-fluorouracil and cisplatin) to achieve a high probability of local tumor control with conservation of normal tissue integrity in many patients who would otherwise have required exenteration to achieve surgical tumor clearance with secure margins.[38] The GOG described results in 71 patients with FIGO stages III or IV vulvar cancer with disease involving or encroaching on functionally important midline anatomic structures and were judged not amenable to initial surgical therapy by standard radical vulvectomy. After preoperative chemoradiation, residual unresectable disease persisted in only 2 patients, and bowel and bladder continence were preserved in all but 3 patients.[38] Using this same approach, the GOG used preoperative chemoradiation to convert approximately 90 percent of a group of 46 patients with initially unresectable groin nodes (N2,3 AJCC 1969 TNM classification) to a resectable or potentially resectable status.[39]

External-beam radiation has been the modality most commonly employed for preoperative radiotherapy. Interstitial or intracavitary brachytherapy may be used to focally apply a higher dose to a limited volume, where an inadequate surgical margin is anticipated.[22]

The observation of complete histologic clearance of malignancy following moderate-dose preoperative irradiation or chemoradiation serves to encourage efforts to control locally advanced cancer of the vulva with radiation-based therapy alone. In circumstances where surgery is technically unfeasible, medically contraindicated, or likely to imply more severe chronic morbidity, radiation-based therapy may be a sensible, nonoperative alternative.

RADICAL RADIOTHERAPY AND CHEMORADIATION

Because vulvar cancer is an uncommon disease, it is unlikely that there will ever be a prospective randomized trial comparing initial radical surgery and selective postoperative radiotherapy with nonoperative, radiation-based management (radiation alone or chemoradiation). Inevitably, comparisons of outcomes employing these very different approaches will be attempted but will be unlikely to yield meaningful information. It should be recalled that the pattern of patient referral is generally a two-step process before a patient comes under the care of a radiation oncologist. Generally, a family practice physician or general gynecologist will refer a vulvar cancer patient to a gynecologic oncologist, not to a radiation oncologist. Thus, with the possible exception of patients in multidisciplinary clinics in large referral centers, vulvar cancer patients arriving for consultation with a radiation oncologist constitute a filtered population. Patients who are favorable candidates for initial operative management may be culled from the pool.

Definitive irradiation has been historically employed to treat patients with medically inoperable or technically unresectable disease, sometimes in circumstances that include both advanced, neglected cancer and major comorbid illnesses. Overall, results have been mediocre, in terms of both tumor control as well as chronic normal tissue tolerance, although the tumor control probability for patients with disease of limited volume has approached that of surgery.[11,12,27,100] With the benefit of hindsight, it is easy to appreciate that historic results were frequently compromised by treatment of inadequate target volumes, using primitive techniques, and employing naive dose/fractionation schemes. Contemporary experience using high-dose radiation alone with sensible technique, equipment, and fractionation is sparse.[27] The superior results obtained from synchronous chemotherapy and irradiation in randomized comparison[101,102] with irradiation alone for the treatment of cancers of the anal canal have prompted widespread extrapolation of this approach to the treatment of cancer of the vulva. Most published experiences have employed 5-fluorouracil, with or without cisplatin or mitomycin-C.[28-37,40-45] Experience with bleomycin has been unfavorable.[103]

Vulvar cancer is a rare disease expected to afflict approximately 3,600 women in the United States in the year 2001. This constitutes 4 percent of cancers in the female reproductive organs and 0.6 percent of cancers in American women.[104] Currently, most patients, including the elderly, will be considered medically operable. Many patients will have cancers that can be treated with surgery alone, or in combination with preoperative or postoperative radiotherapy. The number of unresectable or inoperable patients undergoing individualized, nonoperative management with chemoradiation is, therefore, small. This must temper the strength of any conclusions regarding the relative merits of irradiation alone versus irradiation with synchronous chemotherapy. Retrospective review comparing nonrandomized patients treated with irradiation alone with similar patients treated with chemoradiation at Yale University suggests advantages in both local and regional control as well as survival.[105] Unquestionably, the administration of concurrent chemotherapy augments the acute reaction in normal tissues. Moist desquamation of the vulva and perineum will necessitate treatment interruption in many patients (Figures 14–7 and 14–8). Hybrid dose/ fractionation regimens have been developed to preserve dose intensity and to maximize potential synergistic effects. Twice-daily fractionation has become a popular strategy to exploit the radiation–drug interaction while minimizing the theoretic disadvantages of split-course radiation made necessary by the enhanced acute effects in normal tissues.[38,41,43,44] Frequently, the additional patient and physician efforts necessitated by combined modality therapy will be rewarded by dramatic, rapid tumor regression (Figures 14–9 to 14–12). Protection from late effects in normal tissue has been achieved by reducing dose per fraction as well as the total dose. The fraction size should never exceed 1.8 Gy. A fraction size as low as 1.6 Gy has been recommended to reduce late sequelae.[106] Potential enhancement of late normal tissue

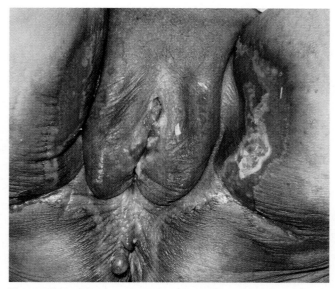

Figure 14–7. Near confluent moist desquamation of the vulva and perineum in a patient with locally advanced vulvar cancer treated with chemoradiation. The patient was photographed 14 days after 36 Gy/20 fractions/4 weeks split-course radiation with 96 hour cycles of infusional 5-fluorouracil administered during the first and fourth week concurrently with twice-daily radiation separated by 6 hours. Helpful remedies may include sitz baths for gentle débridement, topical Silvadene cream, and occlusive dressings in severe cases.

effects, as well as the impossibility of exploiting the skin-sparing effects of megavoltage radiation when treating what is fundamentally a skin cancer, renders it advisable that total dose not exceed approximately 54 Gy/30 fractions, 59.5 Gy/35 fractions, or 64 Gy/40

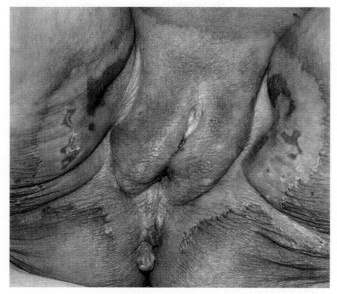

Figure 14–8. The patient in Figure 14–7 with healing vulva and perineum 7 days following previous photograph.

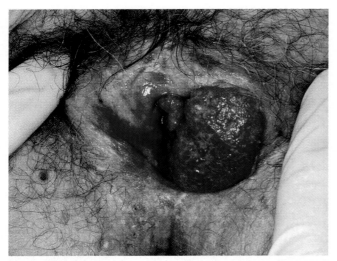

Figure 14–9. Locally advanced vulvar cancer before treatment with chemoradiation.

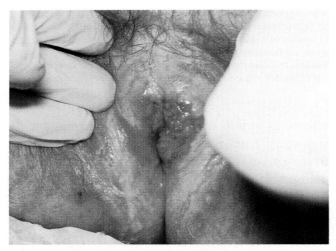

Figure 14–10. Local response of vulvar cancer of the patient in Figure 14–9 photographed 17 days following 18 Gy/10 fractions/ 1 week delivered in twice-daily fractions separated by 6 hours and given synchronously with infusional 5-fluorouracil for 96 hours.

fractions to gross disease when chemoradiation is employed, and that the volume carried to full dose be as small as possible, consistent with inclusion of all areas of initial measurable clinical involvement. Results of 5-fluorouracil–based radical chemoradiation for locally advanced or recurrent cancer of the vulva are compiled in Table 14–7.

ELECTIVE GROIN IRRADIATION

A major contributing factor to perioperative complications and chronic morbidity from the treatment of

vulvar cancer is the dissection of the inguino-femoral nodes. Postoperative wound breakdown is frequent, and chronic lymphedema is a common consequence of radical surgical treatment of the groin.[14,107] For patients with very small, minimally invasive ($\leq$ 1 mm invasion) primary cancers, omission of the node dissection may be prudent. In others, limiting the groin dissection to nodes superficial to the cribriform lamina (if histopathologically neg-

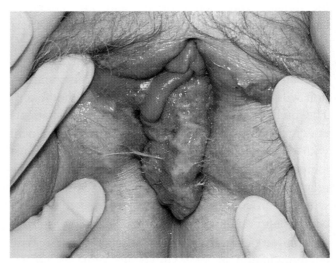

Figure 14–11. Locally advanced T3 vulvar cancer before chemoradiation.

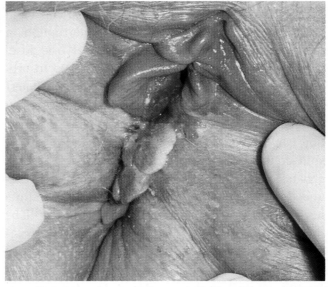

Figure 14–12. Local response of vulvar cancer of the patient in Figure 14–11 photographed 14 days following 18 Gy/10 fractions/ 1 week delivered in twice-daily fractions separated by 6 hours and given synchronously with infusional 5-fluorouracil for 96 hours with bolus cisplatin.

Table 14–7. RESULTS OF RADICAL CHEMORADIATION FOR LOCOREGIONALLY ADVANCED OR RECURRENT CANCERS OF THE VULVA

			Previously Untreated Patients			
Author	Patients Stages (n)	Drugs	Radiation Dose (Gy)	Complete Response	Subsequent Failure*	NED F/U†
Thomas[41]	9 "Advanced"	F,M	40–64	6 (67%)	3 (50%)	N/A
Berek[42]	12 III (8) IV (4)	F,P	44–54	8 (67%)	0	7–60
Russell[43]	18‡ II (1) III (10) IV (6)	F,P M	46.8–56	16 (89%)	2 (13%)	2–52
Koh[44]	14‡ III (4) IV (10)	F,P M	34–63.1	8§ (57%)	1 (17%)	5–75
Cunningham[45]	14 III (9) IV (5)	F,P	50–65	9 (64%)	1 (11%)	7–81
Eifel[35]	12 II (1) III, IV (11)	F,P	40–50	6§ (50%)	1 (16%)	17–37
TOTAL	79			53 (67%)	8 (15%)	
			Patients with Recurrent Disease			
Thomas[41]	15	F,M	40–64	8 (53%)	0	N/A
Russell[43]	7	F,P	54–72	4 (57%)	1 (25%)	2–35
TOTAL	22			12 (55%)	1 (13%)	

Adapted from Russell AH. Vulva. In: Leibel SA, Phillips TL, editors. Textbook of radiation oncology. Philadelphia: W.B. Saunders; 1998.
F = 5-fluorouracil; P = cisplatin; M = mitomycin; N/A = not available; F/U = follow up; NED = no evidence of disease.
*Denotes recurrence within the irradiated volume.
†Length of follow-up in patients continuously cancer free.
‡Includes one patient in each series dying of treatment-related complications (neutropenia and sepsis).
§Includes patients who undergo surgery following completion of chemoradiation because of clinically suspected residual disease. Surgical specimens without residual cancer.

ative) may be an effective strategy to reduce acute and chronic surgical morbidity. Identification of sentinel nodes by lymphatic mapping may ease anxieties occasioned by performing less than a full-node dissection. Elective irradiation of clinically negative groins is an alternative strategy that has the theoretic advantage of treating all the regional nodes rather than leaving all, or some portion, untreated. This approach may also be applicable in patients with locally advanced primaries, for whom less than radical bilateral groin dissections would be inadequate surgical therapy. Several series[22,27,108–112] have reported favorable results with elective or prophylactic groin irradiation (Table 14–8), but frequently in settings where groin nodes would be expected to be histologically uninvolved, if dissected (T1,2 primary tumors of limited extent).[111,112] The GOG

embarked on a prospective randomized trial comparing groin irradiation with groin surgery in selected patients with vulvar cancer.[73] The study was

Table 14–8. RESULTS OF ELECTIVE GROIN IRRADIATION IN PATIENTS WITH VULVAR CANCER AND CLINICALLY NEGATIVE INGUINOFEMORAL LYMPH NODES*

Author	Patients	Groin Failure	Percent
Frankendal[108]	12	0	0
Simonsen[109]	65	11	16.9
Boronow[22]	13	0	0
Perez[27]	39	2	5.1
Lee[110]	16	3	18.8
Petereit[111]	23	2	8.7
Stehman[73]	27	5	18.5
Manavi[112]	65	3	4.6
TOTAL	260	26	10.0

*Patients with AJCC 1969 N0,1 clinically evaluated groin nodes.

terminated early due to an unacceptable rate of groin node failures (5 of 27 patients, 18.5%) observed in the group assigned to irradiation. Technical inadequacies in radiation administration may have inadvertently caused substantial underdosage of inguinofemoral nodes,[74] resulting in the observed failures and serving to emphasize the importance of technique, treatment planning, and proper dosimetry.[70,71] Chemoradiation may be a mechanism to improve the results of elective groin irradiation, but the simplest expedient is to deliver treatment with adequate dose distribution to the tissues at risk.

At Radiological Associates of Sacramento Medical Group, 23 previously untreated patients with locally advanced primary squamous cancers of the vulva (2 T2, 19 T3, 2 T4) but clinically negative groin nodes underwent chemoradiation to a volume electively including the inguinofemoral nodes. No patient underwent subsequent surgical therapy to the groins. With follow-up of 6 to 98 months (mean 45, median 42), no patient relapsed in an irradiated groin.[72] Similarly favorable results have been reported from Loma Linda University.[34] Elective groin irradiation is likely to remain a controversial issue in the therapy of patients with limited-volume operable primaries and clinically negative nodes, in whom radiation may be entirely avoided if the histopathologic results of surgery are favorable. For patients who are already undergoing preoperative or definitive radiation-based therapy because of the extent of the primary tumor, extension of the treatment volume to encompass the regional nodes is a sensible alternative to groin dissection. What role, if any, elective groin irradiation plays in patients with initially operable, low-stage (T1,2) vulvar cancer is presently unclear. Clarification would require a repeat of the GOG study using chemoradiation instead of irradiation alone to treat the groins. This seems unlikely to occur.

RADIATION THERAPY TECHNICAL FACTORS

There is no standard target volume, technique, or dose/fractionation schedule in the radiation treatment of cancer of the vulva. Clinical and histopathologic characteristics of the primary, presence or absence of regional node involvement, anatomic level and extent of node metastases (if present), context (preoperative, postoperative, definitive, salvage), scope and timing of any coordinated surgery, whether or not synchronous chemotherapy will be administered, and the nature and severity of medical comorbidities will influence selection of radiotherapeutic treatment parameters. Individualized, tailored care is the essence of excellence in clinical medicine. Inflexible reliance on a recipe is a formula for catastrophe. What follows is intended to serve as broad guidelines, and not orthodoxy.

TARGET VOLUME

In the assessment of any one patient, particularly an aged individual, the radiation oncologist must first appraise that patient's general health for the presence of coincidental illnesses that may compromise the optimal use of radiation. This will necessitate considering the health of all normal tissues (small and large bowel, blood vessels, nerves, bones, urinary bladder, and skin of the vulva and perineum) that might be included in the treatment volume. Target volume necessarily includes both gross disease and areas of potential microscopic or occult involvement by direct extension. Selection of initial target volume must include appraisal of the risk of embolic involvement of various levels of regional nodes. Sample target volumes are illustrated in Figures 14–13 to 14–16.

VOLUME FOR POSTOPERATIVE IRRADIATION

The target volume in patients undergoing treatment for groin node involvement detected at the time of surgery should, in general, include both groin areas and the caudal external iliac nodes on the side with involved groin nodes. If there has been no surgical assessment of the pelvic nodes, a CT scan or equivalent imaging modality should be used to define whether or not pelvic nodes are grossly enlarged, and a percutaneous needle aspirate performed if suspicious nodes are detected. In the absence of clinical or radiographic pelvic node involvement, the superior border of the treatment volume should encompass the caudal exter-

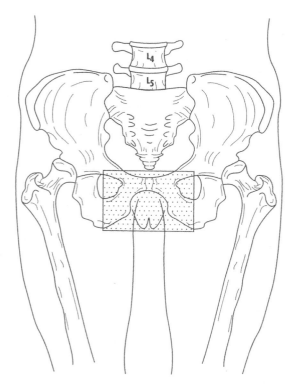

Figure 14–13. Target volume for postsurgical local radiation without groin or pelvic radiation in a patient with risk factors for local recurrence. Volume should be contoured with secondary collimation. Groin and pelvic nodes are not included in the target volume.

nal iliac nodes and should generally not extend more cephalad than the middle of the sacroiliac joints. A 2-cm margin lateral to the medial bony margin of the pelvis will assure adequate coverage of lymphatics that may lie lateral to the external iliac vessels. If there has been invasion of overlying skin, inclusion of at least an additional 5 cm of the skin flaps is prudent to encompass potential contamination of dermal lymphatics. In the groin, the lateral border of the treatment volume should cover the medial 80 percent of the inguinal ligament. If there has been extensive nodal involvement (more than microscopic, subcapsular embolization) the caudal border of the treatment volume should encompass the vertical chain of inguinal lymph nodes in the upper medial thigh between the femoral vein and the saphenous vein. In circumstances dictating irradiation of the groin and pelvic nodes, it will be wise to consider including the primary tumor bed and the adjacent perineal skin. Frequently, patients with multiple groin node metastases will have unfavorable prognostic factors associated with the primary. Substantial risk of recurrence in tissues shielded by a

midline block has been reported when such shielding has been employed during postoperative radiotherapy directed to the groin and pelvic nodes.[61,99] When an infiltrating or "spray" pattern of tumor growth is detected in the primary, wider margins of clinically normal tissue should be included around the tumor bed and perineum. If the primary tumor has grown across the labiocrural fold, treatment volume should include the lymphatics that run through the upper medial thighs. Some patients with histologically negative groin nodes will have indications for local tumor bed irradiation only. A microscopic margin less than 8 mm constitutes an example.[98] Extension of the treatment volume to encompass the groin or pelvic nodes will only increase the risk of subsequent lymphedema and should, therefore, be avoided.

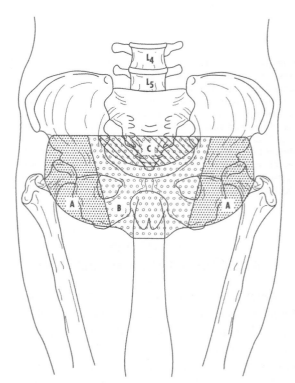

Figure 14–14. Target volume for a patient with locally advanced vulvar cancer with clinically (palpably) and radiographically negative (normal) groin nodes for preoperative radiation to include elective/prophylactic treatment of inguinofemoral nodes. Volume includes obturator and caudal external iliac nodes. Volumes A may be treated with mixed photons and electrons or anterior low-energy photons alone to reduce dose to the femoral necks. Volume B should be treated with opposed anterior and posterior photons. Thermoluminescent dosimetry (TLD) may be useful to assess dose inhomogeneity and potential hot spots on the vulva, and the need for compensators or other dose adjustment interventions. Volume C may be shielded to reduce dose to the intestines and urinary bladder.

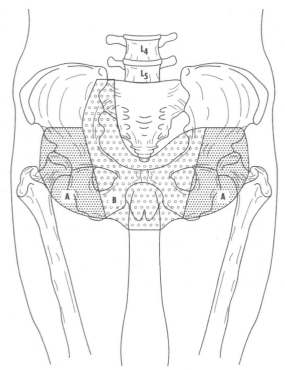

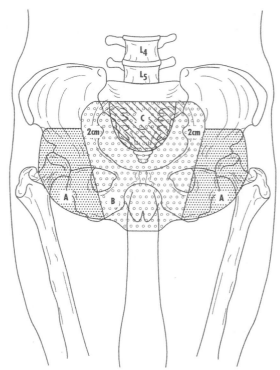

Figure 14–15. Target volume for preoperative irradiation for a patient with advanced vulvar cancer and unilateral groin metastasis. Volume B includes obturator and caudal external iliac nodes on the side opposite to the involved groin but is extended cephalad on the ipsilateral side to encompass the entire external iliac chain. Volumes A may be treated with mixed photons and electrons or anterior low-energy photons alone to reduce dose to the femoral necks. Volume B should be treated with opposed anterior and posterior photons. Thermoluminescent dosimetry may be useful to assess dose inhomogeneity and potential hot spots on the vulva, and the need for compensators or other dose adjustment interventions.

Figure 14–16. Target volume for postoperative radiation for a patient following radical vulvectomy with bilateral occult (microscopic) groin node metastases. Volumes A may be treated with mixed photons and electrons or anterior low-energy photons alone to reduce dose to the femoral necks. Volume B should be treated with opposed anterior and posterior photons. Thermoluminescent dosimetry may be useful to assess dose inhomogeneity and potential hot spots on the vulva, and the need for compensators or other dose adjustment interventions. Volume C may be shielded to reduce radiation dose to the bowel and urinary bladder. However, this volume should not be shielded in patients with significant primary tumor extension up the vagina, in whom hypogastric lymph nodes may be at risk.

VOLUME FOR PREOPERATIVE IRRADIATION

The use of irradiation prior to surgery should be considered either when surgical margins are anticipated to be inadequate (1 cm or less of clinically normal tissue) or when the scope of initial surgery would compromise the functional integrity of important normal tissues (anus, urethra, clitoris, bladder). Usually, such patients will have T3 or T4 primary tumors, but occasional patients, particularly thin individuals, will have predictably inadequate margins with T2 primary tumors. Fixed or matted groin nodes, or nodes invading or ulcerating through overlying skin, are additional indications for preoperative irradiation. If preoperative irradiation is to be employed, the histopathologic status of enlarged groin and pelvic nodes should be

assessed prior to treatment with fine-needle aspiration. Groin nodes exceeding 1 cm in size can be readily studied by excisional biopsy if they are superficial and accessible and fine-needle aspiration biopsy has been inconclusive (Figure 14–17). A CT through the pelvis and the inguinal areas should be used both diagnostically and for treatment planning, with needle-aspiration biopsy assessment of abnormal findings. At Radiological Associates of Sacramento Medical Group, it has become standard practice to include inguinofemoral and caudal external iliac nodes in the initial target volume for most patients undergoing preoperative chemoradiation, even if these nodes are clinically uninvolved. Generally, the extent of the primary lesion will suggest a substantial probability of microscopic nodal contamination. Moderate-dose radiation (36 to 45 Gy) is applied with the intention of sterilizing occult micrometastases, and the groins are not dissected when the primary is removed. If groin nodes are histologically confirmed to be involved, preoperative chemoradiation is administered, and limited dissection of residual palpable nodes is carried out at the same time as removal of the primary. Alternatively, removal of all nodes 1 cm or larger may be accomplished prior to chemoradiation. The anatomic extent of the target volume is determined in a fashion similar to that used to define the target volume for postoperative irradiation. However, a full pelvic node volume is treated if the primary extends to involve the middle or upper vagina, proximal urethra, bladder, or rectum or if the groin nodes are extensively involved (multiple, matted, or ulcerated.)

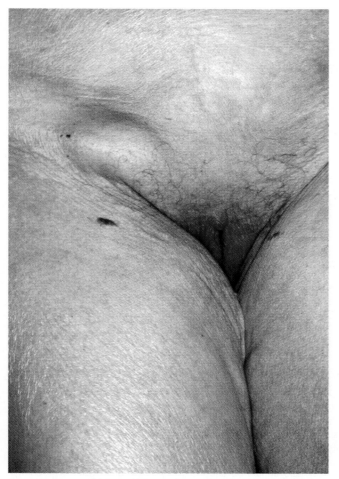

Figure 14–17. Groin node enlargement that is clinically worrisome for metastasis in a patient with locally advanced, infected vulvar cancer and an associated purulent abcess. Fine-needle aspiration of the node retrieved only lymphocytes. Excisional biopsy confirmed a reactive, hyperplastic node without metastasis.

VOLUME FOR RADICAL IRRADIATION

Treatment with radiation alone or with concurrent chemotherapy should be reserved for patients who have advanced locoregional disease that cannot be rendered resectable through preoperative therapy. Although chemoradiation may eventually supplant surgery for many patients in analogy to the evolution of treatment of cancers of the anal canal, surgery remains the standard of care at present. Rarely are technically resectable patients medically inoperable on the basis of severe comorbidities. Patients who are resectable only by exenteration may choose radiation-based therapy as an alternative as well as the sexually active patients among the approximately 15 percent of patients with cancer of the vulva whose primary tumor involves the clitoris. Treatment volume considerations will be similar to those for patients undergoing preoperative irradiation, with the exception that patients who are unresectable because of extensive skin involvement with dermal lymphatic invasion (peau d'orange) or satellite lesions will require inclusion of larger areas of clinically uninvolved skin in order to achieve secure lateral margins.

TECHNIQUE

In addition to the care needed to select appropriate target volumes for gross and microscopic cancers, attention must be directed to the composition and volume of normal tissue unavoidably included. Vulnerable normal tissues include the femoral necks (which lie posterior to lateral inguinal nodes), small bowel, bladder, urethra, clitoris, and anus. For patients who may be undergoing definitive radiation-based therapy, an essential step is meticulous, written recording of the anatomic extent of initial disease involvement. Clinical photographs documenting initial tumor extent will permit accurate volume reductions and sensible selection of limited, high-dose volumes when there has been rapid tumor shrinkage. Available techniques include:

1. Use of a large anterior low-energy photon field (4 MV or 6 MV) designed to encompass the entire target volume, a smaller posterior high-energy photon field (10 to 20 MV) designed to encompass the perineum and pelvic nodes, while

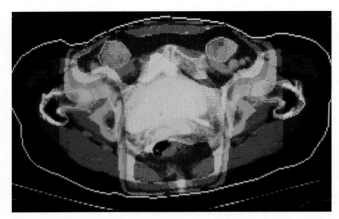

Figure 14–18. Color-wash radiation dose distribution through the pelvic floor and groin in mixed photon electron treatment plan for treating vulvar cancer with bilateral gross groin node metastases. This plan uses 10 MV photons and 15 MeV electrons to treat the groin. The colors purple, red, yellow, green, and blue represent 10 percent dose decrements. (Reproduced with permission from Russell AH. Vulva. In: Leibel SA, Phillips TL, editors. Textbook of radiation oncology. Philadelphia: W.B. Saunders; 1998.)

excluding the femurs, and supplemental anterior electron fields to supplement the dose to the groin areas which overlie the femoral necks[27,43] (Figure 14–18).

2. Alternatively, a large anterior low-energy photon field can be used to encompass the entire target volume and to deliver the full dose to the groin areas, employing a partial transmission block centrally to attenuate the dose to the midplane of the pelvis (central axis) to 50 percent of the intended daily dose. The remaining 50 percent of the daily dose is administered through a smaller

posterior pelvic photon port that excludes the femoral necks[113] (Figure 14–19).

3. Intensity-modulated radiation therapy (IMRT) or proton beam therapy may be future techniques to further optimize radiation dose distribution, but these technologies are not widely available now.

With appropriate technique, dose to the femoral neck should be 10 to 20 percent less than the dose prescribed to the inguinofemoral nodes (Figure 14–20). Because of the contour of the perineum in the sagittal plane, the dose to the vulva and perineum may be as much as 25 percent greater than the central axis midplane dose, depending on the patient's size and the beam energies employed. Thermoluminescent dosimetry (TLD) may be helpful to clarify the magnitude of this effect, and the use of a wedge or tissue compensator may be advisable to minimize dose heterogeneity. Alternatively, the vulva/perineum can be shielded for a portion of each daily treatment to reduce both the total dose and, importantly, the dose per fraction.

Successful use of these techniques mandates that dose to the groin area be applied at an appropriate depth in tissue,[70,71] conventionally defined as the depth of the femoral artery as it passes beneath the inguinal ligament. This will most accurately be mea-

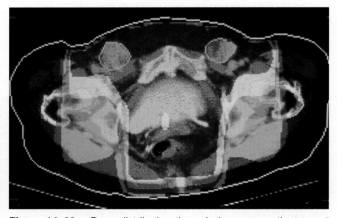

Figure 14–20. Dose distribution through the same patient target volume as in Figure 14–18 employing an anterior partial transmission block technique and 6 MV photons to encompass the groin nodes and the pelvis and posterior 15 MV photons to supplement the dose to the posterior vulva and pelvic floor. Thermoluminescent dosimetry should be used to verify vulvar dose when high-energy photons are employed in an effort to achieve dose homogeneity. The colors purple, red, yellow, green, and blue represent 10 percent dose decrements. (Reproduced with permission from Russell AH. Vulva. In: Leibel SA, Phillips TL, editors. Textbook of radiation oncology. Philadelphia: W.B. Saunders; 1998.)

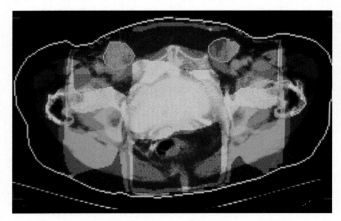

Figure 14–19. Dose distribution through the same patient target volume as in Figure 14–18 employing an anterior partial transmission block technique exclusively with 6 MV photons. The colors purple, red, yellow, green, and blue represent 10 percent dose decrements.

sured by CT and will depend markedly on patient size and whether or not nodes have been dissected or if they are enlarged. Arbitrarily specifying a depth of 3 cm will adequately treat only 18 percent of patients and femoral nodes will be more than 5 cm deep to the skin in more than half the adult women.[70] Boost therapy to grossly contaminated groin nodes should generally be accomplished using electron beam.

A reduced volume encompassing the primary disease can be treated by small, opposed anterior and posterior photon fields. However, more normal tissue will be excluded using an en face perineal electron or orthovoltage port (Figure 14–21). In some patients, it may be feasible to place an obturator in the distal vaginal canal or in the anal canal to physically displace a portion of the vaginal or anal perimeter from the en face boost volume. When disease has extended proximally up the vagina for several centimeters,

interstitial or intracavitary brachytherapy may be useful in lieu of a perineal teletherapy port.

FRACTIONATION AND DOSE

Definitive radiation-based therapy for cancer of the vulva is difficult because of the requirement to administer a high dose to tissue that is frequently moist from perspiration and lack of ventilation and subject to continual friction. Acute radiation dermatitis with moist desquamation and pain is the frequent consequence of a course of continuous, conventionally fractionated radiation. Topical application of Silvadene cream will be soothing to many patients. Gentle débridement with sitz baths, followed by air exposure, will reduce the risk of infection and promote re-epithelialization. Occlusive dressings, such as are used for thermal burn patients, may be helpful to patients with confluent moist desquamation. Interruption of therapy, either mandated by skin reaction or planned to avoid severe acute effects, is common and may prolong the elapsed time required to complete a course of radiation therapy by 2 or more weeks. A compensatory increase in the total dose may not be the best tactic

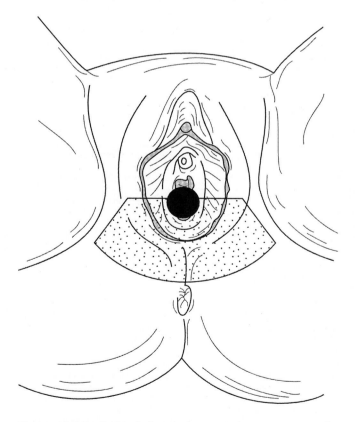

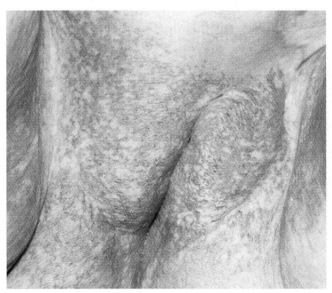

Figure 14–21. Perineal electron boost used to treat a posterior vulvar cancer involving the fourchette with minimal extension to the posterior vagina and perineal skin. Placement of an obturator in the vagina may help in controlling the dose to the anterior vaginal wall and distal urethra.

Figure 14–22. Late skin sequelae on the vulva in a patient with large anteroposterior separation, in whom dose to the vulva may have been 20 to 25 percent greater than to the prescription point at the midplane separation of the central axis of the anterior and posterior fields. (Reproduced with permission from Russell AH. Vulva. In: Leibel SA, Phillips TL, editors. Textbook of radiation oncology. Philadelphia: W.B. Saunders; 1998.)

to address this difficulty. While 63 to 72 Gy can often control gross cancer in the vulva, the predictable late sequelae induced by non–skin-sparing treatment, even when administered in fractions of 1.8 Gy, render such an approach inadvisable. Thin, atrophic skin with prominent telangiectasis may result (Figure 14–22). This tissue is vulnerable to interruption of epithelial integrity with formation of "greasy ulcers" with chronic weeping of serum and infection. Over the years, progressive subcutaneous fibrosis and contracture can be the sequelae of high-dose radiation in this area, resulting in significant disability, if a large volume has been treated. Topical application of a testosterone-containing cream to the vulva may thicken and toughen vulvar skin rendered atrophic by radiation in a fashion analogous to the use of topical estrogen for radiation vaginitis.

For two decades, chemoradiation has been used in an effort to obtain improved cancer control with lesser late sequelae (improved therapeutic ratio), in a fashion extrapolated from its successful use to treat primary cancers of the anal canal. Synchronous administration of chemotherapy complicates the treatment program by substantially potentiating acute radiation effects on all cycling cell systems (cancer and normal epithelia) as well as subjecting the patient to the hazards of systemic treatment. However, the total radiation dose employed can be 15 to 20 percent less than might otherwise be employed using radiation alone, and effects on the infrequently cycling cell populations responsible for late radiation injury do not appear to be as pronounced as effects on cycling cell populations responsible for acute effects. Enhanced acute effects appear to be the price for reduced late sequelae, and treatment interruption is a common consequence. Acute skin reactions, enhanced acute gastrointestinal toxicity, and hematopoietic suppression may all contribute to treatment delay. In an effort to preserve dose intensity by keeping elapsed treatment time as short as possible while minimizing vulnerability to tumor cell repopulation, hybrid fractionation regimens have evolved. Twice-daily fractionation (for all or some portion of the treatment) has been coupled with short, planned treatment interruptions to avoid excessive acute skin toxicity while allowing hematologic recovery.[41,43,44] Multiple daily fractions during chemotherapy infu-

sion will, theoretically, maximize radiation–drug synergism. The chemotherapy agent most commonly employed has been 5-fluorouracil (5-FU), in doses from 750 $mg/m^2/24$ h to 1,000 $mg/m^2/24$ h during 72 to 120 continuous hours. Success has also been reported with low-dose continuous infusion of 5-FU at 250 $mg/m^2/24$ h using 96-hour cycles weekly during 4 weeks of radiotherapy. Cisplatin at 50 mg/m^2 to 100 mg/m^2 has been used as a second agent (renal function permitting), as well as mitomycin-C at 6 mg/m^2 to 12.5 mg/m^2. Continuous infusion cisplatin at 4 $mg/m^2/24$ h has been coordinated with continuous infusion 5-FU.[35] The preoperative fractionation scheme employed by the GOG[38] (Table 14–9) is a rational approach to preserving dose intensity, maxi-

Table 14–9. TIME/DOSE/FRACTIONATION SCHEDULE: GOG PROTOCOL 101. A PHASE II EVALUATION OF PREOPERATIVE CHEMORADIATION* FOR ADVANCED VULVAR CANCER

		Cycle #1										
		Mon–Fri				Sat/Sun		Mon–Fri				
Day	1	2	3	4	5	6	7	8	9	10	11	12
Radiation 1.7 Gy/Fx	R	R	R	R	0	0		R	R	R	R	R
5-Fluorouracil 1,000 mg/m²/24 h		R F	R F	R F	F							
Cisplatin 50 mg/m²		P										

1½–2½ Week Planned Rest

		Cycle #2										
		Mon–Fri				Sat/Sun		Mon–Fri				
Day	1	2	3	4	5	6	7	8	9	10	11	12
Radiation 1.7 Gy/Fx	R	R	R	R	0	0		R	R	R	R	R
5-Fluorouracil 1,000 mg/m²/24 h		R F	R F	R F	F							
Cisplatin 50 mg/m²		P										

Adapted from Moore DH, Thomas GM, Montana GS, et al. Preoperative chemoradiation for advanced vulvar cancer: a phase II study of the Gynecologic Oncology Group. Int J Radiat Oncol Biol Phys 1998;42:79–85.
R = a fraction of external radiation. A 4-hour minimum intertreatment interval is mandatory, but 6 or more hours are suggested, when practically feasible; F = 5-fluorouracil by continuous intravenous infusion; P = bolus cisplatin administration; 0 = no radiation treatment on weekend days; Fx = radiation fraction.
*Patients who are judged to be unresectable following completion of 47.6 Gy preoperative chemoradiation receive additional 20 Gy in fractions of 1.7 to 2.0 Gy, with reduced treatment volume encompassing gross residual disease, or may receive additional radiation dose via brachytherapy. A third cycle of chemotherapy is recommended if teletherapy is employed. The author would suggest restricting the cumulative dose to 59.5 Gy/35 Fx in the interest of avoiding severe late skin effects.

Table 14–10. DOSE GUIDELINES*

Volume	Radiation Alone		Chemoradiation	
	Microscopic	Gross	Microscopic	Gross
Intent				
Preoperative	45–56	45–56	36–48	36–48
Postoperative	45–56	54–64 (+ margin)	36–48	45–56 (+ margin)
Radical	45–56	63–72	36–48	45–64

Reproduced with permission from Russell AH. Vulva. In: Leibel SA, Phillips TL, editors. Textbook of radiation oncology. Philadelphia: W.B. Saunders; 1998. *All doses expressed in Gray. Dose guidelines assume that treatment will be administered in fractions of 1.6 to 1.8 Gy, and that multiple daily fractions may be employed for all or a part of the treatment. Higher total doses imply fraction size of 1.6 Gy, and lower total doses imply fraction size of 1.8 Gy. Dose guidelines should be interpreted in the contexts of tumor bulk, health of normal tissues unavoidably included within the treatment volume, and tolerance and response to treatment. Use of doses in the lower end of the range for gross disease is predicated on a biopsy at the completion of treatment confirming histologic clearance. Doses for gross disease should be applied with progressively shrinking volumes that confine high dose to not more, and possibly less, than the original volume of measurable disease.

mizing radiation–drug synergy, minimizing treatment interruption, and minimizing late effects in normal tissue through the use of reduced dose-per-fraction twice-daily radiation. Guidelines for radiation dose, alone or in combination with concurrent chemotherapy, are summarized in Table 14–10 and are compartmentalized for volume of disease (microscopic versus gross) and treatment intent (preoperative, adjuvant postoperative, or radical). Appropriately fractionated teletherapy, coordinated with synchronous radiopotentiating chemotherapy, and integrated with conservative surgery can achieve both durable cancer control as well as excellent preservation of both function and cosmesis (Figures 14–23 and 14–24).

BARTHOLIN'S GLAND CARCINOMA

Malignancy arising from a Bartholin's gland constitutes approximately 4 to 7 percent of malignancies of the vulva. The criteria established by the Armed Forces Institute of Pathology for the diagnosis of Bartholin's gland carcinoma enjoy the broadest contemporary acceptance.[114] A primary Bartholin's gland cancer should show areas of apparent transition from normal elements to neoplastic ones on histologic study, should be histologically compatible with origin from Bartholin's gland, and should exist without evidence of primary cancer elsewhere. The Bartholin complex comprises a duct lined by squamous epithe-

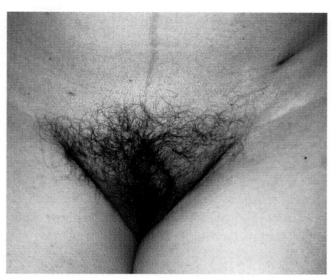

Figure 14–23. Ten-year clinical result in a young, mixed-race, sexually active patient treated for lateralized T2N1 squamous cancer of the vulva arising in the Bartholin's gland area. Therapy was initiated by conservative local excision, with unilateral limited groin dissection followed by postoperative chemoradiation to a volume encompassing the vulva, both groins, and the external iliac nodes on the involved side (see Figure 14–15). Chemoradiation consisted of 45 Gy in 25 fractions with two cycles of synchronous 5-fluorouracil by 96 hour infusion and two doses of bolus cisplatin. Note pubic hair regrowth enabled by use of high-energy photons and low-energy electrons. Scarring in the involved groin is limited to a minor cosmetic defect at the surgical drain site. This result illustrates conservation of structure and cosmesis by the coordinated use of trimodality therapy.

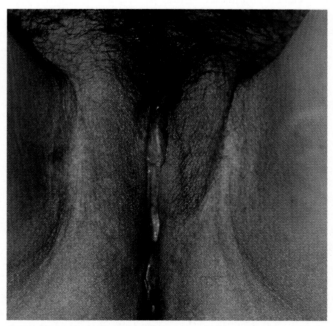

Figure 14–24. Perineal view of the patient in Figure 14–23. Note moderate hyperpigmentation consequent to radiation and a minor asymmetry of the vulva from surgery. This patient remains sexually active with normal bowel and bladder functions and is free of leg lymphedema.

lium as it enters the distal vagina. The more proximal portions of the ductal system are lined with transitional epithelium and may be lined with columnar epithelium before arborization into secretory glandular elements. A variety of histologic tumor types may arise. Squamous carcinoma constitutes approximately 35 to 50 percent of cases, with adenocarcinoma only slightly less common.[114–118] Adenosquamous carcinomas and transitional cell carcinomas are a small minority of cases. Adenoid cystic carcinoma (cylindroma) represents a distinct subset[119] thought to be less likely to spread to regional nodes, and associated with a long natural history and late recurrences that may be either local or hematogenous. Often presenting with a mass deep in the labia with intact overlying skin, a patient with Bartholin's gland carcinoma may experience delay in correct diagnosis due to misdiagnosis as a Bartholin's cyst or abcess, particularly if a patient is young. There is no persuasive evidence that squamous carcinomas of Bartholin's gland origin behave differently or should be managed differently from squamous cancers arising from other structures in the vulva. The roles of radiation will be the same as for other primary sites within the vulva. Patients with other histologic types are so rare that it is not credible to assert standard treatment policies. The majority of patients who fail primary surgical therapy will have at least a component of locoregional recurrence.[117,118] A retrospective review of 36 nonrandomized patients at M.D. Anderson Cancer Center revealed that 6 of 22 patients (27%) treated with surgery alone developed local recurrence, whereas only 1 of 14 higher-risk patients (7%) selected to receive adjuvant radiation manifested local failure.[118]

MELANOMA

Vulvar melanoma[120–127] represents a small minority of female patients with mucocutaneous melanoma (approximately 2%) as well as a minority of patients with primary malignancies of the vulva (10% or less). The Memorial Sloan-Kettering Cancer Center[123] recorded 44 patients between 1934 and 1973 and the Mayo Clinic[124] reported 48 patients between 1950 and 1980. Surgery is the main therapeutic modality to address locoregional disease. A role for radiation therapy has not been established.

CONCLUSION

The management of epidermoid carcinoma of the vulva continues to evolve. The epidemiology of the disease may be changing due to changes in sexual mores. Changed perceptions of the disease (destigmatization) and improved access to health care may be decreasing the average volume and anatomic extent of the disease at the time of diagnosis. The past two decades have seen major modifications in treatment techniques, reflecting alterations in the goals of therapy. Cancer eradication at any price is no longer the sole objective of treatment. Preservation of normal tissue integrity and function has become equally important, as results of therapy have improved. As clinical experience with newer combinations of treatment modalities accumulates and matures, guidelines for patient selection, treatment volume, technique, dose, fractionation, and use of adjunctive therapies are anticipated to become increasingly sophisticated. The optimal coordination of radiation therapy with surgery of variable extent is likely to be an area of continuing research and refinement.

Radiation therapy and surgery are both local modalities of treatment and, in a sense, competitive. But the strengths of each modality complement the other. Local excision is generally easier and more efficacious than reduced volume boost radiotherapy. Radiation therapy deals more efficiently with microscopic or occult disease than surgery. Many patients with cancer of the vulva are elderly and are afflicted with comorbidities that complicate management. This constellation of considerations affords broad opportunities for truly collaborative efforts on the part of gynecologic oncologists, medical oncologists, and radiation oncologists, in which the aggregate result often exceeds the outcome that could be expected from any of the constituent therapies used alone.

REFERENCES

1. Basset A. Traitement chirugical operatoire de l'epitheliome primitif du clitoris. Rev Chir (Paris) 1912; 46:456–552.
2. Taussig FJ. Cancer of the vulva: an analysis of 155 cases. Am J Obstet Gynecol 1940;40:764–79.
3. Way S. The anatomy of the lymphatic drainage of the vulva and its furtherance on the radical operation for carcinoma. Ann R Coll Surg Engl 1948;3:187–209.

4. Way S. Carcinoma of the vulva. Am J Obstet Gynecol 1960;79:692–7.

5. Green TH Jr, Ulfelder H, Meigs JV. Epidermoid carcinoma of the vulva: an analysis of 238 cases. Parts I and II. Am J Obstet Gynecol 1958;73:834–47.

6. Cavanagh D, Shepherd JH. The place of pelvic exenteration in the primary management of advanced carcinoma of the vulva. Gynecol Oncol 1982;13:318–22.

7. Kehrer E. Soll das vulvarkarzinom operiert oder behstrahlt werden? Geburtshilfe Frauenheilkd 1918; 48:346.

8. Lifshitz S, Savage JE, Yates SJ, Buchsbaum HJ. Primary epidermoid carcinoma of the vulva. Surg Gynecol Obstet 1982;155:59–61.

9. Helgason NM, Hass AC, Latourette HB. Radiation therapy in carcinoma of the vulva: a review of 53 patients. Cancer 1972;30:997–1000.

10. Kuipers T. Carcinoma of the vulva. Radiol Clin (Basel) 1975;44:475–83.

11. Frischbier HJ, Thomsen K. Treatment of cancer of the vulva with high energy electrons. Am J Obstet Gynecol 1971;111:431–5.

12. Busch M, Wagener B, Duhmke E. Long-term results of radiotherapy alone for carcinoma of the vulva. Adv Ther 1999;16:89–100.

13. Green TH Jr. Carcinoma of the vulva: a reassessment. Obstet Gynecol 1978;52:462–9.

14. McKelvey JL, Adcock LL. Cancer of the vulva. Obstet Gynecol 1965;26:455–66.

15. Hoffman MS, Roberts WS, LaPolla JP, et al. Carcinoma of the vulva involving the perianal or anal skin. Gynecol Oncol 1989;35:215–8.

16. Andersen BL, Hacker NF. Psychosexual adjustment after vulvar surgery. Obstet Gynecol 1983;62:457–62.

17. Stellman RE, Goodwin JM, Robinson J, et al. Psychological effects of vulvectomy. Psychosomatics 1984;25:779–83.

18. DiSaia PJ, Creasman WT, Rich WM. An alternative approach to early cancer of the vulva. Am J Obstet Gynecol 1979;133:825–32.

19. Iversen T, Abeler V, Aalders J. Individualized treatment of stage I carcinoma of the vulva. Obstet Gynecol 1981;57:85–91.

20. Hacker NF, Berek JS, Lagasse LD, et al. Individualization of treatment for stage I squamous cell vulvar carcinoma. Obstet Gynecol 1984;63:155–62.

21. Boronow RC. Therapeutic alternative to primary exenteration for advanced vulvo-vaginal cancer. Gynecol Oncol 1973;1:233–55.

22. Boronow RC, Hickman BT, Reagan MT, et al. Combined therapy as an alternative to exenteration for locally advanced vulvovaginal cancer. Am J Clin Oncol 1987;10:171–81.

23. Hacker NF, Berek JS, Juillard GJ, Lagasse LD. Preoperative radiation therapy for locally advanced vulvar cancer. Cancer 1984;54:2056–61.

24. Acosta AA, Given FT, Frazier AB, et al. Preoperative radiation therapy in the management of squamous cell carcinoma of the vulva: preliminary report. Am J Obstet Gynecol 1978;132:198–206.

25. Jafari K, Magalotti F, Magalotti M. Radiation therapy in carcinoma of the vulva. Cancer 1981;47:686–91.

26. Fairey RN, MacKay PA, Benedet JL, et al. Radiation treatment of carcinoma of the vulva, 1950–1980. Am J Obstet Gynecol 1985;151:591–7.

27. Perez CA, Grigsby PW, Galakatos A, et al. Radiation therapy in management of carcinoma of the vulva with emphasis on conservation therapy. Cancer 1993;71:3707–16.

28. Kalra JK, Grossman AM, Krumholz BA, et al. Preoperative chemoradiotherapy for carcinoma of the vulva. Gynecol Oncol 1981;12:256–60.

29. Levin W, Goldberg G, Altaras M, et al. The use of concomitant chemotherapy and radiotherapy prior to surgery in advanced stage carcinoma of the vulva. Gynecol Oncol 1986;25:20–5.

30. Whitaker SJ, Kirkbride P, Arnott SJ, et al. A pilot study of chemo-radiotherapy in advanced carcinoma of the vulva. Br J Obstet Gynaecol 1990;97:436–42.

31. Evans LS, Kersh CR, Constable WC, Taylor PT. Concomitant 5–fluorouracil, mitomycin-C, and radiotherapy for advanced gynecologic malignancies. Int J Radiat Oncol Biol Phys 1988;15:901–6.

32. Carson LF, Twiggs LB, Adcock LL, et al. Multimodality therapy for advanced and recurrent vulvar squamous cell carcinoma. A pilot project. J Reprod Med 1990;35:1029–32.

33. Rotmensch J, Rubin SJ, Sutton HG, et al. Preoperative radiotherapy followed by radical vulvectomy with inguinal lymphadenectomy for advanced vulvar carcinomas. Gynecol Oncol 1990;36:181–4.

34. Wahlen SA, Slater JD, Wagner RJ, et al. Concurrent radiation therapy and chemotherapy in the treatment of primary squamous cell carcinoma of the vulva. Cancer 1995;75:2289–94.

35. Eifel PJ, Morris M, Burke TW, et al. Prolonged continuous infusion cisplatin and 5-flourouracil with radiation for locally advanced cancer of the vulva. Gynecol Oncol 1995;59:51–6.

36. Lupi G, Raspagliesi F, Zucali R, et al. Combined preoperative chemoradiotherapy followed by radical surgery in locally advanced vulvar carcinoma. A pilot study. Cancer 1996;77:1472–8.

37. Landoni F, Maneo A, Zanetta G, et al. Concurrent preoperative chemotherapy with 5-flourouracil and mitomycin C and radiotherapy (FUMIR) followed by limited surgery in locally advanced and recurrent vulvar carcinoma. Gynecol Oncol 1996;61:321–7.

38. Moore DH, Thomas GM, Montana GS, et al. Preoperative chemoradiation for advanced vulvar cancer: a phase II study of the Gynecologic Oncology Group. Int J Radiat Oncol Biol Phys 1998;42:79–85.

39. Montana GS, Thomas GM, Moore DH, et al. Preoperative chemo-radiation for carcinoma of the vulva with unresectable lymph nodes: a Gynecologic Oncology Group study. Int J Radiat Oncol Biol Phys 1999;45:208.

40. Roberts WS, Hoffman MS, Kavanagh JJ, et al. Further experience with radiation therapy and concomitant intravenous chemotherapy in advanced carcinoma of the lower female genital tract. Gynecol Oncol 1991;43:233–6.

41. Thomas G, Dembo A, DePetrillo A, et al. Concurrent radiation and chemotherapy in vulvar carcinoma. Gynecol Oncol 1989;34:263–7.

42. Berek JS, Heaps JM, Fu YS, et al. Concurrent cisplatin and 5-flourouracil chemotherapy and radiation therapy for advanced-stage squamous carcinoma of the vulva. Gynecol Oncol 1991;42:197–201.

43. Russell AH, Mesic JB, Scudder SA, et al. Synchronous radiation and cytotoxic chemotherapy for locally advanced or recurrent squamous cancer of the vulva. Gynecol Oncol 1992;47:14–20.

44. Koh WJ, Wallace JH III, Greer BE, et al. Combined radiotherapy and chemotherapy in the management of local-regionally advanced vulvar cancer. Int J Radiat Oncol Biol Phys 1993;26:809–16.

45. Cunningham MJ, Goyer RP, Gibbons SK, et al. Primary radiation, cisplatin, and 5-fluorouracil for advanced squamous carcinoma of the vulva. Gynecol Oncol 1997;66:258–61.

46. Plentl AA, Friedman EA. Lymphatic system of the female genitalia. Philadelphia: W.B. Saunders; 1971.

47. Parry-Jones E. The management of premalignant and malignant conditions of the vulva. Clin Obstet Gynaecol 1976;3:217–28.

48. Iversen T, Aas M. Lymph drainage from the vulva. Gynecol Oncol 1983;16:179–89.

49. Wharton JT, Gallagher S, Rutledge FN. Microinvasive carcinoma of the vulva. Obstet Gynecol 1974;118:159–62.

50. Parker RT, Duncan I, Rampone J, Creasman W. Operative management of early invasive epidermoid carcinoma of the vulva. Am J Obstet Gynecol 1975;123:349–55.

51. Magrina JF, Webb MJ, Gaffey TA, Symmonds RE. Stage I squamous cell cancer of the vulva. Am J Obstet Gynecol 1979;134:453–9.

52. Buscema J, Stern JL, Woodruff JD. Early invasive carcinoma of the vulva. Am J Obstet Gynecol 1981;140:563–9.

53. Curry SL, Wharton JT, Rutledge F. Positive lymph nodes in vulvar squamous carcinoma. Gynecol Oncol 1980;9:63–6.

54. Way S. Aspects and treatment of vulvar cancer. Basel: Karger; 1972. p. 18.

55. Piver MS, Xynos FP. Pelvic lymphadenectomy in women with carcinoma of the clitoris. Obstet Gynecol 1977;49:592–5.

56. Chu J, Tamimi HK, Figge DC. Femoral node metastases with negative superficial inguinal nodes in early vulvar cancer. Am J Obstet Gynecol 1981;140:337–9.

57. Hacker NF, Nieberg RK, Berek JS, et al. Superficially invasive vulvar cancer with nodal metastases. Gynecol Oncol 1983;15:65–77.

58. Hoffman JS, Kumar NB, Morley GW. Microinvasive squamous carcinoma of the vulva: search for a definition. Obstet Gynecol 1983;61:615–8.

59. Morley GW. Infiltrative carcinoma of the vulva. Results of surgical treatment. Am J Obstet Gynecol 1976;124:874–88.

60. Iversen T, Aalders JG, Christensen A, Kolstad P. Squamous cell carcinoma of the vulva: a review of 424 patients, 1956–1974. Gynecol Oncol 1980;9:271–9.

61. Homesley HD, Bundy BN, Sedlis A, Adcock L. Radiation therapy versus pelvic node resection for carcinoma of the vulva with positive groin nodes. Obstet Gynecol 1986;68:733–40.

62. Rutledge F, Smith JP, Franklin EW. Carcinoma of the vulva. Am J Obstet Gynecol 1970;106:1117–30.

63. Dean RE, Taylor ES, Weisbrod DM, Martin JW. The treatment of premalignant and malignant lesions of the vulva. Am J Obstet Gynecol 1974;119:59–68.

64. Morris JM. A formula for selective lymphadenectomy: its application to cancer of the vulva. Obstet Gynecol 1977;50:152–8.

65. Krupp PJ, Bohm JW. Lymph gland metastases in invasive squamous cell carcinoma of the vulva. Am J Obstet Gynecol 1978;130:943–52.

66. Benedet JL, Turko M, Fairey RN, Boyers DA. Squamous carcinoma of the vulva: results of treatment, 1938–1976. Am J Obstet Gynecol 1979;134:201–7.

67. Boyce J, Fruchter RG, Kasambilides E, et al. Prognostic factors in carcinoma of the vulva. Gynecol Oncol 1985;20:364–77.

68. Nicklin JL, Hacker NF, Heintze SW, et al. An anatomical study of inguinal lymph node topography and clinical implications for the surgical management of vulvar cancer. Int J Gynecol Cancer 1995;5:128–33.

69. Borgno G, Micheletti L, Barbero M, et al. Topographic distribution of groin lymph nodes. A study of 50 female cadavers. J Reprod Med 1990;35:1127–9.

70. McCall AR, Olson MC, Potkul RK. The variation in inguinal lymph node depth in adult women and its importance in planning elective irradiation for vulvar cancer. Cancer 1995;75:2286–8.

71. Kalidas H. Influence of inguinal node anatomy on radiation therapy techniques. Med Dosim 1995;20:295–300.

72. Leiserowitz G, Russell AH, Kinney WH, et al. Prophylactic chemoradiation of inguinofemoral lymph

nodes in patients with locally extensive vulvar cancer. Gynecol Oncol 1997;66:509–14.

73. Stehman FB, Bundy BN, Thomas G, et al. Groin dissection versus groin radiation in carcinoma of the vulva: a Gynecologic Oncology Group study. Int J Radiat Oncol Biol Phys 1992;24:389–96.

74. Koh WJ, Chiu M, Stelzer KJ, et al. Femoral vessel depth and the implications for groin node radiation. Int J Radiat Oncol Biol Phys1993;27:969–74.

75. Hunter DJ. Carcinoma of the vulva: a review of 361 patients. Gynecol Oncol 1975;3:117–23.

76. Foye G, Marsh MR, Minkowitz S. Verrucous carcinoma of the vulva. Obstet Gynecol 1969;34:484–8.

77. Gallousis S. Verrucous carcinoma: report of three vulvar cases and review of the literature. Obstet Gynecol 1972;40:502–7.

78. Lucas WE, Benirschke K, Lebherz TB. Verrucous carcinoma of the female genital tract. Am J Obstet Gynecol 1974;119:435–40.

79. Japaze H, Van Dinh T, Woodruff JD. Verrucous carcinoma of the vulva: a study of 24 cases. Obstet Gynecol 1982;60:462–6.

80. Crissman JD, Azoury RS. Microinvasive carcinoma of the vulva. Diagn Gynecol Obstet 1981;3:75–80.

81. Wilkinson EJ, Rico MJ, Pierson KK. Microinvasive carcinoma of the vulva. Int J Gynecol Pathol 1982; 1:29–39.

82. Podratz KC, Symmonds RE, Taylor WF. Carcinoma of the vulva: analysis of treatment failures. Am J Obstet Gynecol 1982;143:340–51.

83. Malfetano J, Piver MS, Tsukada Y. Stage III and IV squamous cell carcinoma of the vulva. Gynecol Oncol 1986;23:192–8.

84. Cavanagh D, Fiorica JV, Hoffman MS, et al. Invasive carcinoma of the vulva: changing trends in surgical management. Am J Obstet Gynecol 1990;163:1007–15.

85. Bryson SCP, Dembo AJ, Colgan TJ, et al. Invasive squamous cell carcinoma of the vulva: defining low and high risk groups for recurrence. Int J Gynecol Cancer 1991;1:25.

86. Tilmans AS, Sutton GP, Look KY, et al. Recurrent squamous carcinoma of the vulva. Am J Obstet Gynecol 1992;167:1383–9.

87. Piura B, Masotina A, Murdoch J, et al. Recurrent squamous cell carcinoma of the vulva: a study of 73 cases. Gynecol Oncol 1993;48:189–95.

88. Jeppesen JT, Sell A, Skjoldborg H. Treatment of cancer of the vulva. Acta Obstet Gynecol Scand 1972;51: 101–7.

89. Prempree T, Amornmarn R. Radiation treatment of recurrent carcinoma of the vulva. Cancer 1984; 54:1943–9.

90. Buchler DA, Kline JC, Tunca JC, Carr WF. Treatment of recurrent carcinoma of the vulva. Gynecol Oncol 1979;8:180–4.

91. Hruby G, MacLeod C, Firth I. Radiation treatment in recurrent squamous cell cancer of the vulva. Int J Radiat Oncol Biol Phys 2000;46:1193–7.

92. Faul CM, Mirmow D, Huang Q, et al. Adjuvant radiation for vulvar carcinoma: improved local control. Int J Radiat Oncol Biol Phys 1997;38:381–9.

93. Goplerud DR, Keettel WC. Carcinoma of the vulva: a review of 156 cases from the University of Iowa Hospitals. Am J Obstet Gynecol 1968;100:550–3.

94. Rutledge FN, Mitchell MF, Munsell MF, et al. Prognostic indicators for invasive carcinoma of the vulva. Gynecol Oncol 1991;42:239–44.

95. Hacker NF, Berek JS, Lagasse LD, et al. Management of regional lymph nodes and their prognostic influence in vulvar cancer. Obstet Gynecol 1983;61:408–12.

96. Homesley HD, Bundy BN, Sedlis A, et al. Assessment of current International Federation of Gynecology and Obstetrics staging of vulvar carcinoma relative to prognostic factors for survival. A Gynecologic Oncology Group study. Am J Obstet Gynecol 1991; 164:997–1004.

97. Boutselis JG. Radical vulvectomy for squamous cell carcinoma of the vulva. Obstet Gynecol 1972;39: 827–36.

98. Heaps JM, Fu YS, Montz FJ, et al. Surgical-pathologic variables predictive of local recurrence in squamous cell carcinoma of the vulva. Gynecol Oncol 1990; 38:309–14.

99. Dusenbery KE, Carlson JW, LaPorte RM, et al. Radical vulvectomy with postoperative irradiation for vulvar cancer: therapeutic implications of a central block. Int J Radiat Oncol Biol Phys 1994;29:989–98.

100. Pirtoli L, Rottoli ML. Results of radiation therapy for vulvar carcinoma. Acta Radiol Oncol 1982;21:45–8.

101. Anal Cancer Trial Working Party. United Kingdom Coordinating Committee on Cancer Research. Epidermoid anal cancer: results from the UKCCCR randomized trial of radiotherapy alone versus radiotherapy, 5-fluorouracil, and mitomycin. Lancet 1996;348:1049–54.

102. Bartelink H, Roelofsen F, Eschwege F, et al. Concomitant radiotherapy and chemotherapy is superior to radiotherapy alone in the treatment of locally advanced anal cancer: results of the European Organization for Research and Treatment of Cancer Radiotherapy and Gastrointestinal Cooperative Groups. J Clin Oncol 1997;15:2040–9.

103. Iversen T. Irradiation and bleomycin in the treatment of inoperable vulval carcinoma. Acta Obstet Gynecol Scand 1982;61:195–7.

104. American Cancer Society. Cancer facts and figures 2001. Atlanta, Georgia: ACS; 2001.

105. Han SC, Kim DH, Kacinski BM. Addition of 5FU + mitomycin C or 5FU + cisplatin decreases the local relapse rate and improves the cause-specific sur-

vival in patients with vulvar cancer. Int J Radiat Oncol Biol Phys 1999;45:208–9.

106. Thomas GM, Dembo AJ, Bryson SC, et al. Changing concepts in the management of vulvar cancer. Gynecol Oncol 1991;42:9–21.

107. Podratz KC, Symmonds RE, Taylor WF, Williams TJ. Carcinoma of the vulva: analysis of treatment and survival. Obstet Gynecol 1983;61:63–74.

108. Frankendal B, Larsson LG, Westling P. Carcinoma of the vulva: results of an individualized treatment schedule. Acta Radiol Ther Phys Biol 1973;12:165–74.

109. Simonsen E, Nordberg UB, Johnsson JE, et al. Radiation therapy and surgery in the treatment of regional lymph nodes in squamous cell carcinoma of the vulva. Acta Radiol Oncol 1984;23:433–42.

110. Lee WR, McCollough WM, Mendenhall WM, et al. Elective inguinal lymph node irradiation for pelvic carcinomas. Cancer 1993;72:2058–65.

111. Petereit DG, Mehta MP, Buchler DA, Kinsella TJ. Inguinofemoral radiation of N0,N1 vulvar cancer may be equivalent to lymphadenectomy if proper radiation technique is used. Int J Radiat Oncol Biol Phys 1993;27:963–7.

112. Manavi M, Berger A, Kucera E, et al. Does T1,N0-1 vulvar cancer treated by vulvectomy but not lymphadenectomy need inguinofemoral radiation? Int J Radiat Oncol Biol Phys 1997;38:749–53.

113. Kalend AM, Park TL, Wu A, et al. Clinical use of a wing field transmission block for the treatment of the pelvis including the inguinal node. Int J Radiat Oncol Biol Phys 1990;19:153–8.

114. Chamlian DK, Taylor HB. Primary carcinoma of Bartholin's gland: a report of 24 patients. Obstet Gynecol 1972;39:489–94.

115. Barclay DL, Collins CG, Macey HB. Cancer of the Bartholin gland: a review and report of 8 cases. Obstet Gynecol 1964;24:329–36.

116. Leuchter RS, Hacker NF, Voet RL, et al. Primary carcinoma of the Bartholin gland: a report of 14 cases and review of the literature. Obstet Gynecol 1982;60:361–8.

117. Wheelock JB, Goplerud DR, Dunn LJ, Oates JF III. Primary carcinoma of the Bartholin gland: a report of ten cases. Obstet Gynecol 1984;63:820–4.

118. Copeland LJ, Sneige N, Gershenson DM, et al. Bartholin gland carcinoma. Obstet Gynecol 1986;67:794–801.

119. Copeland LJ, Sneige N, Gershenson DM, et al. Adenoid cystic carcinoma of Bartholin gland. Obstet Gynecol 1986;67:115–20.

120. Cascinelli N, Di Re F, Lupi G, Balzarini GP. Malignant melanoma of the vulva. Tumori 1970;56:345–52.

121. Fenn ME, Abell MR. Melanomas of vulva and vagina. Obstet Gynecol 1973;41:902–11.

122. Morrow CP, Rutledge FN. Melanoma of the vulva. Obstet Gynecol 1972;39:745–52.

123. Chung AF, Woodruff JM, Lewis JL Jr. Malignant melanoma of the vulva: a report of 44 cases. Obstet Gynecol 1975;45:638–46.

124. Podratz KC, Gaffey TA, Symmonds RE, et al. Melanoma of the vulva: an update. Gynecol Oncol 1983;16:153–68.

125. Brand E, Fu YS, Lagasse LD, Berek JS. Vulvovaginal melanoma. Report of seven cases and literature review. Gynecol Oncol 1989;33:54–60.

126. Tasseron EW, van der Esch EP, Hart AA, et al. A clinicopathologic study of 30 melanomas of the vulva. Gynecol Oncol 1992;46:170–5.

127. Piura B, Egan M, Lopes A, Monaghan JM. Malignant melanoma of the vulva: a clinicopathologic study of 18 cases. J Surg Oncol 1992;50:234–40.

15

Acute Effects of Radiation Therapy

KATHRYN MCCONNELL GREVEN, MD

Although acute effects are common during radiation treatment, they are usually transient, resolving within a few weeks of its completion. Acute toxicity is rarely life threatening, but excessive reactions can delay treatment and decrease the likelihood of its success. Most acute normal tissue effects result from the death and depletion of normal stem cells in the small intestinal epithelium, bone marrow, gonads, basal epidermis, and other tissues. In some tissues, transient vascular effects, characterized by dilated sinusoids and capillaries, edema, and microscopic hemorrhages, may also be prominent. Acute effects are usually confined to the sites of treatment. However, local radiation effects may contribute to systemic symptoms, such as neutropenia, nausea, and fatigue.

The acute effects of radiation may be more severe or more troublesome for patients who have other serious medical problems. Also, patients who have had previous surgery or who receive concurrent chemotherapy may experience more severe side effects than those treated with radiation alone.

Acute effects can begin shortly after the start of radiation therapy and may not completely resolve for 2 to 3 months after treatment. Sequelae that occur or persist after 2 to 3 months are usually referred to as chronic effects. In general, these late effects or chronic normal tissue effects result from a different mechanism and are usually considered to be independent of acute effects. However, if a heavily irradiated area is completely depleted of stem cells, prolonged incomplete healing may result in chronic tissue injury.

EXTERNAL BEAM

Skin

Epithelial tissue is relatively sensitive to radiation; mild skin erythema will begin to appear after a total dose of 20 Gy given with conventional fractionation. With higher doses, this progresses to a brisk erythema and then to a "dry desquamation" characterized by flaking and peeling of the epidermis. After high doses, "wet desquamation" can develop, with complete exposure of the dermis.

The photon beams that are produced with modern linear accelerators deliver a lower dose of radiation to the skin surface than to deeper tissues. This "skin sparing" helps prevent the severe skin reactions that were encountered in the past when treatment was given using lower-energy x-ray machines. The use of multiple fields can also prevent accumulation of an excessive skin dose in treated areas.

However, the skin-sparing effect may be lost in areas where the surface is under skin folds. In particular, reactions tend to be more severe in panicular skin, inguinal folds, or the intergluteal crease. When the vulva is treated with the patient's legs together, there is no skin sparing, and moist desquamation of the skin usually begins to develop before a dose of 40 to 45 Gy is reached (Figure 15–1). Skin folds can sometimes be decreased with careful positioning of the patient during treatment. In particular, placing the patient in a "frog-leg" position or with legs akimbo flattens skin folds and reduces the severity of the vulvar skin reaction (Figure 15–2).

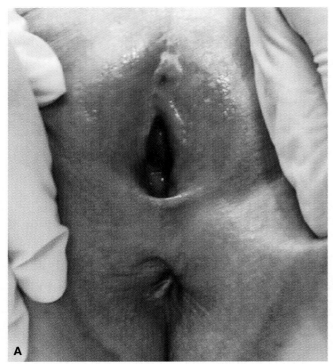

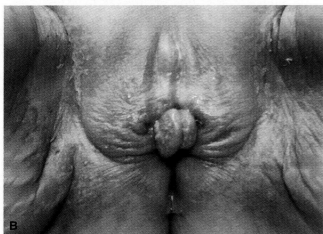

Figure 15–1. *A* and *B*, Acute moist desquamation of the perineal skin in a patient treated with radiation for a cancer that involved the lower vagina.

Skin reactions are treated according to the patient's symptoms and the clinician's experience. In general, patients are advised to maintain good hygiene in the treated areas. However, although clinicians often discourage patients from washing irradiated skin during treatment, some investigators have disagreed with this practice. In a recent randomized study of 99 patients receiving adjuvant radiotherapy to the breast or chest wall, patients who did not wash the irradiated areas tended to have more severe skin reactions than those who were randomized to wash their skin.[1] Sitz baths may be recommended for patients who are treated in the perineal area, although excessive moisture can make the skin more fragile, increasing the risk of break down. Physicians usually discourage patients from using lotions or ointments containing desiccants or perfumes that could irritate the skin. However, aloe, aquaphor, or other "healing" ointments are often recommended. Tight-fitting garments should be avoided and sites of moist desquamation should be exposed to the air as much as possible.

Bowel

Acute bowel reactions are common during pelvic radiotherapy. More than 70 percent have symptoms of acute radiation enteritis, including diarrhea, frequent bowel movements, or abdominal cramping. These effects usually begin approximately 2 weeks into a course of conventionally fractionated radiation (180 to 200 cGy/d). Symptoms may begin earlier or be more severe if treatment is given in larger doses per fraction. After pelvic irradiation is completed, acute effects should diminish over a 2- to 4-week period. Histologic changes that are noted with radiation include progressive shortening of the villi, a decrease in the number of mitotic figures, and abnormal crypt architecture.[2]

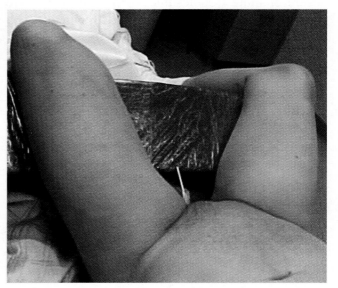

Figure 15–2. Patient set up in the frog-leg position to minimize perineal skin reaction.

Clinicians have explored a number of strategies to reduce the severity of radiation enteritis by decreasing the volume of the small intestine in the radiation area. Oral contrast may be administered so that the small bowel can be visualized at the time of simulation. One retrospective report demonstrated that 93 percent of patients simulated without contrast experienced side effects, compared with 77 percent of patients simulated with contrast (p = .03).[3] This difference seemed to result from alterations of the treatment plan that were made when the small bowel was visualized at the time of simulation. One technique that has been used to reduce the amount of small bowel in the pelvis is the placement of a temporary intrapelvic tissue expander. Herbert and colleagues[4] demonstrated that the use of a tissue expander significantly decreased the incidence of acute radiation enteritis. Positioning patients in a prone position on a "belly-board" may also decrease the volume of small bowel in the pelvis (Figures 15–3 to 15–5). Finally, treating patients with a full bladder may reduce acute complications by displacing bowel out of the pelvis. Treatment techniques that include multiple or rotational fields or that include lateral fields may allow segments of the small bowel to be blocked from the pelvis. Use of a high-energy linear accelerator and computerized dosimetry facilitate normal tissue sparing when a high dose of radiation must be delivered to a pelvic tumor.

The risk of acute bowel complications may be increased in patients with certain characterisitics. Patients with conditions that cause impaired blood supply to the intestine, such as vascular disease, hypertension, and diabetes may have a greater risk of developing radiation complications. Patients who have had prior surgery or pelvic infections may have adhesions and areas of fixed bowel in the pelvis that may be more susceptible to injury. Anecdotal experience has suggested that patients with collagen vascular diseases, such as systemic lupus erythematosus, may be more susceptible to the acute and chronic effects of radiation.[5]

Mild to moderate radiation enteritis is effectively treated with various antidiarrheal medications, such as loperamide or diphenoxylate. To decrease bowel transit times, patients are also advised to follow a low-residue or elemental diet. Patients are frequently advised to omit milk products from their diet during radiation, as it is believed that radiation reduces the intestine's ability to hydrolyze lactose. However, a randomized study failed to demonstrate any difference in the frequency of bowel movements or need for diphenoxylate when patients followed a lactose-

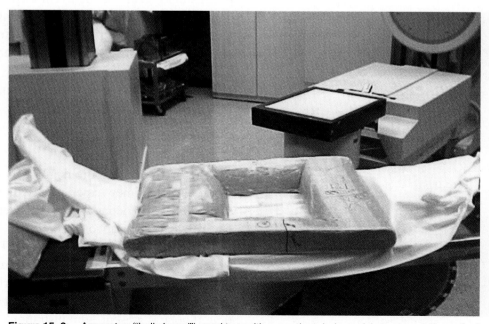

Figure 15–3. Apparatus ("belly board") used to position a patient during pelvic treatment; the patient is placed in the belly board in a prone position, with her abdomen protruding into the cut-out area.

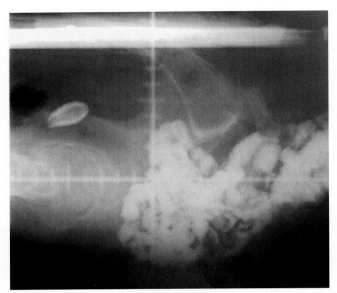

Figure 15–4. Bowel with contrast in the pelvis—patient is in the supine position.

free diet during whole-pelvis radiation.[6] It has been suggested that sucralfate can reduce symptoms of acute radiation enteritis by protecting denuded mucosa, by binding bile acids, or by a direct cyto-protective action. In a randomized prospective trial, patients required less loperamide and had less weight loss, when sucralfate was administered during radiation therapy.[7]

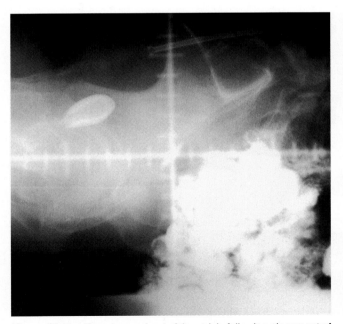

Figure 15–5. Bowel moved out of the pelvis following placement of the patient in the prone position in a "belly board."

Nausea and Vomiting

Patients who are treated with pelvic radiation therapy alone rarely experience nausea and vomiting. In a recent review of treatment-related emesis, a recent panel of the American Society of Clinical Oncology (ASCO) estimated the incidence to be between 0 to 30 percent in patients who received only pelvic irradiation.[8] The risk of nausea seems to be related to the volume of bowel treated with radiation as well as the dose per fraction and pattern of fractionation. Patients who have radiation-related emesis usually begin to experience symptoms 1 to 3 hours after treatment. The symptoms are usually relieved with antiemetics administered on an as-needed basis.

Nausea and vomiting are more frequent when the upper abdomen is included in the treatment field. The ASCO panel considered patients treated with these larger fields to be in an intermediate-risk category and recommended prophylactic use of a dopamine receptor antagonist or serotonin antagonist before each fraction.[8] When very large fields are treated, gastrointestinal toxicity may be less if treatment is delivered at low-dose rates. Theoretically, delivery of radiation at a low-dose rate permits repair of sublethal radiation injury to intestinal crypt cells.[9]

Today, many patients who are treated with radiation therapy for lower female genital tract neoplasms also receive concurrent cisplatin-containing chemotherapy. These patients typically experience nausea and vomiting after administration of their chemotherapy. This should be treated aggressively with antiemetics, dietary counseling, and hydration to prevent weight loss, malnutrition, and harmful treatment delays.

Bladder

Patients who receive more than 30 Gy of fractionated radiation sometimes experience symptoms of radiation cystitis. Cystoscopy may reveal edema of the bladder wall and mucosal congestion after 4 to 6 weeks of conventional fractionated radiation. This can cause spasm of the bladder musculature, producing symptoms of frequency and dysuria. A urinalysis should always be done to rule out concomitant bacterial infection. If none is present, administration of smooth-muscle relaxants or phenazopyridine hydrochloride or phenazopyridine hydrochloride (Pyridium) usually relieves bladder symptoms. When urinary tract symptoms occur, they are rarely a reason to interrupt or abort radiation treatment because they are usually mild and do not occur until the end of the treatment. Irradiation of the introitus may cause urethral irritation and discomfort. When this occurs, the urethra should be carefully inspected and measures instituted to relieve symptoms of local skin irritation. Acute bladder symptoms should resolve 2 to 4 weeks after completion of the radiation treatment.

Systemic Effects

Patients who undergo radiation treatment can experience poor appetite, fatigue, and diminished energy. Anorexia can be related to nausea or acute gastrointestinal effects. This may contribute to fatigue and decreased energy level. However, 10 to 15 percent of patients complain of decreased energy without nausea or anorexia.

The doses of radiation typically used to treat carcinomas of the lower female genital tract are sufficient to deplete bone marrow in the radiation field. The sacrum and pelvis contain approximately 20 percent of the total red marrow in the adult.[10] Changes in the white blood cell or platelet count can be detected after 2 to 3 weeks of conventionally fractionated radiation. However, normally these do not fall below a critical level unless the patient is also receiving concomitant chemotherapy. When chemotherapy is being given, white blood cell and platelet counts should be checked at regular intervals. Treatment-related anemia is rarely seen during radiation; however, many patients require close follow-up of their hemoglobin levels because of bleeding tumors or underlying iron deficiency.

BRACHYTHERAPY

Gynecologic cancer treatment often includes some form of brachytherapy. Treatment with brachytherapy limits the volume of normal tissue that is exposed to radiation, potentially reducing the risk of acute and chronic normal tissue effects. Possible side effects include intraoperative and perioperative complications from the procedure itself and possible acute effects of radiation delivered with the implant.

Possible intraoperative complications include perforation of the uterus by the uterine probe and vaginal laceration. The uterus may be perforated more often than is realized. In a recent study,[11] CT simulation was performed after placement of a CT-compatible intrauterine applicator. Uterine perforation was detected in 8 patients (11%). Only one of these patients appeared to be experiencing unusual discomfort. Most uterine perforations occur in the lower uterine segment (Figure 15–6). Radiographs taken at

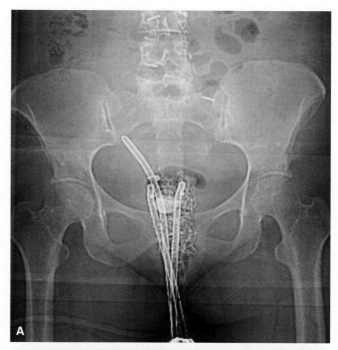

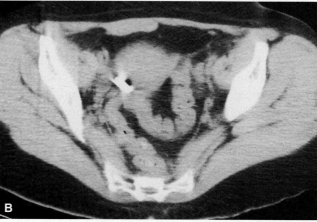

Figure 15–6. *A,* Intraoperative x-ray film of an afterloading applicator in a patient treated for carcinoma of the cervix. The tandem was severely deviated to the right, suggesting possible uterine perforation. *B,* CT scan confirmed that the tandem had perforated the lower uterine segment; the tandem was lying in the peritoneal cavity to the right of the uterus.

the time of intracavitary insertion may suggest uterine perforation, if the tandem is displaced (see Figure 15–6). Intraoperative ultrasonography may assist placement of the tandem in patients with difficult anatomy. If perforation occurs at the time of insertion, the uterine probe may be redirected in order to continue with the procedure. Vaginal lacerations may occur from tearing the vaginal mucosa while placing the colpostats and may require suturing.

Acute perioperative complications of intracavitary brachytherapy are rarely severe. Most patients have some bowel irritability from previous external pelvic irradiation; this is usually controlled with diphenoxylate hydrochloride. In some cases, pain medication, including narcotics, may be needed to control perioperative discomfort. Postanesthesia nausea and vomiting are managed with intravenous hydration and antiemetics. Urinary tract infections may result from the Foley catheter that is left in place during the 24- to 72-hour procedure. Perioperative fever may occur in up to 30 percent of patients, often without any apparent source. Lanciano and colleagues[12] reported that in their patients, temperatures of more than $100.5°F$ were observed during 24 percent of implants; in 96 percent, the fevers were managed successfully without removing the implant.

Deep venous thrombosis (DVT) is a rare but potentially serious complication of gynecologic brachytherapy applications. Dusenbery and colleagues[13] reported three episodes of DVT and one fatal pulmonary embolus (1% complication rate) associated with 462 gynecologic brachytherapy applications. Forty-three percent of their patients received some form of treatment to prevent DVT. Lanciano and colleagues[12] reported no episodes of DVT; 70 percent of their patients received DVT prophylaxis. The DVT prophylaxis may include subcutaneous heparin, graduated compression elastic stockings, and external pneumatic calf compression.

Other rare perioperative complications include exacerbation of chronic obstructive pulmonary disease, change in mental status, congestive heart failure, myocardial infarction, and acute renal failure. These complications are more likely to be observed in a patient population with serious underlying medical illnesses. Lanciano and colleagues[12] reported that 5 percent of patients required emergent removal of the implant secondary to the severity of the acute postoperative event. Univariate analysis of pretreatment and treatment factors revealed that older age and spinal anesthesia were associated with increased perioperative morbidity. However, multivariate analysis did not reveal regional anesthesia to result in more complications because older patients with higher American Society of Anesthesia (ASA) classification tended to receive regional anesthesia. Dusenberry and colleagues reported a 6.4 percent incidence of life-threatening complications and a 1.5 percent mortality rate.[13]

CONCLUSION

In summary, acute reactions are generally self-limiting but may become a problem if radiation delays become necessary because of poor patient tolerance. Patient positioning and optimizing treatment planning may decrease the volume of normal tissue in the radiation field. Weekly monitoring of the patient with early intervention in order to control symptoms may improve patient tolerance.

REFERENCES

1. Campbell IR, Illingworth MH. Can patients wash during radiotherapy to the breast or chest wall? A randomized controlled trial. Clin Oncol 1992;4:78–82.
2. Trier JS, Browning TH. Morphologic response of the mucosa of human small intestine to x-ray exposure. J Clin Invest 1960;45:194–204.
3. Herbert SH, Curran WJ Jr, Soin LJ, et al. Decreasing gastrointestinal morbidity with the use of small bowel contrast during treatment planning for pelvic irradiation. Int J Radiat Oncol Biol Phys 1991;20:835–42.
4. Herbert SH, Solin LJ, Hoffman JP, et al. Volumetric analysis of small bowel displacement from radiation portals with the use of a pelvic tissue expander. Int J Radiat Oncol Biol Phys 1993;25:885–93.
5. DeNaeyer B, DeMeerleer G, Braems S, et al. Collagen vascular diseases and radiation therapy: a critical review. Int J Radiat Oncol Biol Phys 1999;44:975–80.
6. Stryker JA, Bartholomew M. Failure of lactose-restricted diets to prevent radiation-induced diarrhea in patients undergoing whole pelvis irradiation. Int J Radiat Oncol Biol Phys 1986;12:789–92.
7. Hendricksson R, Franzen L, Littbrand B. Effects of sucralfate on acute and late bowel discomfort following radiotherapy of pelvic cancer. J Clin Oncol 1992;10:969–75.

8. Gralla RJ, Osaba D, Kris MG, et al. Recommendations for the use of antiemetics: evidence-based, clinical practice guideline. J Clin Oncol 1999;17:2971–94.

9. Hall EJ. Radiobiology for the radiologist. 2nd edition. Philadelphia: Harper and Row Publishers; 1978.

10. Ellis RE. The distribution of active bone marrow in the adult. Phys Med Biol 1961;5:255.

11. Jones EL, Weeks KJ, Gebara WJ, et al. A three dimensional computed tomography (CT) view of occult uterine perforations in tandem and ovoid implants for cervical carcinoma. Int J Radiat Oncol Biol Phys 1999;45:361.

12. Lanciano R, Corn B, Martin E, et al. Perioperative morbidity of intracavitary gynecologic brachytherapy. Int J Radiat Oncol Biol Phys 1994;29:969–74.

13. Dusenbery, KE, Carson LF, Potish RA. Perioperative morbidity and mortality of gynecologic brachytherapy. Cancer 1991;67:2786–809.

16

Late Complications of Pelvic Radiation Therapy

CHARLES LEVENBACK, MD
PATRICIA J. EIFEL, MD

Locally advanced carcinomas of the cervix, vulva, and vagina can be cured with intensive radiation therapy; however, to achieve the best therapeutic ratio (ie, the highest rate of complication-free cure), some risk of late complications must be allowed. Late effects of radiation therapy can range from relatively minor symptoms, such as occasional diarrhea, to severe tissue necrosis. Although most complications occur within the first 2 to 3 years after treatment, a small risk of complications exists throughout the life of the patient.

The incidence of late complications is correlated with tumor extent, patient characteristics, and treatment technique. Fortunately, serious complications of treatment are rare. When they do occur, skillful management by a gynecologic oncologist who is experienced in the treatment of late radiation effects is critical to maintaining a good quality of life for the patient.

INCIDENCE AND TIME COURSE OF LATE COMPLICATIONS

The most detailed reports of late radiation effects in patients with lower genital tract neoplasms concern patients treated for cervical cancer. For patients with cervical cancer, overall estimates of the risk of major complications of radiation therapy usually range between 5 and 15 percent.[1-4] Crude calculations of incidence in patients who have been followed up for relatively short intervals usually result

in significant underestimates of the true risk of radiation-related side effects. For patients who are treated with radiation for carcinoma of the cervix, the risk of experiencing a late complication is greatest within the first 3 years after treatment (Figure 16–1).[1] However, major complications have been reported as late as 30 years or more after treatment. Because of this long time course, investigators' calculations of incidence are dependent on the duration of follow-up and the method of calculation. Differences in the methods of scoring also complicate comparisons, and tumor, treatment, and patient characteristics that influence the risk of complications make it difficult to generalize results from one experience to another.

More recently, investigators have begun to use actuarial methods to calculate and report complication rates.[1,2,5] Actuarial methods more accurately reflect a surviving patient's risk of experiencing late effects of treatment. However, actuarial methods do not provide an accurate estimate of the prevalence of late side effects, many of which are transient or are managed effectively with medical or surgical interventions.

Lanciano and colleagues[2] reported an overall actuarial rate of major complications of 14 percent at 5 years in a 1992 review of 1,558 patients with cervical cancer treated in more than 100 facilities randomly selected for survey in the 1972 and 1978 Patterns of Care studies. A subsequent review of the 1972 to 1983 surveys suggested that complication

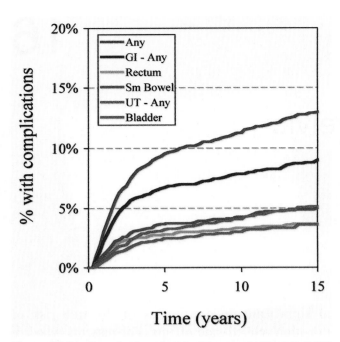

Figure 16–1. Overall rates of major late complications in 3,489 patients with stages I to II carcinomas of the uterine cervix. GI = gastrointestinal; UT = urinary tract; Sm bowel = small bowel.

rates were declining with the advent of more modern radiation therapy techniques and an increase in the use of brachytherapy.[6]

At the University of Texas M.D. Anderson Cancer Center, relatively consistent radiation therapy techniques and a high rate of follow-up have facilitated studies of late radiation-related complications. In a study of more than 1,700 patients with stage Ib cervical cancer treated between 1960 and 1989, Eifel and colleagues[1] reported an overall actuarial risk of major complications (those requiring transfusion, hospitalization, or surgical intervention) of 14.4 percent at 20 years. At 5 years, the incidence was approximately 9.3 percent. Most complications involved the bowel or bladder. The risk of rectal complications was greatest in the first few years after treatment (2.3% at 5 years), but there was also a small, continuous risk of about 0.06 percent per year between 5 and 25 years after treatment. The most frequent urinary tract complication was hematuria; this usually resolved with medical management.[7] The risk of urinary tract complications was greatest during the first 3 years after treatment. However, the complication rate increased from 2.6 percent at 5 years to 6.2 percent at 20 years,

reflecting a time course very different from that of rectal complications (Figure 16–2).

PATHOGENESIS OF LATE COMPLICATIONS

The pathogenesis of late radiation complications is complex and remains incompletely understood. In general, injury results from the direct or indirect killing of critical cells in irradiated normal tissues. Damage to slowly or infrequently proliferating parenchymal stem cells can lead to tissue loss or organ dysfunction.[8] Damage to surrounding stroma, particularly the endothelial cells, can lead to hypovascularity and fibrosis.[9] In addition, tissues that have been damaged by radiation probably release a variety of cytokines and growth factors that contribute to inflammation, edema, and fibrosis.[10]

In some cases, radiation injury is manifested only as a diminished capacity to respond to subsequent injuries. Patients may do well for many years but develop serious side effects after having an incidental pelvic operation. An episode of pelvic inflammatory disease, diverticulitis, or postoperative infection

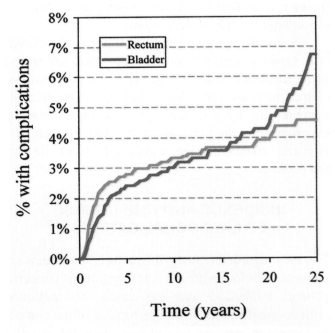

Figure 16–2. Rates of major rectal and bladder complications in 3,489 patients with stages I to II carcinomas of the uterine cervix. All patients were treated with radiation therapy at M.D. Anderson Cancer Center between 1960 and 1994. Major complications were defined as those requiring hospitalization, transfusion, or surgical intervention.

can also precipitate a cascade of events leading to severe tissue fibrosis or necrosis.

Withers and colleagues[11] have suggested a model of normal tissue injury that relates complications to the organizational structure of individual organs. According to their model, the tolerance of an organ to radiation is related to the inherent radiosensitivity of target cells and to the number and arrangement of "functional subunits" in the tissue. They define a functional subunit as the largest unit of cells capable of being regenerated from a surviving clonogenic cell without loss of the specified function. Radiation response is also related to the volume of tissue irradiated and to the functional reserve of the organ.

Followill and colleagues[12] have suggested that two types of late damage occur in the bowel—one type that depends on persistent epithelial denudation and which they refer to as a "consequential late effect," and a second type of late damage that occurs in the absence of mucosal denudation (a true late effect). In their mouse model, higher doses of radiation resulted in mucosal denudation that did not heal completely and led rapidly to "consequential" ulceration and intestinal obstruction. In contrast, true late effects occurred later and were associated with fibrosis without mucosal disruption. These two distinct types of late effects may explain the different time courses of rectal and urinary tract injuries in patients treated with radiation for cervical cancer (see Figure 16–2).[1]

Late complications, which tend to affect slowly proliferating tissues, are not usually correlated with the duration of treatment but are strongly correlated with the dose per fraction of radiation. In contrast, acute effects, which affect rapidly proliferating normal tissues and tumors, tend to be more strongly correlated with the duration of treatment but are little influenced by the fractionation. This fractionation effect is responsible for the advantage of hyperfractionated schedules in clinical settings where late normal tissue reactions are severely dose limiting.[13–15]

FACTORS THAT INFLUENCE THE RISK OF COMPLICATIONS

The risk of late complications from radiation therapy is influenced by treatment technique, patient characteristics, and the extent of disease.

Radiation Therapy Technique

In general, the dose and dose per fraction of external-beam irradiation influence the risk of late complications, as does the volume of tissue irradiated.[2,16] High-energy (more than 15 MV) photon beams are used to treat most patients with deep pelvic tumors because these high-energy beams deliver a homogeneous dose to the central pelvis while sparing more superficial tissues that are unlikely to harbor disease. With these high-energy beams, 40 to 50 Gy can usually be delivered to relatively large pelvic fields without causing major morbidity; however, the risk increases rapidly with higher doses.[16]

In some cases, clinicians can reduce the volume of normal tissue that receives high doses of radiation by using three or more converging beams. Computed tomography (CT)-based treatment planning makes it possible to design complex treatments that deliver a homogeneous dose to the target volume without treating unnecessary tissues. Judicious positioning of the patient also minimizes the volume of tissue exposed to high doses of radiation. For example, in selected patients, the amount of small bowel exposed to a high dose can be decreased by treating the patient in a prone position, by applying abdominal compression, or by treating the patient with a full bladder. In some patients with vaginal or vulvar carcinoma, damage to uninvolved perineal skin can be reduced by treating the patient in an open-leg position.

In the case of gross disease, specialized techniques are needed to deliver the high doses required for disease control. For patients with cervical cancer, intracavitary irradiation permits delivery of a high dose of radiation to the tumor and minimizes the dose to surrounding normal tissues. However, the risk of complications with this technique is dependent on the dose rate or, with high-dose-rate treatment, the dose per fraction. Radiation dose and technique also play a role, but the effect of these factors has been difficult to quantify.[17]

Interstitial brachytherapy, three-dimensional conformal external radiation therapy techniques, and careful application of electron-beam fields permit targeted delivery of a high dose of radiation to a localized tumor volume (Figure 16–3). In carefully selected patients, these techniques reduce the vol-

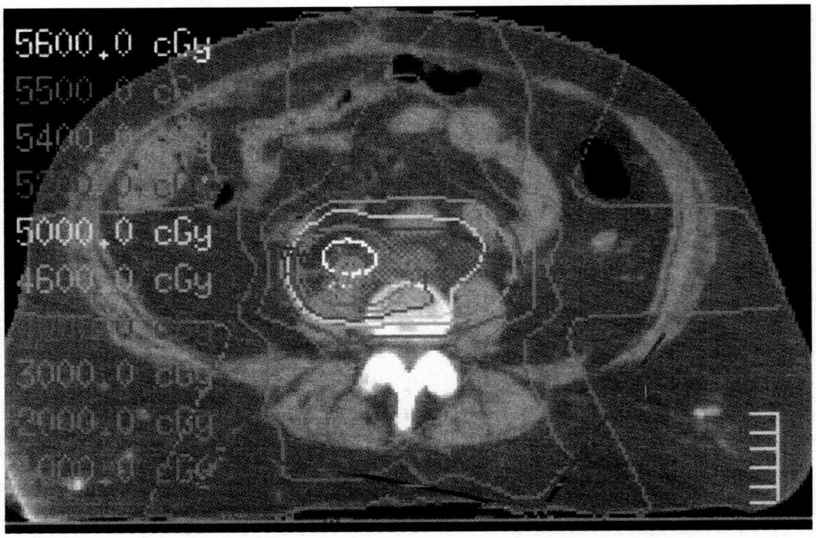

Figure 16–3. Radiation therapy plan used to treat a patient who developed recurrence in the para-aortic lymph nodes 2 years after primary surgery and post-operative pelvic irradiation. The blue cross-hatches represent the initial target volume (target dose 4,600 cGy) and the red cross-hatches represent the boost volume (target dose 5,400 cGy). Using a six-field conformal technique, the target volume was treated to the desired dose, while the dose to most of the small bowel was kept below 30 Gy. In appropriate cases, conformal treatment may significantly decrease the radiation dose to uninvolved normal tissues.

ume of normal tissue that is unnecessarily treated to a high dose.

The brachytherapy techniques that can be used to achieve high local control rates with low risk of complications in patients with neoplasms of the lower genital tract require skill and excellent quality control. Radiographs should be obtained, while the patient is still sedated, to document accurate positioning of the afterloading applicator systems. When films suggest that the positioning of an implant can be improved, the applicators should be repositioned before radioactive sources are inserted. Because lower genital tract neoplasms are relatively rare in the United States and because the required techniques are specialized, patients should be referred to radiation oncologists who have special expertise, whenever possible.[18]

In some cases (eg, cervical cancer with metastases to the aortic nodes), large fields must be used to cover the regions at risk. Although the morbidity of these large fields can sometimes be reduced with multiple-field techniques, the risk of major complications is still greater than for patients who can be treated with smaller pelvic fields.

Surgical Technique

Although small bowel obstruction is an infrequent complication of standard radiation therapy, the risk is increased dramatically in patients who have undergone preirradiation transperitoneal lymph node dis-

sections.[1,2,19] Eifel and colleagues[1] reported a 14.5 percent incidence of major small bowel complications at 10 years in patients who underwent pretreatment laparotomy, compared with only 3.7 percent in those who did not. However, in a retrospective review of the Gynecologic Oncology Group experience, Weiser and colleagues found that the risk of bowel complications could be markedly reduced if pretreatment lymphadenectomy was performed through a retroperitoneal approach.[19] Laparoscopic lymphadenectomy is also being explored as an alternative to laparotomy. This approach has several advantages, including the potential to visualize the entire peritoneal cavity, access to both sides of the pelvis through one set of incisions, a shorter recovery time, and less delay to the start of radiation therapy. Although early results of this approach are encouraging,[20] there are no long-term studies of late complications in patients who have radiation therapy after this procedure. Also, several reports of recurrences in the sites of trocar placement[21,22] suggest that caution is warranted, particularly when gross disease must be resected. Scar implants are extremely rare in patients who are operated on with a retroperitoneal approach.

Several surgical techniques that displace the small intestine from the pelvis have been explored in an effort to reduce the incidence of small bowel complications. These include the use of sigmoid lids, omental pedicled grafts, absorbable mesh slings,[23] rectus abdominis grafts, and saline-filled devices.[24] Although these approaches may reduce the dose of radiation delivered to the small bowel, their effects have not been evaluated in large prospective studies, and these approaches have not gained widespread acceptance.

Patient Characteristics

A number of patient characteristics have been associated with an increased risk of radiation-related complications. Patients who have had major or multiple abdominal surgical procedures may have an increased risk of small bowel complications.[25,26] Patients with diabetes mellitus may have an increased incidence of late complications, but studies investigating this issue have yielded varying conclusions.[27–29] Eifel and colleagues[27] recently reported a strong correlation between smoking history, ethnicity, and the risk of major gastrointestinal complications in patients treated for cervical cancer. The risk of gastrointestinal complications was particularly high for women who smoked more than one pack of cigarettes per day.

Patients who have a history of pelvic inflammatory disease or diverticulitis may also have an increased risk of late complications of radiation therapy.[1,30] Any symptom suggestive of pelvic inflammatory disease (elevated white count, pelvic tenderness, or an adnexal mass) should be carefully evaluated and treated before radiation therapy is initiated. The risk of late complications may also be increased somewhat in patients with collagen vascular disease.[31]

Extent of Disease

The relationship between disease extent and the risk of major complications is difficult to determine from the literature because crude complication rates tend to underestimate the risk in patients with more advanced disease, who are more likely to die of their disease. However, more extensive paracervical tissue destruction, superinfection, and aggressive treatment probably increase the risk of treatment complications in patients with locally advanced disease.[16]

DIAGNOSIS AND MANAGEMENT OF LATE COMPLICATIONS

In many cases, severe complications of radiation therapy are confined to one organ system. However, unless there is an acute emergency, a patient who has a complication involving one of the pelvic organs should have a complete noninvasive work-up to rule out involvement of multiple organ systems before any surgical intervention. Cross-sectional imaging can clarify the nature of complex injuries that involve more than one organ system and can reveal impending problems in other pelvic organs; cross-sectional imaging may also detect recurrent cancer. Traditional contrast imaging studies are also valuable in preoperative planning, particularly to confirm and localize fistulas.

Diagnosis and management of specific late complications of radiation therapy are discussed in the following paragraphs.

Chronic Radiation Enteritis

The symptoms of chronic radiation enteritis can range in severity from a mild intermittent diarrhea that is readily controlled with dietary modifications to a severe syndrome characterized by abdominal pain, diarrhea, nausea, vomiting, anorexia, and weight loss. Patients with mild to moderate enteritis are usually treated on an outpatient basis with a low-residue diet and antimotility agents to control the diarrhea. Patients with severe symptoms may experience temporary improvement with inpatient medical management, but usually surgical intervention is ultimately necessary.

Diagnostic Evaluation

In any patient who has had pelvic radiation therapy, abdominal pain should be evaluated carefully. A physical examination, including a pelvic examination, abdominal radiography, a complete blood count, renal function tests, and measurement of serum electrolytes should be done. However, in patients with radiation injury, peritonitis may be present without the usual signs and symptoms of severe pain, rebound tenderness, fever, and leukocytosis. Thus, clinicians should maintain a high level of concern and a low threshold for hospital admission, even in the face of relatively minor physical signs and laboratory findings. Patients should be admitted to the hospital if abdominal radiographs show an abnormal gas pattern (Figure 16–4).

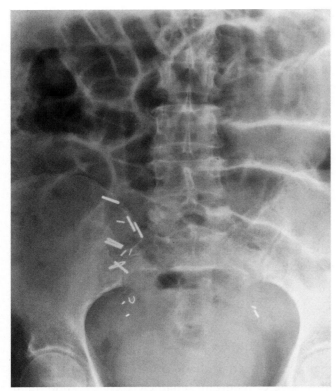

Figure 16–4. Abdominal radiograph from a patient who developed a small bowel obstruction after pelvic radiation therapy. Multiple dilated loops of small bowel are present in the abdomen with no gas in the large bowel.

Chronic radiation enteritis is usually caused by injury to the terminal ileum, which is relatively fixed in the pelvis. The injury can involve one or multiple loops of bowel. In patients with chronic radiation enteritis, CT usually demonstrates thickening of the bowel wall (Figure 16–5). Although an upper gastrointestinal study with small bowel follow-through may demonstrate narrowing or fixation of bowel loops (Figure 16–6), this study tends to be less sensitive than CT for diagnosis of milder cases of radiation enteritis.

Management

In the past, patients with severe symptoms of enteritis were typically managed with hospitalization, bowel rest, nasogastric decompression, and nutritional support. Although few data are available on the long-term results of conservative management of these patients, we have found that bowel rest succeeds only in patients with relatively minor radiation injury and

patients with infectious gastroenteritis. The latter condition usually improves rapidly within 24 to 48 hours. Patients who do not experience improvement within 72 hours usually require surgical intervention. Patients with a history of progressive symptoms and weight loss and who require admission for acute onset of pain, vomiting, or fever should be prepared immediately for laparotomy. On admission, patients should be hydrated and have nothing by mouth. If the patient is febrile, antibiotics should be started after urine and blood cultures are done.

Small bowel obstruction. The operative approach to radiation-related small bowel obstruction has evolved since 1966, when Smith and colleagues[32] emphasized small bowel bypass as the primary surgical intervention. Long-term follow-up of patients treated with this approach revealed a high incidence of infection, abscess, and perforation in the defunctionalized bowel loop. It is now recognized that better results are usually achieved with resection of the injured bowel loop and reanastomosis (Figure 16–7).[33–35] Unirradiated bowel should be used for at least one side of the anastomosis.

Perforation of the small bowel usually presents subacutely with a small bowel obstruction associated with a walled-off abscess.[36] In this situation, resection with reanastomosis is safe if a tension-

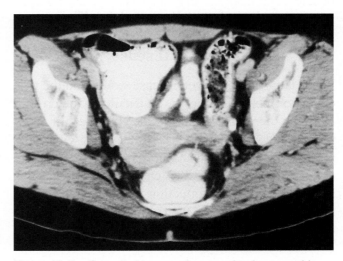

Figure 16–5. Computed tomography scan showing several loops of thickened small bowel anterior to the uterus, 2 years after pelvic radiation therapy for cervical cancer. This patient had diarrhea, crampy abdominal pain, bloating, dyspareunia, and fever after intercourse. She never developed a bowel obstruction, and her symptoms gradually improved. She is now minimally symptomatic 9 years after radiation therapy.

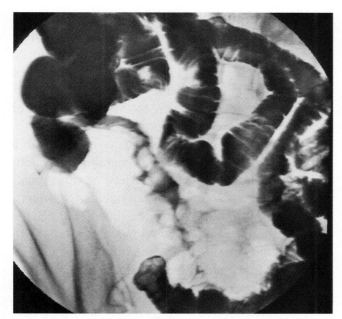

Figure 16–6. Upper gastrointestinal series with small bowel follow-through showing a loop of terminal ileum that is fixed in the pelvis. The lumen of this segment is irregular and narrowed, although the patient does not have an obstruction. This patient underwent ileocolectomy and ileotransverse colostomy with good results.

free, secure anastomosis can be constructed. However, when an acute perforation is associated with generalized peritonitis, ileostomy is the safest alternative; reversal of the ileostomy at a later date is sometimes possible.

Treatment of malnutrition. Patients who are severely malnourished may benefit from a course of total parenteral nutrition (TPN) before the operation. Malnutrition increases a patient's risk of postoperative wound complications. A prospective study of malnourished patients facing major thoracic or abdominal surgery has suggested that patients who have preoperative TPN tend to have more infectious complications and fewer noninfectious complications.[37] Although these effects tended to balance each other for moderately malnourished patients, the most severely malnourished patients appeared to benefit from TPN, with fewer cases of wound infection and major organ dysfunction. Although preoperative TPN may be considered for patients who have lost more that 10 percent of their body weight, in most cases, we prefer not to delay surgery. Instead, we frequently place a feeding gastrostomy or jejunostomy tube at the time of surgery; this may help to rehabilitate small bowel that has atrophied

during the long periods of inadequate nutrition.[38] Three-way gastrostomy tubes permit enteral feedings and keep the stomach decompressed. Although it was once standard practice to delay enteral feedings until there were clinical signs of return of bowel function, the long delay that this required usually worsened intestinal atrophy. More recent data suggest that immediate enteral feeding is safe, even for patients who have been operated on for treatment of perforation and sepsis.[39] We usually prefer to wait for general signs of improvement but do not require complete return of bowel function to begin feedings. If patients are severely malnourished, enteral feeding may be supplemented with TPN to maintain nutritional support.

Anatomic and surgical considerations. In some cases, several loops of bowel may be adherent to the uterus, vaginal cuff, or pelvic side wall. These points of adhesion may be discovered to be several feet away from each other when the bowel is dissected away from the pelvic structures. Placement of ureteral stents sometimes facilitates identification of ureters that may be obscured by adherent bowel and fibrosis. If both the urinary and gastrointestinal tracts are involved in a complex fistula, the urinary and fecal streams should be separated to avoid continued urinary sepsis.[40]

All devitalized tissue, particularly necrotic bowel, should be removed, if possible. Failure to do so usually leads to continuing low-grade sepsis, abscess, and, in some cases, death. However, this must be balanced against the risks of causing further damage to the irradiated pelvic organs and the risk of short bowel syndrome (see the next paragraph). These challenging intraoperative choices demand experience and appropriate consultation with other specialists.

Short bowel syndrome. Short bowel syndrome is a devastating complication that occurs when the digestive and absorptive capacities of the gut are reduced below the threshold required to maintain adequate nutrition. This complication is correlated with the extent and location of the resection, the function of the remaining gastrointestinal tract, and the presence or absence of the ileocecal valve and rectum.[41,42] When the ileum is resected, patients may have problems with bile salt reabsorption and steatorrhea. Resection of the ileocecal valve or rectum reduces transit times. Finally, removal of a portion of the colon reduces reabsorption of fluids and electrolytes. Although any one of these injuries is usually tolerable, a patient who suffers all three is frequently troubled by high-output diarrhea and electrolyte imbalance. Rarely, patients in this category may depend on TPN indefinitely. Because most patients with at least 100 cm of small bowel do not have major symptoms of short bowel syndrome, it is very important that the length of residual bowel be measured in the operating room and documented in the surgeon's report.

Rectosigmoid Complications

The period of greatest risk for rectosigmoid complications is the first 2 years after radiation therapy.[1]

The most common symptoms of radiation proctitis are rectal bleeding and diarrhea; less frequently, patients may have lower abdominal pain and tenesmus. Patients who present with mild symptoms usually respond quickly to simple medical interventions. When there is significant bleeding, proctosigmoidoscopy should be performed to confirm the diagnosis of proctitis and to rule out recurrence or a second primary lesion (Figure 16–8). However, unnecessary

biopsies of the irradiated bowel should be avoided because they can contribute to the risk of ulceration. In some cases, areas of radiation proctitis can be treated with good results using photocoagulation or mechanical dilatation at the time of endoscopy.[43] Barium enema may be useful to diagnose fistulas or rectosigmoid stenoses.

Mild radiation proctitis is usually treated with a low-residue diet, and enemas containing corticosteroids or mesalamine.[44] A variety of other treatments, including short-chain fatty acids,[45,46] sucralfate,[13] and formalin,[14] may be beneficial. Some patients continue to have low-grade symptoms with intermittent flare-ups that respond to medical management. Most patients in this situation learn which foods they cannot tolerate and avoid these foods, although dietary indiscretions, particularly around holidays, can cause increased symptoms.

Symptomatic stricture of the sigmoid colon is an uncommon complication that usually presents with symptoms in the first 2 years after treatment. Patients usually describe progressive constipation and narrowing of the diameter of the stools. Stool softeners should be used to minimize symptoms. In severe cases, obstipation can occur with the signs of a bowel obstruction, including abdominal distention, vomiting, and flatulence.

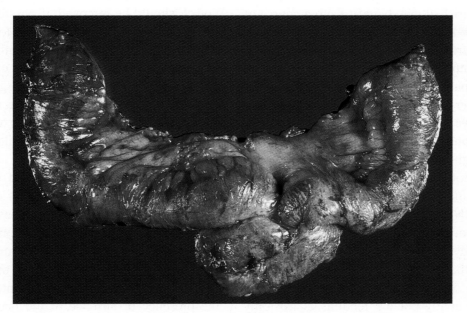

Figure 16–7.   Surgical specimen from a patient who underwent exploratory laparotomy for intestinal obstruction after pelvic irradiation. Note the agglutinated knuckled loop of terminal ileum, which is pale. This loop of ileum was densely adherent in the pelvis.

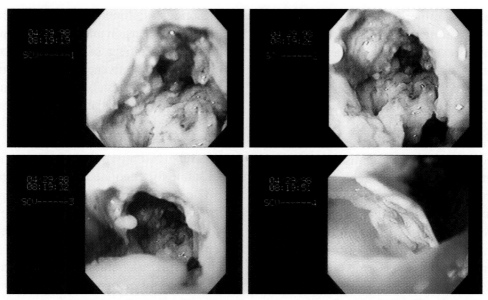

Figure 16–8. Endoscopic views of the sigmoid colon in a patient with severe sigmoiditis after radiation for stage Ib squamous cell carcinoma of the cervix.

Patients whose symptoms do not respond to these treatments may develop mucosal ulceration associated with increasing pain. Although some patients respond to antibiotics and enemas, those who do not or who develop recurrent symptoms of ulceration usually require surgical intervention. Ulceration that penetrates the muscularis can lead to sigmoid perforation, a rare complication that has a high fatality rate. CT is the most sensitive tool for the diagnosis of occult perforations because it can detect small amounts of extraluminal air or contrast (Figure 16–9).

Although sigmoid perforation can present with symptoms of acute abdomen, this complication is often preceded by weeks of low-grade pain, diarrhea (which may be bloody), anorexia, and weight loss. Patients who have these symptoms should be admitted to the hospital immediately for evaluation and possible surgery. Surgical treatment of severe sigmoiditis is most effective if perforation has not yet occurred. In that case, resection of the damaged segment with reanastomosis of the bowel is often successful.[15,47] Circular stapling devices have improved the surgeon's ability to reanastomose the rectum to the descending colon (Figure 16–10).

When the sigmoid has been perforated, the patient may experience a dramatic increase in pain, and there may be a sudden change in the findings on abdominal examination. There is usually evidence of abdominal free air (Figure 16–11) and fecal contamination of the peritoneal cavity. However, patients usually have more insidious symptoms, with a gradual change in physical findings. In these cases, there usually is a walled-off perforation with an associated abscess. If there is a perforation, immediate colostomy is the only surgical option. The patient's eligibility for subsequent reanastomosis of the bowel depends on the length of the involved segment, its distance from the anus, the amount of radiation fibrosis, injury to other organs, and the patient's age and performance status.

Radiation Cystitis

Although most rectal and small bowel complications occur within the first 2 years after treatment, urinary tract complications have a longer time course, with a small but continued risk for at least three decades (see Figure 16–1).[1]

Hematuria, which can be accompanied by lower abdominal pain and dysuria, is the most frequent symptom of radiation cystitis. In most cases, bleeding is associated with a urinary tract infection. In a review of 116 patients treated at M.D. Anderson Cancer Center for hemorrhagic cystitis, 35 percent had laboratory results that indicated a urinary tract infection, and 70 percent received oral antibiotics because of clinical or laboratory suspicion of infection.[7] Most cases of minor hematuria resolve with only antibiotic treatment. If cystoscopy is performed, it usually reveals pale mucosa and telangiectasia, consistent with radiation changes. However, we believe that cystoscopy is not necessary in most cases. If there is persistent bleeding, cystoscopy may be indicated to rule out the small risk of recurrence or a second primary tumor.

Severe bleeding that requires admission or transfusion is rare; Eifel and colleagues[1] reported an actuarial risk of 1 percent at 5 years and 1.4 percent at 10 years. Continuous bladder irrigation should be considered for severe bleeding or if the patient is passing clots, which could cause a urethral obstruction. Continuous bladder irrigation is performed using a large-bore three-way Foley catheter. Special care must be taken to ensure that the drainage rate is equal to the infusion rate; failure to monitor this closely can result in bladder distension and rupture, a catastrophic complication. A number of additives have been used to improve the effectiveness of saline irrigation. These include aluminum salts, prostaglandins, acetic acid, and silver nitrate.[48] Other techniques include hydrostatic tamponade with an intravesical balloon and hyperbaric oxygen therapy.[49] We currently use a solution containing 100 mg of hydrocortisone per liter of normal saline for continuous bladder irrigation.

The last-resort treatment for radiation cystitis is intravesical formalin. This technique is very effective but may lead to reduced bladder capacity and incontinence. These side effects may be reduced if a dilute formalin-containing solution is used.[50] A cystogram should be performed prior to the use of formalin to rule out perforation or ureteral reflux.

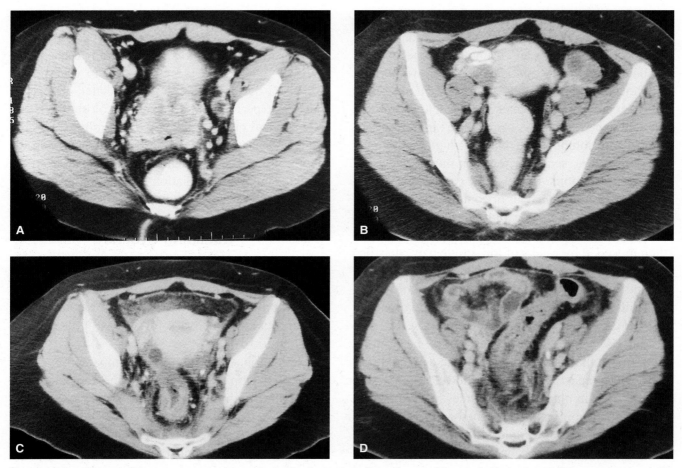

Figure 16–9. Computed tomography scans in a patient with a large stage Ib carcinoma of the cervix. Pretreatment CT scans showing *A*, the tumor adjacent to the normal rectum, and *B*, the normal sigmoid colon. *C* and *D*, Computed tomography scans obtained 12 months after radiation therapy, when the patient presented with symptoms of severe proctitis. *C*, The rectum is visible behind the uterus with a markedly thickened wall. *D*, The sigmoid colon is also seen to have a thickened wall, suggesting severe radiation sigmoiditis.

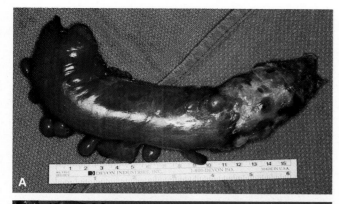

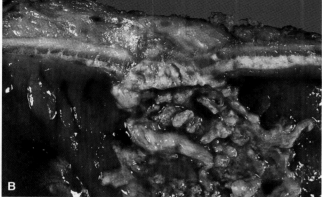

Figure 16–10. Surgical specimen after resection of the sigmoid colon in a patient with an imminent perforation but no abscess or fecal contamination. A Hartmann's pouch and end-sigmoid colostomy were performed at the same time. *A*, Entire surgical specimen. *B*, Close-up of the surgical specimen showing near-full-thickness necrosis of the bowel wall.

In our series of 1,784 patients with cervical cancer treated with radiation therapy, 116 had at least one episode of hematuria; of these, 25 required hospitalization or transfusion.[7] Only 5 patients required surgical intervention: 1 required cystectomy for intractable bleeding, and 4 required urinary diversions for urinary tract complications not associated with hematuria. One patient died of a myocardial infarction that may have been related, in part, to anemia caused by her complication. In very severe cases of bladder necrosis, diversion of the urine is warranted; this reduces the risk of urosepsis by separating the urine from the injured site.

Ureteral Stenosis

Ureteral stenosis is a rare complication of radiation therapy, occurring in fewer than 1 percent of patients who receive moderate doses of pelvic radiation and low-dose-rate intracavitary radiation therapy. Although the distal ureters routinely tolerate radiation doses of 80 Gy or more, some techniques have been associated with an increased risk of ureteral stricture. In particular, high doses of transvaginal orthovoltage irradiation (sometimes used to control bleeding) and external-beam fields that include a narrow midline block have been associated with an increased risk of this complication. Ureteral complications are also more frequent in patients who have combined treatment with surgery and radiation.

Whenever a patient treated for carcinoma of the cervix develops hydronephrosis or hydroureter, an effort should first be made to rule out recurrent disease, usually with a CT scan of the abdomen and pelvis and fine-needle aspiration of any suspicious lesions. The function of the affected kidney should be evaluated with a renal scan. If function is reduced by more than approximately 90 percent, the risk of

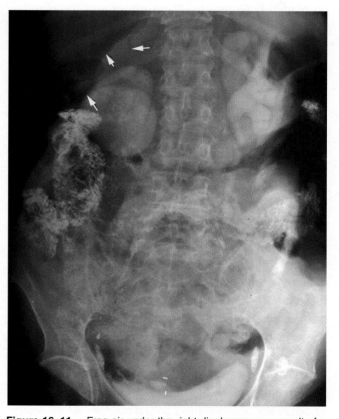

Figure 16–11. Free air under the right diaphragm as a result of a bowel perforation. Patients with previous pelvic radiotherapy and a bowel perforation may not have the classic signs and symptoms of an acute abdomen. Clinicians must have a high index of suspicion for serious bowel injuries when evaluating abdominal pain in irradiated patients.

manipulation usually exceeds the potential benefit. If the kidney is salvageable and the obstruction is not complete, cystoscopic placement of a ureteral stent should be attempted. If this fails, an antegrade stent can sometimes be placed; if this is impossible, a percutaneous nephrostomy is required to drain the kidney. The Silastic stents and nephrostomy tubes used for these procedures are prone to infection and must be replaced approximately every 3 months. The decision to perform a percutaneous nephrostomy should be considered very carefully because the risk of infection is very high if a nephrostomy drainage is discontinued without relieving the ureteral obstruction.

Several surgical options are available for management of ureteral obstruction. If the obstruction is deep in the pelvis, a ureteral neocystostomy with a psoas hitch can be performed. If the damaged segment of ureter is too long for that procedure, bladder lengthening procedures—such as a biori flap—can be employed. Alternatively, a segment of ileum can be placed between the distal ureter and the bladder. The final option is a transureteroneocystostomy, which connects the two ureters. However, this procedure risks a new stenosis obstructing both kidneys. In most cases, ureteroneocystostomy with a psoas hitch is the preferred procedure.

Fistula

Fistulas are rare complications that occur when tissue necrosis results in an abnormal communication between pelvic structures. Rectovaginal (Figure 16–12) and vesicovaginal fistulas are most frequent. Although most cases occur within 2 to 3 years of treatment, fistulas may form in previously asymptomatic patients many years after radiation therapy. However, these late instances usually follow a pelvic operation or infection. Treatment that includes a combination of surgery and radiation therapy can also increase the risk of fistula formation; Eifel and colleagues[1] found that the risk was approximately doubled in patients who underwent pretreatment transperitoneal laparotomy or adjuvant postradiation hysterectomy. At 10 years, the overall risk was 2 percent in their series.

Rectovaginal fistula is usually diagnosed when the patient complains of passing stool or flatus from the vagina. The diagnosis is usually confirmed by

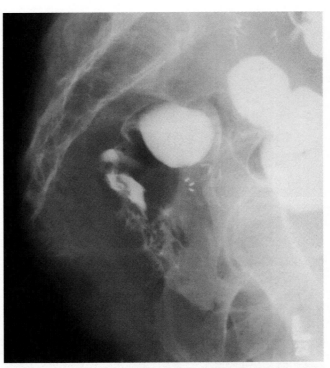

Figure 16–12. Contrast agent appearing in the vagina after a barium enema. This demonstrated the presence of a rectovaginal fistula.

physical examination or barium enema. Because patients with this severe complication frequently have injury to other organs, radiographic studies of the small bowel and urinary tract should be performed before an operation is performed.

Occasionally, very small, well-demarcated fistulas can be repaired using one of a variety of methods that preserve the rectum and anus.[51,52] However, larger fistulas—particularly, those that occur within a year or two of the primary treatment—are usually associated with more extensive necrosis. In these cases, primary repair is usually not successful, and fecal diversion is a safer alternative.

If the lesion may be amenable to repair at a later date, loop colostomy may be preformed to preserve the marginal artery of Drummond. However, loop colostomies tend to prolapse, leak, or spill stool into the descending colon. End-sigmoid colostomy is a better long-term solution that eliminates the risk of spillover and is much easier to fit with an appliance. Although end-sigmoid colostomy requires a laparotomy and may require revisions for peristomal hernias, it is usually the better option for patients with rectovaginal fistula.[53]

Patients with a vesicovaginal fistula usually present with a complaint of bladder incontinence. The diagnosis is easily confirmed by blue staining of an intravaginal tampon after the bladder is filled with a solution of saline and methylene blue. As with rectal fistulas, small defects that have minimal surrounding induration can be repaired locally, using transvaginal multilayer closure techniques with small local flaps as needed. However, larger fistulas usually require urinary diversion to keep the patient dry. Although a Foley catheter combined with bilateral percutaneous nephrostomy tubes can help some patients who are not candidates for surgery, continued leakage usually necessitates the use of perineal pads or adult diapers.

Enterovaginal, enterovesical, and enterocutaneous fistulas are very rare problems that require individualized management. Separation of the urinary and fecal streams and control of infection are important. In a small number of cases, medical interventions, such as TPN or somatostatin, have led to closure of the fistulas.[54] However, this approach is successful only in postsurgical patients who develop a single fistula without evidence of distal obstruction.

Vaginal Effects

Detailed prospective studies of the long-term vaginal and vulvar effects of radiation therapy have not been done in large numbers of patients. The relative contributions of patient, tumor, and treatment factors to post-treatment sexual dysfunction are still incompletely understood. Patients who are treated with radiation for cervical cancer tend to have varying degrees of atrophy, telangiectasia, or scarring of the upper third of the vagina. Bruner and colleagues[55] reported an average reduction in vaginal length of approximately 1 cm during the first 2 years after treatment. However, more severe shortening can occur. Changes may be greater in patients with very extensive tumors and in patients who are elderly, sexually inactive, or hypoestrogenic.[1,55]

Other Complications

Patients who have radiation therapy after lymphadenectomy may have an increased risk of lower

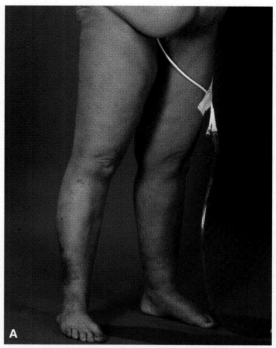
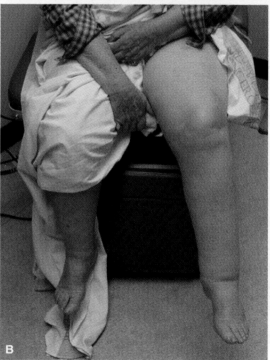

Figure 16–13. *A*, This patient has severe streptococcal lymphangitis, celluliltis, and epidermal necrolysis (lateral aspect of right lower leg). She received pelvic radiotherapy for cervical cancer many years earlier and had been symptom free until she underwent partial radical vulvectomy and bilateral inguinal femoral lymphadenectomy for a new vuvlar cancer. *B*, Another example of chronic lymphedema in a patients treated with radical vulvectomy, lymphadenectomy, and radiation therapy. Modern radiation therapy alone rarely causes lower extremity lymphedema, but it can increase the risk of edema after lymphadenectomy. Cellulitis may develop in patients who have chronic lymphedema; however, infections of the severity shown here are rare.

extremity edema or infection (Figure 16–13). Other, very rare side effects of radiation therapy include neurologic dysfunction, large vessel disease, and pelvic fracture (Figure 16–14). For patients who have these symptoms, the role of radiation therapy is often difficult to differentiate from that of peripheral vascular disease, diabetic neuropathy, or osteoporosis, all of which are associated with aging. Consultation with a symptom management specialist is very helpful.

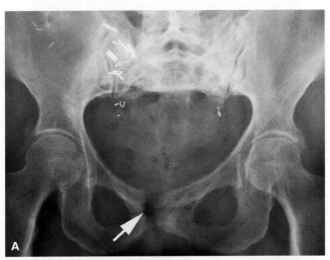

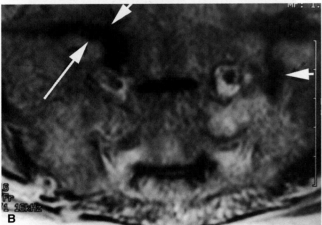

Figure 16–14. *A,* Chronic osteoradionecrosis of the symphysis pubis with osteomyelitis in a patient heavily treated with irradiation. She received initial radiation therapy in 1978 for cervical cancer with 40 Gy to the pelvis and intracavitary irradiation. She had a recurrence in the distal vagina in 1985, for which she received additional external-beam and interstitial radiotherapy. She was free of disease when this radiograph was taken in 1999. *B,* Magnetic resonance image of the same patient. There are diffuse bony changes, including insufficiency fractures of the sacrum (*arrows*) and dural thickening. These findings result in chronic pain that requires consultation with a symptom management specialist.

CONCLUSION

In most women with lower genital tract tumors, the side effects of radiation therapy are far outweighed by the benefits. However, severe complications do occur in a small proportion of patients. Prompt and judicious management is required to minimize the impact of these complications on patients' well being. The risk of late radiation-related complications justifies continued follow-up of irradiated patients by gynecologic oncologists.

REFERENCES

1. Eifel PJ, Levenback C, Wharton JT, Oswald MJ. Time course and incidence of late complications in patients treated with radiation therapy for FIGO stage IB carcinoma of the uterine cervix. Int J Radiat Oncol Biol Phys 1995;32:1289–300.
2. Lanciano RM, Martz D, Montana GS, Hanks GE. Influence of age, prior abdominal surgery, fraction size, and dose on complications after radiation therapy for squamous cell cancer of the uterine cervix. A Patterns of Care Study. Cancer 1992;69:2124–30.
3. Montana GS, Fowler WC. Carcinoma of the cervix: analysis of bladder and rectal radiation dose and complications. Int J Radiat Oncol Biol Phys 1989;16:95–100.
4. Perez CA, Camel HM, Kuske RR, et al. Radiation therapy alone in the treatment of carcinoma of the uterine cervix: a 20-year experience. Gynecol Oncol 1986;23:127–40.
5. Chassagne D, Sismondi P, Horiot JC, et al. A glossary for reporting complications of treatment in gynecological cancers. Radiother Oncol 1993;26:195–202.
6. Komaki R, Brickner TJ, Hanlon AL, et al. Long-term results of treatment of cervical carcinoma in the United States in 1973, 1978, and 1983: Patterns of Care Study (PCS). Int J Radiat Oncol Biol Phys 1995;31:973–82.
7. Levenback C, Eifel PJ, Burke TW, et al. Hemorrhagic cystitis following radiotherapy for stage Ib cancer of the cervix. Gynecol Oncol 1994;55:206–10.
8. Withers HR, Mason KA. The kinetics of recovery in irradiated colonic mucosa of the mouse. Cancer 1974;34 Suppl:896–903.
9. Hopewell J, Withers HR. Proposition: long-term changes in irradiated tissues are due principally to vascular damage in the tissues. Med Phys 1998;25:2265–8.
10. Langberg CW, Hauer-Jensen M, Sung CC, Kane CJM. Expression of fibrogenic cytokines in rat small intestine after fractionated irradiation. Radiother Oncol 1994;32:29–36.

11. Withers HR, Taylor JM, Maciejewski B. Treatment volume and tissue tolerance. Int J Radiat Oncol Biol Phys 1988;14:751–9.

12. Followill DS, Kester D, Travis EL. Histological changes in mouse colon after single- and split-dose irradiation. Radiat Res 1993;136:280–8.

13. Kochhar R, Sriram PV, Sharma SC, et al. Natural history of late radiation proctosigmoiditis treated with topical sucralfate suspension. Dig Dis Sci 1999;44:973–8.

14. Counter SF, Froese DP, Hart MJ. Prospective evaluation of formalin therapy for radiation proctitis. Am J Surg 1999;177:396–8.

15. Palmer JA, Bush RS. Radiation injuries to the bowel associated with the treatment of carcinoma of the cervix. Surgery 1976;80:458–64.

16. Logsdon MD, Eifel PJ. FIGO stage IIIB squamous cell carcinoma of the uterine cervix: an analysis of prognostic factors emphasizing the balance between external beam and intracavitary radiation therapy. Int J Radiat Oncol Biol Phys 1999;43:763–75.

17. Katz A, Eifel PJ. Quantification and correlation of intracavitary brachytherapy parameters in patients with carcinoma of the cervix. Int J Radiat Oncol Biol Phys 2000;48:1417–25.

18. Eifel PJ, Moughan J, Owen JB, et al. Patterns of radiotherapy practice for patients with squamous carcinoma of the uterine cervix. A Patterns of Care Study. Int J Radiat Oncol Biol Phys 1999;43:351–8.

19. Weiser EB, Bundy BN, Hoskins WJ, et al. Extraperitoneal versus transperitoneal selective paraaortic lymphadenectomy in the pretreatment surgical staging of advanced cervical carcinoma (a Gynecologic Oncology Group study). Gynecol Oncol 1989;33:283–9.

20. Possover M, Krause N, Plaul K, et al. Laparoscopic para-aortic and pelvic lymphadenectomy: experience with 150 patients and review of the literature. Gynecol Oncol 1998;71:19–28.

21. Lavie O, Cross PA, Beller U, et al. Laparoscopic port-site metastasis of an early stage adenocarcinoma of the cervix with negative lymph nodes. Gynecol Oncol 1999;75:155–7.

22. Lane G, Tay J. Port-site metastasis following laparoscopic lymphadenectomy for adenosquamous carcinoma of the cervix. Gynecol Oncol 1999;74:130–3.

23. Soper JT, Clarke-Pearson DL, Creasman WT. Absorbable synthetic mesh (910-polyglactin) intestinal sling to reduce radiation-induced small bowel injury in patients with pelvic malignancies. Gynecol Oncol 1988;29:283–9.

24. Hoffman JP, Sigurdson ER, Eisenberg BL. Use of saline-filled tissue expanders to protect the small bowel from radiation [published erratum appears in Oncology (Huntingt) 1998;12(3):421]. Oncology (Huntingt) 1998;12:51–4.

25. Montz FJ, Holschneider CH, Solh S, et al. Small bowel obstruction following radical hysterectomy: risk factors, incidence and operative findings. Gynecol Oncol 1994;53:114–20.

26. Potish RA. Importance of predisposing factors in the development of enteric damage. Am J Clin Oncol 1982;5:189–94.

27. Eifel PJ, Jhingran A, Atkinson HN, et al. Correlation of smoking history and other patient characteristics with major complications of radiation for cervical cancer. Int J Radiat Oncol Biol Phys 2000; 48:S212.

28. Herold DM, Hanlon AL, Hanks GE. Diabetes mellitus: a predictor for late radiation morbidity. Int J Radiat Oncol Biol Phys 1999;43:475–9.

29. Mitchell PA, Waggoner S, Rotmensch J, Mundt AJ. Cervical cancer in the elderly treated with radiation therapy. Gynecol Oncol 1998;71:291–8.

30. Van Nagell JR, Parker JC, Maruyama Y, et al. The effect of pelvic inflammatory disease on enteric complications following radiation therapy for cervical cancer. Am J Obstet Gynecol 1977;128:767–71.

31. Ross JG, Hussey DH, Nayr NA, Davis CS. Acute and late reactions to radiation therapy in patients with collagen vascular diseases. Cancer 1993;71:3744–52.

32. Smith J, Golden P, Rutledge F. The surgical management of intestinal injuries following irradiation for carcinoma of the cervix. Eleventh Annual Clinical Conference on Cancer; 1966; Houston, Texas. Houston: The University of Texas MD Anderson Hospital and Tumor Institute; 1966.

33. Galland RB, Spencer J. Surgical management of radiation enteritis. Surgery 1986;99:133–9.

34. Harling H, Balslev I. Radical surgical approach to radiation injury of the small bowel. Dis Colon Rectum 1986;29:371–3.

35. Hoskins WJ, Burke TW, Weiser EB, et al. Right hemicolectomy and ileal resection with primary reanastomosis for irradiation injury of the terminal ileum. Gynecol Oncol 1987;26:215–24.

36. Levenback C, Lucas K, Morris M, et al. Management of small bowel perforation and necrosis following radiotherapy for gynecologic cancer. Gynecol Oncol 1997;64:331.

37. Anonymous. Perioperative total parenteral nutrition in surgical patients. The Veterans Affairs Total Parenteral Nutrition Cooperative Study Group [see comments]. N Engl J Med 1991;325:525–32.

38. Lo CW, Walker WA. Changes in the gastrointestinal tract during enteral or parenteral feeding. Nutr Rev 1989;47:193–8.

39. Singh G, Ram RP, Khanna SK. Early postoperative enteral feeding in patients with nontraumatic intestinal perforation and peritonitis. J Am Coll Surg 1998;187:142–6.

40. Levenback C, Gershenson DM, McGehee R, et al.

Enterovesical fistula following radiotherapy for gynecologic cancer. Gynecol Oncol 1994;52:296–300.

41. Dudrick SJ, Latifi R, Fosnocht DE. Management of the short-bowel syndrome. Surg Clin North Am 1991; 71:625–43.

42. Rombeau JL, Rolandelli RH. Enteral and parenteral nutrition in patients with enteric fistulas and short bowel syndrome. Surg Clin North Am 1987;67: 551–71.

43. Triadafilopoulos G, Sarkisian M. Dilatation of radiation-induced sigmoid stricture using sequential Savary-Guilliard dilators. A combined radiologic-endoscopic approach. Dis Colon Rectum 1990;33:1065–7.

44. Triantafillidis JK, Dadioti P, Nicolakis D, Mericas E. High doses of 5-aminosalicylic acid enemas in chronic radiation proctitis: comparison with betamethasone enemas [letter]. Am J Gastroenterol 1990;85:1537–8.

45. Pinto A, Fidalgo P, Cravo M, et al. Short chain fatty acids are effective in short-term treatment of chronic radiation proctitis: randomized, double-blind, controlled trial. Dis Colon Rectum 1999;42:788–96.

46. Talley NA, Chen F, King D, et al. Short-chain fatty acids in the treatment of radiation proctitis: a randomized, double-blind, placebo-controlled, crossover pilot trial. Dis Colon Rectum 1997;40:1046–50.

47. Kimose HH, Fischer L, Spjeldnaes N, Wara P. Late radiation injury of the colon and rectum. Surgical management and outcome. Dis Colon Rectum 1989;32:684–9.

48. deVries CR, Freiha FS. Hemorrhagic cystitis: a review. J Urol 1990;143:1–9.

49. Weiss JP, Boland FP, Mori H, et al. Treatment of radiation-induced cystitis with hyperbaric oxygen. J Urol 1985;134:352–4.

50. Fair WR. Formalin in the treatment of massive bladder hemorrhage. Techniques, results, and complications. Urology 1974;3:573–6.

51. Elkins TE, DeLancey JO, McGuire EJ. The use of modified Martius graft as an adjunctive technique in vesicovaginal and rectovaginal fistula repair. Obstet Gynecol 1990;75:727–33.

52. Steichen FM, Barber HK, Loubeau JM, Iraci JC. Bricker-Johnston sigmoid colon graft for repair of postradiation rectovaginal fistula and stricture performed with mechanical sutures. Dis Colon Rectum 1992;35:599–603.

53. Segreti EM, Levenback C, Morris M, et al. A comparison of end and loop colostomy for fecal diversion in gynecologic patients with colonic fistulas. Gynecol Oncol 1996;60:49–53.

54. Torres AJ, Landa JI, Moreno-Azcoita M, et al. Somatostatin in the management of gastrointestinal fistulas. A multicenter trial [see comments]. Arch Surg 1992;127:97–100.

55. Bruner DW, Lanciano R, Keegan M, et al. Vaginal stenosis and sexual function following intracavitary radiation for the treatment of cervical and endometrial carcinoma. Int J Radiat Oncol Biol Phys 1993;27:825–30.

17

Chemotherapy in Curative Management

KEVIN R. BRADER, MD

Although chemotherapy has a central role in the curative management of ovarian cancer, its use in female lower genital tract malignancies has been limited to the palliative treatment of incurable disease. Carcinomas of the cervix, vulva, and vagina are relatively chemorefractory, and few sustained remissions are seen with the use of chemotherapy alone in the treatment of these malignancies. For this reason, chemotherapy *alone* may generally be viewed as a secondary treatment modality for lower genital tract malignancies, reserved for patients who fail primary treatment. Classically, the primary treatment of carcinomas of the cervix, vulva, and vagina has been surgery, radiation, or a combination of the two. Primary chemotherapy is never curative for these tumors. However, recent studies have established that the most important application of chemotherapy to the treatment of lower genital tract malignancies is its concurrent use with curative radiation therapy. Chemoradiation has become the treatment of choice for many patients with cervical cancer and has been investigated for the treatment of advanced vulvar cancer. Although randomized studies are impossible to perform with a malignancy as rare as vaginal cancer, extrapolation of the cervical cancer data makes the use of chemoradiation in this malignancy intuitively appealing.

BASICS

Tumor Biology

Much of the behavior of a tumor, including its response to antineoplastic agents, can be understood by considering several key biologic elements of the tumor cell population. One element involves the concept of *tissue homeostasis*. The loss of normal tissue homeostasis is critical in the development of a malignant neoplasm. Tumors are capable of uncontrolled cellular proliferation as a result of the loss of cell cycle control (Figure 17–1). However, in the presence of functional cellular "guardians," a stimulus that results in uncontrolled proliferation will trigger either cell cycle arrest or programmed cell death (apoptosis). Only through the combined loss of these guardian mechanisms, in concert with uncontrolled proliferation, can the malignant transformation take place. Multiple viral and chemical models of carcinogenesis support this concept.[1]

This concept is particularly relevant when considering the ability of a cytotoxic treatment (chemotherapy or radiation therapy) to eradicate a tumor cell population. These treatments either directly or indirectly cause cellular and molecular alterations that trigger the cell death pathway (Figure 17–2). Clearly, a cytotoxic treatment, regardless of its ability to interact with its primary target, will not kill cells with a faulty cell death pathway. This concept is supported by several observations. First, cells with derangements in factors known to regulate cell death (eg, *P53*) often demonstrate global chemoresistance.[2–4] Additionally, clinical tumor response is often predictable by the status of these cell death factors.[5,6] Finally, preliminary gene therapy studies have shown that the re-introduction of these factors into tumor cells renders them chemosensitive.[7,8]

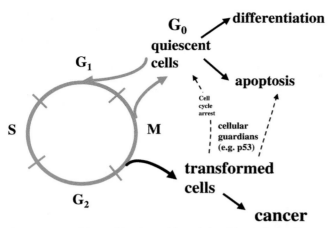

Figure 17–1. The cell cycle and its relationship to the malignant transformation. G_1 = gap phase 1; S = DNA synthesis phase; G_2 = gap phase 2; M = mitosis phase.

The concept of *tumor heterogeneity* must also be considered in order to understand the response of a tumor cell population to a cytotoxic treatment. The uncontrolled nature of tumor cell growth and the resultant genetic instability give rise to the development of a heterogeneous tumor cell population. Now-

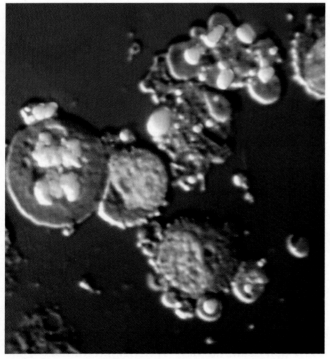

Figure 17–2. Human tumor cell undergoing apoptosis in response to cytotoxic therapy. Note the characteristic compartmentalization and formation of apoptotic bodies. (Courtesy of Zbigniew Darzynkiewicz, MD, PhD, Brander Cancer Research Institute, New York Medical College, Valhalla, New York.)

ell suggested that acquired genetic variability within tumor cell clones, in combination with host selection pressures, lead to several subpopulations of cells with different growth advantage mechanisms.[9] This variability may be at the level of classic resistance mechanisms, cell cycle control, the cell death mechanism, or a combination of these factors. Tumor heterogeneity may, in part, explain the success of chemoradiation over radiation therapy alone in the treatment for lower genital tract malignancies, as some subpopulations within a tumor may be relatively chemosensitive and others may be less sensitive to chemotherapy and more sensitive to radiation.

The development of resistant tumor cell subpopulations by the selection of clones with *defective cell death pathways* explains the cross-resistance seen between radiation therapy and chemotherapy (Figure 17–3). In vitro studies clearly demonstrate that tumor cells that have been irradiated are chemoresistant, and tumor cells that have been treated with chemotherapy are radioresistant.[10,11] Clinically, tumors that recur in an irradiated field are chemoresistant, regardless of the mechanism of action of the antineoplastic agent.[12] This concept also explains the observation that the *sequential* administration of chemotherapy followed by irradiation is no more efficacious than irradiation alone.[13] Chemotherapy could be expected to select for clones that have a defective cell death pathway, rendering them resistant to subsequent radiation therapy. Given the central role of radiation in the treatment for lower genital tract malignancies, an understanding of the cellular and clinical interactions

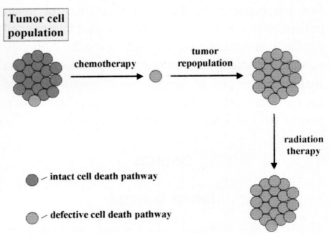

Figure 17–3. Possible mechanism for cross-resistance between chemotherapy and radiation therapy.

between chemotherapy and radiation is crucial to correctly plan treatment.

The concept of a defective cell death pathway may also partially explain the general chemoresistance observed with female lower genital tract malignancies. The common etiologic factor shared by the majority of these malignancies is the human papillomavirus (HPV). Malignant transformation by the HPV virus requires integration into the host genome. Integrated HPV deoxyribonucleic acid (DNA) has been demonstrated in over 90 percent of cervical carcinomas,[14] in 40 to 60 percent of vulvar carcinomas,[15,16] and in 70 percent of vaginal carcinomas.[17] This transformation causes loss of normal *P53* and *RB* function, one of the results of which is a dysfunctional cell death pathway (Figure 17–4). Carcinomas that do not contain integrated HPV DNA frequently have *P53* mutations, again resulting in an aberrant cell death pathway.[18,19] A dysfunctional cell death pathway may be one explanation for the global insensitivity of lower genital tract malignancies to chemotherapy. These tumors are generally radiation sensitive, however, and this may be a result of the relatively higher cell death "triggering" damage that can be delivered with ionizing radiation, compared with chemotherapy. Indeed, cells with a faulty cell death pathway that are resistant to standard-dose chemotherapy do respond when subjected to much higher concentrations of the same agent.[20] Additionally, this concept may partially explain the superiority of chemoradiation, compared with radiation therapy alone, in that the combined treatments are able to bring about a cell death–inducing level of molecular damage that cannot be achieved by either treatment alone.

Applications

Any cancer treatment, including chemotherapy, may be divided into two distinct approaches. The first is curative, with the goal being complete and permanent tumor eradication. The second is noncurative or palliative, where the goal is to prolong survival and improve quality of life. Given these distinctly different treatment goals, the aggressiveness of the treatment and the desired treatment outcomes of these two approaches are quite dissimilar.

Chemotherapy may be used at multiple points in the cancer treatment sequence. For the curative treat-

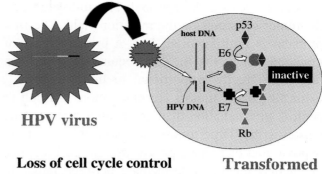

Loss of cell cycle control
Loss of apoptosis
Transformation/carcinogenesis

Figure 17–4. Human papillomavirus (HPV) infection and cellular transformation. Transformation requires infection of the host cell and integration of HPV DNA into the host genome. E6 and E7 counteract the guardian functions of RB and *P53*, allowing transformation to take place.

ment of lower genital tract malignancies, chemotherapy is generally used in three different ways. *Adjuvant* chemotherapy is given to improve survival or tumor control after the primary treatment (surgery or radiation) has been administered. Adjuvant chemotherapy for lower genital tract malignancies has been investigated but should not be considered the standard of care. *Neoadjuvant* chemotherapy refers to the administration of chemotherapy to patients with advanced disease for whom primary surgical or radiation treatment approaches may be less than optimal. An example would be the administration of chemotherapy to patients with advanced-stage cervical cancer in an attempt to render them operative candidates. Another example is the administration of chemotherapy to patients with large cervical tumors to reduce tumor bulk prior to radiation therapy. Although intuitively appealing, this approach has not been demonstrated to be beneficial in the treatment for lower genital tract malignancies. *Chemoradiation* involves the use of chemotherapy concurrently with radiation therapy. Chemoradiation is now the standard of care for most stages of cervical cancer and will be discussed at length below.

Chemoradiation

Failure of radiation therapy to cure lower genital tract malignancies is the result of two factors: (1) failure to sterilize the local disease, and (2) inability to affect the tumor cells outside the radiation field. The first problem is multifactorial. It is a primary tenet of radiation therapy that the dose required to eradicate a tumor is directly proportional to tumor volume.[21] Clinically, bulky tumors are much more difficult to control with radiation than are smaller tumors. One reason is that large tumors are more likely to have hypoxic foci or to have poorly vascularized regions. Oxygen is the key intermediate between radiation and cell injury, and decreased tissue oxygen levels reduce the effectiveness of radiation. Additionally, bulky tumors are more likely to be heterogeneous and harbor cell subpopulations resistant to cytotoxic therapies. The second factor that limits the curative ability of radiation is its inability to treat tumor foci outside the radiation field. Regardless of how localized a tumor appears, some proportion of apparently localized tumors will have micrometastases. Both these limitations are potentially addressed by the use of chemoradiation.

Chemotherapy and radiation interact by "sensitization," whereby a synergistic therapeutic effect is obtained. Strictly speaking, however, few of the currently used agents in chemoradiation are true sensitizers. This term should be reserved for agents that replace oxygen as an intermediate (hypoxic sensitizers) or have metabolites that directly render DNA more sensitive to the damaging effects and increase the relative bioeffectiveness of radiation (Figure 17–5). "Chemoradiation" is generally a more appropriate term than "radiation-sensitizing chemotherapy." In addition to its ability to enhance the response of a tumor to radiation, administration of chemotherapy during primary radiation may sterilize micrometastases that are outside the radiation field.

Numerous mechanisms of chemotherapy-induced radiation sensitization have been proposed. The simultaneous administration of chemotherapy and radiation therapy results in both a decrease in the shoulder and an increase in the slope of the cell survival curve (Figure 17–6). The shoulder represents sublethal damage, and a decrease in the shoulder suggests that chemotherapy inhibits repair of this damage. The increased slope of the curve suggests an approved "efficiency" for the delivered radiation. This may be a result of tumor cell cycle synchroniza-

tion or arrest of the cell cycle at the radiation-sensitive late G_2- and M-phase by chemotherapy. Chemotherapy may also result in the recruitment of nonproliferating cells into the cell cycle. For certain agents, such as hydroxyurea and misonidazole, the specific mechanisms have been fairly well established.[22,23] For other agents, such as cisplatin or 5-fluorouracil (5-FU), the mechanisms are less well understood (Table 17–1).

Although the potential for significant adverse effects exists with the use of combined modality treatment, pelvic chemoradiation is usually well tolerated. The degree of reported acute toxicity from pelvic radiation and concurrent chemotherapy has been quite variable. The concurrent administration of chemotherapy and radiation moderately increases both hematologic and nonhematologic toxicities, the latter manifesting predominantly as acute bowel toxicity. The degree of toxicity is dependent on a number of factors, including radiation dose, fractionation, and schedule; chemotherapeutic agent(s), dose, and schedule; and underlying medical conditions. Importantly, however, the resulting toxicity from the majority of chemoradiation regimens is seldom life threatening, and the benefit from the combined approach far outweighs the toxicity. Even extended-field radiation therapy, which results in greater small bowel irradiation than pelvic radiation, is well tolerated when combined with concurrent chemotherapy.[24]

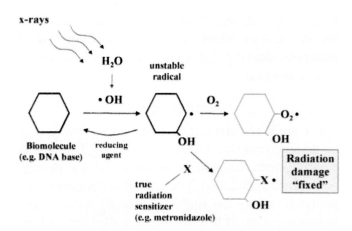

Figure 17–5. Role of oxygen and hypoxic (true) radiation sensitizers in radiation-induced cell injury. The unstable radical intermediate can undergo spontaneous "reversion" to the parent molecule. Oxygen or an electron affinic radiation sensitizer, such as metronidazole, makes permanent or "fixes" the radiation damage. This damage must then be enzymatically repaired or the cell will undergo a mutation and/or cell death.

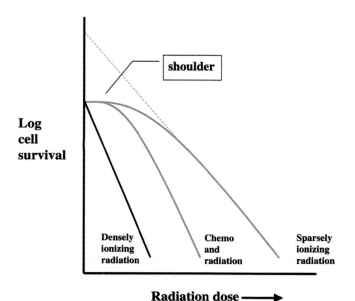

Log cell survival

shoulder

Densely ionizing radiation

Chemo and radiation

Sparsely ionizing radiation

Radiation dose ⟶

Figure 17–6. Survival curves for cells exposed to ionizing radiation. Radiation used for gynecologic malignancies is sparsely ionizing and results in a less steep cell kill slope and a "shoulder" region compared to densely ionizing radiation. The shoulder represents wasted radiation attributable to sublethal damage. The addition of concurrent chemotherapy to radiation reduces the shoulder and increases the slope of the cell survival curve compared to radiation alone.

The most active agents for use with the radiation of lower genital tract malignancies are mitomycin-C,[25] hydroxyurea,[26] 5-FU,[27] and cisplatin,[28] with cisplatin probably being the most important agent for this use. Other potential radiation "sensitizers" include paclitaxel,[29] carboplatin,[30] and gemcitabine.[31] The spe-

cific use of these agents will be discussed under Chemoradiation, below.

APPLICATIONS TO SPECIFIC TUMORS

Carcinoma of the Cervix

Adjuvant Therapy

The value of adjuvant therapy after radical hysterectomy for patients found to have high-risk factors at the time of surgery has been debated for years. Multiple risk factors have been identified, including positive pelvic nodes, positive margins, parametrial invasion, grade, cervical stromal invasion, lymph-vascular space invasion, and tumor size. Depending on the study, patients with one or more of these risk factors appear to be at an increased risk for recurrence.[32-34] Radiation therapy alone in these patients probably reduces the incidence of local and regional recurrences but does not affect survival. Despite the lack of definitive evidence, the standard approach for high-risk patients has been adjuvant pelvic radiation with or without vaginal brachytherapy. However, patients with these risk factors are at an increased risk for early, microscopic metastatic disease that will not be affected by pelvic radiotherapy. This fact underlies the rationale for using chemotherapy as an adjuvant therapy in this situation, either alone or in

Table 17–1. CHEMORADIATION AGENTS			
Agent	**Class**	**Cytotoxic Mechanism**	**Chemoradiation Mechanism**
Misonidazole	Nitroimidazole	Bioreductive agent (not cytotoxic to eukaryotic cells)	Hypoxic sensitizer (substitutes for oxygen in hypoxic tissues; interacts with radiation to form bioreactive radicals)
Mitomycin-C	Antitumor antibiotic	DNA cross-linking, leading to disruption of DNA synthesis	May preferentially kill hypoxic and, therefore, radioresistant cells
Hydroxyurea	Antimetabolite	Ribonucleotide reductase inhibition, leading to disruption of DNA synthesis	1. Cell cycle synchronization 2. Inhibition of radiation-induced DNA damage
5-Fluorouracil	Antimetabolite/pyrimidine antagonist	False pyrimidine inhibits thymidine synthesis, leading to disruption of DNA synthesis	Unknown "Sensitization" may be secondary to radiation enhancement of 5-FU cytotoxic mechanism
Cisplatin	Alkylating-like agent	DNA cross-linking, leading to disruption of DNA synthesis	Unknown Possible mechanisms: inhibition of the repair of sublethal damage; depletion of endogenous radioprotectors; enhancement of DNA cross-linkage

DNA = deoxyribonucleic acid; 5-FU = 5-fluorouracil.

combination with radiation. The majority of trials of adjuvant chemotherapy compare radiation alone versus chemotherapy *followed* by radiation, with the randomized trials showing no benefit with the addition of chemotherapy.[35,36] Conversely, a study comparing chemotherapy alone versus chemotherapy followed by radiation in high-risk surgically treated cervical cancers found no benefit with the addition of radiation therapy.[37] One randomized study compared observation versus radiation versus chemotherapy for high-risk patients after radical hysterectomy and found no improvement in recurrence rates or survival with either adjuvant treatment.[38] Such studies are generally difficult to conduct, as many physicians are hesitant to enroll high-risk patients in a study that has a "no-treatment" arm. Therefore, the true value of any adjuvant treatment for these patients will be difficult to establish.

The most significant study to date involving the use of chemotherapy in the adjuvant setting investigated the use of chemotherapy *concurrently* with radiation in high-risk patients after radical hysterectomy.[39] Patients with positive pelvic nodes, positive margins, or microscopic involvement of the parametria were randomized to radiation therapy alone versus radiation plus concurrent cisplatin/5-FU. Preliminary results have projected a statistically significant improved progression-free survival for the chemoradiation arm, with this survival being equal to historic controls of patients without risk factors. The mature results of this study are pending. However, on the basis of these preliminary data, the current standard of care for adjuvant therapy for patients found to have positive pelvic lymph nodes, positive margins, or microscopically positive parametria is chemoradiation therapy. Whether patients with other risk factors who are treated with radiation benefit from concurrent chemotherapy has not been established. The most appropriate agents and schedule are yet to be defined; on the basis of its central role in the chemoradiation of advanced-stage disease, cisplatin, either alone or in combination therapy, should be given.

Neoadjuvant Therapy

The use of chemotherapy in order to reduce the bulk of a tumor and improve its resectablity for surgery or curability with radiation therapy is attractive. This approach has been applied with varying degrees of success to tumors of the breast, gastrointestinal tract, and head and neck; it is logical to test this approach in carcinoma of the cervix. Neoadjuvant chemotherapy has been applied to carcinoma of the cervix in two different situations. The first is the use of chemotherapy to reduce the bulk of an advanced-stage or bulky early-stage tumor so that it may be surgically resected. When considering this approach, the physician must remember that the standard treatment for such tumors is radiation therapy. It is against this standard that neoadjuvant chemotherapy should be measured. Numerous studies have evaluated the efficacy of chemotherapeutic agents given prior to radical surgery, with the most active agents being cisplatin, ifosfamide, bleomycin, and vincristine, among others.[40] Response rates are in the range of 40 to 60 percent, depending on the tumor stage and the agents used. Most of these are phase II studies, although several randomized studies have also been conducted. Unfortunately, the majority of studies, to date, have not included radiation therapy as the principal modality in the control arm but, instead, have compared neoadjuvant chemotherapy plus radical surgery with radical surgery alone. Not surprisingly, neoadjuvant chemotherapy increases the operability of these tumors.

Several studies have included radiation in the control arm, and their results have been less than definitive. A European study compared chemotherapy followed by surgery and radiation therapy with surgery and radiation alone in stage Ib cervical cancers. The data showed improved survival in the former group for patients with bulky tumors.[41] Two randomized studies have compared neoadjuvant chemotherapy followed by radical surgery with radiation therapy alone in bulky cervical tumors. The first was conducted in stages Ib2 to III patients, and preliminary results have shown a survival benefit in the neoadjuvant chemotherapy surgery arm for patients with stages Ib2 to IIb tumors.[42] These results must be interpreted with caution, as the radiation dose given was low (70 Gy to point A). The results of a second study showed no difference between neoadjuvant chemotherapy/radical surgery and radiation therapy for bulky stage Ib and IIa tumors.[43] Additionally, an argument can be made that neoadjuvant chemotherapy/radical surgery should be compared with chemoradiation and not with radiation alone for these tumors, as this modality is emerging as the standard of care for most stage Ib2 and advanced-stage tumors.

It is important to consider that the need for radical surgery at all in these patients is questionable. Radiation therapy alone results in excellent pelvic control and survival in patients with bulky early-stage tumors, and radical surgery is only justified if it improves outcome, compared with radiation therapy alone. Indeed, radical surgery *followed* by radiation therapy offers no benefit, compared with radiation alone in stage Ib patients, and toxicity may be worsened by a combined approach.[44] Radical surgery also eliminates the ability to administer optimal brachytherapy and theoretically compromises the curative ability of radiation therapy. Until neoadjuvant chemotherapy and radical surgery are clearly shown to be superior to radiation therapy alone, this approach should be considered experimental. In countries where the facility to administer modern radiation therapy is limited, such an approach may be justified.

The second use of neoadjuvant chemotherapy involves the use of chemotherapy to reduce the bulk of an advanced-stage tumor prior to radiation, the rationale being that the ability to treat large tumor volumes is limited by the dose that can be delivered without injuring surrounding normal tissues (Figure 17–7). Numerous studies have shown that neoadjuvant chemotherapy followed by radiation is well tolerated. Unfortunately, these studies have shown this approach to have no benefit over radiation therapy alone. Several well-conducted randomized trials have compared neoadjuvant chemotherapy/radiation with radiation alone, with no improvement in pelvic control or survival with the addition of neoadjuvant chemotherapy.[45–50] Indeed, one study showed a worse outcome for patients in the neoadjuvant chemotherapy/radiation arm.[51] This is not surprising, as chemotherapy may select for tumor clones that are resistant to cell death, resulting in the repopulation of a tumor with cells that will not die in response to radiation therapy. On the basis of the current literature, neoadjuvant chemotherapy fol-

lowed by radiation cannot be recommended for the treatment for advanced-stage cervical cancer.

Chemoradiation

Pelvic radiation has been the standard curative treatment for bulky or locally advanced cervical tumors for over 50 years. The ability to cure patients with extensive, bulky tumors is primarily related to the ability to administer brachytherapy through the vagina. Additionally, cervical cancer has an orderly pattern of dissemination and, unlike many other tumors, does not usually disseminate early in its growth. These factors have led to cure rates as high as 40 percent in patients with stage IIIb disease. Unfortunately, cure rates using radiation therapy have not improved significantly since the introduction of megavoltage radiation in the 1950s. Large cervical tumors often cannot be cured because the dose of radiation required for disease control exceeds the dose that can be delivered according to the limits of normal tissue tolerance. This observation has prompted the development of numerous approaches to improve the efficacy of primary curative radiation therapy, including altered fractionation schedules, heavy particle irradiation, hyperthermia, and the administration of chemotherapy with radiation. The

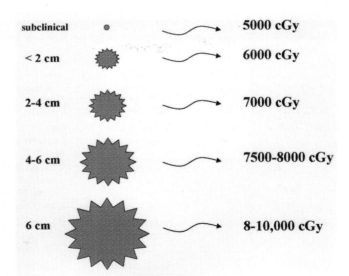

subclinical	5000 cGy
< 2 cm	6000 cGy
2-4 cm	7000 cGy
4-6 cm	7500-8000 cGy
6 cm	8-10,000 cGy

Figure 17–7. Relationship between tumor volume and tumoricidal radiation dose. The doses listed are those required to obtain tumor control 90 percent of the time in the area treated. (Adapted from Wharton JT, Jones HW 3rd, Day TG Jr, et al. Preirradiation celiotomy and extended field irradiation for invasive carcinoma of the cervix. Obstet Gynecol 1977;49:333–8.)

only approach that has thus far been shown to be efficacious is the *concurrent* administration of chemotherapy with radiation (chemoradiation). This approach was initially supported by evidence in several nongynecologic malignancies that chemotherapy may improve the efficacy of radiation therapy. Several studies suggest that chemoradiation improves local control in patients with squamous cell carcinoma of the head and neck,[52,53] and preoperative chemoradiation followed by continence-sparing resection has become the treatment standard for anal carcinomas.[54] Chemoradiation has been extensively studied in cervical cancer, with early studies demonstrating that several chemotherapeutic agents, including cisplatin, 5-FU, mitomycin-C, and hydroxyurea can safely be given concurrently with pelvic radiation.[55–58] However, not until the recent publication of several randomized collaborative trials has chemoradiation moved to the forefront in the treatment of cervical tumors. The results of the five trials (Table 17–2) prompted the National Cancer Institute (NCI) to issue a clinical announcement recommending that "strong consideration should be given to the incorporation of concurrent cisplatin-based chemotherapy with radiation therapy in women who require radiation therapy for the treatment of cervical cancer."[59]

This is all the more significant, considering that the 1996 National Institutes of Health (NIH) Consensus Statement on Cervical Cancer concluded that "there is no evidence that hydroxyurea or any other concomitant chemotherapy agent should be incorporated into standard practice."[60]

The five studies mentioned above have addressed two important questions, the first of which is whether chemoradiation is better than radiation alone. Although an earlier randomized study (Gynecologic Oncology Group [GOG] protocol 4) showed improved survival for patients with stage III and IV disease receiving hydroxyurea and radiation, compared with radiation alone, the study has been criticized because of the low doses of radiation employed.[61] It prompted the further investigation of chemoradiation, but it was not felt to offer sufficient evidence to justify chemoradiation as standard treatment for these patients. The GOG protocol 123 investigated the use of weekly cisplatin in patients with stage Ib2, node-negative cervical cancers and found a statistically significant survival advantage (83% versus 74%) in the chemoradiation arm.[62] Although the radiation dose was somewhat on the low side (75 Gy to point A) in GOG 123, the combined regimen was well tolerated, and the median

Table 17–2. COLLABORATIVE CHEMORADIATION TRIALS FOR CERVICAL CANCER

Study	FIGO Stage	Control Group	Comparison Group Treatment		Relative Risk of Death in Comparison Group
			Agents and Dose	Schedule	
GOG 123[62]	Ib2	Radiation	Cisplatin 40 mg/m²	Weekly (max. 6 cycles)	0.54
GOG 120[65]	IIb–IVa	Radiation plus hydroxyurea	Arm 1 Cisplatin 40 mg/m² Arm 2 1. Cisplatin 50 mg/m² and 5-FU 4,000 mg/m² over 96 hours 2. Hydroxyurea 2 mg/m²	Arm 1 Weekly (max. 6 cycles) Arm 2 1. Every 3 weeks for 2 cycles 2. Twice weekly for 6 weeks	0.61
RTOG 90-01[63]	Ib2–IVa	Extended-field radiation	Cisplatin 75 mg/m² and 5-FU 4,000 mg/m² over 96 hours	Radiation therapy days 1 and 22	0.58
GOG 85[64]	IIb–IVa	Radiation plus hydroxyurea	1. Cisplatin 50 mg/m² 2. 5-FU 4,000 mg/m²	1. Radiation therapy days 1 & 29 2. Radiation therapy days 2 & 30	0.72
SWOG 8797/ GOG 109[39]	Ib, IIa	Radiation	Cisplatin 70 mg/m² and 5-FU 4,000 mg/m² over 96 hours	Every 3 weeks for 4 cycles	0.5

Adapted from Thomas GM. Improved treatment for cervical cancer—concurrent chemotherapy and radiotherapy. N Engl J Med 1999;340:1198–200.
FIGO = International Federation of Gynecology and Obstetrics; 5-FU = 5-fluorouracil.

treatment time was not prolonged (50 days). It is important to recall that prolonged treatment time is a strong independent predictor of negative outcome in patients being treated with radiation for cervical cancer. The Radiation Therapy Onology Group (RTOG) protocol 90-01 randomized patients with stages Ib2 to IVa disease and negative para-aortic lymph nodes to pelvic chemoradiation with cisplatin and 5-FU or extended-field radiation and found improved 5-year survival in the chemoradiation group (73% versus 58%).[63] This study used aggressive doses of radiation (85 Gy to point A). Again, the combined regimen was well tolerated, and the median treatment time was not prolonged. With subset analysis, no difference was observed between treatment arms in patients with stage III and stage IV disease, although the study was not specifically designed to detect a significant difference within different subsets. The final study in this group to compare chemoradiation with radiation alone was the SWOG protocol 8797, which investigated the use of chemoradiation in patients with high-risk factors following radical hysterectomy. As noted in the previous section, the addition of chemotherapy to radiation therapy in these patients improved survival.

The second important question to be addressed in the chemoradiation of cervical cancer is which drugs/regimens, dose, and schedule are the most efficacious. Many agents have been purported to have activity as radiation sensitizers, but GOG 85 and GOG 120 have clearly demonstrated the superiority of cisplatin-containing regimens for the chemoradiation of cervical cancer. On the basis of the results of GOG 4, hydroxyurea had been noted to be an important agent for use in the chemoradiation therapy for cervical cancer. Because of the criticism of this study, GOG 85 sought to compare pelvic radiation and hydroxyurea with pelvic radiation and cisplatin/5-FU in patients with stages IIb to IVa disease.[64] This study showed the latter regimen to be more efficacious. Similarly, GOG 120 compared radiation plus weekly cisplatin versus cisplatin/ 5-fluorouracil/hydroxyurea versus hydroxyurea alone and found improved survival in the cisplatin-containing arms, compared with the hydroxyurea arm.[65] These two studies have established cisplatin as the cornerstone of treatment in the chemoradia-

tion of cervical cancer. Additionally, the poorer survival in the hydroxyurea groups, as well as the increased toxicity seen in the hydroxyurea-containing combination regimens, suggests that this drug should not be used in the chemoradiation therapy of cervical cancer.

The role of 5-FU in the chemoradiation therapy for cervical cancer has yet to be clarified. 5-FU is the cornerstone of chemoradiation therapy for squamous cell carcinomas of the head and neck and carcinomas of the anus. Therefore, its use in cervical cancer is logical. Although the initial studies with bolus 5-FU and radiation therapy failed to demonstrate improved response rates in cervical cancer, there was renewed interest when Byfield and colleagues demonstrated a synergistic effect with 5-FU continuous infusion.[66] They showed that to achieve radiosensitization, cells had to be exposed to 5-FU for at least 48 hours after radiation therapy was administered. This observation has led to the use of prolonged intravenous infusions (PVI) in combination with radiation for the treatment of cervical cancer. The PVI 5-FU is usually administered at a dose of 1,000 $mg/m^2/d$ for 96 hours every 3 to 4 weeks during radiation therapy. Many studies have evaluated chemoradiation with PVI 5-FU, although most centers administer it in combination with other agents. One randomized study evaluated the addition of PVI 5-FU to standard and hyperfractionated radiation therapy and found no benefit from the addition of 5-FU.[67] A subset analysis did demonstrate a statistically significant difference in disease-free survival in patients with stages Ib and IIa who received 5-FU. The GOG 165 is currently attempting to clarify the role of 5-FU in the chemoradiation therapy of cervical cancer. This study compares radiation alone with radiation plus weekly cisplatin and with radiation plus PVI 5-FU. This study is still in the accrual phase, and preliminary results are not yet available. Even if the cisplatin arm is found to be superior, GOG 165 still does not address whether 5-FU with cisplatin is superior to cisplatin alone. Only a randomized trial comparing the two regimens can clarify the issue.

Although continuous infusion has been established as the administration method of choice for 5-FU as a radiation sensitizer, this method is costly and inconvenient and exposes the patient to the risks associated with a long-term, indwelling intravenous catheter. The ability to establish prolonged tissue levels of 5-FU without these drawbacks would, therefore, be desirable. The oral fluoropyrimidine UFT has been approved recently for clinical trials in the United States. This drug is an oral anticancer agent that is a combination of tegafur and uracil in a 1:4 molar ratio. Tegafur is the prodrug of 5-FU and is combined with uracil to inhibit the rapid breakdown of 5-FU. Data from Europe and Japan, as well as preliminary studies from the United States, suggest that UFT is as efficacious as intravenous 5-FU, with fewer side effects.[68,69] The dose-limiting toxicity appears to be diarrhea, and no bone marrow suppression, neurotoxicity, or mucositis is seen. UFT, in combination with leucovorin (Orzel), has been tested as a radiation sensitizer in rectal carcinoma but has yet to be studied in gynecologic malignancies.[70] Evidence, to date, suggests that UFT would be a reasonable radiation sensitizer in cervical cancer and offers improved ease of administration and potentially less toxic side effects.

Despite its central role in the chemoradiation of cervical cancer, the optimal dose and schedule of cisplatin in combination with radiation is yet to be determined. Table 17–2 lists the doses and schedules for the most recent cooperative group trials. Cisplatin is typically administered either weekly at a dose of 40 to 50 mg/m^2 or at 3-week intervals at a dose of 50 to 75 mg/m^2 for two to three cycles. The literature, to date, is not sufficient to establish the optimal dose and schedule of cisplatin. However, the RTOG 90-01 trial used three cycles of a relatively high dose of cisplatin in combination with PVI 5-FU and demonstrated acceptable toxicity. This is despite the fact that aggressive doses of radiation were administered. Given the good tolerance of this aggressive regimen, it is appealing to apply it outside the research setting. Conversely, given the excellent tolerance and the greater ease of administration (less hydration required) of lower-dose weekly cisplatin, this regimen is also attractive. The current literature is unable to clarify this issue; until the appropriate randomized studies are performed, the choice of agent(s), dose, and schedule is based on physician preference.

The role of other chemotherapeutic agents in the chemoradiation of cervical cancer is also unclear. Taxol, carboplatin, and gemcitabine have been shown to be adequate radiation sensitizers, and phase II studies have found the first two agents to be well tolerated in combination with pelvic radiation for cervical cancer.[29,30] Carboplatin is particularly appealing because of its better toxicity profile and ease of administration than those of cisplatin. Gemcitabine is an especially potent radiation sensitizer, so much so that its application as a radiation sensitizer in the treatment of some malignancies has led to unacceptable toxicity.[71] A phase I study using gemcitabine with pelvic radiation for treating cervical cancer is currently under way. Regardless of the activity of these agents, until they are compared directly with cisplatin in a randomized fashion, cisplatin-based chemoradiation remains the standard of care for most patients with cervical cancer.

In conclusion, the following patients should receive cisplatin/cisplatin-based chemotherapy concurrently with radiation:

1. Stage Ib1 or Ib2 patients found to have positive pelvic nodes, positive margins, or positive pelvic lymph nodes after radical hysterectomy
2. Stages Ib2 to IVa patients undergoing primary curative radiation therapy

Carcinoma of the Vulva

The principal application of chemotherapy to the treatment of invasive vulvar cancer is its concurrent administration with radiation therapy. Similar to that for cervical cancer, the primary treatment for vulvar cancer is surgery, radiation, or a combination of the two. However, unlike cervical cancer, the vast majority of vulvar cancers are candidates for primary curative surgical resection, which usually consists of wide radical resection/vulvectomy and inguinal lymph node dissection. Adjuvant radiation is generally reserved for patients with poor prognostic factors determined by surgical staging (eg, positive nodes or positive margins). Radiation therapy is also administered as primary treatment to patients with locally advanced, inoperable disease (Figure 17–8). Other patients may technically be operative candidates, but surgical resection would require urethra/bladder resection or aproctectomy. In these patients, radiation therapy, either alone or followed by surgical resection, offers similar tumor control rates to radical surgery, with the benefit of improved functional outcomes.[72] Given the proven efficacy of chemoradiation in the continence-sparing management of squamous cell carcinoma of the anus, it is logical to extend this approach to locally advanced vulvar cancers.

The use of chemoradiation to treat locally advanced vulvar cancer is not a new concept. Boronow and colleagues first reported the use of radiation alone in the treatment of advanced vulvar cancer in 1987.[73] This was followed by a study by Thomas and colleagues, who administered concurrent 5-FU/mitomycin-C/radiation to advanced vulvar cancer patients and found the regimen to be efficacious and well tolerated.[74] Numerous similar studies have followed, with the vast majority corroborating Thomas' initial finding.[75-78] Specifically,

patients with advanced vulvar cancers (T3 or T4 primary tumors) treated with primary chemoradiation were found to have high response rates (> 80% with 30 to 50% surgical complete responders) and manageable acute toxicity. Importantly, exenterative surgery was avoided in all but a small fraction (< 10%) of patients. Whether survival is improved relative to radical surgery alone has not been clearly established. However, given the improved cosmetic and functional outcome with preoperative radiation/chemoradiation and at least similar survival results to historic controls treated with radical surgery, primary radiation/chemoradiation should be considered the treatment of choice in patients with advanced vulvar cancer.

Whether the addition of concurrent chemotherapy to radiation therapy in these patients is superior to radiation alone has not been established. This question is difficult to answer because of the rarity of advanced vulvar cancers and the subsequent diffi-

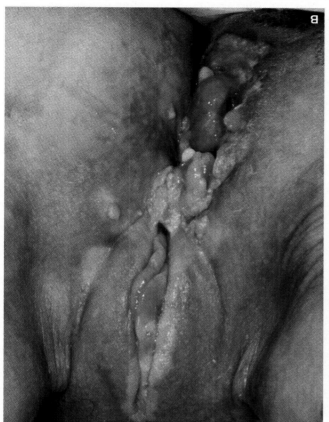
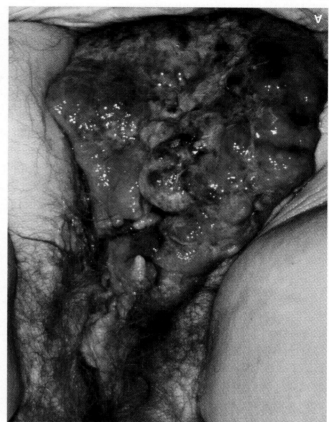

Figure 17-8. Large vulvar cancer before and after chemoradiation. A, Large squamous cell carcinoma of the vulva. The tumor involved the anal verge and distal vagina. B, The same patient 2 weeks after completing 40 Gy to the pelvis, inguinal lymph nodes, and vulva with concurrent cisplatin and 5-fluorouracil.

vagina. Because patients with squamous cell carci-
treatment for squamous cell carcinoma of the
this author that chemoradiation is the preferred
rent chemotherapy and radiation, it is the opinion of
in vaginal cancer. Given the low toxicity of concur-
those conducted for cervical cancer, are not feasible
this malignancy, randomized clinical trials, such as
to chemotherapy.[84,85] Again, because of the rarity of
that untreated, advanced vaginal cancer is sensitive
vagina. Additionally, several case reports suggest
lar results should be expected for carcinoma of the
alone in carcinoma of the cervix suggests that simi-
the superiority of chemoradiation over radiation
them to the treatment of vaginal cancer. Specifically,
data from cervical chemoradiation studies and apply
and vaginal cancers, it is tempting to extrapolate
larities in the biology and natural history of cervical
superior with radiation alone. On the basis of simi-
approach, and functional outcomes are generally
stage II or greater disease requires an exenterative
tum, primary surgical resection of patients with
due to the close proximity of the bladder and the rec-
patients are candidates for conservative surgery, but
interstitial brachytherapy. Selected, early-stage
including both external-beam pelvic radiation and
the majority of vaginal cancers is radiation therapy,
cent of vaginal cancers. The standard treatment for
squamous cell carcinoma, which makes up 90 per-
are lacking. This discussion will be restricted to
the use of chemotherapy in its curative management
This is a very rare malignancy, and data regarding

Carcinoma of the Vagina

tigated before recommending this approach as standard treatment.

ity of chemoradiation needs to be thoroughly inves-
proven adjuvant treatment (radiation). The feasibil-
thereby limiting the curative effectiveness of the
ment delays and possible treatment termination,
problematic. Increased toxicity could result in treat-
tion of chemotherapy to radiation in these patients is
ation therapy following radical resection, the addi-
increased risk of skin and wound toxicity with radi-
of this approach has not been tested. Given the
tion alone in these high-risk patients, the superiority
appealing to give chemoradiation in place of radia-

considered investigational only. Although it is
risk, postresection vulvar cancer patients should be
alone, the use of adjuvant chemotherapy for high
chemoresistance of vulvar cancer to chemotherapy
ting has been well established.[82,83] Given the overall
section. The efficacy of radiation therapy in this set-
the time of radical resection and inguinal node dis-
positive inguinal nodes or positive vulvar margins at
the treatment of choice for patients found to have
been extensively studied. Radiation therapy has been
risk factors at the time of surgical resection has not
setting for early-stage patients found to have high
The use of chemotherapy alone in the adjuvant
cell carcinoma of the vulva.

mended for patients with locally advanced squamous
followed by conservative surgery is strongly recom-
tion therapy with 5-FU and cisplatin/mitomycin-C
Taking all this information as a whole, chemoradia-
carcinoma, the results of which are still pending.
with 5-FU/cisplatin with radiation for treating anal
domized study that compares 5-FU/mitomycin-C
appealing. The RTOG is currently undertaking a ran-
making the choice of the former regimen more
5-FU is generally less toxic than mitomycin-C/5-FU,
nation for either malignancy is unsettled. Cisplatin/
anal and vulvar cancers, and the optimal drug combi-
combination with 5-FU in the chemoradiation of both
latter regimen.[81] Cisplatin is also used extensively in
and mitomycin-C showed improved outcome with the
patients to chemoradiation with 5-FU versus 5-FU
However, a study in anal cancer which randomized
outcome in vulvar cancer has not been established.
Whether the addition of other agents improves the
the chemoradiation studies in vulvar cancer.
anal cancer and has been included in the majority of
is the cornerstone of chemoradiation therapy for
ation therapy of advanced vulvar cancer. PVI 5-FU
ing the chemotherapeutic agents for the chemoradi-
studies in anal cancer have been relied on in choos-
radiation alone.[79,80] Additionally, chemoradiation
free survival with chemoradiation, compared with
demonstrate improved local control and disease-
atively more prevalent disease. These studies clearly
squamous cell carcinoma of the anus, which is a rel-
have been developed by extrapolating from studies of
treatment approaches for advanced vulvar cancer
culty in performing randomized clinical trials. Most

noma of the vagina are generally older than cervical cancer patients, they may not tolerate chemoradiation as well. Therefore, individualization of treatment plans is recommended. Considering the evidence in cervical cancer, cisplatin, either alone or in combination, should be included in the treatment.

The use of chemotherapy in the curative treatment of vaginal cancer should be limited to chemoradiation. Given the lack of efficacy of neoadjuvant chemotherapy/radiation in cervical cancer, this approach cannot be recommended for vaginal cancer. Chemotherapy may be appropriate as primary treatment in patients with advanced vaginal cancer who have contraindications to radiation therapy, but the likelihood of sustained remission is low.

FUTURE DIRECTIONS

Despite improvements in conventional therapy, it is apparent that a relative plateau has been reached in the curative management of lower genital tract malignancies. Although chemoradiation represents a positive step forward, a significant proportion of patients with these malignancies experience treatment failures. Many promising, innovative approaches have been proposed to reduce the failure rate of conventional treatment. These approaches include the use of biologic response modifiers, chemomodulators, molecular mediators/inhibitors, immunotherapy, and gene therapy (see Table 17–2). All these approaches have their own merits but are limited by the same factor that limits traditional therapy. This factor is tumor heterogeneity. As Novell proposed, acquired genetic variability within tumor cell clones, in combination with host selection pressures, lead to several subpopulations of cells with different growth advantage mechanisms. Although each of these alternative approaches potentially addresses mechanisms that are bypassed by traditional therapies, the variety of growth advantage mechanisms within a heterogeneous tumor are unlikely to be addressed by any one treatment. Thus, a singular "cure" for cancer is unlikely.

As has been evidenced by the impact of the Papanicolaou test, efforts to improve screening and early detection are the most important mechanisms to impact the overall death rates from lower genital tract malignancies. Fortunately, adequate screening exists for cervical, vaginal (Pap smear), and vulvar (pelvic examination) cancers. Increased compliance with screening recommendations and improvements in the accuracy of screening mechanisms (eg, ThinPrep Pap smear) are likely to further reduce death rates from these malignancies. Additionally, efforts to develop HPV vaccines are under way, with the hope of someday preventing infection with this virus, which is responsible for the majority of lower genital tract malignancies. In the meantime, the cancer research community will continue to attempt to optimize conventional treatment modalities and integrate them into innovative therapies in order to advance our treatment outcomes beyond our current plateau.

REFERENCES

1. Evan GI, Whyte M, Harrington E. Apoptosis and the cell cycle. Curr Opin Cell Biol 1995;7:825–34.
2. Lotem J, Sachs L. Regulation by *bcl-2, c-myc,* and p53 of susceptibility to induction of apoptosis by heat shock and cancer chemotherapy compounds in differentiation-competent and -defective myeloid leukemic cells. Cell Growth Differ 1993;4:41–7.
3. Hsu B, Marin MC, Brisbay S, et al. Expression of *bcl-2* gene confers multidrug resistance to chemotherapy-induced cell death. Cancer Bull 1994;46:125–9.
4. Siles E, Villabos M, Valenzuela MT, et al. Relationship between p53 status and radiosensitivity in human tumor cell lines. Br J Cancer 1996;73:581–8.
5. Mano Y, Kikuchi Y, Yamamoto K, et al. Bcl-2 as a predictor of chemosensitivity and prognosis in primary epithelial ovarian cancer. Eur J Cancer 1999; 35:1214–9.
6. Krajewski S, Blomqvist C, Franssila K, et al. Reduced expression of proapototic gene BAX is associated with poor response rates to combination chemotherapy and shorter survival in women with metastatic breast adenocarcinoma. Cancer Res 1995;55:4471–8.
7. Gurnani M, Lipari P, Dell J, et al. Adenovirus-mediated p53 gene therapy has a greater efficacy when combined with chemotherapy against human head and neck, ovarian, prostate, and breast cancer. Cancer Chemother Pharmacol 1999;44:143–51.
8. Dorigo O, Turla ST, Lebedeva S, Gjerset RA. Sensitization of rat glioblastoma multiforme to cisplatin in vivo following restoration of wild-type p53 function. J Neurosurg 1998;88:535–40.
9. Nowell PC. The clonal evolution of tumor cell populations. Science 1976;194:23–8.

10. Osmak M, Perovic S. Multiple fractions of gamma rays induced resistance to cis-dichloro-diammineplatinum (II) and methotrexate in human HeLa cells. Int J Radiat Oncol Biol Phys 1989;16:1537–41.

11. Aref A, Mohammad R, Yudelev M, et al. Radiobiological characterization of two human chemotherapy-resistant intermediate grade non-Hodgkin's lymphoma cell lines. Radiol Oncol Invest 1999;7:158–62.

12. Brader KR, Morris M, Levenback C, et al. Chemotherapy for cervical carcinoma: factors determining response and implications for clinical trial design. J Clin Oncol 1998;16:1879–84.

13. Shueng PW, Hsu WL, Jen YM, et al. Neoadjuvant chemotherapy followed by radiotherapy should not be a standard approach for locally advanced cervix cancer. Int J Radiat Oncol Biol Phys 1998;40:889–96.

14. International Agency for Reseach on Cancer. Human papillomaviruses. IARC Monogr Eval Carcinog Risks Hum 1995;64:1–409.

15. Madeline MM, Darling JR, Carter JJ, et al. Cofactors with human papillomavirus in a population-based study of vulvar cancer. J Natl Cancer Inst 1997; 89:1516–23.

16. Iwasawa A, Nieminen P, Lehtinen M, et al. Human papillomavirus in squamous cell carcinoma of the vulva by polymerase chain reaction. Obstet Gynecol 1997;89:81–4.

17. Ikenberg H, Runge M, Goppinger A, et al. Human papillomavirus DNA in invasive carcinoma of the vagina. Obstet Gynecol 1990;76:432–8.

18. Kagie MJ, Kenter GG, Tollenaar RA, et al. P53 overexpression is common and independent of human papillomavirus infection in squamous cell carcinoma of the vulva. Cancer 1997;80:1228–33.

19. Skomedal H, Kristensen G, Helland A, et al. TP53 gene mutations and protein accumulation in primary vaginal carcinoma. Br J Cancer 1995;72:129–33.

20. Griswold DP, Trader MW, Frei E, et al. Response of drug-sensitive and -resistant L1210 leukemias to high-dose chemotherapy. Cancer Res 1987;47:2323–7.

21. Fletcher GH. Clinical dose-response curves of human malignant epithelial tumors. Br J Radiol 1973;6:1–12.

22. Fu KK. Biological basis for the interaction of chemotherapeutic agents and radiation therapy. Cancer 1985;55:2123–30.

23. Lafleur MV, Pluijmackers-Westmijze EJ, Loman H. Effect of radiation-induced reduction of nitroimidazoles on biologically active DNA. Int J Radiat Oncol Biol Phys 1986;12:1211–4.

24. Malfetano JH, Keys H, Cunningham MJ, et al. Extended field radiation and cisplatin for stage IIB and IIIB cervical carcinoma. Gynecol Oncol 1997;67:203–7.

25. Levin W, Goldberg G, Altaras M, et al. The use of concomitant chemotherapy and radiotherapy prior to surgery in advanced stage carcinoma of the vulva. Gynecol Oncol 1986;25:20–5.

26. Hreshchyshyn MM, Aron BS, Boronow RC, et al. Hydroxyurea or placebo combined with radiation to treat stages IIIB and IV cervical cancer confined to the pelvis. Int J Radiat Oncol Biol Phys 1979;5:317–22.

27. Goolsby CD, Daly JW, Skinner OD, et al. Combination of 5-fluorouracil and radiation as primary therapy of carcinoma of the cervix. Obstet Gynecol 1968; 32:674–6.

28. Choo YC, Choy TK, Wong LC, et al. Potentiation of radiotherapy by cis-dichlorodiammine platinum (II) in advanced cervical carcinoma. Gynecol Oncol 1986;23:94–100.

29. Chen MD, Paley PJ, Potish RA, et al. Phase I trial of taxol as a radiation sensitizer with cisplatin in advanced cervix cancer. Gynecol Oncol 1997;67:131–6.

30. Muderspach LI, Curtin JP, Roman LD, et al. Carboplatin as a radiation sensitizer in locally advanced cervical cancer: a pilot study. Gynecol Oncol 1997;65:336–42.

31. Milas L, Fuji T, Hunter N, et al. Enhancement of tumor radioresponse in vivo by gemcitabine. Cancer Res 1999;59:107–14.

32. Fuller AF, Elliott N, Kosloff C, et al. Determinants of increased risk for recurrence in patients undergoing radical hysterectomy for stage IB and IIA carcinoma of the cervix. Gynecol Oncol 1989;33:34–9.

33. Kamura T, Tsukamoto N, Tsuruchi N, et al. Multivariate analysis of histopathologic prognostic factors of cervical cancer in patients undergoing radical hysterectomy. Cancer 1992;69:181–6.

34. Delgado G, Bundy B, Zaino R, et al. Prospective surgical-pathological study of disease-free interval in patients with stage IB squamous cell carcinoma of the cervix: a Gynecologic Oncology Group study. Gynecol Oncol 1990;38:352–7.

35. Tattersall MHN, Ramirez C, Coppleson M. A randomized trial of adjuvant chemotherapy after radical hysterectomy in stage IB-IIA cervical cancer patients with pelvic lymph node metastases. Gynecol Oncol 1992;46:176–81.

36. Kumar L, Kaushal M, Nandy B, et al. Chemotherapy followed by radiotherapy versus radiotherapy alone in locally advanced cervical cancer: a randomized study. Gynecol Oncol 1994;54:307–15.

37. Curtin JP, Hoskins WJ, Venkatraman ES, et al. Adjuvant chemotherapy versus chemotherapy plus pelvic irradiation for high-risk cervical cancer patients after radical hysterectomy and pelvic lymphadenectomy (RH-PLND): a randomized phase III trial. Gynecol Oncol 1996;61:3–10.

38. Lahousen M, Haas J, Pickel H, et al. Chemotherapy versus radiotherapy versus observation for high-risk cervical carcinoma after radical hysterectomy: a randomized, prospective multicenter trial. Gynecol Oncol 1999;73:196–201.

39. Peters WA, Liu PY, Barrett R, et al. Cisplatin, 5-fluorouracil plus radiation therapy are superior to radiation therapy as adjunctive treatment in high-risk, early stage carcinoma of the cervix after radical hysterectomy and pelvic lymphadenectomy: report of a phase III inter-group study. Proc Soc Gynecol Oncol 1999;30:28.

40. Eddy GL Sr. Neoadjuvant chemotherapy before surgery in cervical cancer. Monogr Natl Cancer Inst 1996;21:93–9.

41. Sardi JE, Giaroli A, Sannes C, et al. Long-term follow-up of the first randomized trial using neoadjuvant chemotherapy in stage Ib squamous carcinoma of the cervix: the final results. Gynecol Oncol 1997;67:61–9.

42. Benedetti-Panici P, Landoni F, Greggi S, et al. Neoadjuvant chemotherapy (NACT) and radical surgery (RS) vs. exclusive radiotherapy (RT) in locally advanced squamous cell cervical cancer (LASCCC). Results from the Italian Multicenter Trial. Proc Soc Gynecol Oncol 1999;28:38.

43. Chang TC, Lai CH, Hong JH, et al. Randomized trial of neoadjuvant cisplatin, vincristine, bleomycin, and radical surgery versus radiation therapy for bulky IB and IIA cervical cancer. J Clin Oncol 2000;18:1740–7.

44. Morris M. Early cervical carcinoma: are two treatments better than one? [editorial]. Gynecol Oncol 1994;54:1–3.

45. Chauvergne J, Rohart J, Heron JF, et al. Randomized phase III trial of neo-adjuvant chemotherapy (CT) + radiotherapy (RT) in stage IIB, III carcinoma of the cervix (CACX): a cooperative study of the French oncology centers [abstract]. Proc Am Soc Clin Oncol 1988;7:136.

46. Tobias EJ, Buxton G, Blackledge JJ, et al. Neoadjuvant bleomycin, ifosfamide, and cisplatin in cervical cancer. Cancer Chemother Pharmacol 1990; 26 Suppl:59–62.

47. Souhami L, Gil RA, Allan SE, et al. A randomized trial of chemotherapy followed by pelvic radiation therapy in stage IIIb carcinoma of the cervix. J Clin Oncol 1991;9:970–977.

48. Cardenas J, Olguin A, Figueroa F, et al. Neoadjuvant chemotherapy (CT) + radiotherapy vs. radiotherapy alone in stage IIIb cervical carcinoma: preliminary results [abstract]. Proc Am Soc Clin Oncol 1992;11:232.

49. Kumar L, Kaushal R, Nandy M, et al. Chemotherapy followed by radiotherapy versus radiotherapy alone in locally advanced cervical cancer: a randomized study. Gynecol Oncol 1994;54:307–15.

50. Sundfor K, Trope CG, Hogberg T, et al. Radiotherapy and neoadjuvant chemotherapy for cervical carcinoma: a randomized multicenter study of sequential cisplatin and 5-fluorouracil and radiotherapy in advanced cervical carcinoma stage 3B and 4A. Cancer 1996;77:2371–8.

51. Tattersal MHN, Lorvidhaya V, Vootiprux V, et al. Randomized trial of epirubicin and cisplatin chemotherapy followed by pelvic radiation in locally advanced cervical cancer. J Clin Oncol 1995;13:444–51.

52. Herskovic A, Martz K, Al-Sarraf M, et al. Combined chemotherapy and radiotherapy compared with radiotherapy alone in patients with cancer of the esophagus. N Engl J Med 1992;326:1593–8.

53. Bosset J, Gignoux M, Triboulet J, et al. Chemoradiotherapy followed by surgery compared with surgery alone in squamous-cell cancer of the esophagus. N Engl J Med 1997;337:161–7.

54. Minsky BD, Cohen AM, Enker WE, et al. Pre-operative 5-FU, low dose leucovorin, and concurrent radiation therapy for rectal cancer. Cancer 1993;73:273–8.

55. Choo YC, Choy YK, Wong LC, et al. Potentiation of radiotherapy by cis-dichlorodiammine platinum (II) in advanced cervical carcinoma. Gynecol Oncol 1986;23:94–100.

56. Goolsby CD, Daly JW, Skinner OD, et al. Combination of 5-fluorouracil and radiation as primary therapy of carcinoma of the cervix. Obstet Gynecol 1968; 32:674–6.

57. Ludgate SM, Crandon AJ, Hudson CN, et al. Synchronous 5-fluorouracil, mitomycin-C and radiation therapy in the treatment of locally advanced carcinoma of the cervix. Int J Radiat Oncol Biol Phys 1988;15:893–9.

58. Hreshchyshyn MM. Hydroxyurea with irradiation for cervical carcinoma—a preliminary report. Cancer Chemother Rep 1968;52:601–2.

59. National Cancer Institute. Concurrent chemoradiation for cervical cancer. Clinical Announcement, Washington, D.C., February 22, 1999.

60. National Cancer Institute. Cervical cancer. NIH Consens Statement 1996;14:1–38.

61. Hreshchyshyn MM, Aron BS, Boronow RC, et al. Hydroxyurea or placebo combined with radiation to treat stages IIIB and IV cervical cancer confined to the pelvis. Int J Radiat Oncol Biol Phys 1979;5: 317–22.

62. Keys HM, Bundy BN, Stehman FB, et al. Cisplatin, radiation, and adjuvant hysterectomy compared with radiation and adjuvant hysterectomy for bulky stage Ib cervical carcinoma. N Engl J Med 1999; 340:1154–61.

63. Morris M, Eifel P, Lu J, et al. Pelvic radiation with concurrent chemotherapy compared with pelvic and para-aortic radiation for high-risk cervical cancer. N Engl J Med 1999;340:1137–43.

64. Whitney CW, Sause W, Bundy BN, et al. Randomized comparison of fluorouracil plus cisplatin versus hydroxyurea as an adjunct to radiation therapy in stage IIB-IVA carcinoma of the cervix with negative

para-aortic lymph nodes: a Gynecologic Oncology Group and Southwest Oncology Group study. J Clin Oncol 1999;17:1339–48.

65. Rose PG, Bundy BN, Watkins EB, et al. Concurrent cisplatin-based radiotherapy and chemotherapy for locally advanced cervical cancer. N Engl J Med 1999;340:1144–53.

66. Byfield JE, Calabro-Jones P, Klisak I, et al. Pharmacologic requirements for obtaining sensitization of human tumor cells *in vitro* to combined 5-fluorouracil or ftorafur and x-rays. Int J Radiat Oncol Biol Phys 1982;8:1923–33.

67. Thomas G, Dembo A, Ackerman I, et al. A randomized trial of standard versus partially hyperfractionated radiation with or without concurrent 5-fluorouracil in locally advanced cervical cancer. Gynecol Oncol 1998;69:137–45.

68. Sulkes A, Benner SE, Canetta RM. Uracil-ftorafur: an oral fluoropyrimidine active in colorectal cancer. J Clin Oncol 1998;16:3461–75.

69. Hoff PM, Royce M, Medgyesy D, et al. Oral fluoropyrimidines. Semin Oncol 1999;26:640–6.

70. Hoff PM, Lassere Y, Pazdur R, et al. Preoperative UFT and calcium folinate and radiotherapy in rectal cancer. Oncology (Huntingt) 1999;13:129–31.

71. Lawrence TS, Eisbruch A, McGinn CJ, et al. Radiosensitization by gemcitabine. Oncology (Huntingt) 1999;13:55–60.

72. Nigro ND. An evaluation of combined therapy for squamous cell cancer of the anal canal. Dis Colon Rectum 1984;27:763–6.

73. Boronow RC, Hickman BT, Reagan MT, et al. Combined therapy as an alternative to exenteration for locally advanced vulvovaginal cancer. Am J Clin Oncol 1987;10:171–81.

74. Thomas G, Dembo A, DePetrillo A, et al. Concurrent radiation and chemotherapy in vulvar carcinoma. Gynecol Oncol 1989;34:263–7.

75. Koh W, Wallace HJ, Greer BE, et al. Combined radiotherapy and chemotherapy in the management of local-regionally advanced vulvar cancer. Int J Radiat Oncol Biol Phys 1993;26:809–16.

76. Wahlen SA, Slater JD, Wagner RJ, et al. Concurrent radiation therapy and chemotherapy in the treatment of primary squamous cell carcinoma of the vulva. Cancer 1995;75:2289–94.

77. Eifel PJ, Morris M, Burke TW, et al. Prolonged continuous infusion cisplatin and 5-fluorouracil with radiation for locally advanced carcinoma of the vulva. Gynecol Oncol 1995;59:51–6.

78. Moore, DH, Thomas GM, Montana GS, et al. Preoperative chemoradiation for advanced vulvar cancer: a phase II study of the gynecologic oncology group. Int J Radiat Oncol Biol Phys 1998;42:79–85.

79. UKCCCR Anal Cancer Trial Working Party. Epidermoid anal cancer: results from the UKCCCR randomised trial of radiotherapy alone versus radiotherapy, 5-fluorouracil, and mitomycin. Lancet 1996;348:1049–54.

80. Bartelink H, Roelofsen F, Eschwege F, et al. Concomitant radiotherapy and chemotherapy is superior to radiotherapy alone in the treatment of locally advanced anal cancer: results of a phase III randomized trial of the European Organization for Research and Treatment of Cancer Radiotherapy and Gastrointestinal Cooperative Groups. J Clin Oncol 1997;15:2040–9.

81. Flam M, John M, Pajak TF, et al. Role of mitomycin in combination with fluorouracil and radiotherapy, and of salvage chemoradiation in the definitive nonsurgical treatment of epidermoid carcinoma of the anal canal: results of a phase III randomized intergroup study. J Clin Oncol 1996;14:2527–39.

82. Faul CM, Mirmow D, Huang Q, et al. Adjuvant radiation for vulvar carcinoma: improved local control. Int J Radiat Oncol Biol Phys 1997;38:381–9.

83. Homesley HD, Bundy BN, Sedlis A, et al. Radiation therapy versus pelvic node resection for carcinoma of the vulva with positive groin nodes. Obstet Gynecol 1986;68:733–40.

84. Katib S, Kuten A, Steiner M, et al. The effectiveness of multidrug treatment by bleomycin, methotrexate, and cis-platinum in advanced vaginal cancer. Gynecol Oncol 1985;21:101–2.

85. Kim DS, Moon H, Hwang YY, et al. Histologic disappearance of locally advanced vaginal cancer after combination chemotherapy. Gynecol Oncol 1990;38:144–5.

18

Post-treatment Surveillance

DIANE C. BODURKA, MD

Surveillance following primary cancer therapy is defined as the observation and follow-up of asymptomatic patients who are clinically free of disease. The goal of surveillance strategies is to detect recurrent disease at a point when therapeutic intervention may significantly prolong life. To date, the effectiveness of surveillance programs after treatment of gynecologic malignancies has not been well evaluated, especially in terms of prospective, randomized trials; no standard of care exists for this type of follow-up. This chapter addresses the post-treatment surveillance of carcinomas of the cervix, vagina, and vulva. Rates and patterns of recurrence, surveillance tools, imaging modalities, development of second primary concerns, and options for surveillance strategies will be presented for each tumor site.

CERVIX

The introduction of the Papanicolaou (Pap) smear test in the United States more than 50 years ago has led to a significant decline in both the incidence and number of deaths due to cervical cancer.[1] Nevertheless, this cancer remains one of the most common malignancies in women worldwide. It is estimated that in the year 2001, 12,900 new cervical cancer cases (2% of all new cancer cases in women) and 4,400 deaths due to the disease will occur in the United States.[2]

Rates and Patterns of Recurrence

Approximately 35 percent of patients having invasive cervical cancer will have persistent or recurrent disease after the completion of therapy. Seventy-five percent of cervical cancer recurrences occur within 2 years of the completion of therapy.[3] By the end of 5 years, 95 percent of patients having recurrent disease will have had a relapse.[4] In the great majority of patients, recurrent disease is incurable.

Cervical cancer may recur in one of three sites. Most commonly, it recurs on the sidewall of the pelvis, presumably in lymph node–bearing areas. Recurrence may also be seen in distant sites, such as para-aortic or other distal lymph node metastasis, lung metastasis, or bony metastasis (most commonly to the vertebral bodies). Finally, a small group of patients may have central pelvic recurrence. One of the crucial reasons for careful follow-up after treatment is to identify this last subgroup of patients, as they may be candidates for curative radical surgery. It should be noted that treatment of recurrent disease is based on the type of primary therapy administered.

Surveillance Tools

As mentioned above, the goal of surveillance is to detect disease at a point when intervention would positively impact the life span of the patient. Although a variety of tools exist to help detect recurrent cervical cancer, no single tool or surveillance schema has been proven prospectively to accomplish this goal.

Traditionally, asymptomatic women undergo a physical examination, including a pelvic examination and Pap test every 3 to 6 months (Table 18–1). Laboratory studies, including a complete blood count, blood urea nitrogen (BUN), and creatinine measurements, may be obtained; chest radiographs, intravenous pyelograms, and/or computed tomography (CT) scans may also be obtained. This surveillance schedule is not based on data that prove its efficacy.

Table 18–1. STANDARD SURVEILLANCE PROGRAM FOLLOWING TREATMENT OF CERVICAL CANCER

Year after Treatment	Physical and Pelvic Examinations [n=14]	Pap Test [n=14]	Chest Radiography [n=1]
1	4	4	1
2	3	3	0
3	3	3	0
4	2	2	0
5	2	2	0

The cytologic evaluation of a patient immediately following radiation therapy is often difficult and may be compromised by the anatomic and tissue changes resulting from irradiation (Figures 18–1, A and B, and 18–2).[5] Therefore, a Pap test should not be done until approximately 3 months after the completion of radiation therapy due to the distortion in exfoliated cells produced by irradiation. While some authors have advocated that a Pap test be done at every visit,[6,7] others have stated that the efficacy of a Pap test in the diagnosis of recurrent cervical cancer in an asymptomatic patient has yet to be proven.[8] Our retrospective review of 1,096 patients with International Federation of Gynecology and Obstetrics (FIGO) stage Ib cervical cancer examined the use of the Pap test for surveillance of cervical cancer.[8] In our series, Pap tests did not detect a single asymptomatic recurrence. We do, however, advocate

that a Pap test be obtained a minimum of once a year to screen for dysplasia.[9,10]

The use of routine chest radiography to detect recurrent cervical cancer has not been well evaluated. Retrospective data from Gallousis[11] revealed a 5-year survival rate of 20 to 40 percent after surgical resection of isolated pulmonary metastases from pelvic malignancies (Figure 18–3). In another study, Bodurka-Bevers and colleagues[8] reported a median survival of 3 years in asymptomatic cervical cancer patients who underwent pulmonary resection for recurrent disease. The median survival of symptomatic women who underwent pulmonary resection was only 1 year. Larson and colleagues[6] identified only 2 of 27 women having asymptomatic pulmonary recurrences using chest radiography and did not recommend screening using chest radiography until effective systemic therapy was available. Contrary to this finding, Soisson and colleagues[7] suggested that semiannual chest radiography may be warranted for the surveillance of women having recurrent cervical cancer. As illustrated by this variety of recommendations, no consensus exists regarding the frequency of chest radiography.

The effectiveness of post-therapy surveillance programs after treatment of gynecologic cancers has not been well evaluated. Our study of 1,096 patients with FIGO stage Ib cervical cancer is the largest to date to assess the impact of surveillance

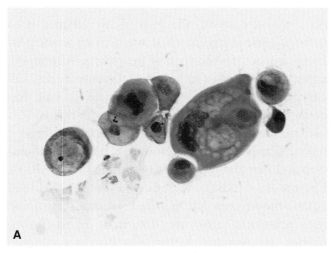

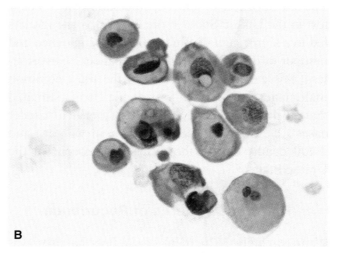

A

B

Figure 18–1. *A,* Pap smear showing radiation effect, increased nuclear size, and irregularity plus hyperchromatic features in keeping with the possibility of squamous carcinoma. However, multinucleation, chromatin's smudged quality, and relative preservation of the nuclear/cytoplasmic ratio suggests radiation effect. *B,* Pap smear with treatment effect. Cytoplasmic vacuolization and synchronous cytoplasmic enlargement mirroring nuclear enlargement not as pronounced as in Figure 18–1A. (Courtesy of Gregg Staerkel, MD.)

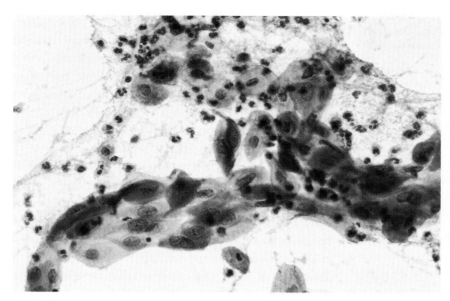

Figure 18–2. Pap smear illustrating difficulty interpreting carcinoma versus treatment effect. This Pap smear also shows radiation changes, although the changes are more generic and less specific to radiation effect. Nuclei are enlarged, but chromatin is not hyperchromatic and nuclear shape is not irregular. Cell shape is somewhat spindled, raising one's concern for squamous carcinoma. Final diagnosis: radiation treatment effect. (Courtesy of Gregg Staerkel, MD.)

after treatment.[8] While retrospective in nature, our study demonstrated that detection of asymptomatic recurrences is associated with prolonged overall survival and survival from time of initial detection of recurrence. On the basis of these data, we proposed a surveillance program that differs from the standard surveillance program in terms of timing of physician visits and the frequency of chest radiography and Pap tests (Table 18–2). Our suggestions for this new surveillance schema are subject to the biases of our study, including its retrospective nature and lead time and length time biases. This schema requires prospective validation and additional investigation, not only to eliminate bias but also to help optimize surveillance strategies after treatment for early cervical cancer.

While the studies described above may be used in the detection of recurrence in asymptomatic women, a different standard exists for women with symptoms. Appropriate studies should be performed to evaluate any symptoms reported by women having a history of invasive cervical cancer. The diagnosis of recurrent cervical cancer must be confirmed histologically. If a patient complains of recurrent bowel symptoms and a diagnosis of recurrent disease has not been established histologically, the possibility of a bowel injury should be considered and addressed appropriately, including the possibility of surgery.

Finally, the use of serum tumor markers to predict the recurrence of cervical cancer is being investigated. Squamous cell carcinoma antigen (SCCA) is a tumor-associated antigen first described by Kato and Torigoe.[12] The biologic mechanism responsible for the release of this antigen into the serum is not well understood. Several investigators have suggested that the level of squamous cell carcinoma antigen may be a useful marker for cervical cancer progression and recurrence.[13,14] Although abnormal SCCA levels have been documented 2 to 7 months prior to clinical detection of recurrence,[15] the clinical benefit of a slightly earlier diagnosis of recurrence has not been evaluated.

In addition to SCCA, investigators have attempted to predict recurrent disease by measuring the levels of CA 125, tissue polypeptide antigen (TPA), and

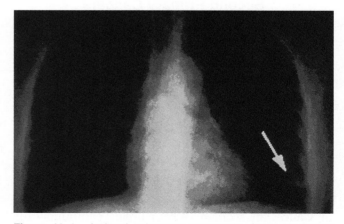

Figure 18–3. Isolated pulmonary metastasis. Chest radiograph illustrating an isolated pulmonary metastasis (*arrow*) amenable to wedge resection.

Table 18–2. PROPOSED SURVEILLANCE PROGRAM FOLLOWING TREATMENT OF CERVICAL CANCER

Year after Treatment	Physical and Pelvic Examinations [n=12]	Pap Test [n=5]	Chest Radiography [n=8]
1	3	1	1
2	3	1	2
3	2	1	2
4	2	1	2
5	2	1	1

carcinoembryonic antigen (CEA).[16,17] While the preliminary data are interesting, prospective studies evaluating the potential clinical utility of tumor markers in the detection of recurrent cervical cancer are needed.

Imaging

Currently, there is no established role for routine diagnostic imaging in the surveillance of patients receiving treatment for invasive cervical cancer.[18] Chest radiography may be used to detect asymptomatic pulmonary recurrences, although the optimal surveillance schedule has not yet been determined. CT and magnetic resonance imaging (MRI) scans may also be used to detect recurrence, although the utility and cost-effectiveness of these modalities has also not been well studied. Diagnostic imaging techniques should be integrated into surveillance studies to determine the efficacy and utility of the various modalities available.

Second Primary Cancers

The possibility of induction of a second primary carcinoma by pelvic radiation therapy is a controversial topic. Spitz and colleagues[19] used incidence data from the Surveillance, Epidemiology, and End Results (SEER) program of the National Cancer Institute (NCI) to evaluate the incidence of second cancers of the buccal cavity following treatment of invasive cervical cancer. Standard incidence ratios were elevated in both Caucasian and African American women, while laryngeal cancer incidence ratios were elevated in Caucasian women only. Human papillomavirus (HPV) transmission was thought to play a role in the paired occurrence of second cancers in these anatom-

ically distinct cancer sites. Lee and colleagues[20] reviewed the records of 1,048 patients having cervical cancer treated with irradiation, alone or combined with surgery. The incidence rate of second primaries was 5.4 per 1,000 person-years, a figure consistent with population-based rates. Conversely, Storm,[21] in an analysis of the population-based Danish Cancer Registry, studied the risk of second malignancy in women who received irradiation for invasive cervical cancer and in situ disease. Storm observed a small increase in the relative risk of lung, bladder, and other cancers, as well as a decrease in the relative risk of breast cancer. Storm concluded that cancers attributable to radiation therapy for invasive disease tended to appear 10 or more years after irradiation, and that the risk remained elevated for more than 30 years. The greater risk of acute lymphocytic leukemia seen in patients who received irradiation for in situ disease was attributed to lower radiation doses, which may have induced more mutations and less cell killing. Lastly, Werner-Wasik and colleagues[22] evaluated the relative risk of second primary cancers in 125 women having FIGO stages I or II cervical carcinoma that was treated using irradiation. They attributed the increased risk of second primary cancers, including breast, bladder, vulval, and thyroid cancers, to an abnormal genetic background and/or a common etiology between the initial or second tumors. The authors also noted that their study was the only study that reported an increased risk of breast cancer in survivors of cervical cancer, attributing this finding to close follow-up of the patients. Clearly, more research must be performed to truly answer this question.

Surveillance Strategies

In 1994, Markman[23] suggested four considerations for the design of a surveillance program after treatment of a primary malignancy. These included the documented effectiveness of salvage treatment regarding survival and/or quality of life, cost of surveillance, cost of potential salvage treatments, and the psychologic impact of pursuing or not pursuing aggressive surveillance. The issue of post-therapy surveillance for cervical cancer in particular is controversial and requires more evaluation. Ansink and colleagues,[24] in a retrospective study of 674 cervical cancer patients who underwent a radical hysterectomy and lymph node dissection, identified 8 patients who were alive without disease at a mean interval of 51 months after receiving a diagnosis of recurrence; 7 of the 8 recurrences were central. The authors concluded that routine surveillance is ineffective in improving the outcome in patients having recurrent cervical cancer in this setting. Conversely, Bodurka-Bevers and colleagues[8] demonstrated that detection and treatment of asymptomatic recurrences were associated with prolonged overall survival (83 months versus 31 months) and survival from the time of the detection of recurrence (42 months versus 11 months). While both these studies were retrospective and subject to potential sources of bias, it is interesting to note that they both identified a subset of women in whom detection and treatment of recurrent cervical cancer may prolong life.

Published cervical cancer surveillance strategies are based on a combination of physical and pelvic examinations, Pap tests, chest radiography, and, occasionally, CT and intravenous pyelograms. The majority of the patients are evaluated every 3 to 4 months for the first 2 years after treatment and then every 6 months for an additional 3 years. The studies described above are the first step in an effort to develop an effective surveillance program for patients treated for invasive cervical cancer. Future efforts should be targeted toward the prospective evaluation of surveillance strategies to assess potential clinical and economic benefits.

VAGINA

Vaginal cancer is one of the least common gynecologic malignancies. It has been estimated that in the year 2001, approximately 2,100 new cases of vaginal cancer and 600 deaths due to the disease will occur in the United States.[2] Due, in part, to the rarity of this disease, no standard post-treatment surveillance program exists for patients treated for vaginal cancer.

Rates and Patterns of Recurrence

Approximately 80 percent of patients having recurrent vaginal cancer have local recurrences, the majority of which occur within 2 years after primary treat-

ment.[25] Distant metastases usually occur later and less frequently. An exception to this may be patients with clear cell adenocarcinoma of the vagina. In 1997, Herbst[26] reported on 588 patients having clear cell adenocarcinoma of the vagina and cervix; 2 patients had a recurrence 7 years after the completion of primary treatment, a longer interval than that reported for the majority of vaginal carcinoma patients. Also, a larger proportion of these carcinomas appeared to metastasize to the supraclavicular area and lungs, compared with squamous cell cancer of the vagina.[27] As with cervical cancer, the majority of patients having recurrent vaginal cancer have a grave prognosis.

Surveillance Tools

There is a paucity of data describing surveillance for recurrent vaginal cancer. As in cervical cancer surveillance, physical and pelvic examinations should be performed. In addition, a Pap test should not be done until 3 months after the completion of radiation therapy. Symptoms suggestive of recurrence should be evaluated appropriately.

Imaging

The routine use of chest radiography and CT or MRI for surveillance after treatment of vaginal cancer has not been reported. However, in studies of symptomatic patients, the accuracy of MRI in the detection of recurrent vaginal carcinoma, compared with clinical or surgical findings, was 82 percent.[28,29]

Surveillance Strategies

Post-treatment surveillance for invasive vaginal cancer is usually modeled after cervical cancer surveillance programs, as there are essentially no data regarding surveillance programs for this disease. As with cervical cancer, patients are usually evaluated every 3 to 4 months for the first 2 years after treatment and then every 6 months for an additional 3 to 5 years. Once an effective surveillance program for cervical cancer has been identified, it would likely also be used for vaginal cancers. Due to the rarity of vaginal cancer, prospective randomized trials to determine optimal surveillance strategies for the disease are not anticipated to occur.

VULVA

Carcinoma of the vulva accounts for approximately 3 to 5 percent of all female genital tract malignancies. It has been estimated that in 2001, 3,600 new cases of vulvar cancer and 800 deaths due to the disease will occur in the United States.[2] Additionally, the majority of vulvar lesions are of squamous histology.

Rates and Patterns of Recurrence

Vulvar cancer recurrences may be local or distant. More than 80 percent of recurrences occur during the first 2 years following treatment, and more than 50 percent of them are local.[25] Although Simonsen[30] reported a 40 percent salvage rate with local recurrence, the prognosis for vulvar cancer patients having recurrent nodal disease or distant metastases is poor. Piura and colleagues[31] reported a 3.7-fold increase in risk for death due to recurrence beyond the vulva over recurrence in the vulva only. Careful follow-up is indicated to identify patients having locally recurrent disease as they may do well after treatment of this type of recurrence.

Surveillance Tools

As with vaginal cancer, there is a paucity of data describing the surveillance for recurrent vulvar cancer. Careful physical and pelvic examinations should be performed, and symptoms should be evaluated appropriately. Additionally, close surveillance using colposcopy and biopsies has been advocated for patients having minimally invasive squamous cell carcinoma of the vulva, defined as 1 mm or less of stromal invasion.[32]

Serum concentrations of squamous cell carcinoma antigen and tissue polypeptide antigen have been evaluated in the follow-up of vulvar cancer patients. Hefler and colleagues[33] reported that the serum concentration of squamous cell carcinoma antigen displayed good sensitivity and specificity characteristics in the surveillance of vulvar cancer patients, with lead-time effects seen in 75 percent and 50 percent of patients having regional and distant recurrent disease, respectively. However, the addition of tissue polypeptide antigen measurement to the sur-

veillance regimen did not improve the sensitivity or duration of lead-time effects in the study group.

Imaging

The routine use of chest radiography, CT, or MRI for surveillance after treatment of vulvar cancer has not been reported.

Surveillance Strategies

Post-treatment surveillance for invasive vulvar cancer is usually modeled after cervical cancer surveillance programs, as there are essentially no data regarding surveillance programs for this disease. As with cervical and vaginal cancers, patients are usually evaluated every 3 to 4 months for the first 2 years after treatment and then every 6 months for an additional 3 to 5 years. Once an effective surveillance program for cervical cancer has been identified, it would likely also be used for vulvar cancer. Due to the relative rarity of vulvar cancer, prospective randomized trials to determine optimal surveillance strategies would probably require an international research setting.

FUTURE DIRECTIONS

Today's health-care market has experienced rapid changes in resource allocation. Increased financial pressure on the medical profession has led to the close scrutiny of patterns of care, particularly in terms of patient outcomes and costs. Surveillance of women following primary treatment of early cervical cancer may improve their overall survival, thereby meeting the demands of such scrutiny. However, surveillance of women following primary treatment of advanced cervical, vaginal, or vulvar cancers has not been well studied. Future surveillance efforts should target the prospective development and evaluation of surveillance programs for women who receive treatment for these malignancies in an effort to optimize the clinical outcomes of these patients.

REFERENCES

1. Kosary CL, Schiffman MH, Trimble EL. Cervix uteri. In: Miller BA, Ries LAG, Hankey BF, et al. editors. SEER cancer statistics review. Bethesda, MD:

United States Department of Health and Human Services; 1993. p. 1973–90.

2. Greenlee RT, Hill-Harmon MB, Murray T, Thun M. Cancer statistics, 2001. CA Cancer J Clin 2001;51:15–36.

3. van Nagell JR Jr, Rayburn W, Donaldson ES, et al. Therapeutic implications of patterns of recurrence in cancer of the uterine cervix. Cancer 1979;44:2354–61.

4. Jampolis S, Andras J, Fletcher G. Analysis of sites and causes of failures of irradiation in invasive squamous cell carcinoma of the intact uterine cervix. Radiology 1975;15:681.

5. Shield PW, Daunter B, Wright RG. Post-irradiation cytology of cervical cancer patients. Cytopathology 1992;3:167–82.

6. Larson DM, Copeland LJ, Malone JM Jr, et al. Diagnosis of recurrent cervical carcinoma after radical hysterectomy. Obstet Gynecol 1988;71:6.

7. Soisson AP, Geszler G, Soper JT, et al. A comparison of symptomatology, physical examination, and vaginal cytology in the detection of recurrent cervical carcinoma after radical hysterectomy. Obstet Gynecol 1990;76:106–9.

8. Bodurka-Bevers D, Morris M, Eifel PJ, et al. Posttherapy surveillance of women with cervical cancer: an outcomes analysis. Gynecol Oncol 1997;64:289.

9. ACOG Committee Opinion. Recommendations on frequency of Pap test screening. Chicago, IL: American College of Obstetricians and Gynecologists; March 1995. No. 152.

10. ACOG Technical Bulletin. Cervical cytology: evaluation and management of abnormalities. Chicago, IL: American College of Obstetricians and Gynecologists; August 1993. No. 183.

11. Gallousis S. Isolated lung metastases from pelvic malignancies. Gynecol Oncol 1979;7:206–14.

12. Kato H, Torigoe T. Radioimmunoassay for tumor antigen of human cervical squamous cell carcinoma. Cancer 1977;40(4):1621–8.

13. Rose PG, Baker S, Fournier L, et al. Serum squamous cell carcinoma antigen levels in invasive cervical cancer: prediction of response and recurrence. Am J Obstet Gynecol 1993;168:942–6.

14. Bolger BS, Dabbas M, Lopes A, Monaghan JM. Prognostic value of preoperative squamous cell carcinoma antigen level in patients surgically treated for cervical carcinoma. Gynecol Oncol 1997;65:309–13.

15. Holloway RW, To A, Moradi M, et al. Monitoring the course of cervical carcinoma with the squamous cell carcinoma serum radioimmunoassay [see comments]. Obstet Gynecol 1989;74(6):944–9.

16. Gocze PM, Vahrson HW, Freeman DA. Serum levels of squamous cell carcinoma antigen and ovarian carcinoma antigen (CA 125) in patients with benign and malignant diseases of the uterine cervix. Oncology 1994;51:430–4.

17. Juang CM, Wang PH, Yen MS, et al. Application of tumor markers CEA, TPA, and SCC-Ag in patients with low-risk FIGO stage IB and IIA squamous cell carcinoma of the uterine cervix. Gynecol Oncol 2000;76:103–6.

18. Russell AH. Integration of diagnostic imaging in the clinical management of cervical cancer. Monogr Natl Cancer Inst 1996;21:35–41.

19. Spitz MR, Sider, JG, Schantz SP, Newell GR. Association between malignancies of the upper aerodigestive tract and uterine cervix. Head Neck 1992;14:347–51.

20. Lee JY, Perez CA, Ettinger N, Fineberg BB. The risk of second primaries subsequent to irradiation for cervix cancer. Int J Radiat Oncol Biol Phys 1981;8:207–11.

21. Storm HH. Second primary cancer after treatment for cervical cancer. Cancer 1988;61:679–88.

22. Werner-Wasik M, Schmid CH, Bornstein LE, Madox-Jones H. Increased risk of second malignant neoplasms outside radiation fields in patients with cervical carcinoma. Cancer 1995;75:2281–5.

23. Markman M. Follow-up of the asymptomatic patient with ovarian cancer. Gynecol Oncol 1994;55:S134–7.

24. Ansink A, de Barros Lopes A, Naik R, Monaghan JM. Recurrent stage 1B cervical carcinoma: evaluation of the effectiveness of routine follow up surveillance. Br J Obstet Gynaecol 1996;10:1156–8.

25. DiSaia PJ, Creasman WT. Clinical gynecologic oncology. 5th ed. St Louis, MO: Mosby; 1997.

26. Herbst AL. Neoplastic diseases of the vagina. In: Mishell DR Jr, Herbst AL, Stenchever MA, Droegemueller W. Comprehensive gynecology. 3rd ed. St. Louis, MO: Mosby; 1997.

27. Robboy SJ, Herbst AL, Scully RE. Clear cell adenocarcinoma of the vagina and cervix in young females: analysis of 37 tumors that persisted or recurred after primary therapy. Cancer 1974;34:606–14.

28. Ebner F, Kressel HY, Mintz MC, et al. Tumor recurrence versus fibrosis in the female pelvis: differentiation with MR imaging at 1.5 T. Radiology 1988;166:333–40.

29. Glazer HS, Lee JK, Levitt RG, et al. Radiation fibrosis: differentiation from recurrent tumor by MR imaging. Radiology 1985;156:721–6.

30. Simonsen E. Treatment of recurrent squamous cell carcinoma of the vulva. Acta Radiol Oncol 1984;23:345–8.

31. Piura B, Masotina A, Murdoch J, et al. Recurrent squamous cell carcinoma of the vulva: a study of 73 cases. Gynecol Oncol 1993;48:187–95.

32. Kelley JL, Burke TW, Tornos C, et al. Minimally invasive vulvar carcinoma: an indication for conservative surgical therapy. Gynecol Oncol 1992;44:240–4.

33. Hefler L, Frischmuth K, Heinze G, et al. Serum concentrations of squamous-cell carcinoma antigen and tissue polypeptide antigen in the follow-up of patients with vulvar cancer. Int J Cancer 1999;83:167–70.

19

Palliative Care

JOHN J. KAVANAGH, MD

The recurrences of cervical, vaginal, and vulvar cancers following definitive surgery and/or radiotherapy are a difficult clinical problem. This is particularly so if chemotherapy has been given as part of the primary regimen. The focus at this point in the patient's care is using therapeutic modalities that will maintain the patient's life with optimum quality. Generally used modalities are radiation therapy at symptomatic sites of recurrence and systemic chemotherapy. Salvage therapy plays a minor role. A comprehensive palliative care approach is often necessary and includes hospice care, spiritual support, and adequate bereavement counseling to families and loved ones.

CERVICAL CANCER

The use of chemotherapy in cervical cancer has been well studied. Cisplatin has been used most frequently, both as a single agent and in combination therapies (Table 19–1). Although a dose response has been demonstrated, the toxicity and poor survival advantage of this agent are thought to be major disadvantages. Response rates to cisplatin are within the range of approximately 20 percent.[1] Carboplatin has also been studied as a single agent. Although, the response rates may be slightly less, its toxicity has been more tolerable. Myelosuppresion can be a problem in patients with extensive prior radiation therapy. Ifosfamide was initially reported to have significant clinical activity. However, this was usually in patients who had had no prior treatment. Later studies of the drug demonstrated lower activity with significant side effects. The drug is now considered modestly active in the disease.

Two relatively newer compounds that have been used are paclitaxel and irinotecan. Both are natural products, with unique mechanisms of action. Paclitaxel produced responses in 9 of 52 patients. This has prompted a randomized trial comparing the drug in combination with cisplatin versus cisplatin alone.[2] Irinotecan is a campothecin that inhibits the topoisomerase enzyme. Responses were reported to be approximately 24 percent by Japanese researchers.[3] Two subsequent studies have also confirmed responses rates of greater than 20 percent.[4] Topotecan, the earlier compound has also been reported to be active in the treatment of this disease. Therefore, the topoisomerase agents appear to have definite activity in the disease.

Although many single agents have been evaluated in clinical trials, the responses are usually partial and relatively short. Therefore, a significant effort is being made to develop combination chemotherapies (Table 19–2). Most of these have been single-arm trials, with relatively small numbers of patients. It has been very difficult to demonstrate survival advantages over the single-agent therapy. One of the more definitive trials was by the Gynecologic Oncology Group, which randomized patients to cisplatin alone versus cisplatin and dibromodulcitol versus cisplatin, ifosfamide, and mesna. The ifosfamide-cisplatin arm had a superior response rate and progression-free survival. However, there was no significant difference in overall survival, and toxicity was more severe.[5] This trial is representative of the problems of treating metastatic cervical cancer, that is, failure to improve survival and lack of quality-of-life data as part of the clinical research. At the moment, the impact of chemotherapy on improving

Table 19–1. SINGLE-AGENT CHEMOTHERAPY FOR CERVICAL CANCER

Agent	Response (%)
Alkylating agents	
Cyclophosphamide	38/251 (15)
Chlorambucil	11/44 (25)
Melphalan	4/20 (20)
Ifosfamide	25/84 (30)
Mitolactol	16/55 (29)
Heavy metal complexes	
Cisplatin	182/785 (23)
Carboplatin	27/175 (15)
Antitumor antibiotics	
Doxorubicin	33/205 (16)
Bleomycin	19/176 (11)
Mitomycin	5/23 (22)
Antimetabolites	
Fluorouracil	29/142 (20)
Methotrexate	17/96 (18)
Hydroxyurea	0/14 (0)
Plant alkaloids	
Vincristine	10/55 (18)
Vinblastine	2/20 (10)
Etoposide	0/31 (0)
Miscellaneous agents	
Altretamine	12/64 (19)
Irinotecan (PCT-11)	13/55 (24)
Paclitaxel	
CCOP*	3/21 (14)
GOG†	9/52 (17)
Docetaxel	1/13 (8)

Reproduced with permission from Lopez A, Kudelka AP, Edwards CL, Kavanagh JJ. Carcinoma of the uterine cervix. In: Pazdur R, editor. Medical oncology: a comprehensive review. Huntington, NY: PRR Inc.; 1995.

CCOP = Community Clinical Oncology Program; GOG = Gynecologic Oncology Group.

*AP Kudelka, Houston, Texas, personal communication, 1995.

†W McGuire, Atlanta, Georgia, personal communication, 1995.

the overall life of patients, as measured with various psychosocial parameters, remains an open area of research. From a pragmatic point of view, a large number of patients have now already received the most active compounds as part of a radiosensitization program. It is unclear whether these patients will have the same chemotherapy responses as reported in earlier literature. The most common approach is to re-expose patients to a platin-type compound, with careful attention to toxicity. Chemotherapy beyond this is highly individualized and of dubious value. The patient who has asymptomatic indolent metastatic disease may be observed and may require judicious intervention, depending on the pace and sites of neoplastic growth.

Two important subsets of patients are those who have pelvic recurrences following either radiation therapy or definitive surgery. The former subset of patients should be evaluated for the possibility of pelvic exenteration. The survival rate following such radical surgery is approximately 34 percent.[6] The latter subset of patients should be considered for definitive radiation therapy. The literature concerning such patients reports survival rates ranging from 10 to 44 percent. Such therapy is highly individualized and often includes interstitial implantation. Although the results may often be disappointing, there is the possibility of palliative improvement in these patients when symptoms of local recurrence are controlled. Therefore, these two subsets of patients require careful evaluations.[7,8]

The treatment of recurrent non–squamous cell carcinoma is usually based on the data of squamous cell carcinoma or very small studies. The tumors most often dealt with are adenocarcinoma or small cell carcinomas. Cisplatin remains the mainstay, but doxorubicin and 5-fluorouracil have also been used. Etoposide is often used on small cell carcinomas.[9,10] There have been no definitive, large single-agent combination chemotherapy studies in this subset of tumors. The usual clinical practice is treating a small cell carcinoma of the cervix similar to the lung counterpart and the adenocarcinoma of the cervix similar to the squamous cell histology.

In summary, the palliative care of recurrent cervical cancer is based on first determining if the patient is a candidate for a radical surgical procedure, such as a pelvic exenteration, or for definitive radiotherapy for a localized recurrence. Systemic chemotherapy is cautiously used, usually with single agents. Careful attention is paid to toxicity. Further research is needed to determine the impact of chemotherapy on quality of life and the sensitivity of patients who have had prior chemotherapy as part of radiation therapy.

VULVAR CANCER

The chemotherapy of vulvar cancer has an extremely narrow focus. The patients are often older with significant concurrent medical illnesses. Frequently, the recurrences are in an area that has been

Table 19–2. COMBINATION CHEMOTHERAPY FOR ADVANCED OR RECURRENT CERVICAL CARCINOMA

Chemotherapy Regimen	Number of Patients	Prior Radiation Therapy (%)	Complete Response Rate (%)	Overall Response Rate (%)
Bleomycin/ifosfamide/cisplatin	49	86	20	69
Bleomycin/ifosfamide/carboplatin	21	49	23	60
Vinblastine/bleomycin/cisplatin	33	66	18	67
Fluorouracil/doxorubicin/vincristine/cyclophosphamide	31	87	9	58

Reproduced with permission from Lopez A, Kudelka AP, Edwards CL, Kavanagh JJ. Carcinoma of the uterine cervix. In: Pazdur R, editor. Medical oncology: a comprehensive review. Huntington, NY: PRR Inc.; 1995.

intensively treated with radiotherapy. The disease is also rare and the squamous cell histology has been the one studied most extensively. The largest trial was with cisplatin,[11] with negative results. There have been anecdotal reports of doxorubicin and bleomycin having activity, however, the trials were too small for definitive statements.[12,13]

Combination chemotherapy has been used in the treatment of this disease. There are two published trials of combination chemotherapy with greater than 20 patients. The combination of bleomycin, mitomycin-C, and cisplatin produced a response rate of 27 percent. The combination of bleomycin, methotrexate, and lomustine (CCNU) produced a response rate of 64 percent. However, in both studies, a significant number of patients had had no prior radiation therapy or chemotherapy.[14,15] Therefore, the question of responses following radiation therapy within the therapy field remains unanswered.

VAGINAL CANCER

Vaginal cancer is a rare neoplasm, therefore, the trials for palliative systemic therapy are small in number and have had a heterogeneous mix of patients. The two compounds that have undergone standard evaluation are etoposide and cisplatin. Neither compound produced positive results, therefore, reports on the systemic therapy of this disease remain largely anecdotal. Any studies on combination therapy or other single agents have too few numbers for a meaningful conclusion.[16,17] In practical terms, in most patients, recurrent vaginal cancers are of a squamous cell histology, and therapy is similar to that for squamous cell carcinoma of the cervix.

PALLIATIVE CARE

Palliative care is essentially aimed at minimizing the distress a patient suffers in the process of dying. It is impossible to completely eliminate distress during this time. However, by approaching the patient's problems in a comprehensive way, very methodical measures may be taken to help the patient cope. One may review the major issues that cause distress (Table 19–3) and develop a plan of response. Yet, the physician alone cannot adequately address many of these problems. A team approach, especially in the hospice setting, is ideal. Most oncologists will focus on the various physical aspects of palliative care, which can range from nausea and vomiting to pain management. Issues, such as the practical problems of the physical environment and the patient's financial issues, spiritual issues, and family problems, are often best handled by a cohesive team.

The triad of adequate palliative care comprises the nature of the patient-physician relationship, adequate control of the symptoms of terminal disease, and the management of the events surrounding the dying process itself (Table 19–4).

The relationship between the patient and the physician, with the interaction of the family, is structured by the nature of the communication process. Several papers have been written emphasizing the importance of the comfort and privacy of the physician's office, direct visual contact, and the importance of understanding the expectations and hopes of the patient. In addition, it is essential for the physician to ask open questions and to be able to understand the concerns of the patient. Giving bad news has a proposed structure (Table 19–5). The interaction with family represents a complex issue. When children are involved in this process, it is often difficult to under-

Table 19–3. CAUSES OF DISTRESS

Practical problems
- Housing
- Insurance
- Work/school
- Transportation
- Child care

Family problems
- Dealing with partner
- Dealing with children

Emotional problems
- Worry
- Sadness
- Depression
- Nervousness

Spiritual/religious concerns
- Relating to God
- Loss of faith
- Other problems

Physical problems
- Pain
- Nausea
- Fatigue
- Sleep
- Getting around
- Bathing/dressing
- Breathing
- Mouth sores
- Indigestion
- Constipation/diarrhea
- Bowel changes
- Changes in urination
- Fevers
- Dry/itchy skin
- Dry/congested nose
- Tingling in hands/feet
- Feeling swollen
- Sexual problems

Adapted from Back AL, Waltzman RJ. Palliative care for patients with lower gastrointestinal malignancies. In: Willet CG, editor. Cancer of the lower gastrointestinal tract. Hamilton, ON: BC Decker Inc.; 2001. p. 214–26.

stand and appreciate the perceptions of children. Often, additional professional advice is necessary. Patients also have important spiritual concerns and needs. The physician should be comfortable with discussing the patient's spiritual attitude and providing easy and efficient access to spiritual counseling. An early part of the dialogue between the physician and the patient will be the decision regarding advanced directives, including the do-not-resuscitate (DNR) order. Although there are significant variations among institutions and countries regarding the legal process, comfortable communication remains the cornerstone of reaching rational decisions on this subject.[18–20]

Table 19–4. PRINCIPLES OF PALLIATIVE CARE

Palliative care is the active total care of patients whose disease is not responsive to curative treatment. Controlling pain and other symptoms as well as managing psychological, social, and spiritual problems is paramount. Ultimately, the goal of palliative care is to achieve the best possible quality of life for patients and their families. Many aspects of palliative care are also applicable earlier in the course of an illness, in conjunction with cancer treatment. Overall, palliative care does the following:
- affirms life and regards dying as a normal process,
- neither hastens nor postpones death,
- provides relief from pain and other distressing symptoms,
- integrates the psychological and spiritual aspects of patient care,
- offers a support system to help patients live as actively as possible until death, and
- offers a support system to help the family cope during both a patient's illness and its own bereavement.

Reproduced with permission from Driver LC, Bruera E. The MD Anderson palliative care handbook. 1st ed. Houston, TX: Department of Symptom Control and Palliative Care. The University of Texas MD Anderson Cancer Center; 2000.

Symptom control is essential to facilitate adequate communication and a comfortable dying process. Control of pain is a frequent aspect of symptom control. Although beyond the scope of this article, the essentials for effective pain control are an adequate history and assessment tool, knowledge of the relative strengths of analgesics, and appropriate consultations with pain specialists in difficult cases.[21,22] The assessment of pain requires a series of steps. The first step is to determine the type and eti-

Table 19–5. GIVING BAD NEWS

Prepare. Choose an appropriate physical location where all participants can be comfortably seated, and verify the important information before sitting down.

Find out how much the patient knows. Getting both patient and physician on the same page at the outset can allow the physician to provide context for the information and to get insight into the patient's emotional state.

Find out how much the patient wants to know. Asking what level of detail is desired by the patient can help the physician tailor the information and give the patient some control over the flow of the information.

Share the information. Avoid medical jargon. Give information in pieces and check for understanding after each piece.

Respond to the patient's feelings. This may need to be done after each piece of information. Allowing the patient to react as the information unfolds can help prevent the patient from being overwhelmed.

Make concrete follow-up plans for the next step.

Reproduced with permission from Back AL, Waltzman RJ. Palliative care for patients with lower gastrointestinal malignancies. In: Willet CG, editor. Cancer of the lower gastrointestinal tract. Hamilton, ON: BC Decker Inc.; 2001. p. 214–26.

ology of the pain. Measuring the intensity of the pain, along with recognizing concurrent symptoms, is the second step; a scale is frequently used to describe the pain. The third step is to consider the pain in terms of the patient's overall condition and environment. At this stage, it is important to ascertain whether there will be any obstacles to pain management, such as cognitive impairment or poor coping strategies. The last step involves a ladder technique of gradually increasing strengths of pain medicines on a scheduled basis. One should not forget the local palliative measures, such as radiotherapy, that may be used for pain relief. Driver and Bruera have written a superb review of palliative care and offer many "pearls if wisdom" regarding pain management (Table 19–6).[20] Nausea and vomiting are treated with standard antiemetics, commonly phenothiazines. The use of ondansetron and granisetron may be useful, but cost represents a barrier to long-term use. Often overlooked is the problem of reflux eosophagitis causing nausea, which may be treated with H_2-blockers.[23,24] The problem of bowel obstruction is often difficult to treat and may require a percutaneous gastrostomy. A diverting colostomy in selected cases may be useful for colon obstruction. Octreotide could be used as a medicinal palliation because of its ability to reduce the volume of intestinal secretions; however, the compound is relatively expensive.[25–27] Constipation requires diligent and systematic treatment with stool softeners and mild stimulants.[20] Infected necrotic lesions are a particular problem in these cancers. These induce malodorous secretions and various degrees of hemorrhage. Fistulas between various pelvic organs also result because of local progression of the tumors. Regular gentle cleaning of the wound areas or douching of the vagina with a weak solution of peroxide is helpful. Also, the use of topical metronidazole may reduce bad odors and discharge.[28] There is no standard policy regarding a surgical intervention for rectovaginal or vesicovaginal fistulas. It depends on the estimated life expectancy of the patient and the effects of the fistula. Nutrition is a uniquely difficult problem. The family members find it difficult to watch their loved one starving and want to give food to show how much they care. Patients are often anorectic and have no particular desire to eat but feel

guilty about not accepting the food given to them by their loved ones. Usually, a practical compromise is the best solution. That entails teaspoons of liquid, such as a mild nutritional supplement or a tasty beverage. Families need to be educated as to the role of nutrition at this point in the illness and the possibility of adding to the suffering of the patients by forcing food on them.[29]

The time of death is often not apparent to the physician. However, there is frequently a change in the emotional tenor in the family as the time approaches. Again, communication among all parties becomes essential. Careful re-emphasis on symptom control and explanations of the nature of the dying process should be made; also, arrange-

Table 19–6. PALLIATIVE PEARLS

- Pain is a multidimensional experience that requires multidimensional assessment.
- Because pain and other symptoms can change rapidly in the advanced cancer patient, regular and frequent assessment is necessary.
- Ask the patient about his or her pain, and believe what he or she reports.
- Reassure the patient and family that most pain can be relieved.
- Reassure the patient and family about their concerns and fears regarding opioids.
- Explain to the patient the differences between physical dependence, addiction, and tolerance.
- Almost all patients with advanced cancer require treatment until death. Thus, concerns about dependence and addiction are irrelevant.
- Encourage normal activity to the fullest extent possible.
- Treat pain promptly and aggressively.
- Rational pain management tailors the regimen to the stage of pain.
- Regular atc opioid administration, with adequate breakthrough dosing and adjuvants as required and proactive antiemetic and laxative regimens, is the hallmark of rational and effective pain management in the cancer patient.
- Optimize opioids before adding adjuvants.
- Because opioid conversion tables are inexact, patients should be observed carefully whenever regimen changes are made.
- Beware of overzealous use of opioids in the patient who is experiencing delirium or somatization.
- Benzodiazepines and phenothiazines are questionable adjuvants. They may cause oversedation and confusion and do not address pain.
- Beware of the pitfalls of polypharmacy.
- Treating the patient who suffers from total pain (nociception, psychologic distress, and spiritual distress) means treating the whole patient (body, mind, and spirit).
- "Pain is a more terrible Lord of mankind than even death itself." — Albert Schweitzer

ments should be made for constant companionship and for carrying out the final wishes of the patient.

After death comes the bereavement process, which is a complex but important aspect of the physician's relationship with the family. Although the primary physicians are not often involved in this, a compassionate and sensitive response to the family with bereavement questions is essential. In addition, if the primary physician senses that the grieving process is disproportionate or difficult, he should make arrangements for the family to receive professional counseling.

CONCLUSION

The recurrences of cervical, vulvar, or vaginal cancer following primary therapy are extremely problematic. Salvage therapy is usually not effective. A balanced approach, with the judicious application of cisplatin-based therapy and a comprehensive palliative care program, would be the wisest course.

REFERENCES

1. Bonomi P, Blessing JA, Stehman FB, et al. Randomized trial of three cisplatin dose schedules in squamous cell carcinoma of the cervix: a Gynecologic Oncology Group study. J Clin Oncol 1985;3:1079.

2. McGuire WP, Blessing JA, Moore D, et al. Paclitaxel has moderate activity in squamous cervix cancer: a Gynecologic Oncology Group study. J Clin Oncol 1996;14:792.

3. Takeuchi S, Noda K. Yakushiji M. Late phase II study of CPT11, topoisomerase I inhibitor in advanced cervical carcinoma (CC) [abstract]. Proc Am Soc Clin Oncol 1992;11:224.

4. Verschraegen CF, Levy T, Kudelka AP, et al. Phase II study of irinotecan in prior chemotherapy-treated squamous cell carcinoma of the cervix. J Clin Oncol 1997;15:625.

5. Omura GA, Blessing JA, Vaccarello L, et al. Randomized trial of cisplatin versus cisplatin plus mitolactol versus cisplatin plus ifosfamide in advanced squamous carcinoma of the cervix: a Gynecologic Oncology Group study. J Clin Oncol 1997;15:165.

6. Rutledge FN, Smith JP, Wharton JT, O'Quinn AG. Pelvic exenteration: an analysis of 296 patients. Am J Obstet Gynecol 1977;129:881.

7. Jobsen JJ, Lee JWH, Cleton FJ, Hermans J. Treatment of locoregional recurrence of carcinoma of the cervix by radiotherapy after primary surgery. Gynecol Oncol 1989;33:368.

8. Friedman M, Pearlman AW. Carcinoma of the cervix: radiation salvage of surgical failures. Radiology 1965;84:801.

9. Slayton RE, Blessing JA, Rettenmaier M, Ball H. Phase II trial of etoposide in the management of advanced or recurrent nonsquamous cell carcinoma of the cervix: a Gynecologic Oncology Group study. Cancer Treat Rep 1984;68:1513.

10. Thigpen JT. Chemotherapy of gynecologic cancer. In: Perry MC, editor. The chemotherapy source book. Baltimore, MD: Williams & Wilkins; 1996. p. 1253.

11. Thigpen JT, Blessing JA, Homesley HD, et al. Phase II trials of cisplatin and piperzinedione in advanced or recurrent squamous cell carcinomas of the vulva: a Gynecologic Oncology Group study. J Clin Oncol 1986;23:358.

12. Deppe G, Bruckner HW, Cohen CJ. Adriamycin treatment of advanced vulvar carcinoma. Obstet Gynecol 1997;50:13.

13. Trope C, Johnsson JE, Larsson G, et al. Bleomycin alone or combined with mitomycin C in the treatment of advanced or recurrent squamous cell carcinoma of the vulva. Cancer Treat Rep 1980;64:639.

14. Belinson JL, Stewart JA, Richards A, et.al. Bleomycin, vincristine, mitomycin C, and cisplatin in the management of gynecologic squamous cell cancer. Gynecol Oncol 1985;20:387.

15. Durrant KR, Mangione C, Lacave AJ, et.al. Bleomycin, methotrexate, and CCNU in advanced inoperable squamous cell carcinoma of the vulva: a phase II study of the EORTC Gynaecological Cancer Cooperative Group (GCCG). Gynecol Oncol 1990;37:359.

16. Slayton RE, Blessing JA, Beecham J, DiSaia PJ. Phase II trial of etoposide in the management of advanced of recurrent squamous cell carcinoma of the vulva and carcinoma of the vagina: a Gynecologic Oncology Group study. Cancer Treat Rep 1987;71:869.

17. Thigpen JT, Blessing JA, Homesley HD, et al. Phase II trial of cisplatin in advanced or recurrent cancer of the vagina: a Gynecologic Oncology Group study. Gynecol Oncol 1986;23:10.

18. Finlay I. End-of-life care in patients dying of gynecologic cancer. Hematol Oncol Clin North Am 1999;13:77–108.

19. Ptacek JT. The patient-physician relationship: breaking bad news. A review of the literature. JAMA 1996;176:496–502.

20. Driver LC, Bruera E. The MD Anderson palliative care handbook. 1st ed. Houston, TX: Department of Symptom Control and Palliative Care. The University of Texas M.D. Anderson Cancer Center; 2000.

21. Bridges J. Management of advanced gynecological malignancies. Br J Hosp Med 1993;49:191–9.

22. Portenoy RK. Management of common opioid side effects during long term therapy of cancer pain. Ann Acad Med 1994;23:160–70.

23. Rousseau P. Antiemetic therapy in adults with terminal disease. A brief review. Am J Hospice Palliat Care 1995;12:13–8.
24. Finlay IG. Rational use of antiemetics in the terminally ill. Postgrad Update 1991;Dec:874–80.
25. Fernandes JR, Seymour RJ, Suissa S. Bowel obstruction in patients with ovarian cancer: a search for prognostic factors. Am J Obstet Gynecol 1988;158:244–9.
26. Khoo D, Hall E, Motson R, et al. Palliation of malignant intestinal obstruction using octreotide. Eur J Cancer 1994;30A:28–30.
27. Riley J, Fallon MT. Octeotide in terminal malignant obstruction of the gastrointestinal tract. Eur J Palliat Care 1993;1:23–5.
28. Finlay IG, Bowyszyc J, Famalu C, et al. The effect of topical 0.75% metronidazole gel on malodorous cutaneous ulcers. J Pain Symptom Manage 1996; 11:1151–61.
29. Ottery FD. Cancer cachexia. Cancer Pract 1994;2: 123–31.

Index

Page numbers followed by f indicate figure. Pages numbers followed by t indicate table.